AMERICA'S
TEST KITCHEN

THE COMPLETE
autumn&winter
COOKBOOK

550+ RECIPES **for** WARMING DINNERS,
HOLIDAY ROASTS, SEASONAL DESSERTS,
BREADS, FOOD GIFTS, **and** MORE

AMERICA'S TEST KITCHEN

Library of Congress Cataloging-in-Publication Data

Names: America's Test Kitchen (Firm), author.
Title: The complete autumn & winter cookbook : 550+ recipes for warming dinners, holiday roasts, seasonal desserts, breads, food gifts, and more / America's Test Kitchen.
Other titles: Complete autumn and winter cookbook
Description: Boston, MA : America's Test Kitchen, [2021] | Includes index.
Identifiers: LCCN 2021016571 (print) | LCCN 2021016572 (ebook) | ISBN 9781948703840 (paperback) | ISBN 9781948703857 (ebook)
Subjects: LCSH: Cooking. | Seasonal cooking. | Autumn. | Winter. | LCGFT: Cookbooks.
Classification: LCC TX714 .A497 2021 (print) | LCC TX714 (ebook) | DDC 641.5/64--dc23
LC record available at https://lccn.loc.gov/2021016571
LC ebook record available at https://lccn.loc.gov/2021016572

AMERICA'S TEST KITCHEN
21 Drydock Avenue, Boston, MA 02210

Printed in Canada
10 9 8 7 6 5 4 3 2 1

Distributed by Penguin Random House Publisher Services
Tel: 800.733.3000

Pictured on Front Cover Pot Roast with Root Vegetables (page 83); Pan-Roasted Pear Salad with Radicchio, Blue Cheese, and Walnuts (page 141); Fluffy Dinner Rolls (page 307); Cranberry-Orange Olive Oil Cake (page 359); Brandied Mulled Cider (page 274)

Pictured on Back Cover Maple Cheesecake (page 262)

Editorial Director, Books Adam Kowit

Executive Food Editor Dan Zuccarello

Deputy Food Editor Stephanie Pixley

Executive Managing Editor Debra Hudak

Senior Editor Sara Mayer

Editor Sara Zatopek

Assistant Editor Emily Rahravan

Editorial Support Christine Campbell, April Poole, and Rachel Schowalter

Design Director, Books Lindsey Timko Chandler

Graphic Designer Molly Gillespie

Photography Director Julie Bozzo Cote

Photography Producer Meredith Mulcahy

Senior Staff Photographers Steve Klise and Daniel J. van Ackere

Staff Photographer Kevin White

Additional Photography Joseph Keller and Carl Tremblay

Food Styling Joy Howard, Catrine Kelty, Chantal Lambeth, Gina McCreadie, Kendra McNight, Ashley Moore, Christie Morrison, Marie Piraino, Elle Simone Scott, Kendra Smith, and Sally Staub

Photoshoot Kitchen Team

    Photo Team and Special Events Manager Alli Berkey

    Lead Test Cook Eric Haessler

    Test Cooks Hannah Fenton, Jacqueline Gochenouer, and Gina McCreadie

    Assistant Test Cooks Hisham Hassan and Christa West

Senior Manager, Publishing Operations Taylor Argenzio

Imaging Manager Lauren Robbins

Production and Imaging Specialists Tricia Neumyer, Dennis Noble, and Amanda Yong

Copy Editor Cheryl Redmond

Proofreader Kelly Gauthier

Indexer Elizabeth Parson

Chief Creative Officer Jack Bishop

Executive Editorial Directors Julia Collin Davison and Bridget Lancaster

contents

welcome to
America's Test Kitchen

This book has been tested, written, and edited by the folks at America's Test Kitchen, where curious cooks become confident cooks. Located in Boston's Seaport District in the historic Innovation and Design Building, it features 15,000 square feet of kitchen space including multiple photography and video studios. It is the home of *Cook's Illustrated* magazine and *Cook's Country* magazine and is the workday destination for more than 60 test cooks, editors, and cookware specialists. Our mission is to empower and inspire confidence, community, and creativity in the kitchen.

We start the process of testing a recipe with a complete lack of preconceptions, which means that we accept no claim, no technique, and no recipe at face value. We simply assemble as many variations as possible, test a half-dozen of the most promising, and taste the results blind. We then construct our own recipe and continue to test it, varying ingredients, techniques, and cooking times until we reach a consensus. As we like to say in the test kitchen, "We make the mistakes so you don't have to." The result, we hope, is the best version of a particular recipe, but we realize that only you can be the final judge of our success (or failure). We use the same rigorous approach when we test equipment and taste ingredients.

All of this would not be possible without a belief that good cooking, much like good music, is based on a foundation of objective technique. Some people like spicy foods and others don't, but there is a right way to sauté, there is a best way to cook a pot roast, and there are measurable scientific principles involved in producing perfectly beaten, stable egg whites. Our ultimate goal is to investigate the fundamental principles of cooking to give you the techniques, tools, and ingredients you need to become a better cook. It is as simple as that.

To see what goes on behind the scenes at America's Test Kitchen, check out our social media channels for kitchen snapshots, exclusive content, video tips, and much more. You can watch us work (in our actual test kitchen) by tuning in to *America's Test Kitchen* or *Cook's Country* on public television or on our websites. Listen to *Proof*, *Mystery Recipe*, and *The Walk-In* (AmericasTestKitchen.com/podcasts) to hear engaging, complex stories about people and food. Want to hone your cooking skills or finally learn how to bake—with an America's Test Kitchen test cook? Enroll in one of our online cooking classes. And you can engage the next generation of home cooks with kid-tested recipes from America's Test Kitchen Kids.

Our community of home recipe testers provides valuable feedback on recipes under development by ensuring that they are foolproof. You can help us investigate the how and why behind successful recipes from your home kitchen. (Sign up at AmericasTestKitchen.com/recipe_testing.)

However you choose to visit us, we welcome you into our kitchen, where you can stand by our side as we test our way to the best recipes in America.

facebook.com/AmericasTestKitchen
twitter.com/TestKitchen
youtube.com/AmericasTestKitchen
instagram.com/TestKitchen
pinterest.com/TestKitchen

AmericasTestKitchen.com
CooksIllustrated.com
CooksCountry.com
OnlineCookingSchool.com
AmericasTestKitchen.com/kids

introduction

Cookies and hot cocoa. Holiday roasts and warming long-cooked braises. Hearty root vegetables, pies and baked goods galore, fresh-picked apples, and endless varieties of squash. Autumn and winter are seasons of bounty, communal eating, and celebration.

And in between the hustle and bustle of the holidays, there are quiet moments, too: Spending a cozy evening in with a book and a cup of steaming chai; sitting down to a simple but satisfying family dinner after a day spent outdoors; baking up a pan of bar cookies as the kitchen fills with the sweet aroma of caramelizing sugar. The recipes in this book span all these occasions, from cocktails, appetizers, and centerpiece mains suitable for the biggest holiday celebrations to one-pot dinners designed to help you eat well on even the most ordinary weeknights. Recipes for artisan-style breads and sky-high layer cakes are perfect for when you're in the mood for a project, while quick and easy recipes for drop biscuits, cookies, quick breads, and more ensure that soul-satisfying baked goods are always within reach.

We think that time spent in the kitchen should be enjoyable, not stressful. Cooking for guests, especially during the holidays, comes with a host of things to consider: what dishes to serve together and how much of each to make; when to buy ingredients; when to begin defrosting or brining or roasting. That's why we break the process down into easy-to-follow steps in Tips for Cooking for a Crowd (pages 6–7), so you'll always know what needs to get done and when. The rest of the book provides several other tools you can use to simplify your planning. Chapters organized by side dishes, celebration-worthy mains, appetizers and festive drinks, and desserts help you plan a menu that you can be proud of. Recipes throughout the book include Make Ahead tags if the bulk of the work can be done at least a day in advance, so you can get the hard part out of the way at a time that's best for you. And plenty of recipes made for the slow cooker or electric pressure cooker free up space on the stove and in the oven and let you focus on other tasks while the appliance does most of the work.

But good food shouldn't be relegated to the holidays. Much of the time it takes to make the dishes in our chapter on Weekend Roasting and Braising is hands-off, perfect for a leisurely day of cooking. On busier nights, you can turn to the Weeknight Dinners chapter to find complete meals that come together in around an hour or less. And no cold-weather cookbook would be complete without a selection of warming soups, stews, and chilis. We dedicated an entire chapter to the subject, with recipes ranging from Chicken and Dumplings (page 32) to a deeply complex Hawaiian oxtail soup you can make in the pressure cooker (page 21).

The abundance of fresh, peak-season produce available in autumn and winter deserves some recognition. The recipes in this book open up the world of cold-weather produce. It's not just root vegetables (though we make ample use of these seasonal stalwarts) but also bright, sharp citrus; sweet and toothsome squash; vividly colored and crisp radicchio and lacy frisée; sweet, pungent onions; hearty greens such as Swiss chard, kale, and their peppery-sweet cousin kohlrabi; and more (far more!). From Unstuffed Shells with Butternut Squash and Leeks (page 67) and Steak Tips with Wilted Spinach, Goat Cheese, and Pear Salad (page 53) to Braised Savoy Cabbage with Pancetta (page 145) and Sautéed Parsnips with Ginger, Maple, and Fennel Seeds (page 152), the recipes in this book will give you new ways to appreciate your favorites and, we hope, help you discover creative ways to use new-to-you ingredients, too.

Whatever the occasion calls for, *The Complete Autumn and Winter Cookbook* will be there to guide you through it all.

a quick guide to autumn & winter produce

These days, you can find just about any fruit or vegetable at the supermarket year-round, but out-of-season produce often tastes bland and listless. Luckily, the autumn and winter months offer just as wide and exciting an array of produce as the other months of the year. With the following list as a guide, we hope you'll have the confidence to seek out and cook with the best of what the season brings.

Root Vegetables

Often taken for granted or even overlooked entirely, root vegetables are wintertime kitchen champions. Ranging in flavor from earthy to sweet, they're especially well-suited for techniques like roasting and braising. Chapter 5 provides plenty of inspiration if you're looking to expand your root vegetable universe or put a twist on classic holiday sides. Try Celery Root Puree for a Crowd (page 145) instead of mashed potatoes; jazz up tender, earthy-sweet beets with citrus and nuts (page 142); and get acquainted with Roasted Turnips, Shallots, and Garlic with Rosemary (page 160). Or change up your chicken plus vegetable weeknight dinner routine by using whole parsnips (page 48).

Hearty Greens

Hearty greens, also called winter greens, are sturdy green-leaved vegetables that are at their best in the colder months. The category includes Swiss chard, collard greens, kale, and spinach (mature, not baby), to name a few. Like all the greens in this category, kale easily stands up to cooking, which tenderizes its somewhat tough leaves and stems. We love it creamed with chestnuts (page 149), braised with garlic and chorizo in the slow cooker (page 150), and cooked into meaty Beef Stew with Parsnips, Kale, and Mushrooms (page 36). Swiss chard, which turns irresistibly silky when cooked slowly, is the star ingredient in Swiss Chard Pie (page 128), a beloved dish from central Italy.

Potatoes

We thought these enormously popular root vegetables deserved their own category. With so many varieties out there, it can be difficult to know which to use when. In this book, we most commonly call for russets, Yukon Golds, red potatoes, and fingerling potatoes. Starchy russets are great for baking; when mashed, they turn out light and fluffy. For a more substantial mash such as our Creamy Mashed Potatoes (page 153), lower-starch Yukon Gold potatoes are ideal. Red and fingerling potatoes are both small varieties with thin skins that are great for cooking whole. Sweet potatoes actually belong to their own family, but don't let that stop you from enjoying them in crispy fritters (page 158) or a classic mash made in the slow cooker (page 158).

Winter Squashes

Winter squashes vary dramatically in size, color, and shape. Immediately recognizable bright-orange butternut squash is one of our favorites, appearing in this book in recipes from chili to salad to baked pasta. The thin, delicate skin of delicata squash is edible, and simple rounds make for a breathtaking side when roasted (page 160). Acorn squash is dense and mildly flavored; stuffed with bulgur, it makes a filling vegetarian main (page 68). And we can't forget about pumpkin: Although many people skip straight to using canned puree, if you can get your hands on a fresh sugar pumpkin, be sure to check out chapter 8 (pages 210–227) for recipes.

Cruciferous Vegetables

This category covers a lot of ground, from broccoli and cauliflower to brussels sprouts, kohlrabi, and underappreciated cabbage. Known for giving off a sulfurous aroma when overcooked, when done right these veggies turn tender, nutty, and even sweet. Brussels sprouts are excellent roasted either on their own or in a supporting role in a dish like Za'atar Chicken with Pistachios, Brussels Sprouts, and Pomegranates (page 47). Or, if you'd like to work a vegetable-centered main into your winter diet, try our Roasted Cabbage Wedges with Stewed Tomatoes and Chickpeas (page 69).

Chicories

Bittersweet and beautiful, multicolored chicories, a category that includes radicchio, endive, and escarole, are related to both lettuce and sunflowers and are at their peak in autumn and winter. Whether curly-leafed or flat-leafed, these "greens" take extremely well to intense flavors. Crisp, bitter, purple-red radicchio is great both in fresh wintertime salads like our Citrus and Radicchio Salad with Dates and Smoked Almonds (page 138) and in cooked applications. Pale-green, slightly sharp escarole stars in our hearty, warming Lentil and Escarole Soup (page 30).

Orchard Fruits

For many, autumn brings to mind fond memories of going apple picking with their families. This book includes an entire chapter of apple recipes (pages 188–209) to help you make use of the season's bounty. Pears, another cold season standby, are also prominently featured. Quince, a fruit once commonplace in American kitchens and now sadly less so, is hard, dry, and astringent when raw, but delicious when cooked. Try it in Mulled Wine Quince Pie (page 371).

Citrus Fruits

Winter is when citrus is in season and tastes its best. We use citrus liberally to add a hit of balancing acidity to rich dishes and to bring a taste of sunshine to overcast days. You'll find dozens of recipes that make use of oranges, lemons, and limes throughout this book. Sweet, floral clementines make their way into a tropical fruit salad (page 287) and adorn Clementine Cake (page 351). Tart grapefruit is a key ingredient in a refreshing mocktail (page 262).

PRODUCE PANTRY STAPLES

Canned and Sun-Dried Tomatoes

We make it a point to keep canned and sun-dried tomatoes on hand. These products deliver the fresh taste of peak-season tomatoes and concentrated, chewy bursts of sweet-savory flavor, respectively, and are especially useful in the cold months when most tomatoes are out-of-season and bland.

Unsweetened Canned Pumpkin

Using canned pumpkin puree is a convenient alternative to roasting and pureeing a pumpkin yourself (though if you'd like to try your hand at homemade, see our recipe for Homemade Pumpkin Puree on page 216). This book includes an entire chapter on pumpkin treats (pages 210–227), so you'll want to stay stocked up.

Dried Fruit

We turn to dried apricots frequently to give sunny sweetness to dishes including stews, warm grain salads, and our Apricot and Cherry Modern Fruitcake (page 357). Raisins, dates, dried cherries, and dried cranberries also pop up throughout the book.

Frozen Vegetables and Berries

Small, relatively uniform fruits and vegetables such as peas, corn, and blueberries are flash-frozen at peak ripeness and taste as good as the stuff you'd find at a summer farmers' market. We actually prefer to use frozen pearl onions in dishes like Stifado (page 35), since the frozen kind come prepeeled, cutting down significantly on prep work.

tips for cooking for a crowd

party planning timeline

Finalize Your Guest List and Menu
When Three weeks ahead
What Figure out how many people you'll be feeding and what you'll be feeding them so you can shop accordingly. If you need help deciding what to serve, see our menus on pages 8–11 for inspiration.

Fill Your Freezer and Pantry
When Two weeks ahead
What Stock up on any necessary frozen ingredients, and prepare dishes that can be frozen for long periods. Load up on pantry ingredients like canned pumpkin, chicken broth, sugar, flour, and oil. Finally, replace over-the-hill spices that have lost their strong fragrance.

Hit the Dairy and Produce Aisles
When A week to a few days ahead
What Pick up enough milk, butter, and cream for all your recipes. You can stock up on hardier vegetables such as root vegetables and squash a week in advance, but hold off on delicate produce like herbs until just a few days in advance.

Build In Time to Defrost and Brine or Salt
When One day to one week ahead
What If you're planning to cook turkey, beware: A 20-pound bird can take up to five days to thaw out in the refrigerator. Plan on one day for every 4 pounds of turkey. No matter your choice of protein, always check your recipe to see the recommended brining or salting time, if any, and take this time into account as well.

pack it up, pack it in

Send Them Packing
Send folks home happy by picking up a few packages of inexpensive plastic containers and letting guests fill them up before hitting the road. We like to set out a few stacks of Gladware Deep Dish ($5.97) containers and Ziploc Brand Freezer Bags with Easy Open Tabs ($5.37 for 28 bags) at the end of the meal.

Save Some for Yourself
Half the pleasure of preparing an exceptional feast for friends and family is enjoying the leftovers the next day. Store the extras in OXO Good Grips 8 Cup Smart Seal Rectangle containers ($14.99), which have a tight seal perfect for preserving food in the refrigerator and are safe for reheating in the microwave.

Hosting a large crowd doesn't have to be anxiety-inducing. You just need to know how to prepare. Our number one lesson: The more you can get done in advance, the less you have to worry about when guests arrive.

stress-free hosting hacks

Stir Together a Batch of Cocktails Ahead of Time

The big-batch cocktails in chapter 10 serve from eight to 16 guests, and many can be made ahead of time—some up to a month in advance!

Serve Make-Ahead (or Last-Minute) Appetizers

Throughout the book, we marked recipes "make ahead" if they could be prepared at least 24 hours in advance. Look through our Appetizers and Starters chapter for recipes you can make ahead and forget about. If your guests are due to arrive any second, you can make any of our last-minute appetizers (page 241) in under 30 minutes—most of them in under 15.

Enlist Your Slow Cooker

Many of the dishes in this book can be made in the slow cooker, but did you know that you can also use your slow cooker to keep dishes warm? Sides like mashed potatoes can be kept warm for hours in a slow cooker set on Low; all they need before they're served is a quick stir.

Make Accompaniments in Advance

Accompaniments like vinaigrettes, Simple Cranberry Sauce (page 132), or All-Purpose Gravy (page 135) can often be made several days in advance with no problem. Just store them covered in the refrigerator until they're needed.

6 make-ahead mains for any occasion

These six recipes give you time to focus on making your sides—or to enjoy a laid-back hosting experience.

- **Faster Coq au Vin** (page 80)
- **Pot Roast with Root Vegetables** (page 83)
- **Braised Short Ribs with Daikon and Shiitakes** (page 85)
- **Turkey and Gravy for a Crowd** (page 108)
- **Braised Brisket with Pomegranate, Cumin, and Cilantro** (page 115)
- **Mushroom and Leek Galette with Gorgonzola** (page 126)

5 best uses for leftover turkey

Move over, turkey sandwiches: These five recipes make the most of Turkey Day leftovers.

- **Simple Turkey Stock** (page 33)
- **Turkey Barley Soup** (page 19)
- **Rustic Turkey Tart** (page 51)
- **Double-Crust Turkey Pot Pie** (page 130)
- **Buffalo Turkey Dip** (page 232)

menus

Food-focused gatherings are a mainstay of autumn and winter: Holiday entertaining, family get-togethers, and friendly social events all often center around sharing food with loved ones. To make it easier for you to plan your festivities, we've created menus for occasions spanning from a family dinner by the fire to game day. Of course, these menus are only a glimpse of the endless menu combinations you can create with this book.

Post–Apple Picking Supper
Caraway-Crusted Pork Tenderloin with Sauerkraut and Apples (page 192) ◆ Sautéed Swiss Chard with Currants and Pine Nuts (page 160) ◆ Quinoa Pilaf with Herbs and Lemon (page 171) ◆ Skillet Apple Crisp (page 198)

Fireside Dinner
Make-Ahead Firesides for Four (page 259) ◆ Creamy Chestnut Soup (page 27) ◆ Pan-Roasted Chicken Breasts with Root Vegetables (page 46) ◆ Baked Wild Rice with Almonds and Cranberries (page 168) ◆ Slow-Cooker White Wine–Poached Pears (page 387)

Cozy French Farmhouse Dinner
French Onion Soup (page 24) ◆ Bibb and Frisée Salad with Apple and Celery (page 190) ◆ Chicken in a Pot with Red Potatoes, Carrots, and Shallots (page 82) ◆ Make-Ahead Individual Chocolate Soufflés (page 380)

Festive Italian Dinner
Sicilian Sojourns (page 266) ◆ Roman Braised Oxtails (page 90) ◆ Polenta with Cheese and Butter (page 174) ◆ Roasted Delicata Squash (page 160) ◆ Tiramisu (page 382)

Intimate Winter Dinner Party for Six
Brandied Mulled Cider (page 274) ◆ Pot Roast with Root Vegetables (page 83) ◆ Pan-Roasted Pear Salad with Radicchio, Blue Cheese, and Walnuts (page 141) ◆ Fluffy Dinner Rolls (page 307) ◆ Cranberry-Orange Olive Oil Cake (page 359)

Vegetarian Harvest Dinner
Bulgur-Stuffed Acorn Squash with Ras El Hanout (page 68) ◆ Roasted Kohlrabi with Crunchy Seeds (page 150) ◆ Slow-Cooker Lentil Salad with Dill, Orange, and Spinach (page 182) ◆ Cranberry-Pecan-Stuffed Baked Apples (page 197)

three ways to do thanksgiving

Whether you're looking to shake things up or need a little help in the inspiration department—or maybe you're cooking for a bigger (or smaller) crowd than you have in the past—here are three menus to get you started.

our favorite autumn & winter equipment

The kitchen sees a lot of action in the autumn and winter months. The right equipment will help you make the most of your time, whether you're baking cookies or preparing to host a party. Below are some of our favorite tools for cold-weather cooking.

For Roasting, Braising & Baking

Dutch Oven

Perhaps the most versatile pot in your kitchen, a Dutch oven can be used to braise, roast, and even bake. We've long loved the **Le Creuset 7¼ Quart Round Dutch Oven** as well as our Best Buy, the **Cuisinart Chef's Enameled Cast Iron Casserole**, both of which hold and distribute heat excellently.

Roasting Pan

What's more iconic than a handsome, heavy-duty roasting pan bearing a holiday roast to the table? We like the **Cuisinart MultiClad Pro Stainless 16" Roasting Pan with Rack**. The included roasting rack fits snugly in the roomy pan, great for roasting a side of vegetables beneath your elevated protein.

Slow Cooker

A slow cooker is your secret weapon when you want an easy, hands-off meal or a way to prepare a hot side dish while other cooking appliances are occupied. The **KitchenAid 6-Quart Slow Cooker With Solid Glass Lid** is our favorite thanks to its even cooking and unambiguous controls.

Electric Pressure Cooker

An electric pressure cooker is a powerful tool, capable of getting a good sear on food as well as speeding up cooking with the pressure cook function. We like how easy it is to use the **Instant Pot Pro 8QT** thanks to its streamlined interface with intuitive digital controls.

Carving Board

The trench around a carving board's perimeter captures the juices that leak out when a roast is cut. We love the **J.K. Adams Maple Reversible Carving Board**, which has deep trenches on both sides as well as a poultry-shaped well on one side that's perfect for steadying a turkey during carving.

13 by 9 Broiler-Safe Baking Dish

Whether you're making cheesy baked pasta or a warm-you-from-the-inside-out casserole, a baking dish that can withstand the heat of the broiler is a must-have. We like that **Mrs. Anderson's Baking Lasagna Pan with Handle (Rose)** has large, looped handles that are easy to grab even with bulky oven mitts, and holds enough food to feed a hungry crowd.

Rimmed Baking Sheet

You need a rimmed baking sheet—or better yet, two— for baking cookies, roasting vegetables, and accomplishing a whole host of other kitchen tasks. A sturdy pan that doesn't warp under high heat is best for evenly cooking foods. The **Nordic Ware Baker's Half Sheet** resists warping and is also the perfect size to fit a standard-size wire rack snugly inside.

Loaf Pan

When cool whether hits, baking season begins. Having a couple of loaf pans on hand opens the door to quick breads like pumpkin and banana bread, pound cake, loaves of sandwich bread, and more. For professional-quality, clean-edged baked goods, we like the **USA Pan Loaf Pan, 1 lb Volume**.

Round Cake Pans

Using the right-size cake pan is essential for a well-baked cake. We usually call for either a 9-inch round cake pan or an 8-inch round cake pan. We like both the **Nordic Ware Naturals Nonstick 9" Round Cake Pan** and its smaller sibling, the **Nordic Ware Naturals Nonstick 8" Round Layer Cake Pan**. It's a good idea to keep two pans of each size on hand for making layer cakes.

Pie Plate

It's difficult to make a great pie without a great pie plate—a pie plate's material, thickness, and color all affect the final product. We prefer to use the **Williams-Sonoma Goldtouch Nonstick Pie Dish**. The gold-hued metal plate bakes crusts beautifully without overbrowning them, and its nonfluted lip allows for maximum crust-crimping flexibility.

Handy Tools & Gadgets

Slicing/Carving Knife

If you're spending time and money on a special meal, it's worth getting the right tool to serve it. Slicing knives are long and straight for smooth, even slicing. The **Victorinox Swiss Army 12" Granton Slicing Knife** produces perfect slices of turkey and roast beef every time.

Carving Fork

A carving fork is the best option for holding the turkey or roast firmly in place when slicing meat tableside. We like carving forks with curved prongs, such as the **Mercer Culinary 6-Inch High-Carbon Carving Fork**, which keeps roasts from budging while staying out of the knife's way.

Digital Instant-Read Thermometer

A perfectly cooked protein requires knowing when to stop the cooking—and the best way to pinpoint the precise moment a roast is medium-rare or turkey thighs are cooked through is to use a digital instant-read thermometer like the **Thermoworks Thermapen Mk4**.

Fat Separator

A fat separator makes it easy to defat stocks and pan juices: You just pour in the liquid, wait a few minutes for the fat to rise to the top, and then pour off the liquid. We appreciate the **OXO Good Grips Good Gravy Fat Separator—4 Cup**'s easy-to-read measurement lines and tightly sealed, leak-free bottom release valve.

Potato Masher

Don't wind up serving lumpy mashed potatoes to company. A good potato masher should do its one job really well. The **Zyliss Stainless Steel Potato Masher** produces an ultracreamy, smooth mash thanks to a plethora of small holes on its mashing plate and a long, sturdy handle made of slip-free plastic.

Apple Corer

Planning to bake a whole bushel of apples into a pie or autumnal crisp? An apple corer is the most efficient tool for prepping the fruit. The **Cuisipro Apple Corer**'s large handle, sharp teeth, and wide barrel allows us to push through even large, firm-fleshed apples with ease.

Pie Server

When serving a pie you spent hours baking, you want to ensure that you end up with picturesque, intact pieces. We like using the **OXO SteeL Pie Server** for this task: Its sharp serrated blade is capable of slicing through all types of pie—even through pecan pie—and it slides neatly under the wedges, making removal quick and tidy.

Bar Cart

Cocktail Shaker

A proper cocktail shaker is essential for preparing shaken drinks. Whether you use a cobbler-style shaker or a Boston-style shaker is a matter of preference, as either can make an excellent cocktail. We like both the cobbler-style **Tovolo Stainless Steel 4-in-1 Cocktail Shaker** (pictured) and the Boston-style **The Boston Shaker Professional Boston Shaker, Weighted**.

Hawthorne Strainer

If you use a Boston shaker to make cocktails, you'll need a separate cocktail strainer to hold back the ice, stray herbs, and citrus wedges as you pour. The Hawthorne strainer is the most commonly used type, essentially a slotted and/or perforated disk with a spring that acts as a filter. The **Cocktail Kingdom Koriko Hawthorne Strainer** filters out all but the tiniest bits of pulp and ice.

Citrus Zester/ Channel Knife

A pretty cocktail presentation goes a long way toward securing you the title of Master Mixologist in the eyes of your guests. A citrus zester/channel knife like the **Norpro 113 Grip-EZ Zester and Stripper** is made to neatly cut long, attractive, pith-free strips of zest from all sorts of citrus, perfect for twisting into curls for garnishing drinks.

Barspoon

A barspoon is an essential tool for mixing up a cocktail with style. It's designed for stirring drinks in tall shakers and for fishing garnishes such as olives and cherries out of their narrow jars. The **Cocktail Kingdom Teardrop Barspoon** is just the right length for most cocktail shakers, and its handle is elegantly twisted from top to bottom, making it easy to grip.

Jigger

When mixing up a cocktail, it's important to get the ingredient proportions right. A jigger is a handy tool used to measure small volumes of liquids. We like the beaker-style **OXO Good Grips Angled Measuring Cup, Clear**, which is clearly marked and has a wide mouth that is easy to fill and a small spout that ensures a clean pour every time.

On the Go

Insulated Food Carrier

Winter is potluck season, and that means you need a way to get your contribution from point A to point B hot and in one piece. In our tests, no other food carrier matched the insulating ability of the **Rachael Ray Expandable Lasagna Lugger**, which keeps food ripping hot for more than 3 hours. What's more, it can expand upward to fit two 13 by 9-inch baking dishes.

Pie Carrier

If you're the one responsible for bringing the pie to your family's Thanksgiving celebration, you'd better make sure it arrives intact. The **Prepworks Collapsible Party Carrier** expands to accommodate even the tallest whipped cream– and meringue-laden pies. It even comes with an insert that can be used as a second tier for transporting two shorter pies at once.

Cake Carrier

Safe, secure transport is what cake carriers are all about, allowing you to take your beautifully frosted cake on the road without fear of disaster. We like that the **Progressive Collapsible Cupcake and Cake Carrier** can fit either 9-inch round or square layer cakes or up to 24 cupcakes and collapse for compact storage when not in use thanks to its flexible design.

soups, stews, & chilis

■ MAKE AHEAD ▪ VEGETARIAN
Photo: Slow-Cooker White Chicken Chili

Classic Chicken Noodle Soup

Serves 8 to 10 | **Total Time** 2¼ hours | MAKE AHEAD

WHY THIS RECIPE WORKS This classic rendition of chicken soup starts the old-fashioned way, by making a broth from scratch. Chicken thighs added intense, meaty flavor to the broth and were easier than using a whole chicken. To cut down on greasiness, we removed the skin after browning and before letting the thighs simmer. Since most people prefer white meat in their chicken soup, we simply poached two boneless, skinless chicken breasts in the simmering broth, removing them when tender to shred and add to the soup at the end. With the broth and the meat taken care of, we rounded out our soup with onion, carrot, celery, and some fresh thyme. As for the noodles, cooking them right in the broth intensified their flavor. Note that the thighs are used to flavor the broth, but once the broth is strained, the meat can be shredded and used for chicken salad or a pot pie. If you prefer dark meat in your soup, you can omit the chicken breasts and add the shredded thigh meat to the soup instead.

BROTH

- 4 pounds bone-in, skin-on chicken thighs, trimmed
- ½ teaspoon plus 1 tablespoon table salt, divided
- ¼ teaspoon pepper
- 1 tablespoon vegetable oil
- 1 onion, chopped
- 12 cups water
- 2 bay leaves
- 1 pound boneless, skinless chicken breasts, trimmed

SOUP

- 1 tablespoon vegetable oil
- 1 onion, chopped fine
- 1 carrot, peeled and sliced thin
- 1 celery rib, halved lengthwise and sliced thin
- 2 teaspoons minced fresh thyme or ½ teaspoon dried
- 6 ounces wide egg noodles
- ¼ cup minced fresh parsley

1. FOR THE BROTH Pat thighs dry with paper towels and sprinkle with ½ teaspoon salt and pepper. Heat oil in Dutch oven over medium-high heat until smoking. Cook half of thighs skin side down until deep golden brown, about 6 minutes. Turn thighs and lightly brown second side, about 2 minutes. Transfer to strainer set in large bowl. Repeat with remaining thighs and transfer to strainer; discard fat in bowl. Pour off fat from pot, add onion, and cook over medium heat until just softened, about 3 minutes. Meanwhile, remove and

Classic Chicken Noodle Soup

discard skin from thighs. Add thighs, water, bay leaves, and remaining 1 tablespoon salt to pot. Cover and simmer for 30 minutes. Add chicken breasts and continue simmering until broth is rich and flavorful, about 15 minutes longer.

2. Strain broth into large container, let settle for at least 10 minutes, then skim off fat. Meanwhile, transfer chicken to cutting board to cool. Once cooled, remove thigh meat from bones, shred, and reserve for another use. (Thighs can be refrigerated for up to 2 days or frozen for up to 1 month). Shred breast meat and reserve for soup. (Cooled broth and shredded breast meat can be refrigerated separately for up to 2 days or frozen for up to 1 month before being used to make soup. To avoid soggy noodles and vegetables, finish soup just before you plan on serving it.)

3. FOR THE SOUP Heat oil in now-empty Dutch oven over medium-high heat until shimmering. Add onion, carrot, and celery and cook until onion has softened, 3 to 4 minutes. Stir in thyme and broth and simmer until vegetables are tender, about 15 minutes. Add noodles and shredded breast meat and simmer until noodles are just tender, about 5 minutes. Off heat, stir in parsley and season with salt and pepper to taste. Serve.

Pressure-Cooker Spiced Chicken Soup with Squash and Chickpeas

Serves 6 to 8 | **Total Time** 1½ hours `MAKE AHEAD`

WHY THIS RECIPE WORKS With the help of a pressure cooker, you can have chicken soup with superflavorful homemade broth on the table in an hour and a half of mostly hands-off time. We amped up the flavor of our chicken soup with a spice mix inspired by hararat (also called Libyan five-spice blend, or bzaar), a North African blend of spices such as cumin, coriander, and allspice. Hearty butternut squash cooked to perfection with the chicken under high pressure, and the canned chickpeas were simply warmed through in the finished soup. Chopped cilantro added herbal freshness. To peel a butternut squash, first cut straight across the top and bottom of the squash and then use a sharp vegetable peeler to remove the peel. This recipe will only work in an electric pressure cooker.

- 2 tablespoons extra-virgin olive oil
- 1 onion, chopped
- 1¾ teaspoons table salt
- 2 tablespoons tomato paste
- 4 garlic cloves, minced
- 1 tablespoon ground coriander
- 1½ teaspoons ground cumin
- 1 teaspoon ground cardamom
- ½ teaspoon ground allspice
- ¼ teaspoon cayenne pepper
- 7 cups water, divided
- 2 (12-ounce) bone-in split chicken breasts, trimmed
- 4 (5- to 7-ounce) bone-in chicken thighs, trimmed
- 1½ pounds butternut squash, peeled, seeded, and cut into 1½-inch pieces (4 cups)
- 1 (15-ounce) can chickpeas, rinsed
- ½ cup chopped fresh cilantro

1. Using highest sauté or browning function, heat oil in pressure cooker until shimmering. Add onion and salt and cook until onion is softened, about 5 minutes. Stir in tomato paste, garlic, coriander, cumin, cardamom, allspice, and cayenne and cook until fragrant, about 30 seconds. Stir in 5 cups water, scraping up any browned bits. Nestle chicken breasts and thighs in pot, then arrange squash evenly around chicken.

2. Lock lid in place and close pressure release valve. Select high pressure cook function and cook for 20 minutes. Turn off pressure cooker and quick-release pressure. Carefully remove lid, allowing steam to escape away from you.

3. Transfer chicken to cutting board, let cool slightly, then shred into bite-size pieces using 2 forks; discard skin and bones.

Pressure-Cooker Spiced Chicken Soup with Squash and Chickpeas

4. Using wide, shallow spoon, skim excess fat from surface of soup, then break squash into bite-size pieces. Stir chicken along with any accumulated juices, chickpeas, and remaining 2 cups water into soup and let stand until heated through, about 3 minutes. Stir in cilantro and season with salt and pepper to taste. Serve. (Soup can be refrigerated for up to 3 days and reheated just before serving.)

Turkey Barley Soup

Serves 6 | **Total Time** 1½ hours

WHY THIS RECIPE WORKS Designed to use up leftover meat and highlight the flavor of our homemade turkey stock, this soup is a soul-satisfying way to put those turkey leftovers to use. Along with leftover turkey meat, we included starchy barley for bulk and chew and just a few vegetables: the classic trio of onion, carrot, and celery. Limiting our seasonings to garlic, fresh thyme, a bay leaf, a squeeze of lemon juice, and salt and pepper allowed the pure turkey stock flavor to shine through. If you don't have turkey fat, you can substitute unsalted butter.

- 2 tablespoons turkey fat
- 1 onion, chopped fine
- 2 teaspoons minced fresh thyme or ¾ teaspoon dried
  Pinch red pepper flakes
- 2 garlic cloves, minced
- 8 cups Simple Turkey Stock (page 33)
- ¾ cup pearl barley
- 1 bay leaf
- 2 celery ribs, cut into ¼-inch pieces
- 2 carrots, peeled and cut into ¼-inch pieces
- 2 cups shredded turkey
- 1 tablespoon lemon juice

1. Heat fat in Dutch oven over medium heat until shimmering. Add onion, thyme, and pepper flakes and cook, stirring occasionally, until onion is softened and translucent, about 5 minutes. Add garlic and cook until fragrant, about 1 minute. Add stock, barley, and bay leaf; increase heat to high and bring to simmer. Reduce heat to medium-low and simmer, partially covered, for 15 minutes.

2. Add celery and carrots and simmer, partially covered, until vegetables start to soften, about 15 minutes.

3. Add turkey and cook until barley and vegetables are tender, about 10 minutes. Off heat, stir in lemon juice and season with salt and pepper to taste. Serve.

Turkey Barley Soup

Kimchi, Beef, and Tofu Soup

Serves 4 | **Total Time** 1 hour

WHY THIS RECIPE WORKS This warming, piquant, and deeply savory soup makes deft use of two proteins: Ground beef imbues the broth with tons of meaty flavor, and firm tofu absorbs all the soup's bold flavors and gives it even more staying power. We added complexity and heat with tangy, spicy kimchi, and a dash of the kimchi's brine amped up its presence. Fresh ginger; mirin, a sweet rice wine; and soy sauce gave the broth more depth of flavor and a fantastic aroma. Using chicken broth instead of beef broth here helped support all those savory flavors without overwhelming them. A drizzle of toasted sesame oil lent pleasing nuttiness, and a sprinkling of scallions added some welcome color. If there's not enough brine in the kimchi jar to yield ¼ cup, add water to compensate. Make sure to use firm (not soft) tofu here.

- 1 pound 85 percent lean ground beef
- ½ teaspoon table salt
- ½ teaspoon pepper
- 1 tablespoon grated fresh ginger
- ½ cup mirin
- 3 cups water
- 3 cups kimchi, drained with ¼ cup brine reserved, chopped coarse
- 2 cups chicken broth
- 8 ounces firm tofu, cut into ½-inch pieces
- 2 tablespoons soy sauce
- 4 scallions, sliced thin
- 1 tablespoon toasted sesame oil

1. Combine beef, salt, and pepper in Dutch oven and cook over medium-high heat, breaking up meat with wooden spoon, until moisture evaporates and beef begins to sizzle, 8 to 10 minutes.

2. Add ginger and cook until fragrant, about 30 seconds. Stir in mirin, scraping up any browned bits. Stir in water, kimchi and reserved brine, broth, tofu, and soy sauce and bring to boil. Reduce heat to low, cover, and simmer to allow flavors to meld, about 15 minutes.

3. Off heat, stir in scallions and oil. Serve.

Pressure-Cooker Hawaiian Oxtail Soup

Serves 4 to 6 | **Total Time** 2¼ hours `MAKE AHEAD`

WHY THIS RECIPE WORKS Oxtail soup is a local Hawaiian favorite attributed to the islands' Chinese, Japanese, Okinawan, and Korean populations. One of the most popular versions draws from Cantonese traditions and boasts a clear broth perfumed by ginger and star anise, sweet-pungent chen pi (aged dried citrus peel), and fruity dried jujubes. The heady aromatics provide a counterpoint to the savory wallop of the oxtails, shiitakes, peanuts, and soy sauce. Peppery gai choy, scallions, and fresh cilantro offer bite. The soup's lightness makes it excellent post-holiday fare; our pressure-cooker version saves some time but delivers lots of flavor. Look for oxtails that are approximately 2 inches thick. If certain ingredients are difficult to find, we suggest some substitutes, but the soup's flavor will be less nuanced as a result: You can substitute dry-roasted peanuts for the raw peanuts, four Medjool dates for the jujubes, 1½ tablespoons dried orange peel or three strips fresh orange zest for the chen pi, and 1 pound stemmed American mustard greens for the gai choi. For a complete Hawaiian-style meal, serve with two scoops of white rice. This recipe will only work in an electric pressure cooker.

Pressure-Cooker Hawaiian Oxtail Soup

- 8 ounces fresh ginger, sliced thin, plus 4 tablespoons peeled and grated for serving
- 5 star anise pods
- ¼ ounce chen pi
- 3 pounds oxtails, thawed if frozen, fat trimmed to ¼ inch or less
- 8 cups water
- ½ cup raw peanuts
- 8 dried jujubes
- 1 ounce dried whole shiitake mushrooms, stemmed and rinsed
- ¼ cup soy sauce, plus extra for serving
- ½ teaspoon table salt
- 1 pound gai choy, trimmed and cut into 2-inch pieces
- 1 cup fresh cilantro leaves
- 4 scallions, sliced thin on bias

1. Bundle sliced ginger, star anise, and chen pi in single layer of cheesecloth and secure with kitchen twine. Add cheesecloth bundle, oxtails, water, peanuts, jujubes, mushrooms, soy sauce, and salt to pressure cooker.

2. Lock lid into place and close pressure release valve. Select high pressure cook function and cook for 60 minutes. Turn off pressure cooker and let pressure release naturally for 30 minutes. Quick-release any remaining pressure, then carefully remove lid, allowing steam to escape away from you.

3. Discard cheesecloth bundle. Using slotted spoon, transfer oxtails, peanuts, and mushrooms to large bowl, tent with aluminum foil, and let rest while finishing soup. Strain broth through fine-mesh strainer into separate large bowl or container, pressing on solids to extract as much liquid as possible; discard solids. Let broth settle for 5 minutes, then, using wide, shallow spoon or ladle, skim excess fat from surface. (Broth and oxtails, peanuts, and mushrooms can be refrigerated separately for up to 4 days. Reheat oxtail mixture in simmering broth before adding gai choy in step 4.)

4. Return defatted broth to now-empty pot. Using highest sauté or browning function, bring broth to simmer, then turn off pressure cooker. Stir in gai choy and cooked, using residual heat, until wilted, about 3 minutes. Season with soy sauce to taste.

5. Thinly slice mushrooms, if desired. Divide oxtails, peanuts, and mushrooms among individual bowls, then ladle hot broth and greens over top. Sprinkle evenly with cilantro and scallions. Serve, passing grated fresh ginger and extra soy sauce separately.

Harira

Miso Soup with Halibut

Harira

Serves 8 | **Total Time** 1¾ hours `MAKE AHEAD`

WHY THIS RECIPE WORKS Harira is an intensely flavored Moroccan soup of lentils, tomatoes, chickpeas, and often chicken or lamb. To make our version we chose lamb shoulder chops as our protein, and, after browning them, we bloomed our aromatics in the rendered fat they left behind. We began with minced onion, next adding a fragrant and warming combination of fresh ginger, cumin, paprika, cinnamon, cayenne, saffron, and black pepper. The result was a sweet, smoky, deeply flavorful base with just a touch of heat. Harissa, a superspicy paste of hot chiles, spices, garlic, and olive oil, is a critical finishing touch to every harira recipe; for the best and most potent flavor, we made our own. Large green or brown lentils work well in this recipe; do not use lentilles du Puy (French green lentils). We prefer to use our homemade Harissa (page 101), but you can substitute store-bought harissa if you wish, though spiciness can vary greatly by brand.

- 1 pound lamb shoulder chops (blade or round bone), 1 to 1½ inches thick, trimmed and halved
- ½ teaspoon table salt
- ½ teaspoon pepper, divided
- 1 tablespoon extra-virgin olive oil
- 1 onion, chopped fine
- 1 teaspoon grated fresh ginger
- 1 teaspoon ground cumin
- ½ teaspoon paprika
- ¼ teaspoon ground cinnamon
- ¼ teaspoon cayenne pepper
  Pinch saffron threads, crumbled
- 1 tablespoon all-purpose flour
- 10 cups chicken broth
- ¾ cup green or brown lentils, picked over and rinsed
- 1 (15-ounce) can chickpeas, rinsed
- 4 plum tomatoes, cored and cut into ¾-inch pieces
- ⅓ cup minced fresh cilantro
- ¼ cup harissa, plus extra for serving

1. Adjust oven rack to lower-middle position and heat oven to 325 degrees. Pat lamb dry with paper towels and sprinkle with salt and ¼ teaspoon pepper. Heat oil in Dutch oven over medium-high heat until just smoking. Brown lamb, about 4 minutes per side; transfer to plate. Pour off all but 2 tablespoons fat from pot.

2. Add onion to fat left in pot and cook over medium heat until softened, about 5 minutes. Stir in ginger, cumin, paprika, cinnamon, cayenne, saffron, and remaining ¼ teaspoon pepper and cook until fragrant, about 30 seconds. Stir in flour and cook for 1 minute. Slowly whisk in broth, scraping up any browned bits and smoothing out any lumps, and bring to boil.

3. Nestle lamb into pot along with any accumulated juices, bring to simmer, and cook for 10 minutes. Stir in lentils and chickpeas, cover, and place pot in oven. Cook until fork slips easily in and out of lamb and lentils are tender, 50 minutes to 1 hour.

4. Transfer lamb to cutting board, let cool slightly, then shred into bite-size pieces using 2 forks, discarding excess fat and bones. Stir shredded lamb into soup and let sit until heated through, about 2 minutes. Stir in tomatoes, cilantro, and harissa and season with salt and pepper to taste. Serve, passing extra harissa separately. (Soup can be refrigerated for up to 3 days and reheated just before serving.)

NOTES FROM THE TEST KITCHEN

STORING AND REHEATING SOUPS, STEWS, AND CHILIS

As tempting as it might seem, do not transfer hot foods straight to the refrigerator. This can increase the fridge's internal temperature to unsafe levels, which is dangerous for all the other food stored there. Letting the pot cool on the countertop for an hour helps its temperature drop to about 75 degrees, at which point you can transfer it safely to the fridge.

To reheat soups, stews, and chilis, we prefer to simmer them gently on the stovetop in a heavy-bottomed pot, but a spin in the microwave works, too. Just be sure to cover the dish to prevent a mess. And note that while most soups, stews, and chilis freeze just fine, those that contain dairy or pasta do not—the dairy curdles as it freezes, and the pasta turns bloated and mushy. Instead, make and freeze the dish without including the dairy or pasta. After thawing the soup, stew, or chili, and heating it through, stir in the uncooked pasta and simmer until just tender, or stir in the dairy and continue to heat gently until hot (do not boil).

Miso Soup with Halibut

Serves 4 | **Total Time** 1¼ hours MAKE AHEAD

WHY THIS RECIPE WORKS Miso soup is a classic Japanese warmer made with its namesake fermented soybean paste that's mixed into dashi, a traditional stock made from dried kelp (kombu) and flakes of shaved, dried, and smoked bonito (a fish in the tuna family). Unlike many other stocks that require long simmering, this stock comes together in a matter of minutes. Miso soup can have a variety of additions, most traditionally tofu and wakame (a type of seaweed) but also seafood and vegetables, like our version with tender, delicately flavored halibut, crisp-tender carrots, and barely wilted spinach. Incorporating the carrots into the broth with the halibut allowed them to both cook through sufficiently, while adding the miso and spinach just before serving preserved the miso's unique sweet-salty flavor and the spinach's freshness. Ladling the finished broth over portions of halibut wasn't just practical—it was an impressive presentation. Drizzle individual servings with sesame oil or chili oil, or sprinkle with crumbled nori or furikake (a fundamental Japanese seasoning blend of dried seaweed, bonito flakes, sesame seeds, sugar, and salt) for additional texture and flavor, if desired.

DASHI
- 6 cups water
- ½ ounce kombu
- 1½ cups dried bonito flakes

SOUP
- 1 tablespoon vegetable oil
- 3 scallions, white and green parts separated and sliced thin
- 1 tablespoon grated fresh ginger
- 3 garlic cloves, minced
- 2 carrots, peeled, halved lengthwise and sliced thin on bias
- 4 (6- to 8-ounce) skinless halibut fillets, 1 inch thick
- ⅓ cup white miso
- 3 ounces (3 cups) baby spinach
- 1 tablespoon sesame seeds, toasted

1. FOR THE DASHI Bring water and kombu to rapid simmer in large saucepan over medium heat. Turn off heat and discard kombu, then stir in bonito flakes and let stand to infuse flavor, about 5 minutes. Strain dashi through fine-mesh strainer, pressing on solids to extract liquid, then return dashi to saucepan. (You should have about 5½ cups dashi. Cooled dashi can be refrigerated for up to 2 days.)

2. FOR THE SOUP Heat oil in Dutch oven over medium heat until shimmering, then add scallion whites, ginger, and garlic and cook until fragrant, about 30 seconds. Add carrots and dashi to pot and bring to simmer.

3. Submerge halibut in dashi and return to simmer. Reduce heat to medium-low, cover, and gently simmer until fish flakes apart when gently prodded with paring knife and registers 130 degrees, 6 to 8 minutes. Transfer halibut to individual serving bowls.

4. Whisk miso into dashi in pot and bring to simmer. Add spinach and cook until wilted, 15 to 30 seconds. Remove from heat, then ladle soup over halibut in bowls. Sprinkle with scallion greens and sesame seeds and serve.

Rich and Velvety Shrimp Bisque

Serves 6 | **Total Time** 1½ hours

WHY THIS RECIPE WORKS This luxurious soup is pure elegance; its silky texture is interrupted only by tender pieces of sweet poached shrimp. For an incomparable base of shrimp flavor, we ground the shrimp shells with half the shrimp, cooked them with the aromatics, simmered them, and then strained them from a broth of clam juice, wine, and tomatoes. Adding the remaining shrimp at the last minute quickly cooked them to plump, juicy perfection. Before flambéing, roll up long sleeves, tie back long hair, and turn off the exhaust fan and lit burners; use a long match or wooden skewer.

  2 pounds large shrimp (26 to 30 per pound), divided
  2 tablespoons vegetable oil
  ⅓ cup brandy or cognac
  1 onion, chopped coarse
  1 carrot, peeled and chopped coarse
  1 celery rib, chopped coarse
  1 garlic clove, peeled
  2 tablespoons unsalted butter
  ½ cup all-purpose flour
  1½ cups dry white wine
  4 (8-ounce) bottles clam juice
  1 (14.5-ounce) can diced tomatoes, drained
  1 cup heavy cream
  1 tablespoon lemon juice
  1 small sprig fresh tarragon
     Pinch ground cayenne
  2 tablespoons dry sherry or Madeira
  2 tablespoons minced fresh chives

1. Peel and devein 1 pound shrimp, reserving shells, and cut each shrimp into 3 pieces; refrigerate until needed.

2. Heat oil in 12-inch skillet over medium-high heat until just smoking. Add remaining 1 pound shrimp and reserved shrimp shells and cook until lightly browned, 3 to 5 minutes. Off heat, add brandy and let warm through, about 5 seconds. Wave lit match over skillet until brandy ignites, then shake pan to distribute flames.

3. When flames subside, transfer shrimp mixture to food processor and process until mixture resembles fine meal, 10 to 20 seconds. Transfer to bowl. Pulse onion, carrot, celery, and garlic in now-empty food processor until finely chopped, about 5 pulses.

4. Melt butter in Dutch oven over medium heat. Add processed shrimp and vegetables, cover, and cook until softened and fragrant, 5 to 7 minutes. Stir in flour and cook for 1 minute.

5. Slowly whisk in wine and clam juice, scraping up any browned bits and smoothing out any lumps. Stir in tomatoes and bring to boil. Reduce heat to medium-low and simmer gently until thickened and flavors meld, about 20 minutes. Strain broth through fine-mesh strainer, pressing on solids to extract as much liquid as possible. Wipe out pot with paper towels.

6. Combine strained broth, cream, lemon juice, tarragon sprig, and cayenne in pot and bring to simmer. Stir in reserved shrimp pieces and gently simmer until shrimp are bright pink, 1 to 2 minutes. Off heat, discard tarragon sprig, stir in sherry, and season with salt and pepper to taste. Sprinkle individual portions with chives before serving.

French Onion Soup

Serves 6 | **Total Time** 2¼ hours **MAKE AHEAD**

WHY THIS RECIPE WORKS The key to this bistro classic is a shortcut-free, hour-long caramelization of the onions. We cooked a mountain of sliced onions covered at first to trap steam and soften them, and then we removed the lid to allow the released liquid to evaporate. Deglazing the pot with wine ensured that all the flavorful browned bits ended up in the soup. Be patient when caramelizing the onions; the entire process takes 55 to 70 minutes. If you don't have ovensafe soup crocks, form six individual piles of croutons on a baking sheet, cover them with the cheese, and broil them on the middle oven rack until the cheese is melted, 1 to 3 minutes. Then use a spatula to transfer the crouton portions to the individual filled soup bowls.

4   tablespoons unsalted butter
4   pounds onions, halved and sliced thin
1¾ teaspoons table salt, divided
1   teaspoon sugar
1   cup dry red wine
8   cups beef broth
4   sprigs fresh thyme
2   bay leaves
¾   teaspoon pepper, divided
6   ounces baguette, cut into 1-inch cubes
3   tablespoons extra-virgin olive oil
8   ounces Gruyère cheese, shredded (2 cups)
1½ ounces Parmesan cheese, shredded (½ cup)

1. Melt butter in Dutch oven over medium-high heat. Stir in onions, 1 teaspoon salt, and sugar. Cover and cook, stirring occasionally, until onions release their liquid and are uniformly translucent, about 20 minutes.

2. Uncover and cook until liquid has evaporated, and browned bits start to form on bottom of pot, 5 to 10 minutes. Reduce heat to medium and continue to cook, uncovered, until onions are caramel colored, 30 to 40 minutes, stirring and scraping with wooden spoon as browned bits form on bottom of pot and spreading onions into even layer after stirring. (If onions or browned bits begin to scorch, reduce heat to medium-low.)

3. Stir in wine, scraping up any browned bits, and cook until nearly evaporated, about 1 minute. Stir in broth, thyme sprigs, bay leaves, ½ teaspoon pepper, and ½ teaspoon salt. Increase heat to high and bring to boil. Reduce heat to medium-low and simmer, uncovered, for 30 minutes. (Soup can be refrigerated for up to 3 days. To reheat, bring soup, covered, to gentle simmer, stirring often, and continue with step 4.)

4. While onions simmer, adjust oven rack to middle position and heat oven to 350 degrees. Toss baguette, oil, remaining ¼ teaspoon salt, and remaining ¼ teaspoon pepper together in bowl. Transfer to rimmed baking sheet and bake until golden and crisp, 15 to 18 minutes. Remove sheet from oven and set aside. Increase oven temperature to 500 degrees.

5. Set six 12-ounce ovensafe crocks on second rimmed baking sheet. Discard thyme sprigs and bay leaves and season soup with salt and pepper to taste. Divide soup evenly among crocks (about 1½ cups each). Divide 1 cup Gruyère evenly among crocks, top with croutons, and sprinkle with remaining Gruyère, then Parmesan. Bake until cheeses are melted and soup is bubbly around edges, 5 to 7 minutes. Let cool for 5 minutes before serving.

French Onion Soup

BROWNING ONIONS

Getting Started
Place sliced onions in pot with butter, salt, and sugar. Cover and cook over medium-high heat. After about 20 minutes, once onions have released most of their liquid, remove lid and turn down heat to medium.

After 55 to 70 Minutes
Periodically scrape fond from bottom of pot. After about 1 hour, fully caramelized onions should be soft, sticky, and deep brown.

Creamless Creamy Tomato Soup

Creamy Chestnut Soup

Creamless Creamy Tomato Soup

Serves 6 to 8 | **Total Time** 50 minutes

MAKE AHEAD VEGETARIAN

WHY THIS RECIPE WORKS Creamy, comforting tomato soup is a rainy-day favorite. To give our creamless soup some body, we blended white sandwich bread into our tomato base. Make sure to purchase canned whole tomatoes in juice, not in puree. If half of the soup fills your blender by more than two-thirds, process the soup in three batches. For an even smoother soup, pass the pureed mixture through a fine-mesh strainer after blending it. To make this dish vegetarian, use vegetable broth. Serve with Classic Croutons (page 28), if desired.

¼ cup extra-virgin olive oil, divided, plus extra
   for serving
1 onion, chopped fine
3 garlic cloves, minced
1 bay leaf
   Pinch red pepper flakes (optional)
2 (28-ounce) cans whole peeled tomatoes
3 slices hearty white sandwich bread, crusts removed,
   torn into 1-inch pieces
1 tablespoon packed brown sugar
2 cups vegetable or chicken broth
2 tablespoons brandy (optional)
¼ cup minced fresh chives

1. Heat 2 tablespoons oil in Dutch oven over medium-high heat until shimmering. Add onion; garlic; bay leaf; and pepper flakes, if using, and cook until onion is softened, about 5 minutes. Stir in tomatoes and their juice. Using potato masher, mash tomatoes until no pieces bigger than 2 inches remain. Stir in bread and sugar and bring to boil. Reduce heat to medium and cook, stirring occasionally, until bread is completely saturated and starts to break down, about 5 minutes. Discard bay leaf.

2. Transfer half of soup to blender. Add 1 tablespoon oil and process until soup is smooth and creamy, 2 to 3 minutes. Transfer to large bowl and repeat with remaining soup and remaining 1 tablespoon oil. Return pureed soup to clean pot. (Soup can be refrigerated for up to 3 days or frozen for up to 1 month. If frozen, thaw completely in refrigerator. To reheat, bring soup, covered, to gentle simmer, whisking often and adjust consistency with hot water as needed and continue with step 3.)

3. Stir in broth and brandy, if using. Return soup to boil and season with salt and pepper to taste. Serve, sprinkling individual bowls with chives and drizzling with extra oil.

Creamy Chestnut Soup

Serves 6 | **Total Time** 1½ hours `MAKE AHEAD`

WHY THIS RECIPE WORKS Earthy, nutty, and silky, chestnut soup is a perfect starter for a cozy winter meal next to a roaring fire. For a supersmooth texture, we simmered chestnuts, leeks, pear, celery, and thyme until they were completely tender before pureeing them. Half-and-half gave the soup just the right amount of creaminess and fat. The sweet pear complemented the subtle sweetness of the chestnuts, and a splash of sherry vinegar brightened the soup. If the soup seems too thick, add extra half-and-half to reach the desired consistency. We prefer our Classic Chicken Stock (page 33) here. If you use store-bought, choose a low-sodium chicken broth.

1 tablespoon unsalted butter
12 ounces leeks, white and light green parts only, halved lengthwise, sliced thin, and washed thoroughly
1 ripe Bartlett or Bosc pear, peeled, halved, cored, and chopped
1 celery rib, chopped
1 teaspoon minced fresh thyme or ¼ teaspoon dried
1 bay leaf
1 teaspoon table salt, divided
4 cups chicken broth
3 cups (14 ounces) peeled cooked chestnuts, chopped
¾ cup half-and-half
2 tablespoons brandy or cognac
½ teaspoon sherry vinegar
Pinch ground nutmeg
¼ teaspoon pepper
¼ cup minced fresh chives

1. Melt butter in large saucepan over medium heat. Add leeks, pear, celery, thyme, bay leaf, and ½ teaspoon salt and cook until leeks just begin to soften, about 3 minutes. Reduce heat to low, cover, and continue to cook, stirring occasionally, until leeks and pear are soft, about 8 minutes.

2. Stir in broth and chestnuts and bring to boil over high heat. Reduce heat to medium-low, cover, and simmer until chestnuts are very tender, about 20 minutes. Discard bay leaf.

3. Working in batches, process soup in blender until very smooth, 30 to 60 seconds per batch. (Alternatively, blend with immersion blender until smooth, about 2 minutes.)

4. Transfer soup to clean saucepan. Stir in half-and-half, brandy, vinegar, nutmeg, pepper, and remaining ½ teaspoon salt. Bring to simmer over medium heat. Season with salt and pepper to taste. (Soup can be refrigerated for up to 3 days and reheated just before serving.) Serve, sprinkled with chives.

Pureed Carrot Soup with Nutmeg

Serves 4 to 6 | **Total Time** 1¼ hours
`MAKE AHEAD` `VEGETARIAN`

WHY THIS RECIPE WORKS We wanted a no-cream carrot soup recipe that produced a smooth and silky soup really tasting like vegetables. Most of the vegetable soup recipes we consulted used equal amounts of vegetables and liquid; in a few cases, there was slightly more liquid than vegetables. We decided to alter this ratio in a big way and cook 4 cups of vegetables in 2 cups of broth. This brought about immediate improvement. By the time the vegetables had cooked, the mixture was thick enough to create a puree with good body. Instead of adding cream to the vegetables as they cooked, we added whole milk to the blender to thin out the puree. This provided just the right amount of dairy fat to provide a smooth and creamy texture without blocking out the vegetable flavor. To make this dish vegetarian, use vegetable broth.

2 tablespoons unsalted butter, vegetable oil, or extra-virgin olive oil
1 onion, 3 shallots, or 1 leek (white and light green parts only), chopped
2 tablespoons dry sherry or white wine
1½ pounds carrots, peeled, halved lengthwise, and sliced thin (about 4 cups)
2 cups vegetable or chicken broth
1 teaspoon table salt
Pinch ground nutmeg
1–1¼ cups whole milk
2 teaspoons minced fresh tarragon, mint, chives, or parsley

1. Melt butter in large saucepan over medium-high heat. Add onion and cook until golden, about 5 minutes. Add sherry and carrots and cook, stirring constantly, until sherry evaporates, about 30 seconds.

2. Add broth, salt, pepper to taste, and nutmeg to saucepan and bring to boil. Reduce heat to simmer, cover and cook until carrots are tender, about 20 minutes.

3. Working in batches, process soup and 1 cup milk in blender until very smooth, 30 to 60 seconds per batch. Return soup to saucepan and cook over low heat until warmed through. If soup is too thick, stir in additional milk to thin consistency. Season with salt and pepper to taste. (Soup can be refrigerated for up to 3 days and reheated just before serving.)

4. Ladle soup into individual bowls. Garnish with minced herbs and serve immediately.

Red Lentil and Squash Soup

Serves 4 | Total Time 1¼ hours

MAKE AHEAD VEGETARIAN

WHY THIS RECIPE WORKS Red lentils cook quickly and disintegrate completely, giving our butternut squash soup velvety body after only a brief simmer. Roasting the squash brought out its sweetness; blooming aromatics and chili powder in oil while the squash roasted deepened the soup's flavor and gave it a pleasantly pronounced spicy kick. A slightly thinned yogurt sauce offered a cooling counterpoint to the soup's heat. To make this dish vegetarian, use vegetable broth. Serve with Classic Croutons (recipe follows), if desired.

2	pounds butternut squash, peeled, seeded, and cut into 1-inch pieces (6 cups)
¼	cup extra-virgin olive oil, divided, plus extra for drizzling
2	teaspoons chili powder, divided, plus extra for serving
1¼	teaspoons table salt, divided
½	teaspoon pepper, divided
1	large shallot, sliced thin
3	garlic cloves, sliced thin
5	cups vegetable or chicken broth
1	cup dried red lentils, picked over and rinsed
¼	cup plain Greek yogurt

1. Adjust oven rack to lower-middle position and heat oven to 425 degrees. Toss squash, 1 tablespoon oil, ½ teaspoon chili powder, ½ teaspoon salt, and ¼ teaspoon pepper together on rimmed baking sheet. Roast until squash is well browned and tender, about 25 minutes.

2. Meanwhile, heat 2 tablespoons oil in Dutch oven over medium heat until shimmering. Add shallot and garlic and cook until lightly browned, about 5 minutes. Add remaining 1½ teaspoons chili powder and cook until fragrant, about 30 seconds. Stir in broth, lentils, ½ teaspoon salt, and remaining ¼ teaspoon pepper and bring to boil. Reduce heat to low; cover; and simmer until lentils are completely broken down, about 15 minutes.

3. Stir squash into lentil mixture; blend soup using immersion blender until smooth (add up to 1 tablespoon water as needed to thin soup). Season with salt and pepper to taste. (Soup can be refrigerated for up to 2 days. Reheat over medium-low heat.) Remove from heat and cover to keep warm. Combine yogurt, 1 tablespoon water, remaining 1 tablespoon oil, and remaining ¼ teaspoon salt in small bowl. Serve soup dolloped with yogurt sauce, sprinkled with extra chili powder, and drizzled with extra oil.

Classic Croutons

Makes 3 cups | Total Time 50 minutes

Stale bread is easier to cut and crisps more quickly in the oven, but either fresh or stale bread can be used.

6	slices hearty white sandwich bread, crusts removed, cut into ½-inch pieces (3 cups)
3	tablespoons unsalted butter, melted, or extra-virgin olive oil

Adjust oven rack to middle position and heat oven to 350 degrees. Toss bread with melted butter, season with salt and pepper to taste, and spread on rimmed baking sheet. Bake until croutons are golden brown and crispy, 20 to 25 minutes, stirring halfway through baking. Let cool before serving. (Croutons can be stored at room temperature for up to 3 days.)

Sweet Potato and Peanut Soup

Serves 4 to 6 | Total Time 1¼ hours

MAKE AHEAD VEGETARIAN

WHY THIS RECIPE WORKS This soup puts sweet potatoes center stage. Onion and garlic offered aromatic backbone; using butter instead of oil to sauté them brought out the alliums' sweet, nutty notes. Creamy peanut butter packed a flavor punch and gave the soup a smoother, more luxurious texture than simply pureeing peanuts into the soup did. We opted for a combination of vegetable broth and water to give the soup a bit of savoriness without overpowering the other flavors. A simple combination of slightly floral coriander and spicy cayenne complemented the sweet potato and brought all the flavors into focus. A bit of fresh cilantro offered bright freshness. This recipe was developed with standard sweet potatoes (called Beauregards), but Jewel and Red Garnet sweet potatoes also work well. Do stick with the orange-fleshed varieties; white- or purple-fleshed sweet potatoes, in conjunction with the peanut butter, will blend to an unappetizing color. For a spicier soup, use the larger amount of cayenne.

2	tablespoons unsalted butter
1	onion, chopped fine
1	teaspoon packed light brown sugar
1	teaspoon table salt

3 garlic cloves, minced

½ teaspoon ground coriander

⅛–¼ teaspoon cayenne pepper

2 pounds sweet potatoes, peeled, quartered lengthwise, and sliced thin

3½ cups vegetable broth, plus extra as needed

2 cups water

3 tablespoons creamy peanut butter

½ cup unsalted dry-roasted peanuts

¼ cup minced fresh cilantro

1. Melt butter in Dutch oven over medium heat. Add onion, sugar, and salt and cook until onion is softened, about 5 minutes. Stir in garlic, coriander, and cayenne and cook until fragrant, about 30 seconds.

2. Add potatoes, broth, water, and peanut butter and bring to simmer. Reduce heat to low, partially cover, and cook until potatoes are tender, 25 to 30 minutes.

3. Working in batches, process soup in blender until smooth, 1 to 2 minutes, then return to clean pot. (Soup can be refrigerated for up to 2 days. Reheat over medium-low heat.)

4. Adjust consistency as needed with extra hot broth. Season with salt and pepper to taste. Sprinkle individual portions with peanuts and cilantro. Serve.

Wild Rice and Mushroom Soup

Serves 6 to 8 | **Total Time** 1¾ hours VEGETARIAN

WHY THIS RECIPE WORKS Supremely comforting, this substantial and hearty—but not heavy—creamy soup is full of earthy, nutty, umami-rich depth thanks to the addition of two kinds of mushrooms. Chewy, nutty wild rice is classically complemented by fresh cremini mushrooms and, for a dose of potent, superconcentrated mushroom flavor, dried shiitake mushrooms. Grinding the shiitakes to a powder ensured that their flavor completely permeated the broth. Simmering the wild rice with baking soda decreased its cooking time by helping break down its tough exterior. We used the rice simmering liquid as the broth for our soup, thus infusing the entire soup with robust wild rice flavor. Some cream stirred in at the end gave the broth a velvety texture and rich mouthfeel. We finished the soup with chives and lemon zest for brightness. We used a spice grinder to process the dried shiitakes, but a blender also works. To make this dish vegetarian, use vegetable broth.

Sweet Potato and Peanut Soup

Wild Rice and Mushroom Soup

¼ ounce dried shiitake mushrooms, rinsed

5 garlic cloves, peeled (1 whole, 4 minced)

1 sprig fresh thyme

1 bay leaf

1½ teaspoons table salt, divided

¼ teaspoon baking soda

1 cup wild rice

4 tablespoons unsalted butter

1 pound cremini mushrooms, trimmed and sliced ¼ inch thick

1 onion, chopped fine

1 teaspoon tomato paste

1 teaspoon pepper

⅔ cup dry sherry

4 cups vegetable or chicken broth

1 tablespoon soy sauce

¼ cup cornstarch

½ cup heavy cream

¼ cup minced fresh chives

¼ teaspoon grated lemon zest

1. Adjust oven rack to middle position and heat oven to 375 degrees. Grind shiitake mushrooms in spice grinder until finely ground (you should have about 3 tablespoons).

2. Bring 4 cups water, whole garlic clove, thyme sprig, bay leaf, ¾ teaspoon salt, and baking soda to boil in medium saucepan over high heat. Add rice and return to boil. Cover, transfer to oven, and bake until rice is tender, 35 to 50 minutes. Strain rice through fine-mesh strainer set in 4-cup liquid measuring cup. Discard garlic, thyme sprig, and bay leaf and set aside rice. Add enough water to reserved cooking liquid to measure 3 cups.

3. Melt butter in Dutch oven over high heat. Add cremini mushrooms, onion, tomato paste, pepper, minced garlic, and remaining ¾ teaspoon salt. Cook, stirring occasionally, until vegetables are browned and dark fond develops on bottom of pot, about 15 minutes. Stir in sherry, scraping up any browned bits, and cook until pot is almost dry, about 2 minutes. Stir in ground shiitake mushrooms, reserved rice cooking liquid, broth, and soy sauce and bring to boil. Reduce heat to low and simmer, covered, until onion and mushrooms are tender, about 20 minutes.

4. Whisk cornstarch with ¼ cup water in small bowl until cornstarch is dissolved. Stir cornstarch mixture into soup, return to simmer, and cook until thickened, about 2 minutes. Off heat, stir in cooked rice, cream, chives, and lemon zest. Cover and let stand for 20 minutes. Season with salt and pepper to taste. Serve.

Lentil and Escarole Soup

Serves 6 | **Total Time** 1¾ hours VEGETARIAN

WHY THIS RECIPE WORKS Tiny, deep green, and fragrant, Umbrian lentils are considered some of the world's best. Soup made with them is a favorite wintertime primo, or first course. Because Umbrian lentils hold their shape particularly well during cooking, the soup remains brothy rather than thick and creamy. As our supporting ingredients, we particularly liked hearty escarole and diced tomatoes. Adding the escarole toward the end of cooking allowed the leaves to retain some of their character. Finally, adding a rind of Parmesan to the simmering soup gave the broth a supersavory backbone. Umbrian lentils are our preferred choice for this recipe, but brown lentils are fine, too (note that cooking time will vary).

¼ cup extra-virgin olive oil, plus extra for drizzling

1 onion, chopped fine

1 carrot, peeled and chopped fine

1 celery rib, chopped fine

½ teaspoon table salt

6 garlic cloves, sliced thin

2 tablespoons minced fresh parsley

4 cups vegetable broth, plus extra as needed

3 cups water

8 ounces (1¼ cups) Umbrian lentils, picked over and rinsed

1 (14.5-ounce) can diced tomatoes

1 Parmesan cheese rind (optional), plus grated Parmesan for serving

2 bay leaves

½ head escarole (8 ounces), trimmed and cut into ½-inch pieces

1. Heat oil in Dutch oven over medium heat until shimmering. Add onion, carrot, celery, and salt and cook until softened and lightly browned, 8 to 10 minutes. Stir in garlic and parsley and cook until fragrant, about 30 seconds. Stir in broth; water; lentils; tomatoes and their juice; Parmesan rind, if using; and bay leaves and bring to simmer. Reduce heat to medium-low and cover, leaving lid slightly ajar. Simmer until lentils are tender, 1 to 1¼ hours.

2. Discard Parmesan rind, if using, and bay leaves. Stir in escarole, 1 handful at a time, and cook until wilted, about 5 minutes. Adjust consistency with extra hot broth as needed. Season with salt and pepper to taste. Drizzle individual portions with extra oil and serve, passing grated Parmesan separately.

Lentil and Escarole Soup

Beet and Wheat Berry Soup with Dill Cream

Serves 6 | **Total Time** 1¾ hours VEGETARIAN

WHY THIS RECIPE WORKS For a lighter, fresh soup inspired by borscht—one that highlighted the flavor of the beets—we used vegetable broth and swapped out starchy potatoes for wheat berries. Toasting the wheat berries gave them a rich, nutty flavor and a pleasant chewy consistency in the soup. To build a flavorful backbone, we sautéed onion, garlic, thyme, and tomato paste before stirring in the broth. Red wine vinegar, red cabbage, and a pinch of cayenne helped to round out the flavor of the beets as well. A dollop of≈ dill-flecked sour cream to finish added tang. You can use the large holes of a box grater or a food processor fitted with a shredding disk to shred the beets and carrot. Do not use presteamed or quick-cooking wheat berries here, as they have a much shorter cooking time; read the package carefully to determine what kind of wheat berries you are using.

DILL CREAM
½ cup sour cream
¼ cup minced fresh dill
½ teaspoon table salt

SOUP
⅔ cup wheat berries, rinsed
3 tablespoons vegetable oil
2 onions, chopped fine
2 tablespoons tomato paste
4 garlic cloves, minced
1 teaspoon minced fresh thyme or ¼ teaspoon dried
¼ teaspoon cayenne pepper
8 cups vegetable broth
3 cups water
1½ cups thinly sliced red cabbage
1 pound beets, trimmed, peeled, and shredded
1 small carrot, peeled and shredded
1 bay leaf
¾ teaspoon pepper
1 tablespoon red wine vinegar
1 teaspoon table salt

1. FOR THE DILL CREAM Combine all ingredients in bowl; refrigerate until ready to serve.

2. FOR THE SOUP Toast wheat berries in Dutch oven over medium heat, stirring often, until fragrant and beginning to darken, about 5 minutes; transfer to bowl.

3. Heat oil in now-empty pot over medium heat until shimmering. Add onions and cook until softened, about 5 minutes. Stir in tomato paste, garlic, thyme, and cayenne and cook until fragrant and darkened slightly, about 2 minutes.

4. Stir in broth, water, cabbage, beets, carrot, bay leaf, pepper, and wheat berries, scraping up any browned bits, and bring to boil. Reduce heat to low and simmer until wheat berries are tender but still chewy and vegetables are tender, 45 minutes to 1¼ hours.

5. Off heat, discard bay leaf and stir in vinegar and salt. Season with additional salt and pepper to taste. Serve, passing dill cream separately.

Chicken and Dumplings

Serves 6 to 8 | **Total Time** 2¼ hours MAKE AHEAD

WHY THIS RECIPE WORKS Full of succulent chicken, creamy broth, and tender biscuits, chicken and dumplings is a rightful cornerstone of American comfort food. Our version is quick but no less satisfying. Replacing the whole chicken (which must be cut up into parts) with boneless, skinless breasts was a good start. To ensure that the meat stayed moist, we poached the breasts in broth and then removed them while we built the rest of the stew. This had the added benefit of enhancing the flavor of the broth. Tasters liked a mix of carrots and onion and welcomed the fresh pop of peas stirred in at the end. Dry sherry, garlic, thyme and bay leaves added flavor. Flour helped thicken the stew base nicely, and cream added richness. Dropped biscuit–style dumplings were easier to make than rolled, noodle-style dumplings, and using a full tablespoon of baking powder ensured that the dumplings were fluffy and not dense. For tender dumplings, the dough should be gently mixed right before the dumplings are dropped onto the stew.

STEW

- 5 cups chicken broth
- 2 pounds boneless, skinless chicken breasts, trimmed
- 5 tablespoons unsalted butter
- 4 carrots, peeled and sliced ¼ inch thick
- 1 large onion, chopped fine
- 1 teaspoon table salt
- 3 garlic cloves, minced
- 6 tablespoons all-purpose flour
- ¾ cup dry sherry
- ⅓ cup heavy cream
- 2 bay leaves
- 2 teaspoons minced fresh thyme or ¾ teaspoon dried
- ½ teaspoon pepper
- 1½ cups frozen peas
- ¼ cup minced fresh parsley

DUMPLINGS

- 2 cups all-purpose flour
- 1 tablespoon baking powder
- ½ teaspoon table salt
- 1⅓ cups heavy cream

1. FOR THE STEW Bring broth to simmer in Dutch oven over high heat. Add chicken and return to simmer. Reduce heat to low, cover, and cook until chicken registers 160 degrees, 10 to 15 minutes. Transfer chicken to cutting board and broth to bowl.

Chicken and Dumplings

2. Melt butter in now-empty Dutch oven over medium-high heat. Add carrots, onion, and salt and cook until softened, about 7 minutes. Stir in garlic and cook until fragrant, about 30 seconds. Stir in flour and cook, stirring frequently, for 1 minute. Stir in sherry, scraping up browned bits and smoothing out any lumps. Stir in cream, bay leaves, thyme, pepper, and reserved broth and bring to boil. Cover, reduce heat to low, and simmer until stew thickens, about 20 minutes. (Stew and poached chicken can be refrigerated separately for up to 24 hours. To cook, bring stew, covered, to gentle simmer, stirring often, and continue with step 3.)

3. FOR THE DUMPLINGS Whisk flour, baking powder, and salt together in large bowl. Stir in cream until incorporated (dough will be very thick and shaggy).

4. Discard bay leaves and return stew to rapid simmer. Shred chicken into bite-size pieces using 2 forks and add to stew along with any accumulated juices, peas, and 3 tablespoons parsley. Using 2 large soupspoons, drop golf ball–size dumplings onto stew about ¼ inch apart (you should have 16 to 18 dumplings). Reduce heat to low, cover, and cook until dumplings have doubled in size, 15 to 18 minutes. Sprinkle with remaining 1 tablespoon parsley and serve.

Stocks and Broth

Simple Turkey Stock

Makes 8 cups
Total Time 3¼ hours, plus 1½ hours cooling

Pick off most of the meat from the carcass and reserve it, but don't pick the carcass clean. The stock will have more flavor if there is some meat and skin still attached. If you have the bones from the drumsticks and thighs, add them to the pot.

  1 carcass from 12- to 14-pound roasted turkey
10 cups water

1. Using chef's knife, remove wings from carcass and separate each wing at joints into 3 pieces. Cut through ribs to separate breastbone from backbone, then cut backbone into 3 or 4 pieces. Using kitchen shears or heavy knife, remove ribs from both sides of breastbone. (You should have roughly 4 pounds of bones broken into 10 to 12 pieces.)

2. Arrange bones in large stockpot or Dutch oven in compact layer. Add water and bring to boil over medium-high heat. Reduce heat to low, cover, and cook for 2 hours, using shallow spoon to skim foam and impurities from surface as needed.

3. Strain stock through fine-mesh strainer into large container; discard solids. Let stock cool slightly, about 20 minutes. Skim any fat from surface (reserve fat for making soup). Let stock cool for 1½ hours before refrigerating. (Stock can be refrigerated for up to 4 days or frozen for up to 2 months.)

Classic Chicken Stock

Makes 8 cups
Total Time 5¾ hours, plus 1½ hours cooling

Ask your butcher for chicken backs, or use all wings if you can't find them. If you have a large pot (at least 12 quarts), you can easily double this recipe to make 1 gallon.

  4 pounds chicken backs and wings
3½ quarts water
  1 onion, chopped
  2 bay leaves
  2 teaspoons table salt

1. Heat chicken and water in large stockpot or Dutch oven over medium-high heat until boiling, skimming off any scum that comes to surface. Reduce heat to low and simmer gently for 3 hours.

2. Add onion, bay leaves, and salt and continue to simmer for 2 hours.

3. Strain broth through fine-mesh strainer into large pot or container, pressing on solids to extract as much liquid as possible. Let broth settle for about 5 minutes, then skim off fat. Let broth cool for 1½ hours before refrigerating. (Broth can be refrigerated for up to 4 days or frozen for up to 2 months.)

Vegetable Broth Base

Makes about 1¾ cups base, enough for 7 quarts broth
Total Time 20 minutes

To make 1 cup of broth, stir 1 tablespoon of fresh or frozen broth base into 1 cup of boiling water. If particle-free broth is desired, let the broth steep for 5 minutes and then strain it through a fine-mesh strainer.

  2 leeks, white and light green parts only, chopped and washed thoroughly (2½ cups or 5 ounces)
  2 carrots, peeled and cut into ½-inch pieces (⅔ cup or 3 ounces)
 ½ small celery root, peeled and cut into ½-inch pieces (¾ cup or 3 ounces)
 ½ cup (½ ounce) parsley leaves and thin stems
  3 tablespoons dried minced onions
  2 tablespoons kosher salt
1½ tablespoons tomato paste
  3 tablespoons soy sauce

Process leeks, carrots, celery root, parsley, minced onions, and salt in food processor, scraping down sides of bowl frequently, until paste is as fine as possible, 3 to 4 minutes. Add tomato paste and process for 1 minute, scraping down sides of bowl every 20 seconds. Add soy sauce and continue to process 1 minute. Transfer mixture to airtight container and tap firmly on counter to remove air bubbles. Press small piece of parchment paper flush against surface of mixture and cover. (Base can be frozen for up to 6 months.)

Doro Wat

Stifado

Doro Wat

Serves 4 | **Total Time** 1¾ hours **MAKE AHEAD**

WHY THIS RECIPE WORKS Stews in Ethiopia are deeply flavored with warm spices and are traditionally served with injera, a type of flatbread that is made from teff and is used as a utensil to eat the stew. One of the most popular is doro wat, a hearty chicken stew garnished with hard-cooked eggs. The meat is cooked in niter kibbeh, a spiced butter flavored with cardamom, garlic, ginger, and cinnamon. It's further seasoned with berbere, a spice blend typically consisting of hot red chiles, paprika, cloves, nutmeg, fenugreek, and cumin. Our version calls for just a few big-impact spices—chili powder, cardamom, nutmeg, and fenugreek. To build more flavor, we started by simply browning our chicken pieces and then sautéed our aromatics—onion, ginger, and garlic—in the chicken's rendered fat before stirring in our spices to bloom their flavor. Cooking tomato paste, an unconventional addition, with the aromatics and spices gave the stew richer color. Basing the broth on a combination of chicken broth and wine gave the stew nice acidity and depth. Keeping the chicken pieces whole rather than shredding the meat gave each bowl a real "wow" factor. A spiced butter seemed superfluous in the highly seasoned stew, but finishing the dish with plain butter gave it a rich lift. Serve with the Ethiopian flatbread injera if you can find it. The stew can alternatively be served with white rice or noodles.

  4 pounds bone-in, skin-on chicken pieces (split breasts cut in half, drumsticks, and/or thighs)
  1 teaspoon table salt
  ½ teaspoon pepper
  2 tablespoons vegetable oil
  1 onion, chopped fine
  2 tablespoons tomato paste
  3 garlic cloves, minced
  1 tablespoon grated fresh ginger
  1 tablespoon chili powder
  ½ teaspoon ground cardamom
  ½ teaspoon ground nutmeg
  ½ teaspoon ground fenugreek
  3 tablespoons all-purpose flour
  2 cups chicken broth
  2 cups dry red wine
1½ cups water
  4 Easy-Peel Hard-Cooked Eggs (recipe follows)
  2 tablespoons unsalted butter, cut into 2 pieces and chilled

1. Pat chicken dry with paper towels and sprinkle with salt and pepper. Heat oil in Dutch oven over medium-high heat until just smoking. Brown half of chicken, 5 to 8 minutes per side, reducing heat if pan begins to scorch. Transfer chicken to plate, leaving fat in pot. Return pot with fat to medium-high heat and repeat with remaining chicken; transfer to plate.

2. Pour off all but 1 tablespoon fat left in pot. Add onion and cook over medium heat, stirring occasionally, until softened, 5 to 7 minutes. Stir in tomato paste, garlic, ginger, chili powder, cardamom, nutmeg, and fenugreek and cook until fragrant, about 30 seconds. Stir in flour and cook for 1 minute. Stir in broth, wine, and water, scraping up any browned bits and smoothing out any lumps.

3. Nestle chicken, along with any accumulated juices, into pot and bring to simmer. Cover, turn heat to medium-low, and simmer until chicken is fully cooked and tender, about 20 minutes for breasts (160 degrees on an instant-read thermometer) or 1 hour for thighs and drumsticks. (If using both types of chicken, simmer thighs and drumsticks for 40 minutes before adding breasts.)

4. Transfer chicken to serving dish, tent with foil, and let rest while finishing sauce. Skim as much fat as possible off surface of sauce and return to simmer until sauce is thickened and measures about 3 cups, about 20 minutes. (Stew can be refrigerated for up to 3 days and reheated just before serving.) Stir in eggs and cook until warmed through, about 1 minute. Off heat, stir in butter and season with salt and pepper to taste. Pour sauce over chicken and serve.

Easy-Peel Hard-Cooked Eggs

Makes 4 eggs | **Total Time** 40 minutes

Be sure to use large eggs that have no cracks and are cold from the refrigerator. This recipe can be doubled.

   4 large eggs

1. Bring 1 inch water to rolling boil in medium saucepan over high heat. Place eggs in steamer basket. Transfer basket to saucepan. Cover, reduce heat to medium-low, and cook eggs for 13 minutes.

2. When eggs are almost finished cooking, combine 2 cups ice cubes and 2 cups cold water in medium bowl. Using tongs or spoon, transfer eggs to ice bath; let sit for 15 minutes. (Eggs can be refrigerated for up to 5 days.) Peel before using.

Stifado

Serves 4 to 6 `MAKE AHEAD`
Total Time 3¼ to 3¾ hours

WHY THIS RECIPE WORKS With ultratender beef and a wine-and-spice-infused tomato sauce, the Greek stew known as stifado offers an intriguing take on beef stew. For creamy caramelized onions, we began by sautéing pearl onions with a pinch of sugar to jump-start the development of flavorful browning. Be sure to buy a chuck-eye roast and cube it yourself. Do not use precubed stew meat. One 14.4-ounce bag of frozen pearl onion contains about 3½ cups. Do not thaw the onions before cooking. Serve over orzo or with pita bread, sprinkling individual portions with chopped fresh parsley and crumbled feta cheese, if desired.

2½ pounds boneless beef chuck-eye roast, trimmed and cut into 1-inch pieces
   2 teaspoons kosher salt, divided
   ½ teaspoon pepper
3½ cups frozen pearl onions
   2 tablespoons extra-virgin olive oil
   ½ teaspoon sugar
   2 tablespoons tomato paste
   3 garlic cloves, minced
   1 teaspoon ground cumin
   ⅛ teaspoon ground allspice
   2 tomatoes, cored and chopped
2¼ cups chicken broth
   ¾ cup dry white wine
   1 cinnamon stick
   2 bay leaves

1. Adjust oven rack to middle position and heat oven to 300 degrees. Sprinkle beef with 1½ teaspoons salt and pepper; set aside.

2. Cook onions, oil, sugar, and remaining ½ teaspoon salt in large Dutch oven over medium-high heat until onions are softened and deeply browned, 10 to 12 minutes. Add tomato paste, garlic, cumin, and allspice and cook until fragrant, about 1 minute. Add tomatoes and cook until tomatoes break down and mixture is darkened and thick, about 5 minutes.

3. Add broth, wine, cinnamon stick, bay leaves, and beef to pot, scraping up any browned bits. Increase heat to high and bring to simmer. Transfer to oven and cook, uncovered, for 1 hour. Remove pot from oven and stir to redistribute beef. Return pot to oven and continue to cook, uncovered, until meat is tender, 1½ to 2 hours longer. Serve. (Soup can be refrigerated for up to 3 days and reheated just before serving.)

Beef Stew with Parsnips, Kale, and Mushrooms

Serves 4 to 6 | **Total Time** 3¾ hours `MAKE AHEAD`

WHY THIS RECIPE WORKS Sometimes we find ourselves craving a beef stew where the vegetables are as hearty as the meat, so we developed this vegetable-heavy stew. The extra vegetables not only added nutrition, they also lent their own clean, fresh, earthy flavors to the gravy. A combination of chicken and beef broths provided meaty flavor but was neutral enough that it didn't overtake the beefiness of the chuck roast or obscure the flavor of the vegetables. Stirred in at the end, peas and parsley contributed verdant freshness. With so many vegetables, this plant-boosted stew was just as filling and satisfying as traditional beef stew. Use a red wine made from a blend of grapes, such as Côtes du Rhône, for this dish.

Beef Stew with Parsnips, Kale, and Mushrooms

  2 pounds boneless beef chuck-eye roast, trimmed and cut into 1½-inch pieces
  ½ teaspoon table salt
  ¼ teaspoon pepper
  5 teaspoons vegetable oil, divided
  1 large portobello mushroom cap, cut into ½-inch pieces
  2 onions, chopped fine
  3 garlic cloves, minced
  1 tablespoon minced fresh thyme or 1 teaspoon dried
  3 tablespoons all-purpose flour
  1 tablespoon tomato paste
1½ cups dry red wine
  2 cups chicken broth
  2 cups beef broth
  2 bay leaves
12 ounces red potatoes, unpeeled, cut into 1-inch pieces
  4 carrots, peeled, halved lengthwise, and sliced 1 inch thick
  4 parsnips, peeled, halved lengthwise, and sliced 1 inch thick
  1 pound kale, stemmed and sliced into ½-inch-wide strips
  ½ cup frozen peas
  ¼ cup minced fresh parsley

1. Adjust oven rack to lower-middle position and heat oven to 300 degrees. Pat beef dry with paper towels and sprinkle with salt and pepper. Heat 1 teaspoon oil in Dutch oven over medium-high heat until just smoking. Brown half of meat on all sides, 5 to 10 minutes; transfer to bowl. Repeat with 1 teaspoon oil and remaining beef; transfer to bowl.

2. Add mushroom pieces to fat left in pot, cover, and cook over medium heat until they've softened and released their liquid, about 5 minutes. Uncover and continue to cook until mushroom pieces are dry and browned, 5 to 10 minutes longer.

3. Stir in remaining 1 tablespoon oil and onions and cook until softened, 5 to 7 minutes. Stir in garlic and thyme and cook until fragrant, about 30 seconds. Stir in flour and tomato paste and cook until flour is lightly browned, about 1 minute.

4. Slowly whisk in wine, scraping up any browned bits and smoothing out any lumps. Slowly whisk in chicken broth and beef broth until smooth. Stir in bay leaves and browned meat and bring to simmer. Cover and transfer pot to oven. Cook for 1½ hours.

5. Stir in potatoes, carrots, and parsnips; cover, return pot to oven, and continue to cook until meat and vegetables are tender, about 1 hour longer. Stir in kale and continue to cook in oven until tender, about 10 minutes longer. Remove stew from oven and remove bay leaves. Stir in peas and parsley and let stew stand for 5 to 10 minutes. Season with salt and pepper to taste. Serve. (Stew can be refrigerated for up to 3 days and reheated just before serving.)

CUTTING STEW MEAT

1. Pull apart roast at its major seams (delineated by lines of fat and silverskin). Use knife as necessary.

2. With knife, trim off excess fat and silverskin. Cut meat into 1- to 2-inch pieces, according to recipe.

Lamb Stew with Turnips and Carrots

Serves 6 | **Total Time** 3 hours   `MAKE AHEAD`

WHY THIS RECIPE WORKS Hearty Irish stew is made from meat and root vegetables in a richly flavored base. The recipe can vary from town to town and household to household, though the traditional meat is lamb. Some versions use only potatoes for the vegetable component, but we think that's a shame and prefer our Irish stew to also incorporate peppery turnips, pungent onions, and sweet carrots. We chose lamb shoulder chops for the meat, because we found that slicing the meat off the bone from a lamb shoulder chop, browning it, and adding the bones and meat to the stewing liquid gave us a great stew with a rich-tasting broth and the velvety texture that only marrow-rich bones can contribute. If possible, try to buy the shoulder chops from a butcher. In most supermarkets, lamb shoulder chops are sold too thin, often only about ½ inch thick. Though we prefer chops cut 1½ inches thick, 1-inch-thick chops will suffice.

4½ pounds lamb shoulder chops (blade or round bone), 1 to 1½ inches thick, trimmed, meat removed from bones and cut into 1½-inch pieces, bones reserved
2½ teaspoons table salt, divided
½ teaspoon pepper
3 tablespoons vegetable oil, divided
2½ pounds onions, chopped
¼ cup all-purpose flour
3 cups water, divided, plus extra as needed
1 teaspoon dried thyme
3 carrots, peeled and sliced ¼ inch thick
8 ounces turnips, peeled and cut into 1-inch pieces
¼ cup minced fresh parsley

1. Adjust oven rack to lower-middle position and heat oven to 300 degrees. Pat lamb dry with paper towels and sprinkle with 1 teaspoon salt and pepper. Heat 1 tablespoon oil in Dutch oven over medium-high heat until just smoking. Brown half of lamb on all sides, about 8 minutes; transfer to bowl. Repeat with 1 tablespoon oil and remaining lamb; transfer to bowl.

2. Add remaining 1 tablespoon oil, onions, and ¼ teaspoon salt to fat left in pot and cook over medium heat until onions are softened and lightly browned, about 8 minutes. Stir in flour and cook until onions are evenly coated, about 1 minute.

3. Stir in 1½ cups water, scraping up any browned bits and smoothing out any lumps. Gradually add remaining 1½ cups water, stirring constantly. Stir in thyme and 1 teaspoon salt and bring to simmer. Add reserved bones and lamb along with any accumulated juices and return to simmer. Cover, transfer pot to oven, and cook for 1 hour.

4. Remove pot from oven and place carrots and turnips on top of lamb and bones. Cover, return pot to oven, and cook until lamb is tender, about 1 hour.

5. Remove pot from oven and discard bones. Stir carrots and turnips into stew. Using large spoon, skim excess fat from surface of stew. (Soup can be refrigerated for up to 3 days and reheated just before serving.) Adjust consistency with extra hot water as needed. Stir in parsley and season with salt and pepper to taste. Serve.

Seafood and Chorizo Stew

Serves 4 | **Total Time** 55 minutes

WHY THIS RECIPE WORKS Seafood stews can seem like grand, celebratory affairs, with their medley of fresh-catch seafood and rich broths, but they don't have to be complicated. We added chorizo, an abundantly spiced pork sausage, as a quick way to flavor our stew. When cooked together with an onion, the chorizo's bold, smoky flavor added heat and interest to sweet shrimp and mild-mannered cod, and a tomato base brought the lively components together. Cutting the cod in our stew into smaller pieces helped it cook at the same quick rate as the shrimp so we could stir them in together, and we liked the way the firm fish maintained its bite-size shape. A drizzle of oil finished off this impressive, multidimensional dish. Black sea bass, haddock, hake, or pollock would make good substitutions for the cod in this stew.

1 tablespoon extra-virgin olive oil, plus extra for serving
6 ounces smoked chorizo sausage, quartered lengthwise and sliced ½ inch thick
1 onion, chopped fine
4 garlic cloves, minced
1 tablespoon chopped fresh oregano, divided
2 (14.5-ounce) cans diced tomatoes
1 (8-ounce) bottle clam juice
1 pound extra-large shrimp (21 to 25 per pound), peeled, deveined, and tails removed
2 (6- to 8-ounce) skinless cod fillets, 1 inch thick, cut into 1-inch pieces
½ teaspoon table salt
¼ teaspoon pepper

1. Heat oil in large saucepan over medium-high heat until shimmering. Add chorizo and onion and cook until lightly browned, 7 to 9 minutes. Stir in garlic and 1 teaspoon oregano and cook until fragrant, about 30 seconds. Add tomatoes and their juice and clam juice, scraping up any browned bits, and bring to simmer. Cook until slightly thickened, about 10 minutes.

2. Pat shrimp and cod dry with paper towels and sprinkle with salt and pepper. Gently stir seafood into stew and cook until cod flakes apart when gently prodded with paring knife and registers 135 degrees and shrimp is opaque throughout, about 5 minutes. Stir in remaining 2 teaspoons oregano and season with salt and pepper to taste. Portion stew into individual serving bowls and drizzle with extra oil. Serve.

Tuscan White Bean Stew

Serves 8 `MAKE AHEAD`
Total Time 2½ hours, plus 8 hours brining

WHY THIS RECIPE WORKS The people of Tuscany are known as mangiafagioli, or "bean eaters," a nod to the prominent role beans play in their cuisine. Cannellini (white kidney) beans are the region's most famous legume, and Tuscan cooks go to extremes to ensure that these beans are cooked perfectly, from simmering them in rainwater to slow-cooking them overnight in a wine bottle in a fire's dying embers. Zuppa di fagioli alla toscana is a quintessential bean dish featuring an aromatic base, hearty greens, tomatoes, pancetta, and, of course, creamy, buttery beans. Soaking the beans overnight was essential to soften them so their interiors cooked up creamy.

And salting the soaking water—essentially brining—softened the skins until they were barely perceptible for ultratender beans. After experimenting with cooking times and temperatures, we found that a vigorous stovetop simmer caused some beans to explode, so we gently cooked them in a 250-degree oven for even results. Adding the tomatoes toward the end of cooking ensured that their acidity wouldn't toughen the beans.

3 tablespoons table salt for brining beans
1 pound (2½ cups) dried cannellini beans, picked over and rinsed
6 ounces pancetta, cut into ¼-inch pieces
1 tablespoon extra-virgin olive oil, plus extra for serving
1 onion, chopped
2 carrots, peeled and cut into ½-inch pieces
2 celery ribs, cut into ½-inch pieces
8 garlic cloves, peeled and smashed
4 cups chicken broth
3 cups water
2 bay leaves
1 pound kale or collard greens, stemmed and chopped
1 (14.5-ounce) can diced tomatoes, drained
1 sprig fresh rosemary

1. Dissolve 3 tablespoons salt in 4 quarts cold water in large container. Add beans and soak at room temperature for at least 8 hours or up to 24 hours. Drain and rinse well.

2. Adjust oven rack to lower-middle position and heat oven to 250 degrees. Cook pancetta and oil in Dutch oven over medium heat, stirring occasionally, until pancetta is lightly browned and fat is rendered, 6 to 10 minutes. Stir in onion, carrots, and celery and cook until softened and lightly browned, 10 to 16 minutes. Stir in garlic and cook until fragrant, about 1 minute. Stir in broth, water, bay leaves, and beans and bring to boil. Cover, transfer pot to oven, and cook until beans are almost tender (very center of beans will still be firm), 45 minutes to 1 hour.

3. Stir in kale and tomatoes, cover, and cook until beans and greens are fully tender, 30 to 40 minutes.

4. Remove pot from oven and submerge rosemary sprig in stew. Cover and let stand for 15 minutes. Discard bay leaves and rosemary sprig and season stew with salt and pepper to taste. If desired, use back of spoon to press some beans against side of pot to thicken stew. (Stew can be refrigerated for up to 3 days and reheated just before serving.) Drizzle individual portions with extra oil before serving.

Swiss Chard and Butternut Squash Stew

Serves 4 to 6 | **Total Time** 1¼ hours VEGETARIAN

WHY THIS RECIPE WORKS Callaloo is a lively, pesto-green stew that's both creamy and spicy, with a rich, coconutty broth studded with leafy greens and other vegetables. The name comes from the main ingredient, callaloo leaves, which are leafy green plants grown throughout the Caribbean. Traditionally the earthy, citrusy greens are enriched with salt pork, chiles, aromatics, and coconut milk. Variations on the stew abound, but we opted to create a vegetarian version to keep the focus right where we wanted it: on the vegetables. First and foremost, we needed to find an appropriate substitute for the callaloo leaves, which can be difficult to find stateside. Swiss chard proved the best option, offering hearty, earthy flavor, a hint of citrus, and a delicate texture. A single habanero chile provided subtle but persistent heat, while some garlic and thyme contributed aromatic backbone. Some callaloo recipes call for pumpkin, but we chose easy-to-find butternut squash instead. A handful of recipes called for a few dashes of angostura bitters, an aromatic alcohol infused with herbs and citrus. While not a must, the bitters gave the stew a uniquely authentic flavor. We pureed a small portion of the stew to give it a thick consistency and bright green color, while leaving most of the greens and squash in large bites. You can substitute delicata or carnival squash for the butternut squash if you prefer. For more spice, do not remove the ribs and seeds from the chiles.

2 tablespoons vegetable oil
2 onions, chopped fine
4 scallions, minced
½ teaspoon table salt
4 garlic cloves, minced
1 habanero or Scotch bonnet chile, stemmed, seeded, and minced
1 teaspoon minced fresh thyme or ¼ teaspoon dried
 Pinch cayenne pepper
3½ cups vegetable broth
2 pounds butternut squash, peeled, seeded, and cut into ½-inch pieces (6 cups)
1 pound Swiss chard, stemmed and cut into 1-inch pieces
1 cup canned coconut milk
 Angostura bitters (optional)

Tuscan White Bean Stew

Swiss Chard and Butternut Squash Stew

1. Heat oil in Dutch oven over medium heat until shimmering. Add onions, scallions, and salt and cook until vegetables are softened, 5 to 7 minutes. Stir in garlic, habanero, thyme, and cayenne and cook until fragrant, about 30 seconds.

2. Stir in broth and squash, scraping up any browned bits. Bring to simmer and cook for 15 minutes. Stir in chard and cook until squash and chard are tender, 10 to 15 minutes. Stir in coconut milk and return to brief simmer.

3. Process 2 cups stew in blender until smooth, about 45 seconds; return to pot. Season with salt and bitters, if using, to taste. Serve.

PREPARING CHILES SAFELY

Wear gloves when working with very hot peppers such as habaneros to avoid direct contact with oils that supply heat. Wash your hands, knife, and cutting board well after prepping chiles.

Hearty Beef and Vegetable Chili

Hearty Beef and Vegetable Chili

Serves 6 | **Total Time** 3½ hours `MAKE AHEAD`

WHY THIS RECIPE WORKS Most chili recipes are either meat-based or vegetarian, but this chili offers the best of both worlds with satisfying chunks of beef and hearty vegetables. We started with beef chuck eye, which transformed from tough to meltingly tender after simmering. Garlic, cumin, chipotle, and chili powder gave our stew depth and heat, balanced by sweet potatoes and red bell pepper. Using a mild beer as the liquid added complexity. For a spicier chili, use the greater amount of chipotle. Serve with your favorite chili garnishes.

3½ pounds boneless beef chuck-eye roast, pulled apart at seams, trimmed, and cut into 1-inch pieces
1¾ teaspoons table salt, divided
½ teaspoon pepper
3 tablespoons vegetable oil, divided
1 onion, chopped
1½ pounds sweet potatoes, peeled and cut into ½-inch pieces, divided
1–2 tablespoons minced canned chipotle chile in adobo sauce
3 garlic cloves, minced
1 tablespoon ground cumin
2 teaspoons chili powder
1 (28-ounce) can diced tomatoes
1½ cups mild lager, such as Budweiser
2 (15-ounce) cans black beans, rinsed
1 red bell pepper, stemmed, seeded, and cut into ½-inch pieces
4 scallions, sliced thin

1. Adjust oven rack to lower-middle position and heat oven to 325 degrees. Pat beef dry with paper towels and sprinkle with ¾ teaspoon salt and pepper. Heat 1 tablespoon oil in Dutch oven over medium heat until shimmering. Brown half of beef on all sides, 8 to 10 minutes; transfer to large bowl. Repeat with 1 tablespoon oil and remaining beef; transfer to bowl.

2. Add onion, ¾ cup sweet potatoes, and remaining 1 tablespoon oil to fat left in pot and cook over medium heat until just beginning to brown, 5 to 7 minutes. Stir in chipotle, garlic, cumin, chili powder, and remaining 1 teaspoon salt and cook until fragrant, about 30 seconds. Stir in tomatoes and their juice and beer, scraping up any browned bits, and bring to simmer. Stir in beans and beef with any accumulated juices, scraping up any browned bits.

3. Cover, transfer pot to oven, and cook, stirring occasionally, until sweet potatoes are broken down and beef is just tender, 1½ to 2 hours. Stir in bell pepper and remaining sweet potatoes and continue to cook, covered, until meat and sweet potatoes are tender, about 20 minutes longer.

4. Remove pot from oven, uncover, and let chili sit until thickened slightly, about 15 minutes. Adjust consistency with hot water as needed. Season with salt and pepper to taste. Sprinkle individual portions with scallions before serving. (Chili can be refrigerated for up to 2 days.)

Pressure-Cooker Easy Beef Chili

Serves 4 to 6 | **Total Time** 50 minutes MAKE AHEAD

WHY THIS RECIPE WORKS Great chili should have bold, long-simmered flavor, even if it's made with convenient ground beef. The pressure cooker achieves this with a minimum of hands-on time. Chili powder, cumin, and garlic gave the chili great spice flavor. We used crushed tomatoes plus chicken broth for a base with the proper consistency. Browning the beef is standard in many chili recipes, and to help prevent the meat from overcooking in the intense heat we mixed it with a panade (a mixture of bread and milk) to help it stay moist, and sautéed the meat just until it lost its pink color. This recipe will only work in an electric pressure cooker. Serve with your favorite chili garnishes.

  1 slice hearty white sandwich bread, torn into 1-inch pieces
  2 tablespoons whole milk
 ¾ teaspoon table salt, divided
 ½ teaspoon pepper
  1 pound 85 percent lean ground beef
  2 tablespoons vegetable oil
  1 onion, chopped fine
  2 tablespoons chili powder
  2 teaspoons ground cumin
  4 garlic cloves, minced
  1 cup chicken broth, plus extra as needed
  2 (15-ounce) cans kidney beans, rinsed
  1 (28-ounce) can crushed tomatoes

1. Mash bread, milk, ½ teaspoon salt, and pepper into paste in large bowl using fork. Add ground beef and knead with your hands until well combined.

2. Using highest sauté or browning function, heat oil in pressure cooker until shimmering. Add onion and remaining ¼ teaspoon salt and cook until onion is softened, about 5 minutes. Stir in chili powder, cumin, and garlic and cook until fragrant, about 30 seconds. Add beef mixture and cook, breaking up meat with wooden spoon, until no longer pink, about 4 minutes. Stir in broth, scraping up any browned bits, then stir in beans and tomatoes.

3. Lock lid in place and close pressure release valve. Select high pressure cook function and cook for 10 minutes. Turn off pressure cooker and quick-release pressure. Carefully remove lid, allowing steam to escape away from you.

4. Adjust chili consistency with extra hot broth as needed. Season with salt and pepper to taste. Serve. (Chili can be refrigerated for up to 2 days.)

Pressure-Cooker Easy Turkey Chili
Be sure to use ground turkey, not ground turkey breast (also labeled 99 percent fat-free), in this recipe. Substitute 1 pound ground turkey for ground beef. Break turkey mixture into pieces no smaller than 1 inch when browning in step 2.

Pressure-Cooker Easy Five-Alarm Chili
For more spice, do not remove the ribs and seeds from the chiles. Add 2 minced jalapeño chiles to pressure cooker with onions. Add ¼ cup minced canned chipotle chile in adobo and 1 teaspoon cayenne pepper to pressure cooker with chili powder.

Slow-Cooker White Chicken Chili

Serves 6 to 8 MAKE AHEAD
Cooking Time 4 to 5 hours on Low

WHY THIS RECIPE WORKS White chicken chili, which gets its vibrant flavor and spiciness from fresh green chiles, is a fresher, lighter cousin of the thick red chili many of us know and love. Its appeal is not surprising; without tomatoes to mask the other flavors, the chiles, herbs, and spices take center stage. To achieve a great white chicken chili in the slow cooker, we needed to build flavor every step of the way. We started by browning boneless chicken thighs to give our chili big chicken flavor. Sautéing the aromatics—including four jalapeño chiles—and spices together in the skillet deepened the flavor, and deglazing the pan ensured that all the rich browned bits we developed ended up in the slow cooker. For convenience, instead of multiple types of chiles, we relied on jalapeño chiles only. For more spice, do not remove the ribs and seeds from the chiles. Serve with your favorite chili garnishes. You will need a 5- to 7-quart slow cooker for this recipe.

  3 cups chicken broth, divided, plus extra as needed
  1 (15-ounce) can white or yellow hominy, rinsed
  3 pounds boneless, skinless chicken thighs, trimmed
  1 teaspoon table salt
  ½ teaspoon pepper
  3 tablespoons vegetable oil, divided
  2 onions, chopped fine
  4 jalapeño chiles, stemmed, seeded, and minced
  6 garlic cloves, minced
  4 teaspoons ground cumin
  2 teaspoons ground coriander
  3 (15-ounce) cans cannellini beans, rinsed
  ¼ cup minced fresh cilantro
  2 tablespoons minced jarred jalapeños
  2 avocados, halved, pitted, and cut into ½-inch pieces

   1. Process 2 cups broth and hominy in blender until smooth, about 1 minute; transfer to slow cooker.
   2. Pat chicken dry with paper towels and sprinkle with salt and pepper. Heat 1 tablespoon oil in 12-inch skillet over medium-high heat until just smoking. Brown half of chicken, about 4 minutes per side; transfer to slow cooker. Repeat with 1 tablespoon oil and remaining chicken; transfer to slow cooker.
   3. Heat remaining 1 tablespoon oil in now-empty skillet over medium heat until shimmering. Add onions and cook until softened and lightly browned, 8 to 10 minutes. Stir in fresh jalapeños, garlic, cumin, and coriander and cook until fragrant, about 30 seconds. Stir in remaining 1 cup broth, scraping up any browned bits; transfer to slow cooker.
   4. Stir beans into slow cooker, cover, and cook until chicken is tender, 4 to 5 hours on low.
   5. Transfer chicken to cutting board, let cool slightly, then pull apart into large pieces using 2 forks. Stir chicken into chili and let stand until heated through, about 5 minutes. Adjust consistency with extra hot broth as needed. (Chili can be refrigerated for up to 2 days and reheated just before serving.) Stir in cilantro and jarred jalapeños and season with salt and pepper to taste. Serve with avocados.

Pressure-Cooker Black Bean Chili

Pressure-Cooker Black Bean Chili

Serves 4 to 6 `MAKE AHEAD` `VEGETARIAN`
Total Time 1¼ hours, plus 8 hours brining

WHY THIS RECIPE WORKS The pressure cooker cuts more than an hour from the time it takes to cook tender black beans for chili. A hands-off overnight soak helped dried beans (which we preferred over canned for their creamier texture) stay intact once cooked. Instead of relying on bacon or ham for flavor, we browned a hefty amount of aromatics and bloomed spices to give this vegetarian chili depth. White mushrooms and bell peppers added body. This recipe will only work in an electric pressure cooker. Serve with your favorite chili garnishes.

  3 tablespoons table salt for brining beans
  1 pound (2½ cups) dried black beans, picked over and rinsed
  3 tablespoons vegetable oil
  1 onion, chopped fine
  9 garlic cloves, minced

2 tablespoons ground cumin
1½ tablespoons chili powder
1 teaspoon minced canned chipotle chile in adobo sauce
1 (28-ounce) can crushed tomatoes
1 cup vegetable broth, plus extra as needed
1 pound white mushrooms, trimmed and halved if small or quartered if large
2 red bell peppers, stemmed, seeded, and cut into ½-inch pieces
2 bay leaves
½ cup minced fresh cilantro
Lime wedges

1. Dissolve 3 tablespoons salt in 4 quarts cold water in large container. Add beans and soak at room temperature for at least 8 hours or up to 24 hours. Drain and rinse well.

2. Using highest sauté or browning function, heat oil in pressure cooker until shimmering. Add onion and cook until softened, 3 to 5 minutes. Stir in garlic, cumin, chili powder, and chipotle and cook until fragrant, about 1 minute. Stir in tomatoes and broth, scraping up any browned bits, then stir in beans, mushrooms, bell peppers, and bay leaves.

3. Lock lid in place and close pressure release valve. Select high pressure cook function and cook for 40 minutes. Turn off pressure cooker and quick-release pressure. Carefully remove lid, allowing steam to escape away from you.

4. Discard bay leaves. (Chili can be refrigerated for up to 2 days and reheated just before serving.) Adjust consistency with extra hot broth as needed. Stir in cilantro and season with salt and pepper to taste. Serve with lime wedges.

Butternut Squash and Peanut Chili with Quinoa

Serves 6 | **Total Time** 1½ hours
MAKE AHEAD VEGETARIAN

WHY THIS RECIPE WORKS This stick-to-your-ribs vegetable chili is aromatic and boldly flavored with coconut milk, garlic, and ginger. It gets its silky body from a combination of blended dry-roasted salted peanuts and squash. We like the convenience of prewashed quinoa; rinsing removes the quinoa's bitter protective coating (called saponin). If you buy unwashed quinoa (or if you are unsure whether it's washed), rinse it and then spread it out over a clean dish towel to dry for 15 minutes before cooking. Serve with hot sauce.

3 pounds butternut squash, peeled, seeded, and cut into ½-inch pieces (9 cups)
2 onions, chopped
6 tablespoons vegetable oil, divided
1 tablespoon table salt, divided
1¼ teaspoons pepper, divided
5 cups water, divided, plus extra as needed
¾ cup dry-roasted salted peanuts, chopped, divided
1 large red bell pepper, stemmed, seeded, and cut into ½-inch pieces
1 jalapeño chile, stemmed, seeded, and minced
3 garlic cloves, minced
2 tablespoons grated fresh ginger
¾ teaspoon ground cinnamon
¾ teaspoon ground coriander
½ teaspoon cayenne pepper
1 (14.5-ounce) can diced tomatoes
1 (14-ounce) can coconut milk
1 cup prewashed white quinoa
¼ cup minced fresh cilantro or parsley

1. Adjust oven racks to upper-middle and lower-middle positions and heat oven to 450 degrees. Toss squash, onions, ¼ cup oil, 1 teaspoon salt, and ½ teaspoon pepper together in bowl to coat. Arrange vegetables in even layer over 2 rimmed baking sheets. Roast vegetables, stirring occasionally, until tender, 45 to 50 minutes, switching and rotating sheets halfway through roasting.

2. Process ½ cup roasted vegetables, 2 cups water, and ¼ cup peanuts in food processor until smooth, about 1 minute.

3. Heat remaining 2 tablespoons oil in Dutch oven over medium-high heat until shimmering. Add bell pepper, jalapeño, and remaining 2 teaspoons salt and cook until peppers begin to soften, about 5 minutes. Stir in garlic, ginger, cinnamon, coriander, cayenne, and remaining ¾ teaspoon pepper, and cook until fragrant, about 30 seconds. (Chili can be prepared through step 3 and refrigerated for up to 3 days. To serve, bring chili, covered, to gentle simmer, stirring often, and continue with step 4.)

4. Stir in remaining 3 cups water, tomatoes and their juice, coconut milk, and quinoa and bring to boil. Reduce heat to low and simmer, stirring occasionally, until quinoa is tender, about 15 minutes.

5. Stir in pureed vegetable mixture and remaining roasted vegetables and cook until warmed through, about 3 minutes. Season with salt and pepper to taste. Adjust consistency with additional hot water as needed. Serve, sprinkling individual portions with cilantro and remaining ½ cup peanuts.

weeknight **dinners**

■ MAKE AHEAD ■ VEGETARIAN
Photo: Garlicky Spaghetti with Basil and Broiled Tomatoes

Pan-Roasted Chicken Breasts with Root Vegetables

Za'atar Chicken with Pistachios, Brussels Sprouts, and Pomegranate

Pan-Roasted Chicken Breasts with Root Vegetables

Serves 4 | **Total Time** 1¼ hours

WHY THIS RECIPE WORKS A smoking-hot skillet creates a great seared crust on juicy, bone-in chicken breasts and is the perfect vessel for roasting a medley of hearty root vegetables to serve on the side. To start, we seared our chicken to crisp the skin to golden brown perfection. After the initial sear, we took the chicken out of the skillet and filled the pan with potatoes, parsnips, carrots, and shallots, all cut into bite-size pieces. We then put the chicken back in the pan on top of the vegetables and moved the whole thing to the oven. Elevating the chicken on top of the vegetables allowed the meat to cook gently while the root vegetables roasted against the hot surface of the pan; the direct heat helped them cook quickly and evenly. Once the chicken was done, we removed it and let it rest while we finished cooking the vegetables. A simple sprinkling of chives was all that was needed to finish our dish. Use small red potatoes measuring 1 to 2 inches in diameter; if your potatoes are larger, cut them into 1-inch pieces to ensure that they cook through properly. You will need a 12-inch ovensafe skillet for this recipe.

- 4 (10- to 12-ounce) bone-in split chicken breasts, trimmed
- 1 teaspoon table salt, divided
- ¾ teaspoon pepper, divided
- 1 tablespoon vegetable oil
- 1 pound small red potatoes, unpeeled, quartered
- 8 ounces parsnips, peeled, halved lengthwise, and cut into 1-inch pieces
- 4 carrots, peeled, halved lengthwise, and cut into 1-inch pieces
- 4 shallots, peeled and quartered
- 1 teaspoon minced fresh rosemary or ¼ teaspoon dried
- 1 tablespoon minced fresh chives

1. Adjust oven rack to middle position and heat oven to 450 degrees. Pound thicker end of chicken breasts between 2 sheets of plastic wrap to ¾- to 1-inch thickness. Pat chicken dry with paper towels and sprinkle with ½ teaspoon salt and ½ teaspoon pepper. Heat oil in 12-inch ovensafe skillet over medium-high heat until just smoking. Place chicken skin side down in skillet and cook until well browned on first side, 5 to 7 minutes. Flip chicken and continue to cook until lightly browned on second side, about 3 minutes longer; transfer to plate.

2. Add potatoes, parsnips, carrots, shallots, rosemary, remaining ½ teaspoon salt, and remaining ¼ teaspoon pepper to fat left in skillet and toss to coat. Place chicken skin side up on top of vegetables, transfer skillet to oven, and roast until chicken registers 160 degrees, 20 to 25 minutes.

3. Using potholders, remove skillet from oven. Transfer chicken to serving platter, tent with aluminum foil, and let rest while finishing vegetables.

4. Being careful of hot skillet handle, stir vegetables, return skillet to oven, and roast until vegetables are tender, about 15 minutes. Stir in chives and season with salt and pepper to taste. Serve chicken with vegetables.

Za'atar Chicken with Pistachios, Brussels Sprouts, and Pomegranate

Serves 4 | **Total Time** 55 minutes

WHY THIS RECIPE WORKS Za'atar, a Mediterranean seasoning made from thyme, sumac, and sesame, gives meaty bone-in chicken breasts irresistible complexity. We skillet-roasted brussels sprouts using the chicken's rendered fat and paired them with pistachios and pomegranate molasses, a perfect match for the earthy flavors of the za'atar. We like to use our homemade Za'atar (page 101), but you can use store-bought if you prefer. We like the convenience of store-bought pomegranate molasses, but if you can't find it you can make our homemade Pomegranate Molasses. Look for brussels sprouts that are similar in size with small, tight heads, and no more than 1½ inches in diameter, as they're likely to be sweeter and more tender than larger sprouts.

- 4 (10- to 12-ounce) bone-in split chicken breasts, trimmed and halved crosswise
- 1 teaspoon table salt, divided
- ¼ teaspoon pepper
- ⅓ cup extra-virgin olive oil, divided
- 2 tablespoons za'atar
- 1 pound small brussels sprouts, trimmed and halved
- ¼ cup shelled pistachios, toasted and chopped
- 2 tablespoons pomegranate seeds
- 1 tablespoon pomegranate molasses
- ½ teaspoon ground cumin
  Lemon wedges

1. Adjust oven rack to lowest position and heat oven to 450 degrees. Pat chicken dry with paper towels and sprinkle with ½ teaspoon salt and pepper. Heat 1 teaspoon oil in 12-inch nonstick skillet over medium-high heat until just smoking. Place chicken skin side down in skillet and cook until well browned, 6 to 8 minutes. Transfer chicken, skin side up, to rimmed baking sheet (do not wipe out skillet).

2. Meanwhile, combine za'atar and 2 tablespoons oil in small bowl. Brush chicken skin with za'atar mixture. Transfer to oven and roast until chicken registers 160 degrees, about 20 minutes. Transfer pieces to platter, tent with aluminum foil, and let rest.

3. Add remaining 3 tablespoons oil to now-empty skillet and arrange brussels sprouts in single layer, cut side down. Cover skillet, place over medium-high heat, and cook until sprouts are bright green and cut sides have started to brown, about 5 minutes. Continue to cook, uncovered, until cut side of sprouts are deeply and evenly browned and paring knife slides in with little to no resistance, 2 to 3 minutes.

4. Off heat, add pistachios, pomegranate seeds, pomegranate molasses, cumin, and remaining ½ teaspoon salt to skillet and stir to coat evenly. Season with salt and pepper to taste. Serve with chicken and lemon wedges.

Pomegranate Molasses

Makes ⅓ cup | **Total Time** 25 minutes

Pomegranate molasses can be whisked into vinaigrette, drizzled over vegetables, brushed onto roasted meats, or pureed into dips. Reducing the pomegranate juice at a simmer, rather than at a boil, drives off fewer flavor compounds and results in fresher, more complex flavor. To speed up evaporation, we use a 12-inch skillet, which offers more surface area.

- 2 cups unsweetened pomegranate juice
- ½ teaspoon sugar
  Pinch table salt

Bring pomegranate juice, sugar, and salt to simmer in 12-inch skillet over high heat. Reduce heat to low and simmer, stirring and scraping thickened juice from sides of skillet occasionally, until mixture is thick and syrupy and measures ⅓ cup, 12 to 15 minutes. Let cool slightly before transferring to container. (Once cooled, syrup can be refrigerated for up to 1 month.)

Pressure-Cooker Chicken with Spiced Whole Parsnips and Scallion-Mint Relish

Serves 4 | **Total Time** 1 hour

WHY THIS RECIPE WORKS Cream-colored parsnips become sweeter when left in the ground just long enough to be exposed to a hard frost, making winter prime parsnip season. We paired this underutilized vegetable with rich, juicy chicken thighs and let the concentrated heat of a pressure cooker do the hard work of braising both simultaneously. Since root vegetables like parsnips do an amazing job of absorbing the taste of whatever liquid they are cooked in, we knew we could infuse them with the flavors of cardamom, allspice, and cinnamon by blooming the spices in the chicken fat rendered from quickly searing the thighs. After nestling the thighs atop the parsnips and adding a splash of chicken broth, we simply turned on the pressure cooker and let it braise both to perfection. A dollop of sweet and tangy scallion-mint relish completed the dish. Use parsnips that measure roughly 1½ inches in diameter at the thickest end; if necessary, larger parsnips can be halved lengthwise. This recipe will only work in an electric pressure cooker.

¼ cup extra-virgin olive oil, divided
2 tablespoons white wine vinegar
1 tablespoon honey
1 teaspoon table salt, divided
4 scallions, sliced thin
4 (5- to 7-ounce) bone-in chicken thighs, trimmed
¼ teaspoon pepper
¾ teaspoon ground cardamom
¼ teaspoon ground cinnamon
⅛ teaspoon cayenne pepper
2 pounds parsnips, peeled, thin ends discarded
¾ cup chicken broth
¼ cup chopped fresh mint
¼ cup whole almonds, toasted and chopped

1. Whisk 3 tablespoons oil, vinegar, honey, and ¼ teaspoon salt in medium bowl until honey has dissolved. Stir in scallions and set aside.

2. Pat chicken dry with paper towels and sprinkle with pepper and ¼ teaspoon salt. Using highest sauté or browning function, heat remaining 1 tablespoon oil in electric pressure cooker until just smoking. Place chicken skin side down in pot and cook until well browned on first side, about 5 minutes; transfer to plate. Turn off electric pressure cooker.

3. Add cardamom, cinnamon, cayenne, and remaining ½ teaspoon salt to fat left in pot and cook, using residual heat, until fragrant, about 30 seconds. Add parsnips and toss to coat with spice mixture. Add broth, scraping up any browned bits, then arrange parsnips in even layer. Place chicken skin side up on top of parsnips along with any accumulated juices. Lock lid into place and close pressure release valve. Select high pressure cook function and cook for 14 minutes.

4. Turn off electric pressure cooker and quick-release pressure. Carefully remove lid, allowing steam to escape away from you. Transfer chicken to serving platter and discard skin, if desired. Using large spoon, gently transfer parsnips to platter with chicken. Stir mint and almonds into scallion mixture and season with salt and pepper to taste. Dollop relish over chicken and parsnips. Serve.

Chicken Schnitzel with Apple-Fennel Rémoulade

Serves 4 to 6 | **Total Time** 1 hour

WHY THIS RECIPE WORKS Chicken schnitzel, defined by its tender cutlets and fine, wrinkly crust that puffs away from the meat during frying, becomes a complete weeknight meal with the easy addition of a tangy-crisp rémoulade featuring in-season apples and fennel. Adding oil to the egg wash we used to anchor the bread crumb crust to the cutlets made the coating slightly elastic, allowing steam to build and puff it away from the meat as the cutlets cooked. Use fine, unseasoned store-bought bread crumbs for this recipe; substituting panko bread crumbs will produce a crust that lacks the proper texture and appearance. The oil must wash over the cutlets in waves to achieve the desired wrinkles and puff, so the ample space provided by a large Dutch oven is necessary; do not attempt to use a smaller pot. Serve with Apple-Fennel Rémoulade (recipe follows).

½ cup all-purpose flour
2 large eggs
1 tablespoon vegetable oil
2 cups plain dried bread crumbs
4 (6- to 8-ounce) boneless, skinless chicken breasts, trimmed
2 tablespoons kosher salt
1 teaspoon pepper
2 cups vegetable oil for frying
Lemon wedges

1. Spread flour in shallow dish. Beat eggs and 1 tablespoon oil in second shallow dish. Place bread crumbs in third shallow dish. Set wire rack in rimmed baking sheet. Line second rimmed baking sheet with double layer of paper towels. Adjust oven rack to middle position and heat oven to 200 degrees.

2. Halve chicken breasts horizontally to form 8 cutlets of even thickness. Place 1 cutlet between 2 sheets of plastic wrap and pound to ½-inch thickness. Repeat with remaining cutlets. Sprinkle each cutlet on both sides with ¾ teaspoon salt and ⅛ teaspoon pepper.

3. Working with 1 cutlet at a time, dredge cutlets thoroughly in flour, shaking off excess, then coat with egg mixture, allowing excess to drip back into dish to ensure very thin coating. Coat evenly with bread crumbs, pressing on crumbs to adhere. Place cutlets on prepared wire rack, taking care not to overlap cutlets. Let coating dry for 5 minutes.

4. Add 2 cups oil to large Dutch oven and heat over medium-high heat to 350 degrees. Lay 2 or 3 cutlets (depending on size) in oil, without overlapping them, and cook, shaking pot continuously and gently, until cutlets are wrinkled and light golden brown on both sides, 1 to 1½ minutes per side. Transfer cutlets to paper towel–lined sheet, flip to blot excess oil, and transfer sheet to oven to keep warm. Repeat with remaining cutlets. Serve immediately with lemon wedges.

Pressure-Cooker Chicken with Spiced Whole Parsnips and Scallion-Mint Relish

Apple-Fennel Rémoulade

Serves 6 to 8 | **Total Time** 15 minutes

- ¼ cup mayonnaise
- 2 tablespoons whole-grain mustard
- 2 tablespoons lemon juice
- 2 tablespoons capers, rinsed, plus 1 tablespoon brine
- 4 celery ribs, sliced thin on bias
- 1 fennel bulb, 1 tablespoon fronds minced, stalks discarded, bulb halved, cored, and sliced thin crosswise
- 1 apple, cored and cut into 2-inch-long matchsticks

Whisk mayonnaise, mustard, lemon juice, and caper brine together in large bowl. Add celery, fennel bulb, apple, and capers and toss to combine. Season with salt and pepper to taste. Top with fennel fronds and serve.

Chicken Schnitzel with Apple-Fennel Rémoulade

Chicken, Spinach, and Artichoke Pot Pie

Thanksgiving Quinoa Bowl

Chicken, Spinach, and Artichoke Pot Pie

Serves 4 | Total Time 1¼ hours **MAKE AHEAD**

WHY THIS RECIPE WORKS This easy pot pie is as quick to make as it is comforting. Thawed frozen spinach and jarred artichokes packed in a serving of vegetables with zero prep work. Boursin cheese was the other key to the recipe's ease, melting into an exceptionally lush sauce when combined with broth and just a splash of cream, which we thickened with finely ground Wondra flour. Last, a buttery sheet of store-bought puff pastry made the perfect top crust. While we prefer the flavor and texture of jarred whole baby artichoke hearts in this recipe, you can substitute 6 ounces frozen artichoke hearts, thawed and patted dry, for the jarred. To thaw frozen puff pastry, let it stand either in the refrigerator for 24 hours or on the counter for 30 minutes to 1 hour. You can substitute all-purpose flour for the Wondra flour, if necessary; however, the sauce will have a pasty, slightly gritty texture.

1¼ pounds frozen spinach, thawed and squeezed dry
1 (5.2-ounce) package Boursin Garlic & Fine Herbs cheese
1 cup jarred whole artichoke hearts packed in water, halved
2 carrots, peeled and shredded
¾ cup chicken broth
½ cup heavy cream
¼ cup capers, rinsed
1 tablespoon Wondra flour
12 ounces boneless, skinless chicken breasts, trimmed and sliced thin
1 teaspoon grated lemon zest
¼ teaspoon table salt
⅛ teaspoon pepper
1 (9½ by 9-inch) sheet puff pastry, thawed
1 large egg, lightly beaten with 2 tablespoons water

1. Adjust oven rack to middle position and heat oven to 425 degrees. Spray 8-inch square baking dish with vegetable oil spray. Stir spinach, Boursin, artichokes, carrots, broth, cream, capers, and flour together in bowl, then transfer to prepared dish.

2. Toss chicken with lemon zest in second bowl, sprinkle with salt and pepper, and spread in even layer over spinach mixture. Cut puff pastry into 8-inch square and place over top of chicken. Cut four 2-inch slits in center of dough, then brush dough with egg wash. (Pot pie, prepared through step 2, can be refrigerated for up to 24 hours. Bake as directed in step 3.)

3. Bake until crust is golden brown and filling is bubbling, 30 to 35 minutes, rotating dish halfway through baking. Remove pot pie from oven and let cool for 10 minutes before serving.

Rustic Turkey Tart

Serves 6 to 8 | **Total Time** 1 hour `MAKE AHEAD`

WHY THIS RECIPE WORKS Thanksgiving dinner is notorious for yielding heaping portions of leftovers—leftover turkey foremost among them. Living off of turkey soup and sandwiches for the next few days is a tried-and-true strategy for making the most of the leftover meat, but these aren't the only options available. If you're looking for more inspiration, we suggest baking some of those leftovers into a savory, flaky tart. Using our recipe for Press-In Tart Dough eliminated the stressful step of transferring a rolled sheet of dough to the tart pan. We loved the balanced interplay that additions of toasted pecans; tart, chewy cranberries; and sweet diced pears brought to the turkey filling. Coupled with the richness and piquancy of crumbled blue cheese and sour cream, the festive flavors of this tart feel like a welcome extension of the holidays. We found that firm pears worked best, as soft pears were too watery and mushy. We recommend buying a chunk of blue cheese and crumbling it just before using.

1½ cups leftover turkey meat, cut into bite-sized pieces
1 cup sour cream
¾ cup crumbled blue cheese, divided
4 firm pears, peeled, cored, and diced
¼ cup pecans, toasted and chopped
¼ cup dried cranberries
3 tablespoons heavy cream
1 tablespoon minced fresh thyme or ¼ teaspoon dried
1 recipe Press-In Tart Dough (page 254), baked and cooled

1. Adjust oven rack to middle position and heat oven to 425 degrees. Combine turkey, sour cream, ½ cup cheese, pears, pecans, cranberries, heavy cream, and thyme in large bowl; season with salt and pepper to taste. Transfer turkey mixture to tart crust, then sprinkle with remaining ¼ cup cheese.

2. Bake until crust is golden brown and cheese is melted, about 20 minutes. Let cool 20 minutes. Serve warm or at room temperature. (Tart can be refrigerated for up to 24 hours. Let come to room temperature before serving.)

Thanksgiving Quinoa Bowl

Serves 4 | **Total Time** 1¼ hours `MAKE AHEAD`

WHY THIS RECIPE WORKS With make-ahead options for its major components (mini turkey meatballs, a nutty grain base, and a creamy sauce that ties it all together), this bowl puts Thanksgiving flavors within reach on a regular weeknight. We riffed on traditional stuffing and cranberry sauce with quinoa and dried cranberries, and the green bean "side" is the easiest ever. Be sure to use ground turkey in this recipe, not ground turkey breast (also labeled 99 percent fat-free). If you buy unwashed quinoa (or if you are unsure whether it's been washed), be sure to rinse it before cooking to remove its bitter protective coating (called saponin). We love the complex flavor of our homemade roasted garlic dressing, but you can substitute store-bought roasted garlic dressing if you like. You can make microwave-fried shallots for a garnish, if desired: Combine thinly sliced shallots with vegetable oil and microwave, stirring frequently, until shallots are golden brown.

1½ cups prewashed white quinoa
1¾ cups water or chicken broth
1⅛ teaspoons table salt, divided
1 slice hearty white sandwich bread, crust removed, torn into ¼-inch pieces
2 tablespoons milk
1 pound ground turkey
¼ cup chopped fresh parsley
1½ teaspoons ground fennel
1½ teaspoons ground sage
½ teaspoon pepper
4 teaspoons vegetable oil, divided
8 ounces green beans, trimmed and halved crosswise
¼ cup Creamy Roasted Garlic Dressing (page 52)
¼ cup dried cranberries

1. Cook quinoa in large saucepan over medium-high heat, stirring frequently, until very fragrant and makes continuous popping sound, 5 to 7 minutes. Stir in water and ½ teaspoon salt and bring to simmer. Reduce heat to low, cover, and simmer until quinoa is tender and water is absorbed, 18 to 22 minutes, stirring once halfway through cooking. (Cooked quinoa can be refrigerated for up to 3 days. Allow to come to room temperature before using.)

2. Mash bread and milk into paste in medium bowl using fork. Break turkey into small pieces over bread mixture and add parsley, fennel, sage, pepper, and ½ teaspoon salt. Lightly knead with your hands until well combined. Pinch off and roll mixture into 18 meatballs (about ½ tablespoon each). (Meatballs can be refrigerated for up to 24 hours.)

3. Heat 1 teaspoon oil in 12-inch nonstick skillet over medium heat until shimmering. Add half of meatballs and cook until well browned and tender, 5 to 7 minutes. Transfer meatballs to plate; cover with aluminum foil to keep warm. Repeat with 1 teaspoon oil and remaining meatballs. Transfer meatballs to plate, cover with foil, and set aside until ready to serve. Heat remaining 2 teaspoons oil in now-empty skillet over medium-high heat until shimmering. Add green beans and remaining ⅛ teaspoon salt and cook until green beans are spotty brown, 2 to 4 minutes.

4. Divide quinoa among individual serving bowls, then top with meatballs and green beans. Drizzle with dressing and sprinkle with cranberries. Serve.

Creamy Roasted Garlic Dressing

Makes 1 cup | **Total Time** 1½ hours

  3 large garlic heads (3 ounces each), outer papery skins removed and top third of heads cut off and discarded
  ¼ cup white wine vinegar
  3 tablespoons water
  2 teaspoons honey
  1 teaspoon Dijon mustard
  1 teaspoon minced fresh thyme
  ¼ teaspoon table salt
  ¼ teaspoon pepper
  ⅓ cup extra-virgin olive oil

1. Adjust oven rack to middle position and heat oven to 350 degrees. Wrap garlic in aluminum foil and roast until golden brown and very tender, 1 to 1¼ hours. Remove garlic from oven and carefully open foil packet. When garlic is cool enough to handle, squeeze cloves from skins (you should have about 6 tablespoons); discard skins.

2. Process garlic, vinegar, water, honey, mustard, thyme, salt, and pepper in blender until smooth, about 45 seconds, scraping down sides of blender jar as needed. With blender running, slowly add oil until combined, about 1 minute. Season with salt and pepper to taste. (Dressing can be refrigerated for up to 1 week; whisk to recombine before serving.)

Steak Salad with Beets, Walnuts, and Creamy Horseradish Dressing

Serves 4 | **Total Time** 35 minutes

WHY THIS RECIPE WORKS We love the sweet, earthy flavor of beets; if you're a fellow beet-lover, chances are one of them is rolling around in your crisper drawer right now. This tangy steak salad is the perfect way to use up that straggling beet. Instead of roasting the beet, we grated it into the salad raw, where it contributed freshness and just the right amount of crunch to make our salad feel substantial. Strip steaks took only a few minutes to cook on the stovetop, and when paired with the beets and crunchy toasted walnuts, they made a hearty dinner-size entrée. Horseradish sauce is a classic match for beef, so we added 2 tablespoons of lemon juice to a mixture of horseradish, sour cream, and chives, loosening up the sauce to just the right consistency for dressing the greens.

  2 (10- to 12-ounce) boneless strip steaks, about 1 inch thick, trimmed
  ½ teaspoon table salt
  ¼ teaspoon pepper
  1 tablespoon vegetable oil
  ¼ cup sour cream
  2 tablespoons lemon juice
  2 tablespoons chopped fresh chives
  1 tablespoon prepared horseradish
  2 romaine lettuce hearts (12 ounces), torn into bite-size pieces
  1 beet, trimmed, peeled, and grated (1½ cups)
  ½ cup walnuts, toasted and chopped

1. Pat steaks dry with paper towels and sprinkle with salt and pepper. Heat oil in 12-inch skillet over medium-high heat until just smoking. Add steaks and cook until meat registers 120 to 125 degrees (for medium-rare), 3 to 5 minutes per side. Transfer to cutting board, tent with aluminum foil, and let rest for 5 minutes.

2. Meanwhile, whisk sour cream, lemon juice, chives, and horseradish together in large bowl.

3. Slice steak thin with grain. Add lettuce, beet, and walnuts to bowl with dressing and toss to coat. Season with salt and pepper to taste. Divide salad among individual plates, top each with sliced steak, and serve.

Steak Tips with Wilted Spinach, Goat Cheese, and Pear Salad

Serves 4 | **Total Time** 30 minutes

WHY THIS RECIPE WORKS Autumn and winter are the seasons for warm salads full of just-wilted greens and extra-hearty add-ins. After searing steak tips, we took advantage of the fond left in the skillet to build a warm dressing for a wilted salad imbued with complex meaty flavor. To make the dressing, we added a bit of oil to the pan and sautéed shallot, garlic, and pistachios. We then tossed tender, sweet baby spinach with our warm dressing to soften the leaves just slightly. A ripe pear was just the thing to liven up this simple salad with sweet crunch, while crumbled goat cheese added a pleasantly tart creaminess. Sirloin steak tips are often sold as flap meat. We prefer to buy flap meat and cut our own steak tips. We prefer steak tips cooked to medium-rare, but if you prefer them more or less done, see our guidelines on page 414.

- 2 pounds sirloin steak tips, trimmed and cut into 2-inch pieces
- ¾ teaspoon table salt, divided
- ¼ teaspoon plus ⅛ teaspoon pepper, divided
- 3 tablespoons extra-virgin olive oil, divided
- 6 ounces (6 cups) baby spinach
- 1 ripe but firm pear, halved, cored, and sliced thin
- 3 tablespoons chopped pistachios
- 1 shallot, halved and sliced thin
- 1 garlic clove, minced
- 1 teaspoon minced fresh thyme or ¼ teaspoon dried
- ½ teaspoon grated lemon zest plus 2 tablespoons juice
- 2 ounces goat cheese, crumbled (½ cup)

1. Pat steak tips dry with paper towels and sprinkle with ½ teaspoon salt and ¼ teaspoon pepper. Heat 1 tablespoon oil in 12-inch skillet over medium-high heat until just smoking. Add steaks and cook until meat registers 120 to 125 degrees (for medium-rare), 3 to 5 minutes per side. Transfer steak tips to serving platter and let rest while finishing salad.

2. Combine spinach and pear in large bowl. Add remaining 2 tablespoons oil, pistachios, shallot, garlic, thyme, remaining ¼ teaspoon salt, and remaining ⅛ teaspoon pepper to now-empty skillet and cook over medium heat until pistachios are toasted and shallot is softened, about 2 minutes. Stir in lemon zest and juice and any accumulated meat juices. Immediately pour warm dressing over spinach and toss gently to wilt. Season with salt and pepper to taste. Sprinkle with goat cheese. Serve with steak tips.

Steak Salad with Beets, Walnuts, and Creamy Horseradish Dressing

Steak Tips with Wilted Spinach, Goat Cheese, and Pear Salad

Pressure-Cooker Steak Tips with Warm Potato and Green Bean Salad

Serves 4 | **Total Time** 1 hour

WHY THIS RECIPE WORKS Steak tips don't need much more than a good sear, so we fast-tracked a hearty dinner of steak tips and potato salad by using our electric pressure cooker. We started by cooking the potatoes for our side. In just a few minutes under pressure the potatoes were nearly tender, so we released the pressure, added a few handfuls of green beans to the pot, and simmered them along with the potatoes until both were perfectly cooked. As for our steak tips, the pressure cooker's sauté function gave them a great sear on all sides and cooked them to a perfect medium-rare in the time it took for our veggies to cool slightly. To finish, we dressed the still-warm potatoes and green beans in a lighter, tangier version of the traditional mayonnaise dressing made with yogurt, whole-grain mustard, and capers. Use potatoes measuring 1 to 2 inches in diameter; if using larger potatoes, cut them into 1½-inch pieces. Sirloin steak tips are often sold as flap meat. We prefer to buy flap meat and cut our own steak tips. This recipe will only work in an electric pressure cooker.

1½ pounds small red potatoes, unpeeled, halved
2 (2-inch) strips lemon zest plus 1 tablespoon juice
¾ teaspoon table salt, divided, plus salt for cooking potatoes
8 ounces green beans, trimmed and cut on bias into 1-inch lengths
1 pound sirloin steak tips, trimmed and cut into 2-inch pieces
¼ teaspoon pepper
1 tablespoon extra-virgin olive oil
¼ cup plain yogurt
¼ cup chopped fresh parsley
1 shallot, minced
2 tablespoons mayonnaise
1 tablespoon whole-grain mustard
2 teaspoons capers, rinsed and minced

1. Add potatoes, 4 cups water, lemon zest, and ½ teaspoon salt to electric pressure cooker. Lock lid into place and close pressure release valve. Select high pressure cook function and cook for 3 minutes. Turn off electric pressure cooker and quick-release pressure. Carefully remove lid, allowing steam to escape away from you.

Pressure-Cooker Steak Tips with Warm Potato and Green Bean Salad

2. Stir green beans into pot with potatoes, partially cover, and cook, using highest sauté or browning function, until beans are crisp-tender, 3 to 5 minutes. Drain potatoes and green beans; discard lemon zest. Let vegetables cool while preparing steak tips.

3. Pat steak tips dry with paper towels and sprinkle with ¼ teaspoon salt and pepper. Using highest sauté or browning function, heat oil in clean, dry electric pressure cooker until just smoking. Add steak tips and cook until well browned on all sides and meat registers 120 to 125 degrees (for medium-rare) or 130 to 135 degrees (for medium), 6 to 8 minutes.

4. Whisk yogurt, parsley, shallot, mayonnaise, mustard, capers, lemon juice, and remaining ½ teaspoon salt together in large bowl. Add vegetables to bowl with dressing and gently toss to combine. Season with salt and pepper to taste. Serve steak tips with salad.

Roasted Pork Chops and Vegetables with Parsley Vinaigrette

Serves 4 | **Total Time** 1¼ hours

WHY THIS RECIPE WORKS Thick-cut bone-in pork chops deliver the succulence of a larger roast but cook in just 10 to 15 minutes, making them perfect weeknight treats. They stand up to high heat and bold flavors, so it was natural to pair them with roasted root vegetables and to season everything well for a memorably flavor-packed meal. Roasting the chops on a rimmed baking sheet meant that there was plenty of room to cook our side at the same time. Since pork chops cook relatively quickly, we partially roasted the vegetables—a rustic mix of thick-sliced Yukon Gold potatoes, carrot spears, and fennel wedges—to give them a head start. For a bold hit of flavor, we tossed them with fresh rosemary and peeled whole garlic cloves, which turned deliciously creamy when roasted. Once the vegetables had softened and taken on some color, we added our pork chops, which we'd seasoned with pepper, salt, paprika, and coriander for a deeply flavored crust. Finally, we whisked together a simple parsley vinaigrette to drizzle over the pork, ensuring that our meal would end on an herbal note.

- 1 pound Yukon Gold potatoes, unpeeled, halved lengthwise, and sliced crosswise ½ inch thick
- 1 pound carrots, peeled and cut into 3-inch lengths, thick ends quartered lengthwise
- 1 fennel bulb, stalks discarded, bulb halved, cored, and cut into ½-inch-thick wedges
- 10 garlic cloves, peeled
- 2 teaspoons minced fresh rosemary or ¾ teaspoon dried
- ⅓ cup extra-virgin olive oil, divided
- 2¾ teaspoons kosher salt, divided
- 1½ teaspoons pepper, divided
- 1 teaspoon paprika
- 1 teaspoon ground coriander
- 4 (12-ounce) bone-in pork rib or center-cut chops, 1 to 1½ inches thick, trimmed
- 2 tablespoons minced fresh parsley
- 4 teaspoons red wine vinegar
- 1 small shallot, minced
- ⅛ teaspoon sugar

Roasted Pork Chops and Vegetables with Parsley Vinaigrette

1. Adjust oven rack to upper-middle position and heat oven to 450 degrees. Toss potatoes, carrots, and fennel with garlic, rosemary, 1 tablespoon oil, 1½ teaspoons salt, and ¼ teaspoon pepper in bowl and spread in single layer on rimmed baking sheet. Roast until beginning to soften, about 25 minutes.

2. Combine 2 teaspoons salt, 1 teaspoon pepper, paprika, and coriander in bowl. Using sharp knife, cut 2 slits, about 2 inches apart, through fat on edge of each pork chop. Pat chops dry with paper towels, rub with 1 teaspoon oil, then sprinkle with spice mixture.

3. Arrange pork chops on top of vegetables and continue to roast until pork registers 145 degrees and vegetables are tender, 10 to 15 minutes, rotating sheet halfway through roasting.

4. Remove sheet from oven and let pork chops rest for 5 minutes. Whisk parsley, vinegar, shallot, sugar, remaining oil, remaining ¼ teaspoon salt, and remaining ¼ teaspoon pepper together in bowl. Drizzle vinaigrette over pork and vegetables. Serve.

Harissa-Glazed Pork Tenderloin with Couscous Salad

Serves 4 | **Total Time** 50 minutes

WHY THIS RECIPE WORKS You can't go wrong when pairing pork with a sweet-spicy glaze, especially when the sweetness comes from floral honey and the spice comes from smoky-savory harissa, a paste made from Aleppo peppers and a blend of earthy-sharp aromatics and spices. To give the pork an attractive crust, we browned two tenderloins on all sides before brushing them with the glaze and roasting; we made use of the pork's hands-off time in the oven to throw together a vibrant side dish of carrots, feta cheese, olives, and super quick-cooking couscous. We prefer to use our homemade Harissa (page 101), but you can substitute store-bought if you wish, though spiciness can vary greatly by brand.

- 2 tablespoons honey
- 4 teaspoons harissa, divided
- 2 (1-pound) pork tenderloins, trimmed
- 1¼ teaspoons table salt, divided
- ½ teaspoon pepper
- 6 tablespoons extra-virgin olive oil, divided
- 1 cup water
- ¾ cup couscous
- 3 carrots, peeled and shredded
- 3 ounces feta cheese, crumbled (¾ cup)
- ½ cup pitted green olives, chopped coarse
- ½ cup fresh parsley leaves

1. Adjust oven rack to middle position and heat oven to 350 degrees. Combine honey and 1 tablespoon harissa in small bowl. Pat pork dry with paper towels and sprinkle with 1 teaspoon salt and pepper. Heat 1 tablespoon oil in 12-inch nonstick skillet over medium-high heat until just smoking. Add pork and cook until well browned on all sides, about 7 minutes. Transfer pork to rimmed baking sheet; brush with honey mixture; and roast until meat registers 135 degrees, about 18 minutes.

2. Meanwhile, bring water, 2 tablespoons oil, remaining 1 teaspoon harissa, and remaining ¼ teaspoon salt to boil in now-empty skillet. Stir in couscous, cover, and remove from heat. Let stand for 5 minutes.

3. Let pork rest for 5 minutes. Stir carrots, feta, olives, parsley, and remaining 3 tablespoons oil into couscous. Slice pork and serve with couscous salad.

Crunchy Parmesan-Crusted Pork Chops with Glazed Winter Squash

Crunchy Parmesan-Crusted Pork Chops with Glazed Winter Squash

Serves 4 | **Total Time** 1¼ hours

WHY THIS RECIPE WORKS Pork is known for pairing spectacularly well with autumnal ingredients such as sweet squash and apple, so it was only natural that we sought to use it in the ultimate one-pan fall supper. For oven-cooked pork chops that delivered maximum crunch sans stovetop sear, we used a coating of Parmesan-seasoned panko. Elevating the pork on a wire rack set in a rimmed baking sheet kept the crust crunchy. We put our microwave through its paces here, using it to pretoast the panko with oil to make sure it became properly crisped and browned. We also used it to jump-start the cooking of rings of acorn squash so they could finish roasting in the oven alongside the chops, and to cook cranberries down into a sweet-tart, couldn't-be-easier sauce. The pork's craggy golden-brown exterior, together with the squash's scalloped edges and the bright red sauce, made this hearty roasted dinner feel like something truly special.

2 cups panko bread crumbs, toasted
3 tablespoons extra-virgin olive oil, divided
¼ cup all-purpose flour
2 large eggs
3 tablespoons Dijon mustard
1¾ teaspoons table salt, divided
¾ teaspoon pepper, divided
2 ounces Parmesan cheese, grated (1 cup)
¼ cup minced fresh parsley
4 (6- to 8-ounce) boneless pork chops,
    ¾ to 1 inch thick, trimmed
1 large acorn squash (2 pounds), sliced into
    ½-inch-thick rings and seeded
1 cup plus 1 tablespoon sugar, divided
12 ounces (3 cups) fresh or thawed frozen cranberries
¼ cup water
¼ teaspoon five-spice powder

1. Adjust oven rack to middle position and heat oven to 425 degrees. Toss panko with 2 tablespoons oil in bowl until evenly coated. Microwave panko, stirring every 30 seconds, until light golden brown, about 5 minutes; let cool slightly. Spread flour in shallow dish. Whisk eggs, mustard, 1 teaspoon salt, and ½ teaspoon pepper together in second shallow dish. Toss panko, Parmesan, and parsley together in third shallow dish.

2. Set wire rack in aluminum foil–lined rimmed baking sheet and spray with vegetable oil spray. Using sharp knife, cut 2 slits, about 2 inches apart, through fat on edge of each pork chop. Pat chops dry with paper towels. Working with 1 chop at a time, dredge in flour, dip in egg mixture, allowing excess to drip off, then coat with toasted panko mixture, pressing gently to adhere. Lay pork chops on 1 side of prepared wire rack, spaced at least ¼ inch apart.

3. Place squash on large plate, brush with remaining 1 tablespoon oil, and sprinkle with ½ teaspoon salt and remaining ¼ teaspoon pepper. Microwave squash until it begins to soften but still holds its shape, 8 to 10 minutes.

4. Place squash on empty side of rack, slightly overlapping if needed, and sprinkle with 1 tablespoon sugar. Roast pork chops and squash until pork registers 145 degrees and squash is lightly tender, 20 to 30 minutes, rotating sheet halfway through roasting. Remove sheet from oven and let rest for 5 minutes.

5. Meanwhile, combine cranberries, water, five-spice powder, remaining ¼ teaspoon salt, and remaining 1 cup sugar in bowl and microwave, stirring occasionally, until cranberries are broken down and juicy, about 10 minutes. Coarsely mash cranberries with fork and serve with pork chops and squash.

Italian Sausage with Grapes and Balsamic Vinegar

Serves 4 to 6 | **Total Time** 45 minutes

WHY THIS RECIPE WORKS This dish originated as a quick yet sustaining meal for Italian vineyard laborers, making use of the plentiful wine grapes of the harvest season. Rich, juicy, and well browned, sweet Italian sausages are a great match for the grapes, which softened and caramelized in the pan. We liked the depth that nontraditional onion added when sautéed with the sausages. Once the sausages were browned, we covered the skillet to allow steam to finish cooking them through, keeping the casings intact and the meat moist. We tied the dish together with a tangy-sweet vinegar-based sauce. Serve with crusty bread for a heartier meal.

1 tablespoon extra-virgin olive oil
1½ pounds sweet Italian sausage
1 pound seedless red grapes, halved lengthwise (3 cups)
1 onion, halved and sliced thin
¼ cup water
¼ teaspoon pepper
⅛ teaspoon table salt
¼ cup dry white wine
1 tablespoon chopped fresh oregano
2 teaspoons balsamic vinegar
2 tablespoons chopped fresh mint

1. Heat oil in 12-inch skillet over medium heat until shimmering. Arrange sausages in skillet and cook, turning once, until browned on 2 sides, about 5 minutes. Tilt skillet and carefully remove excess fat with paper towel. Distribute grapes and onion over and around sausages. Add water and immediately cover. Cook, turning sausages once, until they register between 160 and 165 degrees and onion and grapes have softened, about 10 minutes.

2. Transfer sausages to paper towel–lined plate and tent with aluminum foil. Return skillet to medium-high heat and stir pepper and salt into grape-onion mixture. Spread grape-onion mixture in even layer in skillet and cook without stirring until browned, 3 to 5 minutes. Continue to cook, stirring frequently, until mixture is well browned and grapes are soft but still retain their shape, 3 to 5 minutes. Stir in wine and oregano, scraping up any browned bits, and cook over medium heat until wine is reduced by half, 30 to 60 seconds. Off heat, stir in vinegar.

3. Arrange sausages on serving dish and spoon grape-onion mixture over top. Sprinkle with mint and serve.

Stuffed Veal Cutlets with Prosciutto and Fontina

Serves 4 | **Total Time** 1¼ hours

WHY THIS RECIPE WORKS In the Alpine region of Italy's Valle d'Aosta, food is rich and hearty owing to its climate and history: Substantial foods kept folks sated for the heavy lifting required of mountain living. These stuffed veal cutlets are a prime example of this type of fare, but you don't have to be a mountainside laborer to enjoy them: Supremely tender veal cutlets stuffed with salty prosciutto and tangy melted cheese are a real treat, and their quick cooking time makes them weeknight-ready. While traditional recipes vary in preparation, we followed the simplest approach, pounding a small veal cutlet until it was thin and tender, topping it with cheese and prosciutto, and then placing another thin piece of veal on top. We breaded this veal "sandwich" and then cooked it in butter until its exterior was golden and crispy. Lemon wedges are the only accompaniment this satisfying dish needs, but you can also serve it next to a simple green salad.

- 4 (3-ounce) veal cutlets, about ¼ inch thick, halved crosswise to make 8 cutlets
- 2 ounces fontina cheese, shredded (½ cup)
- 4 thin slices prosciutto (2 ounces)
- 2 large eggs
- 2 tablespoons all-purpose flour
- 1½ cups panko bread crumbs
- 8 tablespoons unsalted butter
  Lemon wedges

1. Pat 2 cutlet halves dry with paper towels and place between 2 layers of plastic wrap. Pound cutlets into rough 5 by 4-inch rectangles, about ⅛ inch thick, using meat pounder. Place 2 tablespoons fontina in center of 1 cutlet half, leaving ¼-inch border around edge. Lay 1 slice prosciutto on top of fontina, folding it as needed to prevent any overhang. Place second cutlet half over prosciutto. Gently press down on cutlets to compress layers, then press along edges to seal. Repeat with remaining cutlet halves, fontina, and prosciutto.

2. Whisk eggs and flour in shallow dish until smooth. Spread panko in second shallow dish. Working with 1 stuffed cutlet at a time, carefully dip in egg mixture, allowing excess to drip off. Dredge in panko to coat both sides, pressing gently so crumbs adhere. Place breaded cutlets in single layer on wire rack set in rimmed baking sheet and let stand for 5 minutes.

3. Melt butter in 12-inch nonstick skillet over medium heat (do not let butter brown). Place cutlets in skillet; cook until deep golden brown and crisp on first side, 3 to 6 minutes.

Stuffed Veal Cutlets with Prosciutto and Fontina

Gently flip cutlets using 2 spatulas and continue to cook until deep golden brown and crispy on second side, about 4 minutes, adjusting burner as needed to prevent scorching. Transfer cutlets to paper towel–lined plate and blot dry. Season with salt and pepper to taste. Serve immediately with lemon wedges.

NOTES FROM THE TEST KITCHEN

BUYING AND CUTTING VEAL CUTLETS
When shopping for veal cutlets, look for those in which no linear striation in the muscle is evident. These lines are an indication that the veal has been cut with the grain instead of against it and will be tough. Instead, the cutlets should have a smooth surface. If you can't find cutlets that have been cut against the grain, consider cutting your own cutlets: Starting with a piece of veal top round roast, use a boning knife to remove the silverskin. Once the silverskin is removed, use a long slicing knife to cut slices from roast on bias and against the grain that are between ¼ and ½ inch thick.

Lamb Meatballs with Orzo, Tomatoes, and Feta

Serves 4 | Total Time 1¼ hours **MAKE AHEAD**

WHY THIS RECIPE WORKS Pasta and meatballs are a perfect match both for one another and for a chilly evening. For a unique spin on this classic duo, we turned to lamb instead of beef or pork, and to orzo instead of spaghetti, and we enhanced the dish with the fresh, bold flavors of mint, oregano, and cinnamon. A panade—a simple paste made from Greek yogurt and panko—kept the meatballs moist and lent the dish welcome tangy flavor. We used our Dutch oven to deeply brown the meatballs and create lots of flavorful fond in the pot. Using some of the rendered fat to cook our aromatics gave our orzo pilaf a supersavory base. After toasting the orzo to golden brown, we added a combination of white wine and chicken broth and cooked the orzo until it was nearly tender. We were then able to simply nestle our seared meatballs back into the pot to cook them through. We finished the dish with a bright topping of cherry tomatoes, more fresh mint, and feta, which cut through the richness for a highly satisfying one-pot meal. Depending on the size of your Dutch oven, you may need to brown the meatballs in two batches rather than one.

Lamb Meatballs with Orzo, Tomatoes, and Feta

½ cup plain whole-milk Greek yogurt
¼ cup panko bread crumbs
3 tablespoons water
1 large egg
2 tablespoons minced fresh mint, plus
  2 tablespoons torn leaves
4 garlic cloves, minced, divided
2 teaspoons minced fresh oregano or
  ½ teaspoon dried
1½ teaspoons table salt, divided
¾ teaspoon ground cinnamon
⅛ teaspoon pepper
1½ pounds ground lamb
2 tablespoons extra-virgin olive oil
1 onion, chopped fine
2 cups orzo
3 cups chicken broth
½ cup dry white wine
8 ounces cherry tomatoes, halved
2 ounces feta cheese, crumbled (½ cup)

1. Mash yogurt, panko, and water together with fork in large bowl to form paste. Stir in egg, minced mint, half of garlic, oregano, 1 teaspoon salt, cinnamon, and pepper until combined. Add ground lamb and knead with your hands until thoroughly combined. Pinch off and roll mixture into eighteen 1½-inch meatballs. (Meatballs can be refrigerated for up to 24 hours.)

2. Heat oil in Dutch oven over medium-high heat until just smoking. Brown meatballs on all sides, 7 to 10 minutes; transfer to plate. Pour off all but 2 tablespoons fat from pot.

3. Add onion and remaining ½ teaspoon salt to fat left in pot and cook over medium heat until onion is softened and lightly browned, 5 to 7 minutes. Stir in remaining garlic and cook until fragrant, about 30 seconds. Add orzo and cook, stirring frequently, until lightly browned and golden, about 5 minutes.

4. Stir in broth and wine, scraping up any browned bits. Bring to simmer and cook, stirring occasionally, until most of liquid has been absorbed and orzo is almost tender, 7 to 10 minutes.

5. Reduce heat to medium-low and nestle meatballs into orzo. Cover and cook until orzo is tender and meatballs are fully cooked through, 5 to 10 minutes. Sprinkle with tomatoes, feta, and torn mint. Serve.

One-Pan Roasted
Salmon with White
Beans, Fennel, and
Tomatoes

Roasted Snapper and
Vegetables with
Mustard Sauce

One-Pan Roasted Salmon with White Beans, Fennel, and Tomatoes

Serves 4 | **Total Time** 1 hour

WHY THIS RECIPE WORKS With a few carefully chosen ingredients, summertime flavor is within reach even in the depths of winter. Cherry tomatoes are available year-round and gave us bright pops of color and acidity; combined with fennel and creamy white beans, they were a delicious side for flaky fillets of roasted salmon. The cherry tomatoes gave off flavorful juices, which, with the addition of butter and some lemon juice, made a luscious sauce. Better yet, all the elements of this one-pan dinner cooked together on a rimmed baking sheet in just an hour. We purchased fennel with the stalks still attached. If you can find only stalkless bulbs, then look for those that weigh around 10 to 12 ounces each. To ensure uniform pieces of salmon that cook at the same rate, buy a whole 2-pound center-cut fillet and cut it into four equal pieces.

2 (1-pound) fennel bulbs, stalks discarded, bulbs halved, cored, and sliced ¼ inch thick

2 tablespoons extra-virgin olive oil, divided

1¼ teaspoons table salt, divided

¾ teaspoon pepper, divided

2 (15-ounce) cans cannellini beans, rinsed

10 ounces cherry tomatoes, halved (2 cups)

¼ cup dry white wine

3 garlic cloves (2 sliced thin, 1 minced)

6 tablespoons unsalted butter, softened

1 teaspoon minced fresh thyme or ¼ teaspoon dried

1 teaspoon grated lemon zest plus 1 tablespoon juice

1 (2-pound) skinless salmon fillet, 1 to 1½ inches thick

2 tablespoons chopped fresh parsley

1. Adjust oven rack to middle position and heat oven to 450 degrees. Toss fennel, 1 tablespoon oil, ¼ teaspoon salt, and ¼ teaspoon pepper together on rimmed baking sheet. Spread fennel into even layer and roast until beginning to brown around edges, about 15 minutes.

2. Meanwhile, toss beans, tomatoes, wine, sliced garlic, ½ teaspoon salt, ¼ teaspoon pepper, and remaining 1 tablespoon oil together in bowl. Combine butter, thyme, lemon zest, and minced garlic in small bowl. Cut salmon crosswise into 4 fillets. Pat salmon dry with paper towels and sprinkle with remaining ½ teaspoon salt and remaining ¼ teaspoon pepper. Spread 1 tablespoon butter mixture on top of each fillet.

3. Remove sheet from oven. Add bean mixture to sheet with fennel, stir to combine, and spread into even layer. Arrange salmon on top of bean mixture, butter side up. Roast until centers of fillets register 125 degrees (for medium-rare), 17 to 20 minutes.

4. Transfer salmon to serving platter. Stir lemon juice and remaining 2 tablespoons butter mixture into bean mixture, transfer to serving platter with salmon, and sprinkle with parsley. Serve.

Roasted Snapper and Vegetables with Mustard Sauce

Serves 4 | **Total Time** 1 hour

WHY THIS RECIPE WORKS Looking for a lighter respite from your cold-weather meat-and-potatoes rut? Try this easy one-pan meal of hearty red snapper, golden potatoes, and charred broccoli. We started by tossing halved red potatoes and broccoli florets with oil, salt, and pepper separately and placing each on one side of a baking sheet to roast in a hot oven. We removed the broccoli once it was just tender and attractively charred, and added our fillets of red snapper to the freed-up side of the sheet, dropping the oven temperature to allow the fish to cook more gently and the browned potatoes to continue cooking through. A simple mix of lemon zest, honey, and paprika brushed on before roasting the fillets added just enough flavor and color to the fish, and paired beautifully with a bright sauce of chives and grainy mustard. Use small red potatoes measuring 1 to 2 inches in diameter.

6 tablespoons plus 2 teaspoons extra-virgin olive oil, divided
¼ cup minced fresh chives
2 tablespoons whole-grain mustard
1 tablespoon honey, divided
1 teaspoon grated lemon zest plus 2 teaspoons juice
1 teaspoon plus pinch table salt, divided
¾ teaspoon plus pinch pepper, divided
1 pound small red potatoes, unpeeled, halved
1 pound broccoli florets, cut into 2-inch pieces
½ teaspoon paprika
4 (6- to 8-ounce) skinless red snapper fillets, 1 inch thick

1. Adjust oven rack to lowest position and heat oven to 500 degrees. Combine 2 tablespoons oil, chives, mustard, 1 teaspoon honey, lemon juice, pinch salt, and pinch pepper in bowl; set mustard sauce aside until ready to serve. Brush rimmed baking sheet with 1 tablespoon oil.

2. Toss potatoes with 1 tablespoon oil, ¼ teaspoon salt, and ¼ teaspoon pepper in bowl. Place potatoes, cut sides down, on half of sheet. In now-empty bowl, toss broccoli with 2 tablespoons oil, ¼ teaspoon salt, and ¼ teaspoon pepper, then place on empty side of sheet. Roast until potatoes are golden brown and broccoli is spotty brown and tender, 12 to 14 minutes, rotating sheet halfway through roasting.

3. While potatoes and broccoli roast, combine paprika, 1 teaspoon oil, lemon zest, remaining 2 teaspoons honey, remaining ½ teaspoon salt, and remaining ¼ teaspoon pepper in small bowl; microwave until bubbling and fragrant, 10 to 15 seconds. Pat red snapper dry with paper towel, brush skinned sides of fillets with remaining 1 teaspoon oil, then brush tops of fillets with honey mixture.

4. Remove sheet from oven and reduce oven temperature to 275 degrees. Transfer broccoli to platter and tent with aluminum foil to keep warm. Place red snapper, skinned side down, on now-empty side of sheet. Continue to roast until fish flakes apart when gently prodded with paring knife and registers 130 degrees, 6 to 8 minutes, rotating sheet halfway through roasting.

5. Transfer potatoes and red snapper to platter with broccoli. Tent with foil and let stand for 10 minutes. Serve with mustard sauce.

Braised Halibut with Coriander, Carrots, and Pearl Couscous

Serves 4 | **Total Time** 1 hour

WHY THIS RECIPE WORKS Braising is a gentle, forgiving cooking method that guarantees moist, succulent fish. It also works particularly well for the sweet carrots and shallots in this dish. Our wine- and butter-enriched cooking liquid becomes a velvety sauce for the fish and couscous. We prefer this recipe with halibut, but another firm-fleshed white fish such as cod, striped bass, or sea bass can be substituted. Look for similarly-shaped fillets that are uniformly 1 inch thick. Pearl couscous is also known as Israeli couscous. You will need a 12-inch skillet with a tight-fitting lid for this recipe.

7 tablespoons unsalted butter, divided
1½ cups pearl couscous
2 cups water
1 teaspoon table salt, divided
5 carrots, peeled and trimmed
4 (6- to 8-ounce) skinless halibut fillets,
   1 to 1½ inches thick
3 shallots, sliced thin
½ teaspoon ground coriander
¾ cup dry white wine
1½ teaspoons lemon juice plus lemon wedges
   for serving
¼ cup chopped fresh cilantro, divided

1. Melt 1 tablespoon butter in medium saucepan over medium heat. Add couscous and cook, stirring frequently, until half of grains are golden, about 5 minutes. Stir in water and ¼ teaspoon salt. Increase heat to high and bring to boil. Reduce heat to low, cover, and simmer until water is absorbed and couscous is tender, 9 to 12 minutes. Off heat, fluff with fork and cover to keep warm.

2. While couscous cooks, shave carrots lengthwise into ribbons with vegetable peeler.

3. Pat halibut dry with paper towels and sprinkle with ½ teaspoon salt. Melt remaining 6 tablespoons butter in 12-inch skillet over low heat. Place halibut in skillet, skinned side up, increase heat to medium, and cook, shaking pan occasionally, until butter begins to brown (fish should not brown), 3 to 4 minutes. Using spatula, carefully transfer halibut to large plate, skinned side down.

4. Add shallots, coriander, carrots, and remaining ¼ teaspoon salt to skillet with butter and cook, stirring frequently, until beginning to soften, 2 to 4 minutes. Add wine and bring to gentle simmer. Place halibut, skinned side down, on top of vegetables. Reduce heat to low, cover, and cook until halibut flakes apart when gently prodded with paring knife and registers 140 degrees, 10 to 14 minutes.

5. Transfer couscous to serving bowl and sprinkle with 3 tablespoons cilantro. When halibut is done, remove from heat and transfer halibut and vegetables to serving platter, leaving sauce in skillet. Tent with aluminum foil.

6. Return skillet with sauce to high heat and cook until sauce is thickened, 2 to 3 minutes. Off heat, stir in lemon juice and season with salt and pepper to taste. Toss couscous with 2 tablespoons sauce and season with salt and pepper to taste. Spoon remaining sauce over fillets and sprinkle with remaining 1 tablespoon cilantro. Serve fillets with couscous and lemon wedges.

Palak Dal

Serves 4 to 6 | **Total Time** 1¼ hours VEGETARIAN

WHY THIS RECIPE WORKS This warmly spiced combination of lentils and spinach is a nutritious favorite in Indian cuisine. For our version, once quick-cooking red lentils had softened, a vigorous whisk transformed them into a rustic, porridge-like stew. Seasoning the lentils with a tadka (whole spices sizzled in ghee with aromatics) right before serving gave the dish loads of complexity. For less heat, remove the ribs and seeds of the serrano. Yellow mustard seeds can be substituted for brown. Monitor the spices and aromatics carefully during frying, reducing the heat if necessary to prevent scorching. Serve the dal with naan and basmati or another long-grain white rice.

4½ cups water
1½ cups (10½ ounces) dried red lentils,
   picked over and rinsed
1 tablespoon grated fresh ginger
¾ teaspoon ground turmeric
6 ounces (6 cups) baby spinach
1½ teaspoons table salt
3 tablespoons ghee
1½ teaspoons brown mustard seeds
1½ teaspoons cumin seeds
1 large onion, chopped
15 curry leaves, roughly torn (optional)
6 garlic cloves, sliced
4 whole dried arbol chiles
1 serrano chile, halved lengthwise
1½ teaspoons lemon juice, plus extra for seasoning
⅓ cup chopped fresh cilantro

1. Bring water, lentils, ginger, and turmeric to boil in large saucepan over medium-high heat. Reduce heat to maintain vigorous simmer. Cook, uncovered, stirring occasionally, until lentils are soft and starting to break down, 18 to 20 minutes.

2. Whisk lentils vigorously until coarsely pureed, about 30 seconds. Continue to cook until lentils have consistency of loose polenta or oatmeal, up to 5 minutes. Stir in spinach and salt and continue to cook until spinach is fully wilted, 30 to 60 seconds. Cover and set aside off heat.

3. Melt ghee in 10-inch skillet over medium-high heat. Add mustard seeds and cumin seeds and cook, stirring constantly, until seeds sizzle and pop, about 30 seconds. Add onion and cook, stirring frequently, until onion is just starting to brown, about 5 minutes. Add curry leaves, if using; garlic; arbols; and serrano and cook, stirring frequently, until onion and garlic are golden brown, 3 to 4 minutes.

4. Add lemon juice to lentils and stir to incorporate. (Dal should have consistency of loose polenta. If too thick, loosen with hot water, adding 1 tablespoon at a time.) Season with salt and extra lemon juice to taste. Transfer dal to serving bowl and spoon onion mixture on top. Sprinkle with cilantro and serve.

NOTES FROM THE TEST KITCHEN

SUBSTITUTING BROWNED BUTTER FOR GHEE
Ghee, pure butterfat with a distinctive, nutty flavor, is traditionally made by simmering fermented cream or butter until browned and then straining out its milk solids. We've found that you can produce a sort of faux ghee with similar nuttiness using browned butter. Here's how to do it: Melt 6 tablespoons butter in 10-inch skillet over medium-high heat. Cook, swirling skillet and stirring constantly with rubber spatula, until butter is dark golden brown and has nutty aroma, 1 to 3 minutes. Slowly pour butter into small heatproof bowl, leaving as much of browned milk solids behind as possible. Using paper towel, wipe solids from skillet and discard.

Palak Dal

Farro, White Bean, and Broccoli Rabe Gratin

Serves 4 to 6 | **Total Time** 1¼ hours
MAKE AHEAD   VEGETARIAN

WHY THIS RECIPE WORKS For a satisfying Italian-inspired gratin, we paired protein-rich farro and white beans with broccoli rabe. Cooking nutty toasted farro in a mixture of water, vegetable broth, and white miso deepened the gratin's flavor. Blanching the broccoli rabe tamed its bite and locked in its vibrant color. We topped it all with a mix of toasted panko and Parmesan for a salty-crunchy finish. Do not substitute pearl, quick-cooking, or presteamed farro for the whole farro in this recipe.

- 3 tablespoons extra-virgin olive oil, divided
- 1 onion, chopped fine
- ¼ teaspoon table salt, plus salt for cooking broccoli rabe
- 1½ cups whole farro
- 2 cups vegetable broth
- 2 tablespoons white miso
- ½ cup panko bread crumbs
- ¼ cup grated Parmesan cheese
- 1 pound broccoli rabe, trimmed and cut into 2-inch pieces
- 6 garlic cloves, minced
- ⅛ teaspoon red pepper flakes
- 1 (15-ounce) can small white beans, rinsed
- ¾ cup oil-packed sun-dried tomatoes, chopped

1. Heat 1 tablespoon oil in large saucepan over medium heat until shimmering. Add onion and ¼ teaspoon salt and cook until softened and lightly browned, 5 to 7 minutes. Stir in farro and cook, stirring occasionally, until lightly toasted, about 2 minutes. Stir in 2½ cups water, broth, and miso; bring to simmer; and cook, stirring often, until farro is just tender and remaining liquid has thickened into creamy sauce, 25 to 35 minutes.

2. Meanwhile, toss panko with 1 tablespoon oil in bowl and microwave, stirring occasionally, until golden brown, 1 to 2 minutes. Stir in Parmesan and set aside.

3. Bring 4 quarts water to boil in Dutch oven. Add broccoli rabe and 1 tablespoon salt and cook until just tender, about 2 minutes. Drain broccoli rabe and set aside. Combine remaining 1 tablespoon oil, garlic, and pepper flakes in now-empty pot and cook over medium heat until fragrant and sizzling, 1 to 2 minutes. Stir in reserved broccoli rabe and cook until hot and well coated, about 2 minutes. Off heat, stir in beans, tomatoes, and farro mixture. Season with salt and pepper to taste. (Gratin can be prepared through step 3 and refrigerated for up to 24 hours. To serve, stir ½ cup water into gratin, cover with aluminum foil, and bake in 400-degree oven on upper-middle rack until hot throughout, about 30 minutes, before continuing with step 4.)

4. Adjust oven rack 10 inches from broiler element and heat broiler. Transfer bean-farro mixture to broiler-safe 3-quart gratin dish (or broiler-safe 13 by 9-inch baking dish) and sprinkle with reserved panko mixture. Broil until lightly browned and hot, 1 to 2 minutes. Serve.

Hoppin' John

Serves 8 | **Total Time** 1¾ hours

WHY THIS RECIPE WORKS In the Lowcountry of South Carolina and Georgia, eating hoppin' John—a slow-cooked dish of rice, black-eyed peas, and ham hocks—at the start of a new year is said to bring good luck. Bacon and boneless ham provided our version with heaps of smoky, meaty depth with minimal simmering; we browned the bacon and then used its rendered fat to brown the ham slices. Convenient frozen black-eyed peas cooked much faster than dried and stayed intact in the dish (unlike canned peas). Rinsing the rice before adding it to the pot rid the grains of excess starch, and covering the hoppin' John with aluminum foil contained the escaping steam—two steps that ensured tender, separate grains of rice. After stirring in the reserved bacon and ham, we served up a one-pot meal that, lucky for us, makes for delicious eating. Small boneless hams are available in the meat case at most supermarkets. If you can't find one, you can substitute an equal weight of ham steak. Covering the surface of the dish with aluminum foil after adding the rice helps ensure that the rice cooks evenly. Serve with hot sauce, if desired.

- 6 slices bacon, chopped
- 1 (1- to 1½-pound) boneless ham, cut into ¾-inch-thick planks
- 1 onion, chopped fine
- 2 celery ribs, minced
- 4 garlic cloves, minced
- ½ teaspoon dried thyme
- 4 cups chicken broth
- 2 pounds frozen black-eyed peas
- 2 bay leaves
- 1½ cups long-grain white rice
- 3 scallions, sliced thin

1. Cook bacon in Dutch oven over medium heat until crispy, 5 to 7 minutes. Using slotted spoon, transfer bacon to paper towel–lined plate. Pour off all but 1 tablespoon fat from pot and brown ham, about 3 minutes per side. Transfer ham to plate with bacon.

2. Add onion and celery to pot and cook until softened, about 5 minutes. Stir in garlic and thyme and cook until fragrant, about 30 seconds. Add broth, peas, bay leaves, and ham and bring to boil. Reduce heat to low and simmer, covered, until peas are just tender, about 20 minutes. Transfer ham to cutting board and cut into ½-inch pieces.

3. Place rice in fine-mesh strainer and rinse under cold running water until water runs clear, about 1 minute. Drain rice well and stir into pot. Place square of aluminum foil directly on surface of simmering liquid. Simmer, covered, until liquid is absorbed and rice is tender, about 20 minutes, stirring and repositioning foil twice during cooking. Remove from heat and let stand, covered, for 10 minutes. Discard bay leaves. Fluff rice with fork. Stir in scallions, bacon, and ham. Serve.

Garlicky Spaghetti with Basil and Broiled Tomatoes

Serves 4 to 6 | **Total Time** 45 minutes VEGETARIAN

WHY THIS RECIPE WORKS One simple technique—broiling—was the key to the unbelievably enticing flavor of this pantry-friendly alternative to the easy dinnertime mainstay of pasta with tomato sauce. Most tomatoes are at their best during a very narrow summertime window, but some, like oblong Roma tomatoes, are of reliably good quality year-round. This is where the broiler came in: Unwilling to settle for good, we combined Roma tomato slices with a little sugar and then popped them under the broiler, where they became sweetly caramelized and lightly crispy, their flavor concentrated and amplified. A generous amount of garlic and a sprinkling of Parmesan and pine nuts were the perfect piquant, nutty foils to the tomatoes. A serrated knife makes quick work of cutting tomatoes. Since broilers vary so much in their output, we included a wide time range to broil the tomatoes. Watch them carefully to get them to a crispy, golden brown without burning. You can substitute 1 pound of linguine or bucatini for the spaghetti, if desired. Note that you'll need 1 cup of basil, so shop accordingly.

- ¼ cup extra-virgin olive oil
- 6 garlic cloves, minced
- ¼ teaspoon red pepper flakes
- 2 ounces Parmesan, grated (1 cup), divided
- 2 tablespoons pine nuts, chopped
- 2 teaspoons grated lemon zest plus 2 tablespoons juice (1 lemon)
- 1 pound spaghetti
- ½ teaspoon table salt plus salt for cooking pasta
- 6 Roma tomatoes, cored and sliced ¼ inch thick crosswise
- ½ teaspoon sugar
- ½ teaspoon pepper
- 1 cup chopped fresh basil, divided

1. Bring 4 quarts water to boil in large pot. Heat oil, garlic, and pepper flakes in 8-inch nonstick skillet over low heat, stirring often, until garlic is pale golden brown, 9 to 12 minutes; remove from heat and set aside. Combine ½ cup Parmesan and pine nuts in bowl and set aside.

2. Add pasta and 1 tablespoon salt to boiling water and cook, stirring occasionally, until al dente. Reserve 1 cup cooking water, then drain pasta and return it to pot.

3. While pasta cooks, adjust oven rack 6 inches from broiler element and heat broiler. Place tomatoes in large bowl. Add sugar, pepper, and ½ teaspoon salt and toss to coat. Arrange tomatoes in even layer on wire rack set in rimmed baking sheet. Top tomatoes evenly with Parmesan–pine nut mixture.

4. Broil tomatoes until topping is golden brown, rotating sheet halfway through cooking, 3 to 6 minutes.

5. Add lemon zest and juice, reserved garlic-oil mixture, and reserved cooking water to pasta. Stir until well coated with oil and no water remains in pot. Add ¾ cup basil and remaining ½ cup Parmesan and toss to combine. Season with salt and pepper to taste. Divide pasta among individual bowls, top with tomatoes, drizzle with extra oil to taste, and sprinkle with remaining ¼ cup basil. Serve.

Hoppin' John

Garlicky Spaghetti with Basil and Broiled Tomatoes

Pasta alla Norcina

Unstuffed Shells with Butternut Squash and Leeks

Pasta with Sautéed Wild Mushrooms

Serves 8 | **Total Time** 1 hour `VEGETARIAN`

WHY THIS RECIPE WORKS The intense flavor of sautéed mushrooms combined with a light cream sauce yields a woodsy, full-flavored pasta dish. We used a combination of cremini and shiitake mushrooms for rich, meaty flavor and texture. We cooked the mushrooms covered until they had released their juices before removing the lid to drive off moisture and maximize browning. A few aromatics rounded out the flavors in a simple sauce of broth, heavy cream, and lemon juice. To make this dish vegetarian, use vegetable broth.

- 4 tablespoons unsalted butter
- 2 tablespoons extra-virgin olive oil
- 1 red onion, chopped fine
- 1 pound shiitake mushrooms, stemmed and sliced ¼ inch thick
- 1 pound cremini mushrooms, trimmed and sliced ¼ inch thick
- ½ teaspoon table salt, plus salt for cooking pasta
- 5 garlic cloves, minced
- 1½ tablespoons minced fresh thyme
- 2 cups vegetable or chicken broth
- ¾ cup heavy cream
- 1½ tablespoons lemon juice
- 1½ pounds farfalle
- 3 ounces Parmesan cheese, grated (1½ cups)
- ¼ cup minced fresh parsley

1. Heat butter and oil in 12-inch skillet over medium heat until butter is melted. Add onion and cook until softened, about 5 minutes. Stir in shiitakes, cremini, and ½ teaspoon salt, cover, and cook until mushrooms have released their liquid, about 8 minutes. Uncover and continue to cook until mushrooms are dry and browned, about 8 minutes. Stir in garlic and thyme and cook until fragrant, about 30 seconds; transfer to bowl and cover to keep warm.

2. Add broth and cream to now-empty skillet and bring to simmer, scraping up browned bits. Off heat, stir in lemon juice and season with salt and pepper to taste. (Sauce can be covered and held at room temperature for up to 2 hours. Add mushrooms, cover, and return to brief simmer over medium-low heat before adding to pasta in step 4.)

3. Meanwhile, bring 6 quarts water to boil in large pot. Add pasta and 1½ tablespoons salt and cook, stirring often, until al dente. Reserve 1 cup cooking water, then drain pasta and return it to pot.

4. Add mushrooms, sauce, Parmesan, and parsley to pasta and toss to combine. Add reserved cooking water as needed to adjust consistency, and serve.

Pasta alla Norcina

Serves 6 to 8 | **Total Time** 1¼ hours

WHY THIS RECIPE WORKS Pasta alla Norcina—fresh sausage in a creamy, cheesy sauce tossed with pasta—is the kind of cozy cold-weather dish that keeps you feeling satiated and warm. The star of the meal is rich, moist, seasoned sausage, traditionally from the Italian region of Umbria. In keeping with tradition, we eschewed regular Italian links and made the sausage ourselves, which turned out to be surprisingly easy (no meat grinder required). We started by combining ground pork with salt and baking soda and letting it sit for 10 minutes. The baking soda raised the meat's pH, improving its ability to hold on to water and thus stay juicy. Rosemary, nutmeg, and garlic rounded out the flavor. We formed our pork into one big patty, browned it on both sides, and chopped it up; the large sausage pieces finished cooking through in the sauce, guaranteeing moist, tender meat. Mushrooms bolstered the dish's earthiness. White mushrooms may be substituted for the cremini. We prefer the flavor and texture of fresh pasta here, but dried can be used as well.

½ teaspoon plus pinch table salt, plus salt for cooking pasta

¼ teaspoon baking soda

8 ounces ground pork

3 garlic cloves, minced, divided

1¼ teaspoons minced fresh rosemary, divided

1¼ teaspoons pepper, divided

⅛ teaspoon ground nutmeg

8 ounces cremini mushrooms, trimmed

7 teaspoons extra-virgin olive oil, divided

1 pound fresh or dried orecchiette

½ cup dry white wine

¾ cup heavy cream

1½ ounces Pecorino Romano cheese, grated (¾ cup)

3 tablespoons minced fresh parsley

1 tablespoon lemon juice

1. Spray large plate with vegetable oil spray. Dissolve ½ teaspoon salt and baking soda in 4 teaspoons water in medium bowl. Gently fold in pork until combined and let stand for 10 minutes. Add one-third of garlic, ¾ teaspoon rosemary,

¾ teaspoon pepper, and nutmeg and smear with rubber spatula until well combined and tacky, 10 to 15 seconds. Transfer sausage mixture to prepared plate and form into rough 6-inch patty. Pulse mushrooms in food processor until finely chopped, 10 to 12 pulses.

2. Heat 2 teaspoons oil in 12-inch skillet over medium-high heat until just smoking. Add patty and cook, without moving it, until browned, 2 to 3 minutes. Flip and continue to cook until well browned on second side, 2 to 3 minutes longer (very center will be raw). Transfer patty to cutting board and chop into ⅛- to ¼-inch pieces.

3. Bring 4 quarts water to boil in large pot. Add pasta and 1 tablespoon salt and cook, stirring often, until al dente. Reserve 1½ cups cooking water, then drain pasta and return it to pot.

4. Meanwhile, heat 1 tablespoon oil in now-empty skillet over medium heat. Add mushrooms and remaining pinch salt and cook, stirring frequently, until browned, 5 to 7 minutes. Stir in remaining garlic, remaining ½ teaspoon rosemary, remaining ½ teaspoon pepper, and remaining 2 teaspoons oil and cook until fragrant, about 30 seconds. Stir in wine, scraping up any browned bits, and cook until completely evaporated, 1 to 2 minutes. Stir in sausage, cream, and ¾ cup pasta cooking water and simmer until meat is no longer pink, 1 to 3 minutes. Off heat, stir in Pecorino Romano until smooth.

5. Add sauce, parsley, and lemon juice to pasta and toss to coat. Adjust consistency with reserved cooking water as needed. Season with salt and pepper to taste. Serve immediately.

Unstuffed Shells with Butternut Squash and Leeks

Serves 4 to 6 | **Total Time** 1 hour `VEGETARIAN`

WHY THIS RECIPE WORKS Stuffed pasta shells, draped in sauce and oozing cheese, are a luxurious Sunday supper–type meal. Unstuffed shells are our quicker weeknight go-to: Instead of individually stuffing uncooked shells, we simply dolloped spoonfuls of a creamy ricotta-Parmesan mixture on top. We stirred the uncooked shells into a thin sauce of butternut squash and leeks (autumn produce superstars), water, and cream, where they absorbed the excess liquid as they cooked. After topping with the cheese mixture, we slid the skillet into the oven for a few minutes until the cheese was bubbly and browned. You will need a 12-inch ovensafe skillet for this recipe. You can substitute large or medium shells, ziti, farfalle, campanelle, or orecchiette for the jumbo shells.

8 ounces (1 cup) whole-milk ricotta cheese
2 ounces Parmesan cheese, grated (1 cup), divided
1 teaspoon grated lemon zest
¾ teaspoon table salt, divided
¼ teaspoon pepper
1 tablespoon extra-virgin olive oil
1½ pounds butternut squash, peeled, seeded, and cut into ½-inch pieces (5 cups)
1 pound leeks, white and light green parts only, halved lengthwise, sliced thin, and washed thoroughly
2 garlic cloves, minced
Pinch cayenne pepper
¼ cup dry white wine
4 cups water
1 cup heavy cream
12 ounces jumbo pasta shells
2 tablespoons chopped fresh basil

1. Adjust oven rack to middle position and heat oven to 375 degrees. Combine ricotta, ½ cup Parmesan, lemon zest, ¼ teaspoon salt, and pepper in bowl; cover and refrigerate until needed.

2. Heat oil in 12-inch ovensafe nonstick skillet over medium heat until shimmering. Add squash, leeks, and remaining ½ teaspoon salt and cook until leeks are softened, about 5 minutes. Stir in garlic and cayenne and cook until fragrant, about 30 seconds. Add wine and cook until almost completely evaporated, about 1 minute.

3. Stir in water and cream, then add pasta. Increase heat to medium-high and cook at vigorous simmer, stirring gently and often, until pasta is tender and liquid is thickened, about 15 minutes.

4. Season with salt and pepper to taste. Sprinkle remaining ½ cup Parmesan over top, then dollop evenly with ricotta mixture. Transfer skillet to oven and bake until Parmesan is melted and spotty brown, about 5 minutes. Remove skillet from oven. Let cool for 10 minutes, then sprinkle with basil and serve.

NOTES FROM THE TEST KITCHEN

THE RIGHT PAN FOR THE JOB

Before using a skillet with a nonstick coating in the oven, check that the manufacturer's recommended maximum temperature is above the temperature at which you'll be cooking. If the handle of your skillet has a silicone grip, keep it safe in the heat by wrapping it in a double layer of wet paper towels followed by a double layer of aluminum foil.

Bulgur-Stuffed Acorn Squash with Ras el Hanout

Serves 4 | **Total Time** 45 minutes VEGETARIAN

WHY THIS RECIPE WORKS Acorn squash halves overflowing with a spiced grain filling bring fall flair to the table and are generous enough to eat as a main course. We first microwaved the squash halves until they were tender. We then scooped some of the softened squash from the skins; mixed it with quickly hydrated bulgur, toasted pine nuts, and ras el hanout; and mounded the mixture back into the squash shells. A few minutes under the broiler produced great browning. Do not use coarse or medium-grind bulgur in this recipe. It is OK if your baking dish does not spin in the microwave. For an accurate measurement of boiling water, bring a full kettle of water to a boil and then measure out the desired amount.

2 acorn squashes (1½ pounds each), halved pole to pole and seeded
1¼ teaspoons table salt, divided
¾ cup boiling water
½ cup fine-grind bulgur
4 tablespoons unsalted butter
½ cup pine nuts or chopped walnuts
2 teaspoons ras el hanout
2 tablespoons pomegranate molasses

1. Adjust oven rack to upper-middle position and heat broiler. Line rimmed baking sheet with aluminum foil and spray with vegetable oil spray. Sprinkle cut sides of squash halves with ¾ teaspoon salt and place cut side down on large plate. Microwave until squash is tender and offers no resistance when pierced with paring knife, 15 to 20 minutes. Transfer squash halves cut side up to prepared sheet and let cool for 5 to 10 minutes.

2. Using spoon, scoop flesh from each squash half into bowl, leaving about ⅛-inch thickness of flesh; set aside.

3. Meanwhile, pour boiling water over bulgur and remaining ½ teaspoon salt in large bowl. Cover and let sit until tender, about 5 minutes. Fluff with fork and set aside.

4. Melt butter in 12-inch skillet over medium heat. Cook, swirling skillet constantly, until butter begins to brown and has nutty aroma, 1 to 2 minutes. Add pine nuts and ras el hanout and cook, stirring constantly, until fragrant and foamy, 1 to 2 minutes. Stir in reserved squash and cook until mixture thickens, 3 to 4 minutes. Gently fold into cooked bulgur in bowl, then mound mixture evenly in squash shells.

5. Broil until beginning to brown, about 5 minutes. Drizzle with pomegranate molasses and serve.

Roasted Cabbage Wedges with Stewed Tomatoes and Chickpeas

Serves 4 | **Total Time** 50 minutes VEGETARIAN

WHY THIS RECIPE WORKS Cut cabbage into wedges and roast it, creating charred, crispy edges with tender, sweet layers underneath, and we guarantee this humble vegetable will be the center of your plate. We covered the curry powder–rubbed cabbage with aluminum foil for the first stage of cooking to steam the wedges. Uncovering the wedges for the last part of cooking and adding another drizzle of oil crisped and browned the upper sides while maximizing browning underneath. While the cabbage roasted, we simmered chickpeas and tomatoes with more curry powder to give our dish bulk and protein for staying power. When slicing the cabbage into wedges, be sure to slice through the core, leaving it intact so the wedges don't fall apart. Smaller 2-pound cabbages work best here; if you have a larger cabbage, you can remove the outer leaves until it weighs about 2 pounds, though it may not brown as well. Serve with Herbed Yogurt Sauce (recipe follows), if you like.

- 7 tablespoons vegetable oil, divided
- 1 tablespoon curry powder, divided
- 1½ teaspoons sugar
- 1 teaspoon table salt
- ¼ teaspoon pepper
- 1 head green cabbage (2 pounds)
- 2 garlic cloves, minced
- 2 teaspoons grated fresh ginger
- 2 (15-ounce) cans chickpeas, undrained
- 10 ounces grape tomatoes, halved
- ¼ cup chopped fresh cilantro

1. Adjust oven rack to lowest position and heat oven to 500 degrees. Combine ¼ cup oil, 2 teaspoons curry powder, sugar, salt, and pepper in small bowl. Halve cabbage through core and cut each half into 4 approximately 2-inch-wide wedges, leaving core intact (you will have 8 wedges).

2. Arrange cabbage wedges in even layer on rimmed baking sheet, then brush cabbage all over with oil mixture. Cover tightly with aluminum foil and roast for 10 minutes. Remove foil and drizzle 2 tablespoons oil evenly over wedges. Return cabbage to oven and roast, uncovered, until cabbage is tender and sides touching sheet are well browned, 12 to 15 minutes.

3. Meanwhile, heat remaining 1 tablespoon oil in 12-inch skillet over medium-high heat until shimmering. Add garlic, ginger, and remaining 1 teaspoon curry powder and cook,

Bulgar-Stuffed Acorn Squash with Ras el Hanout

mashing mixture into skillet, until fragrant, about 30 seconds. Add chickpeas and their liquid and tomatoes and bring to simmer. Cook, stirring frequently, until tomatoes begin to break down and mixture has thickened slightly, 7 to 9 minutes.

4. Divide cabbage among individual plates and spoon chickpea mixture over top. Sprinkle with cilantro and serve.

Herbed Yogurt Sauce

Makes about 1 cup | **Total Time** 35 minutes

- 1 cup plain yogurt
- 2 tablespoons minced fresh cilantro
- 2 tablespoons minced fresh mint
- 1 garlic clove, minced

Whisk all ingredients in bowl until combined. Season with salt and pepper to taste. Let sit until flavors meld, about 30 minutes. (Sauce can be refrigerated for up to 2 days.)

weekend roasting & braising

*For larger-size centerpiece roasts, see pages 104–122.

■ MAKE AHEAD ■ VEGETARIAN
Photo: Pressure-Cooker Boneless Short Rib and Cauliflower Puttanesca

Roast Chicken with Cranberry-Walnut Stuffing

Serves 4 | **Total Time** 2 hours

WHY THIS RECIPE WORKS An herb butter–rubbed chicken boasting a cranberry-walnut stuffing sounds like a meal fit for a holiday table, but this version moves the whole production to a Dutch oven for a fuss-free, one-pot dinner any time. The Dutch oven's tall sides easily contained the chicken and a hefty portion of stuffing. We sautéed aromatics to give the dish a flavor base, then nestled the butter-rubbed chicken into the pot and surrounded it with cubes of sturdy Italian bread. Placing the bread cubes around the chicken rather than underneath it allowed them to toast while soaking up the chicken's flavorful juices. While the chicken rested, we completed the stuffing with a small amount of broth, sweet-tart dried cranberries, buttery toasted walnuts, and fresh parsley.

    4 tablespoons unsalted butter, melted, plus
       1 tablespoon unsalted butter
    4 teaspoons minced fresh sage, divided
    4 teaspoons minced fresh thyme, divided
 1¼ teaspoons table salt, divided
   ¾ teaspoon pepper, divided
    1 (3½- to 4-pound) whole chicken, giblets discarded
    1 onion, chopped coarse
    2 celery ribs, chopped coarse
    5 ounces Italian bread, cut into ½-inch pieces (4 cups)
   ⅓ cup chicken broth
   ⅓ cup dried cranberries
   ¼ cup walnuts, toasted and chopped coarse
    2 tablespoons minced fresh parsley

1. Adjust oven rack to middle position and heat oven to 425 degrees. Combine melted butter, 2 teaspoons sage, 2 teaspoons thyme, 1 teaspoon salt, and ½ teaspoon pepper in bowl. Pat chicken dry with paper towels, tuck wingtips behind back, and rub all over with butter mixture.

2. Melt remaining 1 tablespoon butter in Dutch oven over medium heat. Add onion, celery, remaining ¼ teaspoon salt, and remaining ¼ teaspoon pepper and cook until vegetables are softened, about 5 minutes. Stir in remaining 2 teaspoons sage and remaining 2 teaspoons thyme and cook until fragrant, about 30 seconds.

3. Off heat, place chicken, breast side up, in pot, then tuck bread evenly around sides of chicken. Transfer pot to oven and roast, uncovered, until breast registers 160 degrees and thighs register 175 degrees, about 1 hour, rotating pot halfway through roasting.

Spice-Roasted Chicken with Chili and Oregano

4. Remove pot from oven. Transfer chicken to carving board, brushing any bread pieces back into pot, and let rest for 15 minutes.

5. Meanwhile, stir broth, cranberries, and walnuts into bread mixture and cover to keep warm. Stir parsley along with any accumulated chicken juices into stuffing. Carve chicken and serve with stuffing.

Spice-Roasted Chicken with Chili and Oregano

Serves 4 | **Total Time** 2 hours

WHY THIS RECIPE WORKS One of the simplest—and best—ways to flavor a roast chicken is with a spice rub. This combination lends itself to endless flavor variations through simply switching up the spices used. Here, we rubbed the chicken with oil (which helped the spices stick) and sprinkled on a combination of chili powder, granulated garlic, and dried oregano. The chicken emerged from the oven browned (not burnt) and superflavorful. Roasting at a moderately high temperature helped ensure rendered fat and slightly crispy skin. The skillet captured the seasoned drippings, which (after a quick skim to remove excess fat) became an easy pan sauce for the carved bird. We used a stainless-steel skillet when developing this recipe, but you can also use a 12-inch cast-iron skillet. If using table salt, reduce the amount to 1 teaspoon.

1 tablespoon chili powder
1 tablespoon dried oregano
2 teaspoons kosher salt
1 teaspoon granulated garlic
1 teaspoon pepper
1 (3½- to 4-pound) whole chicken, giblets discarded
2 tablespoons extra-virgin olive oil, divided
1 teaspoon cornstarch
½ cup water
2 teaspoons lemon juice

1. Adjust oven rack to middle position and heat oven to 400 degrees. Combine chili powder, oregano, salt, granulated garlic, and pepper in bowl. Pat chicken dry with paper towels. Transfer chicken, breast side down, to 12-inch ovensafe skillet and rub exposed side with 1 tablespoon oil. Sprinkle with half of spice mixture. Flip chicken breast side up and rub exposed side with remaining 1 tablespoon oil and sprinkle with remaining spice mixture.

2. Transfer skillet to oven and roast until breast registers 160 degrees and thighs register 175 degrees, about 1 hour. Transfer chicken to carving board and let rest, uncovered, for 20 minutes. Reserve drippings in skillet.

3. While chicken rests, dissolve cornstarch in water. Carefully skim as much fat as possible from drippings and discard. Add cornstarch mixture to drippings and place over medium-high heat, whisking to scrape up any browned bits. Cook until mixture is boiling and slightly thickened, about 2 minutes. Off heat, whisk in lemon juice. Carve chicken and serve, passing sauce separately.

Spice-Roasted Chicken with Dill and Garlic

Substitute 1 tablespoon dried dill weed for chili powder and oregano.

Spice-Roasted Chicken with Fennel, Coriander, and Lemon

Substitute 1 tablespoon fennel seeds, 1 tablespoon ground coriander, and 1 tablespoon lemon zest for chili powder and oregano.

One-Pan Roast Turkey
Breast with Herb Stuffing

One-Pan Roast Turkey Breast with Herb Stuffing

Serves 4 to 6
Total Time 2¾ hours, plus 3 hours brining

WHY THIS RECIPE WORKS This one-pan feast makes a festive, flavorful turkey dinner as foolproof as can be. Roasting a turkey breast is a great way to celebrate on a smaller scale or enjoy the flavors of Thanksgiving for Sunday dinner. To start, we sautéed aromatics in a roasting pan before placing an herb butter–rubbed turkey breast on top. There was plenty of room for a side in our pan, so we sprinkled bread cubes around the breast so they could toast as the base for a stuffing, soaking up the turkey's flavorful juices. Starting at a high temperature allowed the turkey breast's juices to render for a deeply browned skin; we later lowered the heat to allow the breast to cook through gently. If using a self-basting turkey breast or kosher turkey, do not brine in step 1, but season with salt after rubbing with butter in step 2. Serve with All-Purpose Gravy (page 135) and Simple Cranberry Sauce (page 132).

½ cup table salt, for brining

1 (6- to 7-pound) bone-in whole turkey breast, trimmed

5 tablespoons unsalted butter, softened, divided

2 tablespoons minced fresh sage, divided

2 tablespoons minced fresh thyme, divided

1¼ teaspoons table salt, divided

¾ teaspoon pepper, divided

1 onion, chopped fine

2 celery ribs, minced

1 pound hearty white sandwich bread, cut into ½-inch cubes

1 cup chicken broth, plus extra as needed

1 tablespoon minced fresh parsley

1. Dissolve ½ cup salt in 1 gallon cold water in large container. Submerge turkey in brine, cover, and refrigerate for 3 to 6 hours; remove from brine and pat dry, inside and out, with paper towels.

2. Adjust oven rack to middle position and heat oven to 425 degrees. Mash 3 tablespoons butter, 1 tablespoon sage, 1 tablespoon thyme, 1 teaspoon salt, and ½ teaspoon pepper together in bowl. Using your fingers, gently separate skin from meat. Spread half of butter mixture under skin directly onto meat. Spread remaining butter mixture evenly over skin.

3. Melt remaining 2 tablespoons butter in large roasting pan over medium heat (over 2 burners, if possible). Add onion, celery, remaining ¼ teaspoon salt, and remaining ¼ teaspoon pepper and cook until vegetables are softened, about 5 minutes. Stir in remaining 1 tablespoon sage and remaining 1 tablespoon thyme and cook until fragrant, about 30 seconds. Off heat, place turkey, skin side up, on top of vegetables and arrange bread around turkey. Roast turkey for 30 minutes.

4. Reduce oven temperature to 325 degrees and continue to roast turkey until breast registers 160 degrees, about 1 hour.

5. Remove pan from oven. Transfer turkey to carving board, tent with aluminum foil, and let rest for 15 minutes. Stir broth and parsley into stuffing left in pan, cover with foil, and let stand for 10 minutes; add extra broth if stuffing is dry. Carve turkey and serve with stuffing.

Deviled Beef Short Ribs

Serves 4 to 6 | **Total Time** 4¼ hours

WHY THIS RECIPE WORKS These rich, ultratender, spicy, crumb-coated short ribs make the perfect late-winter dish. Braising is often the method of choice for short ribs since it allows the connective tissue to break down, making the meat fall-off-the-bone tender. But when we want something different than a saucy braise we turn to this modified slow-roasting technique: It lets us build up great flavor while ensuring completely tender ribs. Roasting the seasoned ribs meat side down in a covered baking dish allowed the meat to cook in its own juices, ensuring that all the fat rendered out. After cranking the heat and pouring off the juices, we brushed the ribs with a sauce of dry and prepared mustards, citrus, brown sugar, and jalapeños. These hot and spicy flavors, typical of "deviled" food, made a perfect counterpoint to the rich meat. A few rounds of brushing and roasting created a browned crust, and for a crunchy finish we coated the ribs with toasted panko. English-style short ribs contain a single rib bone. For a milder sauce, use only one jalapeño and discard the seeds.

⅔ cup yellow mustard

⅓ cup orange juice

⅓ cup packed light brown sugar

1–2 jalapeño chiles, stemmed, seeds reserved, and roughly chopped

5 teaspoons pepper, divided

4 teaspoons dry mustard

1 teaspoon grated lemon zest plus 1 tablespoon juice, divided

1 tablespoon table salt

½ teaspoon cayenne pepper

5 pounds bone-in English-style short ribs, bones 4 to 5 inches long, 1 to 1½ inches of meat on top of bone, trimmed

2 tablespoons unsalted butter

1½ cups panko bread crumbs

1 tablespoon chopped fresh parsley

1. Adjust oven rack to middle position and heat oven to 325 degrees. Process yellow mustard, orange juice, sugar, jalapeños and reserved seeds, 2 teaspoons pepper, dry mustard, and lemon juice in food processor until smooth, scraping down sides of bowl, about 30 seconds; set aside. (Mustard mixture can be refrigerated for up to 1 week.)

2. Combine salt, cayenne, and remaining 1 tablespoon pepper in bowl. Sprinkle ribs all over with spice mixture. Arrange ribs, meat side down, in 13 by 9-inch baking dish. Cover dish tightly with aluminum foil and roast until beef is nearly tender, about 3 hours.

3. Meanwhile, melt butter in 12-inch skillet over medium-high heat. Add panko and cook, stirring often, until golden brown, about 3 minutes. Off heat, stir in parsley and lemon zest and transfer to shallow dish.

4. Remove baking dish from oven and increase oven temperature to 425 degrees; transfer ribs to plate. Discard rendered fat and juices from dish. Brush beef (not bones) all over with one-fourth of mustard sauce and return ribs to dish, meat side up. Roast, uncovered, until beginning to brown, about 10 minutes. Brush beef again with one-third of remaining mustard sauce and continue to roast until well browned and completely tender, 10 to 15 minutes. Transfer ribs to serving dish and let rest for 15 minutes.

5. Brush beef once more with half of remaining mustard sauce and roll in panko mixture, taking care to entirely coat beef. Serve, passing remaining mustard sauce separately.

Maple-Glazed Pork Roast

Serves 4 to 6 | **Total Time** 1¾ hours

WHY THIS RECIPE WORKS An unexpected (and easy) technique yields tender, juicy pork with a rich, clingy glaze that packs pure maple flavor—all in one pan. We used a boneless blade-end loin roast here because it has the most fat and a lot of flavor. Tied into an even bundle, the roast fit into a skillet for a quick sear on the stovetop to build flavor. A maple glaze kept the exterior of the roast from becoming tough and dry. Reducing the glaze in the skillet after the roast was browned ensured that the fond left in the pan contributed meaty flavor. Roasting and turning the pork in the glaze made covering the whole roast easy and kept the pork plenty moist. The blade-end roast is our first choice; however, a center-cut roast will also work in this recipe. In either case, look for a roast with a thin fat cap (about ¼ inch thick) and don't trim this thin layer of fat. We prefer the stronger, richer flavor of grade A maple syrup labeled as "dark, robust" but lighter-colored syrup will work, too. You will need a 10-inch ovensafe skillet for this recipe. For brining instructions, see page 413. For how to tie a roast, see page 77.

- ½ cup maple syrup
- ⅛ teaspoon ground cinnamon
  Pinch ground cloves
  Pinch cayenne pepper
- 1 (2½- to 3-pound) boneless blade-end pork loin roast, tied at 1½ inch intervals and brined if desired
- 1½ teaspoons kosher salt
- ½ teaspoon pepper
- 2 teaspoons vegetable oil

Deviled Beef Short Ribs

Maple-Glazed Pork Roast

1. Adjust oven rack to middle position and heat oven to 325 degrees. Stir maple syrup, cinnamon, cloves, and cayenne together in measuring cup or bowl; set aside. Pat roast dry with paper towels, then sprinkle with salt and pepper.

2. Heat oil in 10-inch ovensafe skillet over medium-high heat until just smoking. Place roast fat side down in skillet and brown roast on all sides, about 10 minutes. Transfer roast to large plate. Reduce heat to medium and pour off fat from skillet; add maple syrup mixture and cook until fragrant, about 30 seconds (syrup will bubble immediately). Off heat, return roast to skillet; using tongs, roll to coat roast with glaze on all sides.

3. Place skillet in oven and roast until pork registers 140 degrees, 35 to 45 minutes, using tongs to roll and spin roast to coat with glaze twice during roasting time (skillet handle will be hot). Transfer roast to carving board; set skillet aside to cool slightly and thicken glaze, about 5 minutes. Pour glaze over roast and let rest for 15 minutes. Remove twine, slice roast ¼ inch thick, and serve.

Maple-Glazed Pork Roast with Orange Essence

Add 1 tablespoon grated orange zest to maple syrup along with spices.

Maple-Glazed Pork Roast with Rosemary

Substitute 2 teaspoons minced fresh rosemary for cinnamon, cloves, and cayenne.

Maple-Glazed Pork Roast with Smoked Paprika

Add 2 teaspoons smoked hot paprika to maple syrup along with spices.

Roast Pork Loin with Sweet Potatoes and Cilantro Sauce

Serves 6 | **Total Time** 1¾ hours

WHY THIS RECIPE WORKS This modern take on a roast pork dinner updates meat and potatoes with fresh flavors: a tender spice-rubbed pork loin, caramelized sweet potatoes, and a lively green herb sauce. And, as an added bonus, it's a one-pan dinner—no piles of dishes to wash on a Sunday night. We roasted the meat in a moderate 375-degree oven and turned it halfway through roasting to ensure juicy, perfectly

Roast Pork Loin with Sweet Potatoes and Cilantro Sauce

cooked pork. A mixture of ground coriander, cumin, and salt gave the pork's exterior color and flavor and complemented a lively cilantro sauce. To complete the meal, we tossed sweet potato chunks with some olive oil and a pinch of cayenne pepper and roasted them along with the pork. By the time the pork was done, the potatoes were tender but a little pale, so we set the pork aside to rest, turned up the heat, and returned the roasting pan to the oven to give the potatoes some extra time to caramelize. A ¼-inch-thick layer of fat on top of the roast is ideal; if your roast has a thicker fat cap, trim it back accordingly. If the pork is enhanced (injected with a salt solution), do not brine but do season with salt in step 1. This sauce uses two entire bunches of cilantro, including the stems. For brining instructions, see page 413. For how to tie a roast, see page 77.

PORK AND POTATOES

1 (2½- to 3-pound) boneless center-cut pork loin roast, trimmed, tied at 1½-inch intervals, brined if desired

1¼ teaspoons table salt, divided

1 teaspoon ground coriander

1 teaspoon ground cumin

3 pounds sweet potatoes, peeled, quartered, and cut into 2-inch pieces

3 tablespoons extra-virgin olive oil

⅛ teaspoon cayenne pepper

¼ teaspoon pepper

CILANTRO SAUCE

2½ cups fresh cilantro leaves and stems, trimmed (2 bunches)

½ cup extra-virgin olive oil

4 teaspoons lime juice

2 garlic cloves, minced

½ teaspoon sugar

1. FOR THE PORK AND POTATOES Adjust oven rack to lower-middle position and heat oven to 375 degrees. Pat roast dry with paper towels. Sprinkle with ¾ teaspoon salt, coriander, and cumin.

2. Toss sweet potatoes in bowl with oil and cayenne, sprinkle with pepper and remaining ½ teaspoon salt, and spread evenly into large roasting pan. Lay roast, fat side up, on top of potatoes. Roast until pork registers 140 degrees, 50 minutes to 1 hour 10 minutes, turning roast over halfway through roasting.

3. FOR THE CILANTRO SAUCE Meanwhile, pulse all ingredients in food processor until cilantro is finely chopped, 10 to 15 pulses, scraping down sides of bowl as needed. Season with salt and pepper to taste.

4. Remove pan from oven. Transfer roast to carving board and let rest for 20 minutes. While roast rests, increase oven temperature to 450 degrees and continue to roast potatoes until nicely browned, about 10 minutes. Remove twine from roast and slice ½ inch thick. Serve with potatoes and cilantro sauce.

TYING A ROAST

Tying a roast helps maintain its shape during cooking so that it cooks evenly. Use double knots to secure pieces of kitchen twine at 1- to 1½-inch intervals (2 to 3 finger widths apart).

Harissa-Rubbed Roast Boneless Leg of Lamb with Warm Cauliflower Salad

Harissa-Rubbed Roast Boneless Leg of Lamb with Warm Cauliflower Salad

Serves 6 to 8 | **Total Time** 2 hours

WHY THIS RECIPE WORKS The robust, smoky, peppery flavor of harissa is a perfect pairing with rich, meaty lamb. We took advantage of the broad surface area of a boneless leg of lamb by rubbing it with harissa paste before rolling it up and tying it to make a compact roast. After searing the roast on all sides to build up some flavorful browning, we rubbed more harissa on the exterior of the roast before moving it to the oven, where it finished roasting to a juicy medium-rare. The pan drippings were so flavorful, we saved some of them to toss with cauliflower florets, which we roasted right in the same pan. Combining the warm cauliflower with shredded carrots, sweet raisins, cilantro, and toasted almonds produced a side that paired perfectly with the fragrant, richly spiced lamb. We prefer to use our homemade Harissa (page 101), but you can substitute store-bought harissa if you wish, though spiciness can vary greatly by brand. Leg of lamb is often sold in elastic netting that must be removed. We prefer this roast cooked to medium-rare, but if you prefer it more or less done, see our guidelines on page 414. For how to tie a roast, see page 77.

- 1 (3½- to 4-pound) boneless half leg of lamb, trimmed and pounded to ¾-inch thickness
- ½ cup harissa, divided
- 2 tablespoons extra-virgin olive oil, divided
- 1 head cauliflower (2 pounds), cored and cut into 1-inch florets
- ½ teaspoon table salt
- ½ teaspoon pepper
- ½ red onion, sliced ¼ inch thick
- 1 cup shredded carrots
- ½ cup raisins
- ¼ cup fresh cilantro leaves
- 2 tablespoons sliced almonds, toasted
- 1 tablespoon lemon juice, plus extra for seasoning

1. Adjust oven rack to lower-middle position and heat oven to 375 degrees. Set V-rack in large roasting pan and spray with vegetable oil spray. Lay roast on cutting board with rough interior side (which was against bone) facing up and rub with 2 tablespoons harissa. Roll roast and tie with kitchen twine at 1½-inch intervals, then rub exterior with 1 tablespoon oil.

2. Heat remaining 1 tablespoon oil in 12-inch skillet over medium-high heat until just smoking. Brown lamb on all sides, about 8 minutes. Brush lamb all over with remaining harissa and place fat side down in prepared V-rack. Roast until thickest part registers 125 degrees (for medium-rare), 50 minutes to 1 hour 10 minutes, flipping lamb halfway through roasting. Transfer lamb to carving board, tent with aluminum foil, and let rest while making salad.

3. Increase oven temperature to 475 degrees. Pour all but 3 tablespoons fat from pan; discard any charred drippings. Add cauliflower, salt, and pepper to pan and toss to coat. Cover with aluminum foil and roast until cauliflower is softened, about 5 minutes.

4. Remove foil and spread onion evenly over cauliflower. Roast until vegetables are tender and cauliflower is golden brown, 10 to 15 minutes, stirring halfway through roasting. Transfer vegetable mixture to serving bowl, add carrots, raisins, cilantro, almonds, and lemon juice and toss to combine. Season with salt, pepper, and lemon juice to taste. Slice leg of lamb ½ inch thick and serve with salad.

Prosciutto-Wrapped Cod with Lemon-Caper Butter

Serves 4 | **Total Time** 45 minutes

WHY THIS RECIPE WORKS You might not guess it from its mild nature, but cod can become a bold dinner party centerpiece when paired with a little pork. Wrapping cod fillets in thin sheets of prosciutto before arranging the fillets in a skillet contributed meaty, salty flavor to the flaky white fish. To get good coloring and crispiness on the prosciutto, we first cooked the wrapped cod on the stovetop before transferring the skillet to the oven to cook the fish through. The prosciutto infused the fish with its salty pork flavor and provided a layer of insulation for the fish during cooking, keeping it supermoist. A warm butter sauce, enlivened by capers, parsley, lemon zest and juice, and garlic, brought the dish together. Do not season the cod with salt before wrapping with the prosciutto; the briny capers and salty prosciutto add plenty of salt to the dish. Black sea bass, haddock, hake, and pollock make good substitutions for the cod. You will need a 12-inch ovensafe nonstick skillet for this recipe.

- 4 (6- to 8-ounce) skinless cod fillets, 1 inch thick
- ½ teaspoon pepper
- 8 thin slices prosciutto (4 ounces)
- 1 tablespoon vegetable oil
- 4 tablespoons unsalted butter, softened
- 2 tablespoons capers, rinsed and minced
- 2 tablespoons minced fresh parsley
- 1 teaspoon grated lemon zest plus 1 tablespoon juice
- 1 garlic clove, minced

1. Adjust oven rack to upper-middle position and heat oven to 450 degrees. Pat cod dry with paper towels and sprinkle with pepper. Wrap each fillet widthwise with 2 overlapping pieces of prosciutto.

2. Heat oil in 12-inch ovensafe nonstick skillet over medium-high heat until just smoking. Brown prosciutto-wrapped cod lightly on both sides, 2 to 4 minutes. Transfer skillet to oven and bake until cod flakes apart when gently prodded with paring knife and registers 135 degrees, about 8 minutes.

3. Using potholders, remove skillet from oven. Transfer cod to serving platter. Being careful of hot skillet handle, add butter, capers, parsley, lemon zest and juice, and garlic to now-empty skillet. Cook over medium heat, swirling skillet, until butter has melted. Spoon butter sauce over cod and serve.

Roasted Salmon with Orange Beurre Blanc

Serves 4 to 6 | **Total Time** 45 minutes

WHY THIS RECIPE WORKS Roasting a center-cut fillet of salmon rather than individual fillets makes serving silky fish for dinner an impressive-looking but almost-hands-off affair. We made our salmon special with a rub of floral, pleasantly bitter juniper berries and fennel seeds. A touch of sugar balanced their bitterness and promoted browning; orange zest added brightness. Transferring the fillet to a preheated baking sheet was easy with a foil sling. Beurre blanc—a classic French butter sauce—offered an elegant accompaniment. We made it while the salmon roasted, reducing wine and vinegar, enriching them with cream and butter, and finishing with orange zest. Use heavy-duty aluminum foil measuring 18 inches wide. You can also make this with arctic char. If using arctic char or wild salmon, cook the fillet until it reaches 120 degrees (for medium-rare) and start checking for doneness early.

SALMON

- 15 juniper berries, toasted
- ¾ teaspoon fennel seeds, toasted
- 1 teaspoon grated orange zest
- ½ teaspoon sugar
- ½ teaspoon table salt
- ½ teaspoon pepper
- 1 (1¾- to 2-pound) center-cut skin-on salmon fillet, 1½ inches thick, pin bones removed
- 1 tablespoon vegetable oil

BEURRE BLANC

- 3 tablespoons dry white wine
- 2 tablespoons white wine vinegar
- 1 small shallot, minced
  Pinch table salt
- 1 tablespoon heavy cream
- 8 tablespoons unsalted butter, cut into 8 pieces and chilled
- ⅛ teaspoon sugar
- ⅛ teaspoon grated orange zest

1. FOR THE SALMON Adjust oven rack to lowest position, place rimmed baking sheet on rack, and heat oven to 500 degrees. Grind juniper berries and fennel seeds in spice grinder until coarsely ground, about 30 seconds. Transfer spices to bowl and stir in orange zest, sugar, salt, and pepper.

2. Cut piece of heavy-duty aluminum foil 12 inches longer than salmon fillet and fold lengthwise into thirds. Make

Prosciutto-Wrapped Cod with Lemon-Caper Butter

8 shallow slashes, about 3 inches long and 1 inch apart, on skin side of salmon, being careful not to cut into flesh. Pat salmon dry with paper towels and lay skin side down on foil. Rub flesh side of salmon with oil, then rub with spice mixture.

3. Reduce oven temperature to 275 degrees. Using foil sling, lay salmon on preheated sheet and roast until center is still translucent when checked with tip of paring knife and registers 125 degrees (for medium-rare), 14 to 18 minutes.

4. FOR THE BEURRE BLANC Meanwhile, bring wine, vinegar, shallot, and salt to simmer in small saucepan over medium heat and cook until about 2 scant tablespoons of liquid remain, 3 to 5 minutes. Reduce heat to medium-low and whisk in cream. Add butter, 1 piece at a time, whisking vigorously after each addition, until butter is incorporated and forms thick, pale yellow sauce, 30 to 60 seconds. Off heat, whisk in sugar. Strain sauce through fine-mesh strainer into bowl. Stir in orange zest and season with salt to taste.

5. Using foil sling, transfer salmon to cutting board or serving platter. Run thin metal spatula between salmon skin and salmon to loosen. Using spatula to hold salmon in place, gently pull foil (and skin) out from underneath salmon. Serve with beurre blanc.

Faster Coq au Vin

Hunter's-Style Chicken

Faster Coq au Vin

Serves 4 to 6 | **Total Time** 1¾ hours `MAKE AHEAD`

WHY THIS RECIPE WORKS Brimming with red wine flavor, this peasant dish remains true to its humble roots, at least in spirit. Our biggest departure was to replace the cut-up whole chicken with boneless thighs, which, after a quick sauté in rendered bacon fat, became fall-apart tender. To develop a fuller, less astringent wine flavor, we simmered our wine with chicken broth in a separate pan while browning our meat and vegetables, a multitasking step that worked beautifully. Use a medium-bodied, fruity red wine such as Pinot Noir or Côtes du Rhône, for this recipe. Avoid bolder wines like Cabernet or very light-bodied wines like Beaujolais. Serve the stew with Creamy Mashed Potatoes (page 153) or egg noodles.

 1 (750-ml) bottle medium-bodied red wine, divided
 2 cups chicken broth
10 sprigs fresh parsley, plus 2 tablespoons minced
 2 sprigs fresh thyme
 1 bay leaf
 4 slices thick-cut bacon, cut crosswise into ¼-inch pieces
2½ pounds boneless, skinless chicken thighs, trimmed and halved
 ¾ teaspoon table salt
 ½ teaspoon pepper, divided
 5 tablespoons unsalted butter, divided
 1 cup frozen pearl onions, thawed, drained, and patted dry
 8 ounces cremini mushrooms, trimmed and halved if small or quartered if large
 2 garlic cloves, minced
 2 tablespoons all-purpose flour
 1 tablespoon tomato paste

1. Set aside 1 tablespoon wine. Bring broth, parsley sprigs, thyme sprigs, bay leaf, and remaining wine to simmer in large saucepan over medium-high heat. Cook until reduced to 3 cups, about 25 minutes. Discard parsley sprigs, thyme sprigs, and bay leaf.

2. While wine mixture reduces, cook bacon in Dutch oven over medium heat until crispy, 5 to 7 minutes. Using slotted spoon, transfer bacon to paper towel–lined plate and set aside. Set aside 2 tablespoons fat, then pour off and discard remaining fat.

3. Sprinkle chicken with salt and ¼ teaspoon pepper. Heat 1 tablespoon reserved fat in now-empty pot over medium-high heat until just smoking. Lightly brown half of chicken, about

2 minutes per side; transfer to plate. Repeat with remaining 1 tablespoon reserved fat and remaining chicken.

4. Melt 3 tablespoons butter in again-empty pot. Add pearl onions and mushrooms and cook, stirring occasionally, until lightly browned, 5 to 8 minutes. Reduce heat to medium, add garlic, and cook until fragrant, about 30 seconds. Add flour and tomato paste; cook, stirring frequently, until well combined, about 1 minute.

5. Add reduced wine mixture, scraping up any browned bits and smoothing out any lumps, then add remaining ¼ teaspoon pepper. Return chicken along with any accumulated juices and reserved bacon to pot; increase heat to high and bring to boil. Reduce heat to medium-low and simmer, covered, until chicken is tender, about 25 minutes, stirring halfway through cooking.

6. Using slotted spoon, transfer chicken to large bowl and tent with aluminum foil. Increase heat to medium-high and simmer until sauce is thick and glossy and measures 3¼ cups, about 5 minutes. Off heat, stir in remaining 2 tablespoons butter and reserved 1 tablespoon wine. Season with salt to taste, then return chicken to pot. (Chicken and sauce can be refrigerated for up to 2 days. To reheat, bring to gentle simmer, covered, and cook until hot throughout, adjusting consistency with hot water as needed.) Sprinkle with minced parsley and serve.

Hunter's-Style Chicken

Serves 4 to 6 | **Total Time** 1¾ hours MAKE AHEAD

WHY THIS RECIPE WORKS In Italy, anything cooked alla cacciatora is cooked "the hunter's way." Hunters would braise their fresh-killed game, typically rabbit or poultry, simply, sautéing it to build flavor and then braising until supertender and enveloped in a savory sauce. In developing our version, we wanted a sauce that wasn't too thick, just substantial enough to cling to the chicken. Tomatoes were in, as we liked their sweetness and acidity, and we chose white wine for its lighter profile. We cut it with chicken broth, which cut the harshness of the wine and rounded the savory flavors. Garlic and rosemary complemented the poultry. For even cooking, we sautéed the chicken on the stove and then transferred it to the oven to finish cooking gently.

- 4 pounds bone-in chicken pieces (2 split breasts cut in half crosswise, 2 drumsticks, and 2 thighs)
- 1 teaspoon table salt
- ½ teaspoon pepper

- 2 tablespoons extra-virgin olive oil
- 1 onion, chopped
- 1 carrot, peeled and chopped
- 1 celery rib, chopped
- 2 garlic cloves, minced
- 1½ teaspoons minced fresh rosemary
- ½ cup dry white wine
- ½ cup chicken broth
- 1 (14.5-ounce) can diced tomatoes, drained
- 1 tablespoon minced fresh parsley

1. Adjust oven rack to middle position and heat oven to 325 degrees. Pat chicken dry with paper towels and sprinkle with salt and pepper. Heat oil in Dutch oven over medium-high heat until just smoking. Brown half of chicken on all sides, 8 to 10 minutes; transfer to plate. Repeat with remaining chicken; transfer to plate.

2. Add onion, carrot, and celery to fat left in pot and cook over medium heat until softened and lightly browned, 6 to 8 minutes. Stir in garlic and rosemary and cook until fragrant, about 30 seconds. Stir in wine, scraping up any browned bits, and cook until almost completely evaporated, about 2 minutes. Stir in broth and tomatoes and bring to simmer.

3. Return chicken to pot along with any accumulated juices. Cover, transfer pot to oven, and cook until breasts register 160 degrees and drumsticks/thighs register 175 degrees, 35 to 40 minutes, turning chicken halfway through cooking.

4. Remove pot from oven. Transfer chicken to large bowl and tent with aluminum foil. Bring sauce to simmer over medium-high heat and cook until reduced to about 2 cups, 5 to 8 minutes. Season with salt to taste, then return chicken to pot. (Chicken and sauce can be refrigerated for up to 2 days. To reheat, bring to gentle simmer, covered, and cook until hot throughout, adjusting consistency with hot water as needed.) Sprinkle with parsley and serve.

Chicken Tagine with Fennel, Chickpeas, and Apricots

Serves 4 to 6 | **Total Time** 1¾ hours MAKE AHEAD

WHY THIS RECIPE WORKS Braising is often associated with cooking large, tough cuts of meat. But it's also great for quicker-cooking proteins like rich, meaty chicken thighs. Here we use them in a tagine that nods to the flavors of Morocco. After browning our chicken pieces and then browning fennel in the rendered fat, we bloomed a blend of spicy, earthy, and warm ground spices and a whole cinnamon stick, which infused the whole dish with flavor as it cooked. A few ribbons of lemon zest gave the tagine a citrus back note.

2 tablespoons extra-virgin olive oil, plus extra as needed
5 garlic cloves, minced
1½ teaspoons paprika
½ teaspoon ground turmeric
½ teaspoon ground cumin
¼ teaspoon ground ginger
¼ teaspoon cayenne pepper
2 (15-ounce) cans chickpeas, rinsed
8 (5- to 7-ounce) bone-in chicken thighs, trimmed
1 large fennel bulb, stalks discarded, bulb halved and cut into ½-inch thick wedges through core
½ teaspoon table salt, divided
¼ teaspoon pepper
3 (2-inch) strips lemon zest, plus lemon wedges for serving
1 cinnamon stick
½ cup dry white wine
1 cup chicken broth
1 cup pitted large brine-cured green or black olives, halved
½ cup dried apricots, halved
2 tablespoons chopped fresh parsley

1. Adjust oven rack to upper-middle position and heat oven to 350 degrees. Combine 1 tablespoon oil, garlic, paprika, turmeric, cumin, ginger, and cayenne in bowl; set aside. Place ½ cup chickpeas in second bowl and mash to coarse paste with potato masher.

2. Pat chicken dry with paper towels and sprinkle with ¼ teaspoon salt and pepper. Heat remaining 1 tablespoon oil in 12-inch ovensafe skillet over medium-high heat until just smoking. Cook chicken skin side down until skin is crisped and well browned, 8 to 10 minutes; transfer chicken skin side up to plate.

3. Pour off all but 2 tablespoons fat from skillet (or, if necessary, add extra oil to equal 2 tablespoons). Heat fat left in skillet over medium heat until shimmering. Arrange fennel cut side down in skillet and sprinkle with remaining ¼ teaspoon salt. Cover and cook until lightly browned, 3 to 5 minutes per side. Push fennel to sides of skillet. Add spice mixture, lemon zest, and cinnamon stick to center and cook, mashing spice mixture into skillet, until fragrant, about 30 seconds. Stir spice mixture into fennel. Stir in wine, scraping up any browned bits, and cook until almost evaporated, about 2 minutes.

4. Stir in broth, olives, apricots, mashed chickpeas, and whole chickpeas and bring to simmer. Nestle chicken skin side up into skillet, keeping skin above liquid. Roast until fennel is tender and chicken registers 185 degrees, 35 to 40 minutes. Using pot holders, carefully remove skillet from oven. Discard lemon zest and cinnamon stick. Season with salt and pepper to taste. (Tagine can be refrigerated for up to 2 days. To reheat, bring to gentle simmer, covered, and cook until hot throughout, adjusting consistency with hot water as needed.) Sprinkle with parsley and serve with lemon wedges.

Chicken in a Pot with Red Potatoes, Carrots, and Shallots

Serves 4 | **Total Time** 2¼ hours

WHY THIS RECIPE WORKS Classic French poulet en cocotte relies on the moist environment of a covered Dutch oven to yield unbelievably tender meat (albeit with soft skin) and a concentrated jus made of the chicken's own juices. To make this dish into a complete meal, we added root vegetables to the pot, but found that they were underdone even after an hour of baking. Adding liquid (a combination of chicken broth and wine) tenderized the vegetables, but the jus lost its appealing intensity. To counter this, we browned the chicken and vegetables to build fond. Browning the bird also crisped its skin slightly, and we wondered if we could preserve and enhance its crispiness by cooking the chicken uncovered. To our satisfaction, the uncovered roasting delivered chicken in a pot that had the best of all worlds: succulent meat, crisped skin, superflavorful vegetables, and a great sauce.

1 (3½- to 4-pound) whole chicken, giblets discarded
1½ teaspoons table salt, divided
½ teaspoon pepper
1 tablespoon vegetable oil
1½ pounds red potatoes, unpeeled, cut into 1-inch pieces
1 pound carrots, peeled and cut into 1-inch pieces
4 shallots, peeled and halved
3 garlic cloves, minced
1 teaspoon minced fresh thyme or ¼ teaspoon dried
½ cup dry white wine
½ cup chicken broth, plus extra as needed
1 bay leaf
2 tablespoons unsalted butter
1 tablespoon lemon juice
1 tablespoon minced fresh parsley

1. Adjust oven rack to lower-middle position and heat oven to 350 degrees. Pat chicken dry with paper towels, tuck wingtips behind back, and sprinkle with 1 teaspoon salt and pepper. Heat oil in Dutch oven over medium-high heat until just smoking. Place chicken, breast side down, in pot and cook until lightly browned, about 5 minutes. Carefully flip chicken breast side up and continue to cook until well browned on second side, 6 to 8 minutes; transfer to large plate.

2. Pour off all but 1 tablespoon fat from pot. Add potatoes, carrots, shallots, and remaining ½ teaspoon salt and cook over medium heat until vegetables are just beginning to brown, 5 to 7 minutes. Stir in garlic and thyme and cook until fragrant, about 30 seconds. Add wine, broth, and bay leaf, scraping up any browned bits.

3. Place chicken, breast side up, on top of vegetables, along with any accumulated juices. Transfer pot to oven and roast, uncovered, until breast registers 160 degrees and thighs register 175 degrees, 55 minutes to 1 hour 5 minutes, rotating pot halfway through roasting. Remove pot from oven. Transfer chicken to carving board, and let rest for 15 minutes. Using slotted spoon, transfer vegetables to serving platter and tent with aluminum foil to keep warm.

4. Discard bay leaf. Pour liquid left in pot into fat separator and let settle for 5 minutes. (You should have ¾ cup defatted liquid; add extra broth as needed to equal ¾ cup.) Return defatted liquid to now-empty pot, bring to simmer over medium-high heat, and cook until it measures ½ cup, 5 to 7 minutes. Off heat, whisk in butter and lemon juice, and season with salt and pepper to taste. Sprinkle vegetables with parsley, carve chicken, and serve with sauce.

Pot Roast with Root Vegetables

Serves 6 | **Total Time** 4¼ hours MAKE AHEAD

WHY THIS RECIPE WORKS A good pot roast should always be tender. For a supremely tender pot roast with a spoonable sauce, we cooked ours for 3 to 3½ hours, adding root vegetables partway through. A chuck-eye roast is our favorite cut for pot roast; opening it along its natural seam into two lobes and trimming excess fat eliminated greasiness and promised more thorough seasoning. A stovetop sear created a caramelized exterior before we moved the roast to the oven where it could braise more evenly. When it emerged, it was so tender a fork met no resistance: Each bite had a silky texture and rich flavor. Use a good-quality, medium-bodied wine, such as a Côtes du Rhône or a Pinot Noir. For how to tie a roast, see page 77.

Chicken Tagine with Fennel, Chickpeas, and Apricots

Chicken in a Pot with Red Potatoes, Carrots, and Shallots

1 (3½- to 4-pound) boneless beef chuck-eye roast,
   pulled into 2 pieces at natural seam, trimmed,
   and tied at 1-inch intervals
1 teaspoon table salt
½ teaspoon pepper
3 tablespoons vegetable oil, divided
1 onion, chopped
1 celery rib, chopped
4 garlic cloves, minced
2 teaspoons sugar
1 teaspoon fresh minced thyme or ¼ teaspoon dried
1 cup chicken broth
1 cup beef broth
1 cup water
1½ pounds carrots, peeled and cut into 3-inch pieces
1½ pounds red potatoes, unpeeled, cut into
   1½-inch pieces
1½ pounds parsnips, peeled and cut into 3-inch pieces
⅓ cup red wine

1. Adjust oven rack to lower-middle position and heat oven to 300 degrees. Pat beef dry with paper towels and sprinkle with salt and pepper. Heat 2 tablespoons oil in Dutch oven over medium-high heat until just smoking. Add both beef roasts and brown on all sides, 7 to 10 minutes; transfer to large plate.

2. Add remaining 1 tablespoon oil, onion, and celery to now-empty pot and cook over medium heat until vegetables are softened, 5 to 7 minutes. Stir in garlic, sugar, and thyme and cook until fragrant, about 30 seconds. Stir in broths and water, scraping up any browned bits.

3. Add browned roasts along with any accumulated juices to pot and bring to simmer. Cover, transfer pot to oven, and cook for 2 hours, flipping roasts halfway through cooking.

4. Remove pot from oven. Nestle carrots into pot around meat and sprinkle potatoes and parsnips over top. Return covered pot to oven and cook until meat and vegetables are very tender, 1 to 1½ hours.

5. Remove pot from oven. Transfer roasts and vegetables to large bowl, season with salt and pepper to taste, and cover to keep warm.

6. Using large spoon, skim any fat from surface of braising liquid. Stir in wine and simmer until sauce measures 2 cups, about 15 minutes. Season with salt and pepper to taste, then return beef and vegetables to pot. (Beef, vegetables, and sauce can be refrigerated for up to 2 days. To reheat, bring to gentle simmer, covered, and cook until hot throughout, adjusting consistency with hot water as needed.) Transfer roasts to

Slow-Cooker
Beef Burgundy

carving board and vegetables to serving platter. Remove twine from roasts, slice meat against grain ¼ inch thick, and serve with vegetables and sauce.

Slow-Cooker Beef Burgundy

Serves 8 | **Cooking Time** 9 to 10 hours on Low or 6 to 7 hours on High

WHY THIS RECIPE WORKS The low, steady heat of a slow cooker is an optimal way to produce a supremely tender, rich-tasting beef burgundy fit for company. We started by browning half the meat in a skillet (we added the other half raw to the slow cooker). Then we boosted the flavor by sautéing bacon with garlic and thyme and adding tomato paste for sweetness and soy sauce for extra meatiness. To keep the flavor of the wine in balance, we added half of it at the outset, reducing the remaining half to mellow its sharpness before adding it at the end. Use a good-quality medium-bodied wine, such as a Côtes du Rhône or Pinot Noir. Serve with Creamy Mashed Potatoes (page 153) or egg noodles.

5 pounds boneless beef chuck-eye roast, pulled apart at seams, trimmed, and cut into 1½-inch pieces

1½ teaspoons table salt

¾ teaspoon pepper

2 tablespoons vegetable oil

4 slices bacon, chopped fine

2 onions, chopped fine

1 carrot, peeled and chopped fine

⅓ cup all-purpose flour

¼ cup tomato paste

6 garlic cloves, minced

1 tablespoon minced fresh thyme or ¾ teaspoon dried

2½ cups dry red wine, divided

1½ cups beef broth, plus extra as needed

⅓ cup soy sauce

2 bay leaves

2 cups frozen pearl onions

½ cup water

3 tablespoons unsalted butter

2 teaspoons sugar

1 pound cremini mushrooms, trimmed and halved if small or quartered if large

2 tablespoons minced fresh parsley

1. Pat beef dry with paper towels and sprinkle with salt and pepper. Heat oil in 12-inch skillet over medium-high heat until just smoking. Brown half of beef on all sides, about 8 minutes; transfer to slow cooker along with remaining uncooked beef.

2. Add bacon to fat left in skillet and cook over medium heat until crisp, 5 to 7 minutes. Stir in onions and carrot and cook until softened and lightly browned, 8 to 10 minutes. Stir in flour, tomato paste, garlic, and thyme and cook until fragrant, about 1 minute. Slowly whisk in 1¼ cups wine, scraping up any browned bits and smoothing out any lumps; transfer to slow cooker.

3. Stir broth, soy sauce, and bay leaves into slow cooker, cover, and cook until beef is tender, 9 to 10 hours on low or 6 to 7 hours on high.

4. About 30 minutes before serving, bring pearl onions, water, butter, and sugar to simmer in 12-inch skillet over medium heat. Cover and cook until onions are fully thawed and tender, 5 to 8 minutes. Uncover and continue to cook until all liquid evaporates, about 4 minutes. Stir in mushrooms and cook until vegetables are browned and glazed, 8 to 12 minutes. Discard bay leaves and stir onion-mushroom mixture into stew.

5. Bring remaining 1¼ cups wine to simmer in now-empty skillet and cook until reduced by half, 6 to 8 minutes; stir into stew. Adjust consistency with extra hot broth as needed. Stir in parsley and season with salt and pepper to taste. Serve.

Braised Short Ribs with Daikon and Shiitakes

Braised Short Ribs with Daikon and Shiitakes

Serves 4 | **Total Time** 3½ hours MAKE AHEAD

WHY THIS RECIPE WORKS Galbi-jjim, beef short ribs braised until tender with chestnuts and jujubes, is considered a special-occasion dish in Korea. In this version, we sautéed the aromatics—scallions, garlic, and ginger—which proved crucial for building flavor. We did not brown the ribs but braised them, along with an Asian pear and a generous handful of earthy shiitake mushrooms, directly in an aromatic liquid seasoned with sake, soy sauce, and rice vinegar. Daikon radishes balanced the rich sweetness of the dish; we stirred them in toward the end of cooking so they kept their crunchy freshness. To finish the dish, we simmered sweet jujubes and nutty chestnuts alongside the radishes. Defatting the cooking liquid ensured that the sauce was rich but not greasy. You can substitute boneless beef chuck-eye roast for the short ribs. If jujubes are unavailable, substitute six Medjool dates. Use a large Dutch oven that holds 6 quarts or more.

6 scallions, white and green parts separated and cut into 1-inch pieces
6 garlic cloves, lightly crushed and peeled
1 (1-inch) piece ginger, sliced thin
1 tablespoon canola oil
1 cup sake or dry white wine
1 cup water
1 Asian pear, halved, cored, and cut into 1-inch pieces
1 ounce dried shiitake mushrooms, stemmed and rinsed
3 tablespoons soy sauce
2 tablespoons sugar
1 tablespoon unseasoned rice vinegar
1 pound boneless beef short ribs, trimmed and cut into 1½-inch pieces
1½ pounds daikon radishes, peeled and cut into 1-inch pieces
1 cup peeled cooked chestnuts, broken into large pieces (optional)
8 dried jujubes, pitted and halved

1. Using highest sauté or browning function, cook scallion whites, garlic, ginger, and oil in electric pressure cooker until fragrant, about 2 minutes. Stir in sake and cook until reduced by half, about 2 minutes.

2. Stir in water, pear, mushrooms, soy sauce, sugar, and vinegar. Nestle short ribs into pot. Lock lid into place and close pressure release valve. Select high pressure-cook function and cook for 40 minutes.

3. Turn off electric pressure cooker and quick-release pressure. Carefully remove lid, allowing steam to escape away from you. Using slotted spoon, transfer beef and mushrooms to serving platter, tent with aluminum foil, and let rest while finishing sauce.

4. Strain braising liquid through fine-mesh strainer into fat separator; discard solids. Let braising liquid settle for 5 minutes, then return defatted liquid to now-empty pot. Stir in radishes; chestnuts, if using; and jujubes. Partially cover pot and cook, using highest sauté or browning function, until radishes are tender and jujubes are plump, 3 to 5 minutes. (Beef, vegetables, and sauce can be refrigerated for up to 2 days. To reheat, bring to gentle simmer, covered, and cook until hot throughout, adjusting consistency with hot water as needed.)

5. Quarter mushrooms if desired. Divide short ribs and mushrooms evenly among serving bowls. Ladle sauce, radishes, chestnuts, and jujubes evenly over short ribs and mushrooms. Sprinkle with scallion greens. Serve.

Braised Steaks with Root Vegetables

Braised Steaks with Root Vegetables

Serves 6 | **Total Time** 3 hours `MAKE AHEAD`

WHY THIS RECIPE WORKS We don't typically think of braising steaks. But tough blade steaks turn meltingly tender when simmered in liquid, which produces an accompanying sauce full of beefy flavor. To achieve this effect, we purposely "overcooked" the meat; a 2-hour braise allowed nearly all of the fat and connective tissue to dissolve, giving each bite a silky texture. We added potatoes, carrots, and parsnips for the final 30 minutes of cooking so we could easily get a full dinner out of one vessel. Finally, we reduced the braising liquid to a spoonable sauce. Top blade steak may sometimes be labeled as "flat iron" steak. Make sure to buy steaks that are about the same size to ensure even cooking.

6 (6-ounce) top blade steaks, ¾ to 1 inch thick, trimmed
¼ teaspoon table salt
⅛ teaspoon pepper

4 teaspoons vegetable oil, divided
2 onions, halved and sliced thin
3 garlic cloves, minced
1 tablespoon minced fresh thyme or 1 teaspoon dried thyme
1½ cups beef broth
1 cup water
½ cup dry white wine
12 ounces red potatoes, cut into ¾-inch pieces
4 carrots, peeled and sliced ½ inch thick
4 parsnips, peeled and sliced ½ inch thick
2 tablespoons minced fresh parsley
1 tablespoon lemon juice

1. Adjust oven rack to lower-middle position and heat oven to 325 degrees. Pat steaks dry with paper towels and sprinkle with salt and pepper. Heat 2 teaspoons oil in Dutch oven over medium-high heat until smoking. Brown steaks well on all sides, 7 to 10 minutes. Transfer steaks to large plate.

2. Add remaining 2 teaspoons oil to pot and heat over medium heat until shimmering. Add onions and cook until softened, 8 to 10 minutes. Stir in garlic and thyme and cook until fragrant, about 30 seconds. Stir in broth, water, and wine, scraping up any browned bits, and bring to simmer.

3. Nestle steaks, along with any accumulated juices, into pot. Spoon sauce over steaks. Return to simmer and cover; transfer pot to oven. Cook for 1½ hours.

4. Add potatoes, carrots, and parsnips to pot and continue to cook until steaks and vegetables are tender, about 30 minutes. Transfer steaks and vegetables to large bowl, tent with aluminum foil, and let rest while finishing sauce.

5. Simmer sauce over medium-high heat until slightly thickened, 2 to 4 minutes. Return steaks and vegetables to pot and season with salt and pepper to taste. (Steaks, vegetables, and sauce can be refrigerated for up to 2 days. To reheat, bring to gentle simmer, covered, and cook until hot throughout, adjusting consistency with hot water as needed.) Off heat, stir in parsley and lemon juice. Serve.

Braised Steaks with Mushrooms and Tomatoes
Omit carrots and parsnips. Before cooking onions in step 3, add 4 chopped portobello mushroom caps and cook, covered, until they begin to soften and release their liquid, about 5 minutes. Remove lid, add onions, and cook until onions and mushrooms are softened and browned, 10 to 12 minutes. Reduce water to ½ cup, substitute 2 teaspoons minced fresh rosemary for thyme, and add one 14.5-ounce can diced tomatoes with their juice with broth.

Pressure-Cooker Boneless Short Rib and Cauliflower Puttanesca

Serves 4 | **Total Time** 1½ hours

WHY THIS RECIPE WORKS The flavors of a classic puttanesca sauce—anchovies, garlic, capers, olives, and tomatoes—were a great fit for boneless short ribs, which became meltingly tender in just 40 minutes in the pressure cooker. For a well-rounded meal, instead of pasta we turned to nutty cauliflower, which cooked beautifully in the leftover braising liquid while the short ribs rested. Gently stirring everything together and drizzling it with olive oil brought this rich-tasting but not at all heavy dish to life. The thickness and marbling of boneless short ribs varies. Look for lean ribs cut from the chuck that are 1½ to 2 inches thick. You can substitute boneless beef chuck-eye roast for the short ribs. This recipe will only work in an electric pressure cooker.

1½ pounds boneless beef short ribs, trimmed and cut into 1½-inch pieces
1 tablespoon extra-virgin olive oil, plus extra for drizzling
5 garlic cloves, minced
6 anchovy fillets, minced
1 tablespoon tomato paste
¼ teaspoon red pepper flakes
1 (28-ounce) can whole peeled tomatoes, drained with ½ cup juice reserved, halved
1½ pounds cauliflower florets, cut into 1½-inch pieces
¼ cup pitted brine-cured black olives, chopped coarse
¼ cup minced fresh parsley
2 tablespoons capers, rinsed

1. Pat short ribs dry with paper towels. Using highest sauté function, heat oil in pressure cooker until just smoking. Brown short ribs on all sides, 6 to 8 minutes; transfer to plate. Turn off pressure cooker.

2. Add garlic, anchovies, tomato paste, and pepper flakes to fat left in pot and cook, using residual heat, until fragrant, about 30 seconds. Stir in tomatoes and reserved tomato juice, scraping up any browned bits. Nestle short ribs into tomato mixture and add any accumulated juices. Lock lid in place and close pressure release valve. Select high pressure cook function and cook for 40 minutes.

3. Turn off pressure cooker and quick-release pressure. Carefully remove lid, allowing steam to escape away from you. Transfer beef to serving platter, tent with aluminum foil, and let rest while finishing cauliflower and sauce.

4. Strain braising liquid through fine-mesh strainer into fat separator; transfer solids to now-empty pot. Let braising liquid settle for 5 minutes, then pour defatted liquid into pot with solids. Stir in cauliflower and bring to simmer using highest sauté function. Partially cover and cook, stirring occasionally, until cauliflower is tender, 4 to 6 minutes. Turn off pressure cooker.

5. Gently stir in beef and any accumulated juices, olives, parsley, and capers. Partially cover and let sit until heated through, about 2 minutes. Season with salt and pepper to taste. Drizzle individual portions with extra oil before serving.

Red-Cooked Beef

Serves 6 | **Total Time** 3¼ hours `MAKE AHEAD`

WHY THIS RECIPE WORKS This classic Chinese style of braising produces ultratender meat napped with a thick, fragrant sauce. Its complexity often comes from braising beef shanks in a sweet-salty sauce deepened by caramelized sugar. We used boneless beef short ribs, which became fork-tender in less time. Some molasses replicated the bitter sweetness of caramelized sugar, while five-spice powder added complexity. If you can find beef shanks, they're fantastic here, though they take more time to become tender. Use cross-cut shanks and cook for 4 hours in step 2; decrease gelatin to 2¼ teaspoons. We prefer to use our homemade Five-Spice Powder (page 101), but you can substitute store-bought five-spice powder if you wish, though flavor can vary greatly by brand. Serve with white rice and steamed vegetables.

    1½ tablespoons unflavored gelatin
    2½ cups plus 1 tablespoon water, divided
    ½   cup Shaoxing wine or dry sherry
    ⅓   cup soy sauce
    3   scallions, white and green parts separated,
        green parts sliced thin on bias
    2   tablespoons hoisin sauce
    2   tablespoons molasses
    1   (2-inch) piece ginger, peeled, halved lengthwise,
        and crushed
    4   garlic cloves, peeled and smashed
    1½ teaspoons five-spice powder
    1   teaspoon red pepper flakes
    3   pounds boneless beef short ribs, trimmed and
        cut into 4-inch lengths
    1   teaspoon cornstarch

1. Sprinkle gelatin over 2½ cups water in Dutch oven and let sit until gelatin softens, about 5 minutes. Adjust oven rack to middle position and heat oven to 300 degrees.

2. Heat softened gelatin over medium-high heat, stirring occasionally, until melted, 2 to 3 minutes. Stir in wine, soy sauce, scallion whites, hoisin, molasses, ginger, garlic, five-spice powder, and pepper flakes. Stir in beef and bring to simmer. Remove pot from heat. Place large piece of aluminum foil over pot and cover tightly with lid; transfer pot to oven. Cook until beef is tender, 2 to 2½ hours, stirring halfway through cooking.

3. Using slotted spoon, transfer beef to cutting board. Let beef cool slightly, then break beef into 1½-inch pieces with 2 forks.

4. Strain sauce through fine-mesh strainer into fat separator. Wipe pot clean with paper towels. Let liquid settle for 5 minutes, then return defatted liquid to now-empty pot. Cook liquid over medium-high heat, stirring occasionally, until thickened and reduced to 1 cup, 20 to 25 minutes. (Beef and sauce can be refrigerated separately for up to 3 days. Return sauce to simmer, covered, before proceeding with recipe.)

5. Whisk cornstarch and remaining 1 tablespoon water together in small bowl. Reduce heat to medium-low, whisk cornstarch mixture into reduced sauce and cook until sauce is slightly thickened, about 1 minute. Return beef to sauce and stir to coat. Cover and cook, stirring occasionally, until beef is heated through, 5 to 10 minutes. Sprinkle scallion greens over top. Serve.

Shizi Tou (Lion's Head Meatballs)

Serves 4 to 6 | **Total Time** 2 hours `MAKE AHEAD`

WHY THIS RECIPE WORKS Served with rice noodles, soft cabbage, and the broth in which they cook, these giant pork meatballs from eastern China are pure comfort, a soothing bowl for a chilly night. (Their name refers to how the greens fringe the spheres like a lion's mane.) Their flavor is umami-rich but subtle. Their texture is a seemingly paradoxical combination of spoon-tenderness with sausage-like spring and juiciness. To achieve this, we first treated ground pork with a baking soda solution, which helped it retain juices during cooking. Traditional recipes call for vigorously working the meat, which causes its sticky proteins to cross-link and bind, trapping fat and moisture. We accomplished this using a stand mixer. Braising the meatballs for 1½ hours broke down the pork's collagen so that the meatballs were tender. Adding the cabbage for the last 30 minutes allowed it to absorb the flavor of the chicken broth without turning mushy. Fully cooked ground pork can retain a slightly pink hue. Don't be concerned if the meatballs develop cracks while cooking. Use a large Dutch oven that holds 6 quarts or more for this recipe.

¾ teaspoon baking soda

½ teaspoon table salt

2 pounds ground pork

1 large egg, lightly beaten

2 scallions, white parts minced, green parts sliced thin

2 tablespoons soy sauce

2 tablespoons Shaoxing wine or dry sherry

4 teaspoons sugar

2 teaspoons grated fresh ginger

½ teaspoon white pepper

4 cups chicken broth

1 small head napa cabbage (1½ pounds), quartered lengthwise, cored, and cut crosswise into 2-inch pieces

4 ounces rice vermicelli

1. Adjust oven rack to lower-middle position and heat oven to 325 degrees. Whisk baking soda, salt, and 2 tablespoons water together in bowl of stand mixer. Add pork and toss to combine. Add egg, scallion whites, soy sauce, Shaoxing wine, sugar, ginger, and pepper. Fit stand mixer with paddle and beat on medium speed until mixture is well combined and has stiffened and started to pull away from sides of bowl and pork has slightly lightened in color, 45 to 60 seconds. Using your wet hands, form about ½ cup (4½ ounces) pork mixture into 3-inch round meatball; repeat with remaining mixture to form 8 meatballs.(Meatballs can be refrigerated for up to 24 hours.)

2. Bring broth to boil in large Dutch oven over high heat. Off heat, carefully arrange meatballs in pot (7 around perimeter and 1 in center; meatballs will not be totally submerged). Cover pot, transfer to oven, and cook for 1 hour.

3. Transfer meatballs to large plate. Add cabbage to pot in even layer and arrange meatballs over cabbage, paler side up. Cover; return pot to oven; and continue to cook until meatballs are lightly browned and cabbage is softened, about 30 minutes.

4. Meanwhile, bring 4 quarts water to boil in large pot. Remove from heat; add noodles; and let sit, stirring occasionally, until tender but not mushy. Drain noodles and distribute evenly among individual bowls.

5. Ladle meatballs, cabbage, and broth into bowls over noodles. Sprinkle with scallion greens and serve.

Red-Cooked Beef

Shizi Tou
(Lion's Head Meatballs)

Roman Braised Oxtails

Milk-Braised Pork Roast

Roman Braised Oxtails

Serves 6 to 8 | **Total Time** 4¾ hours `MAKE AHEAD`

WHY THIS RECIPE WORKS Coda alla vaccinara is a lush braise originally prepared by slaughtermen (vaccinari) who were often paid with the undesirable parts. It's from these parts that they proved the underestimated worth of inexpensive cuts. When simmered slowly, oxtails become meltingly tender and coated in a deeply flavored sauce. Tomatoes, tomato paste, wine, and a soffritto (onion, carrot, and celery) made the base. To be sure our dish didn't turn out greasy, we roasted the oxtails for an hour, which rendered a significant amount of fat. The oxtails then needed 3 hours to braise in a moderate, 300-degree oven to become fork-tender. After braising, we were careful to remove more fat using a fat separator. A sprinkling of pine nuts is common and added crunch and visual appeal. Try to buy oxtails that are approximately 2 inches thick and 2 to 4 inches in diameter. Oxtails can often be found in the freezer section of the grocery store.

- 4 pounds oxtails (thawed if frozen), trimmed
- ¾ teaspoon table salt
- ¼ teaspoon pepper
- 4 cups chicken broth
- 2 tablespoons extra-virgin olive oil
- 1 onion, chopped fine
- 1 carrot, peeled and chopped fine
- 2 celery ribs, cut into 1-inch lengths
- 2 tablespoons tomato paste
- 3 garlic cloves, minced
- ⅛ teaspoon ground cloves
- ½ cup dry white wine
- 1 (28-ounce) can whole peeled tomatoes, drained with juice reserved and chopped
- 2 tablespoons raisins, chopped
- ½ cup pine nuts, toasted

1. Adjust oven rack to lower-middle position and heat oven to 450 degrees. Pat oxtails dry with paper towels and sprinkle with salt and pepper. Arrange oxtails cut side down in single layer in large roasting pan and roast until meat begins to brown, about 45 minutes.

2. Discard any accumulated fat and juices in pan and continue to roast until meat is well browned, 15 to 20 minutes. Transfer oxtails to bowl; set aside. Stir broth into pan, scraping up any browned bits; set aside.

3. Reduce oven temperature to 300 degrees. Heat oil in Dutch oven over medium heat until shimmering. Add onion, carrot, and celery and cook until softened, about 5 minutes.

Stir in tomato paste, garlic, and clove and cook until fragrant, about 30 seconds.

4. Stir in wine and cook until nearly all liquid is evaporated, about 2 minutes. Stir in broth mixture from roasting pan, tomatoes and their juice, and raisins and bring to simmer. Nestle oxtails into pot and bring to simmer. Cover, transfer pot to oven, and cook until oxtails are tender and fork slips easily in and out of meat, about 3 hours. (Oxtails can be refrigerated for up to 2 days. To reheat, bring to gentle simmer, covered, and cook until hot throughout, adjusting consistency with hot water as needed.)

5. Transfer oxtails to serving dish and tent with aluminum foil. Strain braising liquid through fine-mesh strainer into fat separator; return solids to now-empty pot. Let braising liquid settle for 5 minutes, then pour defatted liquid into pot with solids. Season with salt and pepper to taste. Spoon 1 cup sauce over top of oxtails and sprinkle with pine nuts. Serve, passing remaining sauce separately.

Milk-Braised Pork Roast

Serves 4 to 6
Total Time 2 hours, plus 1½ hours brining

WHY THIS RECIPE WORKS Bolognese families often prepare this hearty dish of pork braised in milk on Sundays in the winter. The milk tenderizes the pork and the meat soaks up the flavors of the resulting sweet, nutty sauce. As you'd expect, the milk curdles; Italians don't mind, but we wanted to make the sauce smoother. We minimized curdling (and amped up flavor) by adding a touch of fat from rendered salt pork; the fat coats the casein proteins in milk and prevents them from bonding. A small amount of baking soda raised the sauce's pH to allow for more Maillard browning, a series of reactions that create aromatic compounds. The milk will bubble up when added to the pot. If necessary, remove the pot from the heat and stir to break up the foam before returning it to the heat. We prefer natural pork, but if your pork is enhanced (injected with a salt solution), do not brine.

¼ cup table salt, for brining
½ cup sugar, for brining
1 (2- to 2½-pound) boneless pork loin roast, trimmed
2 ounces salt pork, chopped coarse
3 cups whole milk
5 garlic cloves, peeled
1 teaspoon minced fresh sage
½ teaspoon baking soda

½ cup dry white wine
3 tablespoons chopped fresh parsley, divided
1 teaspoon Dijon mustard

1. Dissolve ¼ cup salt and sugar in 2 quarts cold water in large container. Submerge roast in brine, cover, and refrigerate for at least 1½ hours or up to 2 hours. Remove roast from brine and pat dry with paper towels.

2. Adjust oven rack to middle position and heat oven to 275 degrees. Bring salt pork and ½ cup water to simmer in Dutch oven over medium heat. Simmer until water evaporates and salt pork begins to sizzle, 5 to 6 minutes. Continue to cook, stirring frequently, until salt pork is lightly browned and fat has rendered, 2 to 3 minutes. Using slotted spoon, discard salt pork, leaving fat in pot.

3. Increase heat to medium-high, add roast to pot, and brown on all sides, 8 to 10 minutes. Transfer roast to large plate. Add milk, garlic, sage, and baking soda to pot and bring to simmer, scraping up any browned bits. Cook, stirring frequently, until milk is lightly browned and has consistency of heavy cream, 14 to 16 minutes. Reduce heat to medium-low and continue to cook, stirring and scraping bottom of pot constantly, until milk thickens to consistency of thin batter, 1 to 3 minutes. Remove pot from heat.

4. Return roast to pot, cover, and transfer to oven. Cook until pork registers 140 degrees, 40 to 50 minutes, flipping roast once halfway through cooking. Transfer roast to carving board, tent with aluminum foil, and let rest for 20 to 25 minutes.

5. Once roast has rested, pour any accumulated juices into pot. Add wine and return sauce to simmer over medium-high heat, whisking vigorously to smooth out sauce. Simmer until sauce has consistency of thin gravy, 2 to 3 minutes. Off heat, stir in 2 tablespoons parsley and mustard and season with salt and pepper to taste. Slice roast ¼ inch thick and transfer to serving dish. Spoon sauce over pork, sprinkle with remaining 1 tablespoon parsley, and serve.

Slow-Cooker Pork Loin with Fennel, Oranges, and Olives

Serves 6 to 8 | **Cooking Time** 2 to 3 hours on Low

WHY THIS RECIPE WORKS Fennel, oranges, and olives are a classic combination in Sicily, where the orange harvest begins and fall and runs through the winter. Here we pair these bright, salty-sweet flavors with a tender pork loin roast, letting it braise gently in a slow cooker. To give our pork satisfying color and deep flavor, we first seared it on the stovetop, and used the same skillet to soften fennel before deglazing the pan with white wine and transferring the mixture and pork to the slow cooker. Later, while the roast rested, we stirred orange segments and chopped kalamata olives into the fennel. You will need a 5- to 7-quart oval slow cooker for this recipe. A wider, shorter pork loin (about 8 inches long) will fit best in the slow cooker. We found that leaving a ⅛-inch-thick layer of fat on top of the roast is ideal; if your roast has a thicker fat cap, trim it to be about ⅛ inch thick. For how to tie a roast, see page 77. Check the pork's temperature after 2 hours of cooking and continue to monitor until it registers 140 degrees.

- 1 (3- to 4-pound) boneless center-cut pork loin roast, trimmed and tied at 1-inch intervals
- 1 teaspoon herbes de Provence
- 1 teaspoon table salt
- ½ teaspoon pepper
- 2 tablespoons extra-virgin olive oil, divided
- 3 fennel bulbs, stalks discarded, bulbs halved, cored, and sliced thin
- 2 garlic cloves, minced
- ½ cup dry white wine
- 4 oranges, plus 1 tablespoon grated orange zest
- ½ cup pitted kalamata olives, chopped
- 2 tablespoons minced fresh tarragon

1. Pat pork dry with paper towels, sprinkle with herbes de Provence, salt, and pepper. Heat 1 tablespoon oil in 12-inch skillet over medium-high heat until just smoking. Brown roast on all sides, 7 to 10 minutes; transfer to plate.

2. Heat remaining 1 tablespoon oil in now-empty skillet over medium heat until shimmering. Add fennel and cook until softened and lightly browned, 8 to 10 minutes. Stir in garlic and cook until fragrant, about 30 seconds. Stir in wine, scraping up any browned bits; transfer to slow cooker. Nestle roast, fat side up, into slow cooker, along with any accumulated juices. Cover and cook until pork registers 140 degrees, 2 to 3 hours on low.

3. Transfer roast to carving board, tent with aluminum foil, and let rest for 20 minutes.

4. Cut away peel and pith from oranges. Cut oranges into 8 wedges, then slice wedges crosswise into ½-inch-thick pieces. Stir oranges and zest and olives into fennel mixture and let stand until heated through, about 5 minutes. Stir in tarragon and season with salt and pepper to taste.

5. Remove twine from roast and slice meat ½ inch thick. Serve with fennel-orange mixture.

Goan Pork Vindaloo

Serves 8 | **Total Time** 2½ hours **MAKE AHEAD**

WHY THIS RECIPE WORKS The word "vindaloo" has evolved to indicate a searingly hot curry, but the traditional Goan dish is a brightly flavored but relatively mild pork braise made with dried Kashmiri chiles. Here, we substituted guajillo chiles and added paprika and tea to provide bright color, mild heat, earthy flavor, and a hint of astringency. Vindaloo should have a pronounced vinegary tang, but long cooking in acid can make meat dry. We withheld the vinegar until halfway through cooking so that we could use less but still enjoy the characteristic acidity. Boneless pork butt roast is often labeled Boston butt. If you don't have loose tea, open up two or three black tea bags and measure out 2 teaspoons of tea. Decaffeinated tea can be used if desired. Traditional Goan vindaloo is not very spicy, but if you prefer more heat, add up to ½ teaspoon of cayenne pepper. Serve with white rice, naan, or Goan pao, which are similar to soft white dinner rolls.

- 4 large dried guajillo chiles, wiped clean, stemmed, seeded, and torn into 1-inch pieces (about 1 ounce)
- 1 cup water, divided
- 1 (1½-inch) piece ginger, peeled and sliced crosswise ⅛ inch thick
- 6 garlic cloves, chopped coarse
- 1 tablespoon paprika
- 1 tablespoon ground cumin
- 2 teaspoons loose black tea
- 2 teaspoons table salt
- 1 teaspoon pepper
- ¼–½ teaspoon cayenne pepper (optional)
- ½ teaspoon ground cinnamon
- ½ teaspoon ground cardamom
- ¼ teaspoon ground cloves
- ¼ teaspoon ground nutmeg
- 1 (3- to 3½-pound) boneless pork butt roast, trimmed and cut into 1-inch pieces
- 1 tablespoon vegetable oil
- 1 large onion, chopped fine
- ⅓ cup cider vinegar

1. Combine guajillos and ½ cup water in bowl and microwave until steaming, about 1½ minutes. Let stand until guajillos are softened, about 10 minutes. While guajillos soften, adjust oven rack to middle position and heat oven to 325 degrees. Process guajillo mixture; ginger; garlic; paprika; cumin; tea; salt; pepper; cayenne, if using; cinnamon; cardamom; cloves; and nutmeg in blender on low speed until smooth paste forms,

1 ½ to 2 minutes. With blender running, add remaining ½ cup water. Increase speed to high and process for 1 minute. Add pork to large bowl; pour spice paste over pork and mix thoroughly.

2. Heat oil in Dutch oven over medium heat until shimmering. Add onion and cook, stirring frequently, until soft and golden, 7 to 9 minutes. Add pork mixture and stir to combine. Spread mixture into even layer. Continue to cook until mixture begins to bubble, about 2 minutes. Cover pot, transfer to oven, and cook for 40 minutes. Stir in vinegar. Cover and return pot to oven. Continue to cook until fork inserted into pork meets little or no resistance, 40 to 50 minutes. (Pork and sauce can be refrigerated for up to 2 days. To reheat, bring to gentle simmer, covered, and cook until hot throughout, adjusting consistency with hot water as needed.) Stir and serve.

Goan Pork Vindaloo

Carne Adovada

Serves 6 | **Total Time** 4¼ hours `MAKE AHEAD`

WHY THIS RECIPE WORKS This New Mexican dish of fall-apart chunks of pork in a brick-red chile sauce has endless uses. Serve it with rice and beans, crispy potatoes, or flour tortillas with shredded lettuce or chopped tomato. Pile it into tacos and burritos. Heat leftovers for breakfast: It goes great with eggs, potatoes, warm tortillas, and coffee. Although it takes a while in the oven, it's a very easy dish to prepare. Fruity, relatively mild dried New Mexican chiles are a defining ingredient of the local cuisine and feature prominently here, but you can substitute dried California chiles. Use Mexican oregano if you have it; otherwise, Mediterranean oregano works. Boneless pork butt roast is often labeled Boston butt.

- 1 (3½- to 4-pound) boneless pork butt roast, trimmed and cut into 1½-inch pieces
- 1 tablespoon plus 1 teaspoon kosher salt, divided
- 4 ounces dried New Mexican chiles, wiped clean, stemmed, seeded, and torn into 1-inch pieces
- 4 cups boiling water
- 2 tablespoons honey
- 2 tablespoons distilled white vinegar
- 5 garlic cloves, peeled
- 2 teaspoons dried Mexican oregano
- 2 teaspoons ground cumin
- ½ teaspoon cayenne pepper
- ⅛ teaspoon ground cloves
    Lime wedges

Carne Adovada

1. Pat pork dry with paper towels and toss with 1 tablespoon salt in bowl; refrigerate for 1 hour.

2. Place chiles in medium bowl. Pour boiling water over chiles, making sure they are completely submerged, and let stand until softened, 30 minutes. Adjust oven rack to lower-middle position and heat oven to 325 degrees.

3. Drain chiles and reserve 2 cups soaking liquid (discard remaining liquid). Process chiles, honey, vinegar, garlic, oregano, cumin, cayenne, cloves, and remaining 1 teaspoon salt in blender until chiles are finely ground and thick paste forms, about 30 seconds. With blender running, add 1 cup reserved liquid and process until smooth, 1½ to 2 minutes, adding up to ¼ cup additional reserved liquid to maintain vortex. Add remaining reserved liquid and continue to blend sauce at high speed, 1 minute.

4. Combine pork and chile sauce in Dutch oven, stirring to make sure pork is evenly coated. Bring to boil over high heat. Cover pot, transfer to oven, and cook until pork is tender and fork inserted into pork meets little to no resistance, 2 to 2½ hours.

5. Using wooden spoon, scrape any browned bits from sides of pot and stir until pork and sauce are recombined and sauce is smooth and homogeneous. Let stand, uncovered, for 10 minutes. Season with salt to taste. Serve with lime wedges. (Pork and sauce can be refrigerated for up to 2 days. To reheat, bring to gentle simmer, covered, and cook until hot throughout, adjusting consistency with hot water as needed.)

Choucroute Garnie

Serves 8 | **Total Time** 3¼ hours **MAKE AHEAD**

WHY THIS RECIPE WORKS This country-style dish with roots in Alsace puts the focus on the meat. "Choucroute" means "sauerkraut" in French; the beauty of the dish is how the rich meat is tempered with just enough acidity (from wine and sauerkraut) and contrasting texture (also from sauerkraut) to keep things in balance. Everything is tied together with accents such as thyme, garlic, and caraway. We liked a mix of garlicky kielbasa, herbal bratwurst, smoky ham hock, and rich pork belly. Rinsing the sauerkraut kept its brininess in check. Note that we call for fully cooked bratwurst. We developed this recipe with 12 ounces of bratwurst and 14 ounces of kielbasa, but if you can find only slightly larger packages, it's OK to use the whole package. You can substitute two 8- to 10-ounce bone-in blade-cut pork chops; 1 pound of boneless pork butt, cut in half; or 1 pound of slab bacon for the pork belly. Serve with boiled potatoes with butter and parsley, if desired.

Choucroute Garnie

2 tablespoons lard, bacon fat, or extra-virgin olive oil
1 onion, sliced thin
1 teaspoon kosher salt, divided
1 (12-ounce) smoked ham hock
1 cup dry white wine
5 garlic cloves, smashed and peeled
6 sprigs fresh thyme
1 pound skinless pork belly, cut into 2 equal pieces, fat cap trimmed to ¼ inch
½ teaspoon pepper
2 pounds sauerkraut, rinsed and squeezed dry
1 teaspoon caraway seeds
14 ounces kielbasa sausage, cut into 6 equal pieces (about 3-inch segments)
12 ounces cooked bratwurst, each sausage halved crosswise
Whole-grain mustard

1. Adjust oven rack to middle position and heat oven to 325 degrees. Heat lard in Dutch oven over medium heat until shimmering. Add onion and ¼ teaspoon salt and cook until just softened, about 6 minutes. Remove pot from heat.

2. Add ham hock, wine, garlic, and thyme sprigs to pot. Sprinkle pork belly with pepper and remaining ¾ teaspoon salt, then add to pot. Cover contents of pot with sauerkraut, then sprinkle with caraway seeds. Cover pot, transfer to oven, and cook for 1½ hours.

3. Remove pot from oven and nestle kielbasa and bratwurst into sauerkraut. Cover; return to oven; and continue to cook until sausages are hot throughout and pork belly is tender when pierced with paring knife, about 45 minutes. (Pork, sauce and sauerkraut can be refrigerated for up to 2 days. To reheat, bring to gentle simmer, covered, and cook until hot throughout, adjusting consistency with hot water as needed.)

4. Transfer sauerkraut to shallow platter; place sausages on top. Discard thyme sprigs. Slice pork belly thin crosswise and add to platter. Remove meat from ham hock, slice thin, and add to platter; discard bone. Serve with mustard.

Salmon en Cocotte with Leeks and White Wine

Serves 4 | **Total Time** 1¼ hours

WHY THIS RECIPE WORKS The French method of cooking slowly in a covered pot works with fish as well as chicken. Our goal was moist salmon that flaked in large, buttery chunks. Leeks sautéed and layered in the pot protected the fish from the pan's heat. To ensure that the fillets cook at the same rate, buy a whole center-cut fillet and cut it into four equal pieces. If the fillets are thicker or thinner than 1½ inches, you may need to adjust the cooking time slightly. You can substitute Arctic char or cod, if desired. If using arctic char or wild salmon, cook until the fillets reach 120 degrees (for medium-rare) and start checking for doneness early.

- 1 (1¾- to 2-pound) center-cut skinless salmon fillet, 1½ inches thick, pin bones removed
- ½ teaspoon plus pinch table salt, divided
- ¼ teaspoon pepper
- 2 tablespoons extra-virgin olive oil
- 2 leeks, white and light green parts only, halved lengthwise, sliced thin, and washed thoroughly
- 2 sprigs fresh thyme
- 2 garlic cloves, minced
- ½ cup dry white wine
- 2 tablespoons unsalted butter, cut into 2 pieces

1. Adjust oven rack to lowest position and heat oven to 250 degrees. Trim any whitish fat from belly of fillet, then cut

Salmon en Cocotte with Leeks and White Wine

fish into 4 equal pieces. Pat salmon dry with paper towels and sprinkle with ½ teaspoon salt and pepper.

2. Heat oil in Dutch oven over medium-low heat until shimmering. Add leeks, thyme sprigs, and pinch salt; cover and cook until softened, 8 to 10 minutes. Stir in garlic and cook until fragrant, about 30 seconds. Remove pot from heat.

3. Lay salmon, skinned side down, on top of leeks. Place large piece of aluminum foil over pot and cover tightly with lid; transfer pot to oven. Cook until salmon is opaque and flakes apart when gently prodded with paring knife, 25 to 30 minutes.

4. Transfer fish to serving platter and tent with foil. Stir wine into leeks in pot and simmer over medium-high heat until slightly thickened, about 2 minutes. Off heat, whisk in butter and season with salt and pepper to taste. Spoon sauce over salmon and serve.

Salmon en Cocotte with Celery and Orange

Add 2 thinly sliced celery ribs and 1 teaspoon minced orange zest along with garlic in step 2. Substitute ½ cup orange juice for wine and add 1 orange, peeled and segmented, when thickening sauce in step 4.

Pressure-Cooker Braised Whole Cauliflower with Olives, Raisins, and Pine Nuts

Mediterranean Braised Green Beans with Potatoes and Basil

Pressure-Cooker Braised Whole Cauliflower with Olives, Raisins, and Pine Nuts

Serves 4 | **Total Time** 45 minutes

WHY THIS RECIPE WORKS Whole braised cauliflower is a showstopper and, when done in the pressure cooker, a snap to make. We started by making an intensely savory cooking liquid of garlic, anchovies, spices, and tomatoes. Making deep cuts in the cauliflower's stem helped the fibrous core cook through so the whole head became tender. After releasing the pressure, we removed the cauliflower and thickened the sauce before spooning it on top. We prefer to use our homemade Ras el Hanout (page 101), but you can substitute store-bought ras el hanout if you wish. Serve with couscous, grains, or crusty bread. This recipe only works with an electric pressure cooker.

2 tablespoons extra-virgin olive oil
6 garlic cloves, minced
2 teaspoons ras el hanout
3 anchovy fillets, rinsed and minced (optional)
⅛ teaspoon red pepper flakes
1 (28-ounce) can whole peeled tomatoes, drained with juice reserved, chopped coarse
1 large head cauliflower (3 pounds)
½ cup pitted brine-cured green olives, chopped coarse
¼ cup golden raisins
¼ cup fresh cilantro leaves
¼ cup pine nuts, toasted

1. Using highest sauté or browning function, cook oil; garlic; ras el hanout; anchovies, if using; and pepper flakes in pressure cooker until fragrant, about 3 minutes. Turn off pressure cooker, then stir in tomatoes and reserved juice.

2. Trim outer leaves of cauliflower and cut stem flush with bottom florets. Using paring knife, cut 4-inch-deep cross in stem. Nestle cauliflower stem side down into pot and spoon some of sauce over top. Lock lid in place and close pressure release valve. Select high pressure cook function and cook for 3 minutes.

3. Turn off pressure cooker and quick-release pressure. Carefully remove lid, allowing steam to escape away from you. Using tongs and slotted spoon, transfer cauliflower to serving dish and tent with aluminum foil. Stir olives and raisins into sauce and cook, using highest sauté function, until sauce has thickened slightly, about 5 minutes. Season with salt and pepper to taste. Cut cauliflower into wedges and spoon some of sauce over top. Sprinkle with cilantro and pine nuts. Serve, passing remaining sauce separately.

Mediterranean Braised Green Beans with Potatoes and Basil

Serves 4 to 6 | **Total Time** 1½ hours VEGETARIAN

WHY THIS RECIPE WORKS When slowly braised in a low oven, green beans turn meltingly tender without being mushy. This can take hours, but a pinch of baking soda speeds up the process by dissolving the pectin in the beans' cell walls. Once the beans were partially softened, we stirred in acidic diced tomatoes to add sweet flavor and neutralize the baking soda so the beans wouldn't soften too much. To infuse the beans with bright Mediterranean flavors, we added sautéed garlic and onion plus some bright lemon juice, basil, and a drizzle of olive oil. Finally, to ensure that the beans were hearty enough for dinner, we added chunks of potatoes; 1-inch pieces turned tender in the same amount of time as the beans. Serve with a dollop of plain yogurt and rice or crusty bread.

- 5 tablespoons extra-virgin olive oil, divided
- 1 onion, chopped fine
- 4 garlic cloves, minced
- 2 teaspoons dried oregano
- 1½ pounds green beans, trimmed and cut into 2- to 3-inch lengths
- 1 pound Yukon Gold potatoes, peeled and cut into 1-inch pieces
- 1½ cups water
- ½ teaspoon baking soda
- 1 (14.5-ounce) can diced tomatoes, drained with juice reserved, chopped coarse
- 1 tablespoon tomato paste
- 2 teaspoons table salt
- ¼ teaspoon pepper
- 3 tablespoons chopped fresh basil
  Lemon juice

1. Adjust oven rack to lower-middle position and heat oven to 275 degrees. Heat 3 tablespoons oil in Dutch oven over medium heat until shimmering. Add onion and cook until softened, 5 to 7 minutes. Stir in garlic and oregano and cook until fragrant, about 30 seconds. Stir in green beans, potatoes, water, and baking soda and bring to simmer. Reduce heat to medium-low and cook, stirring occasionally, for 10 minutes.

2. Stir in tomatoes and their juice, tomato paste, salt, and pepper. Cover pot, transfer to oven, and cook until sauce is slightly thickened and green beans can be cut easily with side of fork, 40 to 50 minutes.

3. Stir in basil and season with lemon juice to taste. Transfer to bowl, drizzle with remaining 2 tablespoons oil, and serve.

Stuffed Cabbage Rolls

Serves 4 | **Total Time** 2¼ hours MAKE AHEAD

WHY THIS RECIPE WORKS Cabbage rolls stuffed with a seasoned beef filling and bathed in a light tomato sauce are serious wintertime comfort food. Sautéed onions and garlic provided a savory foundation for both sauce and filling, and ground ginger, cinnamon, and nutmeg added a warm spice flavor. For a sweet-and-sour balance, we preferred brown sugar to white for its complexity, and red wine vinegar to white for its mellow bite. We supplemented the beef with bratwurst, a mild German sausage, to boost meatiness. A panade of milk and bread helped keep the filling soft and moist. If the tops of the cabbage rolls appear dry after the foil is removed in step 5, spoon some of the sauce over them before returning to the oven.

- 1 head green cabbage (2 pounds), cored
- 1 tablespoon vegetable oil
- 1 onion, chopped fine
- 3 garlic cloves, minced
- 1 teaspoon ground ginger
- ½ teaspoon ground cinnamon
- ¼ teaspoon ground nutmeg
- 1 (28-ounce) can tomato sauce
- ¼ cup packed light brown sugar
- 3 tablespoons red wine vinegar
- 1 teaspoon table salt, divided
- ½ teaspoon pepper, divided
- 2 slices hearty white sandwich bread, torn into pieces
- ½ cup milk
- 12 ounces 85 percent lean ground beef
- 12 ounces bratwurst, casings removed

1. Adjust oven rack to middle position and heat oven to 375 degrees. Microwave cabbage in covered bowl until outer leaves are pliable and translucent, 3 to 6 minutes. Using tongs, carefully remove wilted outer leaves; set aside. Cover and repeat until you have 15 to 17 large, intact leaves.

2. Heat oil in Dutch oven over medium heat until shimmering. Add onion and cook until softened, about 5 minutes. Stir in garlic, ginger, cinnamon, and nutmeg and cook until fragrant, about 30 seconds. Transfer half of onion mixture to small bowl; set aside. Off heat, stir tomato sauce, sugar, vinegar, ½ teaspoon salt, and ¼ teaspoon pepper into pot with remaining onion mixture until sugar has dissolved.

3. Process bread and milk in food processor until smooth, about 30 seconds. Add reserved onion mixture, beef, bratwurst, remaining ½ teaspoon salt, and remaining ¼ teaspoon pepper and pulse until well combined, about 10 pulses.

4. Working with 1 cabbage leaf at a time, cut along both sides of rib at base of leaf to form narrow triangle; remove rib. Continue cutting up center of leaf about 1 inch above triangle, then slightly overlap cut ends of cabbage. Place 2 heaping tablespoons of meat mixture on each leaf, about ½ inch from bottom of where cut ends overlap. Fold bottom of leaf over filling and fold in sides. Roll leaf tightly around filling. Repeat with remaining leaves and remaining filling. Arrange rolls, seam side down, in 13 by 9-inch baking dish. (Unbaked rolls can be refrigerated for up to 24 hours.)

5. Pour sauce over cabbage rolls, cover with aluminum foil, and bake until sauce is bubbling and rolls are heated through, about 45 minutes. Remove foil and bake, uncovered, until sauce is slightly thickened and cabbage is tender, about 15 minutes. Serve.

Mushroom Ragu

Serves 4 | **Total Time** 50 minutes

MAKE AHEAD VEGETARIAN

WHY THIS RECIPE WORKS Fresh and dried mushrooms offer a bounty of flavors and textures in this saucy dish, which is ideal for topping pasta or polenta. Dried porcini delivered rich depth, while chanterelles—among the best wild mushrooms available in America—and portobellos provided deep, nutty flavor and meaty texture, respectively. To jump-start the cooking, we microwaved the fresh mushrooms until they released some of their juice. We then added them to the Dutch oven with the dried porcini, along with red wine and tomatoes, and simmered everything until all the flavors melded. You can substitute any wild mushrooms for the chanterelles. Serve over Polenta with Cheese and Butter (page 174) or pasta, or with crusty bread.

18 ounces chanterelle mushrooms, trimmed and halved if small or quartered if large
 1 pound portobello mushroom caps, gills removed, halved and sliced ½ inch thick
 2 tablespoons unsalted butter
 1 onion, chopped fine
 ½ ounce dried porcini mushrooms, rinsed and minced
 ½ teaspoon table salt
 3 garlic cloves, minced
 1 teaspoon minced fresh thyme or ¼ teaspoon dried
 ½ cup dry red wine
 1 (14.5-ounce) can diced tomatoes, drained with juice reserved, chopped
 2 tablespoons minced fresh parsley

1. Microwave chanterelle mushrooms and portobello mushrooms in covered bowl, stirring occasionally, until tender and mushrooms have released their liquid, 6 to 8 minutes. Transfer mushrooms to colander set in bowl and let drain, reserving liquid.

2. Melt butter in Dutch oven over medium heat. Add onion, porcini mushrooms, and salt and cook until softened and lightly browned, 5 to 7 minutes. Add portobello and chanterelle mushrooms and cook, stirring often, until dry and lightly browned, about 5 minutes. Stir in garlic and thyme and cook until fragrant, about 30 seconds.

3. Stir in wine and reserved mushroom liquid, scraping up any browned bits. Stir in tomatoes and their juice, bring to simmer, and cook until ragu is slightly thickened, about 8 minutes. (Mushroom Ragu can be refrigerated for up to 3 days. To reheat, bring to gentle simmer, covered, and cook until hot throughout, adjusting consistency with hot water as needed.) Off heat, stir in parsley and season with salt and pepper to taste. Serve.

Chana Masala

Serves 4 to 6 | **Total Time** 55 minutes

MAKE AHEAD VEGETARIAN

WHY THIS RECIPE WORKS The allure of chana masala is deep: Golden, creamy chickpeas glimmer in an orangey-red tomato sauce, and spices perfume the dish. Onion, chile, and cilantro provide contrasting freshness and crunch. We fried a paste of onion, ginger, and garlic in a bit of oil before stirring in spices. We then added tomatoes, chickpeas, and water and brought the mix to a simmer. Sautéing the spice paste in a full 3 tablespoons of oil added richness. We got even more depth when we included the chickpea liquid from the can rather than draining it away. Sodium contents of canned chickpeas and tomatoes vary; season with additional salt at the end of ooking if desired. If you prefer a spicier dish, leave the seeds in the serrano chiles. Serve with rice or naan.

 1 small red onion, quartered, divided
10 sprigs fresh cilantro, stems and leaves separated
 1 (1½-inch) piece ginger, peeled and chopped coarse
 2 garlic cloves, chopped coarse
 2 serrano chiles, stemmed, halved, seeded, and sliced thin crosswise, divided
 3 tablespoons vegetable oil
 1 (14.5-ounce) can whole peeled tomatoes
 1 teaspoon paprika

1 teaspoon ground cumin
½ teaspoon ground turmeric
½ teaspoon fennel seeds
2 (15-ounce) cans chickpeas, undrained
1½ teaspoons garam masala
½ teaspoon table salt
Lime wedges

1. Chop three-quarters of onion coarse; reserve remaining quarter for garnish. Cut cilantro stems into 1-inch lengths. Process chopped onion, cilantro stems, ginger, garlic, and half of serranos in food processor until finely chopped, scraping down sides of bowl as necessary, about 20 seconds. Combine onion mixture and oil in large saucepan. Cook over medium-high heat, stirring frequently, until onion is fully softened and beginning to stick to saucepan, 5 to 7 minutes.

2. While onion mixture cooks, process tomatoes and their juice in now-empty food processor until smooth, about 30 seconds. Add paprika, cumin, turmeric, and fennel seeds to onion mixture and cook, stirring constantly, until fragrant, about 1 minute. Stir in chickpeas and their liquid and processed tomatoes and bring to boil. Adjust heat to maintain simmer, then cover and simmer for 15 minutes. While mixture cooks, chop reserved onion fine.

3. Stir garam masala and salt into chickpea mixture and continue to cook, uncovered and stirring occasionally, until chickpeas are softened and sauce is thickened, 8 to 12 minutes. Season with salt to taste. (Chana masala can be refrigerated for up to 2 days. To reheat, bring to gentle simmer, covered, and cook until hot throughout, adjusting consistency with hot water as needed.) Transfer to wide, shallow serving bowl. Sprinkle with chopped onion, remaining serranos, and cilantro leaves and serve, passing lime wedges separately.

NOTES FROM THE TEST KITCHEN

TIMING YOUR SPICES
In Indian cooking, coriander, cardamom, cinnamon, and other sweet spices (often combined in garam masala) are valued for their vibrant flavors, so they're often added at the end of cooking and sometimes sprinkled atop a dish before serving. In our Chana Masala, we added stronger cumin, turmeric, paprika, and fennel seeds at the beginning, but held back on adding the garam masala until near the end of the simmering time, which preserved more volatile flavor compounds, giving the sauce more dimension.

Mushroom Ragu

Chana Masala

Savory Spice Blends

Pistachio Dukkah

Makes about ½ cup | **Total Time** 10 minutes

1½ teaspoons coriander seeds, toasted
¾ teaspoon cumin seeds, toasted
½ teaspoon fennel seeds, toasted
2 tablespoons sesame seeds, toasted
3 tablespoons shelled pistachios, toasted and chopped fine
½ teaspoon flake sea salt
½ teaspoon pepper

Process coriander seeds, cumin seeds, and fennel seeds in spice grinder until finely ground, about 30 seconds. Add sesame seeds and pulse until coarsely ground, about 4 pulses; transfer to small bowl. Stir in pistachios, salt, and pepper. (Dukkah can be refrigerated for up to 3 months.)

Hazelnut-Nigella Dukkah

Makes about ½ cup | **Total Time** 15 minutes

This dukkah is a bit warmer from the hazelnuts and more intense from the nigella seeds than sweeter pistachio dukkah. Use it when you want more aggressive flavor. You can find nigella seeds at spice shops and specialty markets.

1 teaspoon fennel seeds, toasted
1 teaspoon coriander seeds, toasted
1½ tablespoons raw sunflower seeds, toasted
1 tablespoon sesame seeds, toasted
1½ teaspoons nigella seeds
3 tablespoons hazelnuts, toasted, skinned, and chopped fine
1½ teaspoons paprika
½ teaspoon flake sea salt

Process fennel seeds and coriander seeds in spice grinder until finely ground, about 30 seconds. Add sunflower seeds, sesame seeds, and nigella seeds and pulse until coarsely ground, about 4 pulses; transfer to small bowl. Stir in hazelnuts, paprika, and salt. (Dukkah can be refrigerated for up to 3 months.)

Five-Spice Powder

Makes about ¼ cup | **Total Time** 10 minutes

- 5 teaspoons fennel seeds
- 4 teaspoons white peppercorns or 8 teaspoons Sichuan peppercorns
- 1 tablespoon whole cloves
- 8 star anise pods
- 1 cinnamon stick, broken into pieces

Process fennel seeds, peppercorns, and cloves in spice grinder until finely ground, about 30 seconds; transfer to small bowl. Process star anise and cinnamon in now-empty spice grinder until finely ground, about 30 seconds; transfer to bowl with other spices and stir to combine. (Five-spice powder can be stored in airtight container for up to 1 month.)

Garam Masala

Makes about 1 cup | **Total Time** 10 minutes

- 3 tablespoons black peppercorns
- 8 teaspoons coriander seeds
- 4 teaspoons cardamom pods
- 2½ teaspoons cumin seeds
- 1½ cinnamon sticks

Process all ingredients in spice grinder until finely ground, about 30 seconds. (Garam masala can be stored at room temperature in airtight container for up to 1 year.)

Ras el Hanout

Makes about ½ cup | **Total Time** 15 minutes

If you can't find Aleppo pepper, you can substitute ½ teaspoon paprika plus ½ teaspoon red pepper flakes.

- 16 cardamom pods
- 4 teaspoons coriander seeds
- 4 teaspoons cumin seeds
- 2 teaspoons anise seeds
- 2 teaspoons ground dried Aleppo pepper
- ½ teaspoon allspice berries
- ¼ teaspoon black peppercorns
- 4 teaspoons ground ginger
- 2 teaspoons ground nutmeg
- 2 teaspoons ground cinnamon

Process cardamom pods, coriander seeds, cumin seeds, anise seeds, Aleppo, allspice, and peppercorns in spice grinder until finely ground, about 30 seconds. Stir in ginger, nutmeg, and cinnamon. (Ras el hanout can be stored in airtight container for up to 1 month.)

Harissa

Makes about ½ cup | **Total Time** 10 minutes

If you can't find Aleppo pepper, you can substitute ¾ teaspoon paprika plus ¾ teaspoon red pepper flakes.

- 6 tablespoons extra-virgin olive oil
- 6 garlic cloves, minced
- 2 tablespoons paprika
- 1 tablespoon ground coriander
- 1 tablespoon ground dried Aleppo pepper
- 1 teaspoon ground cumin
- ¾ teaspoon caraway seeds
- ½ teaspoon table salt

Combine all ingredients in bowl and microwave until bubbling and very fragrant, about 1 minute, stirring halfway through microwaving. Let cool to room temperature. (Harissa can be refrigerated for up to 4 days.)

Za'atar

Makes about ⅓ cup | **Total Time** 10 minutes

- 2 tablespoons dried thyme
- 1 tablespoon dried oregano
- 1½ tablespoons sumac
- 1 tablespoon sesame seeds, toasted
- ¼ teaspoon table salt

Process thyme and oregano using spice grinder until finely ground and powdery. Transfer to bowl and stir in sumac, sesame seeds, and salt. (Za'atar can be stored in airtight container at room temperature for up to 1 year.)

CHAPTER 4
centerpieces
for a crowd

■ MAKE AHEAD   ■ VEGETARIAN

Photo: Best Roast Prime Rib

Twin Roast Chickens with Root Vegetables
and Tarragon Vinaigrette

Boneless Turkey Breast
with Gravy

Twin Roast Chickens with Root Vegetables and Tarragon Vinaigrette

Serves 8 | **Total Time** 2¼ hours

WHY THIS RECIPE WORKS Roasting two whole chickens together yields enough food to feed a hungry crowd and is as simple as cooking one, provided you employ the right method. We scattered a mix of root vegetables into the bottom of a roasting pan before perching the chickens above on a V-rack, allowing the vegetables to soak up flavorful chicken drippings. While the chickens rested we switched the pan to the stovetop where the vegetables finished cooking to perfect tenderness. If you choose to brine the chickens, see page 413 for instructions. If brining the chickens, do not season with salt in step 3. If using self-basting or kosher chickens, do not brine.

1½ pounds red potatoes, unpeeled, cut into 1-inch pieces
 1 pound carrots, peeled and cut into 1-inch pieces
 1 pound parsnips, peeled and cut into 1-inch pieces
 6 shallots, peeled and halved
 5 tablespoons extra-virgin olive oil, divided
1½ teaspoons table salt, divided
 1 teaspoon pepper, divided
 2 (3½- to 4-pound) whole chickens, giblets discarded, brined if desired
 6 tablespoons minced fresh tarragon, divided
⅓ cup minced fresh parsley
 2 tablespoons sherry vinegar
 1 teaspoon Dijon mustard

1. Adjust oven rack to middle position and heat oven to 475 degrees. Toss potatoes, carrots, parsnips, shallots, 1 tablespoon oil, ½ teaspoon salt, and ½ teaspoon pepper together in bowl. Spread vegetables evenly into roasting pan. Spray V-rack with vegetable oil spray and nestle into pan with vegetables.

2. Pat chickens dry with paper towels. Using your fingers or handle of spoon, gently loosen skin covering breasts and thighs. Spread 3 tablespoons tarragon under skin of chickens, directly onto meat. Tie legs together with kitchen twine and tuck wingtips behind back.

3. Sprinkle exterior of chickens with 1 teaspoon salt and ½ teaspoon pepper. Place chickens, breast side down, in prepared V-rack. Roast for 20 minutes.

4. Using 2 large wads of paper towels, flip chickens breast side up and continue to roast until breasts register 160 degrees and thighs register 175 degrees, 50 minutes to 1 hour longer.

5. Remove pan from oven. Transfer chicken to carving board and let rest for 20 minutes. Being careful of hot pan handles, place pan over medium-high heat on stovetop (over 2 burners, if possible) and cook vegetables, stirring gently, until lightly browned and glistening, 8 to 10 minutes.

6. Whisk remaining ¼ cup oil, remaining 3 tablespoons tarragon, parsley, vinegar, and mustard together in small bowl. Carve chickens and serve with vegetables and vinaigrette.

Boneless Turkey Breast with Gravy

Serves 8 to 10
Total Time 4¾ to 5¼ hours, plus 2 hours salting

WHY THIS RECIPE WORKS Rolled and neatly tied, our substantial, golden-skinned boneless roast slices like a dream and is the perfect option for a crowd of white meat–lovers. Starting with a bone-in turkey breast ensured that both breast halves were the same size. To make the joining easier, we used a loaf pan to hold the breast halves together with the skin sides facing out while we tied them into an evenly shaped roast. Refrigerating the salted roast for at least a couple hours ensured that the seasoning penetrated deep into the meat, and cooking in a low 275-degree oven kept the lean meat tender and moist. We made resourceful use of the breastbone, roasting it before simmering with herbs and aromatics to create a deeply flavorful stock that we used as the base for a rich, velvety gravy. We prefer a natural (unbrined) turkey breast here, but both self-basting and kosher also work well. Omit the salt in step 1 if you buy a self-basting or kosher turkey breast. You can make soup with the excess turkey stock, if desired.

TURKEY

- 1 (5- to 7-pound) bone-in turkey breast, trimmed
- 1 tablespoon kosher salt
- 2 teaspoons minced fresh rosemary
- ½ teaspoon pepper
- 1 tablespoon vegetable oil

TURKEY STOCK

- 1 onion, chopped
- 1 carrot, peeled and chopped
- 1 celery rib, chopped
- 6 sprigs fresh rosemary
- 1 bay leaf

GRAVY

- 4 tablespoons unsalted butter
- ¼ cup all-purpose flour
- ⅓ cup dry white wine
- 1½ teaspoons kosher salt
- ½ teaspoon pepper

1. FOR THE TURKEY Position turkey breast skin side up on cutting board. Using sharp knife, remove each breast half from bone by cutting through skin on top of breast on either side of center bone. Continue to work knife along bone until each breast half is removed. Reserve breastbone for stock. Combine salt, rosemary, and pepper in bowl. Sprinkle breasts all over with salt mixture.

2. Lay two 24-inch pieces of kitchen twine crosswise in middle of 8½ by 4½-inch loaf pan, about 1 inch apart. Arrange 1 breast half skin side down in pan on top of twine. Position remaining breast half over first, skin side up, with thick end over tapered end. Tuck turkey into edges of pan to fit if necessary. Tie twine tightly to secure. Remove turkey from pan and continue to tie at 1-inch intervals. Wrap in plastic wrap and refrigerate for at least 2 hours or up to 24 hours.

3. FOR THE TURKEY STOCK Meanwhile, adjust oven rack to middle position and heat oven to 450 degrees. Line rimmed baking sheet with aluminum foil. Place reserved breastbone on prepared sheet and roast until well browned, about 1 hour. Let sit until cool enough to handle, about 15 minutes.

4. Place breastbone in large saucepan (if necessary, use kitchen shears to break down bone to fit). Add onion, carrot, celery, rosemary sprigs, and bay leaf. Add water to cover by 1 inch and bring to boil over high heat. Reduce heat to medium-low and simmer for 1 hour. (Bone should remain covered with water throughout simmer.)

5. Discard breastbone. Strain turkey stock through fine-mesh strainer set over large bowl. Using spoon, press on solids to extract liquid; discard solids. Reserve turkey stock to make gravy when ready.

6. Three hours before serving, adjust oven rack to middle position and heat oven to 275 degrees. Set wire rack in rimmed baking sheet. Heat oil in 12-inch nonstick skillet over medium-high heat until just smoking. Add turkey and cook until well browned on all sides, about 10 minutes. Transfer turkey to prepared wire rack. Roast until turkey registers 160 degrees, 2¼ to 2¾ hours. Transfer turkey to carving board and let rest for 15 minutes.

7. FOR THE GRAVY Meanwhile, melt butter in large saucepan over medium heat. Whisk in flour until smooth. Cook, whisking frequently, until peanut butter–colored, about 5 minutes. Slowly whisk in 3 cups turkey stock, scraping up any browned bits and smoothing out lumps. (Remaining stock can be refrigerated for up to 2 days or frozen for up to 2 months.) Whisk in wine, salt, and pepper and bring to boil. Reduce heat to medium-low and simmer until slightly thickened and reduced to about 2½ cups, 8 to 10 minutes. Off heat, season with salt and pepper to taste. Cover and keep warm.

8. Slice turkey ½ inch thick, removing twine as you slice. Serve, passing gravy separately.

SHAPING TURKEY BREAST ROAST

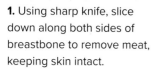

1. Using sharp knife, slice down along both sides of breastbone to remove meat, keeping skin intact.

2. Use loaf pan to keep 2 breast halves in compact, manageable shape while you tie them together.

Two-Hour Turkey and Gravy

Serves 10 to 12
Total Time 2 hours, plus 45 minutes resting

WHY THIS RECIPE WORKS Cooking a whole turkey has never been this quick or easy. Our method requires less than 2 hours of roasting, and we use the resting time to mix up a flavorful gravy from the drippings. Cutting a slit between the turkey thighs and breast exposed more of the dark meat, so it cooked at the same rate as the white meat. Starting in a hot 450-degree oven browned the skin; reducing the temperature to 250 degrees partway through ensured moist, tender meat. Roasting vegetables under the turkey created a base for an easy but richly flavored gravy. If you can't find a self-basting turkey, a kosher turkey can be substituted. Avoid opening the oven too frequently to take the turkey's temperature. If your turkey is on the lower end of the weight range, follow the lower end of the time ranges given, and vice versa.

2 onions, quartered through root end
2 carrots, peeled and cut into 3-inch pieces
1 celery rib, cut into 3-inch pieces
1 (12- to 14-pound) self-basting turkey, neck reserved, giblets discarded
3 tablespoons extra-virgin olive oil
1 tablespoon plus ½ teaspoon kosher salt, divided
2 teaspoons pepper, divided
3 cups water, plus extra as needed
1 tablespoon unsalted butter
¼ cup dry white wine
¼ cup all-purpose flour
4 sprigs fresh thyme
1 sprig fresh sage

1. Adjust oven rack to lowest position and heat oven to 450 degrees. Scatter onions, carrots, celery, and turkey neck in large roasting pan. Set V-rack over vegetables and turkey neck in pan.

2. Pat turkey dry with paper towels and tuck wingtips behind back. Transfer turkey, breast side up, to V-rack. Using sharp knife, slice through skin between breast and leg on each side of turkey to expose entire underside of thigh, without cutting into meat. Combine oil, 1 tablespoon salt, and 1½ teaspoons pepper in small bowl. Brush turkey all over with oil mixture.

3. Roast turkey until thickest part of breast registers 120 degrees and thickest part of thigh registers at least 135 degrees, 1 hour to 1 hour 10 minutes.

4. Reduce oven temperature to 250 degrees and continue to roast turkey until breast registers 160 degrees and thighs register 175 degrees, 35 to 45 minutes. Transfer turkey to carving board and let rest for 45 minutes.

5. While turkey rests, transfer vegetables and turkey neck to bowl, leaving turkey juices in pan.

6. Add water to pan with turkey juices and scrape up any browned bits from pan bottom. Transfer deglazed juices to 4-cup liquid measuring cup; add extra water as needed to equal 4 cups.

7. Melt butter in Dutch oven over medium-high heat. Add vegetables and turkey neck and cook until any liquid has evaporated and browned bits begin to form on bottom of pot, 3 to 5 minutes. Add wine and cook until nearly evaporated, about 2 minutes, scraping up any browned bits.

8. Sprinkle flour over top and cook, stirring constantly, for 1 minute. Add thyme sprigs, sage sprig, deglazed pan juices, remaining ½ teaspoon salt, and remaining ½ teaspoon pepper. Bring to boil, then reduce heat to medium-low and simmer until thickened to gravy consistency, 12 to 15 minutes.

9. Strain gravy through fine-mesh strainer set over medium saucepan; discard solids. Season with salt and pepper to taste. Carve turkey and serve with gravy.

Two-Hour Turkey and Gravy

1 (12- to 14-pound) turkey, neck and giblets removed and reserved for gravy, if desired
¼ cup kosher salt, divided
1 teaspoon pepper
1 teaspoon baking powder
1 tablespoon vegetable oil
1 large disposable aluminum roasting pan (if using charcoal) or 2 disposable aluminum pie plates (if using gas)

1. Place turkey, breast side down, on cutting board. Make two 2-inch incisions below each thigh and breast along back of turkey (4 incisions total). Using your fingers or handle of spoon, gently loosen skin covering breast and thighs. Rub 4 teaspoons salt evenly inside cavity of turkey, 1 tablespoon salt under skin of each breast, and 1 teaspoon salt under skin of each leg.

2. Combine pepper, baking powder, and remaining 1 teaspoon salt in small bowl. Pat turkey dry with paper towels. Evenly sprinkle baking powder mixture all over turkey and rub in with your hands, coating entire surface evenly. Wrap turkey tightly with plastic wrap and refrigerate for 24 to 48 hours.

3. Remove turkey from refrigerator and discard plastic. Tuck wings underneath turkey. Using your hands, rub oil evenly over entire surface.

4A. FOR A CHARCOAL GRILL Open bottom vent halfway and place disposable pan filled with 3 cups water in center of grill. Arrange 1½ quarts unlit charcoal briquettes on either side of pan (3 quarts total) in even layer. Light large chimney starter two-thirds filled with charcoal briquettes (4 quarts). When top coals are partially covered with ash, pour 2 quarts lit coals on top of each pile of unlit coals. Set cooking grate in place, cover, and open lid vent halfway. Heat grill until hot, about 5 minutes.

4B. FOR A GAS GRILL Remove cooking grate and place 2 disposable pie plates, each filled with 2 cups water, directly on 1 burner over which turkey will be cooked. Set grate in place, turn all burners to high, cover, and heat grill until hot, about 15 minutes. Turn primary burner (burner opposite pie plates) to medium and turn off other burner(s). Adjust primary burner as needed to maintain grill temperature of 325 degrees.

5. Clean and oil cooking grate. Place turkey, breast side up, in center of charcoal grill or on cooler side of gas grill, making sure turkey is over disposable pans and not over flame. Cover (positioning lid vents over turkey if using charcoal grill) and cook until breast registers 160 degrees and thighs register 175 degrees, 2½ to 3 hours, rotating turkey after 1¼ hours if using gas grill. Transfer turkey to carving board and let rest for 45 minutes. Carve turkey and serve.

Simple Grill-Roasted Turkey

Serves 10 to 12 | **Total Time** 3½ to 3¾ hours, plus 24¾ hours salting and resting

WHY THIS RECIPE WORKS Grill-roasting a turkey is a great excuse to take the kitchen work outdoors, yielding a bird with crispy bronzed skin and juicy, subtly smoky meat. Bonus: Grilling frees up your oven for other dishes. We set our turkey between two piles of coals, exposing the dark meat of the thighs to more intense, direct heat. A combination of lit coals and unlit briquettes helped our fire burn longer without intervention. Rubbing our turkey all over with salt and giving it a 24-hour rest before grilling ensured that every bite was well seasoned. If using a self-basting turkey or a kosher turkey, don't salt in step 1, but do include the salt in step 2. Check the wings halfway through roasting; if they are getting too dark, slide a small piece of aluminum foil between the wing and the cooking grate to shield the wings from the flame. Serve with Our Favorite Turkey Gravy (page 134) or All-Purpose Gravy (page 135).

Turkey and Gravy for a Crowd

Turkey and Gravy for a Crowd

Serves 18 to 20 | **Total Time** 6¾ to 7¼ hours, plus 24 hours salting and 1 hour cooling `MAKE AHEAD`

WHY THIS RECIPE WORKS A whole turkey large enough to feed 20 is precarious to maneuver in and out of the oven—plus, cooking one requires foresight to account for substantial thawing and resting times. Cooking turkey parts (leg quarters and bone-in breasts) instead of a whole bird is an easy way to simplify the holidays. Our method allowed us to cook the parts separately, braising the leg quarters up to three days ahead and use the braising liquid as a base for a make-ahead gravy. That left us with nothing to do on the big day except roast the breasts and reheat the leg quarters and gravy. If using self-basting or kosher turkey breasts, do not salt in step 7, but season with salt in step 8.

TURKEY LEGS AND GRAVY
- 3 onions, chopped
- 4 celery ribs, chopped
- 4 carrots, peeled and chopped
- 10 garlic cloves, smashed and peeled
- 3 tablespoons unsalted butter, melted, plus extra as needed
- 3 bay leaves
- 10 sprigs fresh thyme
- 10 sprigs fresh parsley
- 1 tablespoon black peppercorns
- 4 cups chicken broth
- 1 cup water
- 1 cup dry white wine
- 4 (1½- to 2-pound) turkey leg quarters, trimmed
- 3 tablespoons kosher salt
- ½ cup all-purpose flour

TURKEY BREASTS
- 2 (5- to 6-pound) bone-in turkey breasts, trimmed
- 2 tablespoons plus 2 teaspoons kosher salt, divided
- 7 tablespoons unsalted butter, melted, divided

UP TO 3 DAYS IN ADVANCE

1. FOR THE TURKEY LEGS AND GRAVY Adjust oven rack to lower-middle position and heat oven to 325 degrees. Toss onions, celery, carrots, garlic, melted butter, bay leaves, thyme sprigs, parsley sprigs, and peppercorns together in large roasting pan; spread into even layer. Place pan over medium heat and cook, stirring occasionally, until vegetables are softened and lightly browned and fond forms on bottom of pan, about 15 minutes. Add broth, water, and wine and bring to simmer, scraping up any browned bits. Remove pan from heat.

2. Cut leg quarters at joints into thighs and drumsticks, sprinkle with salt, and season with pepper to taste. Place pieces skin side up in pan (braising liquid should come about three-quarters of way up legs and thighs). Place 12 by 16-inch piece of parchment paper over turkey pieces. Cover pan tightly with aluminum foil. Place pan in oven and cook until thighs register 170 degrees, 2½ to 3 hours. Remove pan from oven. Transfer turkey pieces to large, shallow container and let cool completely, about 1 hour. Once cool, cover and refrigerate.

3. Using spatula, scrape up any browned bits from bottom and sides of pan. Strain contents of pan through fine-mesh strainer set over large bowl, pressing on solids with spatula to extract as much liquid as possible; discard solids.

4. Transfer liquid to fat separator and let settle for 5 minutes. Reserve ½ cup plus 1 tablespoon fat (if there is not enough fat, add extra melted butter to make up difference) and 8 cups liquid; discard remaining liquid.

5. Heat reserved fat in large saucepan over medium-high heat. Add flour and cook, stirring constantly, until flour is medium golden brown and fragrant, about 5 minutes. Slowly whisk in reserved liquid, scraping up any browned bits and smoothing out any lumps, and bring to boil. Reduce heat to medium-low and simmer, stirring occasionally, until gravy is thickened and reduced to 6 cups, 15 to 20 minutes. Off heat, season gravy with salt and pepper to taste. Transfer to large container and let cool completely, about 1 hour. Once cool, cover and refrigerate.

DAY BEFORE

6. FOR THE TURKEY BREASTS Place breasts on cutting board skin side down. Using kitchen shears, cut through ribs, following vertical lines of fat where breasts meet backs, from tapered ends of breasts to wing joints. Using your hands, bend backs away from breasts to pop shoulder joints out of sockets. Using paring knife, cut through joints between bones to separate backs from breasts.

7. Flip breasts skin side up. Using your fingers, carefully loosen and separate skin from each side of 1 breast. Peel back skin, leaving it attached at top and center of each breast. Rub 1 teaspoon salt onto each side of breast, then place skin back over meat. Rub 1 teaspoon salt onto underside of breast cavity. Repeat with remaining breast. Place breasts on rimmed baking sheet and refrigerate, uncovered, for 24 hours.

SERVING DAY

8. Adjust oven rack to middle position and heat oven to 325 degrees. Measure out 20-inch piece of foil and roll into loose ball. Unroll foil, place on second rimmed baking sheet, and top with wire rack. Place breasts, skin side up, on prepared wire rack; brush with 4 tablespoons melted butter and sprinkle each whole breast with remaining 1 teaspoon salt. Roast until thickest part of breast registers 130 degrees, about 1½ hours.

9. Remove breasts from oven and increase oven temperature to 500 degrees. When oven reaches temperature, return breasts to oven and roast until skin is deeply browned and thickest part of breast registers 160 degrees, 20 to 30 minutes. Transfer to carving board and let rest, uncovered, for 30 minutes. Pour any juices from sheet into bowl and set aside.

10. Adjust oven rack to upper-middle position. Place thighs and drumsticks skin side up on now-empty wire rack set in sheet and brush with remaining 3 tablespoons melted butter. Place in oven and reheat until skin is well browned and thighs register 110 degrees, 18 to 22 minutes. Transfer thighs and drumsticks to large platter.

11. While thighs reheat, bring gravy to simmer in large saucepan over medium-low heat, whisking occasionally. Add any reserved juices from breasts and season with salt and pepper to taste. Cover and keep warm.

12. Carve breasts and transfer to platter with thighs and drumsticks. Serve, passing gravy separately.

Balsamic-Glazed Cornish Game Hens

Serves 8 | **Total Time** 1¾ hours

WHY THIS RECIPE WORKS Cornish game hens are classic dinner party fare and an elegant alternative to chicken; their small size means each guest has one to themselves, making for a stunning presentation. We often use a roasting pan to cook poultry, but the tall sides of this vessel trapped steam next to the petite hens, preventing them from browning. For a foolproof, streamlined recipe, our first step was to ditch the roasting pan in favor of a wire rack set in a rimmed baking sheet; the lower sides of the baking sheet maximized heat exposure and minimized steaming. The sugars in a quick brown sugar–balsamic vinegar glaze caramelized in the hot oven, giving the birds a gorgeous, spotty mahogany hue and adding a sweet and savory complexity to the delicate meat. Try to buy hens that are the same size so they will cook at the same rate; if the hens vary widely in size, be ready to remove them individually from the oven as they finish cooking.

    1⅓ cups packed dark brown sugar
     1   cup balsamic vinegar
     2   teaspoons table salt, divided
     8   (1¼- to 1½-pound) Cornish game
         hens, giblets removed
    ½   teaspoon pepper

1. Adjust oven rack to middle position and heat oven to 450 degrees. Set wire rack in rimmed baking sheet lined with aluminum foil. Whisk sugar, vinegar, and 1 teaspoon salt in 4-cup liquid measuring cup and microwave until thickened and reduced to about 1⅓ cups, 8 to 10 minutes. Measure out and reserve ⅓ cup glaze for serving. Cover remaining glaze to keep warm. (Glaze will thicken as it cools between bastings; rewarm as needed to loosen.)

2. Tuck wings and tie legs of each hen together with kitchen twine. Pat hens dry with paper towels and sprinkle with remaining 1 teaspoon salt and pepper. Arrange hens breast side down, with wings facing out, on prepared wire rack. Roast for 15 minutes.

3. Remove hens from oven and brush with ⅓ cup glaze. Flip hens breast side up with legs facing out, and brush with ⅓ cup glaze. Continue to roast for 20 minutes.

4. Brush hens with remaining ⅓ cup glaze and continue to roast until hens are spotty brown and breasts register 160 degrees and thighs register 175 degrees, 15 to 20 minutes. Transfer hens to carving board and brush with glaze reserved for serving. Let rest for 10 minutes, then serve.

Whole Roast Ducks with Cherry Sauce

Whole Roast Ducks with Cherry Sauce

Serves 8 | Total Time 3 hours, plus 6 hours salting

WHY THIS RECIPE WORKS Roast duck, with its sultry bass-note richness and crackly burnished skin, is a dark meat–lover's best friend, but it requires ingenuity both to render its abundant fat (to prevent greasiness) and to ensure that the legs and breasts cook at the same rate. Our solution: First, we scored the ducks' skin extensively to create channels that would allow rendered fat to escape. Second, we used a two-stage cooking method, half-braising the ducks before roasting them. Submerging just the legs in simmering water in a roasting pan exposed them to lots of direct heat, giving them a head start over the breasts, which we kept above the liquid. Only once the legs were well on their way did we ditch the liquid and move the ducks into the oven to roast. Pekin ducks may also be labeled as Long Island ducks and are typically sold frozen. Thaw the ducks in the refrigerator for 24 hours. Use a roasting pan that measures at least 14 by 12 inches. Do not thaw the cherries before using. If desired, pulse the cherries in a food processor until coarsely chopped. In step 4, the crumpled aluminum foil prevents the rendered fat from smoking. Even when the duck is fully cooked, its juices will have a reddish hue. For carving instructions, see page 111.

DUCKS

- 2 (5½- to 6-pound) Pekin ducks, necks and giblets reserved if making stock
- ¼ cup kosher salt, divided
- 2 tablespoons maple syrup
- 1 tablespoon soy sauce

CHERRY SAUCE

- ⅓ cup maple syrup
- ¼ cup red wine vinegar
- 4 teaspoons soy sauce
- 2 teaspoons cornstarch
- ½ teaspoon pepper
- 2 sprigs fresh thyme
- 18 ounces frozen sweet cherries, quartered

1. FOR THE DUCKS Working with 1 duck at a time, use your hands to remove large fat deposits from bottom of cavity. Using kitchen shears, trim excess neck skin from top of breast; remove tail and first 2 segments from each wing, leaving only

Rosemary-Garlic Top Sirloin Roast

drumette. Arrange duck breast side up. With tip of sharp knife, cut slits spaced ¾ inch apart in crosshatch pattern in skin and fat of breast, being careful not to cut into meat. Flip duck breast side down. Cut parallel slits spaced ¾ inch apart in skin and fat of each thigh (do not crosshatch).

2. Rub 2 teaspoons salt into cavity of 1 duck. Rub 1 teaspoon salt into breast, taking care to rub salt into slits. Rub 1 tablespoon salt into skin of rest of duck. Align skin at bottom of cavity so 1 side overlaps other by at least ½ inch. Use sturdy toothpick to pin skin layers to each other to close cavity. Place duck on rimmed baking sheet. Repeat with second duck. Refrigerate uncovered for 6 to 24 hours.

3. Place ducks breast side up in roasting pan. Add water until at least half of thighs are submerged but most of breasts remain above water, about 14 cups. Bring to boil over 2 burners over high heat. Reduce heat to maintain vigorous simmer. Cook until thermometer inserted into thickest part of drumstick, all the way to bone, registers 145 to 160 degrees, 45 minutes to 1 hour 5 minutes. After 20 minutes of cooking, adjust oven rack to lower-middle position and heat oven to 425 degrees. Stir maple syrup and soy sauce together in bowl.

4. Set V-rack on rimmed baking sheet and spray with vegetable oil spray. Remove roasting pan from heat. Using tongs and spatula, lift ducks from pan one at a time, allow liquid to drain, and transfer to V-rack, breast side up. Brush breasts and tops of drumsticks with approximately one-third of maple syrup mixture. Flip ducks and brush remaining mixture over backs and sides. Transfer braising liquid to pot or large bowl to cool. (Once cool, defat liquid and reserve liquid and/or fat for another use, if desired.) Rinse roasting pan and wipe with wad of paper towels. Crumple 20-inch length of aluminum foil into loose ball. Uncrumple foil and place in roasting pan. Set V-rack on foil. Roast until backs are golden brown and breasts register 140 to 150 degrees, about 20 minutes.

5. Remove roasting pan from oven. Using tongs and spatula, flip ducks breast side up. Continue to roast until breasts register 160 to 165 degrees, 15 to 25 minutes. Transfer ducks to carving board and let rest for 20 minutes.

6. FOR THE CHERRY SAUCE Whisk maple syrup, vinegar, soy sauce, cornstarch, and pepper together in small saucepan. Add thyme sprigs and bring to simmer over medium-high heat, stirring constantly with rubber spatula. Continue to cook, stirring constantly, until mixture thickens, 2 to 3 minutes. Stir in cherries and cook, stirring occasionally, until sauce has consistency of maple syrup, 5 to 8 minutes. Discard thyme sprigs and season with salt and pepper to taste. (Sauce can be refrigerated for up to 24 hours. Let come to room temperature before serving.) Transfer to serving bowl. Carve duck and serve, passing sauce separately.

HOW TO CARVE LEG QUARTERS AND BREASTS FROM DUCK

1. Use tip of knife to cut through skin and fat where leg meets breast.

2. Pull leg quarter away from breast while pushing up on joint. Cut through joint and skin to remove leg quarter. Repeat on other side.

3. Arrange duck so cavity faces you. Draw tip of knife along side of breastbone, making sure knife stays against bone, to separate meat from breastbone.

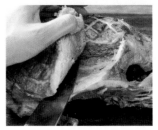

4. Rotate duck 90 degrees. Starting at pointy (cavity) end of breast, draw knife along rib cage, lifting meat as you separate it from ribs. Repeat on other side.

Rosemary-Garlic Top Sirloin Roast

Serves 8 to 10
Total Time 3½ hours, plus 24 hours salting

WHY THIS RECIPE WORKS As a holiday main, a boneless top sirloin center-cut roast supplies beefy flavor and a tender, juicy texture for a very reasonable price, but its irregular shape and lack of a fat cap present some cooking challenges. First, we cut and tied the oddly shaped roast into two even, attractive roasts so they would cook evenly. Refrigerating the salted roasts for at least 24 hours dried out their exteriors so that when we seared them in a smoking-hot skillet they quickly developed allover browning. To boost the richness of this somewhat lean cut and promote even more browning, we then slathered the roasts with a bold paste of garlic, rosemary, and anchovies. As the meat roasted in the oven to cook through, the paste dried out and crisped up to form a deeply browned crust full of concentrated umami flavor. The roast, also called a top sirloin roast, top butt roast, center-cut roast, spoon roast, shell roast, or shell sirloin roast, should not be confused with a whole top sirloin butt roast or top loin roast.

1	(5- to 6-pound) boneless top sirloin center-cut roast
2	tablespoons kosher salt
4	teaspoons plus ¼ cup extra-virgin olive oil, divided
3	tablespoons chopped fresh rosemary
4	garlic cloves, minced
6	anchovy fillets, rinsed and patted dry
1	teaspoon pepper
¼	teaspoon red pepper flakes
	Coarse sea salt

1. Cut roast lengthwise with grain into 2 equal pieces. Rub 1 tablespoon kosher salt evenly over each piece. Transfer roasts to large plate and refrigerate, uncovered, for at least 24 hours or up to 4 days.

2. Adjust oven rack to middle position and heat oven to 225 degrees. Heat 2 teaspoons oil in 12-inch skillet over high heat until just smoking. Brown 1 roast on all sides, 6 to 8 minutes. Return browned roast to plate. Repeat with 2 teaspoons oil and remaining roast. Let roasts cool for 10 minutes.

3. Meanwhile, process rosemary, garlic, anchovies, and remaining ¼ cup oil in food processor until smooth paste forms, about 30 seconds, scraping down sides of bowl as needed. Add pepper and pepper flakes and pulse to combine, 2 or 3 pulses.

4. Using 5 pieces of kitchen twine per roast, tie each roast crosswise at equal intervals into loaf shape. Transfer roasts to wire rack set in rimmed baking sheet and rub roasts evenly with paste.

5. Roast until meat registers 125 degrees (for medium-rare) or 130 degrees (for medium), 2 to 2¼ hours. Remove roasts from oven, leaving them on wire rack, and tent with aluminum foil; let rest for at least 30 minutes or up to 40 minutes.

6. Heat oven to 500 degrees. Remove foil from roasts and cut and discard twine. Return roasts to oven and cook until exteriors are well browned, 6 to 8 minutes.

7. Transfer roasts to carving board. Slice meat ¼ inch thick. Season with sea salt to taste, and serve.

Slow-Roasted Chuck Roast with Horseradish–Sour Cream Sauce

Serves 8 to 10
Total Time 2¼ to 2¾ hours, plus 1 hour salting

WHY THIS RECIPE WORKS Low-and-slow oven roasting transforms chuck into a first-rate, supremely beefy roast. First, we split the roast in half to remove the central layer of fat and then tied the pieces into a single, uniform cylinder for even cooking. A quick sear browned the exterior, and an hour in a 300-degree oven broke its tough connective tissue down into silky gelatin. We then coated the roast in an assertive spice blend of mustard seeds, peppercorns, and chopped fresh rosemary and returned it to the oven for just a few minutes to crisp its crust. A tangy horseradish sauce balanced the roast's richness. For how to tie a roast, see page 77. Start with the smaller amount of prepared horseradish and add more to taste.

1	(4- to 5-pound) boneless beef chuck-eye roast, pulled into 2 pieces at natural seams and trimmed of large pieces of fat
2¾	teaspoons table salt, divided
2	tablespoons vegetable oil
2	teaspoons plus ⅛ teaspoon pepper, divided
2	tablespoons mustard seeds
4	teaspoons black peppercorns
3	tablespoons chopped fresh rosemary
⅔	cup sour cream
¼–½	cup prepared horseradish, drained
1	large egg white

1. Sprinkle beef with 2 teaspoons salt. Tie meat pieces together at 1-inch intervals using kitchen twine to create 1 evenly shaped roast. Transfer to plate, cover with plastic wrap, and refrigerate for at least 1 hour or up to 24 hours.

2. Adjust oven rack to middle position and heat oven to 300 degrees. Heat oil in Dutch oven over medium-high heat until just smoking. Pat roast dry with paper towels and sprinkle with 2 teaspoons pepper. Brown roast on all sides, 8 to 10 minutes. Transfer pot to oven and roast, uncovered, until meat registers 150 degrees, 1 to 1½ hours, flipping roast halfway through roasting.

3. Process mustard seeds and peppercorns in spice grinder until coarsely ground. Transfer to small bowl and stir in rosemary. Whisk sour cream, horseradish, remaining ¾ teaspoon salt, and remaining ⅛ teaspoon pepper together in separate bowl; cover and refrigerate until ready to serve.

4. Remove pot from oven and increase oven temperature to 450 degrees. Transfer roast to rimmed baking sheet. Pour off any fat left in pot. Whisk egg white in medium bowl until frothy. Brush roast with egg white on all sides and sprinkle with mustard seed mixture, rolling roast and pressing on mixture to adhere. Return roast to now-empty pot, transfer pot to oven, and cook, uncovered, until roast is browned and fragrant, about 10 minutes, flipping roast halfway through roasting.

5. Remove pot from oven. Transfer roast to carving board and let rest for 15 minutes. Discard twine and slice roast against grain ½ inch thick. Serve with sauce.

Slow-Roasted Chuck Roast with Horseradish–Sour Cream Sauce

Best Roast Prime Rib

Serves 8 to 10 | **Total Time** 4½ to 6¼hours, plus 24½ hours salting and resting

WHY THIS RECIPE WORKS Roasting lets a prime rib's extraordinary flavor shine. We salted our roast up to four days in advance to dry the exterior so that it developed a deeply browned crust when seared. We removed the meat from the bones to make searing easier and then tied the roast back to the bones to ensure even cooking in the oven. A very low oven temperature allowed the meat's enzymes to act as natural tenderizers, and a quick trip under the broiler restored the crust's glorious crispness. In step 1, a longer salting time is preferable. If the roast has not reached the correct temperature in the time range specified in step 4, reheat the oven to 200 degrees for 5 minutes, shut it off, and continue to cook the roast until it reaches the desired temperature. We prefer this roast cooked to medium-rare, but if you prefer it more or less done, see our guidelines on page 414. Serve with Horseradish Sauce (page 114) or Garlic-Herb Butter (page 329).

1 (7-pound) first-cut beef standing rib roast (3 bones), with ½-inch fat cap
2 tablespoons kosher salt
2 teaspoons vegetable oil
½ teaspoon pepper

1. Using sharp knife, cut beef from bones. Cut slits 1 inch apart in crosshatch pattern in fat cap of roast, being careful not to cut into beef. Rub salt thoroughly over roast and into slits. Place beef back on bones (to save space in refrigerator), and refrigerate, uncovered, for at least 24 hours or up to 4 days.

2. Adjust oven rack to middle position and heat oven to 200 degrees. Heat oil in 12-inch skillet over high heat until just smoking. Remove beef from bones. Sear top and sides of roast until browned, 6 to 8 minutes; do not sear side of roast that was cut from bones.

3. Fit roast back onto bones, let cool for 10 minutes, then tie together with kitchen twine between ribs. Transfer roast, fat side up, to wire rack set in rimmed baking sheet and sprinkle with pepper. Roast until beef registers 110 degrees, 3 to 4 hours.

4. Turn oven off and leave roast in oven, without opening door, until beef registers 120 to 125 degrees (for medium-rare), 30 minutes to 1¼ hours.

5. Remove roast from oven (leave roast on sheet) and let rest for at least 30 minutes or up to 1¼ hours.

6. Adjust oven rack 8 inches from broiler element and heat broiler. Place 3-inch aluminum foil ball under ribs to elevate fat cap. Broil until top of roast is well browned and crisp, 2 to 8 minutes. Transfer roast to carving board, remove twine, and remove beef from ribs. Slice roast ¾ inch thick. Serve with horseradish sauce.

Horseradish Sauce

Makes about 1 cup
Total Time 5 minutes

⅔ cup mayonnaise
2 tablespoons prepared horseradish, drained
2 tablespoons lemon juice

Whisk all ingredients together in bowl. Season with salt and pepper to taste. (Horseradish sauce can be refrigerated for up to 2 days.)

HOW TO HANDLE THE BONES IN PRIME RIB

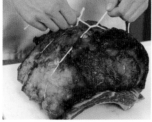

1. Removing bones from prime rib makes it easier to salt thoroughly and sear evenly. Use sharp knife to cut beef from bones.

2. Tying roast back onto bones before roasting helps insulate meat. After searing, fit roast back onto bones, let cool for 10 minutes, then tie together with kitchen twine between bones.

Herb-Crusted Roast Beef Tenderloin

Serves 12 | **Total Time** 1¼ hours, plus 1½ hours salting and cooling

WHY THIS RECIPE WORKS Supremely tender, almost buttery beef tenderloin more than earns its name. Here, an herby crust provides the beef with richness, fresh flavor, and contrasting texture. If exposed to heat for too long, herbs can burn or lose their flavor, so we roasted the tenderloin until its exterior was caramelized before applying the herb paste. Some grated Parmesan cheese added nutty notes to the mix and helped the paste adhere. For how to tie a roast, see page 77. We prefer this roast cooked to medium-rare, but if you prefer it more or less done, see our guidelines on page 414. Serve with Horseradish Sauce, if desired.

1 (6-pound) whole beef tenderloin, trimmed, tail end tucked, and tied at 1½-inch intervals
1 tablespoon kosher salt
1 tablespoon cracked black peppercorns
2 teaspoons sugar
2 slices hearty white sandwich bread, torn into pieces
2½ ounces Parmesan cheese, grated (1¼ cups), divided
½ cup chopped fresh parsley, divided
6 tablespoons extra-virgin olive oil, divided
2 tablespoons plus 2 teaspoons chopped fresh thyme, divided
4 garlic cloves, minced

1. Set wire rack in rimmed baking sheet. Pat roast dry with paper towels. Combine salt, peppercorns, and sugar in small bowl and rub all over roast. Transfer to prepared sheet and let sit at room temperature for 1 hour. (Tenderloin can be trimmed, tied, rubbed with salt mixture, and refrigerated up to 24 hours in advance; allow roast to come back to room temperature before putting in oven.)

2. Meanwhile, pulse bread in food processor to fine crumbs, about 15 pulses. Transfer bread crumbs to medium bowl and toss with ½ cup Parmesan, 2 tablespoons parsley, 2 tablespoons oil, and 2 teaspoons thyme until evenly combined. Wipe out food processor with paper towels and process remaining ¾ cup Parmesan, remaining 6 tablespoons parsley, remaining ¼ cup oil, remaining 2 tablespoons thyme, and garlic until smooth paste forms. Transfer herb paste to small bowl.

3. Adjust oven rack to upper-middle position and heat oven to 400 degrees. Roast beef for 20 minutes, then remove from oven. Remove twine. Coat beef with herb paste, then breadcrumb topping. Roast until beef registers 120 to 125 degrees (for medium-rare) and topping is golden brown, 20 to 25 minutes. (If topping browns before beef reaches preferred internal temperature, lightly cover with aluminum foil for remainder of roasting time and remove foil while beef rests.) Transfer to carving board and let rest for 30 minutes. Slice roast ½ inch thick. Serve.

Herb-Crusted Roast Beef Tenderloin

Braised Brisket with Pomegranate, Cumin, and Cilantro

Serves 6 to 8 `MAKE AHEAD`
Total Time 5½ hours, plus 16 hours salting

WHY THIS RECIPE WORKS Notoriously high in collagen, the main component of tough connective tissue, brisket takes a lot of cooking to become tender—but when the collagen is given the time it needs to break down, the beefy cut transforms into something moist, tender, and beautifully sliceable. The addition of cumin, cardamom, and pomegranate juice to the braising liquid gave our holiday brisket an unexpected but extremely satisfying flavor profile; we then turned the braising liquid into a velvety sauce perfect for spooning over the beef. Serve with boiled or mashed potatoes or buttered noodles.

- 1 (4- to 5-pound) beef brisket, flat cut, fat trimmed to ¼ inch
- 5 teaspoons kosher salt
- 2 tablespoons vegetable oil
- 2 large onions, chopped
- ¼ teaspoon baking soda
- 6 garlic cloves, minced
- 4 anchovy fillets, rinsed, patted dry, and minced to paste
- 1 tablespoon tomato paste
- 1 tablespoon ground cumin
- 1½ teaspoons ground cardamom
- ½ teaspoon pepper
- ⅛ teaspoon cayenne pepper
- ¼ cup all-purpose flour
- 2 cups pomegranate juice
- 1½ cups chicken broth
- 3 bay leaves
- 2 tablespoons unflavored gelatin
- 1 cup pomegranate seeds
- 3 tablespoons chopped fresh cilantro

Braised Brisket with Pomegranate, Cumin, and Cilantro

1. Place brisket, fat side down, on cutting board and cut in half lengthwise with grain. Using paring knife or metal skewer, poke each roast 20 times, pushing all the way through roast. Flip roasts and repeat on second side.

2. Sprinkle each roast evenly on all sides with 2½ teaspoons salt. Wrap each roast in plastic wrap and refrigerate for at least 16 hours or up to 48 hours.

3. Adjust oven rack to middle position and heat oven to 325 degrees. Heat oil in large roasting pan over medium heat until shimmering. Add onions and baking soda and cook, stirring frequently, until onions have started to soften and break down, 4 to 5 minutes. Add garlic and cook until fragrant, about 30 seconds. Stir in anchovies, tomato paste, cumin, cardamom, pepper, and cayenne. Add flour and cook, stirring constantly, until onions are evenly coated and flour begins to stick to pan, about 2 minutes. Stir in pomegranate juice, broth, and bay leaves, scraping up any browned bits and smoothing out any lumps. Stir in gelatin. Increase heat to medium-high and bring to boil.

4. Unwrap roasts and place in pan. Cover pan tightly with aluminum foil, transfer to oven, and cook until meat registers 180 to 185 degrees at center, about 1½ hours. Reduce oven temperature to 250 degrees and continue to cook until fork slips easily in and out of meat, 2 to 2½ hours. Transfer roasts to baking sheet and wrap sheet tightly in foil.

5. Strain braising liquid through fine-mesh strainer set over large bowl, pressing on solids to extract as much liquid as possible; discard solids. Let liquid settle for 10 minutes. Using wide, shallow spoon, skim fat from surface and discard. Wipe roasting pan clean with paper towels and return defatted liquid to pan.

6. Increase oven temperature to 400 degrees. Return pan to oven and cook, stirring occasionally, until liquid is reduced by about one-third, 30 to 40 minutes. Remove pan from oven and use wooden spoon to draw liquid up sides of pan and scrape browned bits around edges of pan into liquid.

7. Transfer roasts to carving board and slice against grain ¼ inch thick; transfer to wide serving platter. Season sauce with salt and pepper to taste, and pour over brisket. Tent platter with foil and let stand for 5 to 10 minutes to warm brisket through. Sprinkle with pomegranate seeds and cilantro and serve.

To make ahead Let sauce and brisket cool completely at the end of step 6. Cover and refrigerate sauce and roasts separately for up to 2 days. To serve, slice each roast against grain ¼ inch thick and transfer to 13 by 9-inch baking dish. Heat sauce in small saucepan over medium heat until just simmering. Pour sauce over brisket, cover dish with aluminum foil, and cook in 325-degree oven until meat is heated through, about 20 minutes.

Pomegranate-Glazed Roast Bone-In Leg of Lamb

Serves 8 to 10
Total Time 2¾ hours, plus 1 hour salting

WHY THIS RECIPE WORKS Talk about a showstopper—a roasted leg of lamb boasts a browned, crusty, gleaming exterior and juicy, ultrarich meat. Because of its large, awkward shape, stovetop searing isn't an option; instead, we used a combination of low-and-slow roasting and an "oven sear," where we cranked the oven temperature up to 450 degrees for the last 20 minutes of cooking. Adding water to the roasting pan during the high-heat finish prevented the pan drippings from smoking. This recipe actually uses a semi-boneless leg of lamb, which is what you most commonly find at the market; if, by chance, the leg has the full bone, have the butcher remove the hipbone and aitchbone for you. We prefer the subtler flavor and larger size of lamb labeled "domestic" or "American," but you may substitute lamb imported from New Zealand or Australia. We prefer this roast cooked to medium-rare, but if you prefer it more or less done, see our guidelines on page 414.

LAMB

1 (6- to 8-pound) semi-boneless leg of lamb, trimmed
1 tablespoon vegetable oil
2 teaspoons kosher salt
½ teaspoon pepper

POMEGRANATE GLAZE

2 cups pomegranate juice
⅓ cup sugar
3 sprigs fresh thyme

1. FOR THE LAMB Pat roast dry with paper towels, rub with oil, and sprinkle with salt and pepper. Cover roast with plastic wrap and let sit at room temperature for at least 1 hour or up to 2 hours.

2. FOR THE POMEGRANATE GLAZE Meanwhile, simmer pomegranate juice, sugar, and thyme sprigs in small saucepan over medium heat until thickened and mixture measures about ½ cup, about 20 minutes. Discard thyme sprigs. Measure out and reserve half of glaze for serving.

3. Adjust oven rack to lowest position and heat oven to 250 degrees. Set wire rack inside aluminum foil–lined rimmed baking sheet. Transfer roast to prepared rack, fat side up, and brush with about half of remaining glaze. Roast until meat registers 100 degrees, about 1¾ hours.

4. Brush roast with remaining glaze and pour ¼ cup water into sheet. Increase oven temperature to 450 degrees and roast until lamb registers 125 degrees (for medium-rare), about 20 minutes. Transfer roast to carving board and brush with half of glaze reserved for serving. Let rest for 30 minutes. Brush with remaining glaze reserved for serving and carve roast. Serve.

Spiced Lamb Pot Roast with Figs

Serves 8 to 10
Total Time 3½ to 4 hours, plus 1 hour salting

WHY THIS RECIPE WORKS Less common (and less expensive) than leg of lamb, a lamb shoulder roast is an intensely flavorful cut that is no less impressive as a showpiece. Slow braising breaks down its collagen and fat, adding flavor and body to the cooking liquid and producing fall-apart tender meat. Simmering the lamb in ruby port along with rosemary and other aromatics elevated this dish. Stirring figs into the defatted braising liquid created a sauce with balanced salty, sweet, and tart notes. We prefer the subtler flavor and larger size of lamb labeled "domestic" or "American," but you may substitute lamb imported from New Zealand or Australia.

Spiced Lamb Pot Roast with Figs

1	tablespoon ground coriander
2	teaspoons ground fennel
1½	teaspoons table salt
1½	teaspoons pepper
1	(4- to 5-pound) boneless lamb shoulder, trimmed
2	tablespoons extra-virgin olive oil
1	onion, chopped fine
5	garlic cloves, minced
2	cups ruby port
2	sprigs fresh rosemary
12	ounces fresh figs, stemmed and quartered
¼	cup chopped fresh parsley

1. Combine coriander, fennel, salt, and pepper in bowl. Place roast with rough interior side (which was against bone) facing up on cutting board and sprinkle with 4 teaspoons spice mixture. Starting from short side, roll roast tightly and tie with kitchen twine at 1-inch intervals. Sprinkle exterior with remaining spice mixture. Transfer to plate, cover, and refrigerate for at least 1 hour or up to 24 hours.

2. Adjust oven rack to lower-middle position and heat oven to 300 degrees. Pat roast dry with paper towels. Heat oil in

Dutch oven over medium-high heat until just smoking. Brown roast on all sides, 8 to 10 minutes; transfer to plate.

3. Pour off all but 1 tablespoon fat from pot. Add onion and cook over medium heat until softened, about 5 minutes. Stir in garlic and cook until fragrant, about 30 seconds. Stir in port, scraping up any browned bits, and bring to simmer. Return roast to pot, adding any accumulated juices. Add rosemary sprigs, cover, and transfer pot to oven. Cook until lamb is tender and fork slips easily in and out of meat, 2¼ to 2¾ hours, flipping roast halfway through cooking.

4. Remove pot from oven. Transfer roast to large bowl. Discard rosemary sprigs and strain braising liquid through fine-mesh strainer into fat separator; reserve solids. Allow braising liquid to settle for 5 minutes. Add defatted braising liquid and reserved solids to now-empty pot and bring to simmer over medium-high heat. Cook until slightly thickened and reduced to 1½ cups, about 10 minutes. (Pot roast can be refrigerated for up to 2 days. To reheat, bring to gentle simmer, covered, and cook until hot throughout, adjusting consistency with hot water as needed.) Stir in figs and cook until heated through, about 2 minutes. Season with salt and pepper to taste, and serve.

Porchetta

Crown Roast of Pork

Porchetta

Serves 8 to 10 `MAKE AHEAD`
Total Time 3 to 3½ hours, plus 6 hours salting

WHY THIS RECIPE WORKS We took Italy's porchetta—aromatic, tender, rich, slow-cooked pork that is traditionally served with pieces of crispy skin on a crusty roll—and turned it into a holiday-worthy roast with a luxurious presentation. For quicker cooking, we cut pork butt roast (instead of the traditional whole pig) into two pieces and tied each into a compact cylinder. To season the meat, we cut slits in the exterior; coated it with salt and an intensely flavored paste of garlic, rosemary, and fennel; and let it sit overnight in the refrigerator. Roasting the pork low and slow in the oven before blasting it with intense 500-degree heat gave us the perfect combination of moist, juicy meat and crispy crust. Pork butt roast is often labeled Boston butt in the supermarket. Look for a roast with a substantial fat cap. If fennel seeds are unavailable, substitute ¼ cup of ground fennel.

    3 tablespoons fennel seeds
    ½ cup fresh rosemary leaves (2 bunches)
    ¼ cup fresh thyme leaves (2 bunches)
    12 garlic cloves, smashed and peeled
    4 teaspoons plus 1 tablespoon kosher salt, divided
    1 tablespoon plus 1 teaspoon pepper, divided
    ½ cup extra-virgin olive oil
    1 (5- to 6-pound) boneless pork butt roast
    ¼ teaspoon baking soda

1. Grind fennel seeds in spice grinder or mortar and pestle until finely ground. Transfer ground fennel to food processor and add rosemary, thyme, garlic, 2 teaspoons salt, and 1 tablespoon pepper. Pulse mixture until finely chopped, 10 to 15 pulses. Add oil and process until smooth paste forms, 20 to 30 seconds.

2. Using sharp knife, cut slits 1 inch apart in crosshatch pattern in fat cap of roast, being careful not to cut into meat. Cut roast in half with grain into 2 equal pieces.

3. Turn each roast on its side so fat cap is facing away from you, bottom of roast is facing toward you, and newly cut side is facing up. Starting 1 inch from short end of each roast, use boning or paring knife to make slit that starts 1 inch from top of roast and ends 1 inch from bottom, pushing knife completely through roast. Repeat making slits, spaced 1 to 1½ inches apart, along length of each roast, stopping 1 inch from opposite end (you should have 6 to 8 slits, depending on size of roast).

4. Turn roast so fat cap is facing down. Rub sides and bottom of each roast with 2 teaspoons salt, taking care to work salt into slits from both sides. Rub herb paste onto sides and bottom of each roast, taking care to work paste into slits from both sides. Flip roast so that fat cap is facing up. Tie each roast with kitchen twine at 1½-inch intervals into compact cylinder.

5. Combine baking soda, remaining 1 tablespoon salt, and remaining 1 teaspoon pepper in small bowl. Rub fat cap of each roast with salt–baking soda mixture, taking care to work mixture into crosshatches. Refrigerate roasts, uncovered, for at least 6 hours or up to 24 hours.

6. Adjust oven rack to middle position and heat oven to 325 degrees. Transfer roasts, fat side up, to large roasting pan, leaving at least 2 inches between roasts. Cover tightly with aluminum foil. Cook until extremely tender and pork registers 180 degrees, 2 to 2½ hours.

7. Remove pan from oven and increase oven temperature to 500 degrees. Carefully remove and discard foil and transfer roasts to large plate. Discard liquid in pan. Line pan with foil. Remove twine from roasts; return roasts to pan, directly on foil; and return pan to oven. Cook until well browned and pork registers 190 degrees, 20 to 30 minutes. Transfer roasts to carving board and let rest for 20 minutes. Slice roasts ½ inch thick. Serve.

READYING TWO ROASTS FOR PORCHETTA

1. After crosshatching surface, halve pork butt, creating 2 smaller roasts.

2. Cut deep slits into sides of roasts, then rub salt and herb paste over roasts and into slits.

3. Flip roasts so that fat cap is facing up. Using kitchen twine, tie each roast at 1½-inch intervals into compact cylinder.

Crown Roast of Pork

Serves 10 to 12
Total Time 2½ hours, plus 6 hours salting

WHY THIS RECIPE WORKS The unique shape of a crown roast of pork makes it the ultimate showstopper, but it requires some forethought to get rosy, perfectly seasoned meat. Most crown roast recipes call for stuffing the roast with vegetables to make an easy side dish, but this practice insulates the pork unevenly and prolongs its cooking. Instead, we cooked the pork in a V-rack atop a mix of potatoes, shallots, and apples, which soaked up the meat's delectable drippings. Roasting the pork upside down for the first hour before flipping it right-side up helped it cook evenly. A crown roast is two bone-in pork loin roasts, with the rib bones frenched and chine bones removed, that have been tied into a crown shape. This can be difficult to do, so ask your butcher to make this roast for you. We wrap extra kitchen twine around the widest part of the roast to provide more support when flipping. Use potatoes that measure 1 to 2 inches in diameter. In step 1, a longer salting time is preferable. We strongly prefer natural pork in this recipe. If the pork is enhanced (injected with a salt solution), omit the salt in step 1.

- 3 tablespoons kosher salt
- 3 tablespoons minced fresh thyme
- 2 tablespoons minced fresh rosemary
- 5 garlic cloves, minced
- 1 tablespoon pepper
- 1 (8- to 10-pound) pork crown roast, trimmed
- 2 pounds small red potatoes, scrubbed
- 10 ounces shallots, peeled and halved
- 2 Golden Delicious apples, peeled, cored, and halved
- 8 tablespoons unsalted butter, melted, divided
- ½ cup apple cider
- 1 cup chicken broth

1. Combine salt, thyme, rosemary, garlic, and pepper in bowl; set aside 2 teaspoons for vegetables. Pat roast dry with paper towels and rub with remaining herb salt. Wrap kitchen twine twice around widest part of roast and tie tightly. Refrigerate roast, covered, for at least 6 hours or up to 24 hours.

2. Adjust oven rack to lower-middle position and heat oven to 475 degrees. Place V-rack inside large roasting pan and spray with vegetable oil spray. Toss potatoes, shallots, apples, 4 tablespoons melted butter, and reserved herb salt in large bowl and transfer to pan. Arrange roast bone side down in V-rack and brush with remaining 4 tablespoons melted butter. Roast until pork is well browned and registers 110 degrees, about 1 hour.

3. Remove roast from oven and reduce oven temperature to 300 degrees. Using 2 wads of paper towels, flip roast bone side up. Add apple cider to pan and return to oven, rotating direction of pan. Roast until pork registers 140 degrees, 30 to 50 minutes. Transfer roast to carving board and let rest for 20 minutes.

4. Transfer apple halves to blender and potatoes and shallots to bowl. Pour pan juices into fat separator, let liquid settle for 5 minutes, and pour into blender, discarding fat. Add broth to blender with apples and pan juices and process until smooth, about 1 minute. Transfer sauce to medium saucepan and bring to simmer over medium heat. Season with salt and pepper to taste. Cover and keep warm. Remove twine from roast and slice between bones. Serve with vegetables and sauce.

COOKING CROWN ROAST OF PORK

When roasted directly on a roasting pan, the perimeter of a crown roast overcooks by the time the interior ring is done. Here's how we solved that problem and produced evenly cooked pork.

Tie Roast
Using kitchen twine, make 2 loops around widest part of roast and tie securely to help crown hold its shape when flipped.

Set Bone Side Down
Place pork bone side down on V-rack and adjust bones to steady roast. Roast about 1 hour, until meat registers 110 degrees.

Flip Bone Side Up
Using paper towels to protect your hands, flip hot roast bone side up and set it back on V-rack to finish cooking in gentle oven.

Pork Pernil

Serves 8 to 12
Total Time 6½ hours, plus 12 hours marinating

WHY THIS RECIPE WORKS A celebratory Puerto Rican classic, this dish of boldly seasoned, long-cooked pork with supremely crispy skin is often eaten on Christmas Eve. The skin is critical; the big crunch of the mahogany-colored pieces is a huge part of what makes the dish so special. We rubbed a bone-in picnic shoulder with an herb-spice paste called a sofrito before cooking the pork skin side down in a roasting pan, covered at first to create steam that would keep the meat moist. When the pork was nearly done, we moved it to a V-rack skin side up and roasted it at 500 degrees just long enough to turn the skin crispy and deep mahogany brown. A quick sauce of pan drippings, cilantro, and lime finished the dish. Crimp the foil tightly over the edges of the roasting pan in step 2 to minimize evaporation. Serve with rice, if desired.

1½ cups chopped fresh cilantro leaves and stems, divided
1 onion, chopped coarse
½ cup extra-virgin olive oil
¼ cup kosher salt
10 garlic cloves, smashed and peeled
2 tablespoons pepper
1 tablespoon dried oregano
1 tablespoon ground cumin
1 (7-pound) bone-in, skin-on pork picnic shoulder roast
1 tablespoon grated lime zest plus ⅓ cup juice (3 limes)

1. Pulse 1 cup cilantro, onion, oil, salt, garlic, pepper, oregano, and cumin in food processor until finely ground, about 15 pulses, scraping down sides of bowl as needed. Pat pork dry with paper towels and rub cilantro mixture all over pork. Wrap pork in plastic wrap and refrigerate for at least 12 hours or up to 24 hours.

2. Adjust oven rack to lower-middle position and heat oven to 450 degrees. Pour 8 cups water into large roasting pan. Unwrap pork and place skin side down in pan. Cover pan tightly with aluminum foil and roast for 1½ hours. Remove foil, reduce oven temperature to 375 degrees, and roast for 2½ hours.

3. Remove pan from oven. Spray V-rack with vegetable oil spray. Gently slide metal spatula under pork to release skin from pan. Using 2 large wads of paper towels, grasp ends of pork and transfer to V-rack, skin side up. Wipe skin dry with paper towels. Set V-rack with pork in roasting pan. If pan looks dry, add 1 cup water. Roast until pork registers 195 degrees, about 1 hour. (Add water as needed to keep bottom of pan from drying out.)

4. Line rimmed baking sheet with foil. Remove pan from oven. Transfer V-rack with pork to prepared sheet, place sheet in oven, and increase oven temperature to 500 degrees. Roast until pork skin is well browned and crispy (when tapped lightly with tongs, skin will sound hollow), 15 to 30 minutes, rotating sheet halfway through roasting. Transfer pork to carving board and let rest for 30 minutes.

5. Meanwhile, pour juices from pan into fat separator. Let liquid settle for 5 minutes, then pour 1 cup defatted juices into large bowl (if necessary, add water to equal 1 cup). Whisk lime zest and juice and remaining ½ cup cilantro into juices.

6. Using sharp knife, remove skin from pork in 1 large piece. Coarsely chop skin into bite-size pieces and set aside. Trim and discard excess fat from pork. Remove pork from bone and chop coarse. Transfer pork to bowl with cilantro-lime sauce and toss to coat. Serve pork, with crispy skin on side.

Glazed Spiral-Sliced Ham

Serves 12 to 14
Total Time 3 to 3½ hours, plus 30 minutes resting

WHY THIS RECIPE WORKS When cooking for a large gathering, a spiral-sliced ham is an appealing choice; you just throw it in the oven, brush on a sweet glaze, and are rewarded with sweet, caramelized edges and juicy, tender meat. Bone-in hams labeled "with natural juices" have the best flavor. Using an oven bag reduced the cooking time and also helped the ham retain moisture. For the perfect savory-sweet lacquer, we determined that it was best to apply our simple, syrupy glaze toward the end of cooking and then again once the ham came out of the oven. Be sure to cut slits in the oven bag so it doesn't burst. This recipe requires a turkey-size oven bag. You can bypass the 1½-hour sitting time, but the roasting time will increase to 18 to 20 minutes per pound for a cold ham.

HAM
  1 (7- to 10-pound) spiral-sliced bone-in ham
  1 turkey-size oven bag

CHERRY-PORT GLAZE
  ½ cup ruby port
  1 cup packed dark brown sugar
  ½ cup cherry preserves
  1 teaspoon pepper

Pork Pernil

Glazed Spiral-Sliced Ham

1. FOR THE HAM Place ham in oven bag. Gather top of bag tightly so bag fits snugly around ham, tie bag with kitchen twine, and trim excess plastic. Set ham, cut side down, in large roasting pan and cut 4 slits in top of bag with paring knife. Let ham sit at room temperature for 1½ hours.

2. Adjust oven rack to lowest position and heat oven to 250 degrees. Roast ham until center registers 100 degrees, 1 to 1½ hours (about 10 minutes per pound).

3. FOR THE CHERRY-PORT GLAZE Simmer port in small saucepan over medium heat until reduced to 2 tablespoons, about 5 minutes. Add sugar, preserves, and pepper and cook, stirring occasionally, until sugar dissolves and mixture is thick, syrupy, and reduced to 1 cup, 5 to 10 minutes; set aside.

4. Remove ham from oven and increase oven temperature to 350 degrees. Cut open oven bag and roll back sides to expose ham. Brush ham with one-third of glaze and return to oven until glaze becomes sticky, about 10 minutes (if glaze is too thick to brush, return to heat to loosen).

5. Remove ham from oven, transfer to carving board, brush entire ham with one-third of glaze, and let rest for 30 minutes. While ham rests, add 4 to 6 tablespoons ham juices to remaining one-third of glaze and cook over medium heat until thick but fluid sauce forms. Carve ham and serve, passing sauce separately.

Roasted Whole Side of Salmon

Roasted Whole Side of Salmon

Serves 8 to 10 | **Total Time** 1 hour, plus 1 hour salting

WHY THIS RECIPE WORKS A whole side of salmon is an elegant, lighter option than beef or turkey for a festive party centerpiece. Even better, it requires only light prep work, cooks quickly, and can be served with nothing more than lemon wedges or dressed up with a sauce. We started by brushing the salmon's surface with honey, which encouraged deeper and more even browning. Broiling the salmon in a preheated oven kickstarted that browning; lowering the heat to 250 degrees after a few minutes allowed the fillet to finish cooking through more gently. The thin, heavily marbled strip known as the belly flap will overcook if left attached to the salmon fillet; trim it by running a sharp knife along the edge of the belly. The surface will continue to brown after the oven temperature is reduced in step 4; if the surface starts to darken too much before the fillet's center registers 125 degrees, shield the dark portion with aluminum foil. If using wild salmon, cook the fillet until it reaches 120 degrees (for medium-rare) and start checking for doneness early. Serve as is or with Grapefruit-Basil Relish (page 134).

1 (4-pound) center-cut skin-on salmon fillet, 1½ inches thick, pin bones removed, and belly fat trimmed
1 tablespoon kosher salt
2 tablespoons honey
  Lemon wedges

1. Sprinkle flesh side of salmon evenly with salt and refrigerate, uncovered, for at least 1 hour or up to 4 hours.

2. Adjust oven rack 7 inches from broiler element and heat oven to 250 degrees. Line rimmed baking sheet with aluminum foil and place wire rack in sheet. Fold 18 by 12-inch piece of foil lengthwise to create 18 by 6-inch sling. Place sling on wire rack and spray with vegetable oil spray.

3. Heat broiler. Pat salmon dry with paper towels and place, skin side down, on foil sling. Brush salmon evenly with honey and broil until surface is lightly but evenly browned, 8 to 12 minutes, rotating sheet halfway through broiling.

4. Return oven temperature to 250 degrees and continue to cook until center of fillet registers 125 degrees, 10 to 15 minutes, rotating sheet halfway through cooking. Using foil sling, transfer salmon to serving platter, then carefully remove foil. Serve, passing lemon wedges separately.

Vegetable Moussaka

Serves 6 to 8 `MAKE AHEAD` `VEGETARIAN`
Total Time 2¼ hours

WHY THIS RECIPE WORKS Our vegetarian interpretation of warmly spiced moussaka, with bulgur and potatoes for a hearty foundation and a bubbly crown of béchamel, will bring guests running to the table. Blooming cinnamon with sautéed onion and garlic built great flavor, as did roasting our eggplant. Bulgur requires only a soak to soften up, so we simply stirred it into the potato-tomato mixture and let it absorb the surrounding liquid and all of its rich flavor. You can swap fine-grind bulgur for the medium-grind in this recipe. Do not substitute low-fat or skim milk in the sauce.

- 4 pounds eggplant, peeled and cut into ¾-inch pieces
- ¼ cup extra-virgin olive oil, divided
- 1½ teaspoons table salt, divided
- ¼ teaspoon pepper
- 1 onion, chopped fine
- 4 garlic cloves, minced
- 1 tablespoon minced fresh oregano or 1 teaspoon dried
- 1 teaspoon ground cinnamon
- ½ cup dry white wine
- 1 pound russet potatoes, peeled and cut into ½-inch pieces
- 2 cups vegetable broth
- 1 (28-ounce) can crushed tomatoes
- 1 cup medium-grind bulgur, rinsed
- 3 tablespoons unsalted butter
- ¼ cup all-purpose flour
- 2 cups whole milk
- 2 ounces Parmesan cheese, grated (1 cup)
  Pinch ground nutmeg
- 2 tablespoons chopped fresh basil

1. Adjust oven racks to upper-middle and lower-middle positions and heat oven to 450 degrees. Line 2 rimmed baking sheets with aluminum foil and spray with vegetable oil spray. Toss eggplant with 3 tablespoons oil, 1 teaspoon salt, and pepper and spread evenly over prepared sheets. Roast until eggplant is light golden brown and tender, 40 to 50 minutes, switching and rotating sheets halfway through roasting. Set eggplant aside to cool. Reduce oven temperature to 400 degrees and adjust oven rack to middle position.

2. Meanwhile, heat remaining 1 tablespoon oil in Dutch oven over medium heat until shimmering. Add onion and remaining ½ teaspoon salt and cook until onion is softened, about 5 minutes. Stir in garlic, oregano, and cinnamon and cook until

Vegetable Moussaka

fragrant, about 30 seconds. Stir in wine, scraping up any browned bits, until nearly all liquid is evaporated, about 2 minutes. Stir in potatoes and broth and bring to simmer. Cover, reduce heat to low, and cook until potatoes are nearly tender, about 15 minutes.

3. Stir in tomatoes and cook, uncovered, until flavors meld, about 5 minutes. Off heat, stir in bulgur and let sit until grains are tender and most of liquid is absorbed, about 15 minutes. Transfer to 13 by 9-inch baking dish and top evenly with roasted eggplant to form compact layer.

4. Melt butter in now-empty pot over medium heat. Stir in flour and cook for 1 minute. Gradually whisk in milk, scraping up any browned bits and smoothing out any lumps, bring to simmer, and cook, whisking often, until sauce thickens and no longer tastes of flour, about 5 minutes. Off heat, whisk in Parmesan and nutmeg and season with salt and pepper to taste. Pour sauce over eggplant and smooth into even layer. (Moussaka can be refrigerated for up to 24 hours. Increase covered baking time to 30 minutes.)

5. Cover with foil and bake until bubbling around edges, about 15 minutes. Uncover and continue to bake until top is light golden brown around edges, about 15 minutes. Let cool for 10 minutes. Sprinkle with basil and serve.

Mushroom Lasagna

4 red onions, chopped

8 ounces white mushrooms, trimmed and halved if small or quartered if large

½ ounce dried porcini mushrooms, rinsed and minced

4 garlic cloves, minced, divided

½ cup dry vermouth

3 tablespoons unsalted butter

3 tablespoons all-purpose flour

3½ cups whole milk

¼ teaspoon ground nutmeg

¼ cup plus 2 tablespoons chopped fresh basil, divided

¼ cup minced fresh parsley, divided

12 no-boil lasagna noodles

8 ounces Italian fontina cheese, shredded (2 cups)

1½ ounces Parmesan cheese, grated (¾ cup)

½ teaspoon grated lemon zest

1. Adjust oven rack to middle position and heat oven to 425 degrees. Toss portobello mushrooms with 2 tablespoons oil, ½ teaspoon salt, and ½ teaspoon pepper and spread onto rimmed baking sheet. Roast until shriveled, about 30 minutes, stirring halfway through roasting; transfer to bowl and let cool.

2. Meanwhile, heat 1 tablespoon oil in 12-inch nonstick skillet over medium heat until shimmering. Add onions, ¼ teaspoon salt, and ¼ teaspoon pepper and cook, stirring occasionally, until onions are softened and lightly browned, 8 to 10 minutes; transfer to bowl with roasted portobellos.

3. Pulse white mushrooms in food processor until coarsely chopped, about 6 pulses. Heat remaining 1 tablespoon oil in now-empty skillet over medium-high heat until shimmering. Add chopped mushrooms and porcini and cook, stirring occasionally, until browned and all moisture has evaporated, 6 to 8 minutes. Stir in 1 tablespoon garlic, remaining 1 teaspoon salt, and remaining 1 teaspoon pepper; reduce heat to medium; and cook, stirring often, until garlic is fragrant, about 30 seconds. Stir in vermouth and cook until liquid has evaporated, 2 to 3 minutes.

4. Add butter and cook until melted. Add flour and cook, stirring constantly, for 1 minute. Stir in 1 cup water, scraping up any browned bits and smoothing out any lumps. Stir in milk and nutmeg and simmer until sauce has thickened and measures 4 cups, 10 to 15 minutes. Off heat, stir in ¼ cup basil and 2 tablespoons parsley.

5. Bring kettle of water to boil. Pour 2 inches boiling water into 13 by 9-inch baking dish. Add noodles one at a time and soak until pliable, about 5 minutes, separating noodles with tip of sharp knife to prevent sticking. Remove noodles from water and place in single layer on clean dish towels; discard water. Dry and grease dish.

Mushroom Lasagna

Serves 8 to 10 | **Total Time** 3 hours

MAKE AHEAD   VEGETARIAN

WHY THIS RECIPE WORKS A great vegetarian mushroom lasagna, brought to the table steaming hot and bursting with savory, earthy, meaty depth, can hold its own against any other special-occasion main. We built our version with hearty roasted portobellos for concentrated mushroom flavor, daintier white mushrooms, and dried porcini mushrooms for complexity and a subtle woodsiness, layering everything with gooey, melty fontina cheese. Using no-boil noodles saved us some time and made assembling our lasagna a breeze, and a creamy, very loose béchamel sauce hydrated the noodles. Whole-milk mozzarella can be used in place of fontina cheese.

2 pounds portobello mushroom caps, gills removed, halved and sliced crosswise ¼ inch thick

¼ cup extra-virgin olive oil, divided

1¾ teaspoons table salt, divided

1¾ teaspoons pepper, divided

6. Combine fontina and Parmesan in bowl. Spread 1 cup mushroom sauce evenly over bottom of prepared dish. Arrange 3 noodles in single layer on top of sauce. Spread ¾ cup sauce evenly over noodles, then sprinkle with 2 cups mushroom-onion mixture and ¾ cup cheese mixture. Repeat layering of noodles, mushroom sauce, mushroom-onion mixture, and cheese mixture 2 more times. Arrange remaining 3 noodles on top, cover with remaining sauce, and sprinkle with remaining cheese.(Lasagna can be refrigerated, covered, for up to 24 hours. Increase covered baking time to 40 minutes.)

7. Cover dish tightly with aluminum foil that has been sprayed with vegetable oil spray and bake until edges are just bubbling, about 20 minutes, rotating dish halfway through baking. Remove foil, increase oven temperature to 500 degrees, and continue to bake until cheese on top is spotty brown, 6 to 8 minutes.

8. Combine remaining garlic, remaining 2 tablespoons basil, remaining 2 tablespoons parsley, and lemon zest together and sprinkle over lasagna. Let cool for 15 minutes before serving.

Simple Cheese Lasagna

Serves 6 to 8 | **Total Time** 1 hour
MAKE AHEAD **VEGETARIAN**

WHY THIS RECIPE WORKS Having a simple lasagna recipe in your back pocket ensures that you're always prepared, whether you need an easy vegetarian main, a dish to bring a friend, or a casserole to round out a holiday spread. Using no-boil lasagna noodles eliminated the multiple steps required to boil and drain conventional noodles. For the requisite layers of creamy cheese, we combined ricotta and Parmesan, plus fresh basil and an egg to help thicken and bind the mixture. Baking the lasagna covered with foil locked in moisture to help soften the noodles; removing the foil for the last 25 minutes of baking allowed the cheeses to brown properly. You will need to buy two 24- to 26-ounce jars of tomato sauce to make 6 cups.

15 ounces whole-milk or part-skim ricotta cheese (1¾ cups)
2½ ounces Parmesan cheese, grated (1¼ cups), divided
½ cup chopped fresh basil
1 large egg, lightly beaten
½ teaspoon table salt
½ teaspoon pepper
6 cups tomato sauce
12 no-boil lasagna noodles (one 8- or 9-ounce package)
1 pound whole-milk mozzarella, shredded (4 cups)

1. Adjust oven rack to middle position and heat oven to 375 degrees. Mix ricotta, 1 cup Parmesan, basil, egg, salt, and pepper in medium bowl with fork until well combined and creamy. Set aside.

2. Spread ¼ cup tomato sauce over bottom of 13 by 9-inch baking dish. Arrange 3 noodles in single layer on top of sauce and dollop 3 tablespoons ricotta mixture down center of each noodle, then spread with spoon to even thickness. Sprinkle evenly with 1 cup mozzarella. Spoon 1½ cups sauce evenly over cheese. Repeat layering of noodles, ricotta, mozzarella, and sauce 2 more times.

3. Arrange 3 remaining noodles on top and spread remaining 1¼ cups sauce over noodles. Sprinkle remaining 1 cup mozzarella over sauce, then sprinkle the remaining ¼ cup Parmesan over mozzarella. Spray large sheet aluminum foil lightly with vegetable oil spray and cover lasagna. (Lasagna can be refrigerated, covered, for up to 24 hours. Increase covered baking time to 30 minutes.)

4. Bake for 15 minutes. Remove foil and continue to bake until cheese is spottily browned and sauce is bubbling, about 25 minutes. Let cool for 10 minutes before serving.

Eggplant Parmesan

Serves 8 | **Total Time** 2 hours **VEGETARIAN**

WHY THIS RECIPE WORKS Italians have their own refined, delicate version of Italian-American eggplant parm: Thin, silky—and unbreaded—eggplant slices are layered with fresh mozzarella and tomato sauce, and topped with Parmigiano Reggiano. Roasting the eggplant slices with just a thin brush of olive oil gave them creamy interiors and golden exteriors ripe for saucing and sprinkling with cheese. Be careful when opening the oven in step 3, as the eggplant will release steam. Fresh mozzarella is key to the success of this recipe; do not substitute low-moisture mozzarella. If using fresh mozzarella packed in water, press the slices between layers of paper towels to remove excess moisture before using. If you can't find Italian eggplants, substitute 4 pounds of small globe eggplants.

TOMATO SAUCE
1 (28-ounce) can crushed tomatoes
1 tablespoon extra-virgin olive oil
2 garlic cloves, minced
⅛ teaspoon red pepper flakes
¼ teaspoon table salt
2 tablespoons chopped fresh basil

EGGPLANT

- ½ cup extra-virgin olive oil, divided
- 8 Italian eggplants (6 to 9 ounces each), sliced lengthwise into ¼-inch-thick planks, divided
- 1 teaspoon table salt, divided
- 8 ounces fresh mozzarella, sliced thin
- 7 tablespoons grated Parmigiano Reggiano, divided
- 10 fresh basil leaves, torn into 1-inch pieces

1. FOR THE TOMATO SAUCE Pulse tomatoes in food processor until smooth, about 10 pulses, scraping down sides of bowl as needed. Cook oil and garlic in large saucepan over medium heat, stirring occasionally, until fragrant, about 2 minutes. Stir in pepper flakes and cook until fragrant, about 30 seconds. Stir in tomatoes and salt, bring to simmer, and cook until thickened slightly, about 10 minutes. Off heat, stir in basil.

2. FOR THE EGGPLANT Adjust oven racks to upper-middle and lower-middle positions and heat oven to 450 degrees. Line 2 rimmed baking sheets with aluminum foil and brush each sheet with 1 tablespoon oil. Arrange half of eggplant in single layer on prepared sheets. Brush tops of eggplant planks with 2 tablespoons oil and sprinkle with ½ teaspoon salt.

3. Roast eggplant until tender and lightly browned, 15 to 20 minutes, switching and rotating sheets halfway through baking. Let eggplant cool slightly on sheets, then transfer, still on foil, to wire racks to cool completely. Line now-empty sheets with additional foil and brush each sheet with 1 tablespoon oil. Repeat brushing with remaining oil, sprinkling with remaining salt, and roasting remaining eggplant; transfer to wire racks.

4. Reduce oven temperature to 375 degrees. Spread ½ cup tomato sauce in bottom of 13 by 9-inch baking dish. Layer one-quarter of eggplant over sauce, overlapping planks as needed to fit. Spread ¼ cup sauce over eggplant, then top with one-third of mozzarella and 1 tablespoon Parmigiano. Repeat layering of eggplant, tomato sauce, mozzarella, and Parmigiano 2 more times.

5. Layer remaining eggplant in dish, spread remaining tomato sauce over top, and sprinkle with remaining ¼ cup Parmigiano. Bake until bubbling around edges, about 25 minutes. Let cool for 10 minutes before sprinkling with basil and serving.

Mushroom and Leek Galette with Gorgonzola

Serves 6 to 8 `MAKE AHEAD` `VEGETARIAN`
Total Time 1 hour, plus 1½ hours chilling

WHY THIS RECIPE WORKS Our main dish–worthy tart has a crust that perfectly straddles the line between sturdy and delicate, and a flavorful, savory filling to match. To enhance the flavor of the crust and keep it tender, we swapped out some of the white flour for nutty whole-wheat, and we used butter rather than shortening. To punch up its flaky texture and introduce more structure, we gave the crust a series of folds to create numerous interlocking layers. And to make the filling both flavorful and easy to slice, we paired earthy mushrooms and sweet, mildly oniony leeks with rich, potent binders like Gorgonzola cheese and crème fraîche, adding a spoonful of Dijon mustard for piquancy. Cutting a few small holes in the dough prevented it from lifting off the pan as it baked. An overturned baking sheet can be used in place of the baking stone. This dough will require a generous amount of flour (up to ¼ cup) to roll out.

DOUGH

- 1¼ cups (6¼ ounces) all-purpose flour
- ½ cup (2¾ ounces) whole-wheat flour
- 1 tablespoon sugar
- ¾ teaspoon table salt
- 10 tablespoons unsalted butter, cut into ½-inch pieces and chilled
- 7 tablespoons ice water
- 1 teaspoon distilled white vinegar

FILLING

- 1¼ pounds shiitake mushrooms, stemmed and sliced thin
- 5 teaspoons extra-virgin olive oil, divided
- 1 pound leeks, white and light green parts only, halved lengthwise, sliced ½ inch thick, and washed thoroughly (3 cups)
- 1 teaspoon minced fresh thyme
- 2 tablespoons crème fraîche
- 1 tablespoon Dijon mustard
- 3 ounces Gorgonzola cheese, crumbled (¾ cup)
- 1 large egg, lightly beaten
- 2 tablespoons minced fresh parsley

1. FOR THE DOUGH Process all-purpose flour, whole-wheat flour, sugar, and salt in food processor until combined, about 5 seconds. Scatter butter over top and pulse until it forms pea-size pieces, about 10 pulses. Transfer mixture to medium bowl.

2. Sprinkle ice water and vinegar over mixture. With rubber spatula, use folding motion to mix until loose, shaggy mass forms with some dry flour remaining (do not overwork). Transfer mixture to center of large sheet of plastic wrap, press gently into rough 4-inch square, and wrap tightly. Refrigerate for 45 minutes.

3. Transfer dough to floured counter. Roll into 11 by 8-inch rectangle with short side of rectangle parallel to edge of counter. Using bench scraper, bring bottom third of dough up, then fold upper third over it, folding like business letter into 8 by 4-inch rectangle. Turn dough 90 degrees counterclockwise. Roll dough again into 11 by 8-inch rectangle and fold into thirds again. Turn dough 90 degrees counterclockwise and repeat rolling and folding into thirds. After last fold, fold dough in half to create 4-inch square. Press top of dough gently to seal. Wrap in plastic and refrigerate for at least 45 minutes or up to 2 days.

4. FOR THE FILLING Microwave mushrooms, covered, until just tender, 3 to 5 minutes. Transfer to colander and let drain; return to bowl. Meanwhile, heat 1 tablespoon oil in 12-inch skillet over medium heat until shimmering. Add leeks and thyme, cover, and cook, stirring occasionally, until leeks are tender and beginning to brown, 5 to 7 minutes. Transfer to bowl with mushrooms. Stir in crème fraîche and mustard. Season with salt and pepper to taste; set aside.

5. Adjust oven rack to lower-middle position, set baking stone on rack, and heat oven to 400 degrees. Line rimmed baking sheet with parchment paper. Remove dough from refrigerator and let stand at room temperature for 15 to 20 minutes. Roll dough into 14-inch circle about ⅛ inch thick on floured counter. (Trim edges as needed to form rough circle.) Transfer dough to prepared sheet. Using straw or tip of paring knife, cut five ¼-inch circles in dough (one at center and four evenly spaced halfway from center to edge of dough). Brush top of dough with 1 teaspoon oil.

6. Spread half of filling evenly over dough, leaving 2-inch border around edge. Sprinkle half of Gorgonzola over filling, cover with remaining filling, and top with remaining Gorgonzola. Drizzle remaining 1 teaspoon oil over filling. Grasp 1 edge of dough and fold outer 2 inches over filling. Repeat around circumference of tart, overlapping dough every 2 to 3 inches; gently pinch pleated dough to secure but do not press dough into filling. Brush dough with egg and sprinkle evenly with kosher salt.

7. Lower oven temperature to 375 degrees. Set sheet on stone and bake until crust is deep golden brown and filling is beginning to brown, 35 to 45 minutes. Let tart cool on sheet on wire rack for 10 minutes. Using offset or wide metal spatula, loosen tart from parchment and carefully slide tart onto cutting board. Sprinkle parsley over filling, cut into wedges, and serve.

Eggplant Parmesan

Mushroom and Leek Galette with Gorgonzola

Swiss Chard Pie

Double-Crust Chicken Pot Pie

Swiss Chard Pie

Serves 12 MAKE AHEAD
Total Time 2¾ hours, plus 2 hours chilling

WHY THIS RECIPE WORKS Hailing from central Italy and locally called erbazzone, this savory winter pie packs several pounds of hearty greens between layers of flaky golden pie crust, with additional flavor provided by pancetta and plenty of Parmigiano Reggiano cheese. We first browned the pancetta and set it aside so we could cook our aromatics and wilt our chard in its flavorful rendered fat. Ricotta is a controversial ingredient in erbazzone; many recipes don't include it, though some sources claim it's not erbazzone without it. We liked the cleaner, earthier taste of the erbazzone without the ricotta, but if you prefer a cheesier filling we've provided the option to include it. A buttery pie crust wrapped the whole thing up in an irresistible package, which we sprinkled with the reserved pancetta so it could finish crisping in the oven. This dough will be moister than most pie doughs; as the dough chills, it will absorb any excess moisture, leaving it supple and workable. To make this dish vegetarian, leave out the pancetta.

CRUST
20 tablespoons (2½ sticks) unsalted butter, chilled
2½ cups (12½ ounces) all-purpose flour, divided
1 teaspoon table salt
½ cup ice water, divided

FILLING
1 tablespoon extra-virgin olive oil
3 ounces pancetta, chopped fine, divided
1 onion, chopped fine
4 garlic cloves, minced
3 pounds Swiss chard, stemmed and cut into 1-inch pieces
4 ounces Parmesan cheese, grated (2 cups)
6 ounces (¾ cup) whole-milk ricotta cheese (optional)
1 large egg, lightly beaten

1. FOR THE CRUST Grate half stick butter using coarse holes on box grater and place in freezer. Cut remaining 2 sticks butter into ½-inch pieces.

2. Pulse 1½ cups flour and salt in food processor until combined, about 4 pulses. Add butter pieces and process until homogeneous dough forms, about 30 seconds. Using your hands, carefully break dough into 2-inch pieces and redistribute evenly around processor blade. Add remaining 1 cup flour and pulse until mixture is broken into pieces no larger than 1 inch (most pieces will be much smaller), 4 or 5 pulses. Empty mixture into medium bowl. Add grated butter and toss until butter pieces are separated and coated with flour.

3. Sprinkle ¼ cup ice water over mixture. Toss with rubber spatula until mixture is evenly moistened. Sprinkle remaining ¼ cup ice water over mixture and toss to combine. Press dough with spatula until dough sticks together. Divide dough in half and transfer to sheets of plastic wrap. Draw edges of plastic wrap over first dough half and press firmly on sides and top to form compact fissure-free mass. Flatten to form 5-inch square. Repeat with second dough half. Refrigerate for at least 2 hours or up to 2 days. Let chilled dough sit on counter to soften slightly, about 10 minutes, before rolling.

4. FOR THE FILLING Adjust oven rack to lower-middle position and heat oven to 400 degrees. Cook oil and ⅓ cup pancetta in Dutch oven over medium-low heat until pancetta is browned and fat is rendered, 5 to 7 minutes. Using slotted spoon, transfer pancetta to bowl. Pour off all but 1 tablespoon fat from pot.

5. Add onion to fat left in pot and cook over medium heat until softened, about 5 minutes. Stir in garlic and cook until fragrant, about 30 seconds. Increase heat to high. Add chard, 1 handful at a time, and cook until beginning to wilt, about 1 minute. Cover and continue to cook, stirring occasionally, until chard is wilted but still bright green, 2 to 4 minutes. Uncover and continue to cook until liquid evaporates, about 5 minutes. Transfer chard to large bowl and let cool completely, about 30 minutes.

6. Grease rimmed baking sheet. Stir Parmesan; ricotta, if using; and cooked pancetta into chard. Roll 1 dough square into 14 by 10-inch rectangle on well-floured counter. Roll dough loosely around rolling pin and unroll it onto prepared sheet. Spread chard mixture evenly over crust, leaving 1-inch border around edges. Brush edges of crust with egg.

7. Roll remaining dough square into 14 by 10-inch rectangle on well-floured counter. Roll dough loosely around rolling pin and unroll it over filling. Press edges of crusts together to seal. Roll edges inward and use your fingers to crimp. Using sharp knife, cut through top crust into 12 equal squares (do not cut through filling). Brush with remaining egg and sprinkle with remaining pancetta.

8. Bake until pie is golden brown and pancetta is crispy, 30 to 35 minutes, rotating sheet halfway through baking. Transfer sheet to wire rack and let pie cool completely, about 30 minutes. Transfer pie to cutting board, cut into squares, and serve.

Double-Crust Chicken Pot Pie

Serves 6 to 8 | **Total Time** 2¾ hours, plus 2¼ hours chilling and resting `MAKE AHEAD`

WHY THIS RECIPE WORKS It's hard to imagine anything more comforting or full of rustic charm than savory chicken and tender vegetables suspended in a velvety, smooth cream gravy and topped with a flaky pie crust. Buttery homemade crust always tastes best, and to make it easier to handle, we incorporated sour cream and egg into the dough, leaving it remarkably malleable. Using already-cooked rotisserie chicken streamlined the process of making the filling, as it needed only to be shredded and stirred in. Cutting the vegetables small allowed the filling to cook quickly. The pie may seem loose when it comes out of the oven; it will set up as it cools.

CRUST
- ½ cup sour cream, chilled
- 1 large egg, lightly beaten
- 2½ cups (12½ ounces) all-purpose flour
- 1½ teaspoons table salt
- 12 tablespoons unsalted butter, cut into ½-inch pieces and chilled

FILLING
- 4 tablespoons unsalted butter
- 1 onion, chopped fine
- 2 carrots, peeled and cut into ¼ inch pieces (⅔ cup)
- 2 celery ribs, cut into ¼-inch pieces (½ cup)
- ½ teaspoon table salt
- ½ teaspoon pepper
- 6 tablespoons all-purpose flour
- 2¼ cups chicken broth
- ½ cup half-and-half
- 1 small russet potato (6 ounces), peeled and cut into ¼-inch pieces (1 cup)
- 1 teaspoon minced fresh thyme
- 1 (2½-pound) rotisserie chicken, skin and bones discarded, meat shredded into bite-size pieces (3 cups)
- ¾ cup frozen peas
- 1 large egg, lightly beaten

1. FOR THE CRUST Combine sour cream and egg in bowl. Process flour and salt in food processor until combined, about 3 seconds. Add butter and pulse until only pea-size pieces remain, about 10 pulses. Add half of sour cream mixture and pulse until combined, about 5 pulses. Add remaining sour cream mixture and pulse until dough begins to form, about 10 pulses.

2. Transfer dough to lightly floured counter and knead briefly until dough comes together. Divide dough in half and form each half into 4-inch disk. Wrap disks tightly in plastic wrap and refrigerate for 1 hour. (Wrapped dough can be refrigerated for up to 2 days or frozen for up to 2 months. If frozen, let dough thaw completely on counter before rolling.)

3. Let chilled dough sit on counter to soften slightly, about 10 minutes, before rolling. Roll 1 disk of dough into 12-inch circle on lightly floured counter. Roll dough loosely around rolling pin and gently unroll it onto 9-inch pie plate, letting excess dough hang over edge. Ease dough into plate by gently lifting edge of dough with your hand while pressing into plate bottom with your other hand.

4. Roll other disk of dough into 12-inch circle on lightly floured counter, then transfer to parchment paper–lined baking sheet; cover with plastic. Refrigerate both doughs for 30 minutes.

5. FOR THE FILLING Meanwhile, adjust oven rack to lowest position and heat oven to 450 degrees. Melt butter in large saucepan over medium heat. Add onion, carrots, celery, salt, and pepper and cook until vegetables begin to soften, about 6 minutes. Add flour and cook, stirring constantly, until golden, 1 to 2 minutes. Slowly stir in broth and half-and-half, scraping up any browned bits and smoothing out any lumps, and bring to boil over medium-high heat.

6. Stir in potato and thyme. Reduce heat to medium and simmer until sauce is thickened and potato is tender, about 8 minutes. Off heat, stir in chicken and peas.

7. Transfer filling to dough-lined pie plate. Roll remaining dough round loosely around rolling pin and gently unroll it onto filling. Trim overhang to ½ inch beyond lip of plate. Pinch edges of top and bottom crusts firmly together. Tuck overhang under itself; folded edge should be flush with edge of plate. Crimp dough evenly around edge of plate using your fingers. Cut four 2-inch slits in top of dough.

8. Brush top of pie with egg. Place pie on rimmed baking sheet. Bake until top is light golden brown, 18 to 20 minutes. Reduce oven temperature to 375 degrees; rotate sheet; and continue to bake until crust is deep golden brown, 12 to 15 minutes. Let pie cool on wire rack for at least 45 minutes. Serve.

Double-Crust Turkey Pot Pie
Substitute shredded cooked turkey for chicken.

Chicken B'stilla

Chicken B'stilla

Serves 10 to 12 | **Total Time** 2½ hours

WHY THIS RECIPE WORKS The most cherished qualities of b'stilla, a Moroccan tart customarily made with pigeon and flavored with almonds and cinnamon sugar, are its contrasts: crisp yet juicy, sweet yet savory, succulent yet wholesome. Our version calls for cooking chicken thighs gently in a spiced broth; the rich cooking liquid formed the base of the pie's traditional custard-like component. Assembling the b'stilla in the same skillet we used to cook the chicken created a wide, thin pie that was easy to serve. We lined the pan with phyllo, added the almond–cinnamon sugar mixture, poured in the chicken-custard mixture, and topped everything with more phyllo. To finish, we dusted the top of the sweet-savory pie with more cinnamon sugar. Phyllo dough is also available in larger 18 by 14-inch sheets; if using, cut them in half to make 14 by 9-inch sheets. Do not thaw the phyllo in the microwave; let it sit in the refrigerator overnight or on the counter for 4 to 5 hours. While working with the phyllo, cover the sheets with plastic wrap and then a damp dish towel to prevent drying. You will need a 12-inch ovensafe nonstick skillet for this recipe.

½ cup extra-virgin olive oil, divided
1 onion, chopped fine
¾ teaspoon table salt
1 tablespoon grated fresh ginger
½ teaspoon pepper
½ teaspoon ground turmeric
½ teaspoon paprika
1½ cups water
2 pounds boneless, skinless chicken thighs, trimmed
6 large eggs
½ cup minced fresh cilantro
1 pound (14 by 9-inch) phyllo, thawed
1½ cups slivered almonds, toasted and chopped
¼ cup confectioners' sugar, divided
1 tablespoon ground cinnamon, divided

1. Heat 1 tablespoon oil in 12-inch ovensafe nonstick skillet over medium heat until shimmering. Add onion and salt and cook until softened, about 5 minutes. Stir in ginger, pepper, turmeric, and paprika and cook until fragrant, about 30 seconds. Add water and chicken and bring to simmer. Reduce heat to low, cover, and cook until chicken registers 175 degrees, 15 to 20 minutes. Transfer chicken to cutting board, let cool slightly, then shred into bite-size pieces using 2 forks; transfer to large bowl.

2. Whisk eggs together in small bowl. Bring cooking liquid to boil over high heat and cook until reduced to about 1 cup, about 10 minutes. Reduce heat to low. Whisking constantly, slowly pour eggs into broth and cook until mixture resembles loose scrambled eggs, 6 to 8 minutes; transfer to bowl with chicken. Stir in cilantro until combined. Wipe skillet clean with paper towels and let cool completely.

3. Adjust oven rack to middle position and heat oven to 375 degrees. Brush 1 phyllo sheet with oil and arrange in bottom of cooled skillet with short side against side of pan. Some phyllo will overhang edge of skillet; leave in place. Turn skillet 30 degrees. Brush second phyllo sheet with oil and arrange in skillet, leaving any overhanging phyllo in place. Repeat turning and layering with 10 more phyllo sheets in pinwheel pattern, brushing each with oil, to cover entire circumference of skillet (you should have total of 12 layers of phyllo).

4. Combine almonds, 3 tablespoons sugar, and 2 teaspoons cinnamon and sprinkle over phyllo in skillet. Lay 2 phyllo sheets evenly across top of almond mixture and brush top with oil. Rotate skillet 90 degrees and lay 2 more phyllo sheets evenly across top; do not brush with oil. Spoon chicken mixture into skillet and spread into even layer.

5. Stack 5 phyllo sheets on counter and brush top with oil. Fold phyllo in half crosswise and brush top with oil. Lay phyllo stack on center of chicken mixture.

6. Fold overhanging phyllo over filling and phyllo stack, pleating phyllo every 2 to 3 inches, and press to seal. Brush top with oil and bake until phyllo is crisp and golden, 35 to 40 minutes.

7. Combine remaining 1 tablespoon sugar and remaining 1 teaspoon cinnamon in small bowl. Let b'stilla cool in skillet for 15 minutes. Using rubber spatula, carefully slide b'stilla out onto cutting board. Dust top with cinnamon sugar, slice, and serve.

ASSEMBLING CHICKEN B'STILLA

1. Brush 1 phyllo sheet with oil and arrange in bottom of skillet with short side against side of pan. Continue layering 11 more phyllo sheets in skillet in pinwheel pattern.

2. Sprinkle almond mixture over phyllo in skillet, then lay 2 phyllo sheets across top and brush with oil. Rotate skillet 90 degrees and lay 2 more phyllo sheets across top.

3. Spoon chicken mixture into skillet and spread into even layer. Stack 5 phyllo sheets and brush with oil. Fold in half, brush top with oil, and lay on chicken mixture.

4. Fold overhanging phyllo over filling and phyllo stack, pleating phyllo every 2 to 3 inches, and press to seal. Brush top with oil before baking.

Simple Cranberry Sauce

Serves 12 (**Makes** about 2¼ cups)
Total Time 20 minutes, plus 2 hours cooling

This sauce makes a great accompaniment to cheese and meat platters. You can also use it to top biscuits and toast, to spread in sandwiches, or to spoon over roasted poultry or pork. If using frozen cranberries, do not defrost them; just add about 2 minutes to the simmering time.

- 1 cup sugar
- ¾ cup water
- ¼ teaspoon table salt
- 1 (12-ounce) bag fresh or frozen cranberries, picked over

Bring sugar, water, and salt to boil in medium saucepan, stirring occasionally to dissolve sugar. Stir in cranberries and return to boil. Reduce to simmer and cook until slightly thickened and about two-thirds of berries have popped open, about 5 minutes. Transfer to bowl and let cool completely, about 2 hours. (Cranberry sauce can be refrigerated for up to 1 week; allow to come to room temperature before serving.)

Simple Cranberry-Orange Sauce
Add 1 tablespoon grated orange zest to sugar mixture. Stir 2 tablespoons Grand Marnier (or other orange liqueur) into cooled sauce.

Simple Cranberry Sauce with Champagne and Currants
Substitute champagne for water, and add 3 tablespoons dried currants to sugar mixture with cranberries.

Cranberry Sauce with Pears and Ginger

Serves 12 (**Makes** 2¼ cups)
Total Time 25 minutes, plus 1 hour chilling

If using frozen cranberries, do not defrost them; just add about 2 minutes to the simmering time.

    1 cup sugar
    ¾ cup water
    1 tablespoon grated fresh ginger
    ¼ teaspoon ground cinnamon
    ¼ teaspoon table salt
    2 pears, peeled, cored, and cut into ½-inch chunks
    1 (12-ounce) bag fresh or frozen cranberries, picked over

Bring sugar, water, ginger, cinnamon, and salt to boil in large saucepan over high heat, stirring occasionally to dissolve sugar. Stir in pears and cranberries. Return to boil, then reduce to simmer and cook until slightly thickened, about two-thirds of berries have popped open, and pears are soft, about 5 minutes. Transfer to serving bowl and refrigerate until thickened, about 1 hour. Serve. (Sauce can be refrigerated for up to 3 days; allow to come to room temperature before serving.)

Spiced Apple Chutney

Serves 32 (**Makes** about 2 cups)
Total Time 25 minutes, plus 2 hours cooling

You can dollop this chutney on top of a finished dish or serve the chutney on the side, as you might do with cranberry sauce.

    1 tablespoon vegetable oil
    3 Granny Smith apples, peeled, cored, and chopped
    1 shallot, minced
    1 tablespoon grated fresh ginger
    ½ teaspoon ground cinnamon
    ¼ teaspoon ground nutmeg
    ½ cup apple jelly
    ⅓ cup white wine vinegar

Heat oil in 12-inch nonstick skillet over medium-high heat until shimmering. Cook apples until lightly browned, about 5 minutes. Stir in shallot, ginger, cinnamon, and nutmeg and cook until fragrant, about 1 minute. Stir in apple jelly and vinegar, bring to simmer, and cook until thickened and measures about 2 cups, about 5 minutes. Transfer to bowl and let cool completely, about 2 hours. (Chutney can be refrigerated for up to 1 week; allow to come to room temperature before serving.)

Pear-Walnut Chutney

Substitute 3 peeled, cored, and chopped pears for apples, and cherry preserves for apple jelly. Stir ¼ cup chopped toasted walnuts in after chutney has cooled.

Cherry-Port Sauce

Serves 8 (**Makes** about 1½ cups)
Total Time 45 minutes, plus 2 hours cooling

This sauce pairs especially well with pork roasts or duck. You can substitute an equal amount of frozen sweet cherries for the fresh cherries; do not defrost them.

    10 ounces fresh sweet cherries, pitted and halved
     2 cups dry red wine
     ¾ cup sugar
     ¼ cup chicken broth
     5 tablespoons red wine vinegar, divided
     ¼ cup ruby port

Bring cherries, wine, sugar, broth, ¼ cup vinegar, and port to simmer in medium saucepan. Cook, stirring occasionally, until thickened and measures about 1½ cups, about 30 minutes. Transfer to bowl and let cool completely, about 2 hours. Stir in remaining 1 tablespoon vinegar. (Cherry sauce can be refrigerated for up to 1 week; allow to come to room temperature before serving.)

Grapefruit-Basil Relish

Serves 16 (**Makes** about 1 cup)
Total Time 40 minutes

This relish is especially good with seafood.

- 2 red grapefruits
- 1 small shallot, minced
- 2 tablespoons chopped fresh basil
- 2 teaspoons lemon juice
- 2 teaspoons extra-virgin olive oil
  Sugar

Cut away peel and pith from grapefruits. Cut grapefruits into 8 wedges, then slice crosswise into ½-inch-thick pieces. Place grapefruits in strainer set over bowl and let drain for 15 minutes; measure out and reserve 1 tablespoon drained juice. Combine reserved juice, shallot, basil, lemon juice, and oil in bowl. Stir in grapefruits and let sit for 15 minutes. Season with salt, pepper, and sugar to taste. (Relish can be refrigerated for up to 2 days.)

Tangerine-Ginger Relish
Substitute 4 tangerines for grapefruits; quarter tangerines before slicing crosswise. Substitute 1½ teaspoons grated fresh ginger for shallot, and 1 thinly sliced scallion for basil.

Onion-Balsamic Relish

Serves 10 (**Makes** about ⅔ cup)
Total Time 50 minutes

This relish makes a great addition to sandwiches. Avoid adding the mint to the relish before it is fully cooled, or the mint will wilt.

- 6 tablespoons extra-virgin olive oil, divided
- 2 red onions, chopped fine
- ½ teaspoon table salt
- 4 garlic cloves, minced
- ¼ cup balsamic vinegar
- ¼ cup minced fresh mint
- ½ teaspoon pepper

1. Heat ¼ cup oil in medium saucepan over medium-low heat until shimmering. Add onions and salt and cook, stirring occasionally, until onions are very soft and lightly browned, about 20 minutes.

2. Stir in garlic and cook until fragrant, about 1 minute. Stir in vinegar and cook until syrupy, 30 to 60 seconds. Transfer onion mixture to bowl and let cool completely, about 15 minutes. Stir in mint, pepper, and remaining 2 tablespoons oil. Season with salt and pepper to taste. (Relish can be refrigerated for up to 1 week; allow to come to room temperature before serving.)

Our Favorite Turkey Gravy

Serves 12 to 16 (**Makes** 4 cups) | **Total Time** 2½ hours

Much of this gravy's flavor is derived from the trimmed skin and fat plus the neck and giblets of a turkey. Use kitchen shears to cut away extra skin from the neck region (leaving enough to cover the opening) and any loose fat from the cavity. Cut large pieces of skin into 1-inch pieces. If your turkey does not have excess skin or fat, use kitchen shears to snip off the tail and cut it into three or four pieces to use as trimmings. Do not use the liver that is packaged with the giblets. The gravy's consistency can be adjusted to suit your taste: Simmer longer for a thicker gravy or thin with additional broth for a thinner gravy. This gravy is better with turkey drippings; you can add them either in step 4 or when reheating the gravy. To double the recipe, double all the ingredients including the trimmings and make the stock in two separate pots.

- 6 cups chicken broth, divided, plus extra as needed
  Reserved turkey neck and giblets
  Reserved turkey trimmings, cut into 1-inch pieces (⅓ cup)
- 1 onion, chopped
- 1 carrot, chopped
- 1 celery rib, chopped
- 8 sprigs fresh parsley
- 2 sprigs fresh thyme
- 2 garlic cloves, peeled
- ½ teaspoon pepper
- ¼ teaspoon table salt
- ⅓ cup dry white wine
- 4 tablespoons unsalted butter
- 5 tablespoons all-purpose flour
- ¼ cup defatted turkey drippings (optional)

1. Bring 2 cups broth, reserved neck and giblets, and reserved trimmings to simmer in Dutch oven over high heat. Cook, adjusting heat to maintain vigorous simmer and stirring occasionally, until all liquid evaporates and trimmings begin to sizzle, about 20 minutes. Continue to cook, stirring frequently, until dark fond forms on bottom of pot, 2 to 4 minutes.

2. Reduce heat to medium-high. Add onion, carrot, celery, parsley sprigs, thyme sprigs, garlic, pepper, and salt. Cook, stirring frequently, until onion is translucent, 8 to 10 minutes.

3. Stir in wine and bring to simmer, scraping up any browned bits. Add remaining 4 cups broth and bring to simmer over high heat. Reduce heat to medium-low, cover, and simmer for 1 hour. Strain stock through fine-mesh strainer set over bowl; discard solids. (You should have 3½ to 4 cups stock. Turkey stock can be refrigerated for up to 2 days.)

4. Melt butter in medium saucepan over medium heat. Add flour and increase heat to medium-high. Cook, stirring constantly, until mixture is deep golden brown, 5 to 8 minutes. Reduce heat to low and slowly whisk in strained stock, scraping up any browned bits and smoothing out any lumps. Increase heat to medium-high and bring to simmer. Simmer until thickened, about 5 minutes. Add drippings, if using, and thin gravy with extra broth, if desired. Season with salt and pepper to taste, and serve. (Gravy can be refrigerated for up to 3 days or frozen for up to 2 weeks; to reheat, bring to simmer over medium-low heat, stirring occasionally.)

Our Favorite Gluten-Free Turkey Gravy

The test kitchen's favorite gluten-free flour blends are King Arthur Gluten-Free All-Purpose Flour and Betty Crocker All-Purpose Gluten Free Rice Flour Blend. Do not use a gluten-free flour made with beans here.

Substitute gluten-free flour blend for all-purpose flour.

Our Favorite Alcohol-Free Turkey Gravy

Substitute ⅓ cup water and 2 teaspoons cider vinegar for wine.

All-Purpose Gravy

Serves 6 to 8 (**Makes** about 2 cups)
Total Time 50 minutes

This gravy pairs well with poultry, pork, and beef. If you would like to double the recipe, use a Dutch oven to give the vegetables ample space for browning and increase the cooking times by roughly 50 percent.

> 3 tablespoons unsalted butter
> 1 small onion, chopped
> 1 small carrot, peeled and chopped
> 1 small celery rib, chopped
> ½ teaspoon pepper
> ¼ cup all-purpose flour
> 4 cups chicken broth
> ¼ cup dry white wine
> 2 sprigs fresh thyme
> 1 bay leaf

1. Heat butter in large skillet or large saucepan until melted. Add onion, carrot, celery, and pepper and cook over medium heat until vegetables are softened and well browned, about 8 minutes. Stir in flour and cook for 1 minute. Slowly whisk in broth and wine, scraping up any browned bits and smoothing out any lumps. Stir in thyme sprigs and bay leaf, bring to simmer, and cook until gravy is thickened and reduced to 3 cups, about 15 minutes.

2. Strain gravy through fine-mesh strainer into bowl, pressing on solids to extract as much liquid as possible; discard solids. Season with salt and pepper to taste, and serve.

To make ahead Leftover gravy can be frozen for up to 1 month. To thaw, place the gravy and 1 tablespoon water in a saucepan over low heat and bring slowly to a simmer. The gravy may appear broken or curdled as it thaws, but a vigorous whisking will recombine it.

Mushroom Gravy

Add ½ ounce dried porcini mushrooms, rinsed and minced, to skillet with onion.

Tarragon-Sherry Gravy

Substitute dry sherry for wine. Stir 2 tablespoons minced fresh tarragon and 2 additional teaspoons dry sherry into strained gravy.

vegetable sides

▪ MAKE AHEAD ▪ VEGETARIAN
Photo: Slow-Cooker Lemon-Herb Fingerling Potatoes

Roquefort Salad with Apple, Celery, and Hazelnuts

Serves 12 | **Total Time** 25 minutes `VEGETARIAN`

WHY THIS RECIPE WORKS Every host needs a crowd-size salad that's simple to make but impressive enough to hold its own against the rest of the dishes on the table, and this one delivers. We started with the classic and sophisticated combination of blue cheese, apples, and nuts. The sweet, crisp apples balanced the salty, soft-crumbly cheese; hazelnuts offered crunch and more richness. Crisp celery, attractively sliced on the bias, provided more textural contrast. A good dose of cider vinegar in the dressing contributed necessary tartness, and a spoonful of honey performed double duty, tempering the acidity of the vinegar and highlighting the saltiness of the cheese. We like to make this salad with sweet red apples such as Braeburn or Fuji, but any apple will do. If you prefer a very mild and mellow blue cheese, substitute Danish blue for the Roquefort; if you prefer a sharp and piquant one, try Stilton.

- 6 tablespoons cider vinegar
- 6 tablespoons extra-virgin olive oil
- 2 tablespoons honey
- ½ teaspoon table salt
- ¼ teaspoon pepper
- 2 apples, cored and sliced very thin
- 4 celery ribs, sliced very thin on bias
- 2 heads red or green leaf lettuce (1 pound), torn into bite-size pieces
- ½ cup fresh parsley leaves, roughly torn
- 12 ounces Roquefort cheese, crumbled (3 cups)
- 1 cup hazelnuts, toasted, skinned, and chopped fine

1. Whisk vinegar, oil, honey, salt, and pepper in small bowl until combined. Toss apples, celery, and 2 tablespoons vinaigrette together in medium bowl; let stand for 5 minutes.

2. Toss lettuce, parsley, and remaining vinaigrette together in large bowl and season with salt and pepper to taste. Divide salad among individual plates; top each with portion of apple-celery mixture, Roquefort, and hazelnuts. Serve immediately.

Roquefort Salad with Fennel, Dried Cherries, and Walnuts

Omit apples and celery. Substitute red wine vinegar for cider vinegar. Reduce honey to 4 teaspoons. In step 1, whisk vinegar and honey in medium bowl. Mix in 1 cup dried sweetened cherries and microwave, covered, until cherries are plump, about 1 minute. Then whisk in oil, salt, and pepper. While still warm, add 2 thinly sliced small fennel bulbs and toss to combine; let cool completely. In step 2, substitute 2 thinly sliced small heads radicchio for parsley. Substitute 1 cup walnuts, toasted and chopped fine, for hazelnuts.

Citrus and Radicchio Salad with Dates and Smoked Almonds

Serves 4 to 6 | **Total Time** 45 minutes `VEGETARIAN`

WHY THIS RECIPE WORKS Brighten up your winter table with this colorful salad. In a reversal of what you might expect, we used sliced grapefruits and oranges as the salad's base (citrus inevitably sinks to the bottom of a salad), topping them with sliced radicchio for an attractive presentation. To tame the bitterness of the grapefruit and prevent its ample juice from overwhelming, we treated the grapefruit (and the oranges) with sugar and salt and let them drain, reserving some of the juice for a vinaigrette. Salty smoked almonds added mellow richness, and dates contributed sweetness. We prefer to use navel oranges, tangelos, or Cara Caras here.

- 2 red grapefruits
- 3 oranges
- 1 teaspoon sugar
- ½ teaspoon table salt
- 3 tablespoons extra-virgin olive oil
- 1 small shallot, minced
- 1 teaspoon Dijon mustard
- 1 small head radicchio (6 ounces), halved, cored, and sliced thin
- ⅔ cup chopped pitted dates, divided
- ½ cup smoked almonds, chopped, divided

1. Cut away peel and pith from grapefruits and oranges. Cut each fruit in half from pole to pole, then slice crosswise ¼ inch thick. Transfer to bowl, toss with sugar and salt, and let sit for 15 minutes.

2. Drain fruit in fine-mesh strainer set over bowl, reserving 2 tablespoons juice. Arrange fruit in even layer on serving platter and drizzle with oil. Whisk reserved citrus juice, shallot, and mustard together in medium bowl. Add radicchio, ⅓ cup dates, and ¼ cup almonds and gently toss to coat. Season with salt and pepper to taste. Arrange radicchio mixture over fruit, leaving 1-inch border of fruit around edges. Sprinkle with remaining ⅓ cup dates and remaining ¼ cup almonds. Serve.

Butternut Squash and Apple Pita Salad

Serves 4 to 6 | **Total Time** 1¼ hours VEGETARIAN

WHY THIS RECIPE WORKS Although pita bread salad, or fattoush, often features summertime produce such as ripe tomatoes and cucumber, we didn't want to give this vibrant dish up for half the year. Our solution: substituting crisp apples, sweet roasted butternut squash, and pleasantly bitter radicchio for the warm-weather produce. A dressing loaded with lemon juice and citrusy sumac delivered bright, punchy flavor to our multidimensional salad.

- 2 (8-inch) pita breads
- ½ cup extra-virgin olive oil, divided
- ⅛ plus ¾ teaspoon table salt, divided
- ⅛ teaspoon pepper
- 2 pounds butternut squash, peeled, seeded, and cut into ½-inch pieces
- 3 tablespoons lemon juice
- 4 teaspoons ground sumac, plus extra for serving
- 1 garlic clove, minced
- 1 apple, cored and cut into ½-inch pieces
- ¼ head radicchio, cored and chopped (1 cup)
- ½ cup chopped fresh parsley
- 4 scallions, sliced thin

1. Adjust oven racks to middle and lowest positions and heat oven to 375 degrees. Using kitchen shears, cut around perimeter of each pita and separate into 2 thin rounds. Cut each round in half. Place pitas smooth side down on wire rack set in rimmed baking sheet. Brush rough side of pitas evenly with 3 tablespoons oil, then sprinkle with ⅛ teaspoon salt and pepper. (Pitas do not need to be uniformly coated with oil.) Bake on middle rack until pitas are crisp and pale golden brown, 10 to 14 minutes. Let cool completely.

2. Increase oven temperature to 450 degrees. Toss squash with 1 tablespoon oil and ½ teaspoon salt. Spread in even layer on rimmed baking sheet and roast on bottom rack until browned and tender, 20 to 25 minutes, stirring halfway through. Set aside to cool slightly, about 10 minutes.

3. Whisk lemon juice, sumac, garlic, and remaining ¼ teaspoon salt together in small bowl and let sit for 10 minutes. Whisking constantly, slowly drizzle in remaining ¼ cup oil.

4. Break cooled pitas into ½-inch pieces and place in large bowl. Add roasted squash, apple, radicchio, parsley, and scallions. Drizzle dressing over salad and toss gently to coat. Season with salt and pepper to taste. Serve, sprinkling individual portions with extra sumac.

Roquefort Salad with Apple, Celery, and Hazelnuts

Citrus and Radicchio Salad with Dates and Smoked Almonds

Pan-Roasted Pear Salad with Watercress, Parmesan, and Pecans

Pressure-Cooker Beet and Watercress Salad with Orange and Dill

Pan-Roasted Pear Salad with Frisée, Goat Cheese, and Almonds

Serves 6 | **Total Time** 1¼ hours `VEGETARIAN`

WHY THIS RECIPE WORKS Adding ripe, juicy pear to a salad is a hit when you use peak-season fruit. But when you pan-roast the pears, even less-than-optimal fruit will taste amazing, as the caramelization heightens the pears' subtle complexity and intensifies their sweetness. Tossing the pears with sugar sped up browning, and cooking them in quarters on the stovetop let us control the heat and avoid overcooking. Since we were using balsamic vinegar in the dressing, we tried adding a couple of extra tablespoons of balsamic vinegar to the hot pan while roasting the pears. The extra vinegar instantly reduced to form a glazy coating on the pears, perfectly matching the flavor of the salad. We prefer Bartlett pears here, but Bosc pears can also be used. The pears should be ripe but firm. Check the flesh at the neck of the pear—it should give slightly when pressed with your finger. Romaine lettuce can be substituted for the green leaf.

1½ pounds pears, quartered lengthwise and cored
2½ teaspoons sugar, divided
¼ teaspoon table salt
⅛ teaspoon pepper
2 tablespoons extra-virgin olive oil, divided
3 tablespoons plus 1 teaspoon balsamic vinegar, divided
1 small shallot, minced
½ small head green leaf lettuce (4 ounces), torn into 1-inch pieces
1 head frisée, torn into 1-inch pieces
1 cup crumbled goat cheese or feta (4 ounces)
¾ cup toasted sliced almonds

1. Toss pears with 2 teaspoons sugar, salt, and pepper. Heat 2 teaspoons oil in 12-inch skillet over medium-high heat until just smoking. Add pears in single layer, cut side down, and cook until golden brown, 6 to 8 minutes, flipping them halfway through cooking.

2. Turn off heat, leaving skillet on burner, and add 2 tablespoons vinegar to skillet. Gently stir until vinegar becomes glazy and coats pears, about 30 seconds. Transfer pears to large plate and let cool completely, about 45 minutes. Cut each pear quarter crosswise into ½-inch pieces if desired.

3. Whisk together remaining 4 teaspoons oil, remaining 4 teaspoons vinegar, shallot, and sugar in large bowl. Add lettuce, radicchio, and cooled pears and toss to combine. Season with salt and pepper to taste, sprinkle with walnuts, and serve.

Pan-Roasted Pear Salad with Watercress, Parmesan, and Pecans

Substitute 4 ounces watercress (4 cups) for frisée; 1 cup shaved Parmesan or Pecorino Romano cheese for goat cheese; and 3 tablespoons chopped and toasted pecans for almonds.

Pan-Roasted Pear Salad with Radicchio, Blue Cheese, and Walnuts

Substitute 1 large head radicchio, quartered, cored, and cut crosswise into ½-inch pieces, for frisée; crumbled blue cheese for goat cheese; and toasted and chopped walnuts for almonds.

Pressure-Cooker Beet and Watercress Salad with Orange and Dill

Serves 4 to 6 | **Total Time** 40 minutes | `VEGETARIAN`

WHY THIS RECIPE WORKS Sweet, earthy beets make a lovely base for a winter salad but cooking them can take a long time. The pressure cooker not only reduces the cook time, but the intense heat also softens the beets' skins, making them undetectable so there is no need to peel these beets. After cooking the beets and releasing pressure, we stirred the potent cooking liquid into some creamy Greek yogurt, turning it a spectacular pink, perfect as a base for some peppery watercress. Orange zest brightened up the beets, and we arranged them on top of the greens. A sprinkling of dill brought out the anise notes of the caraway seeds, and hazelnuts and coarse sea salt added rich crunchiness. Be sure to scrub the beets clean before cooking. To make this into a main dish, add Easy-Peel Hard-Cooked Eggs (page 35) or Easy-Peel Soft-Cooked Eggs (recipe follows) and serve with crusty bread. This recipe will only work in an electric pressure cooker.

- 2 pounds beets, scrubbed, trimmed, and cut into ¾-inch pieces
- ½ cup water
- 1 teaspoon caraway seeds
- ½ teaspoon table salt
- 1 cup plain Greek yogurt
- 1 small garlic clove, minced to paste
- 5 ounces (5 cups) watercress, torn into bite-size pieces
- 1 tablespoon extra-virgin olive oil, divided, plus extra for drizzling
- 1 tablespoon white wine vinegar, divided
- 1 teaspoon grated orange zest plus 2 tablespoons juice
- ¼ cup hazelnuts, toasted, skinned, and chopped
- ¼ cup coarsely chopped fresh dill
  Coarse sea salt

1. Combine beets, water, caraway seeds, and table salt in pressure cooker. Lock lid in place and close pressure release valve. Using highest sauté or browning function, cook for 8 minutes. Turn off pressure cooker and quick-release pressure. Carefully remove lid, allowing steam to escape away from you.

2. Using slotted spoon, transfer beets to plate; set aside to cool slightly. Combine yogurt, garlic, and 3 tablespoons beet cooking liquid in bowl; discard remaining cooking liquid. In large bowl toss watercress with 2 teaspoons oil and 1 teaspoon vinegar. Season with table salt and pepper to taste.

3. Spread yogurt mixture over surface of serving dish. Arrange watercress on top of yogurt mixture, leaving 1-inch border of yogurt mixture. Add beets to now-empty large bowl and toss with orange zest and juice, remaining 2 teaspoons vinegar, and remaining 1 teaspoon oil. Season with table salt and pepper to taste. Arrange beets on top of watercress mixture. Drizzle with extra oil and sprinkle with hazelnuts, dill, and sea salt. Serve.

Easy-Peel Soft-Cooked Eggs

Serves 1 to 6 | **Total Time** 15 minutes
Be sure to use large eggs that have no cracks and are cold from the refrigerator.

1–6 large eggs

1. Bring 1 inch water to rolling boil in medium or large saucepan over high heat. Place eggs in steamer basket and transfer basket to saucepan. Cover, reduce heat to medium-high, and cook eggs for 6½ minutes.

2. When eggs are almost finished cooking, combine 2 cups ice cubes and 2 cups cold water in bowl. Using tongs or slotted spoon, transfer eggs to ice bath and let sit until just cool enough to handle, about 30 seconds. Peel before using. (Unpeeled soft-cooked eggs can be refrigerated for up to 3 days.)

Braised Beets with Lemon and Almonds

Serves 4 to 6 | **Total Time** 1¼ hours VEGETARIAN

WHY THIS RECIPE WORKS This simple treatment for beets maximizes their sweet, earthy flavor—with minimal mess. We partially submerged the beets in just 1¼ cups of water so that they half simmered and half steamed. In just 45 minutes, the beets were tender and their skins slipped off easily. We reduced the braising liquid and added brown sugar and vinegar to make a glossy glaze. Shallot, toasted almonds, fresh mint and thyme, and a little lemon zest finished the dish. Look for beets that are 2 to 3 inches in diameter. You can use an 11-inch straight-sided sauté pan in place of the Dutch oven in this recipe. The beets can be served warm or at room temperature. If serving at room temperature, add the nuts (or seeds, if making the variation with lime and pepitas) and fresh herbs right before serving.

Braised Bok Choy with Shiitake Mushrooms

1½ pounds beets, scrubbed, trimmed, and halved horizontally
1¼ cups water
¾ teaspoon table salt, divided
3 tablespoons distilled white vinegar
1 tablespoon packed light brown sugar
1 shallot, sliced thin
1 teaspoon grated lemon zest
¼ teaspoon pepper
½ cup whole almonds, toasted and chopped
2 tablespoons chopped fresh mint
1 teaspoon chopped fresh thyme

1. Place beets, cut side down, in single layer in Dutch oven. Add water and ¼ teaspoon salt and bring to simmer over high heat. Reduce heat to low, cover, and simmer until beets are tender and can be easily pierced with paring knife, 45 to 50 minutes.

2. Transfer beets to cutting board to cool slightly. Meanwhile increase heat to medium-high and reduce cooking liquid, stirring occasionally, until pan is almost dry, 5 to 6 minutes. Add vinegar and sugar, return to boil, and cook, stirring constantly with heat-resistant spatula, until spatula leaves wide trail when dragged through glaze, 1 to 2 minutes. Remove pan from heat.

3. Once beets are cool enough to handle, rub off skins with paper towels and cut into ½-inch wedges. Add beets, shallot, lemon zest, pepper, and remaining ½ teaspoon salt to glaze and toss to coat. Transfer to platter; sprinkle with almonds, mint, and thyme; and serve.

Braised Beets with Lime and Pepitas
Omit thyme. Substitute lime zest for lemon zest, toasted pepitas for almonds, and cilantro for mint.

Braised Beets with Orange and Walnuts
Substitute orange zest for lemon zest, walnuts for almonds, and parsley for mint.

Braised Beets with Ginger and Cashews
Substitute 4 scallions, white parts sliced thin, for shallot and green parts sliced thin on bias for mint and thyme, 1 teaspoon grated fresh ginger for lemon zest, and cashews for almonds.

Braised Bok Choy with Garlic

Serves 4 to 6 | **Total Time** 25 minutes VEGETARIAN

WHY THIS RECIPE WORKS Larger heads of bok choy take well to being braised in a covered pan with some seasoned liquid, as with kale or other sturdy greens. We first stir-fried the stalks to give them some light color and then added the greens and some broth and let the bok choy simmer away. After a few minutes, the stalks were soft but not mushy, their texture creamy and delicious, and the leaves were completely tender. Best of all, the bok choy's flavor seemed earthier and more robust. This dish is fairly brothy, making it an excellent accompaniment to seared pork chops, sautéed chicken breasts, or a firm fish like cod. You will need a 12-inch nonstick skillet with a tight-fitting lid for this recipe. To make this dish vegetarian, use vegetable broth.

2 tablespoons vegetable oil
1½ pounds bok choy, stalks halved lengthwise then cut crosswise into ½-inch pieces, greens sliced into ½-inch-thick pieces
4 garlic cloves, minced
½ cup vegetable or chicken broth
1 teaspoon unseasoned rice vinegar

1. Heat oil in 12-inch nonstick skillet over high heat until just smoking. Add bok choy stalks and cook, stirring constantly, until edges begin to turn translucent, about 5 minutes. Stir in garlic and cook until fragrant, about 30 seconds. Add broth and bok choy greens. Cover, reduce heat to medium-low, and cook, stirring occasionally, until bok choy is just tender, about 4 minutes.

2. Uncover, increase heat to medium-high, and cook for 2 minutes. Stir in vinegar and season with salt and pepper to taste. Serve.

Braised Bok Choy with Shiitake Mushrooms

Microwave 1 cup water and ¼ ounce dried shiitake mushrooms, covered, until steaming, about 1 minute. Let stand until softened, about 5 minutes. Drain mushrooms in fine-mesh strainer lined with coffee filter, reserve ½ cup strained liquid, and slice mushrooms ¼ inch thick. Substitute 1 tablespoon grated fresh ginger for 2 garlic cloves and substitute mushroom liquid and mushrooms for broth.

Skillet-Roasted Brussels Sprouts with Pomegranate and Pistachios

Skillet-Roasted Brussels Sprouts with Lemon and Pecorino Romano

Serves 4 | **Total Time** 20 minutes VEGETARIAN

WHY THIS RECIPE WORKS In 20 minutes you can make the best brussels sprouts you've ever tasted: deeply browned on one side, bright green on the other, and crisp-tender within. How? Start the sprouts in a cold skillet with plenty of oil and cook them covered. Using the lid created a steamy environment that cooked them through without needing extra moisture. Using enough oil to coat the skillet ensured that all the sprouts made full contact with fat to brown evenly. After a few minutes, we removed the lid and let the sprouts develop a substantial crust on their cut side. Look for brussels sprouts with small, tight heads no more than 1½ inches in diameter, as they're likely to be sweeter and more tender than larger sprouts. If you can find only large brussels sprouts (greater than 1½ inches in diameter), quarter them. You will need a 12-inch nonstick skillet with a tight-fitting lid.

1 pound brussels sprouts, trimmed and halved
5 tablespoons extra-virgin olive oil
1 tablespoon lemon juice
¼ teaspoon table salt
¼ cup shredded Pecorino Romano or Parmesan cheese

1. Arrange brussels sprouts in single layer cut sides down in 12-inch nonstick skillet and drizzle oil evenly over them. Cover skillet, place over medium-high heat, and cook until brussels sprouts are bright green and cut sides have started to brown, about 5 minutes.

2. Uncover and continue to cook until cut sides of brussels sprouts are deeply and evenly browned and paring knife meets little to no resistance, 2 to 3 minutes, adjusting heat and moving brussels sprouts as needed to prevent overbrowning. While brussels sprouts cook, combine lemon juice and salt in bowl.

3. Off heat, add lemon juice mixture to skillet and stir to evenly coat brussels sprouts. Season with salt and pepper to taste. Transfer to platter, sprinkle with Pecorino, and serve.

Skillet-Roasted Brussels Sprouts with Chile, Peanuts, and Mint

Omit lemon juice, pepper, and Pecorino. Combine 1 stemmed, seeded, and minced Fresno chile, 2 teaspoons lime juice, 1 teaspoon fish sauce, and ¼ teaspoon table salt in small bowl. Off heat, add chile mixture to skillet and stir to evenly coat sprouts. Season with salt to taste. Transfer sprouts to large plate, sprinkle with 2 tablespoons finely chopped dry-roasted peanuts and 2 tablespoons chopped fresh mint, and serve.

Skillet-Roasted Brussels Sprouts with Gochujang and Sesame Seeds

Gochujang is a savory Korean red chili paste that can be found in Asian markets or large supermarkets. Substitute 1 tablespoon gochujang and 1 tablespoon unseasoned rice vinegar for lemon juice and 2 teaspoons toasted sesame seeds for Pecorino.

Skillet-Roasted Brussels Sprouts with Mustard and Brown Sugar

Omit Pecorino. Substitute 1 tablespoon Dijon mustard, 1 tablespoon packed brown sugar, 2 teaspoons white wine vinegar, and ⅛ teaspoon cayenne pepper for lemon juice.

Skillet-Roasted Brussels Sprouts with Pomegranate and Pistachios

Substitute 1 tablespoon pomegranate molasses and ½ teaspoon ground cumin for lemon juice. Substitute ¼ cup shelled pistachios, toasted and chopped fine, and 2 tablespoons pomegranate seeds for Pecorino.

Brussels Sprout Gratin

Serves 6 to 8 | **Total Time** 1¼ hours VEGETARIAN

WHY THIS RECIPE WORKS Nutty roasted sprouts, a bubbling cheese sauce, and a crusty topping make for a gratin that will satisfy even those who think they don't like brussels sprouts. But we didn't want to mask the flavor of the sprouts. Instead, we sought to preserve their freshness, ensuring they became rich and nutty, not cabbage-y. To achieve this, we preroasted the brussels sprouts. We next prepared a quick creamy Mornay sauce using a combination of Gruyère and Parmesan cheeses, stirred in the sprouts, and baked them for merely 5 minutes. To add crunch, we topped the gratin with toasted panko bread crumbs and more nutty Gruyère. Look for brussels sprouts with small, tight heads that are no more than 1½ inches in diameter, as they're likely to be sweeter and more tender than larger sprouts. If you can find only large brussels sprouts (greater than 1½ inches in diameter), quarter them. To make this dish vegetarian, use vegetable broth.

2½ pounds brussels sprouts, trimmed and halved
1 tablespoon vegetable oil
¾ teaspoon plus ⅛ teaspoon table salt, divided
¾ teaspoon pepper, divided
3 tablespoons unsalted butter, divided
¼ cup panko bread crumbs
1 shallot, minced
1 garlic clove, minced
1 tablespoon all-purpose flour
1¼ cups heavy cream
¾ cup vegetable or chicken broth
2 ounces Gruyère cheese, shredded (½ cup), divided
1 ounce Parmesan cheese, grated (½ cup)
   Pinch ground nutmeg
   Pinch cayenne pepper

1. Adjust oven rack to middle position and heat oven to 450 degrees. Grease 13 by 9-inch baking dish. Toss brussels sprouts with oil, ½ teaspoon salt, and ¼ teaspoon pepper in

Braised Savoy Cabbage with Pancetta

Braised Savoy Cabbage with Pancetta

Serves 4 to 6 | **Total Time** 1¼ hours

WHY THIS RECIPE WORKS Milder than green or red cabbage with a light, feathery texture, earthy savoy cabbage is beautiful when braised, and its delicate flavor pairs well with subtly spiced pancetta. Our method for this comforting dish was straightforward: We cooked the pancetta to render some of its fat, added the cabbage and broth, and braised until tender and the liquid had evaporated. Sautéed onions bolstered the sweetness and garlic accentuated the cabbage's earthiness.

- 2 tablespoons unsalted butter
- 4 ounces pancetta, chopped fine
- 1 onion, halved and sliced thin
- 4 garlic cloves, sliced thin
- 1 head savoy cabbage (1½ pounds), cored and sliced thin
- 2 cups chicken broth
- 1 bay leaf
- 2 tablespoons fresh parsley

1. Melt butter in Dutch oven over medium heat. Add pancetta and cook until browned and fat is rendered, 5 to 7 minutes. Add onion and cook until softened and lightly browned, 5 to 7 minutes. Stir in garlic and cook until fragrant, about 30 seconds.

2. Stir in cabbage, broth, and bay leaf and bring to boil. Reduce heat to medium-low and cover, leaving lid slightly ajar. Simmer until cabbage is tender and no broth remains, about 45 minutes. Discard bay leaf. Stir in parsley and season with salt and pepper to taste. Serve.

prepared dish. Bake until sprouts are well browned and tender, 30 to 35 minutes. Transfer to wire rack and set aside to cool for at least 5 minutes or up to 30 minutes.

2. Melt 1 tablespoon butter in medium saucepan over medium heat. Add panko and cook, stirring frequently, until golden brown, about 3 minutes. Transfer to bowl and stir in ¼ teaspoon salt and ¼ teaspoon pepper; set aside. Wipe saucepan clean with paper towels.

3. Melt remaining 2 tablespoons butter in now-empty saucepan over medium heat. Add shallot and garlic and cook until just softened, about 1 minute. Stir in flour and cook for 1 minute. Slowly whisk in cream and broth, scraping up any browned bits and smoothing out any lumps, and bring to boil over medium-high heat. Once boiling, remove from heat and whisk in ¼ cup Gruyère, Parmesan, nutmeg, cayenne, remaining ⅛ teaspoon salt, and remaining ¼ teaspoon pepper until smooth.

4. Pour cream mixture over brussels sprouts in dish and stir to combine. Sprinkle evenly with panko mixture and remaining ¼ cup Gruyère. Bake until bubbling around edges and golden brown on top, 5 to 7 minutes. Let cool for 10 minutes before serving.

Celery Root Puree for a Crowd

Serves 10 to 12 | **Total Time** 50 minutes

MAKE AHEAD **VEGETARIAN**

WHY THIS RECIPE WORKS Puree celery root with touches of butter and cream and you have a stand-in for mashed potatoes that brings elegance—and intrigue—to the holiday table. Because the celery undertones fade with prolonged cooking, we processed it into tiny pieces before simmering it with a bit of baking soda to hasten their breakdown, giving us fully tender celery root with a delightful mellow flavor. Incorporating one russet potato provided just enough body. Serve as is or add our Shallot, Sage, and Black Pepper Topping (page 146).

2½–3 pounds celery root, peeled and cut into 2-inch pieces
     1 large russet potato (about 10 ounces), peeled and cut into 2-inch pieces
     2 tablespoons unsalted butter
     2 cups water
     ¾ teaspoon table salt
     ¼ teaspoon baking soda
     ⅔ cup heavy cream
     2 tablespoons minced fresh chives, parsley, chervil, or tarragon

1. Working in 2 batches, pulse celery root in food processor until finely chopped, about 20 pulses per batch; transfer to bowl. Pulse potato in processor until finely chopped, about 10 pulses, and add to bowl with celery root. (You should have about 9 cups chopped vegetables.)

2. Melt butter in large saucepan over medium heat. Stir in celery root–potato mixture, water, salt, and baking soda. Cover and cook, stirring often (mixture will stick but cleans up easily), until vegetables are very soft and translucent and mixture resembles applesauce, about 30 minutes.

3. Uncover and cook, stirring vigorously to further break down vegetables and thicken remaining cooking liquid, about 1 minute. Transfer celery root mixture to clean, dry food processor. Add cream and process until smooth, about 40 seconds. Season with salt to taste. Transfer to bowl, sprinkle with chives, and serve. (Ungarnished puree can be cooled and refrigerated for up to 2 days. Before serving, microwave puree on medium-high power in covered bowl, stirring often, until hot throughout, 7 to 10 minutes.)

Celery Root Puree for a Crowd

PEELING CELERY ROOT

1. Using chef's knife, cut ½ inch from both root end and opposite end of celery root.

2. Turn celery root so 1 cut side rests on board. To peel, cut from top to bottom, rotating celery root while removing wide strips of skin.

Shallot, Sage, and Black Pepper Topping

Makes about 6 tablespoons
Total Time 10 minutes

For the best results, do not substitute dried sage.

     3 tablespoons unsalted butter
     1 small shallot, minced
1½ tablespoons minced fresh sage
     ½ teaspoon pepper
     ¼ teaspoon table salt

Melt butter in 8-inch nonstick skillet over medium-high heat. Add shallot and sage; cook, stirring frequently, until shallot is golden and sage is crisp, about 3 minutes. Off heat, stir in pepper and salt. Sprinkle topping over celery root and serve.

Southern-Style Collard Greens

Serves 6 to 8 | **Total Time** 2¼ hours

WHY THIS RECIPE WORKS This Southern recipe is made by braising collard greens with a salty smoked pork product. Over a long cooking time, the pork and greens intermingle and turn the cooking water into a supersavory pot liquor (or "pot likker"). We found that two smoked ham hocks provided the best deeply smoky pork flavor. Plus, after a long braising time, it was easy to pull the savory little chunks of meat off the hocks to add back to the greens. If you can't find ham hocks, you can substitute six slices of bacon and 3 ounces of ham steak cut into ½-inch pieces. Be sure to remove the rind from the ham before cutting it into pieces. Add the bacon and ham in place of the ham hocks in step 2, but discard the bacon before serving. Do not drain off the cooking liquid before serving. This flavorful, savory pot liquor should be sipped while eating the collards. Any leftover pot liquor can be used as a soup base.

- 2 pounds collard greens
- 2 tablespoons unsalted butter
- 1 onion, chopped
- 6 cups water
- 2 (12-ounce) smoked ham hocks
- 3 garlic cloves, smashed and peeled
- 2¼ teaspoons table salt
- 2 teaspoons sugar
- ⅛ teaspoon red pepper flakes
  Hot sauce

1. Adjust oven rack to lower-middle position and heat oven to 300 degrees. Trim collard stems to base of leaves; discard trimmings. Cut leaves into roughly 2-inch pieces. Place collard greens in large bowl and cover with water. Swish with your hand to remove grit. Repeat with fresh water, as needed, until grit no longer appears in bottom of bowl. Remove collard greens from water and set aside (you needn't dry them).

2. Melt butter in large Dutch oven over medium heat. Add onion and cook until lightly browned, 6 to 8 minutes. Add water, ham hocks, garlic, salt, sugar, and pepper flakes and bring to boil over high heat. Add collard greens (pot may be full) and stir until collard greens wilt slightly, about 1 minute. Cover, transfer to oven, and cook until collard greens are very tender, about 1½ hours.

3. Transfer ham hocks to cutting board and let cool for 10 minutes. Remove meat from ham hocks, chop, and return to pot; discard skin and bones. Season collard greens with salt to taste. Serve with hot sauce.

Corn Pudding

Serves 6 to 8 | **Total Time** 1 hour `VEGETARIAN`

WHY THIS RECIPE WORKS Recipes for this rustic, soufflé-like casserole, a traditional part of many a Thanksgiving spread, often call for boxed corn muffin mix and canned cream corn, but we wanted a fresher take. We swapped out the creamed corn for frozen corn kernels, which are still convenient but have better texture and more flavor than canned. To ensure a silky base brimming with the flavor of sweet corn, we buzzed some of the kernels with cream in a blender. In place of the boxed muffin mix, we simply combined flour, cornmeal, salt, sugar, and a touch of baking soda; for rich flavor and light texture, we added sour cream and melted butter. The sweet spot for baking turned out to be about 35 minutes in a 400-degree oven—this was just enough time to set the pudding without drying it out. Note that the corn is divided after being microwaved. You can substitute 1 pound of fresh corn kernels (from about four cobs) for the frozen corn, if desired. To double this recipe, bake the pudding in a 13 by 9-inch baking dish and increase the baking time to 45 to 50 minutes.

- 1 pound frozen corn
- ¾ cup heavy cream
- ½ cup (2½ ounces) all-purpose flour
- ⅓ cup (1⅔ ounces) cornmeal
- ¼ cup (1¾ ounces) sugar
- 1¼ teaspoons salt
- ¼ teaspoon baking soda
- 1 cup sour cream
- 6 tablespoons unsalted butter, melted
- 1 large egg, lightly beaten

1. Adjust oven rack to upper-middle position and heat oven to 400 degrees. Grease 8-inch square baking dish. Combine corn and ¼ cup water in microwave-safe bowl. Cover and microwave until corn is tender, about 7 minutes. Drain corn in colander.

2. Combine cream and 1½ cups corn in blender and process until coarse puree forms, about 30 seconds. Whisk flour, cornmeal, sugar, salt, and baking soda together in large bowl. Whisk sour cream, melted butter, egg, pureed corn mixture, and remaining corn together in separate bowl. Whisk sour cream mixture into flour mixture until combined. Transfer batter to prepared dish.

3. Bake until edges of pudding are lightly browned and top is slightly puffed, about 35 minutes. Let cool on wire rack for 10 minutes. Serve warm.

Roasted Fennel with Rye Crumble

Serves 4 to 6 | **Total Time** 1¼ hours `VEGETARIAN`

WHY THIS RECIPE WORKS Subtly caramelized wedges of perfectly roasted fennel make an elegant presentation, especially when capped with something a little indulgent and surprising: a hearty rye bread crumble starring a generous amount of earthy caraway seeds and nutty Parmesan. To start, we cut fennel bulbs into 1-inch-thick wedges through the core before tossing them in a mixture of butter, lemon juice, and thyme and shingling them evenly into a baking dish. Covering the dish with aluminum foil for the first half-hour of roasting ensured that the edges didn't dry out. Once the fennel wedges were nearly tender, we uncovered the dish and sprinkled the topping evenly over the top, baking until the crumble was crisped and deep golden brown and the fennel perfectly tender. Do not core the fennel bulb before cutting it into wedges; the core helps to hold the layers of fennel together during cooking.

6 tablespoons unsalted butter, melted, divided
1 tablespoon lemon juice
1¼ teaspoons table salt, divided
½ teaspoon minced fresh thyme or ¼ teaspoon dried
¼ teaspoon plus ⅛ teaspoon pepper, divided
2 fennel bulbs, stalks discarded, bulbs halved and cut into 1-inch wedges
3 ounces rye bread, cut into 1-inch pieces (3 cups)
1 ounce Parmesan cheese, grated (½ cup)
1 teaspoon caraway seeds

1. Adjust oven rack to middle position and heat oven to 425 degrees. Whisk 3 tablespoons melted butter, lemon juice, 1 teaspoon salt, thyme, and ¼ teaspoon pepper together in large bowl. Add fennel and toss to coat. Arrange fennel cut side down in single layer in 13 by 9-inch baking dish. Cover dish with aluminum foil and bake until fennel is nearly tender, 25 to 30 minutes.

2. Meanwhile, pulse bread, Parmesan, caraway seeds, remaining 3 tablespoons melted butter, remaining ¼ teaspoon salt, and remaining ⅛ teaspoon pepper in food processor to coarse crumbs, about 20 pulses; set aside.

3. Remove foil from dish and sprinkle fennel with bread-crumb mixture. Continue to bake, uncovered, until fennel is tender and topping is browned and crisp, 15 to 20 minutes. Let cool for 5 minutes before serving.

Roasted Fennel with Rye Crumble

Extra-Crunchy Green Bean Casserole

Extra-Crunchy Green Bean Casserole

Serves 6 to 8 | **Total Time** 1½ hours `MAKE AHEAD`

WHY THIS RECIPE WORKS For many, the Thanksgiving table is incomplete without green bean casserole, but this old friend could use a new suit. We looked to modernize the dish with a crunchier topping and a sauce with an extra note of complexity. We jump-started the beans in the microwave, which shortened the bake time. For the sauce, we skipped canned soup, browning mushrooms to develop deep flavor and then stirring in broth, cream, and flour. Adding panko to the fried onions gave them crunch, and we didn't bake them with the beans. The onions were crunchier when not saturated with sauce, so we sprinkled them on after baking. White mushrooms can be substituted for cremini.

TOPPING

½ cup panko bread crumbs
1 tablespoon unsalted butter, melted
2½ cups canned fried onions

CASSEROLE

2 pounds green beans, trimmed and cut into 1-inch pieces
3 tablespoons unsalted butter
1 pound cremini mushrooms, trimmed and sliced thin
1 tablespoon minced fresh thyme or 1 teaspoon dried
2 garlic cloves, minced
1½ teaspoons table salt
½ teaspoon pepper
¼ cup all-purpose flour
1½ cups chicken broth
1½ cups heavy cream
½ cup dry white wine

1. FOR THE TOPPING Combine panko and melted butter in bowl. Microwave, stirring occasionally, until panko is golden brown, about 2 minutes. Let cool completely, then stir in fried onions; set aside.

2. FOR THE CASSEROLE Adjust oven rack to middle position and heat oven to 400 degrees. Combine green beans and ½ cup water in large bowl. Cover and microwave until green beans are just tender, about 8 minutes, stirring halfway through microwaving. Drain green beans in colander; set aside.

3. Melt butter in 12-inch nonstick skillet over medium-high heat. Add mushrooms, thyme, garlic, salt, and pepper and cook until liquid is nearly evaporated, 6 to 8 minutes.

4. Stir in flour and cook for 1 minute. Slowly whisk in broth, cream, and wine, scraping up any browned bits and smoothing out any lumps, and bring to boil. Cook, stirring occasionally, until sauce has thickened, 4 to 6 minutes. Transfer green beans to 13 by 9-inch baking dish. Pour sauce over green beans and toss to combine. (After cooling completely, casserole can be covered with foil and refrigerated for up to 24 hours. To serve, bake, covered until green beans are heated through and completely tender, about 40 minutes. Uncover and bake until edges begin to brown, about 10 minutes.)

5. Bake until bubbling and green beans are completely tender, about 25 minutes. Remove from oven, top with fried-onion mixture, and let cool for 10 minutes. Serve.

Creamed Kale with Chestnuts

Serves 8 | **Total Time** 55 minutes

WHY THIS RECIPE WORKS In this luxurious update on creamed spinach, we dress up earthy kale with a rich cream sauce and meaty chestnuts. Wilting the kale little by little allowed us to fit a hefty 3½ pounds into one pot, and using chicken broth to simmer the kale added savory depth. A full 1½ cups of cream gave the kale richness and silky texture, and grated Parmesan thickened the sauce and infused the kale with nutty, cheesy flavor, while fresh nutmeg and a squeeze of lemon added the finishing touches. You will need approximately six bunches of curly kale for this recipe (it cooks down considerably). If you wash the kale before you cook it, be sure to dry it well, as overly wet kale will alter the recipe's cooking times. Buy chestnuts that are roasted and peeled, not packed in water or syrup. This recipe is easily cut in half to serve four; wilting the kale in step 1 will take about half the time.

2¾ cups chicken broth, divided
1¾ teaspoons table salt, divided
3½ pounds curly kale, stemmed and chopped
4 tablespoons unsalted butter
3 cups (14 ounces) peeled cooked chestnuts
5 shallots, sliced into thin rings
1 teaspoon pepper
4 garlic cloves, minced
½ teaspoon red pepper flakes
1½ cups heavy cream
2 ounces Parmesan cheese, grated (1 cup)
¼ teaspoon ground nutmeg
Lemon wedges

1. Bring 2 cups broth and ¾ teaspoon salt to boil in large Dutch oven over high heat. Gradually add kale, covering pot and letting each addition wilt to make room before adding more, using tongs to turn and stir (this will take about 10 minutes). When all kale has been added to pot, reduce heat to medium-high, cover, and cook, stirring occasionally, until kale is fully wilted and bottom of pot is nearly dry, 5 to 10 minutes; transfer kale to bowl. Wipe pot clean with paper towels.

2. Melt butter in now-empty pot over medium heat. Add chestnuts, shallots, pepper, and remaining 1 teaspoon salt and cook, uncovered, until shallots are softened, 5 to 7 minutes. Add garlic and pepper flakes and cook until fragrant, about 30 seconds. Add remaining ¾ cup broth and bring to boil, scraping up any browned bits. Add cream and return to boil.

3. Add kale and cook, stirring occasionally, until slightly thickened, 7 to 9 minutes. Off heat, stir in Parmesan and nutmeg. Season with salt and pepper to taste. Transfer to serving dish. Serve, passing lemon wedges separately.

Roasted Kohlrabi with Crunchy Seeds

Slow-Cooker Braised Kale with Garlic and Chorizo

Serves 4 to 6 | **Cooking Time** 7 to 8 hours on Low or 4 to 5 hours on High

WHY THIS RECIPE WORKS Using the slow cooker to prepare hearty kale helps to turn the sturdy green meltingly tender and tempers its assertive flavor. With the texture right where we wanted it, all we had to do was come up with a few flavorful ingredients to add to the pot. We liked a simple combination of chorizo and garlic, which gave these earthy greens a meaty, spicy kick. You will need a 5- to 7-quart slow cooker for this recipe.

    8 ounces Spanish-style chorizo sausage, halved
       lengthwise and sliced ½ inch thick
    2 garlic cloves, minced
    1 tablespoon extra-virgin olive oil
 1½   cups chicken broth
    ¼ teaspoon table salt
    2 pounds kale, stemmed and cut into 1-inch pieces

1. Lightly coat slow cooker with vegetable oil spray. Microwave chorizo, garlic, and oil in bowl, stirring occasionally, until fragrant, about 1 minute; transfer to prepared slow cooker. Stir in broth and salt.

2. Microwave half of kale in covered bowl until slightly wilted, about 5 minutes; transfer to slow cooker. Stir in remaining kale, cover, and cook until kale is tender, 7 to 8 hours on low or 4 to 5 hours on high. Season with salt and pepper to taste. Serve. (Kale can be held on warm or low setting for up to 2 hours.)

Roasted Kohlrabi with Crunchy Seeds

Serves 4 | **Total Time** 45 minutes VEGETARIAN

WHY THIS RECIPE WORKS Kohlrabi is a member of the turnip family with a flavor reminiscent of broccoli and celery root. A simple, quick roast with a trio of flavorful seeds is an excellent way to bring mild-tasting kohlrabi to the dinner table. A very hot oven browned the kohlrabi beautifully, and the ¾-inch pieces cooked in just 20 minutes. Lining the baking sheet with foil prevented the kohlrabi from sticking to the pan. As the kohlrabi roasts, make sure to shake the pan once or twice to encourage even browning.

2 tablespoons extra-virgin olive oil
2 teaspoons sesame seeds
1 teaspoon poppy seeds
½ teaspoon fennel seeds, cracked
½ teaspoon table salt
¼ teaspoon pepper
2 pounds kohlrabi, trimmed, peeled, and
  cut into ¾-inch pieces

1. Adjust oven rack to middle position and heat oven to 450 degrees. Combine oil, sesame seeds, poppy seeds, fennel seeds, salt, and pepper in large bowl. Add kohlrabi and toss to coat.

2. Spread kohlrabi onto aluminum foil–lined rimmed baking sheet and roast, stirring occasionally, until browned and tender, about 20 minutes. Season with salt and pepper to taste. Serve.

NOTES FROM THE TEST KITCHEN

BUYING AND PREPARING KOHLRABI
Visually striking kohlrabi is hard to overlook, with pale green or lavender bulbs anchoring antenna-like stalks. Look for bulbs about the size of an orange, as larger kohlrabi may be woody or spongy. If you purchase kohlrabi with stalks and leaves attached, separate them before storing both in the refrigerator. To peel the bulbs, use a paring knife, making sure to peel away the outer ⅛ inch so that both the skin and the fibrous green parts underneath the skin are removed and only the white flesh remains.

Sautéed Mushrooms with Red Wine and Rosemary

Serves 4 | **Total Time** 30 minutes

WHY THIS RECIPE WORKS This versatile recipe works for sautéing any variety of mushroom, or a combination. While mushrooms are typically cooked in oil or butter until their moisture releases, we found that mushrooms released their moisture more quickly when first steamed in a small amount of water. The presteamed mushrooms collapsed and didn't absorb much oil; just ½ teaspoon was needed to achieve good browning. And because we used so little fat to sauté the mushrooms, we were able to sauce them with a butter-based reduction without making them overly rich. Use one variety

of mushroom or a combination. Stem and halve portobello mushrooms and cut each half crosswise into ½-inch pieces. Trim white or cremini mushrooms; quarter them if large or medium or halve them if small. Tear trimmed oyster mushrooms into 1- to 1½-inch pieces. Stem shiitake mushrooms; quarter large caps and halve small caps. Cut trimmed maitake (hen-of-the-woods) mushrooms into 1- to 1½-inch pieces.

1¼ pounds mushrooms, trimmed
¼ cup water
½ teaspoon vegetable oil
1 tablespoon unsalted butter
1 shallot, minced
1 teaspoon minced fresh rosemary
¼ teaspoon table salt
¼ teaspoon pepper
¼ cup red wine
1 tablespoon cider vinegar
½ cup chicken broth

1. Cook mushrooms and water in 12-inch nonstick skillet over high heat, stirring occasionally, until skillet is almost dry and mushrooms begin to sizzle, 4 to 8 minutes. Reduce heat to medium-high. Add oil and toss until mushrooms are evenly coated. Continue to cook, stirring occasionally, until mushrooms are well browned, 4 to 8 minutes. Reduce heat to medium.

2. Push mushrooms to sides of skillet. Add butter to center. When butter has melted, add shallot, rosemary, salt, and pepper to center and cook, stirring constantly, until aromatic, about 30 seconds. Add wine and vinegar and stir mixture into mushrooms. Cook, stirring occasionally, until liquid has evaporated, 2 to 3 minutes. Add broth and cook, stirring occasionally, until glaze is reduced by half, about 3 minutes. Season with salt and pepper to taste, and serve.

Sautéed Mushrooms with Mustard and Parsley
Omit rosemary. Substitute 1 tablespoon Dijon mustard for wine and increase vinegar to 1½ tablespoons (liquid will take only 1 to 2 minutes to evaporate). Stir in 2 tablespoons chopped fresh parsley before serving.

Sautéed Mushrooms with Soy, Scallion, and Ginger
Substitute 1 thinly sliced scallion for shallot and grated fresh ginger for rosemary. Omit salt. Substitute 2 tablespoons soy sauce for wine and sherry vinegar for cider vinegar.

Roasted King Trumpet Mushrooms

Serves 4 | **Total Time** 45 minutes VEGETARIAN

WHY THIS RECIPE WORKS King trumpet mushrooms (or king oyster mushrooms) have little aroma or flavor when raw, but when cooked they become deeply savory, with the meaty texture of squid or tender octopus. We wanted to highlight this special quality by preparing these mushrooms almost like a piece of meat. We started by halving and cross-hatching each mushroom, creating attractive "fillets," and then salting them and letting them sit briefly. Roasting the mushrooms cut side down in a hot oven resulted in plump, juicy, well-seasoned mushrooms with a nicely browned exterior crust. These mushrooms are delicious with just a squeeze of lemon. But to gild the lily, we also developed two potent sauces (recipes follow). Look for trumpet mushrooms that are 3 to 4 ounces in size.

1¾ pounds king trumpet mushrooms
½ teaspoon table salt
4 tablespoons unsalted butter, melted
   Lemon wedges

1. Adjust oven rack to lowest position and heat oven to 500 degrees. Trim bottom ½ inch of mushroom stems, then halve mushrooms lengthwise. Cut ¹⁄₁₆-inch-deep slits on cut side of mushrooms, spaced ½ inch apart, in crosshatch pattern. Sprinkle cut side of mushrooms with salt and let sit for 15 minutes.

2. Brush mushrooms evenly with melted butter, season with pepper to taste, and arrange cut side down on rimmed baking sheet. Roast until mushrooms are browned on cut side, 20 to 24 minutes. Transfer to serving platter. Serve with lemon wedges.

NOTES FROM THE TEST KITCHEN

SHOPPING FOR MUSHROOMS

We recommend buying loose rather than packaged mushrooms so you can inspect their condition. Pay close attention to the following four traits: cap size and condition, moisture, texture, and aroma. Caps should be whole and intact with no discoloration or dry, shriveled patches. Exteriors should seem faintly damp but never moist or slimy, and mushrooms should boast a springy, light—not spongy—texture. Finally, fresh mushrooms should smell intensely sweet and earthy; avoid those that smell sour or fishy.

Red Wine–Miso Sauce

Makes about ⅓ cup | **Total Time** 35 minutes

1 cup dry red wine
1 cup vegetable broth
2 teaspoons sugar
½ teaspoon soy sauce
1 tablespoon unsalted butter
5 teaspoons miso

Bring wine, broth, sugar, and soy sauce to simmer in 10-inch skillet over medium heat and cook until reduced to ⅓ cup, 20 to 25 minutes. Off heat, whisk in butter and miso until smooth.

Browned Butter–Lemon Vinaigrette

Makes about 6 tablespoons
Total Time 10 minutes

4 tablespoons unsalted butter
2 tablespoons lemon juice
1 teaspoon Dijon mustard
1 teaspoon maple syrup
¼ teaspoon table salt
⅛ teaspoon pepper

Melt butter in 10-inch skillet over medium heat. Cook, swirling constantly, until butter is dark golden brown and has nutty aroma, 3 to 5 minutes. Off heat, whisk in lemon juice, mustard, maple syrup, salt, and pepper.

Sautéed Parsnips with Ginger, Maple, and Fennel Seeds

Serves 4 | **Total Time** 25 minutes VEGETARIAN

WHY THIS RECIPE WORKS Sautéing parsnips is dead-easy. We cut them into uniform sticks, used a smoking-hot pan, and employed minimal stirring to caramelize and cook the parsnips through in just minutes. Since parsnips have warm spice and licorice-like notes, we made a glaze that brought out those qualities and had the perfect sweet, salty, and tart balance. You can substitute anise seeds for fennel. Look for parsnips no wider than 1 inch at their base, or you may need to remove their fibrous cores before cooking.

2 tablespoons soy sauce
2 tablespoons balsamic vinegar
1 tablespoon maple syrup
1½ teaspoons fennel seeds
2 tablespoons minced fresh ginger
1 teaspoon plus 2 tablespoons vegetable oil, divided
1½ pounds parsnips, peeled and cut into 2-inch-long by ½-inch-wide matchsticks

1. Stir soy sauce, vinegar, maple syrup, and fennel seeds together in bowl; set aside. Combine ginger and 1 teaspoon oil in separate bowl; set aside.

2. Heat remaining 2 tablespoons oil in 12-inch skillet over medium-high heat until just smoking. Add parsnips and cook, stirring occasionally, until well charred and crisp-tender, 5 to 7 minutes.

3. Push parsnips to sides of skillet. Add ginger mixture to center and cook, mashing mixture into pan, until fragrant, about 30 seconds. Stir ginger into parsnips. Add soy mixture and toss to coat parsnips; cook until liquid is reduced to syrupy glaze, about 15 seconds. Serve immediately.

Creamy Mashed Potatoes

Serves 8 to 10 | **Total Time** 45 minutes VEGETARIAN

WHY THIS RECIPE WORKS These potatoes are so lush and creamy, they can stand on their own—no gravy necessary. For a substantial mash, the texture of Yukon Golds was perfect—less fluffy than russets but lighter than red potatoes. When it comes to cooking perfect potatoes, there's a fine line between creamy and gluey. Starting the potatoes in cold water helped them cook evenly, intensifying their creamy texture without releasing too much starch into the water. Returning the boiled and drained potatoes to the Dutch oven for a brief cook over a low flame helped further evaporate any excess moisture. Using 1½ sticks of butter and 1½ cups of heavy cream gave the potatoes luxurious flavor and richness without making the mash too thin. If you prefer an absolutely smooth puree, you can use a food mill or ricer rather than a potato masher in step 2.

4 pounds Yukon Gold potatoes, peeled, quartered, and sliced ¾ inch thick
Table salt for cooking potatoes
1½ cups warm heavy cream
12 tablespoons unsalted butter, melted

Roasted King
Trumpet Mushrooms

Sautéed Parsnips with Ginger, Maple, and Fennel Seeds

1. Place potatoes and 1 tablespoon salt in Dutch oven; add water to cover by 1 inch. Bring to boil, then reduce to simmer and cook until potatoes are fall-apart tender (potatoes break apart when paring knife is inserted and gently wiggled), 20 to 25 minutes.

2. Drain potatoes and return to now-empty pot. Stir over low heat until potatoes are thoroughly dried, 1 to 2 minutes. Using potato masher, mash potatoes until few small lumps remain. Combine warm cream and melted butter in bowl, then gently fold mixture into potatoes with rubber spatula until combined and potatoes are thick and creamy. Season with salt and pepper to taste. Serve.

Cheesy Mashed Potato Casserole

Serves 10 to 12 | **Total Time** 1½ hours, plus 30 minutes cooling   MAKE AHEAD   VEGETARIAN

WHY THIS RECIPE WORKS Typically, mashed potatoes are made and served right away—which can sometimes make them a source of stress when cooking for a high-pressure holiday. But most of the work for a creamy mashed potato casserole can be done ahead of time and, what's more, it comes loaded with cheese and a crisp topping. After boiling and draining a load of potatoes, we added two full sticks of butter and got to mashing. The butter prevented the potatoes from turning gluey (and made them taste phenomenal). To gild the lily, we stirred in melty mozzarella and nutty Gruyère cheese and then topped the dish with bread crumbs and more cheese, which turned crisp and golden in the oven. If made ahead, the casserole will be slightly firmer and more set than a freshly made one; we liked both versions. Leftovers can be gently warmed in a low oven or on the stovetop; they're excellent the next morning with a poached egg on top.

POTATOES
- 4 pounds Yukon Gold potatoes, peeled and sliced ½ inch thick
- 1 teaspoon table salt, plus salt for cooking potatoes
- 16 tablespoons unsalted butter, cut into 16 pieces
- 1½ cups half-and-half
- 1 teaspoon pepper
- 6 ounces Gruyère cheese, shredded (1½ cups)
- 6 ounces whole-milk mozzarella cheese, shredded (1½ cups)
- ½ cup minced fresh chives

Cheesy Mashed Potato Casserole

Potato Galette

TOPPING
¾ cup panko bread crumbs
2 ounces Gruyère cheese, shredded (½ cup)
2 tablespoons unsalted butter, melted

1. FOR THE POTATOES Adjust oven rack to upper-middle position and heat oven to 400 degrees. Place potatoes and 2 tablespoons salt in Dutch oven, add water to cover by 1 inch, and bring to boil over high heat. Reduce heat to medium and simmer until potatoes are tender and can be easily pierced with paring knife, 18 to 20 minutes.

2. Drain potatoes and return them to pot. Add butter and mash with potato masher until smooth and no lumps remain. Stir in half-and-half, pepper, and salt until fully combined. Stir in Gruyère, mozzarella, and chives until incorporated. Transfer potato mixture to 13 by 9-inch baking dish and smooth top with spatula.

3. FOR THE TOPPING Combine bread crumbs, Gruyère, and melted butter in bowl. Sprinkle topping evenly over potato mixture.

4. Bake until casserole is heated through and topping is crisp and golden brown, about 30 minutes. Let cool for 30 minutes. Serve.

To make ahead At end of step 2, let potato mixture cool completely in dish, cover tightly with plastic wrap, and refrigerate for up to 3 days. When ready to bake, remove plastic, cover dish tightly with aluminum foil, and bake for 25 minutes. Remove foil and proceed with step 3.

Cheesy Mashed Potato Casserole for Six
Halve measurements of all ingredients. In step 1, cook potatoes in large saucepan. In step 2, transfer potatoes to 8-inch square baking dish.

Potato Galette
Serves 6 to 8 | **Total Time** 1¼ hours VEGETARIAN

WHY THIS RECIPE WORKS With its crispy, scalloped, golden-brown exterior and layered presentation, a potato galette is a showstopper side or brunch dish. For even cooking and great browning, we began ours on the stovetop and then slid the pan onto the bottom rack of a hot oven. To keep the potato rounds from sliding around when we sliced our galette, we created a binder to hold them together by mixing cornstarch with the butter that coated the potatoes. Compressing the galette using a cake pan filled with pie weights for the first 20 minutes of cooking helped keep the dish cohesive while the cornstarch worked its magic. Slicing the potatoes ⅛ inch thick is crucial for the success of this dish: Use a mandoline, a V-slicer, or a food processor fitted with a ⅛-inch-thick slicing blade. You will need a 10-inch ovensafe nonstick skillet for this recipe. A pound of dried beans or rice can be substituted for the pie weights.

2½ pounds Yukon Gold potatoes, unpeeled, sliced ⅛ inch thick
5 tablespoons unsalted butter, melted, divided
1 tablespoon cornstarch
1½ teaspoons chopped fresh rosemary
1 teaspoon table salt
½ teaspoon pepper

1. Adjust oven rack to lowest position and heat oven to 450 degrees. Place potatoes in large bowl and fill with cold water. Swirl to remove excess starch, then drain in colander. Spread potatoes on towels and dry thoroughly.

2. Whisk 4 tablespoons melted butter, cornstarch, rosemary, salt, and pepper together in large bowl. Add potatoes and toss until thoroughly coated. Add remaining 1 tablespoon melted butter to 10-inch ovensafe nonstick skillet and swirl to coat. Place 1 potato slice in center of skillet, then overlap slices in circle around center slice, followed by outer circle of overlapping slices. Gently place remaining sliced potatoes on top of first layer, arranging so they form even thickness.

3. Place skillet over medium-high heat and cook until potatoes are sizzling and slices around edge of cake start to turn translucent, about 5 minutes. Spray 12-inch square of aluminum foil with vegetable oil spray. Place foil, sprayed side down, on top of potatoes. Place 9-inch round cake pan on top of foil and fill with 2 cups pie weights. Firmly press down on cake pan to compress potatoes. Transfer skillet to oven and bake for 20 minutes.

4. Remove cake pan and foil from skillet. Continue to cook until paring knife can be inserted in center of cake with no resistance, 20 to 25 minutes. Being careful of hot skillet handle, return skillet to medium heat on stovetop and cook, gently shaking pan (skillet handle will be hot), until galette releases from sides of skillet, 2 to 3 minutes. Carefully slide galette onto large plate, place cutting board over galette, and gently invert plate and cutting board together, then remove plate. Using serrated knife, gently cut galette into wedges and serve immediately.

Braised Red Potatoes with Lemon and Chives

Serves 4 to 6 | **Total Time** 50 minutes `VEGETARIAN`

WHY THIS RECIPE WORKS Braising brings out the best in red potatoes, giving them crispy exteriors and creamy interiors. Our stovetop braising method yields a side dish that features the benefits of both boiling and roasting. We first simmered halved small red potatoes in water with some butter, thyme, and garlic cloves—removing the garlic cloves after they'd softened. By the time the water evaporated, the potatoes were creamy on the inside and starting to crisp up on the outside as they began to fry in the butter that was left behind in the pan. To bolster the potatoes' flavor, we then minced the reserved softened garlic cloves and added them back to the pan along with lemon juice and chives for brightness and pepper for a hint of heat. Use small red potatoes measuring 1 to 2 inches in diameter. You will need a 12-inch nonstick skillet with a tight-fitting lid.

1½ pounds small red potatoes, unpeeled, halved
2 cups water
3 tablespoons unsalted butter
3 garlic cloves, peeled
3 sprigs fresh thyme
¾ teaspoon table salt
1 teaspoon lemon juice
¼ teaspoon pepper
2 tablespoons minced fresh chives

1. Arrange potatoes in single layer, cut side down, in 12-inch nonstick skillet. Add water, butter, garlic, thyme sprigs, and salt and bring to simmer over medium-high heat. Reduce heat to medium, cover, and simmer until potatoes are just tender, about 15 minutes.

2. Remove lid and use slotted spoon to transfer garlic to cutting board; discard thyme sprigs. Increase heat to medium-high and simmer vigorously, swirling skillet occasionally, until water evaporates and butter starts to sizzle, 15 to 20 minutes. When cool enough to handle, mince garlic to paste. Transfer paste to bowl and stir in lemon juice and pepper.

3. Continue to cook potatoes, swirling skillet frequently, until butter browns and cut sides of potatoes turn spotty brown, 4 to 6 minutes. Off heat, add chives and garlic mixture and toss to coat thoroughly. Serve.

Braised Red Potatoes with Dijon and Tarragon
Substitute 2 teaspoons Dijon mustard for lemon juice and 1 tablespoon minced fresh tarragon for chives.

Braised Red Potatoes with Miso and Scallions
Reduce salt to ½ teaspoon. Substitute 1 tablespoon red miso paste for lemon juice and 3 thinly sliced scallions for chives.

Slow-Cooker Lemon-Herb Fingerling Potatoes

Serves 4 to 6 | **Cooking Time** 5 to 6 hours on Low or 3 to 4 hours on High `VEGETARIAN`

WHY THIS RECIPE WORKS Cooking small whole potatoes in the slow cooker requires no prep work, frees up your stove, and turns out perfectly tender little spuds. For this supereasy and attractive side dish, we turned to fingerlings. We could put them into the slow cooker without any liquid whatsoever, and they retained their delicate sweetness without a hint of mushiness. To enhance their flavor, we added some olive oil, garlic, and scallions. Unlike with some other slow-cooker potato dishes, they cooked through properly without our having to cover them first with a sheet of parchment paper. Look for fingerling potatoes about 3 inches long and 1 inch in diameter. You will need a 5- to 7-quart slow cooker for this recipe. This recipe can easily be doubled in a 7-quart slow cooker, but you will need to increase the cooking time range by 1 hour. This recipe will only work in a traditional slow cooker.

2 pounds fingerling potatoes, unpeeled
2 tablespoons extra-virgin olive oil, divided
2 scallions, white parts minced, green parts sliced thin
3 garlic cloves, minced
1 teaspoon table salt
¼ teaspoon pepper
1 tablespoon chopped fresh parsley
1 teaspoon grated lemon zest plus 1 tablespoon juice

1. Combine potatoes, 1 tablespoon oil, scallion whites, garlic, salt, and pepper in slow cooker. Cover and cook until potatoes are tender, 5 to 6 hours on low or 3 to 4 hours on high.

2. Stir in parsley, lemon zest and juice, scallion greens, and remaining 1 tablespoon oil. Season with salt and pepper to taste. Serve.

Cider-Glazed Root Vegetables with Apple and Tarragon

Serves 8 | **Total Time** 55 minutes `VEGETARIAN`

WHY THIS RECIPE WORKS Ideally suited for a mixture of seasonal root vegetables, this simple recipe combines the deep flavors of roasting with a lightly sweetened glaze. We started by cutting the carrots slightly smaller than the other vegetables for even cooking. Then, by caramelizing the vegetables in butter and deglazing with hard cider, we created a glaze that tasted bright and flavorful. A final addition of a diced Granny Smith apple and fresh tarragon completed the flavor profile. If you prefer to use an equal amount of nonalcoholic sparkling or regular cider, reduce the sugar to 1 tablespoon.

- 4 tablespoons unsalted butter, divided
- 1 pound carrots, peeled and cut into ½-inch pieces
- 12 ounces parsnips, peeled and cut into ¾-inch pieces
- 12 ounces turnips, peeled and cut into ¾-inch pieces
- 3 shallots, peeled and halved
- 2½ cups hard cider
- 3 tablespoons sugar
- 1½ teaspoons table salt
- 1 Granny Smith apple, cored and cut into ½-inch pieces
- 2 tablespoons chopped fresh tarragon
- 2 teaspoons cider vinegar

1. Melt 1 tablespoon butter in 12-inch skillet over medium-high heat. Add carrots, parsnips, turnips, and shallots and cook until lightly browned, about 5 minutes. Add cider, sugar, salt, and remaining 3 tablespoons butter and bring to boil. Reduce heat to medium-low, cover, and cook until vegetables are just tender, 7 to 10 minutes, stirring occasionally.

2. Uncover, increase heat to medium, and cook until vegetables are fully tender, about 13 minutes, stirring occasionally. Stir in apple and continue to cook until cider is syrupy and apple is just tender, about 2 minutes longer. Off heat, stir in tarragon and vinegar. Season with salt and pepper to taste. Transfer to serving dish and pour any remaining glaze over vegetables. Serve.

Cider-Glazed Root Vegetables with Pomegranate and Cilantro

Substitute chopped fresh cilantro for tarragon and add ¼ cup pomegranate seeds along with cilantro and vinegar.

Slow-Cooker Lemon-Herb Fingerling Potatoes

Cider-Glazed Root Vegetables with Apple and Tarragon

Sweet Potato Fritters with
Feta, Dill, and Cilantro

3 pounds sweet potatoes, peeled and sliced
¼ inch thick
½ cup boiling water, plus extra as needed
1 teaspoon sugar
¾ teaspoon table salt
6 tablespoons half-and-half, warmed
3 tablespoons unsalted butter, melted

1. Combine potatoes, boiling water, sugar, and salt in slow cooker. Press 16 by 12-inch sheet of parchment paper firmly onto potatoes, folding down edges as needed. Cover and cook until potatoes are tender, 5 to 6 hours on low or 3 to 4 hours on high.

2. Discard parchment. Mash potatoes with potato masher until smooth. Stir in warm half-and-half and melted butter and season with salt and pepper to taste. Serve. (Sweet potatoes can be held on warm or low setting for up to 2 hours; adjust consistency with extra hot water as needed before serving.)

CREATING A PARCHMENT SHIELD

Press 16 by 12-inch sheet of parchment paper firmly onto rice or vegetables, folding down edges as needed.

Slow-Cooker Mashed Sweet Potatoes

Serves 6 to 8 | **Cooking Time** 5 to 6 hours on Low or 3 to 4 hours on High VEGETARIAN

WHY THIS RECIPE WORKS Smooth and velvety, and with a rich buttery finish, these mashed sweet potatoes will keep you coming back for more. We used the slow cooker to cook this classic side dish to free up the stovetop for other tasks. Pressing a piece of parchment on top of the potatoes resulted in even cooking, without any dry edges. For an accurate measurement of boiling water, bring a full kettle of water to a boil and then measure out the desired amount. You will need a 5- to 7-quart slow cooker for this recipe. This recipe can easily be doubled in a 7-quart slow cooker; you will need to increase the cooking time range by 1 hour. This recipe will only work in a traditional slow cooker.

Sweet Potato Fritters with Cheddar, Chipotle, and Cilantro

Serves 4 to 6 | **Total Time** 1¼ hours, plus 30 minutes cooling MAKE AHEAD VEGETARIAN

WHY THIS RECIPE WORKS Set out a plate of these lightly crispy fritters and watch them disappear. Instead of boiling the sweet potatoes in an abundance of water to soften then, which would have diluted their flavor, we steamed them in just a small amount of water. When mashing them, we purposefully left a few small chunks for contrasting texture. Adding eggs and flour to the mash made the fritters fluffier, with extra-crunchy edges. Shallow frying was easier to manage—and clean up—than deep frying. Sharp cheddar cheese and smoky chipotle chiles made each bite of these fritters exciting. Using two spatulas to flip the fritters helps prevent splattering. For less spicy fritters, reduce the chipotle chile to 2 teaspoons.

1½ pounds sweet potatoes, peeled and
    sliced ¼ inch thick
¼ cup water
1½ teaspoons table salt
3 ounces sharp cheddar cheese, shredded (¾ cup)
½ cup all-purpose flour
2 large eggs
4 scallions, sliced thin
¼ cup chopped fresh cilantro
2 tablespoons minced canned chipotle chile in
    adobo sauce
1 teaspoon ground cumin
½ teaspoon pepper
½ cup peanut or vegetable oil for frying
    Sour cream
    Lemon or lime wedges

1. Combine potatoes, water, and salt in large saucepan. Cover and cook over medium-low heat, stirring occasionally, until paring knife inserted into potatoes meets no resistance, about 20 minutes.

2. Remove from heat. Using potato masher, mash potatoes until mostly smooth with some small chunks remaining. Let cool until no longer hot to touch, about 30 minutes. (Mashed sweet potatoes can be transferred to bowl, covered with plastic wrap, and refrigerated for up to 2 days.)

3. Set wire rack in rimmed baking sheet and line half of rack with triple layer of paper towels. Stir cheddar, flour, eggs, scallions, cilantro, chipotle, cumin, and pepper into potato mixture until fully combined.

4. Heat oil in 12-inch nonstick skillet over medium heat to 350 degrees (to take temperature, tilt skillet so oil pools on 1 side). Using greased ¼-cup dry measuring cup, place 6 portions of potato mixture in skillet. Press portions into approximate 3-inch disks with back of spoon.

5. Cook fritters until deep brown, 2 to 3 minutes per side, using 2 spatulas to carefully flip. Transfer fritters to paper towel–lined side of prepared rack to drain for 15 seconds on each side, then move to unlined side of rack. Return oil to 350 degrees and repeat with remaining potato mixture. Serve with sour cream and lemon wedges.

Sweet Potato Fritters with Feta, Dill, and Cilantro

Substitute crumbled feta for cheddar, and ¼ cup chopped fresh dill for chipotle chile.

Candied Sweet Potato Casserole

Serves 10 to 12 | **Total Time** 1½ hours VEGETARIAN

WHY THIS RECIPE WORKS Sweet potato casserole is a must-have side on many Thanksgiving tables; a candied topping makes ours a real treat without turning the corner into cloying territory. We steamed the sweet potatoes on the stovetop with butter and brown sugar and kept the other flavors simple—just salt and pepper. For the candied topping, we used whole pecans instead of chopped; this gave the casserole a better texture and a striking rustic appearance. Tossing the nuts with beaten egg white, brown sugar, and a little cayenne and cumin ensured a balanced pecan topping with an inviting sheen and some welcome contrasting heat. For a more intense molasses flavor, use dark brown sugar in place of light.

SWEET POTATOES
8 tablespoons unsalted butter, cut into 1-inch pieces
5 pounds sweet potatoes (about 8 medium),
    peeled and cut into 1-inch pieces
1 cup packed light brown sugar
½ cup water
1½ teaspoons table salt
½ teaspoon pepper

PECAN TOPPING
2 cups pecans
½ cup packed light brown sugar
1 egg white, lightly beaten
⅛ teaspoon table salt
    Pinch cayenne pepper
    Pinch ground cumin

1. FOR THE SWEET POTATOES Melt butter in Dutch oven over medium-high heat. Add sweet potatoes, sugar, water, salt, and black pepper; bring to simmer. Reduce heat to medium-low, cover, and cook, stirring often, until sweet potatoes are tender (paring knife can be slipped into and out of center with very little resistance), 45 minutes to 1 hour.

2. When sweet potatoes are tender, remove lid and bring sauce to rapid simmer over medium-high heat. Continue to simmer until sauce has reduced to glaze, 7 to 10 minutes.

3. FOR THE PECAN TOPPING Meanwhile, mix all ingredients for topping together in medium bowl; set aside.

4. Adjust oven rack to middle position and heat oven to 450 degrees. Pour sweet potato mixture into 13 by 9-inch baking dish (or shallow casserole dish of similar size). Spread topping over potatoes. Bake until pecans are toasted and crisp, 10 to 15 minutes. Serve immediately.

Sautéed Swiss Chard with Currants and Pine Nuts

Serves 4 | **Total Time** 30 minutes `VEGETARIAN`

WHY THIS RECIPE WORKS Swiss chard is a sturdy green with a bitter, beet-like flavor that mellows when cooked. The key to sautéing this hearty vegetable is to get the tougher stems to finish cooking at the same time as the leaves. To encourage the stems to cook efficiently and evenly, we sliced them thin on the bias. We gave the stems a head start, sautéing them with garlic and cumin over relatively high heat to create a crisp-tender texture and lightly caramelized flavor. We introduced the tender leaves later and in two stages, allowing the first batch to begin wilting before adding the rest. This hearty green is often served simply seasoned or with garlic. To introduce some additional flavors and textures, we chose to incorporate sweet currants and crunchy pine nuts, which we stirred in off the heat with some sherry vinegar; the touch of acidity brightened the dish noticeably.

- 2 tablespoons extra-virgin olive oil
- 1 garlic clove, minced
- ¼ teaspoon ground cumin
- 1½ pounds Swiss chard, stems sliced ¼ inch thick on bias, leaves sliced into ½-inch-wide strips, divided
- ⅛ teaspoon table salt
- 2 teaspoons sherry vinegar
- 3 tablespoons dried currants
- 3 tablespoons pine nuts, toasted

1. Heat oil in 12-inch nonstick skillet over medium-high heat until just shimmering. Add garlic and cumin and cook, stirring constantly, until lightly browned, 30 to 60 seconds. Add chard stems and salt and cook, stirring occasionally, until spotty brown and crisp-tender, about 6 minutes.

2. Add two-thirds of chard leaves and cook, tossing with tongs, until just starting to wilt, 30 to 60 seconds. Add remaining chard leaves and cook, stirring frequently, until leaves are tender, about 3 minutes. Off heat, stir in vinegar, currants, and pine nuts. Season with salt and pepper to taste. Serve.

Roasted Turnips, Shallots, and Garlic with Rosemary

Serves 4 | **Total Time** 1 hour `VEGETARIAN`

WHY THIS RECIPE WORKS Roasting transforms turnips (and rutabagas, too), making them dense, creamy, and mildly peppery while adding some caramelization, which we boosted by tossing the turnips with melted butter first. Alongside the turnips we roasted whole peeled shallots and garlic cloves, which softened, mellowed, and browned in the oven. Adding the garlic and rosemary partway through prevented burning.

- 1½ pounds turnips or rutabagas, peeled and cut into 1¼-inch pieces
- 4 shallots, peeled
- 2 tablespoons unsalted butter, melted
- ½ teaspoon table salt
- 12 garlic cloves, peeled
- 2 teaspoons minced fresh rosemary or ¾ teaspoon dried

Heat oven to 375 degrees. Toss turnips and shallots with butter in rimmed baking sheet and sprinkle with salt. Roast, stirring or shaking vegetables every 15 minutes for 30 minutes. Add garlic and rosemary. Increase heat to 425 degrees and roast until tender and evenly browned, 15 to 20 minutes. Sprinkle with pepper to taste. Serve.

Roasted Delicata Squash

Serves 6 to 8 | **Total Time** 1 hour `VEGETARIAN`

WHY THIS RECIPE WORKS Delicata is the easiest winter squash to cook because its prettily striated skin is so thin that it can be eaten: no peeling needed. Roasting intensifies delicata's sweet and earthy flavors but can dry it out, so we covered the squash with foil initially to let it steam before finishing it uncovered. Cooking the squash in oil and butter ensured that it roasted up golden brown. A vinegar-bright herb sauce lent a contrasting punch without overshadowing our vegetable. To ensure even cooking, choose squashes that are similar in size.

HERB SAUCE
- ¼ cup minced fresh parsley or chives
- ¼ cup extra-virgin olive oil
- 2 tablespoons sherry vinegar
- 2 garlic cloves, minced
- 1 teaspoon smoked paprika
- ¼ teaspoon table salt

SQUASH

- 3 delicata squashes (12 to 16 ounces each), ends trimmed, halved lengthwise, seeded, and sliced crosswise ½ inch thick
- 4 teaspoons extra-virgin olive oil
- ½ teaspoon table salt
- 2 tablespoons unsalted butter, cut into 8 pieces

1. FOR THE SAUCE Stir all ingredients together in bowl; set aside for serving.

2. FOR THE SQUASH Adjust oven rack to lowest position and heat oven to 425 degrees. Toss squash, oil, and salt in bowl to coat. Arrange squash in single layer on rimmed baking sheet. Cover tightly with aluminum foil and bake until squash is tender when pierced with tip of paring knife, 18 to 20 minutes.

3. Uncover and continue to bake until side touching baking sheet is golden brown, 8 to 11 minutes. Remove squash from oven and using thin metal spatula, flip slices over. Scatter butter pieces over squash. Return to oven and continue to bake until side touching baking sheet is golden brown, 8 to 11 minutes. Transfer squash to serving platter and drizzle with herb sauce. Serve.

Roasted Delicata Squash

Roasted Kabocha Squash with Maple and Sage

Serves 4 | **Total Time** 1 hour VEGETARIAN

WHY THIS RECIPE WORKS Kabocha looks like a small, squat pumpkin with dark green or red skin and a nutty, earthy flavor (the red variety is noticeably sweeter). When roasted, its flesh becomes creamy and its skin tender enough to eat. Here we used a mix of warm spices (paprika, coriander, and black pepper) to complement the kabocha's sweetness, which we accentuated with a sweet-tart vinaigrette whisked together from maple syrup, cider vinegar, and sage. The warm squash drank up the dressing to achieve a sweet-savory balance.

- 1 kabocha squash (3 pounds), halved lengthwise and seeded
- ¼ cup extra-virgin olive oil, divided
- 1 garlic clove, minced
- 2 teaspoons paprika
- 1 teaspoon ground coriander
- ½ teaspoon table salt
- ½ teaspoon pepper

- 1 tablespoon cider vinegar
- 1 tablespoon maple syrup
- 2 teaspoons minced fresh sage

1. Adjust oven rack to middle position and heat oven to 475 degrees. Line rimmed baking sheet with parchment paper.

2. Cut each squash half into 2½- to 3-inch pieces. Whisk 2 tablespoons oil, garlic, paprika, coriander, salt, and pepper together in large bowl. Add squash and toss until evenly coated. Arrange squash cut side down in single layer on prepared sheet. Roast until bottoms of most pieces are deep golden brown, 15 to 20 minutes.

3. Remove sheet from oven. Gently flip squash and switch outer pieces with inner pieces on sheet. Continue to roast until squash is tender and most pieces are deep golden brown on second side, 15 to 20 minutes.

4. Whisk vinegar, maple syrup, sage, and remaining 2 tablespoons oil together in small bowl. Transfer squash to serving platter and drizzle with vinaigrette. Serve.

CHAPTER 6

grain & bean sides

■ MAKE AHEAD   ▪ VEGETARIAN
Photo: Egg Noodles with Browned Butter and Caraway

Pressure-Cooker Spiced Rice Pilaf with
Sweet Potatoes and Pomegranate

Mexican Red Rice

Walk-Away Herbed White Rice

Serves 8 | **Total Time** 1 hour

MAKE AHEAD   VEGETARIAN

WHY THIS RECIPE WORKS White rice is a kitchen
chameleon, playing an understated but important supporting
role when paired with just about any protein or vegetable.
However, it can be frustratingly difficult to achieve fluffy, fully
hydrated grains without any scorched bits on the bottom when
cooking rice on the stovetop. This version uses the even heat
of the oven to do away with scorched bottoms forever. All we
had to do was pour boiling water over the rice in a baking
dish, cover it with foil, and let the oven do the work. Our rice
emerged perfectly cooked, needing just a quick fluff with a
fork. For good measure, we stirred in a couple tablespoons
of fresh herbs to give our dish more pizzazz than the average
white rice side. Be sure to cover the pot when bringing the
water to a boil in step 1; any water loss due to evaporation
will affect how the rice cooks.

2½ cups long grain white rice, rinsed
3¾ cups water
 1 teaspoon table salt
 2 tablespoons minced fresh parsley, basil,
    chives, cilantro, dill, or tarragon

   1. Adjust oven rack to middle position and heat oven to
375 degrees. Spread rice into 13 by 9-inch baking dish. Combine
water and salt in large saucepan, cover, and bring to boil over
high heat. Immediately pour boiling water over rice and cover
baking dish tightly with double layer of aluminum foil.
   2. Bake rice until tender and no water remains, 30 to
40 minutes. Remove dish from oven, uncover, and gently fluff
rice with fork, scraping up any rice that has stuck to bottom.
Cover dish with clean dish towel and let rice stand for 10 minutes.
Stir in parsley and season with salt and pepper to taste. Serve.
(Rice can be refrigerated for up to 3 days. Allow to come to
room temperature before serving.)

Walk-Away Herbed White Rice for Four

Use 8-inch square baking dish. Reduce rice to 1⅓ cups, water
to 2¾ cups, salt to ½ teaspoon, and minced fresh herbs to
1 tablespoon. Reduce baking time to 20 minutes.

Pressure-Cooker Spiced Rice Pilaf with Sweet Potatoes and Pomegranate

Serves 4 to 6 | **Total Time** 40 minutes `VEGETARIAN`

WHY THIS RECIPE WORKS The rice in this stunning pilaf gets its vibrant color from a mixture of warming spices; when paired with sweet potatoes and jewel-toned pomegranate seeds, the result is a dish that celebrates the best of autumn and pleases all the senses. A pressure cooker is an excellent tool for cooking rice and ensuring that the grains emerge fluffy, not mushy and blown out. We bloomed our spices in oil right in the pot before adding the rice, broth, and sweet potato. Once the rice and sweet potato were cooked to perfect tenderness, we felt that our pilaf could use some textural contrast, so we sprinkled it with toasted pistachios (the green nuts also contributed another pop of color) and glistening pomegranate seeds to add subtle crunch. To brighten the earthiness of the dish, we incorporated minced preserved lemon and a handful of cilantro. We think the fragrant and floral notes of preserved lemon are an important addition to this dish, but if you can't find it, you can substitute 1 tablespoon lemon zest. To make this dish vegetarian, use vegetable broth. This recipe will only work in an electric pressure cooker.

- 2 tablespoons extra-virgin olive oil
- 1 onion, chopped fine
- ½ teaspoon table salt
- 2 garlic cloves, minced
- 1½ teaspoons ground turmeric
- 1 teaspoon ground coriander
- ⅛ teaspoon cayenne pepper
- 2 cups vegetable or chicken broth
- 1½ cups long-grain white rice, rinsed
- 12 ounces sweet potato, peeled, quartered lengthwise, and sliced ½ inch thick
- ½ preserved lemon, pulp and white pith removed, rind rinsed and minced (2 tablespoons)
- ½ cup shelled pistachios, toasted and chopped
- ¼ cup fresh cilantro leaves
- ¼ cup pomegranate seeds

1. Using highest sauté or browning function, heat oil in pressure cooker until shimmering. Add onion and salt and cook until onion is softened, about 5 minutes. Stir in garlic, turmeric, coriander, and cayenne and cook until fragrant, about 30 seconds. Stir in broth, rice, and sweet potato.

2. Lock lid in place and close pressure release valve. Select high pressure cook function and cook for 4 minutes. Turn off pressure cooker and quick-release pressure. Carefully remove lid, allowing steam to escape away from you.

3. Add preserved lemon and gently fluff rice with fork to combine. Lay clean dish towel over pot, replace lid, and let stand for 5 minutes. Season with salt and pepper to taste. Transfer to serving dish and sprinkle with pistachios, cilantro, and pomegranate seeds. Serve.

Mexican Red Rice

Serves 6 to 8 | **Total Time** 1¼ hours
`MAKE AHEAD` `VEGETARIAN`

WHY THIS RECIPE WORKS In northern Mexico, rice is cooked with broth and tomato to make arroz rojo, a dish of distinct, tender, mildly spicy red-hued grains. Since it's the savory, aromatic cooking liquid that infuses the rice with flavor through and through, we started with broth for savory backbone, and enhanced the broth with a mixture of pureed onion and the obligatory tomatoes. Three minced jalapenos (with some of the ribs and seeds removed to help moderate their heat), some garlic, and a tablespoon of tomato paste gave our rice spice, depth, and a deeper red color. Use an ovensafe pot about 12 inches in diameter with a tight-fitting lid so that the rice cooks evenly and in the time indicated. To make this dish vegetarian, use vegetable broth.

- 2 tomatoes, cored and quartered
- 1 onion, root end trimmed, quartered
- 3 jalapeño chiles, stemmed, divided
- ⅓ cup vegetable oil
- 2 cups long-grain white rice, rinsed
- 4 garlic cloves, minced
- 2 cups vegetable or chicken broth
- 1 tablespoon tomato paste
- 1½ teaspoons table salt
- ½ cup minced fresh cilantro
  Lime wedges

1. Adjust oven rack to middle position and heat oven to 350 degrees. Process tomatoes and onion in food processor until smooth, about 15 seconds. Transfer mixture to liquid measuring cup and spoon off excess until mixture measures 2 cups. Remove ribs and seeds from 2 jalapeños and discard; mince flesh and set aside. Mince remaining 1 jalapeño, including ribs and seeds; set aside.

2. Heat oil in Dutch oven over medium-high heat for 1 to 2 minutes. Drop 3 or 4 grains rice in oil; if grains sizzle, oil is ready. Add rice and cook, stirring often, until rice is light golden and translucent, 6 to 8 minutes.

3. Reduce heat to medium. Stir in garlic and reserved seeded jalapeños and cook, stirring constantly, until fragrant, about 1½ minutes. Stir in broth, tomato paste, salt, and tomato-onion mixture. Increase heat to medium-high and bring to boil.

4. Cover pot, transfer to oven, and cook until liquid is absorbed and rice is tender, 30 to 35 minutes, stirring well after 15 minutes. Fold in cilantro and reserved jalapeño with seeds to taste. Serve with lime wedges. (Rice can be refrigerated for up to 3 days. Allow to come to room temperature before serving.)

Chelow (Persian-Style Rice with Golden Crust)

Serves 6 | **Total Time** 1¾ hours VEGETARIAN

WHY THIS RECIPE WORKS Our version of this showpiece Iranian pilaf features a marriage of unusually light, fluffy rice with a crispy golden-brown crust. To ensure well-separated, evenly cooked grains, we soaked the rice in hot water to wash away excess starch and then boiled it briefly. We packed a portion of the parcooked rice (mixed with Greek yogurt and oil) into the bottom of a Dutch oven; the rest we mounded loosely on top before adding a bit of water, covering the pot, and blasting it with heat. The intense heat fried the bottom layer of rice, while steam finished cooking the rest. Next, we placed the hot pot on a damp dish towel to help the bottom grains contract so the crust released from the pot more easily. Instead of unmolding the entire portion of rice at once as is traditional, we found it easier to spoon the steamed rice onto a plate before breaking up the crust and scattering the pieces on top. Texmati or other long-grain rice will work here. For the best results, use a Dutch oven with a bottom diameter between 8½ and 10 inches. It is important not to overcook the rice during parboiling, as it will continue to cook during steaming. Begin checking the rice at the lower end of the time range.

2 cups basmati rice
1 tablespoon table salt for soaking
¼ teaspoon table salt, plus salt for cooking rice
5 tablespoons vegetable oil, divided

Chelow (Persian-Style Rice with Golden Crust)

¼ cup plain Greek yogurt
1½ teaspoons cumin seeds, divided
2 tablespoons unsalted butter, cut into 8 pieces
¼ cup minced fresh parsley, divided

1. Place rice in fine-mesh strainer and rinse under cold running water until water runs clear. Place rice and 1 tablespoon salt in medium bowl and cover with 4 cups hot tap water. Stir gently to dissolve salt; let stand for 15 minutes. Drain rice in fine-mesh strainer.

2. Meanwhile, bring 8 cups water to boil in Dutch oven over high heat. Add rice and 2 tablespoons salt. Boil briskly, stirring frequently, until rice is mostly tender with slight bite in center and grains are floating toward top of pot, 3 to 5 minutes (begin timing from when rice is added to pot).

3. Drain rice in large fine-mesh strainer and rinse with cold water to stop cooking, about 30 seconds. Rinse and dry pot well to remove any residual starch. Brush bottom and 1 inch up sides of pot with 1 tablespoon oil.

4. Whisk yogurt, 1 teaspoon cumin seeds, ¼ teaspoon salt, and remaining ¼ cup oil together in medium bowl. Add 2 cups rice and stir until combined. Spread yogurt-rice mixture evenly over bottom of prepared pot, packing it down well.

5. Stir remaining ½ teaspoon cumin seeds into remaining rice. Mound rice in center of pot on top of yogurt-rice base (it should look like small hill). Poke 8 equally spaced holes through rice mound but not into yogurt-rice base. Place 1 butter cube in each hole. Drizzle ⅓ cup water over rice mound.

6. Wrap pot lid with clean dish towel and cover pot tightly, making sure towel is secure on top of lid and away from heat. Cook over medium-high heat until rice on bottom is crackling and steam is coming from sides of pot, about 10 minutes, rotating pot halfway through for even cooking.

7. Reduce heat to medium-low and continue to cook until rice is tender and fluffy and crust is golden brown around edges, 30 to 35 minutes. Remove covered pot from heat and place on damp dish towel set in rimmed baking sheet; let stand for 5 minutes.

8. Stir 2 tablespoons parsley into rice, making sure not to disturb crust on bottom of pot, and season with salt to taste. Gently spoon rice onto serving platter.

9. Using thin metal spatula, loosen edges of crust from pot, then break crust into large pieces. Transfer pieces to serving platter, arranging evenly around rice. Sprinkle with remaining 2 tablespoons parsley and serve.

Brown Rice Pilaf with Dates and Pistachios

Serves 6 | **Total Time** 1½ hours
MAKE AHEAD   VEGETARIAN

WHY THIS RECIPE WORKS When enriched with just a few judiciously chosen add-ins, simple brown rice pilaf transforms into something memorable. In a Dutch oven, we sautéed a base of onions, stirred in broth, rice, and a bay leaf, and then covered the pot and popped it into the oven to cook in the oven's even heat for about an hour. When the rice was tender, we removed it from the oven, sprinkled sweet chopped dates over the top, covered the pot again, and let it stand for 10 minutes, just enough time for the dates to plump up. After a quick fluff with a fork to incorporate a sprinkling of earthy pistachios and cooling mint, our light, wholesome pilaf was good to go. Medium-grain or short-grain brown rice can be substituted for the long-grain rice. To make this dish vegetarian, use vegetable broth.

1 tablespoon extra-virgin olive oil
1 onion, chopped fine
½ teaspoon table salt
3¼ cups vegetable or chicken broth
1½ cups long-grain brown rice, rinsed
1 bay leaf
1½ ounces pitted dates, chopped (¼ cup)
⅓ cup shelled pistachios, toasted and chopped coarse
¼ cup minced fresh mint

1. Adjust oven rack to middle position and heat oven to 375 degrees. Heat oil in Dutch oven over medium heat until shimmering. Add onion and salt and cook until softened and lightly browned, 5 to 7 minutes.

2. Stir in broth, cover, and bring to boil. Off heat, stir in rice and bay leaf. Cover, transfer pot to oven, and bake until liquid is absorbed and rice is tender, 55 minutes to 1 hour 5 minutes.

3. Remove pot from oven. Sprinkle dates over rice and let stand, covered, for 10 minutes. Discard bay leaf. Fluff rice with fork, stir in pistachios and mint, and season with salt and pepper to taste. Serve. (Pilaf can be refrigerated for up to 3 days.)

Baked Wild Rice

Serves 4 to 6 | **Total Time** 1¾ hours
MAKE AHEAD   VEGETARIAN

WHY THIS RECIPE WORKS The nuttiness and vivid purple-black color of wild rice make it a great savory side dish that's perfect with turkey, pork, and hearty autumn vegetables. However, its chewy outer husk means it can take nearly an hour of babying on the stovetop to cook through. We took a hands-off approach, utilizing the oven to make this dish hassle-free. In a little more than an hour—time we could use to make the rest of our dinner—our evenly cooked, pleasantly chewy wild rice was ready to be removed from the oven, fluffed, and served. The recipe can be doubled easily using a 13 by 9-inch baking dish. Be sure to cover the pot when bringing the water to a boil in step 2; any water loss due to evaporation will affect how the rice cooks. Do not use quick-cooking or presteamed wild rice in this recipe; read the ingredient list on the package carefully to determine this.

1½ cups wild rice, rinsed
3 cups water
2 teaspoons unsalted butter or extra-virgin olive oil
¾ teaspoon table salt

1. Adjust oven rack to middle position and heat oven to 375 degrees. Spread rice into 8-inch square glass baking dish.

2. Bring water, butter, and salt to boil in covered medium saucepan over high heat. Once boiling, stir to combine, then pour immediately over rice. Cover baking dish tightly with aluminum foil and bake until liquid is absorbed and rice is tender, 1 hour 10 minutes to 1 hour 20 minutes.

3. Remove baking dish from oven, uncover, and fluff rice with fork. Re-cover dish with foil and let rice stand for 10 minutes before serving. (Wild rice can be refrigerated for up to 3 days. Allow to come to room temperature before serving.)

Baked Wild Rice with Almonds and Cranberries

Finely chopping the cranberries helps them soften in the steaming rice. Dried cherries can be substituted for the cranberries. In step 2, melt butter in medium saucepan over medium heat. Add 1 finely chopped onion and salt and cook until onion is softened, 5 to 7 minutes. Stir in water. Cover pot, increase heat to high, and bring to boil before pouring over rice. Before re-covering dish with foil in step 3, stir in ¼ cup finely chopped cranberries. Sprinkle with ¼ cup toasted sliced almonds before serving.

Barley with Lemon and Herbs

Serves 6 to 8 | **Total Time** 1 hour

`MAKE AHEAD` `VEGETARIAN`

WHY THIS RECIPE WORKS On a dreary winter day, a warm grain salad tossed with a pleasantly mouth-puckering, citrusy dressing is sure to perk up your senses with a taste of sunshine. We love barley for its nuttiness and light chew. Using the pasta method—boiling the barley in plenty of salted water and then draining it—rid it of the excess starch that causes clumping. An acid-heavy dressing using a 1:1 ratio of lemon juice to oil, plus fragrant lemon zest and sharp Dijon mustard, gave the salad a punch. A few fresh elements—shallot, scallions, and fresh herbs—gave our satisfying winter salad a truly light and lively flavor profile. The cooking time for barley will vary from product to product, so start checking for doneness after 25 minutes. Be sure to cover the pot when bringing the water to a boil in step 1; any water loss due to evaporation will affect how the barley cooks.

1½	cups pearl barley
½	teaspoon table salt, plus salt for cooking barley
3	tablespoons extra-virgin olive oil
2	tablespoons minced shallot
1	teaspoon grated lemon zest plus 3 tablespoons juice
1	teaspoon Dijon mustard
¼	teaspoon pepper
6	scallions, sliced thin on bias
¼	cup minced fresh mint
¼	cup minced fresh cilantro

1. Line rimmed baking sheet with parchment paper and set aside. Bring 4 quarts water to boil in Dutch oven. Add barley and 1 tablespoon salt. Stir and cook, uncovered, adjusting heat to maintain gentle boil, until barley is tender with slight chew, 25 to 45 minutes.

2. While barley cooks, whisk oil, shallot, lemon zest and juice, mustard, pepper, and ½ teaspoon salt together in large bowl.

3. Drain barley. Transfer to prepared sheet and spread into even layer. Let stand until no longer steaming, 5 to 7 minutes. Add barley to bowl with dressing and toss to coat. Add scallions, mint, and cilantro and stir to combine. Season with salt and pepper to taste. Serve. (Barley can be refrigerated for up to 3 days. Allow to come to room temperature before serving.)

Barley with Celery and Miso Dressing

Substitute 3 tablespoons seasoned rice vinegar, 1 tablespoon white miso, 1 tablespoon soy sauce, 1 tablespoon toasted sesame oil, 1 tablespoon vegetable oil, 2 teaspoons grated fresh ginger, 1 minced garlic clove, 1 teaspoon packed brown sugar, and ¼ to ½ teaspoon red pepper flakes for oil, shallot, lemon zest and juice, mustard, salt, and pepper in step 2. Substitute 2 celery ribs, sliced thin on bias, and 2 peeled and grated carrots for scallions. Omit mint and increase cilantro to ½ cup.

Barley with Fennel, Dried Apricots, and Orange

Substitute 3 tablespoons red wine vinegar and ½ teaspoon grated orange zest plus 2 tablespoons juice for lemon zest and juice. Omit mustard. Reduce oil to 2 tablespoons and add 1 minced garlic clove to dressing in step 2. Substitute 20 chopped dried California apricots and 1 small fennel bulb, 2 tablespoons fronds minced, bulb cored, trimmed, and chopped fine, for scallions. Omit mint and substitute parsley for cilantro.

Farro Salad with Butternut Squash, Radicchio, and Blue Cheese

Serves 6 to 8 | **Total Time** 1 hour

`MAKE AHEAD` `VEGETARIAN`

WHY THIS RECIPE WORKS Nutty farro demands bold ingredients that can stand up to its robust flavor, making it a perfect canvas for an autumnal salad. Sweet, meaty pieces of butternut squash; crisp, bitter radicchio; and creamy, pungent blue cheese combined to make a dish that sang with complex layers of flavor and a multitude of textures. We cooked the farro quickly and easily in a large amount of boiling water, draining it once the farro reached the ideal tender-firm balance. A tangy, assertive dressing made with ingredients including acidic cider vinegar, sharp Dijon mustard, and a dash of spicy cayenne pepper offered a counterpoint to the salad's earthy, bitter flavors. Do not use quick-cooking, presteamed, or pearl farro in this recipe; read the ingredient list on the package to determine this. The cooking time for farro can vary greatly among different brands, so we recommend starting to check for doneness after 10 minutes.

Barley with Lemon and Herbs

- 2 pounds butternut squash, peeled, seeded, and cut into ½-inch pieces (3⅓ cups)
- ¼ cup extra-virgin olive oil, divided
- ¾ teaspoon table salt, divided, plus salt for cooking farro
- 1½ cups whole farro, rinsed
- 2 tablespoons cider vinegar, plus extra for seasoning
- 2 tablespoons minced shallot
- 1 teaspoon Dijon mustard
  Pinch cayenne pepper
- 1 cup chopped radicchio
- ½ cup chopped fresh parsley
- 2 ounces blue cheese, crumbled (½ cup)

1. Adjust oven rack to lowest position and heat oven to 500 degrees. Toss squash, 1 tablespoon oil, and ½ teaspoon salt together in bowl. Spread squash in even layer on rimmed baking sheet and roast until tender, 20 to 22 minutes. Push squash to 1 side of sheet and transfer sheet to wire rack to cool.

2. While squash roasts, bring 2 quarts water to boil in large saucepan. Stir in farro and 1 tablespoon salt. Return to boil and cook until farro is tender with slight chew, 15 to 30 minutes. Drain well. Spread on empty side of sheet with squash and let cool for 15 minutes.

Farro Salad with Butternut Squash, Radicchio, and Blue Cheese

Pressure-Cooker Wild
Mushroom Farrotto

Freekeh Pilaf with Dates
and Cauliflower

3. Whisk vinegar, shallot, mustard, cayenne, remaining 3 tablespoons oil, and remaining ¼ teaspoon salt together in large bowl. (Farro, vegetables, and vinaigrette can be prepared through step 3 and refrigerated separately for up to 3 days. To serve, let farro, vegetables, and vinaigrette come to room temperature; whisk vinaigrette to recombine; and continue with step 4.)

4. Add radicchio, parsley, blue cheese, farro, and squash to vinaigrette and toss to combine. Season with salt, pepper, and extra vinegar to taste. Serve. (Salad can be prepared up to 2 hours in advance.)

Pressure-Cooker Wild Mushroom Farrotto

Serves 6 to 8 | **Total Time** 1 hour   VEGETARIAN

WHY THIS RECIPE WORKS Creamy, luxurious risotto is a pleasure to eat in any weather, but it is especially comforting in winter. Farrotto, made with whole-grain farro instead of rice, is extra satisfying. Cracking the farro in a blender freed some of the starch normally trapped inside, giving the farroto its velvety, risotto-like consistency. Using a pressure cooker allowed us to go hands-off; we let the pressure cooker go until the farro was tender and creamy, and then finished the dish with rich, salty Parmesan and fresh lemon juice. Do not use quick-cooking, presteamed, or pearl farro in this recipe; read the ingredient list on the package to determine this. Be sure to use a blender in step 1; the farro will not pulse properly in a food processor. To make this dish vegetarian, use vegetable broth. This dish will only work in an electric pressure cooker.

1½ cups whole farro
 3 tablespoons extra-virgin olive oil, divided, plus extra for drizzling
12 ounces cremini or white mushrooms, trimmed and sliced thin
½ onion, chopped fine
½ teaspoon table salt
¼ teaspoon pepper
 1 garlic clove, minced
¼ ounce dried porcini mushrooms, rinsed and chopped fine
 2 teaspoons minced fresh thyme or ½ teaspoon dried
¼ cup dry white wine
2½ cups vegetable or chicken broth, plus extra as needed

2 ounces Parmesan cheese, grated (1 cup), plus
  extra for serving
2 teaspoons lemon juice
½ cup chopped fresh parsley

1. Pulse farro in blender until about half of grains are broken into smaller pieces, about 6 pulses.

2. Using highest sauté or browning function, heat 2 tablespoons oil in pressure cooker until shimmering. Add cremini mushrooms, onion, salt, and pepper, partially cover, and cook until mushrooms are softened and have released their liquid, about 5 minutes. Stir in garlic, porcini mushrooms, thyme, and farro and cook until fragrant, about 1 minute. Stir in wine and cook until nearly evaporated, about 30 seconds. Stir in broth.

3. Lock lid in place and close pressure release valve. Select high pressure cook function and cook for 12 minutes. Turn off pressure cooker and quick-release pressure. Carefully remove lid, allowing steam to escape away from you.

4. If necessary adjust consistency with extra hot broth, or continue to cook farrotto, using highest sauté or browning function, stirring frequently, until proper consistency is achieved. (Farrotto should be slightly thickened, and spoon dragged along bottom of multicooker should leave trail that quickly fills in.) Add Parmesan and remaining 1 tablespoon oil and stir vigorously until farrotto becomes creamy. Stir in lemon juice and season with salt and pepper to taste. Sprinkle individual portions with parsley and extra Parmesan, and drizzle with extra oil before serving.

Freekeh Pilaf with Dates and Cauliflower

Serves 4 to 6 | **Total Time** 1 hour

MAKE AHEAD VEGETARIAN

WHY THIS RECIPE WORKS For a pilaf that accentuated freekeh's grassy, slightly smoky flavor and chew, we paired it with pan-roasted cauliflower, spices and aromatics, and refreshing mint. Boiling the grain like pasta was the easiest way to achieve a chewy, firm texture. Allowing the cauliflower to soften and brown slightly before adding the remaining ingredients to the pan created the best flavor and texture. Studded with sweet dates and toasted pistachios, this pilaf works brilliantly as a satisfying side dish or a light main. We prefer the texture of whole, uncracked freekeh; cracked freekeh can be substituted, but you will need to decrease the freekeh cooking time in step 1.

1½ cups whole freekeh
½ teaspoon table salt, plus salt for cooking freekeh
¼ cup extra-virgin olive oil, divided, plus extra
  for serving
1 head cauliflower (2 pounds), cored and cut into
  ½-inch florets
¼ teaspoon pepper
3 ounces pitted dates, chopped (½ cup)
1 shallot, minced
1½ teaspoons grated fresh ginger
¼ teaspoon ground coriander
¼ teaspoon ground cumin
¼ cup shelled pistachios, toasted and chopped coarse
¼ cup chopped fresh mint
1½ tablespoons lemon juice

1. Bring 4 quarts water to boil in Dutch oven. Add freekeh and 1 tablespoon salt, return to boil, and cook until grains are tender, 30 to 45 minutes. Drain freekeh, return to now-empty pot, and cover to keep warm.

2. Heat 2 tablespoons oil in 12-inch nonstick skillet over medium-high heat until shimmering. Add cauliflower, pepper, and ½ teaspoon salt, cover, and cook until florets are softened and starting to brown, about 5 minutes.

3. Remove lid and continue to cook, stirring occasionally, until florets turn spotty brown, about 10 minutes. Add dates, shallot, ginger, coriander, cumin, and remaining 2 tablespoons oil and cook, stirring frequently, until dates and shallot are softened and fragrant, about 3 minutes. (Freekeh and cauliflower can be refrigerated, separately, for up to 3 days. To serve, allow freekeh and cauliflower to come to room temperature and continue with step 4.)

4. Reduce heat to low, add freekeh, and cook, stirring frequently, until heated through, about 1 minute. Off heat, stir in pistachios, mint, and lemon juice. Season with salt and pepper to taste, and drizzle with extra oil. Serve.

Quinoa Pilaf with Herbs and Lemon

Serves 4 to 6 | **Total Time** 50 minutes

MAKE AHEAD VEGETARIAN

WHY THIS RECIPE WORKS The key to a quinoa pilaf with light, distinct grains and appealingly nutty flavor is using the right amount of liquid. To cook 1½ cups of quinoa, 1¾ cups of water was the sweet spot for tender grains with a satisfying bite and robust, not washed-out, flavor. Toasting the quinoa in a dry skillet enhanced its natural nuttiness. Fresh herbs and a squeeze of lemon juice rounded out the pilaf's flavor. We like the convenience of prewashed quinoa; rinsing removes the quinoa's bitter protective coating (called saponin). If you buy unwashed quinoa (or if you are unsure whether it's washed), rinse it and then spread it out over a clean dish towel to dry for 15 minutes before cooking.

  1½ cups prewashed white quinoa
   2 tablespoons unsalted butter or extra-virgin olive oil
   1 small onion, chopped fine
   ¾ teaspoon table salt
  1¾ cups water
   3 tablespoons chopped fresh cilantro, parsley, chives, mint, or tarragon
   1 tablespoon lemon juice

  1. Toast quinoa in medium saucepan over medium-high heat, stirring frequently, until quinoa is very fragrant and makes continuous popping sound, 5 to 7 minutes; transfer to bowl.

  2. Add butter to now-empty pan and melt over medium-low heat. Add onion and salt and cook until onion is softened and light golden, 5 to 7 minutes. Stir in water and quinoa, increase heat to medium-high, and bring to simmer. Cover, reduce heat to low, and simmer until grains are just tender and liquid is absorbed, 18 to 20 minutes, stirring once halfway through cooking.

  3. Remove pan from heat and let stand, covered, for 10 minutes. (Quinoa can be refrigerated for up to 3 days. To reheat, microwave quinoa in covered bowl until hot throughout, 3 to 5 minutes, fluffing with fork halfway through microwaving.) Fluff quinoa with fork, stir in herbs and lemon juice, and serve.

Quinoa Pilaf with Apricots, Aged Gouda, and Pistachios

Add ½ teaspoon grated lemon zest, ½ teaspoon ground coriander, ¼ teaspoon ground cumin, and ⅛ teaspoon pepper to pot with onion and salt. Stir in ½ cup coarsely chopped dried apricots before letting quinoa stand for 10 minutes in step 3. Substitute ½ cup shredded aged gouda; ½ cup shelled pistachios, toasted and chopped; and 2 tablespoons chopped fresh mint for herbs.

Quinoa Pilaf with Olives, Raisins, and Cilantro

Add ¼ teaspoon ground cumin, ¼ teaspoon dried oregano, and ⅛ teaspoon ground cinnamon to pot with onion and salt. Stir in ¼ cup golden raisins halfway through cooking quinoa. Substitute ⅓ cup coarsely chopped pimento-stuffed green olives and 3 tablespoons chopped fresh cilantro for herbs. Substitute 4 teaspoons red wine vinegar for lemon juice.

Wheat Berry Salad with Figs, Pine Nuts, and Goat Cheese

Serves 4 to 6 | **Total Time** 1¾ hours

MAKE AHEAD VEGETARIAN

WHY THIS RECIPE WORKS Figs have a growing season that lasts into fall. We chose to feature their jammy texture and honeyed flavor in a grain salad alongside the understated pop of pine nuts, the tang of goat cheese, and the nutty canvas of wheat berries. For the dressing, we chose a zippy vinaigrette made with balsamic vinegar, shallot, mustard, and honey to highlight the figs' natural sweetness. Toasted pine nuts and parsley leaves contributed crunch and fragrance. Do not add more than 1½ teaspoons of salt when cooking the wheat berries; adding more will prevent the grains from softening. Do not use presteamed or quick-cooking wheat berries here, as they have a much shorter cooking time; read the package to determine what kind of wheat berries you are using.

  1½ cups wheat berries
   ¼ teaspoon table salt, plus salt for cooking wheat berries
   2 tablespoons balsamic vinegar
   1 small shallot, minced
   1 teaspoon Dijon mustard
   1 teaspoon honey
   ¼ teaspoon pepper
   3 tablespoons extra-virgin olive oil
   8 ounces fresh figs, cut into ½-inch pieces
   ½ cup fresh parsley leaves
   ¼ cup pine nuts, toasted
   2 ounces goat cheese, crumbled (½ cup)

  1. Bring 4 quarts water to boil in Dutch oven. Add wheat berries and 1½ teaspoons salt, return to boil, and cook until tender but still chewy, 1 hour to 1 hour 10 minutes. Drain wheat berries, spread onto rimmed baking sheet, and let cool completely, about 15 minutes.

2. Whisk vinegar, shallot, mustard, honey, pepper, and ¼ teaspoon salt together in large bowl. Whisking constantly, slowly drizzle in oil. Add wheat berries, figs, parsley, and pine nuts and toss gently to combine. Season with salt and pepper to taste. Transfer to serving platter and sprinkle with goat cheese. Serve. (Salad can be refrigerated for up to 3 days. Allow to come to room temperature before serving.)

Hearty Pearl Couscous with Eggplant, Spinach, and Beans

Serves 6 | **Total Time** 1 hour VEGETARIAN

WHY THIS RECIPE WORKS Pearl couscous, a common ingredient in many Mediterranean cuisines, never fails to put us in mind of warm, sunny days. Here, pearl couscous plus zesty sumac, nutty-sweet fenugreek, and floral cardamom gave our hearty side dish an Israeli-inspired identity. Porous eggplant is prone to holding on to too much oil when cooked, so to avoid this, we salted and microwaved the pieces to collapse their absorbent air pockets. Next, searing the eggplant pieces in a hot skillet built the fond that would be the base of the aromatic broth in which the couscous cooked. White beans and baby spinach made for a more substantial (and colorful) dish. Do not substitute regular couscous in this dish, as it requires a different cooking method and will not work in this recipe. To make this dish vegetarian, use vegetable broth.

- 1 teaspoon ground sumac
- 1 teaspoon ground fenugreek
- ½ teaspoon table salt
- ½ teaspoon pepper
- ¼ teaspoon ground cardamom
- 1 pound eggplant, cut into ½-inch pieces
- 1½ cups pearl couscous
- 5 tablespoons extra-virgin olive oil, divided, plus extra for serving
- 1 onion, chopped
- 3 garlic cloves, minced
- 1 tablespoon tomato paste
- 2 cups vegetable or chicken broth
- 1 (15-ounce) can great Northern beans, rinsed
- 3 ounces (3 cups) baby spinach

1. Combine sumac, fenugreek, salt, pepper, and cardamom in small bowl. Line large plate with double layer of coffee filters and spray with vegetable oil spray. Toss eggplant with ½ teaspoon spice mixture and spread evenly on coffee filters.

Hearty Pearl Couscous with Eggplant, Spinach, and Beans

Microwave eggplant, uncovered, until dry to touch and slightly shriveled, 7 to 10 minutes, tossing halfway through microwaving.

2. Heat couscous and 2 tablespoons oil in 12-inch nonstick skillet over medium heat, stirring frequently, until about half of grains are golden brown, about 5 minutes. Transfer to bowl and wipe skillet clean with paper towels.

3. Toss eggplant with 1 teaspoon spice mixture. Heat 1 tablespoon oil in now-empty skillet over medium-high heat until shimmering. Add eggplant and cook, stirring occasionally, until well browned, 5 to 7 minutes. Transfer to separate bowl.

4. Heat remaining 2 tablespoons oil in again-empty skillet over medium heat until shimmering. Add onion and cook until softened and lightly browned, 5 to 7 minutes. Stir in garlic, tomato paste, and remaining spice mixture and cook until fragrant, about 1 minute.

5. Stir in broth, beans, and couscous and bring to simmer. Reduce heat to medium-low, cover, and simmer, stirring occasionally, until broth is absorbed and couscous is tender, 9 to 12 minutes. Off heat, stir in spinach and eggplant, cover, and let stand for 3 minutes. Season with salt and pepper to taste, and drizzle with extra oil. Serve.

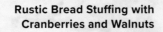
Polenta with Cheese and Butter

Rustic Bread Stuffing with Cranberries and Walnuts

Polenta with Cheese and Butter

Serves 6 to 8 | **Total Time** 55 minutes `VEGETARIAN`

WHY THIS RECIPE WORKS Rich and satisfying, this savory, spoonable polenta makes a perfect companion to braises, meat stews, and myriad other cold-weather dishes. Adding a pinch of baking soda, a nontraditional ingredient, to the cooking liquid broke down the corn's outer layer so it became creamy in less than half the time it would have taken otherwise, needing only occasional stirring. Use coarse-ground cornmeal with grains the size of couscous. If the polenta bubbles or sputters even slightly after the first 10 minutes, the heat is too high and you may need a flame tamer. You can buy one or easily make your own (see "Making a Flame Tamer" for more information). Be sure to cover the pot when bringing the water to a boil in step 1; any water loss due to evaporation will affect how the polenta cooks. Serve with Roman Braised Oxtails (page 90) or Mushroom Ragu (page 98).

7½ cups water
    Table salt for cooking polenta
    Pinch baking soda
1½ cups coarse-ground cornmeal
 4 ounces Parmesan cheese, grated (2 cups), plus extra for serving
 2 tablespoons unsalted butter

1. Bring water to boil in large saucepan over medium-high heat. Stir in 1½ teaspoons salt and baking soda. Slowly pour cornmeal into water in steady stream while whisking constantly and bring to boil. Reduce heat to lowest possible setting, cover, and cook until grains of cornmeal are tender, about 30 minutes, stirring every few minutes. (Polenta should be loose and barely hold its shape; it will continue to thicken as it cools.)

2. Off heat, whisk in Parmesan and butter and season with pepper to taste. Cover and let stand for 5 minutes. Serve, passing extra Parmesan separately.

MAKING A FLAME TAMER

A flame tamer keeps risotto, polenta, and sauces from simmering too briskly. To make one, shape a sheet of heavy-duty aluminum foil into a 1-inch-thick ring of even thickness the size of your burner.

Rustic Bread Stuffing with Cranberries and Walnuts

Serves 6 to 8 | **Total Time** 1½ hours

`MAKE AHEAD` `VEGETARIAN`

WHY THIS RECIPE WORKS Classic holiday side dishes can be on the heavy side. We wanted to introduce a lighter bread stuffing to our repertoire, something loosely textured and a bit less hefty so we had room to enjoy the table's full bounty. Eliminating eggs and cutting back on the moist broth were quick steps to achieving a rustic stuffing. We swapped the usual cubes of toasted white sandwich bread for torn chunks of airy baguette, which retained some crispness and chew even after being combined with the rest of the ingredients, and we stirred the stuffing partway through baking to break up its texture and ensure crispness throughout. In addition to the typical stuffing aromatics, we added dried cranberries for pops of sweetness and scattered earthy walnuts over the top. To make this dish vegetarian, use vegetable broth.

- 2 baguettes (10 ounces each), bottom crust and ends trimmed and discarded
- 3 tablespoons extra-virgin olive oil
- 2 cups vegetable or chicken broth
- 2 tablespoons unsalted butter
- 3 celery ribs, cut into ½-inch pieces
- 1 teaspoon table salt
- ¼ teaspoon pepper
- 2 large onions, cut into ½-inch pieces
- ½ cup dried cranberries
- 3 tablespoons chopped fresh sage
- 3 tablespoons chopped fresh parsley
- ¼ cup walnuts, toasted and chopped

1. Adjust oven rack to upper-middle position and heat oven to 450 degrees. Grease 13 by 9-inch baking dish. Tear baguettes into bite-size pieces (you should have about 12 cups) and spread into even layer on rimmed baking sheet. Drizzle with oil and toss with spatula until oil is well distributed. Toast in oven for 5 minutes. Stir bread, then continue to toast until edges are lightly browned and crisped, about 5 minutes. Transfer sheet to wire rack. Drizzle broth over bread and stir to combine.

2. Melt butter in 10-inch skillet over medium heat. Add celery, salt, and pepper. Cook, stirring frequently, until celery begins to soften, 3 to 5 minutes. Add onions and cook until vegetables are soft but not browned, about 8 minutes. Add cranberries and sage and cook until fragrant, about 1 minute.

3. Add vegetable mixture to bread and toss with spatula until well combined. Transfer stuffing mixture to prepared dish and spread into even layer. (Stuffing can be wrapped in plastic wrap and refrigerated for up to 24 hours; add 5 minutes to baking time.) Bake for 20 minutes. Stir with spatula, turning crisp edges into middle, and spread into even layer. Continue to bake until top is crisp and brown, about 10 minutes. Stir in parsley, sprinkle with walnuts, and serve.

Rustic Bread Stuffing with Dates and Almonds

Substitute 3 tablespoons extra-virgin olive oil for butter (6 tablespoons oil in total). Omit pepper and sage. Substitute ½ cup chopped pitted dates for cranberries. Add 1 minced garlic clove, ½ teaspoon orange zest, ½ teaspoon paprika, ½ teaspoon ground cumin, and pinch cayenne pepper with dates. Substitute toasted sliced almonds for walnuts.

Rustic Bread Stuffing with Fennel and Pine Nuts

Substitute 3 tablespoons extra-virgin olive oil for butter (6 tablespoons in total). Substitute 1 fennel bulb, cored, trimmed, and cut into ½-inch pieces, for celery and increase pepper to ½ teaspoon. Omit cranberries. Substitute 1½ tablespoons chopped fresh rosemary, 1 minced garlic clove, and ½ teaspoon ground fennel for sage. Substitute toasted pine nuts for walnuts.

Classic Sausage-Herb Cornbread Dressing

Serves 10 to 12 | **Total Time** 1¾ hours `MAKE AHEAD`

WHY THIS RECIPE WORKS For a new take on one of our favorite Thanksgiving sides, we looked to wed classic Turkey Day stuffing flavors with a simple Southern-style cornbread dressing, which has a crisp, buttery top and a moist, almost creamy interior. We began by making a simple cornbread using equal parts cornmeal and flour, a touch of sugar, melted butter, eggs, and milk. While the cornbread baked, we sautéed a mix of chopped onions, bell peppers, and celery with rich, porky Italian sausage. After finishing the flavorful sauté with a tablespoon of herby poultry seasoning, we mixed it with our crumbled, warm cornbread and added just enough eggs and savory chicken broth to achieve a cohesive, set dressing. A final brush of melted butter before baking gave the dressing a rich, crisp, golden top. We developed this recipe using Quaker Yellow Cornmeal.

CORNBREAD

1½ cups (7½ ounces) all-purpose flour
1½ cups (7½ ounces) cornmeal
3 tablespoons sugar
1 tablespoon baking powder
1 teaspoon table salt
1¾ cups whole milk
3 large eggs
6 tablespoons unsalted butter, melted

DRESSING

2 tablespoons unsalted butter, plus 4 tablespoons
  unsalted butter, melted
1 pound sweet Italian sausage, casings removed
2 onions, chopped
2 green bell peppers, stemmed, seeded, and chopped
2 celery ribs, chopped
1 tablespoon poultry seasoning
2 garlic cloves, minced
1 teaspoon table salt
1 teaspoon cayenne pepper
3 cups chicken broth
1 cup whole milk
3 large eggs, lightly beaten
¾ cup chopped fresh parsley
½ teaspoon pepper

1. FOR THE CORNBREAD Adjust oven rack to middle position and heat oven to 425 degrees. Grease 13 by 9-inch baking dish.

2. Whisk flour, cornmeal, sugar, baking powder, and salt together in large bowl. Whisk milk, eggs, and melted butter together in second bowl. Whisk milk mixture into flour mixture until just combined. Transfer batter to prepared dish. Bake until cornbread is golden brown and toothpick inserted in center comes out clean, about 20 minutes.

3. FOR THE DRESSING While cornbread bakes, melt 2 tablespoons butter in 12-inch nonstick skillet over medium-high heat. Add sausage, onions, bell peppers, and celery to skillet and cook until vegetables are softened, about 8 minutes. Add poultry seasoning, garlic, salt, and cayenne and cook until fragrant, about 1 minute. Transfer sausage mixture to large bowl.

4. Turn out hot cornbread onto rimmed baking sheet and break into small pieces with 2 forks. (Cooled, crumbled cornbread can be transferred to zipper-lock bag and stored at room temperature for up to 24 hours.)

5. Transfer crumbled cornbread to bowl with sausage mixture. Add broth, milk, eggs, parsley, and pepper and stir to combine. Transfer dressing to now-empty baking dish and spread into even layer (do not pack down). Using side of rubber spatula or wooden spoon, create ridges about ½ inch apart on top of dressing. (Let dressing cool completely if using hot cornbread.)

6. Brush top of dressing with remaining 4 tablespoons melted butter. Bake until browned and crisped on top and heated through, about 35 minutes. Let cool for 10 minutes and serve.

To make ahead After step 5, cover baking dish with plastic wrap and refrigerate for up to 24 hours or wrap in additional layer of aluminum foil and freeze for up to 1 month. To serve, thaw overnight in refrigerator if frozen. Proceed with step 6, extending baking time by 15 minutes and covering with foil for final 10 minutes of cooking if top begins to get too dark.

Dried Fruit and Nut Wild Rice Dressing

Serves 10 to 12 | **Total Time** 2¾ hours
MAKE AHEAD VEGETARIAN

WHY THIS RECIPE WORKS Dramatic wild rice; toasty, slightly sweet pecans; and jewel-like chopped dried fruit combine to make a character-filled holiday stuffing. Since the amount of liquid it takes to cook wild rice varies, we boiled the rice in extra liquid, reserving some of that cooking liquid to use to bind the dressing along with cream and eggs. Using the food processor to chop white bread into bite-size pieces put it into balance with the smaller pieces of rice, fruit, and nuts. Depending on the brand, wild rice absorbs varying quantities of liquid. If you have less than 1½ cups of leftover rice cooking liquid, make up the difference with additional broth. To make this dish vegetarian, use vegetable broth.

2 cups vegetable or chicken broth
2 cups water
1 bay leaf
2 cups wild rice
10 slices hearty white sandwich bread, torn into pieces
4 tablespoons unsalted butter plus 4 tablespoons
  unsalted butter, melted
2 onions, chopped fine
3 celery ribs, minced
4 garlic cloves, minced
1½ teaspoons dried sage

1½ teaspoons dried thyme

1½ cups heavy cream

2 large eggs

¾ teaspoon table salt

½ teaspoon pepper

1½ cups chopped dried apricots, cranberries, or cherries

1½ cups pecans, toasted and chopped

1. Bring broth, water, and bay leaf to boil in medium saucepan over medium-high heat. Add rice, reduce heat to low, and simmer, covered, until rice is tender, 35 to 45 minutes. Strain contents of pan through fine-mesh strainer into 4-cup liquid measuring cup. Transfer rice to bowl; discard bay leaf. Set aside 1½ cups cooking liquid.

2. Adjust oven racks to upper-middle and lower-middle positions and heat oven to 325 degrees. Pulse half of bread in food processor into pea-size pieces, about 6 pulses; transfer to rimmed baking sheet. Repeat with remaining bread and second rimmed baking sheet. Bake bread crumbs until golden, about 20 minutes, stirring occasionally and switching and rotating sheets halfway through baking. Let bread cool completely, about 10 minutes.

3. Melt 4 tablespoons butter in 12-inch skillet over medium heat. Cook onions and celery until softened and golden, 8 to 10 minutes. Add garlic, sage, and thyme and cook until fragrant, about 30 seconds. Stir in reserved cooking liquid, remove from heat, and let cool for 5 minutes.

4. Whisk cream, eggs, salt, and pepper together in large bowl. Slowly whisk in warm broth-vegetable mixture. Stir in rice, toasted bread crumbs, dried apricots, and pecans and transfer to 13 by 9-inch baking dish. (Dressing can be refrigerated for up to 24 hours. To serve, proceed with recipe, increasing baking time by 20 minutes.)

5. Drizzle melted butter evenly over dressing. Cover dish with aluminum foil and bake on lower-middle rack until set, 45 to 55 minutes. Remove foil and let cool for 15 minutes. Serve.

Egg Noodles with Browned Butter and Caraway

Serves 6 | **Total Time** 30 minutes VEGETARIAN

WHY THIS RECIPE WORKS Egg noodles are a no-brainer side dish for hearty meat stews or roasts, but they could do with a little jazzing up. To this end, while our noodles cooked we lightly toasted chopped caraway seeds with butter to deepen their flavor. This also browned the butter, which contributed a nice nutty flavor to the dish when we stirred

Dried Fruit and Nut Wild Rice Dressing

them in with the noodles. Adding some cold butter at the end kept the noodles creamy. Give the caraway seeds a gentle chop with a chef's knife; it brings out their flavor and helps disperse them throughout the dish. Do not use dried dill weed or chives in this recipe; their dusty flavor spoils the noodles.

1 (12-ounce) bag egg noodles
  Table salt for cooking egg noodles

4 tablespoons unsalted butter, cut into 4 pieces, divided

1 teaspoon caraway seeds, chopped

2 tablespoons finely chopped fresh dill or chives

1. Bring 4 quarts water to boil in Dutch oven. Add noodles and 1 tablespoon salt to boiling water and cook until al dente. Drain noodles and return to pot.

2. Meanwhile, melt 3 tablespoons butter in small saucepan over medium-low heat. Add caraway seeds and cook, swirling pan occasionally, until butter is nutty brown and fragrant, about 5 minutes. Add browned butter mixture, herbs, and remaining butter to pot with noodles and toss to combine. Season with salt to taste. Serve.

Creamy Orzo with Peas and Parmesan

Creamy Orzo with Peas and Parmesan

Serves 4 | **Total Time** 40 minutes `VEGETARIAN`

WHY THIS RECIPE WORKS Similar to Arborio rice in size, shape, and starchiness, orzo is in fact a very small pasta. Here, though, we wanted to capitalize on its resemblance to rice by making it the unexpected base of a creamy, risotto-like side dish. Adding extra appeal to our plan was the fact that orzo cooks through much more quickly than Arborio rice, so we could get this side on the table easily even on a busy weeknight. Sweet frozen peas are available year round; we stirred them into the orzo off the heat so they just warmed through but held on to their bright green color. To make our creamy orzo rich and satisfying enough to hold its own next to a savory main, we cooked the pasta in broth and fortified the dish with Parmesan cheese. If the finished orzo is too thick, stir in hot water, a few tablespoons at a time, to adjust the consistency. To make this dish vegetarian, use vegetable broth.

2 tablespoons unsalted butter
1 onion, chopped fine
¼ teaspoon table salt
2 garlic cloves, minced
1 cup orzo
¼ cup dry white wine
3¾ cups vegetable or chicken broth
2 ounces Parmesan cheese, grated (1 cup)
½ cup frozen peas, thawed

1. Melt butter in large saucepan over medium-high heat. Add onion and salt and cook until softened, about 5 minutes. Stir in garlic and cook until fragrant, about 30 seconds. Stir in orzo and cook for 1 minute.

2. Stir in wine and cook until evaporated, about 1 minute. Stir in broth, bring to boil, and cook, stirring often, until orzo is tender and creamy, about 15 minutes. Off heat, vigorously stir in Parmesan until creamy. Stir in peas and let stand off heat until peas are heated through and sauce has thickened slightly, about 2 minutes. Season with salt and pepper to taste, and serve.

Creamy Orzo with Bacon and Scallions

Omit butter, peas, and Parmesan. Cook 3 slices chopped bacon in pot over medium-high heat until crispy, about 5 minutes; transfer to paper towel–lined plate. Add onion to rendered bacon fat and cook as directed. Stir in 2 thinly sliced scallions and sprinkle with bacon before serving.

Make-Ahead Creamy Macaroni and Cheese

Creamy Orzo with Fennel

Omit peas. Add 1 fennel bulb, cored, trimmed, and chopped, to pot with onion in step 1; cook until lightly browned, about 10 minutes. Add ¼ teaspoon fennel seeds and pinch red pepper flakes to pot with garlic.

Make-Ahead Creamy Macaroni and Cheese

Serves 8 to 10 MAKE AHEAD VEGETARIAN
Total Time 2 hours, plus 2 hours cooling

WHY THIS RECIPE WORKS A well-made macaroni and cheese is often the first dish to disappear from a holiday table. And when it comes to cooking for a crowd, whether for a pot-luck or a home gathering, the option to complete most of the work ahead of time is a real boon. Our mac and cheese can be frozen as much as two months (yes, months!) in advance; a quick thaw in the microwave and a stint in the oven is all that's needed to get it ready for company. To keep the pasta from drying out in the freezer, we increased the ratio of sauce to pasta. As for that sauce, heavy cream was less prone to curdling than milk, and cutting the cream with broth made for a uniquely savory mac and cheese light enough to return to for seconds—if there's any left by then. To make this dish vegetarian, use vegetable broth.

- 4 slices hearty white sandwich bread, torn into pieces
- 8 tablespoons unsalted butter, melted, plus 6 tablespoons unsalted butter
- ¼ cup grated Parmesan cheese
- 1 garlic clove, minced
- 1 teaspoon table salt, plus salt for cooking pasta
- 1 pound elbow macaroni
- 6 tablespoons all-purpose flour
- 1 teaspoon dry mustard
- ⅛ teaspoon cayenne pepper
- 4½ cups vegetable or chicken broth
- 1½ cups heavy cream
- 1 pound Colby cheese, shredded (4 cups)
- 8 ounces extra-sharp cheddar cheese, shredded (2 cups)
- ½ teaspoon pepper

1. Pulse bread, 2 tablespoons melted butter, Parmesan, and garlic in food processor until coarsely ground. Transfer crumbs to zipper-lock freezer bag and freeze.

2. Bring 4 quarts water to boil in Dutch oven over high heat. Add 1 tablespoon salt and macaroni and cook until barely softened, about 3 minutes. Drain pasta, then spread out on rimmed baking sheet and let cool.

3. Heat remaining 6 tablespoons butter, flour, mustard, and cayenne in empty pot over medium-high heat, stirring constantly, until golden and fragrant, 1 to 2 minutes. Slowly whisk in broth and cream and bring to boil. Reduce heat to medium and simmer until slightly thickened, about 15 minutes. Off heat, whisk in Colby, cheddar, pepper, and 1 teaspoon salt until smooth.

4. Stir cooled pasta into sauce, breaking up any clumps, until well combined. Transfer pasta mixture to 13 by 9-inch baking dish. Let cool completely, about 2 hours. Wrap dish tightly with plastic wrap, cover with aluminum foil, and freeze for up to 2 months.

5. Adjust oven rack to middle position and heat oven to 375 degrees. Remove foil from casserole and reserve. Microwave casserole until mixture is thawed and beginning to bubble around edges, 7 to 12 minutes, stirring pasta and replacing plastic halfway through cooking. Discard plastic and cover pan with reserved foil. Bake for 20 minutes, then remove foil and sprinkle with frozen bread crumbs. Continue to bake untilcrumbs are golden brown and crisp, about 20 minutes. Let cool for 10 minutes. Serve.

NOTES FROM THE TEST KITCHEN

NO MORE CURDLED CHEESE SAUCE
Since dairy-based dishes can easily become curdled when reheated, it was essential that we find a way to prevent the luscious sauce in our Make-Ahead Creamy Macaroni and Cheese from curdling when we baked this dish after a long stint in the freezer. Curdling occurs when excessive heat causes whey proteins in dairy to denature (or unfold) and bind with casein proteins, forming clumps. Replacing plain milk with heavy cream made for a sauce that was much less prone to curdling because of the larger amount of butterfat (around 36 to 40 percent) found in heavy cream. All that extra fat more thoroughly coats the proteins in the dairy, preventing them from binding together. Plus, with more fat, heavy cream has far fewer proteins to bind together in the first place. All this means rich, decadent, uncurdled cheese sauce is within reach—just add cream.

Savory Noodle Kugel

Serves 8 to 10 | **Total Time** 1¼ hours **MAKE AHEAD**

WHY THIS RECIPE WORKS While sweet kugels are traditionally served with Jewish holiday meals, kugel also has an excellent savory side. Onions caramelized in rendered chicken fat, or schmaltz, built a rich and rounded base of flavor into which we mixed eggs and some parsley. Tossing the egg mixture with just-cooked, still-warm noodles helped thicken the eggs slightly so they clung to the noodles; we then transferred the eggy, oniony noodles to a baking dish and popped the casserole into the oven to set it up. A pass under the broiler gave the kugel its characteristic crunchy top. Use a broiler-safe baking dish for this recipe. Look for rendered chicken fat (schmaltz) in the frozen food section of larger supermarkets. To make this dish vegetarian, use extra-virgin olive oil.

- 3 tablespoons rendered chicken fat (schmaltz) or extra-virgin olive oil
- 3 onions, chopped fine
- 1½ teaspoons table salt, divided, plus salt for cooking noodles
- 6 large eggs
- 2 tablespoons minced fresh parsley
- ¾ teaspoon pepper
- 1 pound wide egg noodles

1. Adjust 1 oven rack to middle position and second rack 6 inches from broiler element. Heat oven to 350 degrees. Grease broilersafe 13 by 9-inch baking dish. Heat rendered chicken fat in 12-inch skillet over medium-low heat. Add onions and ½ teaspoon salt and cook, stirring occasionally, until caramelized, 30 to 40 minutes. Transfer onions to large bowl and let cool for 10 minutes. (Cooled caramelized onions can be refrigerated for up to 3 days.) Whisk eggs, parsley, pepper, and remaining 1 teaspoon salt into onions; set aside.

2. Bring 4 quarts water to boil in large pot. Add noodles and 1 tablespoon salt and cook, stirring often, until al dente. Reserve 3 tablespoons cooking water, then drain noodles and let cool for 5 minutes. Whisk reserved cooking water into onion mixture. Stir still-warm noodles into onion mixture until well combined.

3. Transfer noodle mixture to prepared dish. (Kugel can be refrigerated for up to 24 hours. Increase baking time to 25 minutes.) Bake on middle oven rack until set, about 20 minutes. Remove kugel from oven and heat broiler. Once broiler is hot, broil kugel on upper rack until top noodles are browned and crispy, 1 to 3 minutes, rotating dish as needed for even browning. Serve.

Slow-Cooker Pinto Beans with Chipotle

Serves 6 **VEGETARIAN**
Cooking Time 8 to 9 hours on High

WHY THIS RECIPE WORKS There's a special joy in returning home after a long day and being greeted by the aroma of long-cooked spicy beans wafting from the slow cooker. Since the beans required a full 6 cups of liquid to cook evenly in the slow cooker, we knew that we would need to drain away some of that cooking liquid. To ensure that our beans remained full of flavor despite the loss of that flavorful liquid, we boosted the amount of garlic, oregano, and chili powder. For an extra dimension of flavor, we also added smoky chipotle chiles in adobo sauce and exchanged 1 cup of water for beer. When we stirred 1 cup of reserved cooking liquid back into the tender beans, we created a sauce that was rich and bold. A little bit of brown sugar rounded things out, and a hit of fresh lime juice and cilantro added brightness at the end. You will need a 4- to 7-quart slow cooker for this recipe.

- 1 onion, chopped fine
- 2 tablespoons extra-virgin olive oil, divided
- 4 garlic cloves, minced
- 1 tablespoon minced fresh oregano or 1 teaspoon dried
- 1 tablespoon chili powder
- 2 teaspoons minced canned chipotle chile in adobo sauce
- 1 teaspoon table salt
- 1 pound (2½ cups) dried pinto beans, picked over and rinsed
- 1 cup mild lager, such as Budweiser
- 2 tablespoons minced fresh cilantro
- 1 tablespoon packed brown sugar
- 1 tablespoon lime juice, plus extra for seasoning

1. Microwave onion, 1 tablespoon oil, garlic, oregano, chili powder, chipotle, and salt in bowl, stirring occasionally, until onion is softened, about 5 minutes; transfer to slow cooker. Stir in 5 cups water, beans, and beer. Cover and cook until beans are tender, 8 to 9 hours on high.

2. Drain beans, reserving 1 cup cooking liquid. Return beans and reserved cooking liquid to now-empty slow cooker. Stir in cilantro, sugar, lime juice, and remaining 1 tablespoon oil. Season with salt, pepper, and extra lime juice to taste. Serve. (Beans can be held on warm or low setting for up to 2 hours; adjust consistency with extra hot water as needed before serving.)

Spiced Red Lentils

Serves 6 to 8 | **Total Time** 1 hour `VEGETARIAN`

WHY THIS RECIPE WORKS Dals are spiced lentil stews common throughout India which combine flavor-packed comfort food with absolute ease. In less than a half hour of gentle simmering, the lentils break down to a porridge-like stew perfect for serving next to roast chicken or lamb or as a light main dish when paired with rice or bread. We wanted the spices to contribute warmth and complexity instead of heat, so we used a mix of citrusy coriander, cumin, cinnamon, earthy turmeric, and sweet cardamom, blooming them in oil until they were fragrant. Onion, garlic, and ginger added more fresh, aromatic flavor. Cooking 1¼ cups lentils in 4 cups of water resulted in a pleasingly chunky, not-too-thin puree. A bit of butter stirred in before serving made these warming, creamy lentils sing with richness and layers of flavor. You cannot substitute other types of lentils for the red lentils here; they have a very different texture. Serve over rice if desired.

- 1 tablespoon vegetable oil
- ½ teaspoon ground coriander
- ½ teaspoon ground cumin
- ½ teaspoon ground cinnamon
- ½ teaspoon ground turmeric
- ⅛ teaspoon ground cardamom
- ⅛ teaspoon red pepper flakes
- 1 onion, chopped fine
- 4 garlic cloves, minced
- 1½ teaspoons grated fresh ginger
- 4 cups water
- 8½ ounces (1¼ cups) red lentils, picked over and rinsed
- 1 pound plum tomatoes, cored, seeded, and chopped
- ½ cup minced fresh cilantro
- 2 tablespoons unsalted butter
  Lemon wedges

1. Heat oil in large saucepan over medium-high heat until shimmering. Add coriander, cumin, cinnamon, turmeric, cardamom, and pepper flakes and cook until fragrant, about 10 seconds. Stir in onion and cook until softened, about 5 minutes. Stir in garlic and ginger and cook until fragrant, about 30 seconds.

2. Stir in water and lentils and bring to boil. Reduce heat to low and simmer, uncovered, until lentils are tender and resemble coarse puree, 20 to 25 minutes.

3. Stir in tomatoes, cilantro, and butter and season with salt and pepper to taste. Serve with lemon wedges.

Slow-Cooker Pinto Beans with Chipotle

Spiced Red Lentils

Slow-Cooker Lentil Salad with Dill, Orange, and Spinach

Serves 6 | **Cooking Time** 3 to 4 hours on Low or 2 to 3 hours on High `VEGETARIAN`

WHY THIS RECIPE WORKS Oranges and spinach are two produce stars of autumn and early winter, and together they're a match made in salad heaven. We added French lentils (lentilles du Puy) to the mix for a hearty salad with an impressive presentation that belies its ease. The even heat of the slow cooker made it the ideal hands-off vessel for cooking delicate lentils to perfection; adding salt and vinegar to the water in which we cooked the lentils seasoned them and interacted with their skins to give us beans that were firm and unbroken yet creamy on the inside. The vinegar's tang also helped the earthy lentils shine. To keep the flavors fresh, we added the orange pieces and spinach only once the lentils were cooked and slightly cooled. Toasted pecans added a hint of crunch. We prefer lentilles du Puy for this recipe, but it will work with any type of lentil except red or yellow. You will need a 4- to 7-quart oval slow cooker for this recipe.

- 1 cup lentilles du Puy, picked over and rinsed
- 2½ tablespoons red wine vinegar, divided
- 3 garlic cloves, minced
- 3 (2-inch) strips orange zest, plus 2 oranges
- 1 bay leaf
- ¼ teaspoon table salt, plus salt for cooking lentils
- 4 ounces (4 cups) baby spinach, chopped
- ¼ cup extra-virgin olive oil
- 1 shallot, minced
- 2 tablespoons chopped fresh dill
- 2 tablespoons chopped toasted pecans

1. Combine 4 cups water, lentils, 1 tablespoon vinegar, garlic, orange zest, bay leaf, and ¾ teaspoon salt in slow cooker. Cover and cook until lentils are tender, 3 to 4 hours on low or 2 to 3 hours on high.

2. Cut away peel and pith from oranges. Cut oranges into 8 wedges, then slice wedges crosswise into ¼-inch-thick pieces.

3. Drain lentils, discarding orange zest and bay leaf, and transfer to large serving bowl; let cool slightly. Add oranges, along with any accumulated juices; spinach; oil; shallot; dill; ¼ teaspoon salt; and remaining 1½ tablespoons vinegar and gently toss to combine. Season with salt and pepper to taste, sprinkle with pecans, and serve.

French Lentils with Carrots and Parsley

Serves 6 to 8 | **Total Time** 1¼ hours
`MAKE AHEAD` `VEGETARIAN`

WHY THIS RECIPE WORKS A bowlful of earthy French lentils (also known as lentilles du Puy) is like a hug for your taste buds on a cold winter day. These tiny legumes are wonderfully tender and creamy when cooked properly, and their ability to hold their shape when cooked makes them perfect for a dish in which the lentils take center stage. The backdrop of the nutty lentils provides a great canvas for showcasing the sweeter flavors of carrots and the freshness of herbs. We cooked the carrots with onion and celery to make a classic mirepoix, adding garlic and thyme for bite and a pleasant woodsiness. Using water instead of broth as our cooking liquid allowed the flavors of the vegetables and lentils to come through. We prefer lentilles du Puy for this recipe, but it will work with any type of lentil except red or yellow (note that cooking times will vary depending on the type used).

- 2 carrots, peeled and chopped fine
- 1 onion, chopped fine
- 1 celery rib, chopped fine
- 2 tablespoons extra-virgin olive oil, divided
- ½ teaspoon table salt
- 2 garlic cloves, minced
- 1 teaspoon minced fresh thyme or ¼ teaspoon dried
- 2½ cups water
- 1 cup lentilles du Puy, picked over and rinsed
- 2 tablespoons minced fresh parsley
- 2 teaspoons lemon juice

1. Combine carrots, onion, celery, 1 tablespoon oil, and salt in large saucepan. Cover and cook over medium-low heat, stirring occasionally, until vegetables are softened, 8 to 10 minutes. Stir in garlic and thyme and cook until fragrant, about 30 seconds.

2. Stir in water and lentils and bring to simmer. Reduce heat to low, cover, and continue to simmer, stirring occasionally, until lentils are mostly tender but still slightly crunchy, 40 to 50 minutes. (Lentils can be refrigerated for up to 3 days. To reheat, microwave in covered bowl until hot throughout, 3 to 5 minutes, stirring halfway through microwaving, and continue with step 3.)

3. Uncover and continue to cook, stirring occasionally, until lentils are completely tender, about 8 minutes. Stir in parsley, lemon juice, and remaining 1 tablespoon oil. Season with salt and pepper to taste, and serve.

French Lentils with Carrots and Parsley

6 tablespoons extra-virgin olive oil, divided
2 onions, chopped fine
½ teaspoon table salt
3 garlic cloves, minced
20 ounces curly-leaf spinach, stemmed, divided
2 (14.5-ounce) cans diced tomatoes, drained
¼ cup minced fresh dill
2 slices hearty white sandwich bread, torn into quarters
6 ounces feta cheese, crumbled (1½ cups)
Lemon wedges

1. Dissolve 3 tablespoons salt in 4 quarts cold water in large container. Add beans and soak at room temperature for at least 8 hours or up to 24 hours. Drain and rinse well.

2. Bring beans and 2 quarts water to boil in Dutch oven. Reduce to simmer and cook, stirring occasionally, until beans are tender, 1 to 1½ hours. Drain beans and set aside.

3. Wipe Dutch oven clean with paper towels. Heat 2 tablespoons oil in now-empty pot over medium heat until shimmering. Add onions and salt and cook until softened, about 5 minutes. Stir in garlic and cook until fragrant, about 30 seconds. Stir in half of spinach, cover, and cook until beginning to wilt, about 2 minutes. Stir in remaining spinach, cover, and cook until wilted, about 2 minutes. Off heat, gently stir in beans, tomatoes, dill, and 2 tablespoons oil. Season with salt and pepper to taste.

4. Meanwhile, adjust oven rack to middle position and heat oven to 400 degrees. Pulse bread and remaining 2 tablespoons oil in food processor to coarse crumbs, about 5 pulses. Transfer bean mixture to 13 by 9-inch baking dish. (Dish can be covered with plastic wrap and be refrigerated for up to 24 hours. Allow to come to room temperature before proceeding with recipe.) Sprinkle with feta, then bread crumbs. Bake until bread crumbs are golden brown and edges are bubbling, about 20 minutes. Serve with lemon wedges.

Gigante Beans with Spinach and Feta

Serves 6 to 8 MAKE AHEAD VEGETARIAN
Total Time 1¾ hours, plus 8 hours brining

WHY THIS RECIPE WORKS The size of large lima beans, gigante beans are popular throughout Greece and bring a velvety, creamy texture and welcome earthiness to a variety of dishes. Here, we embraced their Greek heritage by pairing them with spinach and tangy feta cheese. A long saltwater soak was essential for preventing blowouts. To the wilted spinach we added canned diced tomatoes and fresh dill for more bold Greek-inspired flavor. For an impressive presentation, we baked the beans and greens and topped them with bread crumbs and feta for crunch and salty contrast. This dish pairs well with lamb, or with seafood for a lighter dinner. You can substitute flat-leaf spinach; do not substitute baby spinach.

3 tablespoons table salt for brining beans
8 ounces (1½ cups) dried gigante beans, picked over and rinsed

Cannellini Beans with Roasted Red Peppers and Kale

Serves 4 to 6 | **Total Time** 45 minutes
MAKE AHEAD VEGETARIAN

WHY THIS RECIPE WORKS For an easy one-pot take on the classic Italian combination of beans and greens, we paired canned cannellini beans and kale with sweet jarred roasted red peppers. Garlic and hot red pepper flakes added subtle, balancing spiciness. Slicing the kale into thin ribbons and wilting it made it easier to eat. For the liquid, we used water

Cannellini Beans with Roasted Red Peppers and Kale

Basic Black Beans

as a neutral base, adding some white wine for brightness. Parmesan, lemon wedges, and a drizzle of olive oil gave the dish a great finish. Swiss chard can be substituted for the kale. Serve with roast chicken or with bread for a light meal.

- ¼ cup extra-virgin olive oil, plus extra for serving
- 4 garlic cloves, minced
- ¼ teaspoon red pepper flakes
- 1 small red onion, halved and sliced thin
- ¼ teaspoon table salt
- 1 cup jarred roasted red peppers, sliced thin lengthwise
- 1 pound kale, stemmed and sliced thin crosswise
- 2 (15-ounce) cans cannellini beans, rinsed
- ½ cup dry white wine
- ½ cup water
- 1 ounce Parmesan cheese, grated (½ cup)
  Lemon wedges

1. Cook oil, garlic, and pepper flakes in 12-inch skillet over medium-high heat until garlic turns golden brown, about 2 minutes. Stir in onion and salt, reduce heat to medium, and cook until onion is softened, about 5 minutes. Stir in red peppers and cook until softened and glossy, about 3 minutes.

2. Stir in kale, 1 handful at a time, and cook until wilted, about 3 minutes. Stir in beans, wine, and water and bring to simmer. Reduce heat to medium-low, cover, and cook until flavors meld and kale is tender, 15 to 20 minutes. Season with salt and pepper to taste. (Cooled beans can be refrigerated for up to 3 days. Allow to come to room temperature before serving.) Serve with Parmesan, lemon wedges, and extra oil.

Spicy Chickpeas with Turnips

Serves 6 to 8 | **Total Time** 45 minutes
MAKE AHEAD **VEGETARIAN**

WHY THIS RECIPE WORKS We think turnips are underrated. A reliable vegetable to turn to throughout the winter months, they take extremely well to roasting, braising, and different flavor combinations. To turn up the heat on dinner, we combined turnips with chickpeas and dressed them up with a few vibrant ingredients. Sautéed aromatics plus a jalapeño gave us a savory flavor base with a kick, and cayenne pepper added extra spice. Creamy, already-cooked canned chickpeas only needed to be warmed through, and the starchy, seasoned liquid from the cans gave our sauce great flavor and body from the get-go. Turnips added bulk and soaked up all the good flavors we'd developed. A final touch of lemon juice was all this zesty bean dish needed before serving.

    2 tablespoons extra-virgin olive oil
    2 onions, chopped
    2 red bell peppers, stemmed, seeded, and chopped
    ½ teaspoon table salt
    ¼ teaspoon pepper
    ¼ cup tomato paste
    1 jalapeño chile, stemmed, seeded, and minced
    5 garlic cloves, minced
    ¾ teaspoon ground cumin
    ¼ teaspoon cayenne pepper
    2 (15-ounce) cans chickpeas
    12 ounces turnips, peeled and cut into ½-inch pieces
    ¾ cup water, plus extra as needed
    ¼ cup chopped fresh parsley
    2 tablespoons lemon juice, plus extra for seasoning

1. Heat oil in Dutch oven over medium heat until shimmering. Add onions, bell peppers, salt, and pepper and cook until softened and lightly browned, 5 to 7 minutes. Stir in tomato paste, jalapeño, garlic, cumin, and cayenne and cook until fragrant, about 30 seconds.

2. Stir in chickpeas and their liquid, turnips, and water. Bring to simmer and cook until turnips are tender and sauce has thickened, 25 to 35 minutes. (Cooled beans can be refrigerated for up to 2 days. To reheat, bring beans, covered, to gentle simmer, stirring often, and continue with step 3.)

3. Stir in parsley and lemon juice. Season with salt, pepper, and extra lemon juice to taste. Adjust consistency with extra hot water as needed. Serve.

Basic Black Beans

Serves 6 | **Total Time** 3 hours MAKE AHEAD

WHY THIS RECIPE WORKS Every cook needs an easy black bean recipe in their culinary repertoire: Paired with pork chops, chicken, or a simple rice pilaf and vegetable, black beans make for an ultrasatisfying protein-rich meal. We were in pursuit of full-flavored beans that were tender but not mushy. Black beans are commonly cooked with meat to give them a rich, deep flavor, so we chose to simmer ours with a ham hock. For more flavor and to give the beans a touch of Cuban flair, we also decided to add a sofrito—a mix of onion, garlic, and green bell pepper. We sautéed our sofrito in olive

oil, along with some herbs and spices, until the vegetables were soft, and then stirred the mixture into the beans. Mashing a cup of the beans with the sofrito helped to intensify all of the flavors.

BEANS
    12 cups water
    1 pound (2½ cups) dried black beans, picked over and rinsed
    1 smoked ham hock (10 to 12 ounces), rinsed
    1 green bell pepper, stemmed, seeded, and quartered
    1 onion
    6 garlic cloves, minced
    2 bay leaves
    1½ teaspoons table salt

SOFRITO
    2 tablespoons extra-virgin olive oil
    1 onion, chopped fine
    1 green bell pepper, stemmed, seeded, and chopped fine
    8 garlic cloves, minced
    2 teaspoons dried oregano
    ¾ teaspoon table salt
    1½ teaspoons ground cumin
    1 tablespoon lime juice
    ½ cup chopped fresh cilantro

1. FOR THE BEANS Bring all ingredients to boil over medium-high heat in Dutch oven, skimming surface as scum rises. Reduce heat to low and simmer, partially covered, adding more water if cooking liquid reduces to level of beans, until beans are tender but not splitting, about 2 hours. Remove ham hock. When cool enough to handle, remove ham from bone, discard bone and skin, and cut meat into bite-size pieces; set aside. Discard bay leaves.

2. FOR THE SOFRITO Meanwhile, heat oil in 12-inch skillet over medium heat; add onion, bell pepper, garlic, oregano, and salt; and cook until vegetables soften, 8 to 10 minutes. Add cumin; cook until fragrant, about 1 minute.

3. Scoop 1 cup beans and 2 cups cooking liquid into pan with sofrito; mash beans with potato masher or fork until smooth. Simmer over medium heat until liquid is reduced and thickened, about 6 minutes. Return sofrito mixture with meat from ham hock to bean pot; simmer until beans are creamy and liquid thickens to sauce consistency, 15 to 20 minutes. Add lime juice; simmer 1 minute. Stir in cilantro and season with salt and pepper to taste. Serve. (Cooled beans can be refrigerated for up to 3 days.)

Cranberry Beans with Tequila, Green Chiles, and Pepitas

Serves 4 to 6 **MAKE AHEAD** **VEGETARIAN**
Total Time 1¾ hours, plus 8 hours brining

WHY THIS RECIPE WORKS During the coldest months of the year, we often like to take a culinary trip to warmer climes, as with this Mexican-inspired cranberry bean dish. This side also gave us an excuse to turn on the oven and heat up the kitchen, since it makes use of the oven's even heat to cook the delicate pinto-like beans gently. To begin building a flavorful background for our beans, we sautéed onion and garlic with lots of paprika, some cumin seeds, and dried oregano; tequila gave the mix a kick. Once the beans were tender, we stirred in canned chiles and then cooked the beans uncovered for 15 minutes more to allow the sauce to thicken. A garnish of rich sour cream, crunchy pepitas, and quick pickled shallot and radishes nicely balanced the warm flavors of the cranberry beans. If cranberry beans are not available, you can substitute pinto beans.

- 3 tablespoons table salt for brining beans
- 1 pound (2½ cups) dried cranberry beans, picked over and rinsed
- ¼ cup extra-virgin olive oil
- 1 onion, chopped fine
- 1 teaspoon table salt
- 6 garlic cloves, minced
- 1 tablespoon paprika
- ½ teaspoon cumin seeds
- ½ teaspoon dried oregano
- ¼ cup tequila
- 1 tablespoon packed brown sugar
- 1 bay leaf
- ½ cup canned chopped green chiles
- ½ cup roasted pepitas
- ½ cup sour cream or queso fresco
- 1 recipe Quick Pickled Shallot and Radishes

1. Dissolve 3 tablespoons salt in 4 quarts cold water in large container. Add beans and soak at room temperature for at least 8 hours or up to 24 hours. Drain and rinse well.

2. Adjust oven rack to middle position and heat oven to 325 degrees. Heat oil in Dutch oven over medium heat until shimmering. Add onion and 1 teaspoon salt and cook until onion is softened, about 5 minutes. Stir in garlic, paprika, cumin, and oregano and cook until fragrant, about 1 minute. Stir in tequila and cook until evaporated, about 30 seconds.

Stir in 5 cups water, sugar, bay leaf, and cranberry beans; bring to simmer. Cover, transfer pot to oven, and cook until beans are tender, stirring once halfway through cooking, about 1¼ hours.

3. Add green chiles, stirring vigorously. Return pot to oven, uncovered, and cook until sauce is thickened slightly, about 15 minutes. Season with salt and pepper to taste, and serve with pepitas, sour cream, and pickled vegetables. (Cooled beans can be refrigerated for up to 3 days.)

Quick Pickled Shallot and Radishes

Makes about 1 cup | **Total Time** 5 minutes

These quick pickled vegetables add a briny, peppery bite to bean dishes, salads, and more.

- 5 radishes, trimmed and sliced thin
- 1 shallot, sliced thin
- ¼ cup lime juice (2 limes)
- 1 teaspoon sugar
- ⅛ teaspoon table salt

Combine all ingredients in bowl. (Pickled vegetables can be refrigerated for up to 2 days.)

NOTES FROM THE TEST KITCHEN

WHY BRINE YOUR BEANS?
We nearly always recommend brining dried beans before cooking them. The results—intact beans with tender, creamy exteriors—are worth the hands-off time it takes. The reason that soaking dried beans in salt water makes them cook up with softer skins has to do with how the sodium ions in salt water interact with the cells in the beans' skins. As the beans soak in salt water, sodium ions replace some of the calcium and magnesium ions in the skins. Because sodium ions are weaker than these mineral ions, they allow more water to penetrate the skins. This gives the skins themselves a softer, more malleable texture, making them less likely to break apart as the beans swell during cooking.

Black-Eyed Peas with Walnuts and Pomegranate

Serves 4 to 6 | **Total Time** 20 minutes

`MAKE AHEAD` `VEGETARIAN`

WHY THIS RECIPE WORKS Here's a resolution for you: Stop dutifully forcing yourself to eat a few spoonfuls of plain black-eyed peas for luck each New Year's Eve. There are other options just as lucky but with far, far more flavor. Meaty Hoppin' John (page 64) is one: a Southern staple hearty enough to eat as a meal all by itself. Or, if you prefer your luck on the side, try this dish of black-eyed peas with walnuts and pomegranate seeds. We started with convenient and creamy canned black-eyed peas; the crunchy, slightly bitter walnuts and the tart bursts from juicy pomegranate seeds made each bite a textural delight. A punchy dressing of lemon juice and sweet-tart pomegranate molasses (pomegranate juice cooked until reduced to a syrupy consistency) unified the dish and offered balanced acidity and tang. Finally, we incorporated dukkah, a savory nut and seed blend, to give the beans even more textural contrast and a hit of earthy, citrusy flavor. Coming together in a mere 20 minutes, this was now the kind of dish worthy of ringing in an auspicious new year. We prefer to use our homemade Pistachio Dukkah (page 100), but you can substitute store-bought dukkah if you wish, though flavor can vary greatly by brand.

- 3 tablespoons extra-virgin olive oil
- 3 tablespoons dukkah, divided
- 2 tablespoons lemon juice
- 2 tablespoons pomegranate molasses
- ¼ teaspoon table salt
- ⅛ teaspoon pepper
- 2 (15-ounce) cans black-eyed peas, rinsed
- ½ cup walnuts, toasted and chopped
- ½ cup pomegranate seeds
- ½ cup minced fresh parsley
- 4 scallions, sliced thin

Whisk oil, 2 tablespoons dukkah, lemon juice, pomegranate molasses, salt, and pepper in large bowl until smooth. Add peas, walnuts, pomegranate seeds, parsley, and scallions and toss to combine. Season with salt and pepper to taste. (Cooled beans can be refrigerated for up to 3 days. Allow to come to room temperature before serving.) Sprinkle with remaining 1 tablespoon dukkah and serve.

Cranberry Beans with Tequila, Green Chiles, and Pepitas

Black-Eyed Peas with Walnuts and Pomegranate

all things **apple**

■ MAKE AHEAD   ▦ VEGETARIAN
Photo: Apple Cider Doughnuts

Bibb and Frisée Salad with
Apple and Celery

Curried Butternut Squash
and Apple Soup

Bibb and Frisée Salad with Apple and Celery

Serves 4 to 6 | **Total Time** 20 minutes VEGETARIAN

WHY THIS RECIPE WORKS An ideal salad offers a mix of textures, flavors, and colors, and this salad exemplifies that notion. Frilly, crunchy frisée offered a welcome contrast to Bibb lettuce's soft, buttery texture. Thinly slicing the apple and celery allowed us to combine them cohesively with the salad greens. Walnuts added crunch and nuttiness. We chose red wine vinegar as a base for our vinaigrette here since the acid complemented (but didn't overpower) the apple's sweetness and the celery's subtle earthiness. Mayonnaise added creaminess to the dressing and helped emulsify it without imparting any mayonnaise flavor. Use a mandoline to thinly slice the celery and apple. You can use any apple you like in this recipe.

- 1 tablespoon red wine vinegar
- 1½ teaspoons very finely minced shallot
- ½ teaspoon mayonnaise
- ½ teaspoon Dijon mustard
- ⅛ teaspoon table salt
- 3 tablespoons extra-virgin olive oil
- 1 head Bibb or Boston lettuce (8 ounces), torn into bite-size pieces
- 1 small head frisée, torn into bite-size pieces (4 cups)
- 1 apple, cored, halved, and sliced thin
- 1 celery rib, sliced thin
- ⅓ cup walnuts, pecans, or almonds, toasted and chopped coarse, divided

1. Combine vinegar, shallot, mayonnaise, mustard, and salt in medium bowl and season with pepper to taste. Whisk until mixture is milky in appearance and no lumps of mayonnaise remain. Whisking constantly, slowly in drizzle oil until emulsified and lightly thickened.

2. Place lettuce, frisée, apple, celery, and half of walnuts in large bowl. Toss to combine. Drizzle with dressing and toss until greens are evenly coated. Season with salt to taste. Sprinkle with remaining walnuts. Serve immediately.

Bibb and Arugula Salad with Apple and Goat Cheese

Omit celery. Substitute lemon juice for red wine vinegar, arugula for frisée, and ¼ cup toasted pepitas for walnuts. Sprinkle with ¾ cup crumbled goat cheese before serving.

Curried Butternut Squash and Apple Soup

Serves 4 to 6 | **Total Time** 1½ hours

`MAKE AHEAD` `VEGETARIAN`

WHY THIS RECIPE WORKS Butternut squash soup should boast brash orange color, luxurious texture, and unapologetic squash flavor. Unfortunately, many recipes bury the bold flavor of the squash beneath chicken stock, an excess of dairy, or a potpourri of baking spices. Instead of calling for laboriously peeling, chopping, and either sautéing or roasting the squash before incorporating it into the soup (methods that can cause the finished soup to taste gritty or mealy), we steamed the squash for the velvetiest soup. We didn't even need to peel the squash first, since the softened flesh could be scooped from the skin with a spoon after steaming. Plus, using the squash seeds and fibers in the cooking liquid infused the liquid with the squash's essence. After straining, this liquid became an indispensable flavor component. Velvety and permeated with a heady squash flavor, our soup was thick but not custardy, sweet but not pie-like. You can use any apple you like in this recipe. Serve with Classic Croutons (page 28), if desired.

- 4 tablespoons unsalted butter, divided
- 1 large shallot, chopped
- 2½ pounds butternut squash, quartered and seeded, fibers and seeds reserved
- 6 cups water
- 1 teaspoon table salt
- 1 large apple, peeled, cored, and quartered
- ½ cup heavy cream
- 1 teaspoon packed dark brown sugar
- 2 teaspoons curry powder

1. Melt 2 tablespoons butter in Dutch oven over medium heat. Add shallot and cook until softened, 2 to 3 minutes. Stir in squash seeds and fibers and cook until butter turns orange, about 4 minutes.

2. Stir in water and salt and bring to boil. Reduce to simmer, place squash and apple cut side down in steamer basket, and lower basket into pot. Cover and steam until squash is completely tender, 30 to 40 minutes.

3. Using tongs, transfer cooked squash and apple to rimmed baking sheet. Let cool slightly, then scrape cooked squash from skin using soupspoon; discard skins.

4. Strain cooking liquid through fine-mesh strainer into large liquid measuring cup. Working in batches, puree cooked squash and apple with 3 cups strained cooking liquid in blender until smooth, 1 to 2 minutes. (Soup can be refrigerated for up to 3 days or frozen for up to 1 month. If frozen, thaw soup completely in refrigerator. To reheat, bring soup, covered, to gentle simmer, whisking often, and continue with step 5.)

5. Return pureed soup to clean pot and stir in cream, sugar, curry powder, and remaining 2 tablespoons butter. Return to brief simmer, adding additional strained cooking liquid as needed to adjust consistency. Season with salt and pepper to taste, and serve.

Celery Root, Fennel, and Apple Chowder

Serves 6 | **Total Time** 1½ hours `VEGETARIAN`

WHY THIS RECIPE WORKS This sweet-and-savory vegetarian chowder presents a harmony of fall flavors. Grated apple added a fruity counterpoint to the earthy, herbal sweetness of celery root and fennel. White wine, garlic, thyme, and a bay leaf contributed savory notes. Celery root's creamy-but-not-starchy texture made it a wonderful base for a hearty chowder bulked up with chunks of tender red potatoes. Sautéing the fennel along with an onion before simmering brought out its anise flavor. For a bright citrus note, we simmered a strip of orange zest in the broth. Pureeing 2 cups of chowder with a modest amount of cream gave our soup the perfect amount of body. Minced fennel fronds added color to the finished soup. You can use any apple you like in this recipe.

- 2 tablespoons unsalted butter
- 1 onion, chopped
- 1 fennel bulb, 1 tablespoon fronds minced and reserved, stalks discarded, bulb halved, cored, and cut into ½-inch pieces
- 1½ teaspoons table salt
- 6 garlic cloves, minced
- 2 teaspoons minced fresh thyme or ¾ teaspoon dried
- 2 tablespoons all-purpose flour
- ½ cup dry white wine
- 4 cups vegetable broth
- 1½ cups water
- 14 ounces celery root, trimmed, peeled, and cut into ½-inch pieces
- 12 ounces red potatoes, unpeeled, cut into ½-inch pieces
- 1 apple, peeled and shredded
- 1 bay leaf
- 1 (3-inch) strip orange zest
- ¼ cup heavy cream

1. Melt butter in Dutch oven over medium heat. Add onion, fennel, and salt and cook until vegetables are softened, 5 to 7 minutes. Stir in garlic and thyme and cook until fragrant, about 30 seconds. Stir in flour and cook for 1 minute. Stir in wine, scraping up any browned bits and smoothing out any lumps, and cook until nearly evaporated, about 1 minute.

2. Stir in broth, water, celery root, potatoes, apple, bay leaf, and orange zest and bring to boil. Reduce heat to low, partially cover, and simmer gently until stew is thickened and vegetables are tender, 35 to 40 minutes.

3. Off heat, discard bay leaf and orange zest. Puree 2 cups chowder and cream in blender until smooth, about 1 minute, then return to pot. Stir in reserved fennel fronds, season with salt and pepper to taste, and serve.

NOTES FROM THE TEST KITCHEN

SUPERMARKET VERSUS FRESH-PICKED APPLES
Supermarket apple varieties are rarities in the apple world, carefully bred to store well for long periods of time and maintain a consistent taste and texture. The sweetness and firmness of most apple varieties in existence (there are thousands worldwide) change the longer they're stored. Immediately after harvest, most apples contain a large amount of malic acid, making them taste quite tart. But when stored, apples consume that malic acid, making them grow sweeter over time. They also soften as they age, though the rate at which this happens depends on the type of apple and how it's stored.

All this means that you probably won't find many regional or heirloom apple varieties at the super-market, where resistance to spoilage is paramount. But if you have the opportunity to go apple picking at an orchard or to buy fresh-picked apples from your local farmers' market, we recommend doing so: You'll likely discover several exciting new options to try out in recipes like Celery Root, Fennel, and Apple Chowder (page 191), Cider-Braised Pork Roast with Apples (page 193), and Applesauce (page 208).

Caraway-Crusted Pork Tenderloin with Sauerkraut and Apples

Serves 4 | **Total Time** 45 minutes

WHY THIS RECIPE WORKS The caraway seed crust on this pork tenderloin adds crunchy texture to the tender pork and infuses it with aromatic flavor as it sears. For a tart-sweet side dish we paired apples, cooked in the same skillet as the pork until softened, with flavorful sauerkraut. Brown sugar added sweetness to complement the fruit and balance the tangy sauerkraut. Roasting the pork tenderloins on top of the apple-sauerkraut mixture melded their flavors and made this a one-pan dinner. To ensure that the tenderloins don't curl during cooking, be sure to remove the silverskin from the meat. There's no need to peel the apples; we prefer the color of red-skinned Fujis or Galas here, but any sweet apple will do. You will need a 12-inch ovensafe skillet for this recipe.

- 2 (12- to 16-ounce) pork tenderloins, trimmed
- 1 tablespoon caraway seeds
- 1⅛ teaspoons table salt, divided
- ½ teaspoon plus ⅛ teaspoon pepper, divided
- 2 tablespoons vegetable oil, divided
- 2 apples, cored, halved, and cut into ¼-inch-thick slices
- 1 onion, chopped fine
- 1 pound sauerkraut, rinsed and drained
- 2 tablespoons packed light brown sugar
- 2 tablespoons minced fresh dill

1. Adjust oven rack to middle position and heat oven to 475 degrees. Pat pork dry with paper towels and sprinkle with caraway seeds, 1 teaspoon salt, and ½ teaspoon pepper, pressing lightly to adhere. Heat 1 tablespoon oil in 12-inch ovensafe skillet over medium-high heat until just smoking. Cook pork until browned on all sides, 5 to 7 minutes; transfer to plate.

2. Add remaining 1 tablespoon oil, apples, onion, remaining ⅛ teaspoon salt, and remaining ⅛ teaspoon pepper to now-empty skillet and cook over medium heat until softened, about 5 minutes, scraping up any browned bits. Stir in sauerkraut and sugar. Place pork on top of sauerkraut mixture. Bake until pork registers 140 degrees, about 13 minutes.

3. Transfer pork to cutting board, tent with foil, and let rest for 5 minutes. Stir dill into sauerkraut mixture and serve with pork.

Cider-Braised Pork Roast with Apples

Serves 8 | **Total Time** 4 hours, plus 18 hours salting

WHY THIS RECIPE WORKS Pork and apples are a classic combination, so we paired flavorful bone-in pork butt roast with apple cider. Rubbing the meat with a brown sugar–salt mixture and refrigerating it overnight seasoned the pork and helped keep it juicy. A few aromatics and herbs added depth, and apple wedges seared in pork fat united the elements of this hearty roast. Pork butt roast is often labeled Boston butt in the supermarket. You can use any apple you like in this recipe. We like to use our homemade Apple Butter (page 209) in this recipe, but you can use store-bought if you prefer.

- 1 (5- to 6-pound) bone-in pork butt roast
- ¼ cup packed brown sugar, for brining
- ¼ cup kosher salt, for brining
- ½ teaspoon pepper
- 3 tablespoons vegetable oil
- 1 onion, halved and sliced thin
- 6 garlic cloves, smashed and peeled
- 2 cups apple cider, divided
- 6 sprigs fresh thyme
- 2 bay leaves
- 1 cinnamon stick
- 2 apples, cored and cut into 8 wedges each
- ¼ cup apple butter
- 1 tablespoon cornstarch
- 1 tablespoon cider vinegar

1. Using sharp knife, trim fat cap on roast to ¼ inch. Cut 1-inch crosshatch pattern, ¹⁄₁₆ inch deep, in fat cap. Place roast on large sheet of plastic wrap. Combine sugar and ¼ cup salt in bowl and rub mixture over entire roast and into slits. Wrap roast tightly in double layer of plastic, place on plate, and refrigerate for 18 to 24 hours.

2. Adjust oven rack to middle position and heat oven to 275 degrees. Unwrap roast and pat dry with paper towels, brushing away any excess salt mixture from surface. Sprinkle roast with pepper.

3. Heat oil in Dutch oven over medium-high heat until just smoking. Sear roast until well browned on all sides, about 3 minutes per side. Turn roast fat side up. Scatter onion and garlic around roast and cook until fragrant and beginning to brown, about 2 minutes. Add 1¾ cups cider, thyme sprigs, bay leaves, and cinnamon stick and bring to simmer. Cover, transfer to oven, and braise until fork slips easily in and out of meat and meat registers 190 degrees, 2¼ hours to 2¾ hours.

Caraway-Crusted Pork Tenderloin with Sauerkraut and Apples

Cider-Braised Pork Roast with Apples

Apple-Cinnamon Muffins

Apple Cider Doughnuts

4. Transfer roast to carving board, tent with aluminum foil, and let rest for 30 minutes. Strain braising liquid through fine-mesh strainer into fat separator; discard solids and let liquid settle for at least 5 minutes.

5. About 10 minutes before roast is done resting, wipe out pot with paper towels. Spoon 1½ tablespoons of clear, separated fat from top of fat separator into now-empty pot and heat over medium-high heat until shimmering. Season apples with salt and pepper to taste. Space apples evenly in pot, cut side down, and cook until well browned on both cut sides, about 3 minutes per side. Transfer to platter and tent with foil.

6. Wipe out pot with paper towels. Return 2 cups defatted braising liquid to now-empty pot and bring to boil over high heat. Whisk in apple butter until incorporated. Whisk cornstarch and remaining ¼ cup cider together in bowl and add to pot. Return to boil and cook until thickened, about 1 minute. Off heat, add vinegar and season with salt and pepper to taste. Cover sauce and keep warm.

7. To carve roast, cut around inverted T-shaped bone until it can be pulled free from roast (use clean dish towel to grasp bone if necessary). Slice pork and transfer to serving platter with apples. Pour 1 cup sauce over pork and apples. Serve, passing remaining sauce at table.

Apple-Cinnamon Muffins

Makes 12 muffins | **Total Time** 1½ hours
MAKE AHEAD VEGETARIAN

WHY THIS RECIPE WORKS The key to building big apple flavor in a tender muffin lies in the technique. We found that sautéing chopped tart apples in butter with brown sugar and cinnamon before stirring the apples into the batter concentrated the apple flavor and evaporated the excess moisture that would have made the muffins wet and gummy. Replacing traditional buttermilk with a combination of apple cider and plain yogurt added more apple flavor and tang with less moisture to sog out the muffins. For a finishing touch, we added a crunchy topping of cinnamon sugar. Do not substitute apple juice for the apple cider. Make sure to spray the muffin tin thoroughly, inside the cups and on top.

TOPPING
2 tablespoons granulated sugar
2 tablespoons packed brown sugar
¼ teaspoon ground cinnamon

MUFFINS

- 2 tablespoons unsalted butter, plus 4 tablespoons melted
- 2 Granny Smith, Empire, or Braeburn apples, peeled, cored, and cut into ¼-inch pieces (3 cups)
- 2 tablespoons packed brown sugar
- ¾ teaspoon ground cinnamon, divided
- 2½ cups (12½ ounces) all-purpose flour
- 2½ teaspoons baking powder
- ¼ teaspoon baking soda
- 1¼ teaspoons table salt
- 1 cup (7 ounces) granulated sugar
- 2 large eggs
- ¼ cup vegetable oil
- ½ cup apple cider
- ½ cup plain whole-milk yogurt
- 1 teaspoon vanilla extract

1. FOR THE TOPPING Using your fingers, combine granulated sugar, brown sugar, and cinnamon in bowl. Cover and set aside.

2. FOR THE MUFFINS Adjust oven rack to upper-middle position and heat oven to 400 degrees. Spray 12-cup muffin tin generously with vegetable oil spray. Melt 2 tablespoons butter in 12-inch skillet over medium-high heat. Add apples, brown sugar, and ¼ teaspoon cinnamon. Cook, stirring often, until moisture has completely evaporated and apples are well browned, about 9 minutes. Remove pan from heat and let cool for 10 minutes.

3. Meanwhile, whisk flour, baking powder, baking soda, salt, and remaining ½ teaspoon cinnamon together in large bowl. Whisk granulated sugar, eggs, oil, and melted butter together in separate bowl until thick and homogeneous, about 30 seconds. Whisk cider, yogurt, and vanilla into sugar mixture until combined.

4. Fold sugar mixture and cooled apples into flour mixture until just combined. Using greased ⅓-cup dry measuring cup, divide batter evenly among prepared muffin cups (cups will be filled to rim); sprinkle muffin tops evenly with topping.

5. Bake until golden brown and toothpick inserted in center comes out with few crumbs attached, 18 to 22 minutes, rotating muffin tin halfway through baking. Let muffins cool in muffin tin on wire rack for 10 minutes. Remove muffins from muffin tin and let cool on wire rack 5 minutes. Serve. (Muffins can be stored at room temperature for up to 3 days.)

Apple Cider Doughnuts

Makes 12 doughnuts and 12 doughnut holes
Total Time 1 hour VEGETARIAN

WHY THIS RECIPE WORKS These sweet treats are a must-have when visiting apple orchards in the fall. But far too often the apple flavor is lost. For our version, we were able to cut out the time-consuming step of boiling cider by simply stirring tart, intensely flavorful apple juice concentrate right into the dough. A slightly higher ratio of flour to liquid ingredients helped us control the dough's wetness without refrigerating it for hours to tighten it up. Using acidic buttermilk activated the leaveners and gave the doughnuts extra lift and lightness. A bit of cinnamon and nutmeg complemented the doughnuts' sweetness. After frying them, we gave our old-fashioned doughnuts a quick toss in cinnamon sugar seasoned with a touch of salt to add a final layer of flavor and a sugary crunch. Use a Dutch oven that holds 6 quarts or more for this recipe.

COATING

- ½ cup (3½ ounces) sugar
- ⅛ teaspoon ground cinnamon
- Pinch table salt

DOUGHNUTS

- 2½ cups (12½ ounces) all-purpose flour
- 1 teaspoon baking powder
- ½ teaspoon baking soda
- ½ teaspoon ground cinnamon
- ¼ teaspoon ground nutmeg
- ¼ teaspoon table salt
- ½ cup thawed apple juice concentrate
- ⅓ cup (2⅓ ounces) sugar
- ¼ cup buttermilk
- 4 tablespoons unsalted butter, melted and cooled
- 1 large egg
- 2 quarts vegetable oil, for frying

1. FOR THE COATING Whisk sugar, cinnamon, and salt together in medium bowl; set aside.

2. FOR THE DOUGHNUTS Whisk flour, baking powder, baking soda, cinnamon, nutmeg, and salt together in bowl. Whisk apple juice concentrate, sugar, buttermilk, melted butter, and egg together in large bowl. Whisk half of flour mixture into apple juice concentrate mixture until smooth. Add remaining flour mixture; using rubber spatula, use folding motion to mix and press dough until all flour is hydrated and no dry bits remain. (Dough can be covered with plastic wrap and refrigerated for up to 24 hours.)

3. Dust counter heavily with flour. Turn out dough onto floured counter, then dust top of dough with additional flour. Using your floured hands, gently pat dough into ⅓-inch-thick round, 10 to 11 inches in diameter. Using floured 3-inch round cutter, cut out 9 or 10 doughnut rounds. Using 1-inch round cutter, cut hole in center of each round.

4. Lightly dust rimmed baking sheet with flour. Transfer doughnut rounds and holes to prepared sheet. Combine dough scraps, then knead into cohesive ball and pat into ⅓-inch-thick round. Cut out 2 or 3 more doughnut rounds and holes (you should have 12 of each). Transfer to sheet and refrigerate while heating oil.

5. Set wire rack in second rimmed baking sheet and line half of rack with triple layer of paper towels. Add oil to large Dutch oven until it measures about 1½ inches deep and heat over medium-high heat to 350 degrees. Add 6 doughnut rounds and cook, flipping every 30 seconds, until deep golden brown, about 2 minutes. Adjust burner as needed to maintain oil temperature between 325 and 350 degrees.

6. Using spider skimmer or slotted spoon, transfer doughnuts to paper towel–lined side of prepared rack and let sit while frying remaining doughnut rounds. Return oil to 350 degrees and repeat with remaining doughnut rounds.

7. Return oil to 350 degrees and, using spider skimmer or slotted spoon, carefully add doughnut holes to hot oil. Cook, stirring often, until deep golden brown, about 2 minutes. Transfer to paper towel–lined side of wire rack. Lightly toss doughnuts and doughnut holes in coating and transfer to unlined side of wire rack. Serve.

DUST, PAT, AND STAMP
Follow the steps below to shape the dough and cut the doughnut rounds and holes.

1. Dust dough with flour, then use your hands to pat dough into round.

2. Use large and small round cutters to stamp out doughnut rounds and holes.

Apple Fritters

Makes 10 fritters   VEGETARIAN
Total Time 50 minutes

WHY THIS RECIPE WORKS Apple fritters should be crisp on the outside, moist within, and sing out apple flavor. Too often, fritters are leaden, soggy, even undercooked. We found that the best solution was to dry the apples with paper towels and mix them with the dry ingredients, which absorbed the moisture that would otherwise have leached out during frying. As for the batter, replacing the milk with apple cider reinforced the sweet apple flavor. A quick glaze spooned over the warm fritters added another layer of apple flavor. Apple juice doesn't have enough flavor—you really do need the cider.

FRITTERS
2   Granny Smith, Empire, or Braeburn apples, peeled, cored, halved, and cut into ¼-inch pieces
2   cups (10 ounces) all-purpose flour
⅓   cup (2⅓ ounces) granulated sugar
1   tablespoon baking powder
1   teaspoon table salt
1   teaspoon ground cinnamon
¼   teaspoon ground nutmeg
¾   cup apple cider
2   large eggs, lightly beaten
2   tablespoons unsalted butter, melted and cooled
3   cups vegetable oil

GLAZE
2   cups (8 ounces) confectioners' sugar
¼   cup apple cider
½   teaspoon ground cinnamon
¼   teaspoon ground nutmeg

1. FOR THE FRITTERS Spread apples in single layer on paper towel–lined rimmed baking sheet and pat dry thoroughly with more paper towels. Whisk flour, sugar, baking powder, salt, cinnamon, and nutmeg together in large bowl. In separate bowl, whisk cider, eggs, and melted butter together. Add apples to flour mixture to coat, then stir in cider mixture until incorporated.

2. Heat oil in large Dutch oven over medium-high heat to 350 degrees. Set wire rack in clean rimmed baking sheet. Using ⅓-cup dry measure, transfer 5 heaping portions of batter to oil. Press batter lightly with back of spoon to flatten. Fry, adjusting burner as necessary to maintain oil temperature between 325 and 350 degrees, until deep golden brown, 2 to 3 minutes per side.

3. Transfer fritters to prepared wire rack. Return oil to 350 degrees and repeat with remaining batter.

4. FOR THE GLAZE Whisk all ingredients in bowl until smooth. Top each fritter with 1 heaping tablespoon glaze. Let glaze set for 10 minutes before serving.

Cranberry-Pecan-Stuffed Baked Apples

Serves 6 | Total Time 1¼ hours   VEGETARIAN

WHY THIS RECIPE WORKS There's nothing frumpy about these baked apples stuffed with a zesty mixture of nuts and fruit. Removing the skin from everywhere but the top kept the flesh from steaming and turning to mush. A melon baller helped us scoop out a spacious cavity for the brown sugar and pecan filling, which we updated by adding tangy dried cranberries, chewy rolled oats, and diced apple. Before filling the apples, we browned their flat top surface in butter to coax out caramelized flavor. Capping the filled apples with their unpeeled tops protected them from burning. Moving the skillet to the oven, we basted the apples with apple cider and maple syrup to infuse them with flavor and keep them moist. You will need a 12-inch ovensafe nonstick skillet for this recipe. While old-fashioned rolled oats are preferable, quick oats can be substituted; do not use instant oats. Serve with vanilla ice cream, if desired.

 7 large Granny Smith, Empire, or Braeburn apples (8 ounces each)
 6 tablespoons unsalted butter, softened, divided
 ⅓ cup dried cranberries, chopped coarse
 ⅓ cup pecans, toasted and chopped coarse
 ¼ cup packed (1¾ ounces) brown sugar
 3 tablespoons old-fashioned rolled oats
 1 teaspoon finely grated orange zest
 ½ teaspoon ground cinnamon
    Pinch table salt
 ⅓ cup maple syrup
 ⅓ cup plus 2 tablespoons apple cider, divided

1. Adjust oven rack to middle position and heat oven to 375 degrees. Peel, core, and cut 1 apple into ¼-inch dice. Combine diced apple, 5 tablespoons butter, cranberries, pecans, sugar, oats, orange zest, cinnamon, and salt in bowl.

2. Shave thin slice off bottom of remaining 6 apples to allow them to sit flat. Cut top ½ inch off stem end of apples and reserve. Peel apples and use melon baller or small

Apple Fritters

Cranberry-Pecan-Stuffed Baked Apples

Skillet Apple Crisp

Apple Pandowdy

measuring spoon to remove 1½-inch-diameter core, being careful not to cut through bottom of apples.

3. Melt remaining 1 tablespoon butter in 12-inch ovensafe nonstick skillet over medium heat. Add apples, stem side down, and cook until cut surface is golden brown, about 3 minutes. Flip apples, reduce heat to low, and spoon filling inside, mounding excess filling over cavities. Top with reserved apple caps.

4. Add maple syrup and ⅓ cup cider to skillet. Transfer skillet to oven and bake until fork inserted into apples meets little resistance, 35 to 40 minutes, basting every 10 minutes with juices in skillet.

5. Transfer apples to serving dish. Stir up to 2 tablespoons remaining cider into sauce in skillet to adjust consistency. Pour sauce over apples and serve.

Dried Cherry–Hazelnut-Stuffed Baked Apples

Substitute dried cherries for cranberries, skinned hazelnuts for pecans, and pepper for cinnamon.

Dried Fig–Macadamia-Stuffed Baked Apples

Substitute dried figs for cranberries, macadamia nuts for pecans, lemon zest for orange zest, and ¼ teaspoon ground ginger for cinnamon.

Raisin-Walnut-Stuffed Baked Apples

Substitute raisins for cranberries, walnuts for pecans, lemon zest for orange zest, and ¼ teaspoon ground nutmeg for cinnamon.

Skillet Apple Crisp

Serves 8 | **Total Time** 1¼ hours VEGETARIAN

WHY THIS RECIPE WORKS For a lush sweet-tart apple crisp we started by reducing apple cider to a syrupy consistency full of intense fruity depth. We then cooked our apples on the stovetop in the same skillet we'd used to reduce the cider. This allowed us to stir the apples periodically so they would cook evenly. The stovetop's heat drove away extra moisture that might otherwise sog out the crisp topping and allowed the fruit and butter to caramelize and lend a sweet richness to the filling. Combining the softened apples with the cider before baking the crisp ensured that the dessert was juicy (but not soggy) and bursting with apple flavor. A topping made with a combination of white and brown sugars, cinnamon, salt, chopped pecans, and—for extra texture—chewy rolled oats brought depth and crunch to our apple crisp. We prefer rolled oats in the topping, but quick oats can be substituted. Serve with vanilla ice cream or whipped cream.

TOPPING

- ¾ cup (3¾ ounces) all-purpose flour
- ¾ cup pecans, chopped fine
- ¾ cup old-fashioned rolled oats
- ½ cup (3½ ounces) packed light brown sugar
- ¼ cup (1¾ ounces) granulated sugar
- ½ teaspoon ground cinnamon
- ½ teaspoon table salt
- 8 tablespoons unsalted butter, melted and cooled

FILLING

- 1½ cups apple cider
- 1 tablespoon lemon juice
- 4 pounds Golden Delicious, Jonagold, or Honeycrisp apples, peeled, cored, halved, and cut into ½-inch-thick wedges
- ⅓ cup (2⅓ ounces) granulated sugar
- ¼ teaspoon ground cinnamon
- 2 tablespoons unsalted butter

1. FOR THE TOPPING Adjust oven rack to middle position and heat oven to 450 degrees. Combine flour, pecans, oats, brown sugar, granulated sugar, cinnamon, and salt in medium bowl. Stir in butter until thoroughly moistened and crumbly.

2. FOR THE FILLING Bring cider to simmer in 12-inch skillet over medium heat and cook until reduced to ¾ cup, about 7 minutes. Transfer to liquid measuring cup and stir in lemon juice.

3. Toss apples with sugar and cinnamon in bowl. Melt butter in now-empty skillet over medium heat. Add apples and cook, stirring often, until they begin to soften and become translucent, 10 to 15 minutes. (Do not fully cook apples.) Off heat, gently stir in cider mixture.

4. Transfer apple mixture to 13 by 9-inch casserole dish. Sprinkle evenly with topping, breaking up any large chunks. Bake until fruit is tender and topping is deep golden brown, about 20 minutes.

5. Let crisp cool slightly on wire rack, about 15 minutes. Serve warm or at room temperature. (Crisp can be held at room temperature for up to 2 hours; if desired, reheat in 425-degree oven until slightly warm, about 5 minutes, before serving.)

Apple Pandowdy

Serves 6 to 8 VEGETARIAN
Total Time 2¼ hours, plus 1 hour chilling

WHY THIS RECIPE WORKS More rustic than an apple pie, this comforting dessert features just one pastry crust placed on top of a spiced apple filling. During baking, the crust is pressed into the filling so the juices flood over the top crust and caramelize in the oven, a process called "dowdying," which leaves a dowdy-looking but eminently delicious result. Although pandowdies are often baked in a skillet, we found that a Dutch oven had two advantages: We could use it as a mixing bowl for our apples, cutting down on dishes, and the dowdying process was easier and neater, since the Dutch oven's high sides kept the juices in the pot. We started the filling on the stovetop to encourage even cooking, then topped the apples with squares of dough to allow steam to escape during baking and prevent the apples from overcooking. Do not use store-bought pie dough in this recipe; it yields gummy results. Serve with vanilla ice cream.

DOUGH

- 3 tablespoons ice water
- 1 tablespoon sour cream
- ⅔ cup (3⅓ ounces) all-purpose flour
- 1 teaspoon granulated sugar
- ½ teaspoon table salt
- 6 tablespoons unsalted butter, cut into ½-inch pieces and frozen for 15 minutes

FILLING

- 6 tablespoons unsalted butter
- 5 pounds Golden Delicious, Jonagold, or Honeycrisp apples, peeled, cored, halved, and cut into ½-inch-thick wedges
- ½ cup packed (3½ ounces) light brown sugar
- 1 teaspoon ground cinnamon
- ½ teaspoon table salt
- 1½ cups apple cider
- 2 tablespoons cornstarch
- 4 teaspoons lemon juice

TOPPING

- 1 tablespoon granulated sugar
- ¼ teaspoon ground cinnamon
- 1 large egg, lightly beaten

1. FOR THE DOUGH Combine ice water and sour cream in bowl. Process flour, sugar, and salt in food processor until combined, about 3 seconds. Scatter butter over top and pulse until size of large peas, 6 to 8 pulses. Add sour cream mixture and pulse until dough forms large clumps and no dry flour remains, 3 to 6 pulses, scraping down sides of bowl as needed.

2. Form dough into 4-inch disk, wrap tightly in plastic wrap, and refrigerate for 1 hour. (Wrapped dough can be refrigerated for up to 2 days or frozen for up to 1 month. If frozen, let dough thaw completely on counter before rolling.)

3. Adjust oven rack to middle position and heat oven to 400 degrees. Let chilled dough stand at room temperature to soften slightly, about 5 minutes. Roll dough into 10-inch circle on lightly floured counter. Using pizza cutter, cut dough into four 2½-inch-wide strips, then make four 2½-inch-wide perpendicular cuts to form squares. (Pieces around edges of dough will be smaller.) Transfer dough pieces to parchment paper–lined baking sheet, cover with plastic, and refrigerate until firm, at least 30 minutes.

4. FOR THE FILLING Meanwhile, melt butter in Dutch oven over medium heat. Add apples, sugar, cinnamon, and salt and toss to coat. Cover and cook, stirring occasionally, until apples become slightly pliable and release their juice, about 10 minutes.

5. Whisk cider, cornstarch, and lemon juice in bowl until no lumps remain, then stir mixture into apples. Bring to simmer and cook, uncovered, stirring occasionally, until sauce is thickened, about 2 minutes. Off heat, press apples into even layer.

6. FOR THE TOPPING Combine sugar and cinnamon in small bowl. Working quickly, shingle dough pieces over filling until mostly covered, overlapping as needed. Brush dough pieces with egg and sprinkle with cinnamon-sugar mixture. Transfer pot to oven and bake, uncovered, until crust is slightly puffed and beginning to brown, 15 to 20 minutes.

7. Remove pot from oven. Using back of large spoon, press down in center of crust until juices come up over top of crust. Repeat 4 more times around pot. Make sure all apples are submerged and return pot to oven. Bake, uncovered, until crust is golden brown, 35 to 40 minutes.

8. Remove pot from oven and transfer to wire rack. Let pandowdy cool for 20 minutes. Serve, drizzling extra sauce over top.

French Apple Cake

Serves 8 to 10 VEGETARIAN
Total Time 2 hours, plus 2 hours cooling

WHY THIS RECIPE WORKS The French have a remarkable apple cake featuring butter-soft apple slices that are tender yet perfectly intact surrounded by a rich—but not the least bit heavy—custard base. Perched above the rich custard sits a layer of airy cake with a golden, crisp top. While producing such a cake might seem tricky, it's refreshingly simple: You divide the batter, adding egg yolks to one portion to make the custardy base and a bit more flour to the rest to form the cakey layer. For apples, we opted for tart apples such as Granny Smith; their tartness provided a nice foil to the sweet cake. To ensure that the apple slices softened fully, we gave them a head start in the microwave. Sprinkling the top with granulated sugar just before baking gave the cake an appealingly crisp top. The microwaved apples should be pliable but not completely soft. Take one apple slice and try to bend it. If it snaps in half, it's too firm; microwave it for an additional 30 seconds and test again. White rum can be substituted for the Calvados or apple-flavored brandy.

1½ pounds Granny Smith, Empire, or Braeburn apples, peeled, cored, cut into 8 wedges, and sliced ⅛ inch thick crosswise
1 tablespoon Calvados or apple-flavored brandy
1 teaspoon lemon juice
1 cup (5 ounces) plus 2 tablespoons all-purpose flour, divided
1 cup (7 ounces) plus 1 tablespoon granulated sugar, divided
2 teaspoons baking powder
½ teaspoon table salt
1 cup vegetable oil
1 cup whole milk
1 large egg plus 2 large yolks, divided
1 teaspoon vanilla extract
 Confectioners' sugar

1. Adjust oven rack to lower-middle position and heat oven to 325 degrees. Spray 9-inch springform pan with vegetable oil spray. Place prepared pan on aluminum foil–lined rimmed baking sheet. Place apples in pie plate, cover, and microwave until apples are pliable and slightly translucent, about 3 minutes. Toss apples with Calvados and lemon juice and let cool for 15 minutes.

2. Whisk 1 cup flour, 1 cup granulated sugar, baking powder, and salt together in bowl. Whisk oil, milk, whole egg, and vanilla in second large bowl until smooth. Add flour mixture to milk mixture and whisk until just combined. Transfer 1 cup batter to third bowl and set aside.

3. Add egg yolks to remaining batter and whisk to combine. Using spatula, gently fold in cooled apples. Transfer batter to prepared pan; using offset spatula, spread batter evenly to pan edges, gently pressing on apples to create even, compact layer and smooth surface.

4. Whisk remaining 2 tablespoons flour into reserved batter. Pour over batter in pan, spread batter evenly to pan edges, and smooth surface. Sprinkle remaining 1 tablespoon granulated sugar evenly over cake. Bake until center of cake is set, toothpick inserted in center comes out clean, and top is golden brown, about 1¼ hours. Let cake cool in pan on wire rack for 5 minutes. Run thin knife around edge of pan to loosen cake, then let cool completely, 2 to 3 hours. Remove sides of pan and slide thin metal spatula between cake bottom and pan bottom to loosen, then slide cake onto platter. Dust cake lightly with confectioners' sugar before serving.

French Apple Cake

Cider-Glazed Apple Bundt Cake

Serves 12   MAKE AHEAD   VEGETARIAN
Total Time 1¾ hours, plus 2½ hours cooling

WHY THIS RECIPE WORKS If you're making an apple cake, there's a very good reason—one that's backed by science—to bake it in a Bundt pan: efficient energy transfer. Apple flavor is relatively mellow, so you really have to pack in a ton of fruit for it have any real presence. To accommodate all that moisture, apple cake batters have to be pretty thick and stiff, which means it takes longer for the oven's heat to penetrate from the outside to the middle. The central hole in a Bundt pan eliminates the problematic middle; plus, it allows heat to flow through the center, producing a more evenly baked apple cake. To bolster the flavor of a hefty 1½ pounds of apples, we made an apple cider reduction and used it three ways: added to the batter, brushed onto the exterior of the baked cake, and stirred into a glaze. For the sake of efficiency, begin boiling the cider before assembling the rest of the ingredients. Reducing the cider to exactly 1 cup is important; if you over-reduce it, make up the difference with water. You can shred the apples with the shredding disk of a food processor or on the large holes of a paddle or box grater. You can bake this cake in a decorative 10-cup Bundt pan; place a baking sheet under the Bundt pan.

Cider-Glazed Apple Bundt Cake

Apple Turnovers

Apple Strudel with Pine Nuts

- 4 cups apple cider
- 3¾ cups (18¾ ounces) all-purpose flour
- 1½ teaspoons table salt
- 1½ teaspoons baking powder
- ½ teaspoon baking soda
- ¾ teaspoon ground cinnamon
- ¼ teaspoon ground allspice
- ¾ cup (3 ounces) confectioners' sugar
- 16 tablespoons unsalted butter, melted
- 1½ cups packed (10½ ounces) dark brown sugar
- 3 large eggs
- 2 teaspoons vanilla extract
- 1½ pounds Granny Smith, Empire, or Braeburn apples, peeled and shredded (3 cups)

1. Bring cider to boil in 12-inch skillet over high heat; cook until reduced to 1 cup, 20 to 25 minutes. While cider is reducing, adjust oven rack to middle position and heat oven to 350 degrees. Spray 12-cup nonstick Bundt pan with baking spray with flour. Whisk flour, salt, baking powder, baking soda, cinnamon, and allspice in large bowl until combined. Place confectioners' sugar in small bowl.

2. Add 2 tablespoons cider reduction to confectioners' sugar and whisk to form smooth icing. Cover with plastic wrap and set aside. Set aside 6 tablespoons cider reduction.

3. Pour remaining ½ cup cider reduction into large bowl; add melted butter, brown sugar, eggs, and vanilla and whisk until smooth. Pour cider mixture over flour mixture and stir with rubber spatula until almost fully combined (some streaks of flour will remain). Stir in apples and any accumulated juice until evenly distributed. Transfer mixture to prepared pan and smooth top. Bake until skewer inserted in center comes out clean, 55 minutes to 1 hour 5 minutes, rotating pan halfway through baking.

4. Transfer pan to wire rack set in rimmed baking sheet. Brush exposed surface of cake lightly with 1 tablespoon reserved cider reduction. Let cake cool for 10 minutes. Invert cake onto rack, remove pan, and brush top and sides of cake with remaining 5 tablespoons reserved cider reduction. Let cake cool for 20 minutes. Stir icing to loosen, then drizzle evenly over cake. Let cake cool completely, at least 2 hours, before serving. (Cake can be stored at room temperature for up to 3 days.)

Apple Turnovers

Serves 8 | **Total Time** 1¼ hours

MAKE AHEAD | **VEGETARIAN**

WHY THIS RECIPE WORKS These handheld pastries have a ton of appeal—puff pastry dough folded over sweet apple filling and baked until golden brown, flaky, and crisp. We started with good-quality frozen store-bought dough, which we thawed before using. A quick filling, made of thick, savory-sweet apple butter and freshly grated apples, gave our turnovers complex apple flavor. Draining excess moisture from the filling before dolloping it on the pastry reduced the threat of leakage. Chilling the assembled turnovers in the freezer for about 20 minutes before baking them guaranteed that the pastries rose high. To thaw frozen puff pastry, let it sit either in the refrigerator for 24 hours or on the counter for 30 minutes to 1 hour.

- 1½ pounds Granny Smith, Empire, or Braeburn apples, peeled and shredded (3 cups)
- ¼ cup (1¾ ounces) plus 2 tablespoons sugar, divided
- ⅛ teaspoon table salt
- 2 (9½ by 9-inch) sheets puff pastry, thawed
- ½ cup apple butter
- ½ teaspoon ground cinnamon

1. Combine apples, ¼ cup sugar, and salt in bowl and stir to thoroughly combine. Let stand for 5 minutes.

2. Unfold puff pastry sheets onto lightly floured counter and roll each into 10-inch square. Cut each sheet into four 5-inch squares.

3. Drain apples in fine-mesh strainer set over bowl and press gently with rubber spatula to extract about ⅓ cup juice (do not extract more than ⅓ cup juice or volume of apples will decrease too much). Set aside juice.

4. Transfer apples to now-empty bowl. Add apple butter to apples and stir to combine. Mound 3 level tablespoons of apple mixture in center of each dough square. Brush edges of each dough square with some of reserved juice. Fold each square from corner to corner, forming triangle. Cup your hands around apple mixture and gently press on dough triangle to seal. Using tines of fork, crimp outer ½-inch edge of each triangle. Using tip of paring knife, cut two 1-inch slits in center of each triangle. Place turnovers on 2 large plates and freeze until firm, about 20 minutes.

5. Adjust oven rack to middle position and heat oven to 400 degrees. Line rimmed baking sheet with parchment paper. Combine cinnamon and remaining 2 tablespoons sugar in bowl. With turnovers still on plates, brush tops of turnovers with remaining reserved juice and sprinkle with cinnamon sugar. Transfer turnovers to prepared sheet and bake until well browned, 22 to 24 minutes. Let turnovers cool on wire rack for 10 minutes before serving.

To make ahead After step 4, transfer turnovers to zipper-lock bag and freeze for up to 1 month. Freeze juice separately. When ready to bake, thaw juice completely, then proceed with recipe from step 5. Do not thaw turnovers—baking time will not change.

Apple Strudel with Pine Nuts

Serves 6 | **Total Time** 1¾ hours **VEGETARIAN**

WHY THIS RECIPE WORKS Apple strudel may be more recognizable as a classic Austrian dessert, but it's also made in Italy's Alpine region of Trentino–Alto Adige, where it features pine nuts in its filling along with chopped apples and dried fruit. Store-bought phyllo was convenient and produced crisp layers. For the filling, to ensure that the apples didn't end up mushy, we parcooked the apple pieces in the microwave, which caused the pectin in the fruit to set, ensuring that the pieces would hold their shape. The apples also released some of their liquid, which we captured to brush on the strudel just before baking. Some panko bread crumbs absorbed any extra moisture. Finally, slicing each strudel into thirds after baking allowed excess steam to escape so that the phyllo remained flaky. Phyllo dough is also available in larger 18 by 14-inch sheets; if using, cut them in half to make 14 by 9-inch sheets. To thaw frozen phyllo, let it stand either in the refrigerator for 24 hours or on the counter for 4 to 5 hours; don't thaw it in the microwave.

- 1¾ pounds Golden Delicious, Jonagold, or Honeycrisp apples, peeled, cored, and cut into ½-inch pieces
- 3 tablespoons granulated sugar
- ½ teaspoon grated lemon zest plus 1½ teaspoons juice
- ¼ teaspoon ground cinnamon
- ¼ teaspoon table salt, divided
- ½ cup pine nuts, toasted and chopped
- 3 tablespoons golden raisins
- 1½ tablespoons panko bread crumbs
- 7 tablespoons unsalted butter, melted
- 14 (14 by 9-inch) phyllo sheets, thawed
- 1 tablespoon confectioners' sugar, divided, plus extra for serving

1. Toss apples, granulated sugar, lemon zest and juice, cinnamon, and ⅛ teaspoon salt together in large bowl. Cover and microwave until apples are warm to touch, about 2 minutes, stirring once halfway through microwaving. Let apples stand, covered, for 5 minutes. Transfer apples to colander set in second bowl and let drain, reserving liquid. Combine apples, pine nuts, raisins, and panko in now-empty bowl.

2. Adjust oven rack to upper-middle position and heat oven to 375 degrees. Spray rimmed baking sheet with vegetable oil spray. Stir remaining ⅛ teaspoon salt into melted butter.

3. Place 16½ by 12-inch sheet of parchment paper on counter with long side parallel to counter edge. Place 1 phyllo sheet on parchment with long side parallel to counter edge. Place 1½ teaspoons confectioners' sugar in fine-mesh strainer (rest strainer in bowl to prevent making a mess). Lightly brush sheet with melted butter and dust sparingly with confectioners' sugar. Repeat with 6 more phyllo sheets, melted butter, and confectioners' sugar, stacking sheets one on top of the other as you go.

4. Arrange half of apple mixture in 2½ by 10-inch rectangle 2 inches from bottom of phyllo and about 2 inches from each side. Using parchment, fold sides of phyllo over filling, then fold bottom edge of phyllo over filling. Brush folded portions of phyllo with reserved apple liquid. Fold top edge over filling, making sure top and bottom edges overlap by about 1 inch. (If they do not overlap, unfold, rearrange filling into slightly narrower strip, and refold.) Press firmly to seal. Using thin metal spatula, transfer strudel to 1 side of prepared sheet, facing seam toward center of sheet. Lightly brush top and sides of strudel with half of reserved apple liquid. Repeat process with remaining phyllo, melted butter, confectioners' sugar, filling, and apple liquid. Place second strudel on other side of prepared sheet, with seam facing center of sheet.

5. Bake until golden brown, 27 to 35 minutes, rotating sheet halfway through baking. Using thin metal spatula, immediately transfer strudels to cutting board. Let cool for 3 minutes. Slice each strudel into thirds and let cool for at least 20 minutes. Serve warm or at room temperature, dusting with extra confectioners' sugar before serving.

NOTES FROM THE TEST KITCHEN

WORKING WITH PHYLLO DOUGH
Paper-thin phyllo dries out very quickly. As soon as you remove the phyllo from its plastic sleeve, unfold the sheets and carefully flatten them with your hands. Cover with plastic wrap, then a damp kitchen towel.

Classic Apple Tarte Tatin

Serves 8 | **Total Time** 1½ hours VEGETARIAN

WHY THIS RECIPE WORKS Burnished, buttery, caramelized wedges of apple shine like jewels atop tarte Tatin, the classic French dessert with a reputation for being notoriously difficult to execute. After all, it involves arranging dough over (perfectly cooked) apples in a smoking-hot skillet of caramel and, once baked, inverting the tart. But in reality, turning out the ideal tarte Tatin doesn't require the finesse of a French chef. To start, we melted butter in a skillet and then sprinkled sugar evenly over the bottom of the pan before arranging the apples; this approach meant we could avoid making a caramel in advance because the caramel formed right in the pan. Chilling the dough before placing it over the caramelized apples avoided a melty skillet mess and resulted in a tart with clean edges once flipped. Our stick-free tart was easy to flip out once we loosened the edges with a paring knife. And if some apples did stick, we simply popped them back into place and covered the tart with the sweet juices left in the pan for gleam. You will need a 10-inch ovensafe non-stick skillet for this recipe. We don't recommend substituting other apple varieties for the Granny Smith apples in this recipe. Crème fraîche is a traditional accompaniment, but you can serve the tart with vanilla ice cream or Whipped Cream (page 368) if you prefer.

1 recipe Classic Tart Dough (page 389)
8 tablespoons unsalted butter
¾ cup (5¼ ounces) sugar
⅛ teaspoon table salt
6 large Granny Smith apples (8 ounces each), peeled, cored, and quartered
Crème fraîche

1. Roll dough into 11-inch circle on floured counter, then transfer to parchment paper–lined rimmed baking sheet; cover loosely with plastic wrap and refrigerate until fully chilled and firm, about 30 minutes. Adjust oven rack to upper-middle position and heat oven to 375 degrees.

2. While dough chills, melt butter in 10-inch ovensafe nonstick skillet over medium heat. Off heat, sprinkle sugar and salt evenly over surface, then arrange apples cut side down in tight pinwheel around edge of skillet, overlapping as needed. Arrange remaining apples cut side down in center of skillet.

3. Place skillet over high heat and cook until butter mixture is amber-colored, about 10 minutes. Off heat, using paring knife or fork, flip apples browned side up, rearranging into tight pinwheel as needed. Return skillet to high heat and cook for 5 minutes.

4. Off heat, carefully transfer chilled dough to skillet, centering over top of apples. Being careful of hot skillet, gently fold excess dough up against skillet wall. Transfer skillet to oven and bake until crust is golden brown, about 25 minutes. Transfer skillet to wire rack and let cool for 20 minutes.

5. Run paring knife around edge of crust to loosen. Using dish towels or potholders, carefully place serving platter on top of skillet, and, holding platter and skillet firmly together, invert tart onto serving platter. Transfer any apples that stick to skillet to tart and drizzle any remaining juices in skillet over top. Serve with crème fraîche.

MAKING CLASSIC APPLE TARTE TATIN

1. Arrange apples cut side down in tight pinwheel around edge of skillet, overlapping as needed, placing remaining apples in center.

2. Cook over high heat until butter mixture is amber-colored, about 10 minutes. Off heat, flip apples browned side up, rearranging into tight pinwheel. Return skillet to high heat and cook for 5 minutes.

Classic Apple Tarte Tatin

Deep Dish Apple Pie

Deep Dish Apple Pie

Serves 8 | **Total Time** 2¾ hours, plus 4 hours cooling

MAKE AHEAD VEGETARIAN

WHY THIS RECIPE WORKS If you find yourself with a surplus of fruit after a fall apple-picking extravaganza, we recommend you enjoy them in a towering deep-dish pie. This method circumvents common apple pie pitfalls such as unevenly cooked apples, pools of juice, a soggy bottom crust, and a large gap below the top crust. Each slice is dense with juicy, tender apples and framed by a buttery, flaky crust. Precooking the apples allowed us to cram in lots of apples (a mix of tart and sweet); it also solved the shrinking problem and minimized excess liquid, thereby protecting the bottom crust. The gentle cooking also converted the pectin in the apples to a heat-stable form, which kept them from becoming mushy when cooked further in the oven. In the end, our sky-high apple pie emerged golden brown and chock-full of tender, sweet, intact apples.

1 recipe Foolproof All-Butter Double-Crust Pie Dough (page 389)

2½ pounds Granny Smith, Empire, or Braeburn apples, peeled, cored, and sliced ¼ inch thick

2½ pounds Golden Delicious, Jonagold, or Honeycrisp apples, peeled, cored, and sliced ¼ inch thick

½ cup (3½ ounces) plus 1 tablespoon granulated sugar, divided

¼ cup packed (1¾ ounces) light brown sugar

½ teaspoon grated lemon zest plus 1 tablespoon juice

¼ teaspoon table salt

⅛ teaspoon ground cinnamon

1 large egg, lightly beaten with 1 tablespoon water

1. Roll 1 disk of dough into 12-inch circle on well-floured counter. Roll dough loosely around rolling pin and gently unroll it onto 9-inch pie plate, letting excess dough hang over edge. Ease dough into plate by gently lifting edge of dough with your hand while pressing into plate bottom with your other hand. Leave any dough that overhangs plate in place. Wrap dough-lined plate loosely in plastic wrap and refrigerate until firm, about 30 minutes. Roll other disk of dough into 12-inch circle on well-floured counter, then transfer to parchment paper–lined baking sheet; cover with plastic and refrigerate for 30 minutes.

2. Meanwhile, toss apples, ½ cup granulated sugar, brown sugar, lemon zest, salt, and cinnamon together in Dutch oven. Cover and cook over medium heat, stirring frequently, until apples are tender when poked with fork but still hold their shape, 15 to 20 minutes.

3. Spread apples and their juices on rimmed baking sheet and let cool completely, about 30 minutes.

4. Adjust oven rack to lowest position and heat oven to 425 degrees. Drain cooled apples thoroughly in colander set over bowl, reserving ¼ cup of juice. Stir lemon juice into reserved juice.

5. Spread apples into dough-lined plate, mounding them slightly in middle, and drizzle with lemon juice mixture. Roll remaining dough round loosely around rolling pin and gently unroll it onto filling.

6. Trim overhang to ½ inch beyond lip of plate. Pinch edges of top and bottom dough firmly together. Tuck overhang under itself; folded edge should be flush with edge of plate.

7. Crimp dough evenly around edge of plate. Cut four 2-inch slits in top of dough. Brush surface with egg wash and sprinkle evenly with remaining 1 tablespoon granulated sugar. (Unbaked pie can be frozen until firm, then wrapped in double layer of plastic wrap followed by aluminum foil and frozen for up to 2 weeks; to bake, continue with step 5, increasing baking time at 375 degrees to 40 to 50 minutes.)

8. Place pie on aluminum foil–lined rimmed baking sheet and bake until crust is light golden brown, about 25 minutes. Reduce oven temperature to 375 degrees, rotate sheet, and continue to bake until juices are bubbling and crust is deep golden brown, 30 to 40 minutes. Let pie cool on wire rack until filling has set, about 4 hours. Serve. (Baked pie can be held at room temperature for up to 8 hours or refrigerated for up to 24 hours; to serve, refresh in 350 degree oven for 10 to 15 minutes. Note that crust will be less crisp.)

NOTES FROM THE TEST KITCHEN

KNOW YOUR APPLES: SWEET VERSUS TART
We often use a mixture of sweet and tart apples in a recipe for balanced flavor and texture. In general, more tart apples—Braeburn, Empire, Granny Smith— hold their shape. Meanwhile, Golden Delicious, Honeycrisp, and Jonagold apples are all sweeter, and are more prone to breaking down in the oven. (There are exceptions: McIntosh apples, although tart, fall apart and become very watery when baked.)

Golden Delicious   Honeycrisp   Jonagold

MORE SWEET

Braeburn   Empire   Granny Smith

MORE TART

Salted Caramel Apple Pie

Serves 8 `VEGETARIAN`
Total Time 2 hours, plus 4 hours cooling

WHY THIS RECIPE WORKS This stunning pie recalls the flavors of caramel apples at a county fair but looks like an edible bouquet. Rather than stewing the apples beneath a top crust, we reimagined our apple slices and used them as a fancy garnish topping a caramel custard pie. We made the salted caramel filling by whisking basic custard components into homemade caramel. A surprising ingredient—white miso— deepened the caramel flavor dramatically so it stood out from the dairy and prevented our filling from being too sweet. To adorn the custard, we softened thin apple slices with sugar and a little lemon juice so they could be bent and formed into beautiful roses that gave our pie showstopping visual appeal. Carefully tilt the saucepan to pool the caramel to get a more consistent temperature reading. For best results, use a mandoline to slice the apples paper-thin.

- 1 recipe Foolproof All-Butter Single-Crust Pie Dough (page 388)
- 1½ cups (10½ ounces) plus 2 tablespoons sugar, divided
- 3 large eggs
- ¼ cup (1 ounce) cornstarch
- 2 tablespoons white miso
- ½ teaspoon vanilla extract
- ¼ teaspoon table salt
- 2 tablespoons water
- 1 cup heavy cream, divided
- 1½ cups whole milk
- 3 Golden Delicious, Jonagold, or Honeycrisp apples, cored, quartered, and sliced very thin lengthwise
- 2 tablespoons lemon juice
  Flake sea salt

1. Roll dough into 12-inch circle on well-floured counter. Roll dough loosely around rolling pin and gently unroll it onto 9-inch pie plate, letting excess dough hang over edge. Ease dough into plate by gently lifting edge of dough with your hand while pressing into plate bottom with your other hand.

2. Trim overhang to ½ inch beyond lip of plate. Tuck overhang under itself; folded edge should be flush with edge of plate. Crimp dough evenly around edge of plate. Wrap dough-lined plate loosely in plastic wrap and refrigerate until firm, about 30 minutes. Adjust oven rack to middle position and heat oven to 350 degrees.

Salted Caramel Apple Pie

3. Line chilled pie shell with double layer of aluminum foil, covering edges to prevent burning, and fill with pie weights. Bake on foil-lined rimmed baking sheet until edges are set and just beginning to turn golden, 25 to 30 minutes, rotating sheet halfway through baking. Remove foil and weights, rotate sheet, and continue to bake crust until golden brown and crisp, 10 to 15 minutes. Transfer sheet to wire rack. (Crust must still be warm when filling is added.)

4. Whisk ¾ cup sugar, eggs, cornstarch, miso, vanilla, and table salt together in bowl; set aside. Bring ¾ cup sugar and water to boil in large saucepan over medium-high heat. Cook, without stirring, until mixture is straw-colored, 4 to 6 minutes. Reduce heat to low and continue to cook, swirling saucepan occasionally, until caramel is amber-colored and registers 360 to 370 degrees, 2 to 5 minutes.

5. Off heat, carefully stir in ¼ cup cream; mixture will bubble and steam. Whisk vigorously, being sure to scrape corners of saucepan, until mixture is completely smooth, at least 30 seconds. Gradually whisk in remaining ¾ cup cream and milk, then bring to simmer over medium heat. Slowly whisk 1 cup hot caramel mixture into egg mixture to temper, then slowly whisk tempered egg mixture into remaining caramel mixture in saucepan. Cook, whisking constantly, until mixture is thickened and bubbling and registers 180 degrees, 4 to 6 minutes (mixture should have consistency of thick pudding). Strain mixture through fine-mesh strainer into clean bowl.

6. With pie still on sheet, pour filling into warm crust, smoothing top with clean spatula into even layer. Bake until center of pie registers 160 degrees, 14 to 18 minutes. Let pie cool completely on wire rack, about 4 hours.

7. Before serving, combine apple slices, remaining 2 tablespoons sugar, and lemon juice in bowl. Microwave until apples are pliable, about 2 minutes, stirring halfway through microwaving. Drain apples, then transfer to paper towel–lined sheet and pat dry with paper towels. Shingle 5 apple slices, peel side out, overlapping each slice by about ½ inch on cutting board or counter. Starting at 1 end, roll up slices to form rose shape; place in center of pie. Repeat, arranging apple roses decoratively over top of pie. Sprinkle with sea salt and serve.

MAKING APPLE ROSETTES

1. Combine apple slices, 2 tablespoons sugar, and lemon juice in bowl. Microwave until apples are pliable, about 2 minutes, stirring halfway through microwaving.

2. Drain apples and pat dry with paper towels. Shingle 5 apple slices, peel side out, overlapping each slice by about ½ inch.

3. Starting at 1 end, roll up slices to form rose shape.

Applesauce

Makes 4 cups | **Total Time** 45 minutes

MAKE AHEAD **VEGETARIAN**

WHY THIS RECIPE WORKS A beautifully colored, deeply flavored applesauce benefits from cooking the sauce with the apple peels and cores. By cooking those separately, we avoided having to use a food mill to process our fruit. We peeled and cored the apples and then cooked the peels and cores with 1 cup of water, mashing them occasionally to coax out their flavors and pigments. We then cooked the quartered apples in a separate saucepan with a small amount of water and sugar and a pinch of salt. We mashed the cooked apples, strained the pulpy peel-and-core mixture over the mashed apple mixture, and then stirred it all together. Enjoy the straightforward apple flavor of this sauce as is or add a pinch of cinnamon for a lightly spiced version. You can use almost any apple you like except for Red or Golden Delicious, which were either too sweet or never broke down, in this recipe. Keep in mind: Crisp, dense apples take longer to break down, and green or yellow apples make a beige sauce. You may mash this applesauce until it's smooth or leave it chunky for a more rustic effect.

3 pounds apples, peeled and cored, peels and cores reserved
1½ cups water, divided
¼ cup sugar, plus extra to taste
Pinch table salt
Pinch ground cinnamon (optional)

1. Bring reserved peels and cores and 1 cup water to boil in small saucepan over medium-high heat. Reduce heat to medium, cover, and cook, mashing occasionally with potato masher, until mixture is deep pink and cores have broken down, about 15 minutes.

2. While peels and cores cook, cut apples into quarters and place in large saucepan. Add sugar; salt; cinnamon, if using; and remaining ½ cup water and bring to boil over medium-high heat. Reduce heat to medium, cover, and cook, stirring occasionally with rubber spatula, until all apples are soft and about half are completely broken down, about 15 minutes. Using potato masher, mash apples to desired consistency.

3. Transfer peel-and-core mixture to fine-mesh strainer set over saucepan of mashed apple mixture. Using rubber spatula, stir and press peel-and-core mixture to extract pulp; discard solids. Stir to combine. Sweeten with extra sugar to taste. Serve warm, at room temperature, or chilled. (Applesauce can be refrigerated for up to 1 week.)

Apple Butter

Makes two 1-cup jars `MAKE AHEAD` `VEGETARIAN`
Total Time 1¾ hours, plus 1 hour cooling

WHY THIS RECIPE WORKS Apple butter should be full of real apple flavor, but too often it's overspiced and underwhelming. Since apple butter is essentially applesauce cooked long enough for the apples to caramelize into a dark paste, we saw no reason to add an excess of seasonings. Instead, we wanted to intensify the apples into a lush butter that needed no embellishments. Many recipes call for peeling the apples before cooking; however, much of the apples' flavor is in the skins. By simmering the apples with their skins, not only were we able to extract more flavor, but the apples also softened enough that the flesh separated from the skins when passed through a food mill or mesh strainer. We cooked the apples in apple cider to reinforce their flavor, along with Calvados for complexity. To sweeten the mixture, replacing a portion of granulated sugar with brown sugar added extra depth. After about an hour, the puree had darkened to a rich brown color and thickened enough to leave a solid trail behind the path of a spatula. You can use any apple you like in this recipe.

2½ pounds apples, cored, quartered, and cut into 1-inch pieces
⅔ cup apple cider
⅔ cup Calvados or applejack
½ cup granulated sugar
⅓ cup packed light brown sugar
2 tablespoons lemon juice
¼ teaspoon table salt

1. Bring apples, cider, and Calvados to boil in large saucepan over medium-high heat. Reduce heat to medium-low, cover, and simmer, stirring occasionally, until apples are very soft, about 30 minutes.

2. Working in batches, process mixture through food mill fitted with medium disk set over bowl; alternatively, use rubber spatula to work mixture through fine-mesh strainer set over bowl. Return puree to clean saucepan.

3. Stir in granulated sugar, brown sugar, lemon juice, and salt. Cook over low heat, stirring occasionally, until mixture is browned and thickened and rubber spatula leaves distinct trail when dragged across bottom of pot, 45 minutes to 1 hour.

4. Let apple butter cool slightly. Using funnel and spoon, portion apple butter into two 1-cup jars, then let cool to room temperature, about 1 hour. Cover, refrigerate, and serve. (Apple butter can be refrigerated for up to 1 month.)

Applesauce

Apple Butter

everyone loves
pumpkin

■ MAKE AHEAD   ▣ VEGETARIAN

Photo: Pumpkin Pie

Pumpkin Seed Dip

Slow-Cooker Creamy
Pumpkin-Chai Soup

Pumpkin Seed Dip

Makes about 3 cups `MAKE AHEAD` `VEGETARIAN`
Total Time 1 hour, plus 2 hours cooling

WHY THIS RECIPE WORKS The ancient Mayans knew a better use for pumpkin seeds than simply snacking by the handful: They ground the seeds with tomatoes and spicy habanero chiles to make an earthy, toasty dip known as sikil p'ak. The dip features the perfect balance of spicy, tart, and roasty pumpkin seed flavors, perfect for passing around on game day or simply for taking snack time to the next level. The dip is traditionally made with unhulled pumpkin seeds, which are still encased in their white shells. Since unhulled pumpkin seeds are almost always sold roasted and salted, we found it crucial to rinse off the salt before we used the seeds. We then toasted the seeds to a rich golden hue in a hot oven before processing them in a blender, which worked better than a food processor to break down the tough hulls into a smooth, scoopable dip. If using unsalted pumpkin seeds, skip the rinsing and drying in step 1 and go directly to toasting.

1½ cups roasted, unhulled pumpkin seeds
 1 pound plum tomatoes, cored and halved
¼ cup extra-virgin olive oil, divided
 1 onion, chopped
 2 tablespoons lime juice
 1 habanero chile, stemmed, seeded, and chopped
 2 ounces queso fresco, crumbled (½ cup)
 2 tablespoons chopped fresh cilantro

1. Adjust 1 oven rack to middle position and second rack 6 inches from broiler element. Heat oven to 400 degrees. Rinse pumpkin seeds under warm water and dry thoroughly. Spread seeds on rimmed baking sheet, place sheet on lower rack, and toast seeds until golden brown, stirring occasionally, 12 to 15 minutes. Set aside to cool slightly and heat broiler.

2. Line second rimmed baking sheet with aluminum foil. Toss tomatoes with 1 tablespoon oil and arrange cut side down on prepared sheet. Place sheet on upper rack and broil until tomatoes are spotty brown, 7 to 10 minutes. Transfer tomatoes to blender and let cool completely.

3. Add onion, lime juice, habanero, pumpkin seeds, and remaining 3 tablespoons oil to blender and process until smooth, about 1 minute, scraping down sides of jar as needed. Transfer dip to serving bowl and refrigerate until completely chilled, at least 2 hours or up to 24 hours. Season with salt and pepper to taste. Sprinkle with queso fresco and cilantro before serving.

Slow-Cooker Creamy Pumpkin-Chai Soup

Serves 6 | **Cooking Time** 4 to 6 hours on Low or 3 to 5 hours on High **MAKE AHEAD**

WHY THIS RECIPE WORKS This warming pumpkin soup, made with readily available canned pumpkin puree, is perfect for chilly fall days. Brown sugar brought out the sweetness of pumpkin puree, and cream added richness. Simmering a chai tea bag in the broth infused the soup with complex, warm chai flavor. You can substitute ¼ teaspoon of ground cinnamon, ¼ teaspoon of ground ginger, ¼ teaspoon of ground cardamom, and ¼ teaspoon of ground cloves for the chai tea bag. You will need a 4- to 7-quart slow cooker for this recipe. Be sure to buy unsweetened canned pumpkin, not pumpkin pie filling, which is preseasoned and sweetened.

    1 onion, chopped
    3 garlic cloves, minced
    1 tablespoon vegetable oil
    6 cups chicken broth, plus extra as needed
    1 (29-ounce) can unsweetened pumpkin puree
    ½ cup packed brown sugar
    1 chai tea bag
    ½ cup heavy cream

1. Combine onion, garlic, and oil in bowl and microwave, stirring occasionally, until onion is softened, about 5 minutes; transfer to slow cooker. Stir in broth, pumpkin, sugar, and tea bag. Cover and cook until flavors meld, 4 to 6 hours on low or 3 to 5 hours on high.

2. Discard tea bag. Working in batches, process soup in blender until smooth, about 2 minutes. Return soup to slow cooker, stir in cream, and let stand until heated through, about 5 minutes, adjusting consistency with extra hot broth as needed. Season with salt and pepper to taste, and serve. (Soup can be refrigerated for up to 3 days and reheated just before serving.)

Pumpkin Cappellacci

Serves 6 | **Total Time** 2½ hours
MAKE AHEAD **VEGETARIAN**

WHY THIS RECIPE WORKS Is there any more accomplished feeling than the one you get when presenting your family with a plate of homemade stuffed fresh pasta? Pumpkin is the traditional filling in Italian cappellacci di zucca ("zucca" means "pumpkin"), which are similar in shape to jumbo

tortellini but with pointed tops. Italians typically make the pasta using sweet, elongated violina pumpkins, but we found that fresh sugar pumpkin worked nicely in its stead. To make the filling, we microwaved the pumpkin pieces until they were tender and then processed them with butter and Parmigiano-Reggiano until smooth. We used a pasta machine to roll the sheets of fresh pasta thin enough to see the outline of our hands through, which ensured that even the bulkiest folded parts of the pasta cooked up tender and supple in a matter of minutes. Sugar pumpkins are about 8 to 10 inches in diameter and usually have a darker orange exterior than jack-o'-lantern pumpkins. Their flesh is also denser and drier. You will need about 1 pound of sugar pumpkin for this dish; if you prefer to use another winter squash, such as butternut, you will need 1½ pounds.

PUMPKIN FILLING

    3½ cups 1-inch sugar pumpkin or winter squash pieces
     6 tablespoons unsalted butter
    2½ ounces Parmigiano-Reggiano cheese,
         grated (1¼ cups)
     ¼ teaspoon table salt
     ⅛ teaspoon pepper
         Pinch ground nutmeg

CAPPELLACCI

    2 cups (10 ounces) all-purpose flour
    3 large eggs, beaten
    6 tablespoons unsalted butter
    1 tablespoon minced fresh sage
    ½ teaspoon table salt
        Balsamic vinegar
        Shaved Parmigiano-Reggiano cheese

1. FOR THE PUMPKIN FILLING Microwave pumpkin in covered bowl until very soft and easily pierced with fork, 15 to 18 minutes, stirring halfway through microwaving. Carefully remove cover, allowing steam to escape away from you, and drain pumpkin.

2. Process pumpkin, butter, Parmigiano, salt, pepper, and nutmeg in food processor until smooth, about 1 minute, scraping down sides of bowl as needed. Transfer filling to bowl and refrigerate for 30 minutes. (Filling can be refrigerated for up to 24 hours.)

3. FOR THE CAPPELLACCI Pulse flour in food processor to evenly distribute. Add eggs; process until dough forms rough ball, about 30 seconds. (If dough resembles small pebbles, add water, ½ teaspoon at a time; if dough sticks to side of bowl, add flour, 1 tablespoon at a time, and process until dough forms rough ball.) Turn dough ball and small bits out onto dry work surface; knead until dough is smooth, 1 to 2 minutes. Cover with plastic wrap and set aside for at least 15 minutes or up to 2 hours to relax.

4. Transfer dough to clean counter, divide into 6 pieces, and cover with plastic wrap. Flatten 1 piece of dough into ½-inch-thick disk. Using pasta machine with rollers set to widest position, feed dough through rollers twice. Bring tapered ends of dough toward middle and press to seal. Feed dough seam side first through rollers again. Repeat feeding dough tapered ends first through rollers set at widest position, without folding, until dough is smooth and barely tacky. (If dough sticks to fingers or rollers, lightly dust with flour and roll again.)

5. Narrow rollers to next setting and feed dough through rollers twice. Continue to progressively narrow rollers, feeding dough through each setting twice, until dough is paper thin, transparent, and delicate. (Pasta sheet should be about 5 inches wide; if not, fold sheet in half crosswise and roll again.) Transfer sheet of pasta to liberally floured sheet of parchment paper. Cover with second sheet of parchment, followed by damp kitchen towel, to keep pasta from drying out. Repeat rolling with remaining 5 pieces of dough, stacking pasta sheets between floured layers of parchment.

6. Liberally dust rimmed baking sheet with flour. Using pizza cutter or sharp knife, cut 1 pasta sheet into 5-inch squares on lightly floured counter (keep remaining sheets covered); discard scraps. Place 1 rounded tablespoon filling in center of each square. Working with 1 pasta square at a time, lightly brush edges with water. With 1 corner of pasta square facing you, fold bottom corner of pasta over filling until flush with top corner to form triangle shape. Press to seal edges flush to filling. Trim any uneven edges.

7. With folded edge of filled pasta facing you, pull corners together below filling until slightly overlapped to create cappellacci with cupped outer edge and dimpled center. Press to seal overlapping edges and transfer to prepared sheet. Repeat cutting and filling remaining pasta (you should have about 18 cappellacci). Let cappellacci sit uncovered until dry to touch and slightly stiffened, about 30 minutes. (Cappellacci can be wrapped with plastic and refrigerated for up to 4 hours or chilled in freezer until firm, then transferred to zipper-lock bag and frozen for up to 1 month. If frozen, do not thaw before cooking; increase simmering time to 6 to 8 minutes.)

8. Melt butter in 12-inch skillet over medium heat. Off heat, stir in sage and salt; set aside. Bring 4 quarts water to boil in large pot. Add half of cappellacci and 1 tablespoon salt and simmer gently, stirring often, until edges of cappellacci are al dente, 4 to 6 minutes. Using slotted spoon, transfer cappellacci

Pumpkin Cappellacci

to skillet, gently toss to coat, and cover to keep warm. Return cooking water to boil and repeat cooking remaining cappellacci; transfer to skillet and gently toss to coat. Drizzle individual portions with balsamic vinegar and top with Parmigiano-Reggiano before serving.

SHAPING CAPPELLACCI

1. Fold bottom corner of pasta over filling until flush with top corner to form triangle shape. Press to seal edges flush to filling.

2. Pull corners together below filling until slightly overlapped to create cappellacci with cupped outer edge and dimpled center. Press to seal overlapping edges.

Roasted Sugar Pumpkin Wedges

Serves 6 to 8 | **Total Time** 40 minutes `VEGETARIAN`

WHY THIS RECIPE WORKS Small, sweet, and excellently suited for cooking, sugar pumpkins are in season for only a short period. So for those times when we had one on hand, we wanted a recipe that would truly make the most of its dense, buttery, sweet flesh and gorgeous color. Preparing roasted wedges of pumpkin brushed with the warming spice blend ras el hanout kept the focus on the squash. After half an hour in the oven the wedges were deeply browned and ready to shine as a side dish for a savory, rich cut of meat. We prefer to use our homemade Ras el Hanout (page 101), but you can substitute store-bought ras el hanout if you wish, though spiciness and flavor can vary greatly by brand. Sugar pumpkins are about 8 to 10 inches in diameter and usually have a darker orange exterior than jack-o'-lantern pumpkins.

  1 (3 to 4-pound) sugar pumpkin, stemmed, halved
    through root end, and seeded
  3 tablespoons vegetable oil
  2 teaspoons ras el hanout
  1½ teaspoons table salt
  ½ teaspoon pepper

1. Adjust oven rack to upper-middle and lower-middle positions and heat oven to 475 degrees. Cut each pumpkin half into 1½ inch pieces. Whisk oil, ras el hanout, salt, and pepper together in large bowl. Add pumpkin and toss until evenly coated. Arrange pumpkin cut side down in single layer on 2 rimmed baking sheets.

2. Roast until bottoms of most pieces are deep golden brown, about 15 minutes. Remove sheets from oven. Gently flip pumpkin and switch outer pieces with inner pieces on sheet. Continue to roast until pumpkin is tender and most pieces are deep golden brown on second side, 5 to 10 minutes. Serve.

Mashed Spiced Pumpkin

Serves 4 to 6 | **Total Time** 1¾ hours `VEGETARIAN`

WHY THIS RECIPE WORKS A simple sweet-and-spiced sugar pumpkin mash pairs well with any roasted meat, a fun alternative to the butternut squash side dishes often served during the holidays. We roasted our halved pumpkin until its flesh was tender and then simply used a potato masher to produce a rustic, textured mash. Butter, brown sugar, and

warm spices rounded out the dish's flavor. Sugar pumpkins are about 8 to 10 inches in diameter and usually have a darker orange exterior than jack-o'-lantern pumpkins.

  1 (4 to 4½-pound) sugar pumpkin, stemmed, halved
    through root end, and seeded
  4 tablespoons unsalted butter
  1 onion, chopped fine
  ¾ teaspoon table salt
  1 garlic clove, minced
  ¾ teaspoon ground cumin
  ¾ teaspoon ground coriander
  ¼ teaspoon ground cinnamon
  ⅛ teaspoon cayenne pepper
  3 tablespoons packed brown sugar

1. Adjust oven rack to middle position and heat oven to 375 degrees. Line rimmed baking sheet with aluminum foil and place pumpkin halves cut side down on sheet. Roast until flesh can be easily pierced with skewer, 45 minutes to 1 hour. Flip pumpkin and continue to roast for 30 minutes longer. Let pumpkin cool slightly, then scoop flesh into bowl; discard skins. Mash pumpkin with potato masher until almost smooth.

2. Melt butter in large saucepan over medium heat. Add onion and salt and cook until softened, about 5 minutes. Stir in garlic, cumin, coriander, cinnamon, and cayenne and cook until fragrant, about 30 seconds. Add sugar and pumpkin and cook, stirring frequently, until mixture is heated through, about 2 minutes. Adjust consistency with water as needed. Season with salt and pepper to taste. Serve.

HALVING A SUGAR PUMPKIN

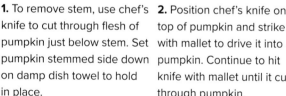

1. To remove stem, use chef's knife to cut through flesh of pumpkin just below stem. Set pumpkin stemmed side down on damp dish towel to hold in place.

2. Position chef's knife on top of pumpkin and strike with mallet to drive it into pumpkin. Continue to hit knife with mallet until it cuts through pumpkin.

Chicken with Pumpkin Seed Sauce

Serves 4 | **Total Time** 1¼ hours

WHY THIS RECIPE WORKS Pumpkin seeds are woefully underappreciated, most often eaten plain as a rather boring snack. We put nutty toasted pumpkin seeds to better use in pipian verde, or pumpkin seed sauce, a traditional Pueblan sauce that's excellent served with chicken. Our first move was to toast sesame seeds and pumpkin seeds (we chose pepitas over unhulled pumpkin seeds for a smoother sauce) in a skillet, which we then used to build our sauce. Onion, garlic, and thyme gave the sauce an aromatic base, while fresh jalapeño contributed lively spice. We chopped tomatillos before stirring them into the sauce to soften and break down. Poaching the chicken right in the sauce kept our recipe streamlined and guaranteed moist, flavorful chicken. Once the chicken was done, we pureed the sauce in the blender; lime juice, cilantro, and a pinch of sugar rounded out the flavors and added brightness. Serve with rice.

⅓ cup pepitas
¼ cup sesame seeds
2 tablespoons vegetable oil
1 onion, chopped fine
1 teaspoon table salt, divided
1 jalapeño chile, stemmed, seeded, and chopped
3 garlic cloves, minced
1 teaspoon minced fresh thyme or ¼ teaspoon dried
6 ounces tomatillos, husks and stems removed, rinsed well, dried, and chopped
1½ cups chicken broth
4 (6- to 8-ounce) boneless, skinless chicken breasts, trimmed
¼ teaspoon pepper
1 cup fresh cilantro leaves
1 tablespoon lime juice
Pinch sugar

1. Toast pepitas and sesame seeds in 12-inch nonstick skillet over medium heat until seeds are golden and fragrant, about 15 minutes; transfer to bowl. Reserve 1 tablespoon seeds for garnish.

2. Add oil, onion, and ½ teaspoon salt to now-empty skillet and cook over medium-high heat until softened, 5 to 7 minutes. Stir in jalapeño, garlic, and thyme and cook until fragrant, about 30 seconds. Stir in tomatillos, broth, and toasted seeds; cover; and cook until tomatillos begin to soften, about 10 minutes.

3. Sprinkle chicken with pepper and remaining ½ teaspoon salt, then nestle into mixture in skillet. Cover, reduce heat to medium-low, and cook until chicken registers 160 degrees, 10 to 15 minutes, flipping halfway through cooking. Transfer chicken to platter, tent with aluminum foil, and let rest for 5 to 10 minutes.

4. Carefully transfer mixture left in skillet to blender. Add cilantro, lime juice, and sugar to blender and process until mostly smooth, about 1 minute. Season with salt and pepper to taste. Spoon some of sauce over chicken and sprinkle chicken with reserved seeds. Serve with remaining sauce.

Homemade Pumpkin Puree

Makes 12 to 16 ounces `MAKE AHEAD` `VEGETARIAN`
Total Time 1¾ hours, plus 1 hour draining

WHY THIS RECIPE WORKS Most of us turn to canned pumpkin puree to add the requisite squashy sweetness to autumnal treats. But if you have a sugar pumpkin on hand, making your own puree is a fun project. For an incredibly fresh homemade puree with a texture comparable to that of canned, we roasted a halved sugar pumpkin until it was completely tender and caramelized and then pureed its flesh (which is sweeter and more intense in flavor than that of other pumpkin varieties) in a food processor. Draining the cooked pumpkin in a fine-mesh strainer let excess liquid drip away so the puree was lusciously thick. Sugar pumpkins are about 8 to 10 inches in diameter and usually have a darker orange exterior than jack-o'-lantern pumpkins. You can substitute this puree for an equal amount of canned product in recipes; 1¾ cups is equal to one 15-ounce can.

1 (3 to 4-pound) sugar pumpkin, stemmed, halved through root end, and seeded

1. Adjust oven rack to middle position and heat oven to 375 degrees. Line rimmed baking sheet with aluminum foil and place pumpkin halves cut side down on sheet. Roast until flesh can be easily pierced with a skewer, 45 minutes to 1 hour.

2. Flip pumpkin and continue to roast for 30 minutes longer. Let pumpkin cool slightly, then scoop flesh from skins and puree in food processor until smooth. Transfer puree to fine-mesh strainer set over bowl and allow to drain for at least 1 hour; reserve drained liquid.

3. To test puree's consistency, pack puree into small drinking glass, then unmold it onto plate. Puree should slump gently toward base but otherwise hold its shape. Loosen as necessary with reserved liquid, or return puree to strainer and continue to drain if too loose. Puree can be refrigerated for up to 4 days or frozen in airtight container with parchment pressed on its surface for up to 2 months.

Pumpkin Bread

Serves 16 (Makes 2 loaves) `MAKE AHEAD` `VEGETARIAN`
Total Time 1½ hours, plus 1¾ hours cooling

WHY THIS RECIPE WORKS Moist, dense but not heavy, lightly spiced and deeply pumpkiny, and studded with toasty nuts: This, in our opinion, is the description of the ideal loaf of pumpkin bread. First, to concentrate the rich, earthy flavor of pumpkin puree, we cooked it on the stovetop just until its sugars began to caramelize. To replace some of the moisture lost during this step and add a counterpoint to the bread's sweetness, we stirred tangy buttermilk and softened cream cheese into the mix. A crisp streusel topping contributed textural contrast to this craveable loaf. The test kitchen's preferred loaf pan measures 8½ by 4½ inches; if using a 9 by 5-inch loaf pan, start checking for doneness 5 minutes early. Be sure to buy unsweetened canned pumpkin, not pumpkin pie filling, which is preseasoned and sweetened.

TOPPING

 5 tablespoons packed (2¼ ounces) light brown sugar
 1 tablespoon all-purpose flour
 1 tablespoon unsalted butter, softened
 1 teaspoon ground cinnamon
 ⅛ teaspoon table salt

BREAD

 2 cups (10 ounces) all-purpose flour
1½ teaspoons baking powder
 ½ teaspoon baking soda
 1 (15-ounce) can unsweetened pumpkin puree
 1 teaspoon table salt
1½ teaspoons ground cinnamon
 ¼ teaspoon ground nutmeg
 ⅛ teaspoon ground cloves
 1 cup (7 ounces) granulated sugar
 1 cup packed (7 ounces) light brown sugar
 ½ cup vegetable oil
 4 ounces cream cheese, cut into 12 pieces
 4 large eggs
 ¼ cup buttermilk
 1 cup walnuts, toasted and chopped fine

Chicken with Pumpkin Seed Sauce

Pumpkin Bread

Pumpkin Spice Muffins

Pumpkin Spice Waffles

1. FOR THE TOPPING Using your fingers, mix all ingredients in bowl until well combined and topping resembles wet sand; set aside.

2. FOR THE BREAD Adjust oven rack to middle position and heat oven to 350 degrees. Grease two 8½ by 4½-inch loaf pans. Whisk flour, baking powder, and baking soda together in bowl.

3. Combine pumpkin puree, salt, cinnamon, nutmeg, and cloves in large saucepan over medium heat. Cook mixture, stirring constantly, until reduced to 1½ cups, 6 to 8 minutes. Remove saucepan from heat; stir in granulated sugar, brown sugar, oil, and cream cheese until combined. Let mixture stand for 5 minutes. Whisk until no visible pieces of cream cheese remain and mixture is homogeneous.

4. Whisk eggs and buttermilk together in bowl. Add egg mixture to pumpkin mixture and whisk to combine. Using silicone spatula, fold flour mixture into pumpkin mixture until combined (some small lumps of flour are OK). Fold walnuts into batter. Divide batter evenly between prepared pans. Sprinkle topping evenly over top of loaves. Bake until skewer inserted in center of loaf comes out clean, 45 to 50 minutes. Let loaves cool in pans on wire rack for 20 minutes. Remove loaves from pans and let cool for at least 1½ hours. Serve warm or at room temperature. (Cooled loaves can be stored at room temperature for up to 3 days.)

Pumpkin Bread with Candied Ginger

Substitute ½ teaspoon ground ginger for cinnamon in topping. Fold ⅓ cup minced crystallized ginger into batter after flour mixture has been added in step 4.

Pumpkin Spice Muffins

Makes 12 muffins | **Total Time** 1¼ hours

MAKE AHEAD VEGETARIAN

WHY THIS RECIPE WORKS When pumpkin spice–flavored treats start showing up in full force in coffee shops and on store shelves, you know autumn has arrived. We stand firmly in the pumpkin spice–appreciation camp, and made it our mission to pack its warming, friendly flavor into the batter of our sweet, almost dessert-worthy muffins as well as the lightly crisp streusel topping. The moisture from canned pumpkin puree turns to steam when heated in the oven, providing superior binding and lift in cakey baked goods such as muffins. That characteristic meant that all we had to do here was whisk it right into the batter. The result: Tall, light, pumpkiny muffins that spoke of fall in every bite. One 15-ounce can of pumpkin puree is more than enough for this recipe. You can transfer the leftover pumpkin to a zipper-lock bag and freeze it for up to a month.

TOPPING

- ½ cup (2½ ounces) all-purpose flour
- 5 tablespoons (2¼ ounces) sugar
- 1 teaspoon pumpkin pie spice
- Pinch table salt
- 4 tablespoons unsalted butter, melted

MUFFINS

- 2½ cups (12½ ounces) all-purpose flour
- 2 cups (14 ounces) sugar
- 1 tablespoon pumpkin pie spice
- 2 teaspoons baking powder
- ¾ teaspoon table salt
- 1 cup canned unsweetened pumpkin puree
- 8 tablespoons unsalted butter, melted
- 2 large eggs
- ¼ cup milk
- 2 teaspoons vanilla extract

1. Adjust oven rack to middle position and heat oven to 375 degrees. Generously spray 12-cup muffin tin, including top, with baking spray with flour.

2. FOR THE TOPPING Combine flour, sugar, pie spice, and salt in bowl. Add melted butter and stir until evenly moistened and mixture resembles wet sand; set aside.

3. FOR THE MUFFINS Whisk flour, sugar, pie spice, baking powder, and salt together in bowl. Whisk pumpkin, melted butter, eggs, milk, and vanilla together in separate bowl. Stir flour mixture into pumpkin mixture until just combined.

4. Using greased ⅓-cup dry measuring cup, portion heaping ⅓ cup batter into each muffin cup (cups will be filled to rim). Sprinkle topping evenly over batter, about 1 tablespoon per muffin.

5. Bake muffins until golden brown and toothpick inserted in center comes out with few crumbs attached, 22 to 25 minutes, rotating muffin tin halfway through baking. Let muffins cool in muffin tin on wire rack for 10 minutes. Remove muffins from muffin tin and let cool on rack for 5 minutes. Serve. (Muffins can be stored at room temperature for up to 2 days.)

Pumpkin Spice Waffles

Makes five 7-inch Belgian waffles
Total Time 45 minutes VEGETARIAN

WHY THIS RECIPE WORKS While we love a crisp-on-the-outside, soft-on-the-inside plain waffle, it didn't take much arm twisting to convince tasters to try a sunset-orange spiced pumpkin version. To avoid an overly wet batter, we used paper towels to absorb the excess moisture from canned pumpkin puree. Oat flour, bolstered by a little all-purpose flour for structure, gave the waffles whole-grain nuttiness. Yogurt provided richness and tang, while cinnamon, nutmeg, cardamom, and fresh ginger added complex notes of warmth and subtle spice. We prefer using store-bought oat flour, as it has a very fine grind and creates the best waffles, but you can make your own in a pinch. Grind 2½ cups (7½ ounces) old-fashioned rolled oats in a food processor to a fine meal, about 2 minutes; note that the waffles will be denser if using ground oats. Do not use toasted oat flour in this recipe. Serve with maple syrup and fresh fruit. Be sure to buy unsweetened canned pumpkin, not pumpkin pie filling, which is preseasoned and sweetened.

- 2½ cups (7½ ounces) oat flour
- ½ cup (2½ ounces) all-purpose flour
- 1 teaspoon ground cinnamon
- 1 teaspoon baking powder
- ½ teaspoon baking soda
- ¾ teaspoon table salt
- ¼ teaspoon ground nutmeg
- ¼ teaspoon ground cardamom
- 1 (15-ounce) can unsweetened pumpkin puree
- 1¼ cups plain yogurt
- 2 large eggs
- ¼ cup vegetable oil, plus extra for brushing
- ¼ cup (1¾ ounces) sugar
- 1 teaspoon grated fresh ginger

1. Adjust oven rack to middle position and heat oven to 200 degrees. Whisk oat flour, all-purpose flour, cinnamon, baking powder, baking soda, salt, nutmeg, and cardamom together in large bowl.

2. Line rimmed baking sheet with triple layer of paper towels. Spread pumpkin on paper towels in even layer. Cover pumpkin with second triple layer of paper towels and press firmly until paper towels are saturated. Peel back top layer of towels and discard. Grasp bottom towels and fold pumpkin in half; peel back towels. Transfer pumpkin to separate bowl (puree will separate easily from towels) and discard towels. Whisk in yogurt, eggs, oil, sugar, and ginger until combined.

Whisk pumpkin mixture into flour mixture until well combined and smooth. Set wire rack in now-empty baking sheet and place in oven.

3. Heat waffle iron according to manufacturer's instructions and brush well with additional oil. Add scant 1 cup batter to waffle iron and cook according to manufacturer's instructions until each waffle is deep golden and has crisp, firm exterior. Serve immediately or transfer to wire rack in oven. Repeat with remaining batter, brushing waffle iron with additional oil.

Pumpkin–Chocolate Chip Snack Cake

Serves 16   MAKE AHEAD   VEGETARIAN
Total Time 40 minutes, plus 1¼ hours cooling

WHY THIS RECIPE WORKS Sweet, water-rich pumpkin puree incorporated into a basic snack cake batter results in a moist and flavorful snack cake that can be whipped up in under an hour. To avoid overdeveloping the batter's gluten (which would lead to a tough crumb), we stirred together the dry and wet ingredients separately before mixing the two together until just combined. Pumpkin pie spice added warm autumnal flavor, and mini chocolate chips punctuated each bite with pops of melty richness. We prefer mini chocolate chips here, but you can substitute standard-size semisweet chocolate chips, if desired. One 15-ounce can of pumpkin puree is more than enough for this recipe. You can transfer the leftover pumpkin to a zipper-lock bag and freeze it for up to a month.

    1 cup (5 ounces) all-purpose flour
    1 tablespoon pumpkin pie spice
    1 teaspoon baking powder
    ½ teaspoon baking soda
    ¼ teaspoon table salt
    1 cup canned unsweetened
       pumpkin puree
    1 cup (7 ounces) sugar
    ½ cup vegetable oil
    2 large eggs
    ½ cup (3 ounces) mini semisweet
       chocolate chips

1. Adjust oven rack to middle position and heat oven to 350 degrees. Grease and flour 8-inch square baking pan. Whisk flour, pumpkin pie spice, baking powder, baking soda, and salt together in large bowl. Whisk pumpkin, sugar, oil, and eggs together in second bowl.

2. Stir pumpkin mixture into flour mixture until just combined. Stir in chocolate chips until just incorporated. Transfer batter to prepared pan and smooth top with rubber spatula. Bake until paring knife inserted in center comes out clean, about 35 minutes.

3. Let cake cool in pan on wire rack for 20 minutes. Remove cake from pan and let cool completely on rack, about 1 hour. Serve. (Cooled cake can be wrapped in plastic wrap and stored at room temperature for up to 2 days.)

Maple-Pumpkin Stack Cake

Serves 10 to 12   VEGETARIAN
Total Time 1½ hours, plus 1¼ hours cooling

WHY THIS RECIPE WORKS We wanted a sky-high pumpkin showstopper that would inspire instant admiration when brought out at the end of a meal. We started with four layers of tender, moist, gently spiced pumpkin cake (which we baked in two batches). We like pumpkin pie served with whipped cream, so we decided to follow suit with this cake, sandwiching billows of maple syrup–sweetened whipped cream between the cake layers. We topped the whole thing off with more maple whipped cream and a sprinkling of crunchy pecans—another autumn favorite—that we toasted to bring out their warm, rich depth. Leaving the sides uncovered allowed us to appreciate all the layers of this stunning multitiered cake. Be sure to buy unsweetened canned pumpkin, not pumpkin pie filling, which is preseasoned and sweetened.

CAKE
    1½ cups (7½ ounces) all-purpose flour
    2   teaspoons pumpkin pie spice
    1   teaspoon baking powder
    1   teaspoon baking soda
    1   teaspoon table salt
    8   tablespoons unsalted butter,
        melted and cooled
    1¼ cups (8¾ ounces) sugar
    3   large eggs
    1   (15-ounce) can unsweetened
        pumpkin puree

WHIPPED CREAM
    1½ cups heavy cream, chilled
    ¼   cup maple syrup

    ¼   cup pecans, toasted and chopped

1. FOR THE CAKE Adjust oven rack to middle position and heat oven to 350 degrees. Grease two 8-inch round cake pans, line with parchment paper, grease parchment, and flour pans.

2. Whisk flour, pie spice, baking powder, baking soda, and salt together in bowl. Using stand mixer fitted with paddle, beat melted butter, sugar, and eggs on medium-high speed until pale and fluffy, about 3 minutes. Reduce speed to low, add pumpkin, and mix until incorporated. Slowly add flour mixture and mix until only few small flour streaks remain, about 30 seconds.

3. Spread about 1 cup of batter in even layer in each prepared pan. Bake until toothpick inserted in center comes out clean, 12 to 14 minutes, switching and rotating pans halfway through baking. Let cakes cool in pans on wire rack for 10 minutes. Remove cakes from pans, discarding parchment, and let cool completely on lightly greased rack. Reline pans with parchment, grease parchment, and flour pans. Repeat process with remaining batter.

4. FOR THE WHIPPED CREAM Using clean, dry mixer bowl and whisk attachment, whip cream and maple syrup on medium speed until stiff peaks form, about 3 minutes.

5. Place 1 cake round on platter, then spread one-quarter of whipped cream (scant 1 cup) evenly over top. Repeat with remaining cake layers and whipped cream. Sprinkle pecans over top. Serve.

Pumpkin–Chocolate Chip Snack Cake

Maple-Pumpkin Stack Cake

Pumpkin Pie

Serves 8 MAKE AHEAD VEGETARIAN
Total Time 1¾ hours, plus 4 hours cooling

WHY THIS RECIPE WORKS This pumpkin pie sets the standard: It's velvety smooth, perfectly spiced, and packed with pumpkin flavor thanks to a surprising extra ingredient. We found that adding both sweet potato and pumpkin puree to our filling actually made the pie taste more like pumpkin than when we made the filling with pumpkin alone. Pouring the hot filling directly into a still-warm prebaked crust helped the custard firm up quickly in the oven and prevented it from soaking into the crust. Starting the pie in a hot oven and then dropping the temperature partway through baking prevented the custard from curdling. If candied sweet potatoes or yams are unavailable, regular canned sweet potatoes or yams can be substituted. When the pie is properly baked, the center 2 inches of the pie should look firm but jiggle slightly. Be sure to buy unsweetened canned pumpkin, not pumpkin pie filling, which is preseasoned and sweetened.

1 recipe Foolproof All-Butter Single-Crust Pie Dough (page 388)

1 cup heavy cream

1 cup whole milk

3 large eggs plus 2 large yolks

1 teaspoon vanilla extract

1 (15-ounce) can unsweetened pumpkin puree

1 cup drained candied sweet potatoes or yams

¾ cup (5¼ ounces) sugar

¼ cup maple syrup

2 teaspoons grated fresh ginger

1 teaspoon table salt

½ teaspoon ground cinnamon

¼ teaspoon ground nutmeg

1. Roll dough into 12-inch circle on well-floured counter. Roll dough loosely around rolling pin and gently unroll it onto 9-inch pie plate, letting excess dough hang over edge. Ease dough into plate by gently lifting edge of dough with your hand while pressing into plate bottom with your other hand.

2. Trim overhang to ½ inch beyond lip of plate. Tuck overhang under itself; folded edge should be flush with edge of plate. Crimp dough evenly around edge of plate. Wrap dough-lined plate loosely in plastic wrap and refrigerate until firm, about 30 minutes. Adjust oven rack to middle position and heat oven to 350 degrees.

3. Line pie shell with double layer of aluminum foil, covering edges to prevent burning, and fill with pie weights. Bake on foil-lined rimmed baking sheet until edges are set and just beginning to turn golden, 25 to 30 minutes, rotating sheet halfway through baking.

4. Remove foil and weights, rotate sheet, and continue to bake crust until golden brown and crisp, 10 to 15 minutes. Transfer sheet to wire rack. (Crust must still be warm when filling is added.) Increase oven temperature to 400 degrees.

5. While crust is baking, whisk cream, milk, eggs and yolks, and vanilla together in bowl; set aside. Bring pumpkin, sweet potatoes, sugar, maple syrup, ginger, salt, cinnamon, and nutmeg to simmer in large saucepan over medium heat and cook, stirring constantly and mashing sweet potatoes against sides of saucepan, until thick and shiny, 15 to 20 minutes.

6. Remove saucepan from heat and whisk in cream mixture until fully incorporated.

7. Strain mixture through fine-mesh strainer into bowl, using back of ladle or spatula to press solids through strainer.

8. Whisk mixture, then, with pie still on sheet, pour into warm crust. Bake for 10 minutes. Reduce oven temperature to 300 degrees and continue to bake until edges of pie are set and

Pumpkin Pie

center registers 175 degrees, 20 to 35 minutes, rotating sheet halfway through baking. Let pie cool completely on wire rack, about 4 hours. Serve. (Baked pie can be held at room temperature for up to 8 hours or refrigerated for up to 2 days; if refrigerated, allow to come to room temperature before serving. Note that crust will be less crisp if refrigerated.)

Rum Pumpkin Chiffon Pie

Serves 8 MAKE AHEAD
Total Time 1½ hours, plus 4 hours cooling

WHY THIS RECIPE WORKS Pumpkin chiffon pie is an airy and elegant version of the old Thanksgiving standard. It consists of a gelatin-stabilized pumpkin custard lightened by meringue and sometimes whipped cream. We eliminated the cooked egg custard step found in many chiffon recipes. Instead, we simply whipped up a meringue and folded it into a smooth mixture of pumpkin, sugar, and cinnamon. Crunchy gingersnap cookies sprinkled over the whipped cream–covered pie and a healthy glug of rum turned this dessert into a festive showstopper. The filling for this pie is not cooked; if you prefer to use pasteurized egg whites, use ½ cup and increase the whipping time in step 4 to 5 to 6 minutes. Be sure to buy unsweetened canned pumpkin, not pumpkin pie filling, which is preseasoned and sweetened.

CRUST

- 9 whole graham crackers, broken into 1-inch pieces
- 3 tablespoons granulated sugar
- ½ teaspoon ground ginger
- 5 tablespoons unsalted butter, melted

FILLING

- 1 tablespoon unflavored gelatin
- ¼ cup dark rum
- 1 (15-ounce) can unsweetened pumpkin puree
- ⅓ cup packed (2⅓ ounces) dark brown sugar
- 1 teaspoon ground cinnamon
- ¾ teaspoon table salt
- ½ cup heavy cream
- 4 large egg whites
- ⅓ cup (2⅓ ounces) granulated sugar
- 1 recipe Whipped Cream (page 368)
- 4 gingersnap cookies, crushed into ¼-inch pieces

1. FOR THE CRUST Adjust oven rack to middle position and heat oven to 325 degrees. Process cracker pieces, sugar, and ginger in food processor to fine, even crumbs, about 30 seconds. Sprinkle melted butter over crumbs and pulse to incorporate, about 8 pulses. Sprinkle mixture into 9-inch pie plate. Using bottom of dry measuring cup, press crumbs into even layer on bottom and sides of pie plate. Bake until crust is fragrant and beginning to brown, 12 to 18 minutes. Let crust cool completely on wire rack, about 30 minutes.

2. FOR THE FILLING Sprinkle gelatin over rum in large bowl and let stand until gelatin softens, about 5 minutes. Microwave until mixture is bubbling around edges and gelatin dissolves, about 30 seconds. Let cool until slightly warm, about 110 degrees. (Mixture will be syrupy.)

3. Meanwhile, microwave pumpkin in bowl until heated to 110 degrees, 30 seconds to 1 minute. Process pumpkin, brown sugar, cinnamon, and salt in food processor until completely smooth, about 1 minute. Scrape down sides of bowl; process until no streaks remain, 10 to 15 seconds. Transfer pumpkin mixture to bowl with gelatin mixture; stir to combine. Stir in cream.

4. Using stand mixer fitted with whisk attachment, whip egg whites on medium-low speed until foamy, about 1 minute. Increase speed to medium-high and whip whites to soft,

Rum Pumpkin Chiffon Pie

billowy mounds, about 1 minute. Gradually add granulated sugar and whip until glossy, stiff peaks form, 2 to 3 minutes. Whisk one-third of meringue into pumpkin mixture until smooth. Using rubber spatula, fold remaining meringue into pumpkin mixture until only few white streaks remain.

5. Spoon filling into center of crust. Gently spread filling to edges of crust, leaving mounded dome in center. Refrigerate pie for at least 4 hours or up to 24 hours. Spread whipped cream evenly over pie, following domed contours. Sprinkle gingersnaps over top. Serve.

Pumpkin-Pecan Cookies

Makes about 40 cookies VEGETARIAN
Total Time 1¾ hours, plus 30 minutes drying

WHY THIS RECIPE WORKS Add pumpkin puree to cookies, and they'll usually come out cakey. That's because when treats made with watery pumpkin hit the oven, all that moisture turns to steam and provides lift. We wanted a pumpkin cookie that was thin, crisp, and shortbread-like. To get rid of the

Pumpkin-Pecan Cookies

Pumpkin Cheesecake Bars

pumpkin puree's problematic excess moisture, we spread it between layers of paper towels, allowing the paper towels to drink up that moisture until the puree reduced in volume from 1 cup to a mere ⅓ cup. Adding this thickened paste to the dough, along with a few spices to give the flavor a lift, resulted in pumpkiny, fine-crumbed cookies: a complete success. One 15-ounce can of pumpkin puree is more than enough for this recipe. You can transfer the leftover pumpkin to a zipper-lock bag and freeze it for up to a month.

  1 cup canned unsweetened pumpkin puree
2¾ cups (13¾ ounces) all-purpose flour
  ¾ cup (5¼ ounces) superfine sugar
  2 teaspoons ground cinnamon, divided
  ½ teaspoon ground ginger
  ½ teaspoon ground nutmeg
  ¼ teaspoon table salt
 16 tablespoons unsalted butter, cut into
     16 pieces and softened
1¼ cups pecans, toasted and chopped fine
1½ ounces cream cheese, softened, divided
  2 teaspoons vanilla extract
  2 tablespoons milk
1½ cups (6 ounces) confectioners' sugar

1. Line rimmed baking sheet with triple layer of paper towels. Spread pumpkin on paper towels in even layer. Cover pumpkin with second triple layer of paper towels and press firmly until paper towels are saturated. Peel back top layer of towels and discard. Grasp bottom towels and fold pumpkin in half; peel back towels. Transfer pumpkin to separate bowl (puree will separate easily from towels) and discard towels. Repeat if needed to reduce paste to ⅓ cup.

2. Using stand mixer fitted with paddle, mix flour, superfine sugar, 1½ teaspoons cinnamon, ginger, nutmeg, and salt on low speed until combined. Add butter, 1 piece at a time, and mix until dough looks crumbly and slightly wet, 1 to 2 minutes. Add pecans, 2 tablespoons cream cheese, vanilla, and pumpkin and beat until dough just begins to form large clumps, about 30 seconds. Transfer dough to counter; knead just until it forms cohesive mass, then divide in half. Form each half into disk, wrap disks tightly in plastic wrap, and refrigerate for 30 minutes.

3. Adjust oven rack to middle position and heat oven to 375 degrees. Line 2 baking sheets with parchment paper. Working with 1 disk of dough at a time, roll dough ⅛ inch thick between 2 large sheets of parchment paper. Transfer dough, still between parchment, to refrigerator and let chill for 10 minutes. Using 2½-inch cutter, cut dough into shapes;

space shapes 1½ inches apart on prepared sheets. Gently reroll scraps, cut into shapes, and transfer to prepared sheets.

4. Bake, 1 sheet at a time, until cookies are light golden brown, about 10 minutes, rotating sheet halfway through baking. Let cookies cool on sheet for 3 minutes, then transfer to wire rack and let cool completely. Whisk milk, remaining ½ teaspoon cinnamon, and remaining 1 tablespoon cream cheese in bowl until combined. Add confectioners' sugar and whisk until smooth. Spread glaze evenly onto cookies and let dry for at least 30 minutes before serving.

Pumpkin Cheesecake Bars

Makes 24 bars MAKE AHEAD   VEGETARIAN
Total Time 1¾ hours, plus 5 hours cooling

WHY THIS RECIPE WORKS Tangy, rich, and velvety, a basic cheesecake is a base well-suited to variation. Our favorite take on the concept might just be pumpkin cheesecake. The cream cheese's tang offsets the sweet pumpkin flavor, and when enhanced with warm pumpkin pie spice the result is pure comfort food. Wanting more of this dessert in our lives, we set out to create a streamlined version in the form of a pumpkin cheesecake bar. The challenge was to remove enough water from the moisture-rich pumpkin puree to maintain the cheesecake layer's structural integrity. We first reduced the puree by cooking it on the stovetop, concentrating its flavor and enhancing its sweetness. Adding the pumpkin pie spice at this stage bloomed and deepened its flavor. A crust made from gingersnap cookies baked up tooth-breakingly hard, so instead, we jazzed up a traditional graham cracker crust with ground ginger for similar flavor. For more information on making a foil sling, see "Making a Foil Sling." Be sure to buy unsweetened canned pumpkin, not pumpkin pie filling, which is preseasoned and sweetened.

- 1 (15-ounce) can unsweetened pumpkin puree
- 2 teaspoons pumpkin pie spice
- ½ teaspoon table salt
- 15 whole graham crackers, broken into 1-inch pieces
- ¼ cup (1¾ ounces) plus 1⅓ cups (9⅓ ounces) sugar, divided
- 1 teaspoon ground ginger
- 8 tablespoons butter, melted
- 1 pound cream cheese, softened
- 1 tablespoon lemon juice
- 2 teaspoons vanilla extract
- 4 large eggs, room temperature

1. Cook pumpkin puree, pumpkin pie spice, and salt in small saucepan over medium heat, stirring constantly, until reduced to 1½ cups, 6 to 8 minutes. Let pumpkin mixture cool for 1 hour.

2. Adjust oven rack to middle position and heat oven to 325 degrees. Make foil sling for 13 by 9-inch baking pan by folding 2 long sheets of aluminum foil; first sheet should be 13 inches wide and second sheet should be 9 inches wide. Lay sheets of foil in pan perpendicular to each other, with extra foil hanging over edges of pan. Push foil into corners and up sides of pan, smoothing foil flush to pan. Grease foil.

3. Process graham crackers, ¼ cup sugar, and ginger in food processor to fine crumbs, about 15 seconds. Add melted butter and pulse until combined, about 5 pulses. Sprinkle mixture into prepared pan and press firmly into even layer. Bake until just starting to brown, 15 to 18 minutes. Let crust cool completely in pan on wire rack.

4. Using stand mixer fitted with paddle, beat cream cheese and remaining 1⅓ cups sugar on medium-low speed until smooth, about 2 minutes. Add lemon juice, vanilla, and pumpkin mixture and beat until combined. Increase speed to medium; add eggs, one at a time, and beat until incorporated. Pour filling over crust and spread into even layer.

5. Bake until edges are slightly puffed and center is just set, 45 to 50 minutes. Let cheesecake cool completely in pan on wire rack, about 2 hours. Refrigerate until thoroughly chilled, at least 3 hours or up to 24 hours. Using foil overhang, lift cheesecake from pan. Cut into 24 pieces before serving.

MAKING A FOIL SLING

1. Line baking pan with 2 sheets of aluminum foil placed perpendicular to each other with extra foil hanging over edges of pan. Push foil into corners and smooth flush to pan.

2. Use foil handles to lift baked bar cookies from pan.

Pumpkin–Cream Cheese Brownies

Makes 16 brownies MAKE AHEAD VEGETARIAN
Total Time 1¼ hours, plus 2 hours cooling

WHY THIS RECIPE WORKS A fudgy, ultrachocolaty brownie doesn't need anything else to be a great dessert— but it's true that a couple of well thought-out flourishes can take regular brownies soaring to new heights. Considering the popularity of cream cheese brownies and our success pairing cream cheese with pumpkin in our Pumpkin Cheesecake Bars (page 225), we decided to combine all three for new levels of craveable decadence. When mixing up the batter, we liked the way whole-wheat flour's subtly bitter earthiness balanced the sweetness and richness of our other ingredients. As the aromas of warm chocolate and pumpkin wafted from the kitchen, the hardest step by far was waiting for the brownies to cool before digging in. For more information on making a foil sling, see page 225. To accurately test the doneness of the brownies, be sure to stick the toothpick into the brownie portion, not the pumpkin layer. One 15-ounce can of pumpkin puree is more than enough for this recipe. You can transfer the leftover pumpkin to a zipper-lock bag and freeze it for up to a month.

PUMPKIN FILLING

- 4 ounces cream cheese, cut into 4 pieces
- ¾ cup canned unsweetened pumpkin puree
- 2 tablespoons sugar
- 1 tablespoon whole-wheat flour
- ¼ teaspoon pumpkin pie spice

BROWNIE BATTER

- ⅔ cup (3⅔ ounces) whole-wheat flour
- ½ teaspoon baking powder
- ½ teaspoon table salt
- 4 ounces unsweetened chocolate, chopped fine
- 1¼ cups (8¾ ounces) sugar
- 6 tablespoons vegetable oil
- 2 large eggs
- 2 tablespoons milk
- 1 teaspoon vanilla extract

1. Adjust oven rack to middle position and heat oven to 350 degrees. Make foil sling for 8-inch square baking pan by folding 2 long sheets of aluminum foil so each is 8 inches wide. Lay sheets of foil in pan perpendicular to each other, with extra foil hanging over edges of pan. Push foil into corners and up sides of pan, smoothing foil flush to pan. Grease foil.

2. FOR THE PUMPKIN FILLING Microwave cream cheese in bowl until soft, 20 to 30 seconds. Whisk in pumpkin puree, sugar, flour, and pumpkin pie spice until combined.

3. FOR THE BROWNIE BATTER Whisk flour, baking powder, and salt together in small bowl and set aside. Microwave chocolate in large bowl at 50 percent power, stirring occasionally, until melted, about 2 minutes. Let cool slightly.

4. Whisk sugar, oil, eggs, milk, and vanilla into melted chocolate until incorporated. Using rubber spatula, fold flour mixture into chocolate mixture to combine. Measure out ⅓ cup batter and set aside. Spread remaining batter in prepared pan. Gently spread pumpkin filling evenly over batter.

5. Microwave reserved ⅓ cup batter until warm and fluid, 15 to 30 seconds. Using spoon, dollop softened batter over pumpkin filling, 6 to 8 dollops. Using knife, swirl batter through pumpkin filling, making marbled pattern, 10 to 12 strokes, leaving ½-inch border around edges.

6. Bake until toothpick inserted in center comes out with few moist crumbs attached, 35 to 40 minutes, rotating pan halfway through baking. Let brownies cool in pan on wire rack for 1 hour.

7. Using foil overhang, lift brownies out of pan. Return brownies to wire rack and let cool completely, about 1 hour. Cut into squares and serve. (Cooled brownies can be wrapped in plastic wrap, then foil, and refrigerated for up to 5 days.)

Pumpkin Streusel Bars

Makes 24 bars MAKE AHEAD VEGETARIAN
Total Time 1½ hours, plus 1 hour cooling

WHY THIS RECIPE WORKS It's a classic Thanksgiving dilemma: If you like pecans and you like pumpkin, which slice of pie do you go for? We envisioned a homey bar cookie that would turn these two dessert table rivals into allies and deliver the best of both worlds in every bite. These sturdy bar cookies were the result, sandwiching a thick layer of gooey spiced pumpkin between a pecan-based cookie crust and a buttery streusel topping. For ease, we mixed together the cookie crust first, reserving a portion and adding melted butter and extra pecans to make the streusel. For the pumpkin filling, sweetened condensed milk acted as both the dairy component and the sweetener. These holiday-ready bars are the perfect base for a scoop of vanilla ice cream. Be sure to buy unsweetened canned pumpkin, not pumpkin pie filling, which is preseasoned and sweetened. For more information on making a foil sling, see page 225.

1½ cups pecans, toasted

2 cups (10 ounces) all-purpose flour

1¼ cups packed (8¾ ounces) brown sugar, divided

1 teaspoon table salt, divided

12 tablespoons unsalted butter, cut into ½-inch pieces and chilled, plus 2 tablespoons melted

½ cup (1½ ounces) rolled oats

4 teaspoons pumpkin pie spice, divided

1 (15-ounce) can unsweetened pumpkin puree

1 (14-ounce) can sweetened condensed milk

1 large egg plus 1 large yolk

2 teaspoons vanilla extract

1. Adjust oven rack to middle position and heat oven to 325 degrees. Make foil sling for 13 by 9-inch baking pan by folding 2 long sheets of aluminum foil; first sheet should be 13 inches wide and second sheet should be 9 inches wide. Lay sheets of foil in pan perpendicular to each other, with extra foil hanging over edges of pan. Push foil into corners and up sides of pan, smoothing foil flush to pan. Grease foil.

2. Pulse pecans in food processor until coarsely chopped, 5 to 7 pulses; transfer ½ cup pecans to medium bowl and set aside.

3. Add flour, 1 cup sugar, and ½ teaspoon salt to processor and process until pecans are finely ground, about 10 seconds. Scatter butter pieces over flour mixture and pulse until mixture resembles damp sand, about 20 pulses.

4. Measure 1½ cups flour mixture into bowl with pecans and set aside; distribute remaining flour mixture evenly in bottom of prepared pan. Using your hands or flat-bottomed measuring cup, firmly press mixture into even layer to form bottom crust. Bake until edges begin to brown, 25 to 30 minutes.

5. While crust is baking, add oats, 1 teaspoon pie spice, melted butter, and remaining ¼ cup sugar to reserved flour mixture; toss to combine until small clumps form. In now-empty processor, combine pumpkin, condensed milk, egg and yolk, vanilla, remaining ½ teaspoon salt, and remaining 1 tablespoon pie spice and process until smooth and slightly thickened, about 30 seconds.

6. Spread filling evenly over hot crust; sprinkle streusel topping evenly over filling (do not press streusel into filling). Return pan to oven and bake until topping is golden brown, edges have puffed up, and center is set, 35 to 40 minutes. Let cool in pan on wire rack for at least 1 hour. Using foil over-hang, lift bars out of pan. Cut into 24 pieces. Serve warm or at room temperature. (Cooled bars can be refrigerated uncovered in pan for up to 2 days; crust and streusel topping will soften.)

Pumpkin–Cream Cheese Brownies

Pumpkin Streusel Bars

appetizers & starters

■ MAKE AHEAD ▪ VEGETARIAN
Photo: Crispy Potato Latkes

Herbed Spinach Dip

Slow-Cooker
Creamy Crab Dip

Parsnip Hummus

Makes about 2 cups MAKE AHEAD VEGETARIAN
Total Time 20 minutes, plus 30 minutes resting

WHY THIS RECIPE WORKS Hummus is a welcome addition to any party spread. To keep it interesting, here we traded chickpeas for hearty winter parsnips, which contribute an earthy sweetness that takes well to the typical flavorings of tahini, olive oil, garlic, and lemon juice. The ideal cooking method for the parsnips turned out to be microwaving, which was easy and resulted in flavor nearly as intense as roasting. Just ¼ cup of tahini was enough to stand up to the parsnips without overwhelming the hummus. To round out the parsnips' earthy, floral flavors, we added warm spices: paprika, coriander, and cumin. Smoky chipotle chile powder and garlic tempered the sweetness of the parsnips, while lemon juice brought the flavors into focus. Look for tender, thin parsnips for this hummus, as large parsnips can turn bitter. Serve with crackers, chips, or crudités.

- 1 pound parsnips, peeled, cut into 1-inch lengths, and thick ends halved lengthwise
- ¼ cup tahini
- 3 tablespoons extra-virgin olive oil, plus extra for drizzling
- ¾ cup water
- 2 tablespoons lemon juice
- 1 garlic clove, minced
- 1 teaspoon paprika
- ¾ teaspoon table salt
- ½ teaspoon ground coriander
- ¼ teaspoon ground cumin
- ¼ teaspoon chipotle chile powder
- 1 tablespoon toasted sesame seeds

1. Microwave parsnips in covered bowl until tender, about 10 minutes. Combine tahini and oil in small bowl.

2. Process parsnips, water, lemon juice, garlic, paprika, salt, coriander, cumin, and chile powder in food processor until completely smooth, about 1 minute, scraping down sides of bowl as needed. With processor running, add tahini mixture in steady stream and process until hummus is smooth and creamy, about 15 seconds, scraping down bowl as needed. Season with salt and pepper to taste.

3. Transfer hummus to bowl, cover with plastic wrap, and let stand at room temperature until flavors meld, about 30 minutes. Drizzle with extra oil and sprinkle with sesame seeds. Serve. (Hummus can be refrigerated for up to 5 days; stir in 1 tablespoon warm water to loosen if necessary before serving.)

Herbed Spinach Dip

Serves 4 to 6 `MAKE AHEAD` `VEGETARIAN`
Total Time 15 minutes, plus 1 hour chilling

WHY THIS RECIPE WORKS A simple spinach dip works as well with chips for a casual snack as it does with crostini for a holiday party. But spinach dips made with soup mixes are flat, overly salty, and stale-tasting. We decided to ditch the mix and create a rich and creamy spinach dip brimming with flavors. We were surprised to discover that frozen spinach made a dip with a vibrant, more intense flavor than fresh spinach. Instead of thawing the spinach completely, we partially thawed it, allowing the chunks of icy spinach to cool the dip. We used a food processor to chop the spinach and then enriched it with sour cream, mayonnaise, and a mixture of fresh herbs and seasonings. You can skip step 1 and let the frozen spinach thaw at room temperature for 1½ hours before squeezing it dry if you prefer. The garlic must be minced before going into the food processor; otherwise, the dip will contain large chunks of garlic. We used Frank's RedHot Original Cayenne Pepper Sauce, but other hot sauces can be used. Serve with crudités, chips, and/or Crostini (see page 236).

- 10 ounces frozen chopped spinach
- ½ red bell pepper, chopped fine
- ½ cup sour cream
- ½ cup mayonnaise
- ½ cup fresh parsley leaves
- 3 scallions, sliced thin
- 1 tablespoon minced fresh dill
- 1 garlic clove, minced
- ½ teaspoon table salt
- ¼ teaspoon pepper
- ¼ teaspoon hot sauce

1. Microwave spinach at 40 percent power for 3 minutes. Edges should be thawed but not warm; center should be soft enough to be broken into icy chunks. Squeeze spinach to release excess liquid.

2. Process spinach, bell pepper, sour cream, mayonnaise, parsley, scallions, dill, garlic, salt, pepper, and hot sauce in food processor until well combined, about 1 minute, scraping down sides of bowl as needed. Transfer to serving bowl, cover, and refrigerate until flavors meld, at least 1 hour or up to 3 days. Season with salt and pepper to taste. Serve. (Dip can be refrigerated for up to 24 hours. To serve, let come to room temperature and season with salt and pepper to taste.)

Slow-Cooker Creamy Crab Dip

Serves 6 to 8
Cooking Time 1 to 2 hours on Low

WHY THIS RECIPE WORKS Warm crab dip is a decadent party pleaser and an especially convenient option when made in a slow cooker, which will keep it warm for several hours and can even double as a serving vessel. For a dip that tasted first and foremost of crab, we included a full pound of crabmeat and limited the amount of filler. Patting the crabmeat dry was key to ensuring that the dip was creamy but not watery, and adding some traditional Old Bay seasoning balanced the sweet richness of the crabmeat. We tried adding raw onions to the slow cooker but they never turned tender, so we softened them first in the microwave. A combination of cream cheese and mayonnaise gave the dip mild tanginess and rich texture. Finishing with a sprinkle of chives instead of the traditional cheese layer gave our creamy dip a lighter, fresher flavor. You will need a 1½- to 7-quart slow cooker for this recipe. Do not substitute imitation crabmeat here. Serve with crusty bread, crackers, and/or Crostini (page 236).

- 1 small onion, chopped fine
- 2 tablespoons unsalted butter
- 2 teaspoons Old Bay seasoning
- 8 ounces cream cheese, softened
- ¼ cup mayonnaise
- ¼ teaspoon pepper
- 1 pound lump crabmeat, picked over for shells and pressed dry between paper towels
- 2 tablespoons minced fresh chives

1. Microwave onion, butter, and Old Bay in large bowl, stirring occasionally, until onion is softened, about 5 minutes. Whisk in cream cheese, mayonnaise, and pepper until well combined. Gently fold in crabmeat.

2A. FOR 1½- TO 5-QUART SLOW COOKER Transfer mixture to slow cooker, cover, and cook until heated through, 1 to 2 hours on low.

2B. FOR 5½- TO 7-QUART SLOW COOKER Transfer mixture to 1½-quart soufflé dish. Set dish in slow cooker and pour water into slow cooker until it reaches about one-third up sides of dish (about 2 cups water). Cover and cook until heated through, 1 to 2 hours on low. Remove dish from slow cooker, if desired.

3. Gently stir dip to recombine. Sprinkle with chives and serve. (Dip can be held on warm or low setting for up to 2 hours.)

Buffalo Chicken Dip

Serves 10 to 15 | **Total Time** 35 minutes

WHY THIS RECIPE WORKS Perfect for a crowd on game night or any night, Buffalo Chicken Dip has all the lip-tingling, tangy flavor of good buffalo wings, but with less messy fingers. Shredding the meat from a rotisserie chicken kept the dip quick to assemble. Cream cheese provided a smooth base for the dip, and microwaving it with hot sauce loosened it so that stirring in chunky ingredients (chicken and blue cheese) was a snap. A cup of ranch dressing, a couple of teaspoons of Worcestershire sauce, and a sprinkling of cheddar cheese and scallions heightened the dip's zesty tang. If you have only a 2-quart baking dish, extend the baking time to 45 minutes. We used Frank's RedHot Original Cayenne Pepper Sauce, but other hot sauces can be used.

- 1 pound cream cheese
- ¾ cup hot sauce
- 1 (2½-pound) rotisserie chicken, skin and bones discarded; meat shredded into bite-size pieces (3 cups)
- 1 cup ranch dressing
- 4 ounces blue cheese, crumbled (1 cup)
- 2 teaspoons Worcestershire sauce
- 4 ounces sharp cheddar cheese, shredded (1 cup)
- 2 scallions, sliced thin
  Tortilla chips
  Carrot sticks
  Celery sticks

1. Adjust oven rack to middle position and heat oven to 350 degrees. Combine cream cheese and hot sauce in medium bowl and microwave until cream cheese is very soft, about 2 minutes, whisking halfway through microwaving. Whisk until smooth and no lumps of cream cheese remain. Stir in chicken, dressing, blue cheese, and Worcestershire until combined (visible bits of blue cheese are OK).

2. Transfer dip to shallow 3-quart baking dish and bake for 10 minutes. Remove dish from oven, stir dip, and sprinkle dip with cheddar. Return dish to oven and continue to bake until cheddar is melted and dip is bubbling around edges, about 10 minutes. Sprinkle with scallions. Serve with chips, carrots, and celery.

Buffalo Turkey Dip
Substitute shredded cooked turkey for chicken.

Slow-Cooker Beer and Cheddar Fondue

Serves 8 to 10 VEGETARIAN
Cooking Time 1 to 2 hours on Low

WHY THIS RECIPE WORKS Cheese fondue is a party in a pot. And this slow-cooker version is also fuss-free: no need for a chafing dish, no incessant stirring or fear of it breaking. For our cheese, sharp cheddar tasted great but turned grainy. We switched to mild cheddar and highly meltable American cheese for creaminess, but our fondue still turned grainy. To stabilize it, we added cornstarch and cream cheese, giving us a fondue that stayed creamy without constant stirring. For characteristic malty flavor, we added mild lager—we preferred its less bitter flavor over other styles of beer. This fondue tastes best with block cheese you shred yourself; you can find block American cheese at the deli counter. Preshredded cheese will work, but the fondue will be much thicker. For dipping we like to use bread, apple slices, steamed broccoli and cauliflower florets, and cured meats. Be sure to have long skewers on hand for easy dipping. You will need a 1½- to 7-quart slow cooker for this recipe.

- 1 cup mild lager, such as Budweiser
- 4 ounces cream cheese
- 1 tablespoon cornstarch
- 1 garlic clove, minced
- 1 teaspoon dry mustard
- ¼ teaspoon pepper
- 8 ounces mild cheddar cheese, shredded (2 cups)
- 8 ounces American cheese, shredded (2 cups)

1. Microwave beer, cream cheese, cornstarch, garlic, mustard, and pepper in large bowl, whisking occasionally, until smooth and thickened, about 5 minutes. Stir in cheddar and American cheeses until combined.

2A. FOR 1½- TO 5-QUART SLOW COOKER Transfer mixture to slow cooker, cover, and cook until cheese is melted, 1 to 2 hours on low.

2B. FOR 5½- TO 7-QUART SLOW COOKER Transfer mixture to 1½-quart soufflé dish. Set dish in slow cooker and pour water into slow cooker until it reaches about one-third up sides of dish (about 2 cups water). Cover and cook until cheese is melted, 1 to 2 hours on low. Remove dish from slow cooker, if desired.

3. Whisk fondue until smooth. Serve. (Fondue can be held on warm or low setting for up to 2 hours. Adjust consistency with hot water as needed, adding 2 tablespoons at a time.)

THE COLOR OF CHEDDAR

If you live in the Midwest, your cheddar is probably orange. If you live in the Northeast, your cheddar is definitely white. Our test cooks, too, have strong opinions about which color cheese tastes better. To settle the matter, we blindfolded 10 cooks and editors and had them taste two national brands of sharp white and orange (sometimes labeled yellow) cheddar, plain and in macaroni and cheese. Only one taster was able to distinguish flavor differences between the two colors of cheddar (and was that just blind luck?). Orange cheddars are colored with ground annatto seeds. These seeds, called achiote in Latin cooking, are used to color butter and margarine, too. Don't let regionalism color your perception: Color has no flavor.

Buffalo Chicken Dip

Cheddar Cheese Log with Everything Bagel Blend

Serves 8 to 10 | **Total Time** 25 minutes, plus 2½ to 3 hours chilling and resting MAKE AHEAD VEGETARIAN

WHY THIS RECIPE WORKS This cheddar cheese log has a creamy, spreadable center—no shattered crackers here! We used a spiced coating to offer visual and textural appeal and cut through some of the richness, and for our goat cheese and blue cheese variations we added a sweet or savory drizzle for a complementary touch. Combining cream cheese with our primary cheese yielded a smooth, spreadable log. Serve with baguette slices or mild crackers.

- 6 ounces extra-sharp yellow cheddar cheese, shredded (1½ cups)
- 6 ounces cream cheese
- ¼ cup mayonnaise
- 1 tablespoon drained prepared horseradish
- 2 teaspoons Worcestershire sauce
- 1 small garlic clove, minced
- ½ teaspoon pepper
- ⅓ cup Everything Bagel Blend (page 234)

1. Process cheddar cheese, cream cheese, mayonnaise, horseradish, Worcestershire, garlic, and pepper in food processor until smooth, scraping down sides of bowl as needed, about 1 minute.

Slow-Cooker Beer and Cheddar Fondue

2. Lay 18 by 11-inch sheet of plastic wrap on counter with long side parallel to counter edge. Transfer cheese mixture to center of plastic and shape into approximate 9-inch log with long side parallel to counter edge. Fold plastic over log and roll up. Pinch plastic at ends of log and roll on counter to form tight cylinder. Tuck ends of plastic underneath and freeze until completely firm, 1½ to 2 hours.

3. Unwrap cheese log and let stand until outside is slightly tacky to touch, about 10 minutes. Spread everything bagel blend into even layer on large plate and roll cheese log in everything bagel blend to coat evenly, pressing gently to adhere. (Garnished cheese log can be tightly wrapped in plastic and refrigerated for up to 2 days.) Transfer to serving platter and let stand at room temperature until softened, about 1 hour. Serve.

Goat Cheese Log with Hazelnut-Nigella Dukkah

Substitute 1½ cups goat cheese for cheddar cheese and ⅓ cup Hazelnut-Nigella Dukkah (page 100) for Everything Bagel Blend. Drizzle with 2 tablespoons extra-virgin olive oil before serving.

Blue Cheese Log with Pistachio Dukkah and Honey

Omit mayonnaise, horseradish, and Worcestershire sauce. Substitute 1 cup soft, mild blue cheese for cheddar. Increase cream cheese to 8 ounces. Substitute Pistachio Dukkah (page 100) for Everything Bagel Blend. Drizzle with 2 tablespoons honey before serving.

Everything Bagel Blend

Makes about ½ cup | **Total Time** 10 minutes

A trendy newcomer in non-bagel contexts, this blend gives everything you sprinkle it on appealing crunch and the aroma of everyone's favorite bagel.

- 2 tablespoons sesame seeds, toasted
- 2 tablespoons poppy seeds
- 1 tablespoon caraway seeds, toasted
- 1 tablespoon kosher salt
- 1 tablespoon dried minced onion
- 1 tablespoon dried minced garlic

Combine all ingredients in bowl. (Blend can be stored in airtight container for up to 3 months.)

Blue Cheese Log with Pistachio Dukkah and Honey

Baked Brie en Croûte with Mango-Peach Chutney

Serves 6 to 8 ▐ MAKE AHEAD ▐ ▐ VEGETARIAN ▐
Total Time 1½ hours, plus 30 minutes cooling

WHY THIS RECIPE WORKS The combination of warm, creamy Brie encased in a flaky puff pastry crust with sweet fruit topping sets a rich, refined tone for any cold-weather fest. And while this cheese plate centerpiece is impressive, it could hardly be easier to prepare. Rather than turning to the standard preserves to top our baked Brie, we opted for a sophisticated Mango-Peach Chutney, which offered the sweetness of typical preserves but also provided complex acidity. Working with a firm wheel of cheese promised gooey cheese that still held its shape. Freezing the pastry-wrapped Brie for 20 minutes kept it from melting too much during baking. Adding the chutney after baking kept the flavor bright. Use a firm, fairly unripe Brie for this recipe. To thaw frozen puff pastry, let it stand either in the refrigerator for 24 hours or on the counter for 30 minutes to 1 hour. Serve with crackers or bread.

1 (9½ by 9-inch) sheet puff pastry, thawed
1 large egg, lightly beaten
1 (8-ounce) wheel firm Brie cheese
¼ cup Mango-Peach Chutney

1. Line rimmed baking sheet with parchment paper. Roll puff pastry into 12-inch square on lightly floured counter. Using pie plate or other round guide, trim pastry to 9-inch circle with paring knife. Brush edges lightly with beaten egg. Place Brie in center of pastry and lift pastry up over cheese, pleating it at even intervals and leaving opening in center where Brie is exposed, leaving small circle of Brie exposed on top. Press pleated edge of pastry up into rim. Brush pastry with egg and transfer to prepared baking sheet. (Wrapped Brie can be refrigerated for up to 24 hours or frozen for up to 1 month.)

2. Freeze Brie for 20 minutes. Adjust oven rack to middle position and heat oven to 425 degrees. Bake wrapped cheese until pastry is deep golden brown, 20 to 25 minutes.

3. Transfer to wire rack. Spoon chutney into exposed center of Brie and let cool for about 30 minutes. Serve.

Mango-Peach Chutney

Makes about 2 cups
Total Time 30 minutes, plus 2 hours cooling

1 tablespoon vegetable oil
2 ripe but firm mangos, peeled, pitted, and chopped (3 cups)
1 shallot, minced
1 tablespoon grated fresh ginger
⅓ cup white wine vinegar
½ cup peach preserves
¼ cup minced fresh cilantro

Heat oil in 12-inch nonstick skillet over medium-high heat until shimmering. Cook mangos until lightly browned, about 5 minutes. Stir in shallot and ginger and cook until fragrant, about 1 minute. Stir in vinegar and peach preserves, bring to simmer, and cook until thickened and measures about 2 cups, about 5 minutes. Transfer to bowl and let cool to room temperature, about 2 hours. Stir in cilantro. (Chutney can be refrigerated for up to 1 week; bring to room temperature before serving.)

Baked Brie en Croûte with Mango-Peach Chutney

WRAPPING BRIE IN PUFF PASTRY

1. Lift pastry up over cheese, pleating it at even intervals and leaving opening in center where Brie is exposed.

2. Press pleated edge of pastry up into rim, which will later be filled with chutney.

Chicken Liver Pâté

Serves 8 to 10 | **Total Time** 30 minutes, plus 6½ hours chilling and resting | **MAKE AHEAD**

WHY THIS RECIPE WORKS A great chicken liver pâté has a smooth, mellow flavor and a velvety texture that seems to melt on the tongue, but bad renditions are all too common. Our recipe circumvents all the potential pitfalls and results in a pâté that is buttery, rich, and very easy to make. Searing the livers to develop their flavor and then gently poaching them in vermouth ensured a moist pâté. A bit of brandy unified the flavors. It is important to cook the livers until just rosy in the center in order to avoid the telltale chalky flavor that results from overcooking. Pressing plastic wrap flush against the surface of the pâté minimizes any discoloration due to oxidation. Because livers are highly perishable (as are all organ meats), this pâté is best when eaten soon after it is made. Serve with Crostini, slices of baguette, or crackers.

- 8 tablespoons unsalted butter
- 3 large shallots, sliced
- 1 tablespoon minced fresh thyme
- ¼ teaspoon table salt
- 1 pound chicken livers, rinsed, patted dry, and trimmed
- ¾ cup dry vermouth
- 2 teaspoons brandy

1. Melt butter in 12-inch skillet over medium-high heat. Add shallots, thyme, and salt and cook until shallots are lightly browned, about 5 minutes. Add chicken livers and cook, stirring constantly, about 1 minute. Add vermouth and simmer until livers are cooked but still have rosy interiors, 4 to 6 minutes.

2. Using slotted spoon, transfer livers to food processor, leaving liquid in skillet. Continue to simmer liquid over medium-high heat until slightly syrupy, about 2 minutes, then add to processor.

3. Add brandy to processor and process mixture until very smooth, about 2 minutes, stopping to scrape down sides of bowl as needed. Season with salt and pepper to taste, then transfer to bowl and smooth top. Press plastic wrap flush against surface of pâté and refrigerate until firm, at least 6 hours or up to 2 days. Let soften at room temperature for 30 minutes before serving. (Pâté can be wrapped tightly in plastic wrap and refrigerated for up to 2 days.)

Chicken Liver Pâté

Crostini

Makes 25 to 30 toasts | **Total Time** 35 minutes

Crostini taste best straight from the oven.

- 1 large (12- to 15-inch) baguette, sliced ½ inch thick on bias
- 1 garlic clove, peeled and sliced in half
- 2 tablespoons extra-virgin olive oil

Adjust oven rack to middle position and heat oven to 400 degrees. Arrange bread in single layer on baking sheet. Bake bread until dry and crisp, about 10 minutes, flipping slices over halfway through baking. Rub garlic clove over 1 side of each piece of toasted bread, then brush with oil. Season with salt and pepper to taste, and serve.

Cheese Straws

Serves 6 (**Makes** 13 straws) `MAKE AHEAD` `VEGETARIAN`
Total Time 45 minutes

WHY THIS RECIPE WORKS Crisp, salty cheese straws are quick to disappear from a party platter. We kept things simple by using store-bought frozen puff pastry, which bakes up buttery and flaky. To incorporate as much bold cheese flavor as possible, we grated nutty Parmesan, sprinkled a substantial layer over our thawed puff pastry, and then used a rolling pin to firmly press the cheese into the pastry. Incorporating a bit of parsley into the cheese filling added some visual interest to our straws, as did twisting them into corkscrew shapes before baking. To thaw frozen puff pastry, let it stand either in the refrigerator for 24 hours or on the counter for 30 minutes to 1 hour.

 1 (9 by 9½-inch) sheet frozen puff pastry, thawed
 2 ounces Parmesan or aged Asiago cheese, grated (1 cup)
 1 tablespoon minced fresh parsley
 ¼ teaspoon table salt
 ⅛ teaspoon pepper

1. Adjust oven racks to upper-middle and lower-middle positions; heat oven to 425 degrees. Line rimmed baking sheet with parchment paper. Lay puff pastry on second sheet of parchment and sprinkle with Parmesan, parsley, salt, and pepper. Top with third sheet of parchment. Using rolling pin, press cheese mixture into pastry, then roll pastry into 10-inch square.

2. Remove top sheet of parchment and cut pastry into thirteen ¾-inch-wide strips with sharp knife or pizza wheel. Gently twist each strip of pastry and space about ½ inch apart on prepared baking sheet. (Cheese straws can be made through step 2, thoroughly chilled, gently wrapped in aluminum foil, and frozen for up to 1 month. Do not thaw before baking. It may be necessary to add a few minutes to the baking time.)

3. Bake on top rack until straws are fully puffed and golden brown, about 10 minutes, switching baking sheet to bottom rack halfway through baking. Let cheese straws cool completely on baking sheet. (Cheese straws can be wrapped in plastic wrap and stored at room temperature for up to 24 hours before serving.)

Everything Straws

Omit Parmesan, parsley, salt, and pepper. Sprinkle dough with 2½ teaspoons Everything Bagel Blend (page 234) in step 1.

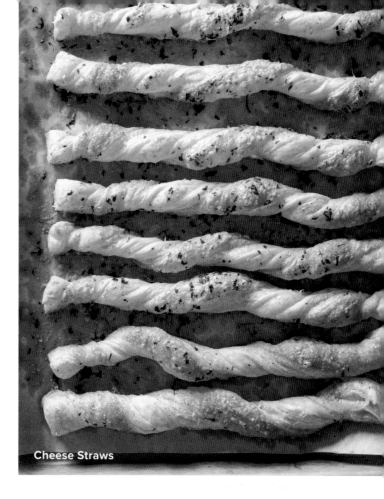

Cheese Straws

Horseradish and Grainy Mustard Straws

Omit Parmesan, parsley, salt, and pepper. Combine 2 tablespoons prepared horseradish, well drained, and 2 tablespoons whole-grain mustard in small bowl. Substitute horseradish mixture for Parmesan mixture.

Olive, Feta, and Oregano Cheese Straws

Omit Parmesan, parsley, salt, and pepper. Combine ½ cup kalamata olives, pitted and chopped fine; ¼ cup crumbled feta; and 1 tablespoon minced fresh oregano in small bowl. Substitute olive mixture for Parmesan mixture.

Fines Herbes Straws

Omit Parmesan, parsley, salt, and pepper. Combine 1 tablespoon minced fresh parsley, 1 tablespoon minced fresh chervil, 1 tablespoon minced fresh tarragon, 1 tablespoon minced fresh chives, ¼ teaspoon table salt, and ⅛ teaspoon pepper in small bowl. Substitute herb mixture for Parmesan mixture.

Slow-Cooker Party Mix

Herbed Deviled Eggs

Slow-Cooker Party Mix

Serves 10 to 12 **MAKE AHEAD**
Cooking Time 3 to 4 hours on High

WHY THIS RECIPE WORKS Crunchy, salty, and irresistible, homemade party snack mix is guaranteed to disappear quickly at any gathering. But after making a back-of-the-box party mix recipe, we felt there was room for improvement. We decided to sidestep the conventional oven method in favor of using the slow cooker to create a perfectly toasted party mix every time. We started with the classic combination of Corn, Rice, and Wheat Chex cereals, to which we added pita chips, mini pretzels, and dry-roasted peanuts. Tasters preferred the nutty sweetness of melted butter to the flavors of margarine or olive oil, each of which left a greasy finish. Worcestershire sauce was integral to getting that trademark party mix flavor, so we decided to add a generous amount to ensure that its flavor didn't become muted in the slow cooker. We also doubled the usual amount of garlic powder and added a little cayenne pepper for subtle heat. To help release excess moisture and ensure that our mix wouldn't get soggy, we removed the lid every hour to stir, which also redistributed the mix so it wouldn't burn. To finish, we spread the mix out on a rimmed baking sheet to dry and crisp. You can use any combination of cereal here; just be sure to have 9 cups of cereal in total. You will need a 4 to 7 quart oval slow cooker for this recipe.

9 cups (10 ounces) Corn, Rice, and/or
Wheat Chex cereal
2 ounces pita chips, broken into
1-inch pieces (1 cup)
1 cup (1½ ounces) mini pretzels
1 cup (5 ounces) dry-roasted peanuts
8 tablespoons unsalted butter, melted
¼ cup Worcestershire sauce
1½ teaspoons garlic powder
¼ teaspoon cayenne pepper

1. Combine cereal, pita chips, mini pretzels, and peanuts in slow cooker. Whisk melted butter, Worcestershire, garlic powder, and cayenne together in bowl. Drizzle butter mixture over cereal mixture and gently toss until evenly coated. Cover and cook, stirring every hour, until cereal mixture is toasted and fragrant, 3 to 4 hours on high.

2. Transfer cereal mixture to rimmed baking sheet and spread into even layer. Let cool completely, about 20 minutes. Serve. (Party mix can be stored at room temperature for up to 1 week.)

Spiced Nuts

Serves 8 `MAKE AHEAD` `VEGETARIAN`
Total Time 1¼ hours, plus 30 minutes cooling

WHY THIS RECIPE WORKS Unassuming spiced nuts pack a double punch of flavor and protein. Most recipes are made with a sugared syrup that causes the nuts to clump and leaves your hands a sticky mess. Tossing the nuts in a mixture of egg white, water, and salt gave them a nice crunch when baked and helped the spices adhere. If you can't find superfine sugar, process granulated sugar in a food processor for 1 minute.

- 1 large egg white
- 1 tablespoon water
- 1 teaspoon table salt
- 1 pound pecans, raw cashews, walnuts, or whole unblanched almonds, or a combination
- ⅔ cup superfine sugar
- 2 teaspoons cumin
- 1 teaspoon cayenne pepper
- 1 teaspoon paprika

1. Adjust oven racks to upper-middle and lower-middle positions and heat oven to 275 degrees. Line 2 rimmed baking sheets with parchment paper. Whisk egg white, water, and salt together in medium bowl. Add nuts and toss to coat. Let nuts drain in colander for 5 minutes.

2. Mix sugar, cumin, cayenne, and paprika together in clean medium bowl. Add nuts and toss to coat. Spread nuts evenly over prepared baking sheets. Bake until nuts are dry and crisp, about 50 minutes, stirring occasionally. Let nuts cool completely on baking sheets, about 30 minutes. Break nuts apart and serve. (Spiced nuts can be stored in airtight container for up to 1 week.)

Herbed Deviled Eggs

Serves 18 (**Makes** 36 filled egg halves)
Total Time 45 minutes `MAKE AHEAD` `VEGETARIAN`

WHY THIS RECIPE WORKS The best deviled eggs start with the best hard-cooked eggs, and this method helps you prepare eggs for a crowd with nary a green ring among them. For perfect hard-cooked eggs with just-cooked, still-yellow yolks, we brought a dozen and a half eggs and water to a boil and then immediately removed the pot from the heat. The residual heat of the water cooked the eggs in exactly 10 minutes. Pressing the yolks through a fine-mesh strainer guaranteed an extra-creamy filling. We mixed the yolks with mayonnaise as well as sour cream for flavor and silkiness, plus white wine vinegar and Dijon mustard for tang and a small amount of sugar for balance. To give this classic party dish a fresh twist, we added chopped tarragon, parsley, and chives to the filling. We find it easiest to pipe the filling into the eggs, but you can use a spoon to fill them if desired. Be sure to use a large pot and plenty of water for cooking the eggs in step 1, or they will not cook correctly.

- 18 large eggs
- ⅓ cup mayonnaise
- ¼ cup sour cream
- 2 tablespoons minced fresh tarragon
- 2 tablespoons minced fresh parsley
- 2 tablespoons minced fresh chives
- 1½ teaspoons white wine vinegar
- 1½ teaspoons Dijon mustard
- ¾ teaspoon sugar
- ½ teaspoon table salt
- ¼ teaspoon pepper

1. Place eggs in large pot, cover with 1 inch water, and bring to boil over high heat. Remove pot from heat, cover, and let stand for 10 minutes. Fill large bowl halfway with ice and water. Pour off water from pot, then gently shake pot back and forth to lightly crack shells. Transfer eggs to ice bath; let cool for 5 minutes, then peel. (Peeled eggs can be refrigerated for up to 2 days.)

2. Halve eggs lengthwise. Transfer yolks to fine-mesh strainer set over medium bowl and arrange whites on large serving platter. Using spatula, press yolks through strainer into bowl, then stir in mayonnaise, sour cream, tarragon, parsley, chives, vinegar, mustard, sugar, salt, and pepper until smooth. Transfer yolk mixture to pastry bag fitted with star tip (or zipper-lock bag with corner snipped off) and pipe mixture into whites. Serve. (Filled deviled eggs can be refrigerated in an airtight container for up to 24 hours; garnish just before serving.)

NOTES FROM THE TEST KITCHEN

FILLING DEVILED EGGS
A piping bag makes quick work of filling deviled eggs. But if you don't have one, simply substitute a zipper-lock bag. Spoon the filling into the bag and push it down into one corner. Use scissors to snip off the corner of the bag, then squeeze the filling into each egg.

Easy Charcuterie Board

Building the Perfect Board
A charcuterie board takes the concept of a classic cheese board to the next level by putting delectable cured meats front and center. Hugely versatile, a charcuterie board is ideal for entertaining, allowing your guests to choose their own culinary adventure and feast their eyes as well as their palates. But with so many options to choose from when it comes to the meats and supporting elements alike, the idea of putting one together can be overwhelming. Following these simple pointers will keep you feeling confident and stress-free the next time it's your turn to host a crowd.

Choose your meats
Start by choosing three to five meats for your board. As a rule of thumb, try to include at least one sliced cured meat, such as prosciutto, and one more-substantial offering your guests can slice themselves, such as smoked sausage or a hard salami. A spreadable element like our buttery-smooth Chicken Liver Pâté (page 236) is another excellent option. And remember, there's a whole world of meats to explore beyond just those listed here, so have fun with it!

Curate your accompaniments
Visual and textural variety is key to a stunning, palate-pleasing plate. Cheeses, crackers, bread, pickles, olives, fresh and/or dried fruit, condiments, and nuts are all common supporting players, but there's no need to rush to the store to buy one of everything. We think there are four boxes your charcuterie board extras should check: crunch, creaminess, tang, and a pop of color. One type of cracker, a cheese, a pickled vegetable, and a jewel-toned fruit are all it takes to tick them all. Of course, if you're feeling ambitious you can get as creative—and as abundant—with your accompaniments as you like.

Add something homemade
If you're looking to wow your guests with a personal touch, we suggest adding one or two easy apps that you made yourself. Any of the superquick appetizers on the following page would fit the bill nicely. Our Boursin–Cheddar Cheese Spread and Baked Goat Cheese with Olive Oil and Herbs both make bold statements and require just a few minutes of hands-on work.

Cheddar and Chutney Canapés with Walnut Bread

Serves 8 | **Total Time** 10 minutes

- 1 loaf artisanal-style walnut bread or similar fruit or nut bread
- 8 ounces farmhouse cheddar
- ½ cup apple chutney or apple butter

Cut bread into canapé-size pieces (about 3 inches). Slice cheddar into similar-size pieces. Spread apple chutney over one side of bread, top with cheddar, and serve.

Easy Melted Brie with Honey and Herbs

Serves 8 | **Total Time** 10 minutes

- 1 (8-ounce) wheel firm Brie cheese
- 2 tablespoons honey
- ½ teaspoon chopped fresh thyme or rosemary
  Crackers or thinly sliced baguette.

1. Using serrated knife, carefully slice rind off top of Brie; leave rind on sides and bottom. Place Brie, cut side up, on microwave-safe platter.

2. Drizzle honey over top. Sprinkle thyme over honey. Microwave until cheese is warm and just begins to bubble, 1 to 2 minutes. Serve immediately with crackers or thinly sliced baguette.

Boursin–Cheddar Cheese Spread

Serves 8 | **Total Time** 10 minutes

- 1 (5.2-ounce) package Boursin Garlic and Fine Herbs cheese
- 4 ounces extra-sharp cheddar cheese, shredded (1 cup)
- 2 tablespoons mayonnaise
- 1½ teaspoons Worcestershire sauce
  Pinch cayenne pepper
- 2 tablespoons minced chives
  Crackers or thinly sliced baguette

Process Boursin, cheddar, mayonnaise, Worcestershire, and cayenne in food processor until smooth, scraping down sides as needed, about 1 minute. Transfer cheese mixture to serving bowl, sprinkle with chives, and serve with crackers or thinly sliced baguette.

Sun-Dried Tomato Tapenade with Farmer's Cheese

Serves 8 | **Total Time** 15 minutes

- 1 cup oil-packed sun-dried tomatoes, rinsedand patted dry
- ¼ cup extra-virgin olive oil
- 1 cup pitted kalamata olives
- ¼ cup coarsely chopped fresh parsley
- 1 tablespoon capers, rinsed
- 8 ounces farmer's cheese or goat cheese
  Crackers or thinly sliced baguette

Pulse tomatoes with oil in food processor until finely chopped, about 25 pulses; transfer to small serving bowl. Pulse olives, parsley, and capers in food processor until finely chopped, about 10 pulses; stir into chopped tomatoes. Season with salt and pepper to taste, and serve with farmer's cheese and crackers or thinly sliced baguette.

Baked Goat Cheese with Olive Oil and Herbs

Serves 8 | **Total Time** 25 minutes

- 12 ounces goat cheese, chilled
- ⅓ cup extra-virgin olive oil
- 2 teaspoons honey
- ½ teaspoon grated orange or lemon zest
- ½ teaspoon dried herbes de Provence
- ¼ teaspoon table salt
- ⅛ teaspoon pepper
- ⅛ teaspoon red pepper flakes
  Crackers or thinly sliced baguette

Heat oven to 400 degrees. Using dental floss, slice goat cheese into ⅓-inch-thick rounds. Shingle cheese into small casserole dish or shallow ovensafe bowl. Combine oil, honey, orange zest, herbes de Provence, salt, pepper, and pepper flakes in small bowl, then pour mixture over cheese. Bake cheese until oil is bubbling and cheese begins to brown around edges, 10 to 15 minutes. Serve warm with crackers or thinly sliced baguette.

Stuffed Mushrooms

Serves 4 to 6 (**Makes** 24 mushrooms)
Total Time 1 hour `MAKE AHEAD` `VEGETARIAN`

WHY THIS RECIPE WORKS Forget about leathery, dried-out stuffed mushrooms with bland, watery filling; these are meaty bites full of great savory flavor. To get rid of excess moisture before stuffing, we roasted the mushrooms gill side up until their juice was released and they were browned; we then flipped them gill side down to let the liquid evaporate. To create the filling, we chopped the mushroom stems in the food processor and sautéed them with garlic and wine. Parmesan cheese bound the filling together.

24 large white mushrooms (1¾ to 2 inches in diameter), stems removed and reserved
¼ cup extra-virgin olive oil, divided
¼ teaspoon table salt
¼ teaspoon pepper, divided
1 small shallot, minced
2 garlic cloves, minced
¼ cup dry white wine
1 ounce Parmesan cheese, grated (½ cup)
1 teaspoon minced fresh thyme
1 teaspoon lemon juice
1 teaspoon minced fresh parsley

1. Adjust oven rack to middle position and heat oven to 425 degrees. Line rimmed baking sheet with aluminum foil. Toss mushroom caps with 2 tablespoons oil, salt, and ⅛ teaspoon pepper in large bowl. Arrange caps gill side up on prepared sheet and roast until juice is released, about 20 minutes. Flip caps and roast until well browned, about 10 minutes; set aside.

2. Meanwhile, pulse shallot, garlic, reserved stems, and remaining ⅛ teaspoon pepper in food processor until finely chopped, 10 to 14 pulses. Heat remaining 2 tablespoons oil in 8-inch nonstick skillet over medium heat until shimmering. Add stem mixture to skillet and cook until golden brown and moisture has evaporated, about 5 minutes. Add wine and cook until nearly evaporated and mixture thickens slightly, about 1 minute. Transfer to bowl and let cool slightly, about 5 minutes. Stir in Parmesan, thyme, and lemon juice. Season with salt and pepper to taste. Flip caps gill side up. Divide stuffing evenly among caps. (Stuffed caps can be refrigerated for 24 hours before baking. Increase baking time to 10 to 15 minutes.)

3. Return caps to oven and bake until stuffing is heated through, 5 to 7 minutes. Sprinkle with parsley and serve.

Shrimp Cocktail with Horseradish Cocktail Sauce

Serves 6 `MAKE AHEAD`
Total Time 1 hour, plus 1 hour chilling

WHY THIS RECIPE WORKS Our take on this party staple boasts tender, sweet shrimp and a lively, horseradish-forward cocktail sauce. We poached the shrimp gently in water flavored with Old Bay seasoning for depth. To avoid overcooking, we brought the water and aromatics to a boil, took the pot off the heat, and then added the shrimp, leaving them to poach for 7 minutes. This method delivered perfectly tender, not rubbery, shrimp every time. We used Frank's RedHot Original Cayenne Pepper Sauce, but other hot sauces can be used.

SHRIMP
2 teaspoons lemon juice
2 bay leaves
1 teaspoon table salt
1 teaspoon black peppercorns
1 teaspoon Old Bay seasoning
1 pound extra-large shrimp (21 to 25 per pound), peeled and deveined

HORSERADISH COCKTAIL SAUCE
1 cup ketchup
2 tablespoons lemon juice
2 tablespoons prepared horseradish, plus extra for seasoning
2 teaspoons hot sauce, plus extra for seasoning
⅛ teaspoon table salt
⅛ teaspoon pepper

1. FOR THE SHRIMP Bring lemon juice, bay leaves, salt, peppercorns, Old Bay, and 1 quart water to boil in medium saucepan for 2 minutes. Remove pan from heat and add shrimp. Cover and steep off heat until shrimp are firm and pink, about 7 minutes.

2. Meanwhile, fill large bowl halfway with ice and water. Drain shrimp, plunge immediately into ice bath to stop cooking, and let stand until cool, about 2 minutes. Drain shrimp and transfer to bowl. Cover and refrigerate until thoroughly chilled, at least 1 hour. (Cooked shrimp can be refrigerated for up to 24 hours)

3. FOR THE COCKTAIL SAUCE Stir all ingredients together in small bowl and season with additional horseradish and hot sauce as desired. (Cocktail sauce can be refrigerated for up to 24 hours.) Arrange shrimp and sauce on serving platter and serve.

Garlicky Roasted Shrimp with Parsley and Anise

Serves 4 to 6 | **Total Time** 45 minutes

WHY THIS RECIPE WORKS Poaching isn't the only way to cook shrimp for a finger-food platter. Roasting deepens and concentrates the shellfish's sweet flavor. Aiming for the ideal balance of profound flavor and perfect doneness, we guarded against overcooking by brining hefty jumbo shrimp, which also seasoned them thoroughly. Butterflying the shrimp offered an easy route to flavor-infused flesh, and although we sliced through the shells, we didn't remove them, as they enhanced flavor while insulating the meat against the oven's heat. After tossing the shrimp in melted butter and olive oil boosted with garlic, spices, and herbs, we elevated them on a wire rack set in a rimmed baking sheet and slid them under the broiler until tender and deeply fragrant. Don't use smaller shrimp here; they will be overseasoned and prone to overcooking.

- ¼ cup table salt for brining
- 2 pounds shell-on jumbo shrimp (16 to 20 per pound)
- 4 tablespoons unsalted butter, melted
- ¼ cup extra-virgin olive oil
- 6 garlic cloves, minced
- 1 teaspoon anise seeds
- ½ teaspoon red pepper flakes
- ¼ teaspoon pepper
- 2 tablespoons minced fresh parsley
  Lemon wedges

1. Dissolve salt in 1 quart cold water in large container. Using kitchen shears or sharp paring knife, cut through shell of each shrimp and devein but do not remove shell. Using paring knife, continue to cut shrimp ½ inch deep, taking care not to cut in half completely. Submerge shrimp in brine, cover, and refrigerate for 15 minutes.

2. Adjust oven rack 4 inches from broiler element and heat broiler. Combine melted butter, oil, garlic, anise seeds, pepper flakes, and pepper in large bowl. Remove shrimp from brine and pat dry with paper towels. Add shrimp and parsley to butter mixture; toss well, making sure butter mixture gets into interior of shrimp. Arrange shrimp in single layer on wire rack set in rimmed baking sheet.

3. Broil shrimp until opaque and shells are beginning to brown, 2 to 4 minutes, rotating sheet halfway through broiling. Flip shrimp and continue to broil until second side is opaque and shells are beginning to brown, 2 to 4 minutes longer, rotating sheet halfway through broiling. Transfer shrimp to serving dish and serve with lemon wedges.

Stuffed Mushrooms

Garlicky Roasted Shrimp with Parsley and Anise

**Broiled Bacon-Wrapped
Sea Scallops**

Broiled Bacon-Wrapped Sea Scallops

Serves 6 to 8 | **Total Time** 30 minutes

WHY THIS RECIPE WORKS Bacon-wrapped anything is always a party hit, but bacon's smoky flavor pairs especially well with sweet, succulent scallops. The challenges are making sure that the bacon crisps, and that the balance between bacon and scallop is right. It was easy to wrap pliable bacon straight from the package around the scallops, but the scallops finished cooking before the bacon had time to brown and crisp. To even out the timing, we parcooked the bacon in the microwave (which had the added benefit of rendering some of the bacon fat to get rid of grease) and finished cooking the bacon-wrapped scallops in the broiler. When buying scallops, be sure to buy large sea scallops rather than the small bay scallops. Also make sure to remove and discard the side muscle attached to each scallop before using.

- 4 slices bacon
- 24 large sea scallops, tendons removed
- ¼ teaspoon table salt
- ⅛ teaspoon pepper
  Pinch cayenne pepper
- 2 tablespoons minced fresh chives

1. Adjust oven rack 6 inches from broiler element and heat broiler. Set wire rack in rimmed baking sheet.

2. Slice each piece of bacon lengthwise into 2 long, thin strips, then cut each strip into 3 short pieces (total of 24 bacon pieces). Spread bacon pieces out over 4 layers of paper towels on plate, then cover with 2 more layers of paper towels. Microwave until bacon fat begins to render but bacon is still pliable, 1 to 2 minutes.

3. Meanwhile, place scallops in bowl. Sprinkle salt, pepper, and cayenne over scallops and toss to coat.

4. Wrap 1 piece of microwaved bacon around center of each scallop and place, seam side down, on prepared wire rack. Broil until sides of scallops are firm and edges of bacon are brown, rotating sheet halfway through cooking, 3 to 4 minutes. Skewer scallops with toothpicks, transfer to serving platter, and sprinkle with chives. Serve immediately.

Broiled Bacon-Wrapped Shrimp
Substitute 1 pound extra-large shrimp (21 to 25 per pound), peeled and deveined, for scallops.

**Fried Brussels Sprouts with
Lemon-Chive Dipping Sauce**

Fried Brussels Sprouts with Lemon-Chive Dipping Sauce

Serves 6 to 8 **MAKE AHEAD**
Total Time 40 minutes

WHY THIS RECIPE WORKS Fried brussels sprouts at restaurants can be delightfully crispy, nutty, and salty. Yet when we tried making them at home, the brussels sprouts splattered every time they hit the hot oil. Instead, we tried submerging the sprouts in cold oil and heating the oil and the sprouts together over high heat. As long as we cooked the brussels sprouts until they were deep brown, this method produced beautifully crisped sprouts. An easy stir-together lemon-chive sauce offered a vibrant creamy counterpoint, perfect for dipping. Stir gently and not too often in step 2; excessive stirring will cause the leaves to separate from the sprouts.

DIPPING SAUCE

- ½ cup mayonnaise
- 2 tablespoons minced fresh chives
- 1 teaspoon grated lemon zest plus 1 tablespoon juice
- 1 teaspoon Worcestershire sauce
- 1 teaspoon Dijon mustard
- ¼ teaspoon garlic powder

BRUSSELS SPROUTS

- 2 pounds brussels sprouts, trimmed and halved
- 1 quart peanut or vegetable oil
  Kosher salt

1. FOR THE DIPPING SAUCE Whisk all ingredients together in bowl. Cover and refrigerate until ready to serve. (Sauce can be refrigerated for up to 3 days.)

2. FOR THE BRUSSELS SPROUTS Line rimmed baking sheet with triple layer of paper towels. Combine brussels sprouts and oil in Dutch oven. Cook over high heat, gently stirring occasionally, until dark brown throughout and crispy, 20 to 25 minutes.

3. Using wire strainer or slotted spoon, transfer brussels sprouts to prepared sheet. Roll gently so paper towels absorb excess oil. Season with salt to taste. Serve immediately with sauce.

Fried Brussels Sprouts with Sriracha Dipping Sauce

Whisk ½ cup mayonnaise, 1½ tablespoons sriracha, 2 teaspoons lime juice, and ¼ teaspoon garlic powder together in bowl. Substitute for lemon-chive dipping sauce.

Cauliflower Buffalo Bites

Serves 4 to 6 | **Total Time** 1 hour **VEGETARIAN**

WHY THIS RECIPE WORKS These crunchy, tangy, spicy cauliflower bites will be the new star of your game day table. A mixture of cornstarch and cornmeal gave us an ultracrispy exterior. But because cauliflower is not naturally moist (like chicken), the mixture didn't stick, so first we dunked the florets in canned coconut milk, which had just the right viscosity. We got decent results when we baked our bites, but we absolutely flipped over the crackly crust and tender interior we achieved through frying. An herby ranch dressing was a cooling foil to the kick of the bites. We used Frank's RedHot Original Cayenne Pepper Sauce, but other hot sauces can be used. Use a Dutch oven that holds 6 quarts or more for this recipe. When you open the can of coconut milk, you may notice that it's separated—there may be a more solid mass above the watery liquid. If so, be sure to mix it together before measuring.

BUFFALO SAUCE

- 4 tablespoons unsalted butter, cut into 4 pieces
- ½ cup hot sauce
- 1 tablespoon packed dark brown sugar
- 2 teaspoons cider vinegar

CAULIFLOWER

- 1–2 quarts peanut or vegetable oil
- ¾ cup cornstarch
- ¼ cup cornmeal
- ½ teaspoon table salt
- ¼ teaspoon pepper
- ⅔ cup canned coconut milk
- 1 tablespoon hot sauce
- 1 pound cauliflower florets, cut into 1½-inch pieces
- 1 recipe Ranch Dressing (page 246)

1. FOR THE BUFFALO SAUCE Melt butter in small saucepan over low heat. Whisk in hot sauce, brown sugar, and vinegar until combined. Remove from heat and cover to keep warm; set aside.

2. FOR THE CAULIFLOWER Line platter with triple layer of paper towels. Add oil to large Dutch oven until it measures about 1½ inches deep and heat over medium-high heat to 400 degrees. While oil heats, combine cornstarch, cornmeal, salt, and pepper in small bowl. Whisk coconut milk and hot sauce together in large bowl. Add cauliflower; toss to coat well. Sprinkle cornstarch mixture over cauliflower; fold with rubber spatula until thoroughly coated.

3. Fry half of cauliflower, adding 1 or 2 pieces to oil at a time, until golden and crispy, gently stirring as needed to prevent pieces from sticking together, about 3 minutes. Using slotted spoon, transfer fried cauliflower to prepared platter.

4. Return oil to 400 degrees and repeat with remaining cauliflower. Transfer ½ cup sauce to clean large bowl, add cauliflower, and gently toss to coat. Serve immediately with ranch dressing and remaining sauce.

Ranch Dressing

Makes ¾ cup | **Total Time** 10 minutes

½ cup mayonnaise
2 tablespoons plain yogurt
1 teaspoon white wine vinegar
1½ teaspoons minced fresh chives
1½ teaspoons minced fresh dill
¼ teaspoon garlic powder
⅛ teaspoon table salt
⅛ teaspoon pepper

Whisk all ingredients in bowl until smooth. Refrigerate until serving. (Dressing can be refrigerated for up to 4 days.)

Slow-Cooker Swedish Meatballs

Serves 10 to 12
Cooking Time 4 to 5 hours on Low

WHY THIS RECIPE WORKS Swedish meatballs have long been standard cocktail party fare, but rolling and browning dozens of little meatballs and then building a sauce leaves little time to get everything (including the host) ready before company arrives. Enter our recipe—prepared in the slow cooker. To avoid a greasy sauce, we put our meatballs in the oven for 15 minutes, allowing much of their fat to render away. Cooking our meatballs in the oven also allowed us to brown them before adding them to the slow cooker. For a sauce, we started with a base of flour-and-butter roux and beef broth, which cooked down to the perfect consistency to coat the meatballs. Soy sauce gave our sauce a meaty backbone without overpowering it. Lingonberry preserves are a traditional accompaniment for Swedish meatballs. If you can't find lingonberry preserves, cranberry preserves can be used. You will need a 4- to 7-quart slow cooker for this recipe.

6 tablespoons unsalted butter, divided
2 onions, chopped fine
4 slices caraway-rye bread, crusts removed, torn into 1-inch pieces
3½ cups beef broth, divided
1 cup sour cream, divided
2 large egg yolks
½ teaspoon ground allspice
½ teaspoon table salt
¼ teaspoon ground nutmeg
¼ teaspoon pepper
1 pound 90 percent lean ground beef
1 pound ground pork
½ cup all-purpose flour
2 tablespoons soy sauce
2 teaspoons minced fresh dill, plus extra for serving

1. Adjust oven rack to middle position and heat oven to 475 degrees. Set wire rack in aluminum foil–lined rimmed baking sheet and coat with vegetable oil spray. Melt 1 tablespoon butter in 12-inch skillet over medium heat. Add onions and cook until softened, about 8 minutes; transfer to large bowl. Add bread, ¼ cup broth, ¼ cup sour cream, egg yolks, allspice, salt, nutmeg, and pepper and mash with fork until smooth. Add ground beef and ground pork and knead with your hands until well combined.

2. Pinch off and roll meat mixture into tablespoon-size meatballs (about 60 meatballs) and arrange on prepared rack. Bake until lightly browned, about 15 minutes. Transfer meatballs to slow cooker.

3. Melt remaining 5 tablespoons butter in now-empty skillet over medium heat. Add flour and cook, whisking often, until beginning to brown, about 3 minutes. Slowly whisk in remaining 3¼ cups broth, smoothing out any lumps, and bring to simmer; transfer to slow cooker. Cover and cook until meatballs are tender and sauce is slightly thickened, 4 to 5 hours on low.

4. Using large spoon, skim excess fat from surface of sauce. Whisk ½ cup sauce, soy sauce, dill, and remaining ¾ cup sour cream together in bowl (to temper), then gently stir mixture back into slow cooker. Season with salt and pepper to taste. Sprinkle with extra dill and serve. (Meatballs can be held on warm or low setting for up to 2 hours. Adjust sauce consistency with hot water as needed, adding 2 tablespoons at a time.)

Baked Jalapeño Poppers

Makes 24 poppers MAKE AHEAD
Total Time 1¼ hours

WHY THIS RECIPE WORKS With all due respect to stuffed, breaded, and fried jalapeño poppers, we wanted an easier option to bring this bar snack to the home kitchen. But perfecting baked jalapeño poppers took a few tricks. First, roasting the halved chiles cut side down let us control the texture of the peppers and drove off excess moisture. For a flavorful filling that wasn't chalky, equal parts cream cheese, cheddar, and Monterey Jack were our cheeses of choice, while panko bread crumbs and an egg yolk helped it stay put. Finally, for a filling that stood up to the fiery jalapeños, we added scallions, cilantro, cumin, lime, and bacon. Use a small spoon to scrape the seeds and ribs from the halved chiles.

 6 slices bacon
12 jalapeño chiles, halved lengthwise with stems left intact, ribs and seeds removed
 4 ounces mild cheddar cheese, shredded (1 cup)
 4 ounces Monterey Jack cheese, shredded (1 cup)
 4 ounces cream cheese, softened
 3 tablespoons minced fresh cilantro
 2 scallions, sliced thin
 2 tablespoons panko bread crumbs
 1 large egg yolk
 2 teaspoons lime juice
 1 teaspoon ground cumin

1. Adjust oven rack to upper-middle position and heat oven to 500 degrees. Set wire rack in rimmed baking sheet. Cook bacon in 12-inch nonstick skillet over medium heat until crispy, 7 to 9 minutes. Transfer to paper towel–lined plate. When bacon is cool enough to handle, chop fine and set aside.

2. Season jalapeños with salt to taste and place cut side down on prepared wire rack. Bake until just beginning to soften, about 5 minutes. Remove sheet from oven and reduce oven temperature to 450 degrees. When cool enough to handle, flip jalapeños cut side up.

3. Mix cheddar, Monterey Jack, cream cheese, cilantro, scallions, panko, egg yolk, lime juice, cumin, and bacon in bowl until thoroughly combined. Divide cheese mixture among jalapeños, pressing into cavities. (Filled and unbaked jalapeños can be covered and refrigerated for up to 24 hours. If refrigerating, add 3 minutes to baking time.)

4. Bake until jalapeños are tender and filling is lightly browned, 9 to 11 minutes. Let cool for 5 minutes. Serve.

Slow-Cooker Swedish Meatballs

Baked Jalapeño Poppers

Korean Fried Chicken Wings

Serves 6 to 8 | **Total Time** 1½ hours `MAKE AHEAD`

WHY THIS RECIPE WORKS One bite of this exceptionally crunchy, sweet-spicy style of fried chicken and you'll be hooked. The biggest challenge is preventing the sauce from destroying the crispy coating; a traditional double-frying method ensures that these wings stay crispy even when tossed with sticky sauce. We tried different coatings for our chicken—plain cornstarch; a light batter of flour, cornstarch, and water; and a heavy batter of eggs, cornstarch, and water. We preferred the flour, cornstarch, and water batter, which yielded the lightest, most crackly crust. The Korean chile paste gochujang gave the sauce spicy, fermented notes, while sugar tempered the spice and ginger and garlic provided depth. You can tailor the heat level of your wings by adjusting the amount of gochujang. If you can't find gochujang, substitute an equal amount of sriracha and add only 2 tablespoons of water to the sauce. If you buy chicken wings that are already split, with the tips removed, you will need only 2½ pounds.

Korean Fried Chicken Wings

  1 tablespoon toasted sesame oil
  1 teaspoon garlic, minced to paste
  1 teaspoon grated fresh ginger
1¾ cups water, divided
  3 tablespoons sugar
2–3 tablespoons gochujang
  1 tablespoon soy sauce
  2 quarts vegetable oil
  1 cup all-purpose flour
  3 tablespoons cornstarch
  3 pounds chicken wings, cut at joints,
     wingtips discarded

1. Combine sesame oil, garlic, and ginger in large bowl and microwave until mixture is bubbly and garlic and ginger are fragrant but not browned, 40 to 60 seconds. Whisk in ¼ cup water, sugar, gochujang, and soy sauce until smooth; set aside.

2. Heat vegetable oil in Dutch oven over medium-high heat to 350 degrees. While oil heats, whisk flour, cornstarch, and remaining 1½ cups water in second large bowl until smooth. Set wire rack in rimmed baking sheet and set aside.

3. Place half of wings in batter and stir to coat. Using tongs, remove wings from batter one at a time, allowing any excess batter to drip back into bowl, and add to hot oil. Increase heat to high and cook, stirring occasionally to prevent wings from sticking, until coating is light golden and beginning to crisp, about 7 minutes. (Oil temperature will drop sharply after adding wings.)

4. Transfer wings to prepared rack. Return oil to 350 degrees and repeat with remaining wings. Reduce heat to medium and let second batch of wings rest for 5 minutes.

5. Heat oil to 375 degrees. Carefully return all wings to oil and cook, stirring occasionally, until deep golden brown and very crispy, about 7 minutes. Return wings to rack and let stand for 2 minutes. (Fried wings can be held in 200-degree oven for up to 2 hours.)

6. Add wings to reserved sauce and toss until coated. Return wings to rack and let stand for 2 minutes to allow coating to set. Transfer to platter and serve.

To make ahead Fried wings and sauce, prepared through step 5, can be refrigerated separately for up to 24 hours; to reheat, place wings on wire rack set in baking sheet, let stand at room temperature for 30 minutes, then reheat in 400-degree oven until hot, 8 to 10 minutes; microwave sauce until hot, about 1 minute, before tossing with reheated wings.

Oven-Fried Chicken Wings

Serves 8 to 10 | **Total Time** 1¾ hours

WHY THIS RECIPE WORKS If you don't deep-fry, can you have wings that are crispy on the outside and moist and tender within? We cooked more than 200 pounds of wings to find out. The first challenge was how to dry out the skin. Baking powder proved to be our secret weapon; it breaks down the proteins within the skin and aids in browning. After tossing the wings with baking powder and salt, we started them in a low oven on a wire rack to dry the skin and begin rendering fat. Then we cranked the oven to finish roasting the wings and crisping the skin. If you buy chicken wings that are already split, with the tips removed, you will need only 3½ pounds.

- 4 pounds chicken wings, cut at joints, wingtips discarded
- 2 tablespoons baking powder
- ¾ teaspoon table salt
- 1 recipe wing sauce

1. Adjust oven racks to upper-middle and lower-middle positions and heat oven to 250 degrees. Set wire rack in aluminum foil–lined rimmed baking sheet. Pat wings dry with paper towels and transfer to 1-gallon zipper-lock bag. Combine baking powder and salt, add to wings, seal bag, and toss to evenly coat.

2. Arrange wings, skin side up, in single layer on prepared wire rack. Bake wings on lower-middle oven rack for 30 minutes. Move wings to upper-middle rack, increase oven temperature to 425 degrees, and roast until wings are golden brown and crispy, 40 to 50 minutes, rotating sheet halfway through baking. Remove sheet from oven and let stand for 5 minutes. Transfer wings to bowl with wing sauce, toss to coat, and serve.

PREPPING CHICKEN WINGS

1. Using chef's knife, cut through joint between drumette and wingette.

2. Cut off and discard wingtip.

Buffalo Wing Sauce

Makes about ¾ cup | **Total Time** 5 minutes

We use Frank's RedHot Original Cayenne Pepper Sauce here, but other hot sauces can be used.

- ½ cup hot sauce
- 4 tablespoons unsalted butter, melted
- 1 tablespoon molasses

Combine all ingredients in large bowl. (Sauce can be refrigerated for up to 24 hours. Microwave sauce until hot, about 1 minute, before tossing with reheated wings.)

Smoky Barbecue Wing Sauce

Makes about ¾ cup | **Total Time** 10 minutes

- ¼ cup chicken broth
- ¼ cup ketchup
- 1 tablespoon molasses
- 1 tablespoon cider vinegar
- 1 tablespoon minced canned chipotle chile in adobo sauce
- ¼ teaspoon liquid smoke

Combine all ingredients in large bowl. (Sauce can be refrigerated for up to 24 hours. Microwave sauce until hot, about 1 minute, before tossing with reheated wings.)

Sweet and Spicy Wing Sauce

Makes about ¾ cup | **Total Time** 20 minutes

- ½ cup packed brown sugar
- ¼ cup lime juice (2 limes)
- 1 tablespoon toasted sesame oil
- 1 teaspoon red pepper flakes
- 1 garlic clove, minced
- 2 tablespoons fish sauce

Combine sugar, lime juice, oil, pepper flakes, and garlic in small saucepan; bring to simmer over medium heat. Cook until slightly thickened, about 5 minutes. Off heat, stir in fish sauce. Transfer to large bowl. (Sauce can be refrigerated for up to 24 hours. Microwave sauce until hot, about 1 minute, before tossing with reheated wings.)

Pizza Monkey Bread

Serves 6 to 8 | **Total Time** 2½ hours

WHY THIS RECIPE WORKS Akin to sweet monkey bread, this savory monkey bread consists of balls of dough stuffed with salty, gooey pepperoni pizza fixings and baked into a ring meant for pulling apart and eating with your hands. For ease, we started off with store-bought pizza dough. Instead of shaping and filling each ball individually, we rolled up logs stuffed with the fillings and cut them into pieces. After we pinched the ends shut, the balls were ready for the pan. Instead of shredded cheese, string cheese turned out to be the perfect shape to roll up in the dough and had great mozzarella flavor. Microwaving the pepperoni before using it prevented greasy dough, and brushing a bit of the pepperoni's rendered fat onto the outside of the balls created a deeply browned crust. A simple tomato sauce for dipping was the final touch. If the dough becomes slack or difficult to work with, refrigerate it for 10 minutes. Seal the open ends of the filled dough after each cut in order to keep the filling from leaking out. If your string cheese sticks are longer than 4½ inches, trim any overhang once you've placed the cheese on the dough.

- 2 (1-pound) balls pizza dough
- 4 ounces sliced pepperoni
- 3 tablespoons extra-virgin olive oil
- 1½ ounces Parmesan cheese, grated (¾ cup)
- ½ teaspoon dried oregano
- 8 (4½-inch-long) sticks mozzarella string cheese, divided
- 1 recipe Tomato Sauce

1. Line baking sheet with parchment paper and dust with flour. Roll each dough ball into 10 by 6-inch rectangle on lightly floured counter, then transfer to prepared sheet. Cover with plastic wrap and let stand for 15 minutes. Microwave pepperoni in bowl until fat is rendered, 60 to 90 seconds, stirring halfway through microwaving. Using tongs, transfer pepperoni to paper towel–lined plate, reserving pepperoni oil in bowl (you should have about 1 tablespoon).

2. Pat pepperoni dry with paper towels. Stir olive oil into pepperoni oil. Brush 12-cup nonstick Bundt pan with 2 teaspoons oil mixture. Combine Parmesan and oregano in separate bowl. Working with 1 dough rectangle at a time, return to lightly floured counter and roll into 18 by 9-inch rectangle with long edge parallel to counter edge, stretching corners as needed to make neat rectangle. Starting 2 inches from long edge of dough nearest you, shingle half of pepperoni parallel to long edge.

3. Place 4 mozzarella sticks end to end on top of pepperoni. Sprinkle half of Parmesan mixture alongside mozzarella. Fold bottom 2-inch section of dough over filling and roll tightly toward opposite edge. Pinch seam and ends to seal. Repeat with remaining dough rectangle, remaining pepperoni, remaining 4 mozzarella sticks, and remaining Parmesan mixture. Cut each log in half and pinch open ends to seal. Cut each log in half again, pinching open ends to seal. Cut each log into thirds, pinching open ends closed as you go.

4. Place single layer of stuffed dough balls (about six) ½ inch apart in prepared pan and brush tops and sides with one-quarter of remaining oil mixture. Layer remaining dough balls in pan, brushing tops and sides with remaining oil mixture as you go. Cover pan with plastic and let dough rise at room temperature until slightly puffed, about 30 minutes. Adjust oven rack to lower-middle position and heat oven to 400 degrees.

5. Bake monkey bread until well browned, about 40 minutes, rotating pan halfway through baking. Transfer pan to wire rack and let cool for 10 minutes. Place serving platter on top of pan and invert. Let cool for 10 minutes. Serve monkey bread with tomato sauce.

Tomato Sauce

Makes about 2 cups | **Total Time** 30 minutes

- 2 tablespoons extra-virgin olive oil
- 4 garlic cloves, minced
- 1 (28-ounce) can crushed tomatoes
- ½ teaspoon dried oregano
- ½ teaspoon table salt
- ½ teaspoon pepper

Heat oil in small saucepan over medium heat until shimmering. Add garlic and cook until beginning to brown, about 90 seconds. Add tomatoes, oregano, salt, and pepper and bring to boil. Reduce heat to medium-low and simmer until slightly thickened, about 10 minutes. Remove from heat, cover, and set aside.

Oysters on the Half Shell with Ginger Mignonette Sauce

Serves 6 to 8 | **Total Time** 30 minutes

WHY THIS RECIPE WORKS We traded out the traditional mignonette sauce for orange juice and rice vinegar infused with fresh ginger. It's crucial to serve oysters ice cold; nestle them in crushed ice to maintain a chilled temperature. They should also be opened very carefully in order to preserve as much of the brine (or liquor) that surrounds the oyster meat as possible. In addition to the mignonette sauce, serve the oysters with lemon wedges, prepared horseradish, and hot sauce, if desired.

⅔ cup unseasoned rice vinegar

1 shallot, minced

2 scallions, minced

1 teaspoon grated fresh ginger

1 teaspoon grated orange zest plus
⅔ cup juice (2 oranges)

½ teaspoon pepper

½ teaspoon sugar

36 large oysters, well scrubbed

1. Whisk vinegar, shallot, scallions, ginger, orange zest and juice, pepper, and sugar together in bowl and set aside.

2. Line large serving platter with ½-inch layer of crushed ice. Using oyster knife and dish towel, carefully pry off and discard flat-sided shell from top of each oyster. Run knife underneath oyster in bottom shell to loosen completely, then nestle into crushed ice. Serve with sauce.

SHUCKING AN OYSTER

1. Hold oyster flat shell down in dish towel. Push blade into hinge, wiggling it back and forth to pry open shell; you will hear and feel pop. Move blade between shells to loosen, then twist to pry open.

2. Without spilling liquor that surrounds oyster, slide knife under oyster to sever muscle that holds meat to bottom shell.

Pizza Monkey Bread

Oysters on the Half Shell with Ginger Mignonette Sauce

Crispy Potato Latkes

Buckwheat Blini with
Smoked Salmon

Crispy Potato Latkes

Makes 10 latkes | **Total Time** 1¼ hours

MAKE AHEAD VEGETARIAN

WHY THIS RECIPE WORKS Great latkes are delicate and light, with a creamy, soft interior surrounded by a shatteringly crispy shell. To achieve this and avoid greasiness, we removed as much water as possible by wringing out the potato shreds in a dish towel. We then microwaved them briefly, causing the starches in the potatoes to form a gel that held on to their moisture so it didn't leach out during cooking. When fried, these latkes crisped up quickly and absorbed minimal oil. We shredded the potatoes using the shredding disk of a food processor, but you can use the large holes of a box grater if you prefer. Serve with applesauce and sour cream. For a special topping, make the brilliantly colored Savory Applesauce with Beets and Horseradish (recipe follows).

2	pounds russet potatoes, unpeeled, shredded
½	cup grated onion
1	teaspoon table salt
2	large eggs, lightly beaten
2	teaspoons minced fresh parsley
¼	teaspoon pepper
	Vegetable oil

1. Adjust oven rack to middle position, place rimmed baking sheet on rack, and heat oven to 200 degrees. Toss potatoes, onion, and salt together in bowl. Working in 2 batches, wrap potato mixture in clean dish towel and wring tightly to squeeze out as much liquid as possible into measuring cup, reserving drained liquid. Let liquid stand until starch settles to bottom, 5 to 10 minutes.

2. Return potato mixture to bowl, cover, and microwave until just warmed through but not hot, 1 to 2 minutes, stirring mixture with fork every 30 seconds. Spread potato mixture evenly over second rimmed baking sheet and let cool for 10 minutes.

3. Pour off water from reserved potato liquid, leaving potato starch in measuring cup. Whisk in eggs until smooth. Return cooled potato mixture to bowl. Add parsley, pepper, and potato starch mixture and toss to combine.

4. Set wire rack in clean rimmed baking sheet and line with triple layer of paper towels. Add oil to 12-inch skillet until it measures ¼ inch deep and heat over medium-high heat until shimmering. Place ¼-cup mound of potato mixture in oil and press with nonstick spatula into ⅓-inch-thick disk. Repeat until 5 latkes are in skillet.

5. Cook, adjusting heat so oil bubbles around latke edges, until golden brown on both sides, about 6 minutes. Let latkes drain briefly on paper towels, then transfer to sheet in oven. Repeat with remaining potato mixture, adding oil between batches as needed to maintain ¼-inch depth. Season with salt and pepper to taste. Serve. (Cooled latkes can be frozen on baking sheet until firm, transferred to zipper-lock bag, and frozen for up to 1 month. Reheat in 375-degree oven until crispy and hot, 6 minutes per side.)

Savory Applesauce with Beets and Horseradish

Makes about 2 cups | **Total Time** 45 minutes

Nearly any tart apple variety will work here.

- 1¼ pounds McIntosh apples, peeled and cored, peels and cores reserved
- 1½ cups water, divided
- 1 beet, peeled and grated (1 cup)
- 2 tablespoons sugar, plus extra to taste
- ¼ teaspoon table salt
- 2 teaspoons prepared horseradish

1. Bring reserved peels and cores and 1 cup water to boil in small saucepan over medium-high heat. Reduce heat to medium, cover, and cook, mashing occasionally with potato masher, until mixture is deep pink and cores have broken down, about 15 minutes.

2. While peels and cores cook, cut apples into quarters and place in large saucepan. Add beet, sugar, salt, and remaining ½ cup water and bring to boil over medium-high heat. Reduce heat to medium, cover, and cook, stirring occasionally with rubber spatula, until all apples are soft and about half are completely broken down (beet will not completely soften), about 15 minutes. Using potato masher, mash apples to desired consistency.

3. Transfer peel-and-core mixture to fine-mesh strainer set over saucepan of mashed apple mixture. Using rubber spatula, stir and press peel-and-core mixture to extract pulp; discard solids. Stir to combine. Stir in horseradish and season with salt to taste. Serve warm, at room temperature, or chilled. (Applesauce can be refrigerated for up to 1 week.)

Buckwheat Blini with Smoked Salmon

Serves 12 to 14 (Makes about 60 blini)
Total Time 50 minutes MAKE AHEAD

WHY THIS RECIPE WORKS These silver dollar–size buckwheat pancakes with an earthy, tangy flavor make an excellent and refined hors d'oeuvre when served with a briny smoked salmon topping. We leavened ours with baking powder and baking soda instead of yeast to save time, adding buttermilk for extra tang. The gluten from a bit of all-purpose flour gave the blini enough structure to prevent them from falling apart.

- ½ cup (2½ ounces) all-purpose flour
- ½ cup (2¼ ounces) buckwheat flour
- 1 tablespoon sugar
- ½ teaspoon table salt
- ½ teaspoon baking powder
- ¼ teaspoon baking soda
- ¾ cup buttermilk
- ½ cup whole milk
- 1 large egg
- 2 tablespoons unsalted butter, melted and cooled, plus extra for cooking blini
- 1 cup sour cream
- 1 pound sliced smoked salmon, cut into 2-inch lengths
- ½ cup capers, drained and rinsed
- 2 large shallots, minced
- ½ cup minced fresh chives

1. Whisk all-purpose flour, buckwheat flour, sugar, salt, baking powder, and baking soda together in large bowl. Whisk buttermilk, milk, egg, and melted butter together in second bowl. Whisk buttermilk mixture into flour mixture until just combined (do not overmix).

2. Brush bottom and sides of 12-inch nonstick skillet very lightly with extra melted butter; heat skillet over medium heat until butter stops sizzling. Using scant 1 tablespoon batter each, scoop 6 to 8 blini into skillet. Cook until large bubbles begin to form on tops of blini, 1½ to 2 minutes. Flip blini and cook until second side is golden, about 1½ minutes.

3. Transfer blini to wire rack. Repeat with additional butter and remaining batter. Let blini cool slightly. (Blini can be stacked between individual sheets of parchment paper, wrapped in plastic wrap, and frozen for up to 1 week. Thaw in refrigerator for 24 hours, then spread out on baking sheet and warm in 350-degree oven for about 5 minutes.) To serve, arrange blini on serving platter and top with sour cream, salmon, capers, shallots, and chives.

Smoked Salmon and Leek Tart

Serves 8
Total Time 50 minutes, plus 2 hours cooling

WHY THIS RECIPE WORKS Unexpected and elegant, this savory tart makes a stunning presentation as either a brunch dish or a holiday starter. It features a trio of flavors and textures in every bite: flaky pastry; creamy, leek-filled custard; and briny, smoky salmon. The pink salmon and green leeks blanketing the pale custard created a beautiful color contrast. Using half-and-half in the leek and custard filling added flavor and richness. Chopping up the salmon, rather than layering it on in slices, made the tart easier to both slice and eat. Buy smoked salmon that looks bright and glossy and avoid salmon that looks milky and dry. Serve either at room temperature or chilled, with lemon wedges if you like.

1 tablespoon unsalted butter
1 pound leeks, white and light green parts only, halved lengthwise, sliced thin, and washed thoroughly
½ teaspoon table salt
2 large eggs
½ cup half-and-half
1 tablespoon minced fresh dill
¼ teaspoon pepper
1 recipe Press-In Tart Dough, baked and cooled
6 ounces thinly sliced smoked salmon, cut into ¼-inch pieces
1 tablespoon extra-virgin olive oil
1 tablespoon minced fresh chives

1. Heat oven to 375 degrees. Melt butter in 10-inch skillet over medium heat. Add leeks and salt and cook, covered, stirring occasionally, until leeks are softened, about 10 minutes. Remove pan from heat and let leeks cool, uncovered, for 5 minutes.

2. Whisk eggs, half-and-half, dill, and pepper together in bowl. Stir in leeks until just incorporated. Place cooled tart shell on rimmed baking sheet and place in oven. Carefully pour egg mixture into cooled shell and bake until filling has set and center feels firm to touch, 20 to 25 minutes. Transfer sheet to wire rack and let tart cool completely, at least 2 hours.

3. Just before serving, toss salmon, oil, and chives together in bowl and season with salt and pepper to taste before sprinkling evenly over cooled tart. Slice and serve.

Press-In Tart Dough

Makes enough for one 9-Inch tart
Total Time 1½ hours

1¼ cups (6¼ ounces) all-purpose flour
1 tablespoon sugar
½ teaspoon table salt
8 tablespoons unsalted butter, cut into ½-inch pieces and chilled
2–4 tablespoons ice water

1. Spray 9-inch tart pan with removable bottom with vegetable oil spray. Pulse flour, sugar, and salt in food processor until combined, about 4 pulses. Scatter butter pieces over top and pulse until mixture resembles coarse sand, about 15 pulses. Add 2 tablespoons ice water and continue to process until clumps of dough just begin to form and no powdery bits remain, about 5 seconds. If dough doesn't clump, add remaining ice water, 1 tablespoon at a time, and pulse to incorporate, about 4 pulses. (Dough can be refrigerated for up to 2 days or frozen for up to 1 month; let chilled/frozen dough stand on counter until very soft before using.)

2. Press two-thirds dough into bottom of prepared pan. Press remaining one-third dough into fluted sides of pan. Lay plastic wrap over dough and smooth out any bumps or shallow areas using your fingertips. Place pan on plate and freeze dough until firm, about 30 minutes. (Unbaked dough-lined tart pan can be frozen for up to 1 month.) Meanwhile, adjust oven rack to middle position and heat oven to 375 degrees.

3. Place frozen tart shell on rimmed baking sheet. Gently press piece of greased aluminum foil against dough and over edges of tart pan. Fill tart pan with pie weights and bake until top edge of dough just starts to color and surface of dough no longer looks wet, about 30 minutes.

4. Remove sheet from oven and carefully remove foil and weights. Return sheet to oven and continue to bake until tart shell is golden brown, 5 to 10 minutes. Set sheet with tart shell on wire rack and let cool.

Camembert, Sun-Dried Tomato, and Potato Tart

Serves 8 | **Total Time** 1½ hours `VEGETARIAN`

WHY THIS RECIPE WORKS The star of this tart is a wheel of soft, melty cheese, cut into wedges and arranged over the tart. As the tart bakes, the rind forms a crisp crust and the cheese melts out into the filling's crevices, binding the filling and buttery tart crust together. Creamy, pungent Camembert cheese, Yukon Gold potatoes, and sun-dried tomatoes offered concentrated, salty-sweet flavor and satisfying texture. If you can't find a wheel of Camembert, look for wedges that you can slice in half. Depending on the ripeness and style of the cheese used, the cheese may melt less and range in mildness of flavor.

- 2 tablespoons unsalted butter
- 1 onion, halved and sliced ¼ inch thick
- 1 pound Yukon Gold potatoes, peeled and sliced ¼ inch thick
- 2 teaspoons minced fresh thyme
- 1 teaspoon table salt
- ¼ teaspoon pepper
- ½ cup oil-packed sun-dried tomatoes, rinsed, patted dry, and chopped coarse
- 1 recipe Press-In Tart Dough (page 254), baked and cooled
- 1 (8-ounce) wheel Camembert cheese

1. Adjust oven rack to middle position and heat oven to 375 degrees. Melt butter in 12-inch nonstick skillet over medium heat. Add onion and cook, stirring often, until golden brown, about 10 minutes. Stir in potatoes, thyme, salt, and pepper and cook, stirring occasionally, until potatoes are completely tender and lightly browned, 8 to 10 minutes. Stir in sun-dried tomatoes.

2. Spread potato mixture evenly into tart shell. Cut Camembert wheel in half horizontally to make 2 thin wheels, then cut each half into 4 wedges. Arrange wedges of cheese, rind side up, over top of tart. (Assembled tart, prepared through step 2, can be refrigerated for up to 24 hours.)

3. Bake tart on rimmed baking sheet until golden and cheese is melted and bubbling, 25 to 35 minutes, rotating sheet halfway through baking.

4. Let tart cool on baking sheet for at least 10 minutes. To serve, remove outer metal ring of tart pan, slide thin metal spatula between tart and tart pan bottom, and carefully slide tart onto serving platter or cutting board. Serve warm. (Baked tart can be held at room temperature for 4 hours; to serve, reheat in 400-degree oven for 5 to 10 minutes.)

Smoked Salmon and Leek Tart

Camembert, Sun-Dried Tomato, and Potato Tart

festive drinks

▪ MAKE AHEAD   ▪ VEGETARIAN
Photo: Holiday Punch

Autumn in New England

Autumn in New England

Makes 1 cocktail | **Total Time** 10 minutes VEGETARIAN

WHY THIS RECIPE WORKS There are times when cocktails showcase interesting and unexpected combinations and then there are ingredients that, when combined, taste like they were always meant to be together. Apple and sage are one such pairing. The piney, slightly astringent notes of the sage are mellowed and made whole by the bright sweetness of apples. We gently muddled just a couple of sage leaves in maple syrup to infuse our sweetener with herbal flavor. Then we shook this up with some apple cider (which offered subtly fermented flavor) and smoky, caramel-y bourbon. As is, this was too sweet, and so we sought something acidic to balance things out. Cider vinegar's clean, bracing acidity worked perfectly, adding another touch of savoriness to this round, juicy cocktail. Garnish with sage and, if you like, a slice of apple. If your sage leaves are longer than 2 inches, use the lesser amount.

2–4 fresh sage leaves, plus small
     sage sprig for garnishing
 ¼ ounce maple syrup
 2 ounces bourbon
 1 ounce apple cider
 ¼ ounce cider vinegar

Add sage leaves and syrup to base of cocktail shaker and muddle until fragrant, about 30 seconds. Add bourbon, apple cider, and vinegar, then fill shaker with ice. Shake mixture until just combined and chilled, about 5 seconds. Double-strain cocktail into chilled old-fashioned glass half-filled with ice. Garnish with sage sprig and serve.

Make-Ahead Autumn in New Englands for Four

Muddle 6 sage leaves with 1 ounce maple syrup in bowl until fragrant, about 1 minute. Combine syrup mixture, 8 ounces bourbon, 4 ounces apple cider, 2 ounces water, and 1 ounce vinegar in serving pitcher or large container. Cover and refrigerate until flavors meld and mixture is well chilled, at least 2 hours or up to 24 hours. Stir to recombine. Serve as above. Makes 4 cocktails.

NOTES FROM THE TEST KITCHEN

MEASURE IN OUNCES, NOT CUPS

When cooking, we're accustomed to measuring liquids in cup measures. However, greater precision is required for measuring the smaller amounts of liquids needed for cocktails. For the most consistent results, we developed our recipes using ounce measurements for liquid ingredients. A cocktail jigger makes it easy to measure this way.

Think of cocktail making as similar to baking: Just as weighing the ingredients used in baking recipes provides more precise measurements and results in better baked goods, measuring liquids in ounces results in well-made, balanced cocktails every time. (We do use teaspoon measurements for amounts less than ¼ ounce.)

Fireside

Makes 1 cocktail | **Total Time** 10 minutes `VEGETARIAN`

WHY THIS RECIPE WORKS We love to serve—and sip—this cocktail during the autumn months; it just seems appropriate when the leaves are falling and the air has turned chilly. The drink is, essentially, a warmly spiced version of a brandy old-fashioned, a gentler version of the traditional whiskey-based cocktail. To make our Fireside, we first replaced the bourbon in a standard old-fashioned recipe with brandy (for a luxe version, you could even use cognac). The cinnamon, clove, and allspice in our Spiced Syrup emphasized the brandy's dried-fruit and subtle warm spice notes. Citrus bitters provided zingy brightness—think of it as not unlike the lemon juice that's added to the very best spiced apple pie fillings. The optional Pumpkin Pie Spice Rim Sugar will further bump up the spiced elements and add a little sweetness. If you like, garnish each drink with a strip of orange peel instead of (or in addition to) the apple slice.

¼ cup Pumpkin Pie Spice Rim Sugar (optional)
  Orange wedge (optional, if using sugar)
2 ounces brandy or cognac
1 teaspoon Spiced Syrup (page 261)
⅛ teaspoon citrus bitters
1 apple slice

1. Spread sugar, if using, into even layer on small saucer. Moisten about ½ inch of chilled old-fashioned glass rim by running orange wedge around outer edge; dry any excess juice with paper towel. Roll moistened rim in sugar to coat. Remove any excess sugar that falls into glass; set aside.

2. Add brandy, spiced syrup, and bitters to mixing glass, then fill three-quarters full with ice. Stir until mixture is fully combined and well chilled, about 30 seconds. Fill prepared glass halfway with ice. Strain cocktail into glass. Garnish with apple slice and serve.

Make-Ahead Firesides for Four

Combine 8 ounces brandy, 2 ounces water, 4 teaspoons Spiced Syrup, and ¼ teaspoon citrus bitters in serving pitcher or large container. Cover and refrigerate until flavors meld and mixture is well chilled, at least 2 hours or up to 24 hours. Stir to recombine. Serve as above. Makes 4 cocktails.

Fireside

Pumpkin Pie Spice Rim Sugar

Makes about ½ cup | **Total Time** 5 minutes
This recipe can easily be doubled.

½ cup sugar
2 teaspoons ground cinnamon
1 teaspoon ground ginger
½ teaspoon ground nutmeg
½ teaspoon ground allspice

Whisk all ingredients in bowl until combined. (Sugar can be stored in an airtight container for up to 1 month. Occasionally sugar can clump together during storage; break up any clumps before using.)

Highlander

Makes 1 cocktail | **Total Time** 10 minutes VEGETARIAN

WHY THIS RECIPE WORKS There are classic cocktails, and then there are those cocktails that taste like classics at first sip. The Highlander falls into this latter group. Scotch whiskey is shaken with our Chamomile Liqueur and sweetened with a touch of thyme herb syrup. The floral, faintly earthy chamomile picks up the grassy quality of the thyme, suggesting heather-laden Scottish Highlands. A more neutral blended Scotch preserved the drink's freshness better than a smokier Islay-type whiskey. We generally like serving our shaken drinks straight up in a cocktail glass, as shaking a cocktail will usually dilute the cocktail sufficiently. Here, however, we liked how the cocktail evolved and relaxed over ice in a rocks glass, with the drink starting off powerful and concentrated before unwinding in the glass over time. In addition to the lemon peel, you can garnish your cocktails with fresh thyme sprigs, if desired. We strongly prefer our homemade Chamomile Liqueur (page 408) but you can use store-bought elderflower liqueur, though the cocktail's flavor will be much different.

- 1½ ounces Scotch
- ¾ ounce Chamomile Liqueur (page 408)
- ½ ounce lemon juice, plus strip of lemon peel for garnishing
- ¼ ounce Herb Syrup with thyme (page 261)

Add Scotch, liqueur, lemon juice, and herb syrup to cocktail shaker, then fill with ice. Shake mixture until just combined and chilled, about 5 seconds. Strain cocktail into chilled old-fashioned glass half-filled with ice. Pinch lemon peel over drink and rub outer edge of glass with peel, then garnish with lemon peel and serve.

Make-Ahead Highlanders for Four

Combine 6 ounces scotch, 2 ounces water, 3 ounces Chamomile Liqueur, 2 ounces lemon juice, and 1 ounce Herb Syrup with thyme in serving pitcher or large container. Cover and refrigerate until flavors meld and mixture is well chilled, at least 2 hours or up to 24 hours. Stir to recombine. Serve as above. Makes 4 cocktails.

Highlander

NOTES FROM THE TEST KITCHEN

A WORD ON SCALING
We developed most of our drink recipes with a single cocktail in mind, but many of them can be scaled to make as many servings as you like simply by proportionally increasing all the ingredients and preparing the cocktails one at a time. For these recipes, we noted "This recipe can be easily scaled to make multiple cocktails." Some recipes require a few modifications when scaled up, so for these we provided variations to help you scale them to serve four. Because these bigger-batch cocktails are chilled in the refrigerator (meaning they can be made up to a day ahead of time) rather than being stirred or shaken with ice, we added a measured amount of water to them to ensure the perfect level of dilution. Finally, some recipes, like Big-Batch Boulevardiers or House Punch, lend themselves exceptionally well to large batches and advance preparation (making them perfect for serving at large gatherings), so we wrote these recipes to make anywhere from eight to 16 servings per batch.

Cocktail Syrups

Simple Syrup

Makes about 8 ounces | **Total Time** 20 minutes

¾ cup sugar
5 ounces warm tap water

Whisk sugar and warm water together in bowl until sugar has dissolved. Let cool completely, about 10 minutes, before transferring to airtight container. (Syrup can be refrigerated for up to 1 month. Shake well before using.)

Herb Syrup

Makes about 8 ounces | **Total Time** 40 minutes

¾ cup sugar
5 ounces water
½ cup fresh herb leaves (basil, dill, mint, or tarragon), 12 fresh thyme sprigs, or 1 fresh rosemary sprig

Heat sugar and water in small saucepan over medium heat, whisking often, until sugar has dissolved, about 5 minutes; do not boil. Stir in herb and let cool completely, about 30 minutes. Strain syrup through fine-mesh strainer into airtight container; discard solids. (Syrup can be refrigerated for up to 1 month. Shake well before using.)

Citrus Syrup

Makes about 8 ounces | **Total Time** 40 minutes

¾ cup sugar
5 ounces water
2 teaspoons grated grapefruit, lemon, lime, or orange zest

Heat sugar, water, and zest in small saucepan over medium heat, whisking often, until sugar has dissolved, about 5 minutes; do not boil. Let cool completely, about 30 minutes. Strain syrup through fine-mesh strainer into airtight container; discard solids. (Syrup can be refrigerated for up to 1 month. Shake well before using.)

Spiced Syrup

Makes about 8 ounces | **Total Time** 40 minutes

¾ cup sugar
5 ounces water
1 cinnamon stick
8 allspice berries, lightly crushed
4 whole cloves

Heat sugar, water, cinnamon stick, allspice berries, and cloves in small saucepan over medium heat, whisking often, until sugar has dissolved, about 5 minutes; do not boil. Let cool completely, about 30 minutes. Strain syrup through fine-mesh strainer into airtight container; discard solids (Syrup can be refrigerated for up to 1 month. Shake well before using.)

Ginger Syrup

Makes about 8 ounces | **Total Time** 50 minutes, plus 12 hours chilling

8 ounces fresh ginger, unpeeled, chopped coarse
¾ cup sugar
5 ounces water
½ teaspoon ground ginger
2 teaspoons lemon juice

1. Process ginger in food processor until finely chopped, about 30 seconds, scraping down sides of bowl as needed.

2. Heat sugar and water in small saucepan over medium heat, whisking often, until sugar has dissolved, about 5 minutes; do not boil. Off heat, stir in chopped ginger and ground ginger and let cool to room temperature, about 30 minutes. Cover and refrigerate for at least 12 hours or up to 24 hours.

3. Set fine-mesh strainer over medium bowl and line with triple layer of cheesecloth that overhangs edges. Transfer ginger mixture to prepared strainer and let drain until liquid no longer runs freely, about 10 minutes. Pull edges of cheesecloth together to form pouch, then firmly squeeze pouch to extract as much syrup from pulp as possible; discard pulp. Stir in lemon juice. (Syrup can be refrigerated in airtight container for up to 1 month. Shake gently before using.)

Grapefruit-Rosemary Spritzer

Makes 1 nonalcoholic cocktail
Total Time 10 minutes VEGETARIAN

WHY THIS RECIPE WORKS With its citrus and herbal flavors, this simple but sophisticated and not-too-sweet nonalcoholic cocktail is perfect for brightening up your wintry holiday table. The three ingredients—freshly squeezed grapefruit juice, seltzer, and rosemary simple syrup—added up to far more than just the sum of their parts. The simple syrup's piney flavor tempered the grapefruit's tartness and gave the drink intriguing savory notes. Before we were done we created a sweeter variation using orange juice and herby thyme syrup. We prefer to use fresh juice for this spritzer (feel free to use yellow, pink, or red grapefruit, as you prefer); however, you can substitute unsweetened store-bought juice, if you like. Garnish the spritzers with a rosemary sprig in addition to the grapefruit twist, if you like. This recipe can be easily scaled to make multiple cocktails.

4 ounces grapefruit juice, plus strip grapefruit peel for garnishing
½ ounce Herb Syrup with rosemary (page 261)
4 ounces seltzer, chilled

Fill chilled collins glass halfway with ice. Add grapefruit juice and herb syrup and stir to combine using bar spoon. Add seltzer and, using spoon, gently lift grapefruit mixture from bottom of glass to top to combine. Top with additional ice. Pinch grapefruit peel over drink and rub outer edge of glass with peel, then garnish with grapefruit peel and serve.

Orange-Thyme Spritzer

Substitute orange juice for grapefruit juice and Herb Syrup with thyme (page 261) for rosemary syrup. Substitute orange peel for grapefruit peel.

Grapefruit-Rosemary Spritzer with Spirits

Add 1 ounce blanco tequila, vodka, or London dry gin to glass with juice.

New Englander

Makes 1 nonalcoholic cocktail
Total Time 1 hour MAKE AHEAD VEGETARIAN

WHY THIS RECIPE WORKS A tart, vivid red New Englander is the perfect thing to serve alongside the rich fare so many of us gravitate toward in wintertime: It's elegant, festive, and sure to perk up your taste buds. The star of the drink is our cranberry shrub syrup. Cranberries are the ideal fruit to receive the sweet-tart shrub treatment; the syrup's luscious flavor shines when mixed with seltzer and a bit of lime juice. We found the syrup sweet enough that we did not need to add any additional sweetener. This recipe makes enough shrub syrup for up to four cocktails. To make additional cocktails, increase lime juice and seltzer accordingly and repeat step 3.

CRANBERRY SHRUB SYRUP
2 cups fresh or frozen cranberries
1 cup sugar
6 ounces water
1 ounce white wine vinegar

NEW ENGLANDER
¼ ounce lime juice, plus lime twist for garnishing
6 ounces seltzer, chilled

1. FOR THE CRANBERRY SHRUB SYRUP Bring cranberries, sugar, and water to boil in large saucepan over high heat. Reduce heat to medium-low, cover, and simmer until cranberries are beginning to break down, about 5 minutes.

2. Remove saucepan from heat and use potato masher to crush cranberries. Set fine-mesh strainer over medium bowl and line with triple layer of cheesecloth that overhangs edges. Transfer cranberry mixture to prepared strainer and let drain until liquid no longer runs freely and mixture is cool enough to touch, about 30 minutes. Pull edges of cheesecloth together to form pouch, then gently squeeze pouch to extract as much syrup as possible; discard solids. Whisk in vinegar. (Shrub syrup can be stored in airtight container for up to 1 month. Shake well before using.)

3. FOR THE NEW ENGLANDER Fill chilled collins glass halfway with ice. Add 2 ounces shrub syrup and lime juice and stir to combine using bar spoon. Add seltzer and, using spoon, gently lift shrub mixture from bottom of glass to top to combine. Top with additional ice and garnish with lime twist. Serve.

New Englander with Vodka

Add 1 ounce vodka to glass with shrub syrup.

Cocochai

Makes 1 nonalcoholic cocktail | **Total Time** 1½ hours, plus 1 hour chilling `MAKE AHEAD` `VEGETARIAN`

WHY THIS RECIPE WORKS Shaking helps incorporate air into a cocktail's body, transforming a heavy, oily cocktail to something light but mouth-filling. Inspired by Vietnamese coffee, a drink in which lower-density coffee naturally floats above higher-density condensed milk, we created an "upside-down" mocktail version with coconut milk layered on top of spiced black tea. When shaken, the coconut milk created gorgeous open bubbles with a rich but light frothy texture. Wanting more complexity, we brewed our own chai by simmering black tea with ginger, cinnamon, cardamom, peppercorns, and cloves. All together, this blend made for a pantry-friendly, highly gluggable spirit-free cocktail for any time of day or night. This recipe makes enough chai for up to four cocktails. To make additional cocktails, increase the simple syrup, coconut milk, and vanilla accordingly and repeat steps 2 and 3.

18	ounces water
3	black tea bags
1	(1-inch) piece ginger, sliced thin
½	cinnamon stick, plus extra for garnishing
5	green cardamom pods, lightly crushed
5	peppercorns
3	whole cloves
1	ounce Simple Syrup (page 261)
4	ounces coconut milk
¼	teaspoon vanilla extract

1. Bring water to simmer in small saucepan over medium-high heat. Stir in tea bags, ginger, cinnamon stick, cardamom pods, peppercorns, and cloves and simmer for 5 minutes. Strain chai through fine-mesh strainer into small bowl, gently pressing on tea bags to extract as much liquid as possible; discard solids. Let chai cool completely, then transfer to airtight container and refrigerate until chilled, at least 1 hour or up to 1 week.

2. Fill chilled collins glass halfway with ice. Add simple syrup and 3 ounces of chai and stir to combine using bar spoon. Top with additional ice, leaving room for coconut milk.

3. Add coconut milk and vanilla to cocktail shaker, then fill with ice. Shake mixture until frothy, about 15 seconds. Arrange spoon concave side down near surface of ice. Gently pour coconut mixture onto back of spoon and into cocktail. Grate extra cinnamon stick over top and serve.

Grapefruit-Rosemary Spritzer

Cocochai

Champagne Cocktails

Quick Differences between Champagne, Prosecco, and Cava Champagne, of course, is the gold standard of sparkling wine. It must be made in Champagne, France, using specific grapes and the region's traditional production method. But even the least expensive bottle of Champagne costs about $40. Great alternatives include the widely produced sparkling wines prosecco ($8 to $30) and cava ($10 to $30).

Prosecco is made with an Italian grape using a different method that makes it less carbonated. It tends to have more residual sugar and a slightly lower acidity.

Cava, a Spanish sparkler, is produced with grapes indigenous to Spain using the same method used to produce Champagne. It features similar levels of carbonation, acidity, and residual sugar.

When to Splurge on Champagne Champagne is essential in a Champagne cocktail—and not just to make it true to its name. Made by pouring the wine over a sugar cube drenched in Angostura bitters and garnished with a twist of lemon zest, this cocktail evolves from the first sip to the last—and the flavors of the Champagne are primary until the very end. First, bursting bubbles aromatize lemon oils from the twist to make the initial sip bright and citrusy. Then the Champagne's flavors and aromas take over, with whispers of the orange-and-spice-scented Angostura. Only in the final sips, when the sugar cube has fully dissolved to create a bitters-infused syrup at the bottom of the glass, does the Angostura supersede the Champagne. For the best experience, Champagne is a must.

When a Budget Bubbly Will Do In virtually all other sparkling wine cocktails, it's fine to substitute a less expensive sparkling wine. In mimosas, most tasters found an $8 prosecco to be perfectly acceptable, since the orange juice and liqueur hid the nuances of the wine. Prosecco is the traditional choice for Bellinis, which are sweetened with peach juice and peach schnapps, and we wouldn't hesitate to use an inexpensive bottle to mix that drink either.

Champagne Cocktail

Makes 4 cocktails | **Total Time** 10 minutes

We started our champagne cocktail with an Angostura bitters–soaked sugar cube in the bottom of a chilled flute. Then we filled the glass with Champagne and garnished it with a lemon twist, resulting in a cocktail that evolved from first sip to last. We strongly prefer Champagne here, but you can use another quality sparkling wine as long as it's brut or extra brut. Tilt the glass to a 45-degree angle and pour the wine down the side of the glass to minimize foaming. The amount of Champagne called for here is slightly less than a full 750-milliliter bottle. Use a channel knife to make the lemon twist (see page 270 for more information).

- 4 sugar cubes
- 1 teaspoon Angostura bitters
- 22 ounces (2¾ cups) Champagne, chilled
- 4 lemon twists

Place sugar cubes in small bowl. Add bitters to sugar cubes. Transfer soaked sugar cubes to 4 chilled champagne flutes. Add 5½ ounces champagne to each flute and garnish with lemon twists. Serve.

Mimosa

Makes 4 cocktails | **Total Time** 10 minutes

The festive, bubbly, brunch-friendly mimosa is one of our favorite sparkling wine–based cocktails. We used freshly squeezed orange juice and a slightly greater ratio of sparkling wine to juice to ensure that our beverage was wine-forward. (Using prosecco or cava instead of more expensive Champagne resulted in no loss in quality.) A little orange liqueur boosted the orange flavor and added complexity. We also liked to garnish our Mimosa with an orange slice or twist (see page 270 for more information).

- 10 ounces fresh orange juice, plus
  - 4 orange twists for garnishing
- 1 ounce orange liqueur
- 12 ounces dry sparkling wine, such as prosecco or cava, chilled

Add 2½ ounces orange juice and ¼ ounce liqueur to 4 chilled wine glasses or flute glasses and stir to combine using bar spoon. Add 3 ounces wine to each glass and, using spoon, gently lift juice mixture from bottom of glass to top to combine. Garnish with orange twists and serve.

Bellini

Substitute peach juice for orange juice, and peach schnapps for orange liqueur. Omit orange twists and garnish with 4 fresh peach slices, if desired.

Royal Berry

We strongly prefer our Fruits of the Forest liqueur (page 408) but you can use store-bought raspberry liqueur, such as Chambord. Add 1 blackberry, raspberry, or halved strawberry to bottom of each flute glass. Substitute 6 ounces Fruits of the Forest Liqueur (page 408) for orange juice and orange liqueur. Increase wine to 16 ounces. Omit orange twists.

DIY Bitters Sugar Cubes

Makes 64 cubes | **Total Time** 10 minutes, plus 24 hours drying

You can use any type of bitters you like here.

- ¾ cup sugar
- 2 tablespoons bitters

Stir sugar and bitters in bowl until well combined. Transfer mixture to large piece of parchment paper and press into 4-inch square. Use chef's knife to cut sugar into ½-inch cubes, being careful not to cut parchment. Transfer sugar square to rimmed baking sheet and let sit uncovered in cool, dry place for 24 hours. Sugar cubes can be stored in airtight container for up to 2 days.

NOTES FROM THE TEST KITCHEN

THE PHYSICS OF FIZZ

The carbonated bubbles that give sparkling wines their tongue-tingling bite start with carbon dioxide. The gas stays dissolved in the wine under pressure until the bottle is opened. Then, when the carbon dioxide finds a nucleation point (a scratch, a fleck of dust, a sugar cube), a bubble is incited to come out of solution, growing in size as it rises. This process repeats itself over and over, creating a trail of effervescence up to the surface of the wine.

Sicilian Sojourn

Espresso Martini

Sicilian Sojourn

Makes 1 nonalcoholic cocktail
Total Time 10 minutes VEGETARIAN

WHY THIS RECIPE WORKS In the depths of winter, when the already limited variety of available fruit all seems so pale and tasteless, citrus is one of the bright spots in the produce section. Blood oranges are a particularly beautiful and flavorful winter standout. When juiced, these oranges, which feature prominently in Sicilian cuisine, make for a striking dark magenta drink with flavor notes of raspberries and just a touch of grapefruit-style bitterness. We muddled fresh tarragon (a classic pairing for citrus in many Mediterranean dishes) in our Simple Syrup and then added this herb-spiked syrup along with a touch of lemon juice to our freshly squeezed blood orange juice. The result was a refreshing nonalcoholic cocktail striking enough to brighten even the darkest winter day. You can substitute fresh basil for tarragon, if you like. If you can't find blood oranges, you can substitute navel oranges.

2 tablespoons fresh tarragon leaves, plus tarragon sprig for garnishing
1 ounce Simple Syrup (page 261)
3½ ounces blood orange juice (3 oranges)
¼ ounce lemon juice
4 ounces seltzer, chilled

1. Add tarragon leaves and simple syrup to base of cocktail shaker and muddle until fragrant, about 30 seconds. Add orange juice and lemon juice, then fill shaker with ice. Shake mixture until just combined and chilled, about 5 seconds.

2. Double-strain cocktail into chilled collins glass half-filled with ice. Add seltzer and, using bar spoon, gently lift juice mixture from bottom of glass to top to combine. Top with additional ice and garnish with tarragon sprig. Serve.

Make-Ahead Sicilian Sojourns for Four

Muddle ½ cup fresh tarragon leaves with 4 ounces simple syrup in bowl until fragrant, about 1 minute. Combine syrup mixture, 14 ounces blood orange juice, 2 ounces water, and 1 ounce lemon juice in serving pitcher or large container. Cover and refrigerate until flavors meld and mixture is well chilled, at least 2 hours or up to 24 hours. Stir in 16 ounces seltzer. Serve as above. Makes 4 cocktails.

Espresso Martini

Makes 1 cocktail | **Total Time** 10 minutes VEGETARIAN

WHY THIS RECIPE WORKS Drinks based on combinations of coffee and spirits abound throughout the world, but perhaps none is quite as elegant as the espresso martini. Traditionally consisting of vodka, espresso, and coffee liqueur, this style of "martini" is shaken (not stirred) to create a thin layer of foam, just as one would find on a hot espresso. Served in a martini glass with a garnish of three floating espresso beans, this drink was the height of sophistication when it was developed in the 1980s in London. Our take on this modern classic swaps out the vodka for smooth aged rum. We also added Bénédictine, a French liqueur with notes of warm spice, honey, and vanilla. After combining these two ingredients with brewed espresso and coffee liqueur, we felt our cocktail was equally appealing as an after-dinner sip or as a cocktail hour pick-me-up before a special evening out. This cocktail tastes best with freshly made and chilled espresso, but you can substitute ½ teaspoon instant espresso powder dissolved in 1 ounce hot water, if necessary.

 1½ ounces aged rum
 1 ounce brewed espresso, chilled, plus
   espresso beans for garnishing
 ¾ ounce Bénédictine
 ½ ounce coffee liqueur

 Add rum, espresso, Bénédictine, and liqueur to cocktail shaker, then fill with ice. Shake mixture until fully combined and well chilled, about 15 seconds. Double-strain cocktail into chilled cocktail glass. Garnish with espresso beans and serve.

Espresso Lattetini
Add ½ ounce heavy cream to shaker with rum.

Make-Ahead Espresso Martinis for Four
Combine 6 ounces aged rum, 4 ounces espresso, 4 ounces water, 3 ounces Bénédictine, and 2 ounces coffee liqueur in serving pitcher or large container. Cover and refrigerate until flavors meld and mixture is well chilled, at least 2 hours or up to 24 hours. Stir to recombine. Serve as above. Makes 4 cocktails.

Whiskey Sour

Makes 1 cocktail | **Total Time** 10 minutes VEGETARIAN

WHY THIS RECIPE WORKS At its simplest, a whiskey sour is whiskey, lemon juice, and simple syrup, shaken with ice. The mouth-puckering quality of the lemon juice that gives the drink its name is balanced by the sweetness of the whiskey and simple syrup. Egg white is another traditional ingredient that has gone in and out of style over the years. For simplicity's sake, we decided to leave the egg white out, simply shaking our three ingredients vigorously to combine them before pouring them into a glass and garnishing with bright red cherries. Our twist, the Amaretto Sour, is one of those often-mocked, trendy/not trendy sort of cocktails. But as we learned, a well-made amaretto sour is shockingly delicious. We prefer the spiciness of rye in our Whiskey Sour, but Tennessee whiskey or bourbon also works well. If using one of those alternatives, decrease the Simple Syrup to ¼ ounce.

 2 ounces rye
 ½ ounce Simple Syrup (page 261)
 ½ ounce lemon juice
   Cocktail cherries

 1. Add rye, simple syrup, and lemon juice to cocktail shaker and vigorously shake until mixture is foamy, 30 to 45 seconds.
 2. Fill shaker with ice, then shake mixture until fully combined and well chilled, about 15 seconds. Strain cocktail into chilled cocktail glass. Garnish with cherries and serve.

Amaretto Sour
Substitute amaretto for rye. Omit Simple Syrup and increase lemon juice to 1 ounce. Add ½ teaspoon cherry bitters such as Peychaud's to shaker with amaretto.

Make-Ahead Whiskey Sours for Four
Combine 8 ounces rye, 4 ounces water, 2 ounces Simple Syrup, and 2 ounces lemon juice in serving pitcher or large container. Cover and refrigerate until flavors meld and mixture is well chilled, at least 2 hours or up to 24 hours. Stir to recombine. Serve as above. Makes 4 cocktails.

Old Poblano

Makes 1 cocktail | **Total Time** 10 minutes VEGETARIAN

WHY THIS RECIPE WORKS Alcohol is well known for creating an illusion of warmth thanks to the way it causes blood vessels just under the skin to dilate (in fact making the body lose heat faster). To really warm up on a cold night, we wanted a cocktail that could truthfully be described as "hot." Enter the Old Poblano, another take on the endlessly customizable template of the old-fashioned. First, we replaced the bourbon in a classic old-fashioned with aged rum, which has a nuanced complexity from its time spent in oak barrels, often featuring slightly smoky aromas and vanilla or even raisiny notes. To bring the heat, we turned to the slow-burn spiciness of chile liqueur; we preferred liqueur made from subtle ancho chiles over those made with more in-your-face jalapeños. We strongly prefer our Ancho Chile Liqueur (page 409) here, but you can use any store-bought dark chile liquor.

1½ ounces aged rum
1 ounce dark chile liqueur
⅛ teaspoon citrus bitters
Strip of lime peel

Add rum, liqueur, and bitters to mixing glass, then fill three-quarters full with ice. Stir until mixture is just combined and chilled, about 15 seconds. Strain cocktail into chilled old-fashioned glass half-filled with ice. Pinch lime peel over drink and rub outer edge of glass with peel, then garnish with lime peel and serve.

Make-Ahead Old Poblanos for Four

Combine 6 ounces aged rum, 4 ounces dark chile liqueur, 2 ounces water, and ¼ teaspoon citrus bitters in serving pitcher or large container. Cover and refrigerate until flavors meld and mixture is well chilled, at least 2 hours or up to 24 hours. Stir to recombine. Serve as above. Makes 4 cocktails.

Moscow Mule

Makes 1 cocktail | **Total Time** 10 minutes VEGETARIAN

WHY THIS RECIPE WORKS The exact origins of the Moscow Mule are up for some debate, but one truth is that this cocktail has been credited for significantly increasing the popularity of vodka in the United States in the mid-20th century. The key to a great mule is to add enough potent ginger flavor to temper the strength of the vodka. To that end, we created a spicy, not-too-sweet Ginger Syrup (page 261) using both fresh and ground ginger. A splash of lime juice increased the overall brightness of the cocktail by enhancing the gingery snap. We strongly prefer 1½ ounces of our Ginger Syrup plus 5 ounces of seltzer here, but you can substitute 6½ ounces of any premium store-bought ginger beer for the Ginger Syrup and seltzer. This recipe can be easily scaled to make multiple cocktails.

2 ounces vodka
1½ ounces Ginger Syrup (page 261)
½ ounce lime juice, plus lime slice for garnishing
5 ounces seltzer, chilled

Fill chilled collins glass or mule mug halfway with ice. Add vodka, ginger syrup, and lime juice and stir to combine using bar spoon. Add seltzer and, using spoon, gently lift vodka mixture from bottom of glass to top to combine. Top with additional ice and garnish with lime slice. Serve.

HOW TO STIR A COCKTAIL

1. Assemble ingredients in mixing glass. Add ice as directed in recipe. Insert bar spoon into mixing glass with outer curved side positioned against wall of glass.

2. Loosely grasp stem of spoon between your thumb and forefinger, similar to holding a pencil. Pivot wrist of hand holding spoon to guide convex side of spoon around wall of glass.

3. Once cocktail is combined and chilled, fit julep or Hawthorne strainer into mixing glass and decant drink into chilled serving glass.

Negroni

Makes 1 cocktail | **Total Time** 10 minutes `VEGETARIAN`

WHY THIS RECIPE WORKS The Negroni, with its distinct, crisp bitterness, is considered a classic aperitivo, or palate opener, even though the addition of gin makes it stronger than many of the other cocktails in this category. It pairs perfectly with such savory and piquant appetizers as olives and cheese. Like the Americano cocktail from which it was born, the alcoholic ingredients for the Negroni—gin, Campari, and sweet vermouth—are mixed in equal parts, and we found it best to stick with tradition in this case for the most balanced experience. A single large (2-inch) ice cube looks dramatic in the rocks glass, but alternatively, you can fill the glass halfway with smaller ice cubes of your choice. A single strip of orange peel, its citrus oils carefully expressed into the cocktail just before serving, is the perfect (and classic) garnish.

1 ounce London dry gin
1 ounce Campari
1 ounce sweet vermouth
  Strip of orange peel

Add gin, Campari, and vermouth to mixing glass, then fill three-quarters full with ice. Stir until mixture is just combined and chilled, about 15 seconds. Strain cocktail into chilled old-fashioned glass half-filled with ice. Pinch orange peel over drink and rub outer edge of glass with peel, then garnish with orange peel and serve.

Negroni Sbagliato

Substitute chilled, dry sparkling wine, such as prosecco or cava, for gin. Add Campari and sweet vermouth to chilled wine glass or flute glass and stir to combine using bar spoon. Add wine and, using spoon, gently lift Campari mixture from bottom of glass to top to combine. Garnish with orange peel and serve.

Make-Ahead Negronis for Four

Combine 4 ounces London dry gin, 4 ounces Campari, 4 ounces sweet vermouth, and 2 ounces water in serving pitcher or large container. Cover and refrigerate until flavors meld and mixture is well chilled, at least 2 hours or up to 24 hours. Stir to recombine. Serve as above. Makes 4 cocktails.

Negroni

Practically Clear Ice

Makes about 7 cups | **Total Time** 25 minutes, plus 8½ hours cooling and freezing

6 cups distilled water

1. Fold 3 dish towels in half widthwise, then stack in 13 by 9-inch baking dish, allowing towels to overhang edges. Arrange two 6½ by 4½-inch silicone ice cube trays in center of prepared dish. Roll up additional towels and tuck into sides of dish as needed to ensure that trays are packed snugly.

2. Bring water to boil in saucepan and boil for 1 minute. Working in batches, carefully transfer water to 4-cup liquid measuring cup, then pour into trays. Let cool completely, about 30 minutes; you may have extra water. Place baking dish in freezer and let sit, uncovered, until ice is completely frozen, at least 8 hours.

Big-Batch Boulevardiers

Makes 8 cocktails MAKE AHEAD VEGETARIAN
Total Time 10 minutes, plus 2 hours chilling

WHY THIS RECIPE WORKS This cocktail is a godsend to busy party hosts: Our recipe allows you to mix up a large batch up to a month ahead of time, freeing you to mingle with your guests rather than spend the night taking drink orders. What's more, the measured added water ensures the perfect amount of dilution, meaning you don't even need to add ice cubes before serving. To keep the assertive Campari from overwhelming the rye, we added a greater amount of rye. This allowed the drink to walk the fine line between bitter and sweet while maintaining a rich, lush texture. We prefer our homemade Sweet Vermouth (page 405) in this recipe, but you can use store-bought sweet vermouth instead, if you like.

**Big-Batch
Boulevardiers**

12 ounces rye or bourbon
 8 ounces Campari
 8 ounces sweet vermouth
 8 ounces water
 8 orange twists

1. Combine rye, Campari, vermouth, and water in serving pitcher or large container. Cover and refrigerate until well chilled, at least 2 hours.

2. Stir cocktail to recombine, then serve in chilled cocktail glasses, garnishing individual portions with orange twists. (Boulevardiers may be refrigerated for up to 1 month.)

HOW TO GARNISH WITH CITRUS ZEST

A1. To make citrus zest twist, use channel knife to remove 3- to 4-inch strand, working around circumference of citrus in spiral pattern to ensure continuous piece.

A2. To garnish with citrus twist, curl strand tightly to establish uniform twist, then place in cocktail or on edge of glass.

B1. To make citrus zest peel, use Y-shaped vegetable peeler to remove 2- to 3-inch strip, working from pole to pole and avoiding as much white pith as possible.

B2. To garnish with citrus peel, hold strip horizontal, pith side facing you, near surface of cocktail, with index finger and thumb of each hand. Pinch zest to express oils onto cocktail. Rub outer edge of glass with peel, then place in cocktail.

House Punch

Makes 8 cocktails `MAKE AHEAD` `VEGETARIAN`
Total Time 10 minutes, plus 2 hours chilling

WHY THIS RECIPE WORKS This sweet-sour punch, with
its nutty, spiced flavor undertones, is our more sophisticated
take on the zombie cocktail. Many interpretations of the
zombie end up being a kitchen-sink amalgamation of whatever
the barkeep has on hand, possibly the cause of the more
imaginative tales about its madness-inducing properties. While
we can't claim ours to be mind-altering, combining smooth
aged rum with just two juices, nutty orgeat, and warmly
spiced syrup ensured that this drink does go down easy. We
prefer to use our homemade Orgeat Syrup (page 409) here;
however, store-bought orgeat will work. Freshly grated nutmeg
is the more aromatic and flavorful choice, but preground
nutmeg will also work. Fresh pineapple wedges make a nice
additional garnish, if you like.

- 16 ounces aged rum
- 6 ounces pineapple juice
- 6 ounces lime juice (6 limes)
- 4 ounces Orgeat Syrup (page 409)
- 3 ounces Spiced Syrup (page 261)
- 1 teaspoon old-fashioned aromatic bitters
  Ground nutmeg

1. Combine rum, pineapple juice, lime juice, orgeat syrup,
spiced syrup, and bitters in serving pitcher or large container.
Cover and refrigerate until well chilled, at least 2 hours or up
to 3 days.

2. Stir punch to recombine. Serve in chilled old-fashioned
glasses or tiki cups half-filled with ice or containing 1 large ice
cube, sprinkling individual portions with nutmeg.

Holiday Punch

Makes 16 cocktails `VEGETARIAN`
Total Time 10 minutes

WHY THIS RECIPE WORKS When the holidays roll
around, having a sophisticated, elegant party punch recipe
that serves a lot of people is crucial. For our punch, we wanted
a clean, simple recipe with a bit of sweetness but without too
much muddled flavor. For a neutral yet flavorful juice, we
chose white grape. Our Fruits of the Forest Liqueur gave this
drink a deep, mysterious berry flavor as well as a pretty color.

House Punch

Holiday Punch

Bloody Marys for a Crowd

A hint of orange liqueur rounded out the fruity sweetness. We preferred prosecco or cava in developing this recipe, but you can use Champagne instead, if you like. If you plan to let the punch sit in the bowl for longer than 30 minutes, we recommend adding six large (2-inch) ice cubes to the bowl to keep it properly chilled. We prefer our Fruits of the Forest liqueur (page 408) but you can use store-bought raspberry liqueur, such as Chambord.

- 3 (750-ml) bottles dry sparkling wine, such as prosecco or cava, chilled
- 12 ounces white grape juice, chilled
- 6 ounces Fruits of the Forest Liqueur (page 408)
- 6 ounces orange liqueur
- 5 ounces (1 cup) blackberries, blueberries, and/or raspberries
- 5 ounces strawberries, hulled and quartered (1 cup)
- ½ cup fresh mint leaves

Combine all ingredients in large punch bowl. Serve in chilled old-fashioned glasses or punch cups.

Bloody Marys for a Crowd

Makes 12 cocktails `MAKE AHEAD`
Total Time 10 minutes, plus 2 hours chilling

WHY THIS RECIPE WORKS A pitcher of Bloody Marys is a ubiquitous brunch-time classic. But because vodka is a flavorless spirit, it's easy to add too much, which will put you under the table (faster than you might like). We decided that a 3:1 ratio of tomato juice to vodka was the best for both the cocktail's potency and its flavor balance. We liked a fair amount or Worcestershire—more than the dash or two specified in most recipes. A Bloody Mary just doesn't taste right without a fairly significant burst of spicy heat, so we added both a generous grind of pepper and a dash of hot sauce. We prefer to use Campbell's Tomato Juice in this recipe, though V8 can be substituted. Do not use horseradish cream here. Garnish with pickled green beans, olives, cocktail onions, and/or cornichons in addition to the celery ribs, if desired.

- 48 ounces tomato juice
- 16 ounces vodka
- 4 ounces lemon juice (3 lemons)
- 1 ounce Worcestershire sauce

Eggnog

4 teaspoons prepared horseradish
2 teaspoons pepper
½–1 teaspoon hot sauce
12 celery ribs

1. Whisk tomato juice, vodka, lemon juice, Worcestershire, horseradish, pepper, and hot sauce together in serving pitcher or large container. Cover and refrigerate until flavors meld and mixture is well chilled, at least 2 hours or up to 24 hours.

2. Stir Bloody Marys to recombine, then serve in chilled collins glasses filled with ice, garnishing individual portions with celery rib.

Eggnog

Makes 8 cocktails MAKE AHEAD VEGETARIAN
Total Time 1 hour, plus 2 hours chilling

WHY THIS RECIPE WORKS Winter activities practically demand eggnog, whether it's served to enliven a holiday party or as a reward for getting out there and shoveling snow. Cooking our eggnog resulted in a velvety texture and put to rest any safety concerns about serving uncooked eggs. We preferred black rum, such as Gosling's Black Seal, in our nog. Freshly grated nutmeg is best, but preground nutmeg will also work.

24 ounces whole milk
¼ teaspoon table salt
12 ounces heavy cream, divided
6 large egg yolks
6 tablespoons sugar
4 ounces black rum
¼ teaspoon ground nutmeg, plus extra for garnishing

1. Bring milk and salt to simmer in medium saucepan over medium-high heat, stirring occasionally. Whisk 6 ounces cream, egg yolks, and sugar in medium bowl until thoroughly combined and pale yellow, about 30 seconds.

2. Fill large bowl halfway with ice and water. Slowly whisk 1 cup of warm milk mixture into yolk mixture to temper, then slowly whisk tempered yolk mixture into remaining milk mixture in saucepan. Cook over medium-low heat, whisking constantly, until eggnog registers 160 degrees, 1 to 2 minutes.

3. Immediately pour eggnog into clean medium bowl and stir in rum and nutmeg. Set bowl with eggnog into prepared ice bath and let stand, stirring occasionally, until chilled to room temperature, about 30 minutes. Remove eggnog from ice bath, cover, and refrigerate until well chilled, at least 2 hours or up to 24 hours.

4. Just before serving, using stand mixer fitted with whisk attachment, whip remaining 6 ounces cream on medium-low speed until foamy, about 1 minute. Increase speed to high and whip until soft peaks form, 1 to 3 minutes. Whisk whipped cream into chilled eggnog. Serve in chilled old-fashioned glasses or punch cups, sprinkling individual portions with extra nutmeg.

Nonalcoholic Eggnog
Reduce total amount of heavy cream to 6 ounces and sugar to ¼ cup and substitute root beer for rum. In step 1, whisk 3 ounces cream together with other ingredients. Proceed with steps 2 and 3. In step 4, whip remaining 3 ounces cream as directed and then proceed with recipe as directed.

Mulled Cider

Makes 12 nonalcoholic cocktails | **Total Time** 1 hour
MAKE AHEAD VEGETARIAN

WHY THIS RECIPE WORKS Bubbling away on the stovetop, mulled cider fills the kitchen with a fantastic aroma. In our version, brandy and spices complement the rounded, sweet-and-tart apple cider flavor. To crack the spices, rock the bottom edge of a skillet over them on a cutting board. The amount of brown sugar will vary depending on the sweetness of the apple cider; start with the lesser amount and add more as needed. Cinnamon sticks and apple slices also make great garnishes. This recipe can easily be doubled.

1 cinnamon stick, broken into pieces
½ teaspoon black peppercorns, cracked
½ teaspoon coriander seeds, cracked
7 whole cloves
2 quarts apple cider
4 (3-inch) strips orange zest, plus
12 orange slices for garnishing
1–3 tablespoons packed brown sugar

1. Toast cinnamon stick pieces, peppercorns, coriander seeds, and cloves in large saucepan over medium heat, shaking saucepan occasionally, until fragrant, 1 to 3 minutes. Add cider, orange zest, and sugar. Bring to simmer and cook until flavors meld, about 30 minutes, using wide, shallow spoon to skim off any foam that rises to surface.

2. Line fine-mesh strainer with coffee filter and set over large bowl. Strain cider mixture through prepared strainer; discard solids. Return cider mixture to now-empty saucepan. (Mulled cider can be refrigerated for up to 1 week; bring to brief simmer before serving.) Serve in warmed mugs, garnishing individual portions with orange slice.

Brandied Mulled Cider

Feel free to substitute bourbon or aged rum for the brandy. Add 16 ounces brandy to saucepan along with strained cider mixture in step 2.

Mulled Cider

Mulled Wine

Makes 8 cocktails `MAKE AHEAD` `VEGETARIAN`
Total Time 1¾ hours

WHY THIS RECIPE WORKS Mulled wine is an ancient alcoholic mixed drink; Roman soldiers in the 2nd century used to heat their wine to fortify themselves against the cold winters, adding sweeteners and other ingredients to make their ration of poorly made wine taste better. We wanted to create a warm, fruity, not-too-sweet wine with a mild alcohol kick and deep spice notes. We toasted a careful balance of cinnamon sticks, cloves, peppercorns, and allspice berries to unlock their full flavor and then simmered, rather than boiled, the wine, spices, and a modest amount of sugar for a full hour to ensure a full-flavored drink that didn't taste raw. A couple of spoonfuls of brandy stirred in just before serving added a fresh, boozy kick. Kept covered in the saucepan, the mulled wine will stay warm for about 30 minutes. Any medium- to full-bodied wine, such as Pinot Noir, Côtes du Rhône, or Merlot, works well. To crack the spices, rock the bottom edge of a skillet over them on a cutting board. Extra cinnamon sticks also make great garnishes, if you like.

> 3 cinnamon sticks, broken into pieces
> 10 whole cloves
> 1 teaspoon allspice berries, cracked
> ½ teaspoon black peppercorns, cracked
> 2 (750-ml) bottles red wine
> ½ cup sugar, plus extra for seasoning
> 4 (3-inch) strips orange zest, plus
>   8 orange slices for garnishing
> 2 ounces brandy

1. Toast cinnamon stick pieces, cloves, allspice berries, and peppercorns in large saucepan over medium heat, shaking saucepan occasionally, until fragrant, 1 to 3 minutes. Add wine, sugar, and orange zest and bring to simmer. Reduce heat to low and partially cover. Simmer gently, stirring occasionally, until flavors meld, about 1 hour.

2. Line fine-mesh strainer with coffee filter and set over large bowl. Strain wine mixture through prepared strainer; discard solids. Return wine mixture to now-empty saucepan, stir in brandy, and season with extra sugar to taste. (Mulled wine can be refrigerated for up to 1 week; bring to brief simmer before serving.) Serve in warmed mugs, garnishing individual portions with orange slice.

Irish Coffee

Makes 1 cocktail `VEGETARIAN`
Total Time 10 minutes

WHY THIS RECIPE WORKS Maybe it's the convivial Irish spirit, or maybe it's because ultimately this is an alcoholic coffee drink decadently topped with whipped cream, but Irish coffee has a tendency to veer toward excess. The best Irish coffees have balanced flavors, in this case a combination of coffee, Irish whiskey, and sugar. We started by comparing ratios of coffee to whiskey, from 2:1 to 4:1. Surprisingly, tasters agreed that a 4:1 ratio offered the best balance of rich coffee to heady whiskey. We preferred the cream whipped enough to float over the drink, but not so stiff that it failed to easily incorporate into the coffee mixture while being enjoyed. Whipping the cream by hand worked best and also provided the best control of thickness. Irish whiskey is traditional here, but rye and Tennessee whiskey also work well. Or take your spiked coffee in a Caribbean or Italian direction by trying one of our twists. We prefer to serve this in a glass mug to highlight the layers of whipped cream and coffee. This recipe can be easily scaled to make multiple cocktails.

- 2 ounces heavy cream
- ¾ ounce Simple Syrup (page 261), divided
- 4 ounces brewed hot coffee
- 1 ounce Irish whiskey

1. Whisk cream and ¼ ounce simple syrup in chilled bowl until soft peaks just begin to form, about 30 seconds; set aside.

2. Add coffee, whiskey, and remaining ½ ounce syrup to warmed mug and stir to combine. Dollop whipped cream over top. Serve.

Caribbean Coffee
Substitute Orgeat Syrup (page 409) for Simple Syrup, and aged rum for whiskey.

Italian Coffee
Substitute Citrus Syrup (page 261) with lemon for Simple Syrup, and an amaro, such as Averna, for whiskey.

Mulled Wine

Irish Coffee

Hot Toddy

Hot Toddy

Makes 1 cocktail VEGETARIAN
Total Time 10 minutes

WHY THIS RECIPE WORKS Toddies have been hailed as a cure-for-what-ails-you for hundreds of years. Arguably the king of hot drinks, the toddy essentially comprises a spirit, hot water, sometimes citrus or spices, and a sweetener (often honey). We don't think a hot toddy should be reserved as only a cold or cough remedy. Made well, it is a delicious cup of comfort that can be enjoyed all winter long. We preferred toddies made with brandy (though bourbon and Tennessee whiskey also worked) and a modest hand when it came to the ratio of brandy to water. As for the lemon juice and honey, we opted for a balanced approach and used an equal amount of each. Be sure to measure the water after boiling it, since even in the short amount of time it takes to boil, you will lose some to evaporation. In addition to the lemon slice, garnish your toddy with a cinnamon stick, if desired. This recipe can be easily scaled to make multiple cocktails.

  5 ounces boiling water
1½ ounces brandy
  ½ ounce lemon juice, plus lemon slice for garnishing
  1 tablespoon honey

Using bar spoon, stir all ingredients in warmed mug until combined and honey has dissolved. Garnish with lemon slice and serve.

Scotch Hot Toddy
Substitute brewed hot black tea for water and Scotch for brandy.

Make-Ahead Hot Chocolate

Makes 10 chocolate balls MAKE AHEAD   VEGETARIAN
Total Time 20 minutes, plus 2 hours chilling

WHY THIS RECIPE WORKS You might think there are only two options for hot chocolate: a dusty packet or a luxurious cup of drinking chocolate that takes more time than you have in the morning to prepare. But with our make-ahead alternative, you can have hot chocolate in your thermos just as easily as you can coffee or tea. Taking inspiration from ganache frosting, we combined semisweet chocolate chips (for crowd-pleasing flavor) with cream to create our base. We then

Masala Chai

rolled this mixture into large truffle-like balls that can be kept in the refrigerator. When it was time to make a cup of cocoa, we simply microwaved one of our ganache balls with the appropriate amount of milk—2 minutes to bliss.

2 cups (12 ounces) semisweet chocolate chips
1 cup heavy cream
¼ teaspoon table salt

1. Microwave chocolate chips, cream, and salt in large bowl at 50 percent power, stirring occasionally, until melted and smooth, about 2 minutes. Refrigerate until firm, about 2 hours.

2. Working with 3 tablespoons chilled chocolate mixture at a time, roll into 2-inch balls. Wrap balls individually in plastic wrap and transfer to zipper-lock bag. (Balls can be refrigerated for up to 5 days or frozen for up to 2 months.)

3. TO MAKE 1 CUP OF HOT CHOCOLATE Place 1 unwrapped chocolate ball and 1 cup milk in mug. Microwave, stirring occasionally, until smooth, about 2 minutes. Serve.

Masala Chai

Makes about 4 cups concentrate (**Serves** 6 to 8)
Total Time 1¼ hours, plus 30 minutes chilling
`MAKE AHEAD` `VEGETARIAN`

WHY THIS RECIPE WORKS Sipping a steaming cup of masala chai (meaning "spiced tea" in Hindi) is a visceral pleasure. To coax out our spices' flavor, we crushed and then simmered them, plus some brown sugar, in water for a full 10 minutes before adding the tea leaves. The resulting concentrate was sweet, spiced, and bracing enough to stand up to plenty of milk. A boldly flavored tea such as Assam is ideal for this recipe; alternatively, use Irish or English breakfast tea. If desired, crush the spices using a mortar and pestle. This recipe makes enough concentrate for multiple masala chais. To make multiple masala chais at once, proportionally scale up the amounts of concentrate and milk called for in step 3.

MASALA CHAI CONCENTRATE
3 (2-inch) cinnamon sticks
1 star anise pod
15 green cardamom pods
2 teaspoons whole cloves
¾ teaspoon black peppercorns
5 cups water
¼ cup (1¾ ounces) packed brown sugar
1 tablespoon finely chopped fresh ginger
Pinch table salt
3 tablespoons loose black tea

MASALA CHAI
½–⅔ cup Masala Chai Concentrate
⅓–½ cup milk

1. FOR THE MASALA CHAI CONCENTRATE Place cinnamon sticks and star anise on cutting board. Using bottom of heavy skillet, press down firmly until spices are coarsely crushed. Transfer to medium saucepan. Crush cardamom pods, cloves, and peppercorns and add to saucepan. Toast spices over medium heat, stirring frequently, until fragrant, 1 to 2 minutes.

2. Add water, sugar, ginger, and salt and bring to boil. Cover saucepan, reduce heat, and simmer mixture for 10 minutes. Stir in tea, cover, and simmer for 10 minutes. Remove from heat and let tea and spices steep for 10 minutes. Strain mixture through fine-mesh strainer. Let cool completely and refrigerate for up to 1 week. Stir before using.

3A. FOR HOT MASALA CHAI Stir ½ cup concentrate and ½ cup milk together in saucepan and heat to desired temperature or combine in mug and heat in microwave.

3B. FOR ICED MASALA CHAI Pour ⅔ cup concentrate and ⅓ cup milk over ice in glass; stir to combine.

NOTES FROM THE TEST KITCHEN

TOASTING SPICES
We've long advocated for blooming herbs and spices in oil or fat before adding liquid, a technique that unlocks their potential by encouraging the release of flavor compounds. But the flavor of many spices can also be enhanced by dry-roasting them without any added fat, as we call for in our recipe for Masala Chai. The flavors of the cinnamon, star anise, cardamom, cloves, and peppercorns used in the chai are drawn out and intensified through exposure to heat, giving the chai a fuller, rounder profile. Crushing the whole spices before simmering them in water also helps them release their flavors. When toasting spices, it's important to stir them or shake the pan occasionally to prevent scorching. You'll know your spices are toasty and flavorful when they start to release a fragrant aroma, which usually takes just a minute or two.

brunch

■ MAKE AHEAD ■ VEGETARIAN
Photo: Gravlax

Broccoli and Feta Frittata

Serves 4 to 6 | **Total Time** 40 minutes

`MAKE AHEAD` `VEGETARIAN`

WHY THIS RECIPE WORKS Frittatas offer an easy route to a satisfying brunch, and ours is brimming with vegetables and oozy bites of cheese. For a vegetable filling that remained suspended in the eggs, we chopped broccoli florets into small pieces before browning it. Whisking milk into the eggs kept their proteins from binding too tightly and turning the eggs rubbery when cooked. Stirring and scraping the mixture as it cooked distributed the curds evenly for a tender frittata. As soon as the skillet was filled with partially cooked curds, we smoothed out the surface and transferred the frittata to the gentler heat of the oven to finish it off. This recipe requires a 12-inch ovensafe nonstick skillet. When the spatula leaves a trail in the skillet that fills in slowly, it's time to transfer the pan to the oven. If it fills in quickly, not enough egg has coagulated and the frittata will contain pockets of undercooked egg. The frittata can be served warm or at room temperature.

Broccoli and Feta Frittata

12 large eggs

⅓ cup whole milk

¾ teaspoon table salt, divided

1 tablespoon extra-virgin olive oil

12 ounces broccoli florets, cut into ½-inch pieces (4 cups)

Pinch red pepper flakes

3 tablespoons water

½ teaspoon grated lemon zest plus ½ teaspoon juice

4 ounces feta cheese, crumbled into ½-inch pieces (1 cup)

1. Adjust oven rack to middle position and heat oven to 350 degrees. Whisk eggs, milk, and ½ teaspoon salt in bowl until well combined.

2. Heat oil in 12-inch ovensafe nonstick skillet over medium-high heat until shimmering. Add broccoli, pepper flakes, and remaining ¼ teaspoon salt; cook, stirring frequently, until broccoli is crisp-tender and spotty brown, 7 to 9 minutes. Add water and lemon zest and juice; continue to cook, stirring constantly, until broccoli is just tender and no water remains in skillet, about 1 minute.

3. Add feta and egg mixture and cook, using rubber spatula to stir and scrape bottom of skillet until large curds form and spatula leaves trail through eggs but eggs are still very wet, about 30 seconds. Smooth curds into even layer and cook, without stirring, for 30 seconds. Transfer skillet to oven and bake until frittata is slightly puffy and surface bounces back when lightly pressed, 6 to 9 minutes. Using rubber spatula, loosen frittata from skillet and transfer to cutting board. Let stand for 5 minutes before slicing and serving. (Frittata can be refrigerated for up to 2 days.)

Spicy Chilaquiles with Fried Eggs

Serves 4 | **Total Time** 1½ hours `VEGETARIAN`

WHY THIS RECIPE WORKS This Mexican breakfast food began as a way to use up leftover tortillas and sauce: The tortillas were lightly fried, simmered in the sauce, and served with fried eggs on top. Here, we baked our tortillas with a little oil to ensure that they crisped up and then stirred them into a quick but deeply aromatic chile sauce flavored with chili powder and chipotle in adobo just before serving. To fry enough eggs for four people at once, we developed a simple trick: We cracked eight eggs into two small bowls so we could add them to the pan all at once, guaranteeing that they cooked at the same rate. A final sprinkle of tangy queso fresco and fresh cilantro rounded out the dish nicely. Proper timing is crucial so that the sauced tortillas don't sit for too long and soften up; make sure to coat the crisped tortillas in the sauce just as the eggs finish cooking. For the best texture, we prefer to use 100 percent corn tortillas in this recipe. To make this dish vegetarian, use vegetable broth.

- 16 (6-inch) corn tortillas, cut into 8 wedges
- 6 tablespoons plus 2 teaspoons extra-virgin olive oil, divided
- ¼ teaspoon table salt
- 1 onion, chopped fine
- 2 tablespoons chili powder
- 3 garlic cloves, minced
- 1 teaspoon minced canned chipotle chile in adobo sauce
- 2 (8-ounce) cans tomato sauce
- 1½ cups vegetable or chicken broth
- 8 large eggs
- 1 tablespoon unsalted butter, cut into 4 pieces
- 4 ounces queso fresco, crumbled (1 cup)
- 2 tablespoons chopped fresh cilantro

1. Adjust oven racks to upper-middle and lower-middle positions and heat oven to 425 degrees. Spread tortillas evenly over 2 rimmed baking sheets. Drizzle each sheet with 2 tablespoons oil, sprinkle with salt, and toss until evenly coated. Bake, stirring occasionally, until tortillas are golden brown and crispy, 15 to 20 minutes, switching sheets halfway through baking.

2. Heat 2 tablespoons oil in Dutch oven over medium heat until shimmering. Add onion and cook until softened, about 5 minutes. Stir in chili powder, garlic, and chipotle and cook

Spicy Chilaquiles with Fried Eggs

until fragrant, about 30 seconds. Add tomato sauce and broth, bring to simmer, and cook, stirring occasionally, until flavors meld, about 10 minutes. Remove pot from heat.

3. Heat remaining 2 teaspoons oil in 12- or 14-inch nonstick skillet over low heat for 5 minutes. Meanwhile, crack eggs into 2 small bowls (4 eggs per bowl) and season with salt and pepper.

4. Increase heat to medium-high and heat until oil is shimmering. Add butter and quickly swirl to coat skillet. Working quickly, pour 1 bowl of eggs in 1 side of skillet and second bowl of eggs in other side. Cover and cook for 2 minutes.

5. Remove skillet from heat and let stand, covered, about 2 minutes for runny yolks (white around edge of yolk will be barely opaque), about 3 minutes for soft but set yolks, and about 4 minutes for medium-set yolks.

6. While eggs finish cooking, return sauce to brief simmer over medium-high heat. Off heat, stir in tortillas, cover, and let sit until tortillas have softened slightly, 2 to 5 minutes. Divide tortilla mixture among individual plates and sprinkle with queso fresco. Slide eggs on top, sprinkle with cilantro, and serve immediately.

FRYING MULTIPLE EGGS AT ONCE

1. While skillet heats, crack eggs into 2 small bowls.

2. Working quickly, pour 1 bowl of eggs in 1 side of skillet and second bowl of eggs in other side. Cover skillet and cook for 2 minutes.

Green Shakshuka

24-Hour "Omelet"

Green Shakshuka

Serves 4 | **Total Time** 50 minutes `VEGETARIAN`

WHY THIS RECIPE WORKS This twist on shakshuka swaps out the traditional long-cooked red sauce for a vibrant sauce loaded with greens. For the greens, we settled on savory Swiss chard and easy-to-prep baby spinach. We cooked a cup of sliced chard stems (any more and their vegetal flavors overwhelmed the dish) with onion to create an aromatic base. For spices, citrusy coriander and mild Aleppo pepper allowed the greens' flavors to stay center stage. Cooking the shakshuka in a Dutch oven rather than a skillet allowed us to wilt a large volume of greens easily. We blended a cup of the greens mixture with broth to give the sauce a creamy, cohesive texture and then added frozen peas for pops of sweetness. To finish, we poached eight eggs directly in the sauce, covering the pot to contain the heat for even cooking. If you can't find Aleppo pepper, you can substitute ⅛ teaspoon of paprika and ⅛ teaspoon of finely chopped red pepper flakes. The Dutch oven will seem crowded at first but the greens will wilt down. Avoid removing the lid during the first 5 minutes of cooking in step 3; it will increase the total cooking time of the eggs. Serve with toasted pita or crusty bread to mop up the sauce.

2	pounds Swiss chard, stems removed and reserved, leaves chopped
¼	cup extra-virgin olive oil, divided
1	large onion, chopped fine
¾	teaspoon table salt
4	garlic cloves, minced
2	teaspoons ground coriander
11	ounces (11 cups) baby spinach, chopped
½	cup vegetable broth
1	cup frozen peas
1½	tablespoons lemon juice
8	large eggs
½	teaspoon ground dried Aleppo pepper
2	ounces feta cheese, crumbled (½ cup)
2	tablespoons chopped fresh dill
2	tablespoons chopped fresh mint

1. Slice chard stems thin to yield 1 cup; discard remaining stems or reserve for another use. Heat 2 tablespoons oil in Dutch oven over medium heat until shimmering. Add chard stems, onion, and salt and cook until vegetables are softened and lightly browned, 5 to 7 minutes. Stir in garlic and coriander and cook until fragrant, about 1 minute.

2. Add spinach and chard leaves. Increase heat to medium-high, cover, and cook, stirring occasionally, until wilted but still bright green, 3 to 5 minutes. Off heat, transfer 1 cup chard mixture to blender. Add broth and process until smooth, about 45 seconds, scraping down sides of blender jar as needed. Stir peas, lemon juice, and pureed chard mixture into pot.

3. Make 4 shallow indentations (about 2 inches wide) in surface of greens using back of spoon. Crack 2 eggs into each indentation, sprinkle with Aleppo pepper, and season with salt. Cover and cook over medium-low heat until edges of egg whites are just set, 5 to 10 minutes. Off heat, let sit, covered, until whites are fully set and yolks are still runny, 2 to 4 minutes. Sprinkle with feta, dill, and mint and drizzle with remaining 2 tablespoons oil. Serve immediately.

24-Hour "Omelet"

Serves 6 to 8 MAKE AHEAD VEGETARIAN
Total Time 1½ hours, plus 8 hours chilling

WHY THIS RECIPE WORKS Despite its name, this "omelet" is nothing like the filling-stuffed egg dish you expect at brunch. This cheesy, puffed casserole consists of a rich custard, bread, and cheese and yields a melt-in-your-mouth texture that rivals even the fluffiest scrambled eggs. While similar to a strata, a 24-hour omelet is more about the eggs than the bread. To keep the eggs' flavor at the fore, we prepared a milk-based custard. Buttered hearty white sandwich bread, cut into bite-size pieces and layered with cheddar cheese in a baking dish, absorbed and melded with the custard but possessed just enough structure not to completely dissolve. Grated onion, dry mustard, and hot sauce added just enough complexity to the creamy eggs. Refrigerating the assembled omelet overnight melded the flavors and saturated the bread, so all we had to do before brunch was bake it.

3 tablespoons unsalted butter, softened
10 slices hearty white sandwich bread
12 ounces cheddar cheese, shredded (3 cups)
3 cups whole milk
8 large eggs
1 small onion, grated
1 teaspoon table salt
1 teaspoon dry mustard
½ teaspoon hot sauce
½ teaspoon pepper

1. Grease 13 by 9-inch baking dish. Spread butter evenly over 1 side of bread slices, then cut bread into 1-inch pieces. Scatter half of bread evenly in prepared dish and sprinkle with half of cheddar. Repeat with remaining bread and cheddar.

2. Whisk milk, eggs, onion, salt, mustard, hot sauce, and pepper in bowl until well combined. Pour egg mixture evenly over bread and lightly press on bread to submerge. Wrap dish tightly in plastic wrap and refrigerate for at least 8 hours. (Omelet can be refrigerated for up to 24 hours.)

3. Adjust oven rack to middle position and heat oven to 350 degrees. Unwrap casserole and bake until puffed and golden, about 1 hour. Serve immediately.

Savory Bread Pudding with Turkey Sausage and Kale

Serves 4 to 6 | **Total Time** 2 hours

WHY THIS RECIPE WORKS Studded with pieces of savory sausage and bright kale, this tender bread pudding is perfect for a relaxed brunch at home. To make sure this casserole came out rich but not overbearing, we chose leaner turkey sausage instead of pork and banned soggy bread by toasting torn baguette pieces, enriching their flavor and ensuring that they would hold their shape. Microwaving the kale with aromatics and oil eliminated excess water and added more savory depth. Our simple custard used 3 parts cream to 2 parts milk for measured richness, and we stabilized it against curdling by using just egg yolks rather than whole eggs. After layering the custard-soaked bread and kale with the sausage, we baked our bread pudding covered at first to set the filling and then uncovered for the last 20 minutes for some appealing browning.

1 (18- to 20-inch) baguette, torn or cut into 1-inch pieces (10 cups)
1 pound kale, stemmed and chopped
4 shallots, sliced thin
2 garlic cloves, minced
1 teaspoon extra-virgin olive oil
3 cups heavy cream
2 cups whole milk
8 large egg yolks
1 tablespoon Dijon mustard
1 pound turkey sausage, casings removed
¼ cup grated Parmesan cheese
2 tablespoons minced fresh chives

1. Adjust oven rack to middle position and heat oven to 450 degrees. Arrange bread in even layer in 13 by 9-inch baking dish. Bake, stirring occasionally, until bread is crisp and browned, about 12 minutes; let cool for 10 minutes. Reduce oven temperature to 400 degrees.

2. Meanwhile, combine kale, shallots, garlic, and oil in bowl and microwave, stirring occasionally, until kale is wilted, about 5 minutes. Wrap kale mixture in clean dish towel and wring tightly to squeeze out as much liquid as possible.

3. Whisk cream, milk, egg yolks, and mustard together in large bowl. Stir in bread and kale mixture until well combined.

4. Spray now-empty baking dish with vegetable oil spray. Pour half of bread mixture into prepared dish. Crumble half of sausage into ½-inch pieces over top. Top with remaining bread mixture and remaining sausage. Sprinkle with Parmesan.

5. Cover tightly with greased aluminum foil and bake for 45 minutes. Uncover and continue to bake until custard is just set and top is browned, about 20 minutes longer.

6. Remove dish from oven and let cool for 10 minutes. Sprinkle with chives before serving.

Leek and Goat Cheese Quiche

Serves 6 to 8 **MAKE AHEAD** **VEGETARIAN**
Total Time 3¼ hours, plus 1 hour cooling

WHY THIS RECIPE WORKS In this appealing quiche, the tender, buttery crust embraces an eggy custard that's rich with sweet, oniony leeks and tangy goat cheese. To prevent the crust from sogging out under the wet filling, we parbaked it before adding the custard. To avoid spillage, we set the parbaked crust in the oven before pouring the custard into the pastry. Baking temperature was important: 350 degrees was low enough to set the custard gently, yet hot enough to brown the top without drying out the filling. For perfectly baked quiche every time, pull it out of the oven when it is still slightly soft, which allows it to set up properly as it cools. Be sure to add the custard to the parbaked crust while the crust is still warm so that the quiche will bake evenly. You can substitute thyme, parsley, or marjoram for the chives. You can also substitute store-bought pie crust.

1 recipe Foolproof All-Butter Single-Crust Pie Dough (page 388)
2 tablespoons unsalted butter
1 pound leeks, white and light green parts only, chopped fine and washed thoroughly
5 large eggs
2 cups half-and-half
¼ teaspoon table salt
¼ teaspoon pepper
4 ounces goat cheese, crumbled (1 cup)
1 tablespoon minced fresh chives

1. Roll dough into 12-inch circle on well-floured counter. Roll dough loosely around rolling pin and gently unroll it onto 9-inch pie plate, letting excess dough hang over edge. Ease dough into plate by gently lifting edge of dough with your hand while pressing into plate bottom with your other hand. Trim overhang to ½ inch. Tuck overhang under itself; folded edge should be flush with edge of plate. Crimp dough evenly around edge of plate using your fingers. Wrap dough-lined plate loosely in plastic and refrigerate until dough is firm, about 30 minutes.

2. Adjust oven rack to middle position and heat oven to 400 degrees. Line chilled pie crust with double layer of aluminum foil, covering edges to prevent burning, and fill with pie weights. Bake until pie dough looks dry and is pale in color, 25 to 30 minutes.

3. Adjust oven rack to lower-middle position and reduce oven temperature to 350 degrees. Melt butter in 10-inch skillet over medium-high heat. Add leeks and cook until softened, about 6 minutes; transfer to bowl. Whisk eggs, half-and-half, salt, and pepper into bowl with leeks. Stir in goat cheese.

4. Place warm pie shell on rimmed baking sheet and place in oven. Carefully pour egg mixture into warm shell until it reaches about ½ inch from top edge of crust (you may have extra egg mixture).

5. Bake quiche until top is lightly browned, center is set but soft, and knife inserted about 1 inch from edge comes out clean, 40 to 50 minutes. Let quiche cool for at least 1 hour. Sprinkle with chives and serve warm. (Baked quiche can be refrigerated for up to 2 days, although crust will be less crisp. To reheat, bake in 400-degree oven for 10 to 15 minutes until hot throughout.)

Spinach and Feta Quiche
Omit leeks and substitute crumbled feta for goat cheese. Stir one 10-ounce package frozen chopped spinach, thawed and squeezed dry, into eggs with cheese. Omit chives.

Shrimp Skewers with Cheesy Grits

4½ cups chicken or vegetable broth
1½ cups old-fashioned grits
¾ cup whole milk
3 scallions, white parts minced, green parts sliced thin on bias, divided
2 garlic cloves, minced
½ teaspoon plus ⅛ teaspoon table salt, divided
1½ pounds jumbo shrimp (16 to 20 per pound), peeled and deveined
4 tablespoons unsalted butter, melted, divided
2 teaspoons chili powder, divided
¼ teaspoon pepper
6 ounces sharp cheddar cheese, shredded (1½ cups)
1 teaspoon chipotle chile powder
Lime wedges

1. Adjust oven rack to middle position and heat oven to 350 degrees. Spray 13 by 9-inch baking dish with vegetable oil spray. Combine broth, grits, milk, scallion whites, garlic, and ¼ teaspoon salt in prepared dish, cover tightly with aluminum foil, and bake until grits are tender, 50 minutes to 1¼ hours.

2. Toss shrimp with 1 tablespoon melted butter, 1 teaspoon chili powder, pepper, and ¼ teaspoon salt. Working with 1 shrimp at a time, thread tail onto one 12-inch skewer, and head onto second 12-inch skewer. Repeat with remaining shrimp, alternating direction of heads and tails, packing 6 to 8 shrimp tightly onto each pair of skewers.

3. Remove grits from oven, uncover, and increase oven temperature to 450 degrees. Stir cheddar into grits and season with salt and pepper to taste. Lay shrimp skewers widthwise across baking dish so that shrimp hover over grits. Continue to bake grits and shrimp until shrimp are opaque throughout and grits have thickened slightly, about 10 minutes.

4. Meanwhile, microwave remaining 3 tablespoons melted butter, remaining 1 teaspoon chili powder, remaining ⅛ teaspoon salt, and chipotle chile powder until fragrant, about 20 seconds.

5. Carefully remove dish from oven and transfer shrimp skewers to plate. Stir grits thoroughly, then portion into serving bowls. Remove shrimp from skewers and place on top of grits. Drizzle with spiced butter, sprinkle with scallion greens, and serve with lime wedges.

Shrimp Skewers with Cheesy Grits

Serves 4 to 6 | **Total Time** 1½ hours

WHY THIS RECIPE WORKS The much-loved combination of Lowcountry-style shrimp and creamy grits doesn't immediately conjure up images of a casserole dish, but this vessel is remarkably useful in turning out a hands-off version of this comfort classic. The grits bake in the casserole while rows of seasoned shrimp suspended on skewers roast above. Baking the grits until tender before adding cheddar cheese kept the cheese from breaking down and becoming oily. At the point when we added our cheese, we also laid our skewered shrimp (tossed with melted butter and chili powder) on top. After 10 minutes in the oven, the shrimp emerged tender and spicy above the now-thickened grits. To give our shrimp a sauce, we created a simple, fragrant mixture of butter, chili powder, and smoky chipotle chile powder to drizzle over our meal and tie it together. The grits' cooking time in step 1 will depend on the brand of grits. You will need eight 12-inch metal or bamboo skewers for this recipe.

Gravlax

1. Combine sugar and salt. Place salmon, skin side down, in 13 by 9-inch glass baking dish. Drizzle with brandy, making sure to cover entire surface. Rub salmon evenly with sugar mixture, pressing firmly on mixture to adhere. Cover with dill, pressing firmly to adhere.

2. Cover salmon loosely with plastic wrap, top with square baking dish, and weight down with several large, heavy cans. Refrigerate until salmon feels firm, about 3 days, basting salmon with liquid released into baking dish once a day. (Gravlax, prepared through step 2, can be wrapped tightly in plastic wrap and refrigerated for up to 1 week.)

3. Scrape dill off salmon. Remove fillet from dish and pat dry with paper towels. Slice salmon crosswise on bias into very thin pieces and serve.

Carrot and Smoked Salmon Salad

Serves 4 to 6 | **Total Time** 1¼ hours

WHY THIS RECIPE WORKS A stunning addition to any spread, this carrot salad incorporates two classic brunch ingredients—buttery smoked salmon and sweet-tart grapefruit—for a playful mix of textures, tones, and flavors. We chose carrots with their greens attached because they taste sweeter than bagged carrots and the feathery, slightly bitter greens could be used as a garnish. For variety, we quick-pickled some of the carrots, shaved into ribbons, for a sweet and punchy bite. The rest we roasted until tender and caramelized. Tossing the roasted carrots with a Dijon-dill vinaigrette while slightly warm allowed them to absorb a lot of flavor. Finally, we added raw endive for its crisp bitterness and color contrast, and a sprinkle of chopped carrot greens. If you can't find carrots with the greens attached, you can substitute parsley for the carrot greens. You should have about 1½ pounds of carrots after trimming the greens.

2   pounds carrots with greens attached, divided, ¼ cup greens chopped
5   tablespoons cider vinegar, divided
1   tablespoon sugar
⅛   teaspoon plus ¾ teaspoon table salt, divided
¼   cup extra-virgin olive oil, divided
¼   teaspoon pepper
1   red grapefruit
2   tablespoons chopped fresh dill
2   teaspoons Dijon mustard
2   heads Belgian endive (4 ounces each), halved, cored, and sliced ½ inch thick
8   ounces smoked salmon

Gravlax

Serves 8 to 10 **MAKE AHEAD**
Total Time 25 minutes, plus 3 days salting

WHY THIS RECIPE WORKS Homemade gravlax sounds like it would require an extravagant amount of work, but in fact it's a supereasy and fun project that is a natural choice for making ahead. For evenly moist, tender, and consistently salted gravlax, we soaked the salmon in brandy; coated it in brown sugar, salt, and dill; and then pressed and refrigerated it. The salt drew liquid from the fish and cured it, while the brown sugar countered the harshness of the salt and added deep flavor. The brandy helped the rub adhere and added flavor. We basted the fish just once a day to keep it moist. The gravlax is ready when the fish is no longer translucent and its flesh is firm, with no give.

⅓   cup packed light brown sugar
¼   cup kosher salt
1   (1-pound) skin-on salmon fillet
3   tablespoons brandy
1   cup coarsely chopped fresh dill

1. Adjust oven rack to lowest position and heat oven to 450 degrees. Peel and shave 4 ounces carrots into thin ribbons with vegetable peeler; set aside. Peel and slice remaining carrots on bias ¼ inch thick; set aside.

2. Microwave ¼ cup vinegar, sugar, and ⅛ teaspoon salt in medium bowl until simmering, 1 to 2 minutes. Stir in shaved carrots and let sit, stirring occasionally, for 45 minutes. (Drained pickled carrots can be refrigerated for up to 5 days.)

3. Toss sliced carrots, 1 tablespoon oil, pepper, and ½ teaspoon salt together in bowl to coat. Spread carrots in single layer on rimmed baking sheet, cut side down. Roast until tender and bottoms are well browned, 15 to 25 minutes. Let cool slightly, about 15 minutes.

4. Meanwhile, cut away peel and pith from grapefruit. Quarter grapefruit, then slice crosswise into ¼-inch-thick pieces.

5. Whisk dill, mustard, remaining 1 tablespoon vinegar, and remaining ¼ teaspoon salt together in large bowl. Whisking constantly, slowly drizzle in remaining 3 tablespoons oil until emulsified. Add endive, carrot greens, roasted carrots, pickled carrots, and grapefruit and toss to combine; season with salt and pepper to taste. Arrange salmon around edge of serving platter, then transfer salad to center of platter. Serve.

Carrot and Smoked Salmon Salad

Mango, Orange, and Jicama Salad

Serves 4 to 6 VEGETARIAN
Total Time 35 minutes, plus 20 minutes cooling

WHY THIS RECIPE WORKS A tropical fruit salad is just the thing to bring cheer to the winter months. Here, we paired sunny mangos and oranges with a sweet-and-spicy lime syrup and jicama, a mild, crisp vegetable common in Mexico. Softening the jicama slightly in the warm syrup allowed the vegetable to add texture to the salad without masking the bright fruit flavor. Our equally bright variation substituted chayote, a member of the gourd family, for the jicama; sweet papayas for the mangos; and delicate clementines for the oranges. Allow the syrup to cool before pouring it over the fruit.

- 3 tablespoons sugar
- ¼ teaspoon grated lime zest plus 3 tablespoons juice (2 limes)
- ¼ teaspoon red pepper flakes
  Pinch table salt
- 12 ounces jicama, peeled and cut into ¼-inch dice
- 2 oranges
- 2 mangos, peeled, pitted, and cut into ½-inch dice

1. Bring sugar, lime zest and juice, pepper flakes, and salt to simmer in small saucepan over medium heat, stirring constantly, until sugar is dissolved, 1 to 2 minutes. Remove pan from heat, stir in jicama, and let syrup cool for 20 minutes.

2. Meanwhile, cut away peel and pith from oranges. Slice into ½-inch-thick rounds, then cut rounds into ½-inch pieces. Place oranges and mangos in large bowl.

3. When syrup is cool, pour over oranges and mangos and toss to combine. Refrigerate for 15 minutes before serving.

Papaya, Clementine, and Chayote Salad

Chayote, also called mirliton, is often sold with other tropical fruits. If you can't find chayote, use jicama instead. Substitute 2 teaspoons grated fresh ginger for red pepper flakes; 1 chayote, peeled, halved, pitted, and cut into ¼-inch dice, for jicama; 3 clementines, peeled and each segment cut into 3 pieces, for oranges; and 2 large papayas, peeled, seeded, and cut into ½-inch dice, for mangos.

Home Fries

Serves 6 to 8 | **Total Time** 1 hour VEGETARIAN

WHY THIS RECIPE WORKS Rather than prepare batch after batch of skillet-fried potatoes, we moved our cooking to a rimmed baking sheet, which allowed us to prepare several pounds of potatoes in one go. Parboiling russets with a touch of baking soda roughed up their exteriors, turning them starchy for speedy browning. Tossing the drained potatoes with salt over low heat further released that exterior starch so when the spuds hit the baking sheet—preheated in a superhot oven to mimic the sear of a skillet—they quickly developed a browned crust surrounding light, fluffy interiors. Because all good home fries are served with sweet bites of onion stirred in, we added diced onions to the center of the pan partway through roasting. Don't skip the baking soda here—it's critical for home fries with just the right crispy texture.

3½ pounds russet potatoes, peeled and cut into ¾-inch pieces
½ teaspoon baking soda
3 tablespoons unsalted butter, cut into 12 pieces
2 teaspoons kosher salt, divided
Pinch cayenne pepper
3 tablespoons vegetable oil, divided
2 onions, cut into ½-inch pieces
3 tablespoons minced chives

1. Adjust oven rack to lowest position, place rimmed baking sheet on rack, and heat oven to 500 degrees.

2. Bring 2½ quarts water to boil in Dutch oven over high heat. Add potatoes and baking soda. Return to boil and cook for 1 minute. Drain potatoes. Return potatoes to pot and place over low heat. Cook, shaking pot occasionally, until any surface moisture has evaporated, about 2 minutes. Off heat, add butter, 1½ teaspoons salt, and cayenne; using rubber spatula, mix until potatoes are coated with thick, starchy paste, about 30 seconds.

3. Remove sheet from oven and drizzle with 2 tablespoons oil. Transfer potatoes to sheet and spread into even layer. Roast for 15 minutes. While potatoes roast, combine onions, remaining ½ teaspoon salt, and remaining 1 tablespoon oil in bowl.

4. Remove sheet from oven. Using thin, sharp metal spatula, scrape and turn potatoes. Clear about 8 by 5-inch space in center of sheet and add onion mixture. Roast for 15 minutes.

5. Scrape and turn again, mixing onions into potatoes. Continue to roast until potatoes are well browned and onions are softened and beginning to brown, 5 to 10 minutes longer. Stir in chives and season with salt and pepper to taste. Serve immediately.

Sheet-Pan Hash Browns

Serves 4 to 6 | **Total Time** 1¼ hours VEGETARIAN

WHY THIS RECIPE WORKS As with our home fries, we enlisted a rimmed baking sheet to make one batch of hash browns that could serve up to six people. Starchy potatoes made for chewy hash browns, so to keep them crispy and creamy, we used only moderately starchy Yukon Gold potatoes and soaked the shreds to remove excess starch before wringing them out to eliminate excess moisture. To avoid a stuck-on mess, we greased the baking sheet with vegetable oil spray. Packing the shreds down on the sheet flattened them into a potato cake, not hash browns, so we lightly distributed the shreds in an even layer on the sheet to keep their integrity. Instead of trying to flip the whole hash at once, we simply flipped sections of the hash browns with a metal spatula and returned the sheet to the oven for a crispy result. We prefer to use the shredding disk of a food processor to shred the potatoes, but you can also use the large holes of a box grater.

3 pounds Yukon Gold potatoes, unpeeled
6 tablespoons extra-virgin olive oil
1 teaspoon table salt
¼ teaspoon pepper

1. Adjust oven rack to middle position and heat oven to 450 degrees. Fit food processor with shredding disk. Halve or quarter potatoes as needed to fit through processor hopper, then shred potatoes. Transfer potatoes to large bowl and cover with cold water. Let sit for 5 minutes.

2. One handful at a time, lift potatoes out of water and transfer to colander; discard water. Rinse and dry bowl.

3. Place one-quarter of shredded potatoes in center of clean dish towel. Gather ends of towel and twist tightly to wring out excess moisture from potatoes. Transfer dried potatoes to now-empty bowl. Repeat 3 more times with remaining potatoes.

4. Add oil, salt, and pepper to potatoes and toss to combine. Lightly spray 16 by 11-inch rimmed baking sheet with vegetable oil spray. Distribute potatoes in even layer on sheet, but do not pack down. Bake until top of potatoes is spotty brown, 32 to 35 minutes.

5. Remove sheet from oven. Flip hash browns with metal spatula. Return sheet to oven and continue to bake until deep golden brown on top, 6 to 8 minutes longer. Season with salt and pepper to taste. Serve.

Oven-Fried Bacon

Serves 4 to 6 | **Total Time** 30 minutes

WHY THIS RECIPE WORKS This bacon-making method is a brunch game changer. Baking the bacon in the oven eliminates the need to cook (and monitor) multiple batches on the stovetop and the greasy splatter that comes with it. The sides of a broad rimmed baking sheet proved just high enough to contain the rendered fat while promoting even exposure to heat. The steady blast from the oven cooked the bacon so evenly that, rather than flipping the strips, we simply rotated the pan at the halfway mark. A large rimmed baking sheet is important here to contain the rendered bacon fat. This recipe is easy to double: Simply double the amount of bacon and use two rimmed baking sheets, rotating and switching their oven positions once halfway through cooking. You can use thin- or thick-cut bacon here, though the cooking times will vary.

12 slices bacon

Adjust oven rack to middle position and heat oven to 400 degrees. Arrange bacon on rimmed baking sheet. Cook until fat begins to render, 5 to 6 minutes; rotate sheet. Continue cooking until bacon is crispy and brown, 5 to 6 minutes for thin-cut bacon or 8 to 10 minutes for thick-cut bacon. Transfer bacon to paper towel–lined plate, drain, and serve.

Maple-Glazed Oven-Fried Bacon

After roasting, pour off most of grease and drizzle maple syrup over each strip (¼ cup total). Return sheet to oven and continue cooking for 2 to 3 minutes, or until maple syrup begins to bubble. Transfer with tongs to paper towel–lined plate, drain, and serve.

Classic Buttermilk Pancakes

Serves 4 to 6 VEGETARIAN
Total Time 40 minutes

WHY THIS RECIPE WORKS A stack of fluffy pancakes is a great starting place for brunch, and these have a distinct sweet tang and an open, airy texture. Buttermilk is a must—it contributes to the pancakes' flavor and creates pancakes with better texture. For even more tang, we whisked in sour cream. To keep our pancakes as light and fluffy as possible, we avoided overmixing the batter, which would overdevelop the gluten and make the pancakes tough, and let the batter rest

Sheet-Pan Hash Browns

Oven-Fried Bacon

briefly to relax the gluten before portioning it into a hot skillet. Keep the pancakes in a warm oven while you finish the remaining batches. Getting the skillet hot enough before making the pancakes is key. An electric griddle set to 350 degrees can also be used to cook the pancakes.

- 2 cups (10 ounces) all-purpose flour
- 2 tablespoons sugar
- 1 teaspoon baking powder
- ½ teaspoon baking soda
- ½ teaspoon table salt
- 2 cups buttermilk
- ¼ cup sour cream
- 2 large eggs
- 3 tablespoons unsalted butter, melted and cooled slightly
- 1–2 teaspoons vegetable oil

1. Adjust oven rack to middle position and heat oven to 200 degrees. Set wire rack in rimmed baking sheet and place in oven.

2. Whisk flour, sugar, baking powder, baking soda, and salt together in large bowl. In separate bowl, whisk buttermilk, sour cream, eggs, and melted butter together. Make well in center of dry ingredients and pour in wet ingredients; gently stir until just combined (batter should be lumpy with few streaks of flour). Do not overmix. Let batter stand for 10 minutes before cooking.

3. Heat 1 teaspoon oil in 12-inch nonstick skillet over medium heat until shimmering. Using paper towels, carefully wipe out oil, leaving thin film on bottom and sides of pan.

4. Using ¼-cup measure, portion batter into pan in 4 places. Cook until edges are set, first side is golden brown, and bubbles on surface are just beginning to break, 2 to 3 minutes. Using thin, wide spatula, flip pancakes and continue to cook until second side is golden brown, 1 to 2 minutes. Transfer to wire rack in oven and repeat with remaining batter, using remaining oil as necessary. Serve.

Blueberry Buttermilk Pancakes
Sprinkle 1 tablespoon fresh blueberries over each pancake before flipping. (If using frozen berries, thaw and rinse berries and spread them out on paper towels to dry.)

Graham Buttermilk Pancakes
Substitute 1 cup graham cracker crumbs plus 2 tablespoons cornmeal for 1 cup flour.

Classic Buttermilk Pancakes

NOTES FROM THE TEST KITCHEN

MORE GREAT BRUNCH RECIPES

Syrups and Other Toppings

Butter-Pecan Maple Syrup

Makes about 2 cups | **Total Time** 10 minutes

1½ cups maple syrup
2 tablespoons unsalted butter
½ cup pecans, toasted and chopped
¼ teaspoon vanilla extract
Pinch table salt

Simmer all ingredients in small saucepan over medium-low heat until slightly thickened, about 5 minutes.

Apple-Cinnamon Maple Syrup

Makes about 1¾ cups | **Total Time** 10 minutes

1½ cups maple syrup
⅓ cup apple jelly
¼ teaspoon ground cinnamon
Pinch table salt

Simmer all ingredients in small saucepan over medium-low heat until slightly thickened, 5 to 7 minutes.

Berry Maple Syrup

Makes about 1¾ cups | **Total Time** 15 minutes

½ cup frozen blueberries, strawberries, or raspberries
1½ cups maple syrup
¼ teaspoon grated lemon zest
Pinch table salt

Mash berries in small saucepan over medium heat until moisture has evaporated, about 5 minutes. Whisk in maple syrup, lemon zest, and salt; reduce heat to medium-low and cook until slightly thickened, 5 to 7 minutes.

Apple-Cranberry Topping

Makes 2½ to 3 cups | **Total Time** 10 minutes

3 Golden Delicious apples, peeled, halved, and cored
¼ cup dried cranberries
1 tablespoon sugar
1 teaspoon cornstarch
Pinch table salt
Pinch ground nutmeg

Cut apples into ¼-inch pieces. Combine apples, cranberries, sugar, cornstarch, salt, and nutmeg in bowl and microwave until fruits are softened but not mushy and juices are slightly thickened, 4 to 6 minutes, stirring once halfway through microwaving. Remove from microwave and stir.

Maple Butter

Makes ¼ cup | **Total Time** 5 minutes

4 tablespoons unsalted butter, softened
1 tablespoon maple syrup
¼ teaspoon table salt

Whisk butter, maple syrup, and salt in bowl until combined. (Maple butter can be refrigerated, covered, for up to 1 week.)

NOTES FROM THE TEST KITCHEN

SYRUP DISPENSERS

Keeping your syrup in a dispenser reduces mess when pouring the sweet stuff over pancakes, waffles, and French toast. Typically designed as a small pitcher with a covered spout operated by a lever, a good syrup dispenser allows you to easily pour controlled amounts without undue dripping. Of the models we tested, the American Metalcraft Beehive Syrup Dispenser, 6 oz ($7.80) proved easiest to fill and clean, and its spring-loaded spout cover made pouring neat and precise.

Savory Dutch Baby with
Burrata and Prosciutto

Yeasted Waffles

Savory Dutch Baby with Burrata and Prosciutto

Serves 4 | **Total Time** 45 minutes

WHY THIS RECIPE WORKS Dutch babies are having a welcome renaissance, especially savory versions. The edge of the skillet-size specialty puffs dramatically to form a tall, crispy rim with a texture similar to that of a popover while the base remains flat, custardy, and tender, like a thick crêpe. This alluring treat is far easier to prepare than its pomp and circumstance would suggest. We simply poured a stir-together batter of flour, egg, and milk into a skillet and baked it. Just before serving, we added our toppings: in one version, a tangle of peppery arugula, salty prosciutto, and burrata; in others, a mix of smoked salmon and creamy avocado or mushrooms and crisp celery. You can use whole or low-fat milk instead of skim, but the Dutch baby won't turn out as crisp. If burrata is unavailable, substitute fresh mozzarella. You can garnish and serve the Dutch baby right in the skillet if you like.

DUTCH BABY
- ¼ cup extra-virgin olive oil, divided
- 1¼ cups (6¼ ounces) all-purpose flour
- ½ teaspoon table salt
- 4 large eggs
- 1 cup skim milk
- 2 tablespoons chopped fresh basil, oregano, thyme, parsley, and/or tarragon, plus extra for sprinkling

BURRATA AND PROSCIUTTO TOPPING
- 4 ounces burrata cheese, room temperature
- ¾ cup baby arugula
- ½ teaspoon extra-virgin olive oil, plus extra for drizzling
- ½ teaspoon balsamic vinegar, plus extra for drizzling
- 1 ounce thinly sliced prosciutto, torn into bite-size pieces

1. FOR THE DUTCH BABY Adjust oven rack to middle position and heat oven to 450 degrees. Grease 12-inch cast-iron skillet with 2 tablespoons oil, place skillet in oven, and heat until oil is shimmering, about 10 minutes.

2. Meanwhile, whisk flour and salt together in large bowl. In separate bowl, whisk eggs until frothy, then whisk in milk, basil, and remaining 2 tablespoons oil until incorporated. Whisk one-third of milk mixture into flour mixture until no lumps remain. Slowly whisk in remaining milk mixture until smooth.

3. Quickly pour batter into skillet and bake until Dutch baby puffs and turns golden brown (edges will be dark brown), about 20 minutes, rotating skillet halfway through baking.

4. FOR THE BURRATA AND PROSCIUTTO TOPPING
Meanwhile, tear burrata into bite-size pieces over plate, collecting creamy liquid. Toss arugula with oil and vinegar and season with salt and pepper to taste.

5. Using potholders, remove skillet from oven. Being careful of hot skillet handle, transfer Dutch baby to cutting board using spatula. Top Dutch baby with arugula mixture, followed by prosciutto and burrata along with any accumulated liquid. Drizzle with extra oil and vinegar and sprinkle with pepper. Slice into wedges and serve immediately.

Savory Dutch Baby with Smoked Salmon and Avocado

Omit burrata and prosciutto topping. While Dutch baby bakes, combine ½ shallot, sliced thin; 1 tablespoon extra-virgin olive oil; 1 teaspoon lemon juice; ¼ teaspoon sugar; and pinch table salt in small bowl and let stand for 10 minutes. Top Dutch baby with 4 ounces smoked salmon; 1 avocado, sliced ¼ inch thick; and shallot mixture. Drizzle with extra oil and sprinkle with 1 teaspoon minced fresh parsley or chives before slicing and serving.

Savory Dutch Baby with Shaved Mushroom and Celery Salad

If your celery came without its leaves, you can substitute fresh parsley leaves. Slice the mushrooms and celery as thinly as possible. Omit burrata and prosciutto topping. While Dutch baby bakes, combine 4 cremini or white mushrooms, stemmed and sliced thin; ½ shallot, sliced thin; 1 tablespoon extra-virgin olive oil; 1 teaspoon lemon juice; pinch table salt; and pinch pepper in small bowl and let stand for 10 minutes. Stir in 1 celery rib, sliced thin on bias, and ½ cup celery leaves. Top Dutch baby with mushroom-celery mixture and ¼ cup shaved Parmesan cheese. Drizzle with extra oil before slicing and serving.

Yeasted Waffles

Serves 2 to 4 `MAKE AHEAD` `VEGETARIAN`
Total Time 50 minutes, plus 12 hours chilling

WHY THIS RECIPE WORKS Raised waffles might sound old-fashioned, and do require advance planning, but the wait is worth it for waffles that are refined, complex, and airy, with crispy edges and creamy centers. We settled on all-purpose flour, found the right amount of yeast to provide a pleasant tang, and added a full stick of melted butter for rich flavor.

Refrigerating the batter overnight kept the growth of the yeast under control and produced waffles with superior flavor. All we had to do in the morning was heat up the waffle iron. While the waffles can be eaten as soon as they are removed from the iron, they will have a crispier exterior if rested in a warm oven for 10 minutes. (This method also makes it possible to serve everyone at the same time.)

1¾ cups milk
8 tablespoons unsalted butter, cut into 8 pieces
2 cups (10 ounces) all-purpose flour
1 tablespoon sugar
1½ teaspoons instant or rapid-rise yeast
1 teaspoon table salt
2 large eggs
1 teaspoon vanilla extract

1. Heat milk and butter in small saucepan over medium-low heat until butter is melted, 3 to 5 minutes. Let mixture cool until warm to touch.

2. Whisk flour, sugar, yeast, and salt together in large bowl. In separate bowl, whisk eggs and vanilla together. Gradually whisk warm milk mixture into flour mixture until smooth, then whisk in egg mixture. Scrape down bowl with rubber spatula, cover tightly with plastic wrap, and refrigerate for at least 12 hours. (Waffle batter can be refrigerated for up to 24 hours.)

3. Adjust oven rack to middle position and heat oven to 200 degrees. Set wire rack in rimmed baking sheet and place in oven. Heat waffle iron according to manufacturer's instructions. Remove batter from refrigerator when waffle iron is hot (batter will be foamy and doubled in size). Whisk batter to recombine (batter will deflate).

4. Spray preheated waffle iron with vegetable oil spray. Add ⅔ cup batter to waffle iron and cook according to manufacturer's instructions until crisp, firm, and golden, 4 to 6 minutes. Serve immediately or transfer to wire rack in oven. Repeat with remaining batter.

Blueberry Yeasted Waffles

We found that frozen wild blueberries—which are smaller than conventional blueberries—work best here. Larger blueberries release too much juice, which burns and becomes bitter when it comes in contact with the waffle iron. After removing waffle batter from refrigerator in step 2, gently fold 1½ cups frozen blueberries into batter using rubber spatula. Bake waffles as directed.

French Toast Casserole

Serves 6 to 8 `MAKE AHEAD` `VEGETARIAN`
Total Time 2 hours, plus 8 hours chilling

WHY THIS RECIPE WORKS This tempting casserole takes traditional French toast to new heights, delivering a sweet, custardy dish that satisfies a crowd. To bind soft yet sturdy bread with a rich custard, we had to look beyond the ingredients we used in our standard recipe for French toast. Though challah is perfect for stovetop versions, here we found that only the dense texture and thin, chewy crusts of French and Italian loaves could stand up to a moist, heavy custard. We added extra insurance by "staling" the bread in the oven, allowing it to dry and toast slightly before assembling the dish. For the custard, we settled on eight whole eggs and a little less than twice as much whole milk as heavy cream, which gave us a rich and custardy but not cloying result. (This is brunch, after all, not dessert.) The assembled casserole needed an extended stay in the refrigerator for the flavors to meld and the bread to soak up the rich custard. All we had left to do before baking was sprinkle on a crunchy pecan topping. Rich, just sweet enough, and make-ahead friendly—what more could you ask for? Do not substitute low-fat or skim milk in this recipe. Supermarket-style French or Italian loaf bread with a thin crust and fluffy crumb works best here.

- 1 pound French or Italian bread, torn into 1-inch pieces
- 2½ cups whole milk
- 8 large eggs
- 1½ cups heavy cream
- 1 tablespoon granulated sugar
- 2 teaspoons vanilla extract
- ½ teaspoon ground cinnamon
- ½ teaspoon ground nutmeg
- 1⅓ cups packed (9⅓ ounces) light brown sugar
- 8 tablespoons unsalted butter, softened
- 3 tablespoons light corn syrup
- 2 cups pecans, chopped coarse

1. Adjust oven racks to upper-middle and lower-middle positions and heat oven to 325 degrees. Spread bread over 2 rimmed baking sheets and bake until dry and light golden, about 25 minutes, switching and rotating sheets halfway through baking. Let bread cool completely.

2. Grease 13 by 9-inch baking dish, then pack bread into dish. Whisk milk, eggs, cream, granulated sugar, vanilla, cinnamon, and nutmeg together in bowl. Pour egg mixture evenly over bread and lightly press on bread to submerge. Wrap dish tightly with plastic wrap and refrigerate for at least 8 hours.

3. Stir brown sugar, butter, and corn syrup in bowl until smooth, then stir in pecans. (Assembled casserole and topping can be refrigerated separately for up to 24 hours.)

4. Adjust oven rack to middle position and heat oven to 350 degrees. Unwrap casserole and sprinkle evenly with brown sugar mixture, breaking apart any large clumps. Place casserole on rimmed baking sheet and bake until puffed and golden, about 1 hour. Let casserole cool for 10 minutes before serving.

Blueberry Swirl Muffins with Frozen Blueberries

Makes 12 muffins `VEGETARIAN`
Total Time 1¼ hours

WHY THIS RECIPE WORKS A great brunch demands great blueberry muffins. Lucky for us, blueberries freeze exceptionally well and high-quality frozen berries are available in stores year-round. By swirling a combination of whole berries and an intense stovetop jam into each cup, this recipe delivers loads of blueberry flavor along with the liquid burst that only whole berries can provide. For finely grated lemon zest, use a rasp grater. If buttermilk is unavailable, substitute ¾ cup of plain whole-milk or low-fat yogurt thinned with ¼ cup of milk.

LEMON-SUGAR TOPPING
- ⅓ cup (2⅓ ounces) sugar
- 1½ teaspoons grated lemon zest

MUFFINS
- 10 ounces (2 cups) frozen blueberries, divided
- 1 teaspoon plus 1⅛ cups (7¾ ounces sugar), divided
- 2½ cups (12½ ounces) all-purpose flour
- 2½ teaspoons baking powder
- 1 teaspoon table salt
- 2 large eggs
- 4 tablespoons unsalted butter, melted and cooled
- ¼ cup vegetable oil
- 1 cup buttermilk
- 1½ teaspoons vanilla extract

1. **FOR THE LEMON-SUGAR TOPPING** Combine sugar and lemon zest in small bowl and set aside.

2. **FOR THE MUFFINS** Adjust oven rack to upper-middle position and heat oven to 425 degrees. Spray 12-cup muffin tin with vegetable oil spray. Bring 1 cup blueberries and 1 teaspoon sugar to simmer in small saucepan over medium heat. Cook, mashing berries with spoon several times and stirring frequently, until berries have broken down and mixture is thickened and reduced to ¼ cup, about 6 minutes. Transfer to small bowl and let cool completely, 10 to 15 minutes. Rinse remaining 1 cup berries under cold running water and dry well.

3. Whisk flour, baking powder, and salt together in large bowl. Whisk remaining 1⅛ cups sugar and eggs in medium bowl until thick and homogeneous, about 45 seconds. Slowly whisk in melted butter and oil until combined. Whisk in buttermilk and vanilla until combined. Using rubber spatula, fold sugar-egg mixture and whole blueberries into flour mixture until just moistened. (Batter will be very lumpy with few spots of dry flour; do not overmix.)

4. Using ice cream scoop or large spoon, divide batter evenly among prepared muffin tin cups (batter should completely fill cups and mound slightly). Spoon 1 teaspoon cooked berry mixture into center of each mound of batter. Using chopstick or skewer, gently swirl berry filling into batter using figure-eight motion. Sprinkle lemon-sugar topping evenly over muffins.

5. Bake until muffins are golden brown and toothpick inserted in center comes out with few crumbs attached, 17 to 19 minutes, rotating muffin tin halfway through baking. Let muffins cool in tin on wire rack for 10 minutes. Remove muffins from tin and let cool for at least 10 minutes before serving.

ADDING THE BLUEBERRY SWIRL

1. Cook berries until broken down, thickened, and reduced to ¼ cup.

2. Place 1 teaspoon of jam in center of batter-filled cup; use chopstick or skewer to swirl jam using "figure-eight" motion to spread berry flavor throughout muffin.

French Toast Casserole

Blueberry Swirl Muffins with Frozen Blueberries

Mixed Berry Scones

Ultimate Banana Bread

Mixed Berry Scones

Makes 8 scones | **Total Time** 1 hour

MAKE AHEAD   VEGETARIAN

WHY THIS RECIPE WORKS These scones are a flaky, honey-glazed delight, brimming with juicy berries in a buttery, rich crumb. We achieved a perfectly crumbly texture by incorporating the butter in two ways, processing some with the dry ingredients for even distribution and some into pea-size pieces that became rich butter pockets. Tossing frozen berries with confectioners' sugar prevented them from bleeding into the dough. A simple glaze of butter and honey added a nice finish to the scones. Work the dough just until it comes together; do not overmix. For the best results, work quickly to keep the butter and berries as cold as possible. If your berry mix contains strawberries, cut them in half before tossing them with the confectioners' sugar in step 1.

SCONES

8¾ ounces (1¾ cups) frozen mixed berries
  3 tablespoons confectioners' sugar
  3 cups (15 ounces) all-purpose flour
12 tablespoons unsalted butter, cut into ½-inch pieces and chilled, divided
  ⅓ cup (2⅓ ounces) granulated sugar
  1 tablespoon baking powder
1¼ teaspoons table salt
  ¾ cup plus 2 tablespoons whole milk
  1 large egg plus 1 large yolk

GLAZE

  2 tablespoons unsalted butter, melted
  1 tablespoon honey

1. FOR THE SCONES Adjust oven rack to upper-middle position and heat oven to 425 degrees. Line rimmed baking sheet with parchment paper. Toss berries with confectioners' sugar in bowl until evenly covered; freeze until needed.

2. Process flour, 6 tablespoons butter, granulated sugar, baking powder, and salt in food processor until butter is fully incorporated, about 15 seconds. Add remaining 6 tablespoons butter and pulse until butter is reduced to pea-size pieces, 10 to 12 pulses. Transfer mixture to large bowl. Stir in berries.

3. Beat milk and egg and yolk together in separate bowl. Make well in center of flour mixture and pour in milk mixture. Using rubber spatula, gently stir, scraping from sides of bowl and folding inward until very shaggy dough forms and some bits of flour remain. Do not overmix.

4. Turn out dough onto well-floured counter and, if necessary, knead briefly until dough just comes together, about 3 turns. Using your floured hands and bench scraper, shape dough into 12 by 4-inch rectangle, about 1½ inches thick. Using knife or bench scraper, cut dough crosswise into 4 equal rectangles. Cut each rectangle diagonally into 2 triangles (you should have 8 triangles total). Transfer triangles to prepared sheet. Bake until scones are lightly golden, 16 to 18 minutes, rotating sheet halfway through baking.

5. FOR THE GLAZE While scones bake, combine melted butter and honey in small bowl.

6. Remove sheet from oven and brush tops of scones evenly with glaze. Return sheet to oven and continue to bake until scones are golden brown, 5 to 8 minutes. Transfer scones to wire rack and let cool for at least 10 minutes before serving.

To make ahead After cutting dough into triangles, transfer scones to parchment paper–lined baking sheet and freeze. Transfer frozen scones to zipper-lock freezer bag and freeze for up to 2 months. When ready to bake, heat oven to 375 degrees and extend baking time in step 4 to 23 to 26 minutes. Baking time in step 6 does not change.

Ultimate Banana Bread

Makes 1 loaf (**Serves** 10) | **Total Time** 2 hours

MAKE AHEAD VEGETARIAN

WHY THIS RECIPE WORKS This banana bread puts all others to shame because it harnesses maximum banana flavor while still delivering a tender, moist (not soggy) bread. The secret behind bringing as many bananas into play as possible? Moisture management. We microwaved five bananas to concentrate their flavor, draining and reserving the liquid, which we simmered until reduced before incorporating it into the batter. We used brown sugar instead of granulated and swapped out oil for the nutty richness of butter. Toasted walnuts gave our banana bread recipe a pleasing crunch, and a sixth banana sliced thin and caramelized on top of the loaf gave our banana bread an enticingly crisp, crunchy top. Our preferred loaf pan measures 8½ by 4½ inches; if using a 9 by 5-inch loaf pan, start checking for doneness 5 minutes early.

1¾ cups (8¾ ounces) all-purpose flour
 1 teaspoon baking soda
 ½ teaspoon table salt
 6 very ripe large bananas (2¼ pounds), peeled
 8 tablespoons unsalted butter, melted and cooled
 2 large eggs
 ¾ cup packed (5¼ ounces) light brown sugar
 1 teaspoon vanilla extract
 ½ cup walnuts, toasted and chopped coarse (optional)
 2 teaspoons granulated sugar

1. Adjust oven rack to middle position and heat oven to 350 degrees. Grease 8½ by 4½-inch loaf pan. Whisk flour, baking soda, and salt together in large bowl.

2. Place 5 bananas in separate bowl, cover, and microwave until bananas are soft and have released liquid, about 5 minutes. Drain bananas in fine-mesh strainer set over medium bowl, stirring occasionally, for 15 minutes; you should have ½ to ¾ cup liquid.

3. Transfer drained liquid to medium saucepan and cook over medium-high heat until reduced to ¼ cup, about 5 minutes. Return drained bananas to bowl. Stir reduced liquid into bananas and mash with potato masher until mostly smooth. Whisk in melted butter, eggs, brown sugar, and vanilla.

4. Pour banana mixture into flour mixture and stir until just combined, with some streaks of flour remaining. Gently fold in walnuts, if using. Scrape batter into prepared loaf pan and smooth top. Slice remaining 1 banana on bias ¼ inch thick and shingle down both sides of loaf pan, leaving center clear to ensure even rise. Sprinkle granulated sugar over top.

5. Bake until skewer inserted in center comes out clean, 55 minutes to 1¼ hours, rotating pan halfway through baking. Let loaf cool in pan for 15 minutes, then turn out onto wire rack and continue to cool. Serve warm or at room temperature. (The texture is best when the loaf is eaten fresh, but it can be cooled completely and stored, covered tightly with plastic wrap, for up to 3 days.)

NOTES FROM THE TEST KITCHEN

THE BEST WAY TO RIPEN BANANAS
Strategies for speeding ripening in bananas abound, from freezing to roasting, but as we worked our way through more than eight cases of fruit we found that most of them do little to encourage the necessary conversion of starch to sugar. The best way to ripen bananas is to enclose them in a paper bag for a few days. The bag will trap the ethylene gas that hastens ripening while still allowing some moisture to escape. Since fully ripe fruit emits the most ethylene, placing a ripe banana or other ripe fruit in the bag will speed the process along by a day or two.

New York–Style Crumb Cake

Serves 8 to 10   MAKE AHEAD   VEGETARIAN
Total Time 1½ hours, plus 30 minutes cooling

WHY THIS RECIPE WORKS Cut with your fork through the thick, soft, crumb layer down into the buttery cake layer of a New York crumb cake and you've got a fantastic bite to enjoy with your first sips of coffee—a near-perfect start to any brunch. To recreate the best bakery-style versions, we modified our yellow cake recipe by reducing the butter so the richness wouldn't overwhelm. Less butter can mean a dry texture; we compensated by adding buttermilk and leaving out an egg white. For the top layer, we wanted our crumb to be soft and cookie-like, not a streusel, so we mixed granulated and brown sugars with melted butter for a dough-like consistency, plus a little cinnamon for familiar warmth and spice. Broken into substantial pieces, our topping held together during baking and created a thick layer of moist crumbs with golden edges. Do not substitute all-purpose flour for the cake flour or the cake will be tough and dry. If you don't have buttermilk, you can substitute an equal amount of plain low-fat yogurt. Take care to not push the crumbs into the batter. This recipe can be doubled and baked in a 13 by 9-inch pan. If doubling, increase the baking time to about 45 minutes.

CRUMB TOPPING

- 8 tablespoons unsalted butter, melted
- ⅓ cup (2⅓ ounces) granulated sugar
- ⅓ cup packed (2⅓ ounces) dark brown sugar
- ¾ teaspoon ground cinnamon
- ⅛ teaspoon table salt
- 1¾ cups (7 ounces) cake flour

CAKE

- 1¼ cups (5 ounces) cake flour
- ½ cup (3½ ounces) granulated sugar
- ¼ teaspoon baking soda
- ¼ teaspoon table salt
- 6 tablespoons unsalted butter, cut into 6 pieces and softened
- ⅓ cup buttermilk
- 1 large egg plus 1 large yolk
- 1 teaspoon vanilla extract
  Confectioners' sugar

New York–Style Crumb Cake

1. Adjust oven rack to upper-middle position and heat oven to 325 degrees. Cut 16-inch length of parchment paper (or aluminum foil) and fold lengthwise to 7-inch width. Spray 8-inch square baking pan with vegetable oil spray and fit parchment into pan, pushing it up sides; allow excess to hang over edges of pan.

2. FOR THE CRUMB TOPPING Whisk melted butter, granulated sugar, brown sugar, cinnamon, and salt together in medium bowl to combine. Add flour and stir with rubber spatula or wooden spoon until mixture resembles thick, cohesive dough; set aside to cool to room temperature, 10 to 15 minutes.

3. FOR THE CAKE Using stand mixer fitted with paddle, mix flour, granulated sugar, baking soda, and salt on low speed to combine. With mixer running, add softened butter 1 piece at a time. Continue beating until mixture resembles moist crumbs, with no visible butter pieces remaining, 1 to 2 minutes. Add buttermilk, egg and yolk, and vanilla and beat on medium-high speed until light and fluffy, about 1 minute, scraping down bowl as needed.

4. Transfer batter to prepared pan. Using rubber spatula, spread batter into even layer. Break apart crumb topping into large pea-size pieces and spread in even layer over batter, beginning with edges and then working toward center. (Cake can be wrapped tightly with plastic wrap and refrigerated for up to 24 hours. To bake, continue with step 5, increasing baking time to 40 to 45 minutes)

5. Bake until crumbs are golden and toothpick inserted in center of cake comes out clean, 35 to 40 minutes, rotating pan halfway through baking. Let cool on wire rack for at least 30 minutes. Remove cake from pan by lifting parchment overhang. Dust with confectioners' sugar just before serving.

Ultimate Cinnamon Buns

Makes 8 buns `MAKE AHEAD` `VEGETARIAN`
Total Time 1½ hours, plus 3½ hours rising and cooling

WHY THIS RECIPE WORKS When you want to go all out at brunch—whether for a holiday, a snowy weekend in, or no reason—these cinnamon buns are how you do it. We set our sights on a mammoth breed of cinnamon bun—sweet, gooey, softball-size—with soft, buttery, yeasted dough; abundant filling; and a thick, tangy glaze. A buttery, tender brioche dough proved to be the best base. Adding cornstarch to all-purpose flour in the dough made the buns especially tender. For a filling with deep caramel flavor, we combined a generous amount of cinnamon with brown sugar. Spreading softened butter over the dough before sprinkling on the cinnamon sugar kept the filling from spilling out. Baked together, the butter and cinnamon sugar turned rich and gooey. For a thick spread of icing, we topped the buns with a tangy glaze of cream cheese, confectioners' sugar, and milk. For more information on making a foil sling, see page 225. For smaller cinnamon buns, cut the dough into 12 pieces in step 3.

DOUGH
- ¾ cup warm whole milk (110 degrees)
- 2¼ teaspoons instant or rapid-rise yeast
- 3 large eggs, room temperature
- 4¼ cups (21¼ ounces) all-purpose flour, plus extra as needed
- ½ cup (2 ounces) cornstarch
- ½ cup (3½ ounces) granulated sugar
- 1½ teaspoons table salt
- 12 tablespoons unsalted butter, cut into 12 pieces and softened

Ultimate Cinnamon Buns

FILLING
- 1½ cups packed (10½ ounces) light brown sugar
- 1½ tablespoons ground cinnamon
- ¼ teaspoon table salt
- 4 tablespoons unsalted butter, softened

GLAZE
- 1½ cups (6 ounces) confectioners' sugar
- 4 ounces cream cheese, softened
- 1 tablespoon whole milk
- 1 teaspoon vanilla extract

1. FOR THE DOUGH Make foil sling for 13 by 9-inch baking pan by folding 2 long sheets of aluminum foil; first sheet should be 13 inches wide and second sheet should be 9 inches wide. Lay sheets of foil in pan perpendicular to each other, with extra foil hanging over edges of pan. Push foil into corners and up sides of pan, smoothing foil flush to pan. Grease foil. Whisk milk and yeast in 2-cup liquid measuring cup until yeast dissolves, then whisk in eggs.

2. Adjust oven rack to middle position and place loaf pan or cake pan on bottom of oven. Bring kettle of water to boil. Using stand mixer fitted with dough hook, mix flour, cornstarch, sugar, and salt on low speed until combined. Add milk mixture in steady stream and mix until dough comes together, about 1 minute. With mixer running, add butter, 1 piece at a time, and mix until incorporated. Continue to mix until dough is smooth and comes away from sides of bowl, about 10 minutes (if dough is still wet and sticky, add up to ¼ cup extra flour, 1 tablespoon at a time, until it clears sides of bowl). Transfer dough to counter and knead by hand to form smooth, round ball. Transfer dough ball to greased medium bowl, cover bowl tightly with plastic wrap, and transfer to middle oven rack. Pour 3 cups boiling water into loaf pan in oven, close oven door, and let dough rise until doubled in size, about 2 hours.

3. FOR THE FILLING Combine sugar, cinnamon, and salt in small bowl. Remove dough from oven and transfer to lightly floured counter. Roll dough into 18-inch square and, leaving ½-inch border around edges, spread with butter, then sprinkle evenly with sugar mixture and lightly press sugar mixture into dough. Roll dough away from you into tight cylinder, pinch lightly to seal seam, and cut into 8 pieces. Transfer pieces, cut side up, to prepared pan. Cover pan tightly with plastic. (Wrapped pan can be refrigerated for up to 24 hours. When ready to bake, let dough sit at room temperature for 1 hour, then bake as directed in step 4.) Let dough rise in oven until doubled in size, about 1 hour.

4. FOR THE GLAZE Whisk all ingredients in medium bowl until smooth. Remove dough and pan with water from oven and heat oven to 350 degrees. Remove plastic and bake until buns are deep golden brown and filling is melted, 35 to 40 minutes, rotating pan halfway through baking. Transfer pan to wire rack, top buns with ½ cup glaze, and let cool for 30 minutes. Using foil overhang, lift buns out of pan. Top with remaining glaze and serve.

FORMING CINNAMON BUNS

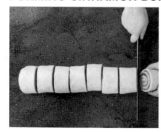

Roll dough away from you into firm cylinder, keeping roll taught by tucking it under itself as you go. Pinch seam closed. Use serrated knife to cut 8 pieces.

Chocolate Babka

Chocolate Babka

Serves 12 | **Total Time** 1½ hours, plus 7¼ to 8¼ hours rising and cooling VEGETARIAN

WHY THIS RECIPE WORKS A decadent chocolate babka is a brunch treat, but it can be hard to get your hands on a great one. For that reason, we decided to devise a foolproof recipe for our own kitchens. By definition, babka dough is rich and tender, akin to brioche. But go too far in that direction and the dough will collapse under the weight of the chocolate filling, leaving large gaps in the bread. To add richness yet preserve the loaf's structural integrity, we cut back on the butter found in most traditional recipes and substituted two egg yolks for one whole egg. For the filling, a combination of bittersweet chocolate and cocoa powder provided the full, rounded chocolate flavor and appealingly fudgy texture we wanted. To make sure the filling stayed put and didn't sink to the bottom of the loaf, we also mixed in confectioners' sugar and an egg white, which helped stiffen it up. Our preferred loaf pan measures 8½ by 4½ inches; if using a 9 by 5-inch loaf pan, increase the shaped rising time by 20 to 30 minutes and start checking for doneness 10 minutes earlier than advised in the recipe. We do not recommend mixing this dough by hand. If the dough becomes too soft to work with at any point, refrigerate it until it's firm enough to easily handle.

DOUGH

- 2 cups (10 ounces) all-purpose flour
- 1½ teaspoons instant or rapid-rise yeast
- ½ teaspoon table salt
- ½ cup (4 ounces) whole milk, room temperature
- ¼ cup (1¾ ounces) granulated sugar
- 2 large egg yolks, room temperature
- 1 teaspoon vanilla extract
- 8 tablespoons unsalted butter, softened

FILLING

- 2 ounces bittersweet chocolate, chopped
- 4 tablespoons unsalted butter
- 3 tablespoons unsweetened cocoa powder
- ¼ cup (1 ounce) confectioners' sugar
- 1 large egg white
- 1 large egg, lightly beaten with 1 tablespoon water and pinch table salt

1. FOR THE DOUGH Whisk flour, yeast, and salt together in bowl of stand mixer. Whisk milk, sugar, egg yolks, and vanilla in 4-cup liquid measuring cup until sugar has dissolved. Fit mixer with dough hook and mix on low speed, slowly adding milk mixture to flour mixture until cohesive dough starts to form and no dry flour remains, about 2 minutes, scraping down bowl as needed.

2. Increase speed to medium-low; add butter, 1 tablespoon at a time, and knead until butter is fully incorporated, about 4 minutes. Continue to knead until dough is smooth and elastic and clears sides of bowl, 10 to 12 minutes.

3. Transfer dough to lightly floured counter and knead by hand to form smooth, round ball, about 30 seconds. Place dough seam side down in lightly greased large bowl or container, cover tightly with plastic wrap, and let rise until increased in size by about half, 1½ to 2 hours. Place in refrigerator until dough is firm, at least 1 hour (Dough can be refrigerated for up to 24 hours; if dough is chilled longer than 1 hour, let rest at room temperature for 15 minutes before rolling out in step 5.)

4. FOR THE FILLING Microwave chocolate, butter, and cocoa in bowl at 50 percent power, stirring occasionally, until melted and smooth, 1 to 2 minutes. Stir in sugar until combined; let cool completely. Whisk in egg white until fully combined and mixture turns glossy. Measure out and reserve 1 tablespoon filling.

5. Grease 8½ by 4½-inch loaf pan. Press down on dough to deflate, then transfer to lightly floured counter. Press and roll dough into 18 by 14-inch rectangle, with long side parallel to counter edge. Spread remaining filling over dough, leaving ½-inch border around edges.

6. Roll dough away from you into firm cylinder, keeping roll taut by tucking it under itself as you go. Pinch seam closed, then reshape cylinder as needed to be 18 inches in length with uniform thickness. Position cylinder seam side up and spread reserved filling over top. Fold cylinder on top of itself and pinch ends to seal.

7. Gently twist double cylinder twice to form double figure 8. Place loaf in prepared pan, pressing dough gently into corners. Cover loosely with greased plastic and let rise until loaf is level with lip of pan, 1½ to 2 hours.

8. Adjust oven rack to lower-middle position and heat oven to 350 degrees. Gently brush loaf with egg mixture and bake until deep golden brown and loaf registers 190 to 195 degrees, 40 to 45 minutes, rotating pan halfway through baking. Let loaf cool in pan for 15 minutes. Remove loaf from pan and let cool completely on wire rack, about 3 hours, before serving.

HOW TO SHAPE BABKA

1. Press and roll dough into 18 by 14-inch rectangle with long side parallel to counter edge. Spread remaining filling over dough, leaving ½-inch border around edges.

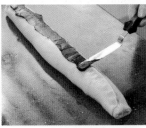

2. Roll dough away from you into firm cylinder. Position seam side up and spread reserved filling over top. Fold cylinder on top of itself and pinch ends to seal.

3. Gently twist double cylinder twice to form double figure 8. Place in prepared pan, pressing dough gently into corners.

breads

■ MAKE AHEAD　▦ VEGETARIAN

Photo: Oatmeal-Raisin Bread

Easiest-Ever Biscuits

Makes 10 biscuits | **Total Time** 30 minutes

MAKE AHEAD   VEGETARIAN

WHY THIS RECIPE WORKS A fresh, warm biscuit instantly doubles the coziness of practically anything you serve it with. These dropped cream biscuits, or "dream biscuits," sport a tender, cake-like, and subtly layered crumb. The key was to use cream instead of butter, and to heat the cream before stirring it into the dry ingredients. This liquefied the cream's fat particles, allowing them to thoroughly incorporate with the dry ingredients. The looser consistency of dough made with warm cream also meant that we could scoop and drop portions right onto a baking sheet, no rolling or cutting required. Baking powder and baking soda gave the biscuits lift, and a couple tablespoons of melted butter brushed on at the last second gave each biscuit a burnished sheen. These biscuits come together very quickly, so in the interest of efficiency, start heating your oven before gathering your ingredients. We like these biscuits brushed with a bit of melted butter, but you can skip that step if you're serving the biscuits with a rich accompaniment such as gravy.

> 3 cups (15 ounces) all-purpose flour
> 4 teaspoons sugar
> 1 tablespoon baking powder
> ¼ teaspoon baking soda
> 1¼ teaspoons table salt
> 2 cups heavy cream
> 2 tablespoons unsalted butter, melted (optional)

1. Adjust oven rack to upper-middle position and heat oven to 450 degrees. Line rimmed baking sheet with parchment paper. In medium bowl, whisk together flour, sugar, baking powder, baking soda, and salt. Microwave cream until just warmed to body temperature (95 to 100 degrees), 60 to 90 seconds, stirring halfway through microwaving. Stir cream into flour mixture until soft, uniform dough forms.

2. Spray ⅓-cup dry measuring cup with vegetable oil spray. Drop level scoops of batter 2 inches apart on prepared sheet (biscuits should measure about 2½ inches wide and 1¼ inches tall). Respray measuring cup after every 3 or 4 scoops. If portions are misshapen, use your fingertips to gently reshape dough into level cylinders. Bake until tops are light golden brown, 10 to 12 minutes, rotating sheet halfway through baking. Brush hot biscuits with melted butter, if using. Serve warm. (Biscuits can be stored in zipper-lock bag at room temperature for up to 24 hours. Reheat biscuits in 300-degree oven for 10 minutes.)

Pat-in-the-Pan Buttermilk Biscuits

Makes 9 biscuits | **Total Time** 1¼ hours

MAKE AHEAD   VEGETARIAN

WHY THIS RECIPE WORKS The exceptionally fluffy interior crumb of these rich and tangy biscuits is achieved thanks to the interplay between buttermilk and a combination of baking powder and baking soda. The heat of the oven and acidity of the buttermilk activated the two leaveners to create tons of rise and a superlight texture. Cake flour also contributed to the biscuits' tenderness, as the low-protein flour didn't form a strong gluten network. Cold butter cut into the dough created steam and even more lift as it melted in the oven's heat. A final brush with softened butter added more delicious buttery flavor for the crusty exterior to soak up. This recipe can easily be doubled to yield 15 biscuits: Use a 13 by 9-inch baking pan and extend the baking time by about 15 minutes. We developed this recipe using a metal baking pan.

> 12 tablespoons unsalted butter, divided
> 4 cups (16 ounces) cake flour, plus extra for sprinkling
> 2 teaspoons baking powder
> ½ teaspoon baking soda
> 2 teaspoons table salt
> 2 cups buttermilk, chilled

1. Adjust oven rack to middle position and heat oven to 450 degrees. Grease 8-inch square baking pan with 1 tablespoon butter. Cut 10 tablespoons butter into ½-inch pieces and freeze until chilled, about 15 minutes. Let remaining 1 tablespoon butter sit at room temperature to soften.

2. Whisk flour, baking powder, baking soda, and salt together in bowl. Add chilled butter to flour mixture and smash butter between your fingertips into pea-size pieces. Gently stir in buttermilk until no dry pockets of flour remain. Using rubber spatula, transfer dough to prepared pan.

3. Lightly sprinkle extra flour evenly over dough to prevent sticking. Using your floured hands, pat dough into even layer and into corners of pan. Using bench scraper sprayed with vegetable oil spray, cut dough into 9 equal squares (2 cuts by 2 cuts), but do not separate. Bake until golden brown on top, about 30 minutes.

4. Let biscuits cool in pan for 5 minutes. Using thin metal spatula, slide biscuits onto wire rack. Brush tops with softened butter. Let cool for 10 minutes. Pull biscuits apart at cuts and serve warm. (Biscuits can be stored in zipper-lock bag at room temperature for up to 24 hours. Reheat biscuits in 300-degree oven for 10 minutes.)

Parker House Rolls

Makes 24 rolls MAKE AHEAD VEGETARIAN
Total Time 2 hours, plus 2 to 3 hours rising

WHY THIS RECIPE WORKS These thin-crusted, fluffy-crumbed, glossy rolls are pillowy soft, a little sweet, and packed with butter. Luxurious as the dough is, the folded shape and buttery shellac are the hallmarks of these rolls. We found that the best way to shape the dough was to press a crease into the center of flattened dough disks before folding them in half. To ensure that the rolls didn't puff open during baking, we kept the edges of the dough thicker than the center so that they adhered to each other when the dough rose. Arranging the rolls on a baking sheet rather than crowded into a baking dish allowed them to bake evenly since they were all exposed to the same amount of heat. Brushing the rolls with melted butter gave them their requisite gleaming crust.

4	cups (20 ounces) all-purpose flour
2¼	teaspoons instant or rapid-rise yeast
1½	teaspoons table salt
1¼	cups whole milk, room temperature
14	tablespoons unsalted butter, melted, divided
1	large egg, room temperature
2	tablespoons sugar

1. Whisk flour, yeast, and salt together in bowl of stand mixer. Whisk milk, 8 tablespoons melted butter, egg, and sugar in 4-cup liquid measuring cup until sugar has dissolved.

2. Fit mixer with dough hook. Slowly add milk mixture to flour mixture on low speed and mix until cohesive dough starts to form and no dry flour remains, about 2 minutes, scraping down bowl as needed. Increase speed to medium-low and knead until dough is smooth and elastic and clears sides of bowl but sticks to bottom, about 8 minutes.

3. Transfer dough to lightly floured counter and knead by hand to form smooth, round ball, about 30 seconds. Place dough seam side down in lightly greased large bowl or container; cover tightly with plastic wrap; and let rise until doubled in size, 1 to 1½ hours.

4. Line 2 rimmed baking sheets with parchment paper. Press down on dough to deflate. Transfer dough to clean counter and use bench scraper or chef's knife to divide in half. Stretch each half into even 12-inch log, cut each log into 12 equal pieces (about 1½ ounces each), and cover loosely with greased plastic. Working with 1 piece of dough at a time (keep remaining pieces covered), form into rough ball by stretching dough with your thumbs and pinching edges together on bottom so top is smooth. Place ball seam side

Easiest-Ever Biscuits

Pat-in-the-Pan Buttermilk Biscuits

Parker House Rolls

Fluffy Dinner Rolls

down on clean counter and, using your cupped hand, drag in small circles until dough feels taut and round. Cover dough balls loosely with greased plastic and let rest for 15 minutes.

5. Working with few dough balls at a time, press balls into ¼-inch-thick rounds. Using thin handle of wooden spoon or dowel, firmly press down across width of rounds to create crease in center. Brush tops of rounds with 3 tablespoons melted butter. Fold in half along crease and gently press edges to seal.

6. Arrange rolls on prepared sheets, spaced about 2 inches apart. Cover loosely with greased plastic and let rise until nearly doubled in size and dough springs back minimally when poked gently with your knuckle, 1 to 1½ hours. (Unrisen rolls can be refrigerated for at least 8 hours or up to 16 hours; let rolls stand at room temperature for 1 hour before baking.)

7. Adjust oven racks to upper-middle and lower-middle positions and heat oven to 350 degrees. Gently brush rolls with remaining 3 tablespoons melted butter, then mist with water. Bake until golden brown, 20 to 25 minutes, switching and rotating sheets halfway through baking. Transfer rolls to wire rack and let cool for 15 minutes. Serve warm or at room temperature.

To make ahead Rolls can be stored in zipper-lock bag at room temperature for up to 24 hours. Wrapped in foil before being placed in bag, rolls can be frozen for up to 1 month. To reheat rolls, wrap them (thawed if frozen) in aluminum foil, place on rimmed baking sheet, and bake in 350-degree oven for 10 minutes.

SHAPING PARKER HOUSE ROLLS

1. Working with few dough balls at a time, press balls into ¼-inch-thick rounds. Using thin handle of wooden spoon or dowel, firmly press down across width of rounds to create crease in center.

2. Lightly brush tops of rounds with melted butter, then fold in half along creases and gently press edges to seal.

Fluffy Dinner Rolls

Makes 12 rolls   `MAKE AHEAD`   `VEGETARIAN`
Total Time 2 hours, plus 1¾ hours rising

WHY THIS RECIPE WORKS Passing a plate of hot, fluffy dinner rolls around the table is a quintessential ritual of hospitality. But because most rolls are at their best for only a few hours after emerging from the oven, baking dinner rolls is often a hectic last-minute affair. To make rolls that tasted fresh-baked even after more than a day, we used a bread-making technique known as tangzhong, in which extra moisture is added to the dough in the form of a flour paste. To support the weight of the extra moisture, we built a strong gluten structure by adding a resting period during which gluten strands formed and withholding the butter until the gluten network was firmly established. The shaping method, inspired by Japanese milk bread, was also important. Flattening each portion of dough and rolling it up in a spiral organized the gluten strands into coiled layers, which baked up into feathery sheets. The slight tackiness of the dough aids in flattening and stretching it in step 5, so do not dust your counter with flour.

FLOUR PASTE
½ cup water
3 tablespoons bread flour

DOUGH
½ cup cold milk
1 large egg
2 cups (11 ounces) bread flour
1½ teaspoons instant or rapid-rise yeast
2 tablespoons sugar
1 teaspoon table salt
4 tablespoons unsalted butter, cut into 4 pieces and softened, plus ½ tablespoon melted
Vegetable oil spray

1. FOR THE FLOUR PASTE Whisk water and flour in small bowl until no lumps remain. Microwave, whisking every 20 seconds, until mixture thickens to stiff, smooth, pudding-like consistency that forms mound when dropped from end of whisk into bowl, 40 to 80 seconds.

2. FOR THE DOUGH In bowl of stand mixer, whisk flour paste and milk until smooth. Add egg and whisk until incorporated. Add flour and yeast. Fit stand mixer with dough hook and mix on low speed until all flour is moistened, 1 to 2 minutes. Let stand for 15 minutes.

3. Add sugar and salt and mix on medium-low speed for 5 minutes. With mixer running, add softened butter, 1 piece at a time. Continue to mix on medium-low speed for 5 minutes, scraping down dough hook and sides of bowl occasionally (dough will stick to bottom of bowl).

4. Transfer dough to very lightly floured counter. Knead briefly to form ball and transfer, seam side down, to lightly greased bowl; lightly coat surface of dough with oil spray and cover with plastic wrap. Let rise until doubled in volume, about 1 hour.

5. Grease 9-inch round cake pan and set aside. Transfer dough to counter. Press dough gently but firmly to expel all air. Pat and stretch dough to form 8 by 9-inch rectangle with short side facing you. Using bench scraper or chef's knife, cut dough lengthwise into 4 equal strips and cut each strip crosswise into 3 equal pieces. Working with 1 piece at a time, stretch and press dough gently to form 8 by 2-inch strip. Starting on short side, roll dough to form snug cylinder. Arrange shaped rolls seam side down in prepared pan, placing 10 rolls around edge of pan, pointing inward, and remaining 2 rolls in center. Cover with plastic and let rise until doubled, 45 minutes to 1 hour.

6. When rolls are nearly doubled, adjust oven rack to lowest position and heat oven to 375 degrees. Bake rolls until deep golden brown, 25 to 30 minutes. Let rolls cool in pan on wire rack for 3 minutes; invert rolls onto rack, then reinvert. Brush tops and sides of rolls with melted butter. Let rolls cool for at least 20 minutes before serving.

To make ahead Rolls can be stored in zipper-lock bag at room temperature for up to 24 hours. To reheat rolls, wrap them in aluminum foil, place on rimmed baking sheet, and bake in 350-degree oven for 15 minutes.

NOTES FROM THE TEST KITCHEN

WHAT IS TANGZHONG?
The tangzhong method calls for briefly cooking a portion of the bread's flour and water to make a paste, which is then combined with the rest of the ingredients. By heating this paste, we can actually add more liquid to the dough because flour can absorb twice as much hot water as cold water. The superhydrated dough yields rolls that are not just moist but also fluffy because the water converts to steam in the oven, creating rise. The extra water also increases gluten development, giving the bread the structure it needs to contain the steam rather than let it escape.

Oatmeal Dinner Rolls

Makes 12 rolls MAKE AHEAD VEGETARIAN
Total Time 1½ hours, plus 1¾ hours rising

WHY THIS RECIPE WORKS Dinner rolls that boast nutty whole-grain flavor and are also fluffy and moist? Yes, it's possible. We started by soaking old-fashioned rolled oats in hot water. During a short rest the oats absorbed most of the water, effectively locking it away. Whole-wheat flour boosted the nutty flavor profile, while some white bread flour added structure. Adding even more water made for a highly hydrated dough that was still easy to handle. Nestling the dough balls close together ensured that they supported each other in upward rather than outward expansion. That mutual support, along with the transformation of water to steam during the bake, yielded dinner rolls that contained the best of both worlds: light, soft, plush texture along with whole-grain complexity. For an accurate measurement of boiling water, bring a kettle of water to a boil and then measure out the desired amount. Avoid blackstrap molasses here, as it's too bitter. If you prefer, you can portion the rolls by weight in step 2 (2¼ ounces of dough per roll). To make 24 rolls, double this recipe and bake the rolls in two 9-inch round cake pans.

- ¾ cup (2¼ ounces) old-fashioned rolled oats, plus 4 teaspoons for sprinkling
- ⅔ cup boiling water, plus ½ cup cold water
- 2 tablespoons unsalted butter, cut into 4 pieces
- 1½ cups (8¼ ounces) bread flour
- ¾ cup (4⅛ ounces) whole-wheat flour
- ¼ cup molasses
- 1½ teaspoons instant or rapid-rise yeast
- 1 teaspoon table salt

- 1 large egg, lightly beaten with 1 teaspoon water and pinch table salt

1. Stir ¾ cup oats, boiling water, and butter together in bowl of stand mixer and let stand until butter is melted and most of water has been absorbed, about 10 minutes. Add bread flour, whole-wheat flour, cold water, molasses, yeast, and salt. Fit mixer with dough hook and mix on low speed until flour is moistened, about 1 minute (dough may look dry). Increase speed to medium-low and mix until dough clears sides of bowl (it will still stick to bottom), about 8 minutes, scraping down dough hook halfway through mixing (dough will be sticky). Transfer dough to counter, shape into ball, and transfer to lightly greased bowl. Cover with plastic wrap and let rise until doubled in volume, 1 to 1¼ hours.

Oatmeal Dinner Rolls

2. Grease 9-inch round cake pan and set aside. Transfer dough to lightly floured counter, reserving plastic. Pat dough gently into 8-inch square of even thickness. Using bench scraper or chef's knife, cut dough into 12 pieces (3 rows by 4 rows). Working with 1 piece of dough at a time, form into rough balls by stretching dough with your thumbs and pinching edges together on bottom so top is smooth. (To round, set piece of dough on unfloured counter. Loosely cup your lightly floured hand around dough and, without applying pressure to dough, move your hand in small circular motions. Tackiness of dough against counter and circular motion should work dough into smooth ball.) Arrange seam side down in prepared pan, placing 9 dough balls around edge of pan and remaining 3 dough balls in center. Cover with reserved plastic and let rise until rolls are doubled in size and no gaps are visible between them, 45 minutes to 1 hour.

3. When rolls are nearly doubled in size, adjust oven rack to lower-middle position and heat oven to 375 degrees. Brush rolls with egg wash and sprinkle with remaining 4 teaspoons oats. Bake until rolls are deep brown and register at least 195 degrees at center, 25 to 30 minutes. Let rolls cool in pan on wire rack for 3 minutes; invert rolls onto rack, then reinvert. Let rolls cool for at least 20 minutes before serving. (Rolls can be wrapped in foil and stored in zipper-lock bag and frozen for up to 1 month. To reheat rolls, thaw them at room temperature, then place on rimmed baking sheet and bake in 350-degree oven for 8 minutes.)

Really Good Garlic Bread

Serves 8 | **Total Time** 30 minutes VEGETARIAN

WHY THIS RECIPE WORKS Unlike squishy, steamy premade loaves, homemade garlic bread is toasty-crisp on the outside, moist on the inside, and brimming with buttery, garlicky flavor. We started with a loaf of supermarket Italian bread since its soft crust would crisp without toughening. We microwaved fresh grated garlic with butter to tame its bite, adding garlic powder for sweet, roasty notes and some solid butter to make a spreadable paste. Compressing the bread halves between two rimmed baking sheets put every inch into contact with the hot sheets, crisping and browning the crust all over. A 12 by 5-inch loaf of supermarket Italian bread works best here. Do not use a rustic or crusty artisan-style loaf. A rasp-style grater makes quick work of turning the garlic into a paste. The amount of time needed to brown the bread after flipping it in step 3 depends on the color of your baking sheet. If you use a dark-colored sheet, the browning time will be on the shorter end of the range.

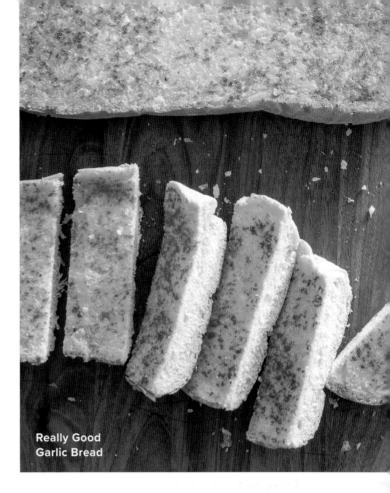

Really Good Garlic Bread

- 1 teaspoon garlic powder
- 1 teaspoon water
- 8 tablespoons unsalted butter, divided
- ½ teaspoon table salt
- ⅛ teaspoon cayenne pepper
- 4–5 garlic cloves, minced to paste (1 tablespoon)
- 1 (1-pound) loaf soft Italian bread, halved horizontally

1. Adjust oven rack to lower-middle position and heat oven to 450 degrees. Combine garlic powder and water in medium bowl. Add 4 tablespoons butter, salt, and cayenne to bowl; set aside.

2. Place remaining 4 tablespoons butter in small bowl and microwave, covered, until melted, about 30 seconds. Stir in garlic and microwave, covered, until mixture is bubbling around edges, about 1 minute, stirring halfway through microwaving. Transfer melted butter mixture to bowl with garlic powder–butter mixture and whisk until homogeneous loose paste forms. (If mixture melts, set aside and let solidify before using.)

3. Spread cut sides of bread evenly with butter mixture. Transfer bread, cut sides up, to rimmed baking sheet. Bake until butter mixture has melted and seeped into bread, 3 to 4 minutes. Remove sheet from oven. Flip bread cut sides down, place second rimmed baking sheet on top, and gently press. Return sheet to oven, leaving second sheet on top of bread, and continue to bake until cut sides are golden brown and crisp, 4 to 12 minutes, rotating sheet halfway through baking. Transfer bread to cutting board. Using serrated knife, cut each half into 8 slices. Serve immediately.

Southern-Style Skillet Cornbread

Makes one 10-inch loaf (**Serves** 12)
Total Time 1 hour VEGETARIAN

WHY THIS RECIPE WORKS In the South, savory, flour-free, skillet-baked cornbread reigns supreme. In our version, we used yellow cornmeal rather than the typical white, finding that it had a more potent corn flavor. We also skipped the customary bacon fat, instead using butter (for its flavor) and vegetable oil (for its ability to withstand high heat). Hydrating toasted cornmeal in a sour cream–milk mixture ensured that our bread had a fine, moist crumb; the sour cream also added pleasing tang. Preheating the skillet before adding the batter delivered the crisp, distinctly Southern crust we were after. We prefer a cast-iron skillet, but any ovensafe 10-inch skillet will work. You can substitute any type of fine- or medium-ground cornmeal; do not use coarse-ground cornmeal.

2¼ cups (11¼ ounces) stone-ground cornmeal
1½ cups sour cream
½ cup whole milk
¼ cup vegetable oil
5 tablespoons unsalted butter, cut into 5 pieces
2 tablespoons sugar
1 teaspoon baking powder
1 teaspoon baking soda
¾ teaspoon table salt
2 large eggs

1. Adjust oven rack to middle position and heat oven to 450 degrees. Toast cornmeal in 10-inch cast-iron skillet over medium heat, stirring frequently, until fragrant, about 3 minutes.

2. Transfer cornmeal to large bowl and whisk in sour cream and milk; set aside.

3. Wipe skillet clean with paper towels. Add oil to now-empty skillet, place skillet in oven, and heat until oil is shimmering, about 10 minutes. Using potholders, remove skillet from oven, carefully add butter, and gently swirl pan to melt.

4. Being careful of hot skillet handle, pour all but 1 table-spoon oil-butter mixture into cornmeal mixture and whisk to incorporate. Whisk sugar, baking powder, baking soda, and salt into cornmeal mixture until combined, then whisk in eggs.

5. Quickly transfer batter to skillet and smooth top. Transfer skillet to oven and bake until top begins to crack and sides are golden brown, 12 to 15 minutes, rotating skillet halfway through baking.

6. Let bread cool in skillet for 15 minutes. Remove bread from skillet and transfer to wire rack. Serve warm or at room temperature.

Spicy Southern-Style Skillet Cornbread

Whisk 2 minced jalapeño chiles and 2 teaspoons grated lime zest into cornmeal mixture with eggs in step 4.

Cranberry-Walnut Loaf

Makes 1 loaf (**Serves** 10)
Total Time 1¼ hours, plus 5 to 6 hours rising and cooling
MAKE AHEAD **VEGETARIAN**

WHY THIS RECIPE WORKS We wanted to bring the seasonal flavors of tart dried cranberries and rich walnuts to a sturdy yet moist sandwich bread. Whole-wheat flour complemented the earthy flavor of the walnuts, while bread flour provided structure. To prevent the bottom of the loaf from getting too dark, we baked it on a stacked set of two baking sheets for insulation. This left us with an evenly browned loaf that we could happily top with leftover turkey or ham or serve on the side to dress up any lunch.

2¼ cups (12⅓ ounces) bread flour
10 tablespoons (3½ ounces) whole-wheat flour
¾ cup dried cranberries
¾ cup walnuts, toasted and chopped
2 teaspoons instant or rapid-rise yeast
2 teaspoons table salt
1¼ cups water, room temperature
2 tablespoons packed light brown sugar
1 tablespoon vegetable oil

1 large egg, lightly beaten with 1 tablespoon water and pinch table salt

1. Whisk bread flour, whole-wheat flour, cranberries, walnuts, yeast, and salt together in bowl of stand mixer. Whisk water, sugar, and oil in 4-cup liquid measuring cup until sugar has dissolved. Using dough hook on low speed, slowly add water mixture to flour mixture and mix until cohesive dough starts to form and no dry flour remains, about 2 minutes, scraping down bowl as needed.

2. Increase speed to medium-low and knead until dough is smooth and elastic and clears sides of bowl, about 8 minutes.

3. Transfer dough to lightly floured counter and knead by hand to form smooth, round ball, about 30 seconds. Place dough seam side down in lightly greased large bowl or container, cover tightly with plastic wrap, and let rise until doubled in size, 1½ to 2 hours.

4. Stack 2 rimmed baking sheets and line with aluminum foil. Press on dough to deflate. Turn dough out onto lightly floured counter (side of dough that was against bowl should now be facing up). Press and stretch dough into 6-inch square.

5. Fold top corners of dough diagonally into center of square and press gently to seal. Stretch and fold upper third of dough toward center and press seam gently to seal.

6. Stretch and fold dough in half toward you to form rough 8 by 4-inch loaf and pinch seam closed. Roll loaf seam side down. Gently slide your hands underneath each end of loaf and transfer to prepared sheet. Reshape loaf as needed, tucking edges under to form taut torpedo shape. Cover loosely with greased plastic and let rise until loaf increases in size by about half and dough springs back minimally when poked gently with your knuckle, 30 minutes to 1 hour.

7. Adjust oven rack to middle position and heat oven to 450 degrees. Using sharp paring knife or single-edge razor blade, make one ½-inch-deep slash with swift, fluid motion lengthwise along top of loaf, starting and stopping about ½ inch from ends.

8. Gently brush loaf with egg mixture and bake for 15 minutes. Reduce oven temperature to 375 degrees and continue to bake until dark brown and loaf registers 205 to 210 degrees, 30 to 35 minutes, rotating sheet halfway through baking. Transfer loaf to wire rack and let cool completely, about 3 hours, before serving. (Bread can be stored cut side down on cutting board at room temperature for up to 24 hours.)

Southern-Style Skillet Cornbread

FORMING A TORPEDO-SHAPED LOAF

1. Fold top corners of dough diagonally into center of square and press gently to seal. Stretch and fold upper third of dough toward center and press seam gently to seal.

2. Stretch and fold dough in half toward you to form rough 8 by 4-inch loaf and pinch seam closed. Roll loaf seam side down and transfer to prepared baking sheet.

3. After letting loaf rise, use sharp paring knife or single-edge razor blade to make one ½-inch-deep slash lengthwise along top of loaf, starting and stopping about ½ inch from ends.

Cranberry-Walnut Loaf

English Muffin Bread

Almost No-Knead Bread

English Muffin Bread

Makes 2 loaves (**Serves** 20) `MAKE AHEAD` `VEGETARIAN`
Total Time 45 minutes, plus 2 hours rising and cooling

WHY THIS RECIPE WORKS A good loaf of English muffin bread has the same chewy crumb and porous texture as individual English muffins—and it takes a fraction of the time to make. Our recipe makes two loaves so you can freeze one for later (or, if you're feeling generous, you can give one away to a friend). Bread flour gave the loaves their chewy yet light consistency, and because it absorbs more water than all-purpose flour, it resulted in a wet, sticky dough that baked into loaves full of consistently sized holes. A dusting of cornmeal gave the crust that signature English muffin crunch. The test kitchen's preferred loaf pan measures 8½ by 4½ inches; if using 9 by 5-inch pans, check for doneness 5 minutes early. English muffin bread is designed to be toasted after it is sliced.

    Cornmeal
  5 cups (27½ ounces) bread flour
1½ tablespoons instant or rapid-rise yeast
  1 tablespoon sugar
  2 teaspoons table salt
  1 teaspoon baking soda
  3 cups warm whole milk (120 degrees)

1. Grease two 8½ by 4½-inch loaf pans and dust with cornmeal. Combine flour, yeast, sugar, salt, and baking soda in large bowl. Stir in warm milk until combined, about 1 minute. Cover dough with greased plastic wrap and let rise in warm place for 30 minutes, or until dough is bubbly and has doubled in size.

2. Stir dough and divide between prepared pans, pushing into corners with greased rubber spatula. (Pans should be about two-thirds full.) Cover pans with greased plastic and let dough rise in warm place until it reaches edges of pans, about 30 minutes. Adjust oven rack to middle position and heat oven to 375 degrees.

3. Discard plastic and transfer pans to oven. Bake until bread is well browned and registers 200 degrees, about 30 minutes, switching and rotating pans halfway through baking. Turn bread out onto wire rack and let cool completely, about 1 hour. Slice, toast, and serve.

To make ahead Bread can be sliced (place parchment paper between slices), wrapped in aluminum foil, placed in a zipper-lock bag, and frozen for up to 1 month. To thaw frozen slices for toasting, place slices on plate and microwave uncovered on high for 15 to 25 seconds.

Almost No-Knead Bread

Makes 1 loaf (**Serves** 10)
Total Time 1¼ hours, plus 12½ to 13 hours rising and cooling `MAKE AHEAD` `VEGETARIAN`

WHY THIS RECIPE WORKS Nothing beats a loaf of fresh-baked bread for sopping up every last bit of a savory sauce or for making a heartier meal out of a warm winter salad. Using a high proportion of liquid to dry ingredients and an extended resting period promoted gluten formation so that it took just 1 minute of kneading to form a smooth, elastic dough. Since the bread got only a relatively short 8-hour room-temperature rise, we added some beer and a splash of white vinegar to the dough to enhance the bread's yeasty tang. We baked the dough in a covered Dutch oven, turning on the heat only after placing the pot in the oven. This contributed to the bread's open, airy crumb by giving the dough more time to expand before the heat set up the crust. We prefer to use a mild American lager, such as Budweiser, here; strongly flavored beers will make the bread taste bitter. Use a Dutch oven that holds 6 quarts or more. In step 5, start the 30-minute timer as soon as you put the bread in the cold oven.

　3　cups (15 ounces) all-purpose flour
1½　teaspoons table salt
　¼　teaspoon instant or rapid-rise yeast
　¾　cup water, room temperature
　½　cup mild lager, room temperature
　1　tablespoon distilled white vinegar

1. Whisk flour, salt, and yeast together in large bowl. Whisk water, beer, and vinegar together in 4-cup liquid measuring cup. Using rubber spatula, gently fold water mixture into flour mixture, scraping up dry flour from bottom of bowl, until dough starts to form and no dry flour remains. Cover bowl tightly with plastic wrap and let stand at room temperature for at least 8 hours or up to 18 hours.

2. Lay 18 by 12-inch sheet of parchment paper on counter and lightly spray with vegetable oil spray. Transfer dough to lightly floured counter and knead by hand until smooth and elastic, about 1 minute.

3. Shape dough into ball by pulling edges into middle, then transfer seam side down to center of prepared parchment.

4. Using parchment as sling, gently lower loaf into Dutch oven (let any excess parchment hang over pot edge). Cover tightly with plastic and let rise until loaf has doubled in size and dough springs back minimally when poked gently with your knuckle, 1½ to 2 hours.

5. Adjust oven rack to middle position. Using sharp paring knife or single-edge razor blade, make two 5-inch-long, ½-inch-deep slashes with swift, fluid motion along top of loaf to form cross. Cover pot and place in oven. Turn oven to 425 degrees and bake loaf for 30 minutes (start timing as soon as bread goes in oven).

6. Remove lid and continue to bake until loaf is deep golden brown and registers 205 to 210 degrees, 25 to 30 minutes. Using parchment sling, remove loaf from pot and transfer to wire rack; discard parchment. Let cool completely, about 3 hours, before serving. (Bread can be wrapped in foil and stored at room temperature for up to 2 days. To reheat, place on rimmed baking sheet and bake in 350-degree oven for 10 minutes.)

Almost No-Knead Whole-Wheat Bread

Substitute 1 cup whole-wheat flour for 1 cup all-purpose flour. Stir 2 tablespoons honey into water before adding it to flour mixture in step 1.

SHAPING ROUND LOAVES (BOULES)

1. Press and stretch dough into a round.

2. Working around circumference of dough, fold edges toward center of round until ball forms.

3. Flip dough ball seam side down and, using your cupped hands, drag dough in small circles until dough feels taut and round.

Oatmeal-Raisin Bread

Makes 1 loaf (**Serves** 10)
Total Time 1½ to 2 hours, plus 5¾ to 6¼ hours rising and cooling `MAKE AHEAD` `VEGETARIAN`

WHY THIS RECIPE WORKS This bread, flavored with oatmeal, sweet raisins, and just a touch of brown sugar, is great toasted up for breakfast or enjoyed with coffee as an afternoon snack. Mixing the oatmeal into the dough toward the end of kneading proved the perfect way to incorporate it without creating big clumps of oats. Replacing a small amount of the bread flour with whole-wheat flour complemented the oats' earthy whole-grain flavor. To give the loaf a pretty finish, we misted it with water and then sprinkled more oats on top. Do not substitute quick or instant oats in this recipe. Use a Dutch oven that holds 6 quarts or more.

  1 cup (3 ounces) old-fashioned rolled oats, divided
  ¾ cup water, room temperature
  2 cups (11 ounces) bread flour
  ½ cup (2¾ ounces) whole-wheat flour
  2 teaspoons instant or rapid-rise yeast
  1½ teaspoons table salt
  1 cup whole milk, room temperature
  3 tablespoons unsalted butter, melted
  ½ cup raisins

1. Microwave ¾ cup oats and water in large covered bowl, stirring occasionally, until oats are softened and water is completely absorbed, about 5 minutes; let cool completely before using.

2. Whisk bread flour, whole-wheat flour, yeast, and salt together in bowl of stand mixer. Whisk milk and melted butter together in 2-cup liquid measuring cup. Using dough hook on low speed, slowly add milk mixture to flour mixture and mix until cohesive dough starts to form and no dry flour remains, about 2 minutes, scraping down bowl as needed.

3. Increase speed to medium-low and knead until dough is smooth and elastic and clears sides of bowl, about 6 minutes. Reduce speed to low, slowly add raisins, then slowly add oatmeal, 2 tablespoons at a time, and mix until mostly incorporated, about 3 minutes. Transfer dough to lightly greased large bowl or container, cover tightly with plastic, and let rise for 30 minutes.

4. Using greased bowl scraper (or your fingertips), fold dough over itself by gently lifting and folding edge of dough toward middle. Turn bowl 45 degrees and fold dough again; repeat turning bowl and folding dough 6 more times (total of 8 folds). Cover tightly with plastic and let rise for 30 minutes.

Repeat folding and rising every 30 minutes, 2 more times. After third set of folds, cover bowl tightly with plastic and let dough rise until nearly doubled in size, 45 minutes to 1¼ hours.

5. Lay 18 by 12-inch sheet of parchment paper on counter; spray with vegetable oil spray. Transfer dough to lightly floured counter. Using your lightly floured hands, press and stretch dough into 10-inch round; deflate any gas pockets larger than 1 inch. Working around circumference of dough, fold edges toward center until ball forms. Flip dough ball seam side down and, using your cupped hands, drag in small circles on counter until dough feels taut and round and all seams are secured on underside of loaf. Mist loaf with water on all sides and sprinkle with remaining ¼ cup oats, pressing gently on sides of loaf to adhere.

6. Place loaf, seam side down, in center of prepared parchment and cover loosely with greased plastic wrap. Let rise until loaf increases in size by about half and dough springs back minimally when poked gently with your knuckle, 30 minutes to 1 hour.

7. Thirty minutes before baking, adjust oven rack to lower-middle position, place Dutch oven (with lid) on rack, and heat oven to 500 degrees. Holding sharp paring knife or single-edge razor blade at 30-degree angle to loaf, make two 5-inch-long, ½-inch-deep slashes with swift, fluid motion along top of loaf to form cross. Discard any exposed raisins on top of loaf.

8. Carefully transfer pot to wire rack and uncover. Using parchment as sling, gently lower dough into Dutch oven. Cover pot, tucking any excess parchment into pot, and return to oven. Reduce oven temperature to 425 degrees and bake loaf for 15 minutes. Uncover and continue to bake until loaf is deep golden brown and registers 205 to 210 degrees, about 20 minutes. Using parchment sling, remove loaf from pot and transfer to wire rack; discard parchment. Let cool completely, about 3 hours, before serving. (Bread can be wrapped in double layer of plastic wrap and stored at room temperature for up to 3 days.)

NOTES FROM THE TEST KITCHEN

WHY BAKE BREAD IN A DUTCH OVEN?
The enclosed environment of a Dutch oven is perfect for trapping steam. Why is this important? Steam keeps the crust soft for longer as the bread bakes, allowing for a higher rise and a more open crumb. Plus, steam condensing on the surface of the bread dissolves some of the natural sugars in the dough; when the steam evaporates, these sugars caramelize to produce a crisp artisan-style crust.

No-Knead Brioche

Makes 1 loaf (**Serves** 8) | **Total Time** 1½ hours, plus 20¾ to 21¾ hours rising and cooling

`MAKE AHEAD` `VEGETARIAN`

WHY THIS RECIPE WORKS Tender, golden, buttery brioche is great on its own, made into a cozy bread pudding, or transformed into French toast. We turned the classic method for brioche on its head: Instead of kneading softened butter into the dough in increments, we used melted butter along with our technique for Almost No-Knead Bread (page 313). To give the highly enriched bread more structure, we used higher-protein bread flour. A series of folds encouraged the formation of a sturdy gluten network. Instead of shaping the dough into a single long loaf, we divided it in two and shaped each half into a ball. Placed side by side in the pan and rested before baking, the two balls merged to form a single loaf with a fine crumb. The test kitchen's preferred loaf pan measures 8½ by 4½ inches; if using a 9 by 5-inch loaf pan, increase the shaped rising time by 20 to 30 minutes and start checking for doneness 10 minutes earlier than advised in the recipe.

No-Knead Brioche

1⅔ cups (9⅛ ounces) bread flour
1¼ teaspoons instant or rapid-rise yeast
¾ teaspoon table salt
3 large eggs, room temperature
8 tablespoons unsalted butter, melted
¼ cup water, room temperature
3 tablespoons sugar

1 large egg, lightly beaten with 1 tablespoon water and pinch table salt

1. Whisk flour, yeast, and salt together in large bowl. Whisk eggs, melted butter, water, and sugar in second bowl until sugar has dissolved.

2. Using rubber spatula, gently fold egg mixture into flour mixture, scraping up dry flour from bottom of bowl, until cohesive dough starts to form and no dry flour remains. Cover bowl tightly with plastic wrap and let dough rest for 10 minutes.

3. Using greased bowl scraper (or your fingertips), fold dough over itself by gently lifting and folding edge of dough toward middle. Turn bowl 90 degrees and fold dough again; repeat turning bowl and folding dough 2 more times (total of 4 folds). Cover tightly with plastic and let rise for 30 minutes. Repeat folding and rising every 30 minutes, 3 more times. After fourth set of folds, cover bowl tightly with plastic and refrigerate for at least 16 hours or up to 2 days.

NOTES FROM THE TEST KITCHEN

SLASHING BREAD LOAVES
Slashing a loaf cuts through its gluten sheath, creating designated weak spots in a loaf's surface which allow the loaf to expand in the right direction in the oven. Act quickly and decisively and slash with a swift, fluid motion; otherwise, your paring knife or single-edge razor blade will drag, creating messy lines.

Round Loaves (Boules): The most basic slashing style for a boule is a cross. Make two slashes along the top of the loaf to form an X.

Torpedo-Shaped Loaves: Wide, long loaves can be scored with three evenly spaced slashes across the width of the loaf, or with a single lengthwise slash, as in our Classic Italian Bread (page 316).

4. Transfer dough to well-floured counter, divide in half, and cover loosely with greased plastic. Using your well-floured hands, press 1 piece of dough into 4-inch round (keep remaining piece covered). Working around circumference of dough, fold edges toward center until ball forms. Repeat with remaining piece of dough.

5. Flip each dough ball seam side down and, using your cupped hands, drag in small circles on counter until dough feels taut and round and all seams are secured on underside. (If dough sticks to your hands, lightly dust top of dough with flour.) Cover dough rounds loosely with greased plastic and let rest for 5 minutes.

6. Grease 8½ by 4½-inch loaf pan. Flip each dough ball seam side up, press into 4-inch disk, and repeat folding and rounding steps.

7. Place rounds seam side down, side by side, into prepared pan. Press dough gently into corners. Cover loosely with greased plastic and let rise until loaf reaches ½ inch below lip of pan and dough springs back minimally when poked gently with your knuckle, 1½ to 2 hours.

8. Adjust oven rack to middle position and heat oven to 350 degrees. Gently brush loaf with egg mixture and bake until deep golden brown and loaf registers 190 to 195 degrees, 35 to 40 minutes, rotating pan halfway through baking. Let loaf cool in pan for 15 minutes. Remove loaf from pan and let cool completely on wire rack, about 3 hours, before serving. (Bread can be wrapped in foil and stored at room temperature for up to 2 days. To reheat, place bread on rimmed baking sheet and bake in 350-degree oven for 10 minutes.)

Classic Italian Bread

Makes 1 loaf (**Serves** 10) `MAKE AHEAD` `VEGETARIAN`
Total Time 1 hour, plus 5 to 6 hours rising and cooling

WHY THIS RECIPE WORKS A cozy Italian American Sunday supper is incomplete without a loaf of fresh-baked bread. Our homemade bread is inspired by a classic supermarket Italian loaf, soft-crusted and chewy yet tender. We wanted to shorten the dough's rising time, but that meant we would also be reducing the fermentation time, which is what provides much of the flavor in an artisan bread. To make up for this loss, we added yeasty tang by using beer as the main liquid component in our dough. Setting the dough on a preheated baking stone gave the bread a nicely browned but not tough crust. Misting the loaf with water before baking helped the exterior of the bread stay supple and encouraged additional rise and a light, tender crumb. We prefer to use a mild American lager, such as Budweiser, here; strongly flavored beers will make the bread taste bitter. You will need a baking peel for this recipe.

    3 cups (16½ ounces) bread flour
    1½ teaspoons instant or rapid-rise yeast
    1½ teaspoons table salt
    1 cup mild lager, room temperature
    6 tablespoons water, room temperature
    2 tablespoons extra-virgin olive oil

1. Whisk flour, yeast, and salt together in bowl of stand mixer. Whisk beer, water, and oil together in 4-cup liquid measuring cup.

2. Using dough hook on low speed, slowly add beer mixture to flour mixture and mix until cohesive dough starts to form and no dry flour remains, about 2 minutes, scraping down bowl as needed. Increase speed to medium-low and knead until dough is smooth and elastic and clears sides of bowl, about 8 minutes.

3. Transfer dough to lightly floured counter and knead by hand to form smooth, round ball, about 30 seconds. Place dough seam side down in lightly greased large bowl or container, cover tightly with plastic wrap, and let rise until doubled in size, 1 to 1½ hours.

4. Line baking peel with 16 by 12-inch piece of parchment paper, with long edge of paper perpendicular to handle. Gently press down on dough to deflate any large gas pockets. Turn dough out onto lightly floured counter (side of dough that was against bowl should now be facing up) and press and stretch dough into 10-inch square.

5. Fold top corners of dough diagonally into center of square and press gently to seal. Stretch and fold upper third of dough toward center and press seam gently to seal. Stretch and fold dough in half toward you to form rough loaf and pinch seam closed.

6. Starting at center of dough and working toward ends, gently and evenly roll and stretch dough until it measures 15 inches long by 4 inches wide. Roll loaf seam side down. Gently slide your hands underneath each end of loaf and transfer seam side down to prepared pizza peel.

7. Reshape loaf as needed, tucking edges under to form taut torpedo shape. Cover loosely with greased plastic and let rise until loaf increases in size by about half and dough springs back minimally when poked gently with your knuckle, 30 minutes to 1 hour.

8. One hour before baking, adjust oven rack to lower-middle position, place baking stone on rack, and heat oven to 450 degrees. Using sharp paring knife or single-edge razor blade, make one ½-inch-deep slash with swift, fluid motion lengthwise along top of loaf, starting and stopping about 1½ inches from ends.

9. Mist loaf with water and slide parchment with loaf onto baking stone. Bake until crust is golden brown and loaf registers 205 to 210 degrees, 25 to 30 minutes, rotating loaf halfway through baking. Transfer loaf to wire rack; discard parchment. Let cool completely, about 3 hours, before serving. (Bread can be stored cut side down on cutting board at room temperature for up to 24 hours.)

Fig and Fennel Bread

Makes 1 loaf (**Serves** 10) | **Total Time** 4 to 4½ hours, plus 9 hours rising and cooling `VEGETARIAN`

WHY THIS RECIPE WORKS If you want to wow company, just set a loaf of this novel artisan-style bread on the table. The sophisticated combination of sweet, earthy figs; complementary fennel; and rye flour gave this grown-up loaf its distinguished flavor profile, ideally suited for accompanying cheese and charcuterie plates. To bolster the flavor and structure of our rye-enhanced loaf, we started by making a sponge: a mixture of flour, water, and yeast that we allowed to rest at room temperature for at least 6 hours. This rest kickstarted the dough's fermentation, developing subtle sour and nutty flavors. The acid developed during this rest also strengthened the bread's gluten network, so it baked up with an open crumb and appealing chew. Finally, to give the crust crunch and a rustic appearance, we dusted the loaf with cornmeal before baking it. Use a Dutch oven that holds 6 quarts or more. While any variety of dried figs will work, we especially like the flavor of Calimyrna figs. Use light or medium rye flour; dark rye flour is overpowering. Toast the fennel seeds in a dry skillet over medium heat until fragrant (about 1 minute), and then remove the pan from the heat so the fennel seeds don't scorch.

SPONGE
- 1 cup (5½ ounces) bread flour
- ¾ cup water, room temperature
- ⅛ teaspoon instant or rapid-rise yeast

Classic Italian Bread

DOUGH
- 1 cup plus 2 tablespoons (6¼ ounces) bread flour
- 1 cup (5½ ounces) light or medium rye flour
- 1 tablespoon fennel seeds, toasted
- 2 teaspoons table salt
- 1½ teaspoons instant or rapid-rise yeast
- 1 cup water, room temperature
- 1 cup dried figs, stemmed and chopped coarse
  Cornmeal

1. FOR THE SPONGE Stir flour, water, and yeast in 4-cup liquid measuring cup with wooden spoon until well combined. Cover tightly with plastic wrap and let sit at room temperature until sponge has risen and begins to collapse, about 6 hours (sponge can sit at room temperature for up to 24 hours).

2. FOR THE DOUGH Whisk bread flour, rye flour, fennel seeds, salt, and yeast together in bowl of stand mixer. Stir water into sponge with wooden spoon until well combined. Using dough hook on low speed, slowly add sponge mixture

Fig and Fennel Bread

Rosemary Focaccia

to flour mixture and mix until cohesive dough starts to form and no dry flour remains, about 2 minutes, scraping down bowl as needed.

3. Increase speed to medium-low and continue to knead until dough is smooth, elastic, and slightly sticky, about 5 minutes. Reduce speed to low; slowly add figs, ¼ cup at a time; and mix until mostly incorporated, about 1 minute. Transfer dough to lightly greased large bowl or container, cover tightly with plastic, and let rise for 30 minutes.

4. Using greased bowl scraper (or your fingertips), fold dough over itself by gently lifting and folding edge of dough toward middle. Turn bowl 45 degrees and fold dough again; repeat turning bowl and folding dough 6 more times (total of 8 folds). Cover tightly with plastic; let rise for 30 minutes. Repeat folding and rising every 30 minutes, 2 more times. After third set of folds, cover bowl tightly with plastic and let rise until nearly doubled in size, 45 minutes to 1¼ hours.

5. Lay 18 by 12-inch sheet of parchment paper on counter, lightly spray with vegetable oil spray, and dust evenly with cornmeal. Transfer dough to lightly floured counter. Using your lightly floured hands, press and stretch dough into 10-inch round, deflating any gas pockets larger than 1 inch.

6. Working around circumference of dough, fold edges toward center until ball forms. Flip dough ball seam side down and, using your cupped hands, drag in small circles on counter until dough feels taut and round and all seams are secured on underside of loaf.

7. Place loaf, seam side down, in center of prepared parchment and cover loosely with greased plastic wrap. Let rise until loaf increases in size by about half and dough springs back minimally when poked gently with your knuckle, about 30 minutes.

8. Thirty minutes before baking, adjust oven rack to lower-middle position, place Dutch oven (with lid) on rack, and heat oven to 500 degrees. Holding sharp paring knife or single-edge razor blade at 30-degree angle to loaf, make two 5-inch-long, ½-inch-deep slashes with swift, fluid motion along top of loaf to form cross. Dust top of loaf with cornmeal.

9. Carefully transfer pot to wire rack and uncover. Using parchment as sling, gently lower dough into Dutch oven. Cover pot, tucking any excess parchment into pot, and return to oven. Reduce oven temperature to 425 degrees and bake loaf for 15 minutes. Uncover and continue to bake until loaf is deep golden brown and registers 205 to 210 degrees, about 20 minutes.

10. Using parchment sling, remove loaf from pot and transfer to wire rack; discard parchment. Let cool completely, about 3 hours, before serving.

Rosemary Focaccia

Makes two 9-inch round loaves (**Serves** 12)
Total Time 1¼ hours, plus 8¾ to 9¼ hours rising and cooling MAKE AHEAD VEGETARIAN

WHY THIS RECIPE WORKS Rosemary adds piney pungency to our airy focaccia. Focaccia is traditionally loaded with olive oil and then coated with more oil before baking, giving the bread its characteristic crisp, golden exterior and soft, supple crumb. A pre-ferment, or sponge, gave us the flavor benefits of fermentation without the need to give the dough a 24-hour (or longer) rest: Allowing a mixture of flour, water, and yeast to sit at room temperature rapidly developed a strong yeasty flavor. We used an almost no-knead mixing method, giving the mixed dough a 15-minute rest before adding salt; this short period gave the dough a chance to form lots of gluten strands before the gluten-inhibiting salt was introduced. Folding the dough at regular intervals as it rose aligned those strands into a resilient network that would trap plenty of air to yield the bubbly interior focaccia is known for. You will need a baking stone for this recipe.

SPONGE

- ½ cup (2½ ounces) all-purpose flour
- ⅓ cup water, room temperature
- ¼ teaspoon instant or rapid-rise yeast

DOUGH

- 2½ cups (12½ ounces) all-purpose flour
- 1¼ cups water, room temperature
- 1 teaspoon instant or rapid-rise yeast
- 1 tablespoon kosher salt, divided
- ¼ cup extra-virgin olive oil
- 2 tablespoons chopped fresh rosemary

1. FOR THE SPONGE Stir flour, water, and yeast in large bowl with wooden spoon until well combined. Cover tightly with plastic wrap and let stand at room temperature until sponge has risen and begins to collapse, about 6 hours (sponge can stand at room temperature for up to 24 hours).

2. FOR THE DOUGH Stir flour, water, and yeast into sponge with wooden spoon until well combined. Cover bowl tightly with plastic; let dough rest for 15 minutes.

3. Stir 2 teaspoons salt into dough with wooden spoon until thoroughly incorporated, about 1 minute. Cover bowl tightly with plastic and let dough rest for 30 minutes.

4. Using greased bowl scraper or rubber spatula, fold dough over itself by gently lifting and folding edge of dough toward middle. Turn bowl 45 degrees and fold dough again; repeat turning bowl and folding dough 6 more times (total of 8 folds). Cover tightly with plastic and let rise for 30 minutes. Repeat folding and let dough rise for 30 minutes. Fold dough one final time, then cover bowl tightly with plastic and let dough rise until nearly doubled in size, 30 minutes to 1 hour.

5. One hour before baking, adjust oven rack to upper-middle position, place baking stone on rack, and heat oven to 500 degrees. Coat two 9-inch round cake pans with 2 table-spoons oil each. Sprinkle each pan with ½ teaspoon salt. Transfer dough to lightly floured counter and dust top with flour. Divide dough in half and cover loosely with greased plastic. Working with 1 piece of dough at a time (keep remaining piece covered), shape into 5-inch round by gently tucking under edges.

6. Place dough rounds seam side up in prepared pans. Coat tops and sides with oil, then flip rounds so seam side is down. Cover loosely with greased plastic and let dough rest for 5 minutes.

7. Using your fingertips, gently press each dough round into corners of pan, taking care not to tear dough. (If dough resists stretching, let it relax for 5 to 10 minutes before trying to stretch it again.) Using fork, poke surface of dough 25 to 30 times, popping any large bubbles. Sprinkle 1 tablespoon rosemary evenly over top of each loaf; cover loosely with greased plastic; and let dough rest until slightly bubbly, about 10 minutes.

8. Place pans on baking stone and reduce oven temperature to 450 degrees. Bake until tops are golden brown, 25 to 30 minutes, rotating pans halfway through baking. Let loaves cool in pans for 5 minutes. Remove loaves from pans and transfer to wire rack. Brush tops with any oil remaining in pans and let cool for 30 minutes. Serve warm or at room temperature. (Bread can be wrapped in double layer of plastic wrap and stored at room temperature for up to 2 days.)

Focaccia with Caramelized Red Onion, Pancetta, and Oregano

Cook 4 ounces finely chopped pancetta in 12-inch skillet over medium heat, stirring occasionally, until well rendered, about 10 minutes. Using slotted spoon, transfer pancetta to medium bowl. Add 1 chopped red onion and 2 tablespoons water to fat left in skillet and cook over medium heat until onion is softened and lightly browned, about 12 minutes. Transfer onion to bowl with pancetta and stir in 2 teaspoons minced fresh oregano; let mixture cool completely before using. Substitute pancetta mixture for rosemary.

Za'atar Bread

Serves 6 to 8 VEGETARIAN
Total Time 1 hour, plus 26 hours rising

WHY THIS RECIPE WORKS Inspired by mana'eesh, a round Arabic flatbread covered with a thick coating of za'atar (a spice blend including thyme, sumac, and sesame seeds) and olive oil, we set out to develop our own recipe for irresistibly seasoned bread ideal for snacking or rounding out a warmly spiced meal. Letting the dough rise slowly for at least 24 hours in the refrigerator made for uniformly sized air bubbles and created more flavor. Before baking, we coated the bottom of a rimmed baking sheet with olive oil; gently pressed the dough into an even, dimpled layer across the sheet; and then spread za'atar and more oil across the dough's surface. The oil essentially fried the exterior of the flatbread as it baked, resulting in a crisp, golden base that contrasted with the plush, soft crumb. We prefer to use our homemade Za'atar (page 101), but you can substitute store-bought za'atar if you wish, though salt content can vary greatly by brand.

3½ cups (19¼ ounces) bread flour
2½ teaspoons instant or rapid-rise yeast
2½ teaspoons sugar
1⅓ cups ice water

2 tablespoons plus ½ cup extra-virgin olive oil, divided
2 teaspoons table salt
⅓ cup za'atar
    Coarse sea salt

1. Pulse flour, yeast, and sugar in food processor until combined, about 5 pulses. With processor running, slowly add ice water and process until dough is just combined and no dry flour remains, about 10 seconds. Let dough rest for 10 minutes.

2. Add 2 tablespoons oil and salt to dough and process until dough forms satiny, sticky ball that clears sides of bowl, 30 to 60 seconds. Transfer dough to lightly floured counter and knead by hand to form smooth, round ball, about 30 seconds. Place dough seam side down in lightly greased large bowl or container, cover tightly with plastic wrap, and refrigerate for at least 24 hours or up to 3 days.

3. Remove dough from refrigerator and let stand at room temperature for 1 hour. Coat rimmed baking sheet with 2 tablespoons oil. Gently press down on dough to deflate any large gas pockets. Transfer dough to prepared sheet and, using your fingertips, press out to uniform thickness, taking care not to tear dough. (Dough may not fit snugly into corners.) Cover loosely with greased plastic and let dough rest for 1 hour.

4. Adjust oven rack to lower-middle position and heat oven to 375 degrees. Using your fingertips, gently press dough into corners of sheet and dimple entire surface.

5. Combine remaining 6 tablespoons oil and za'atar in bowl. Using back of spoon, spread oil mixture in even layer over entire surface of dough to edge.

6. Bake until bottom crust is evenly browned and edges are crisp, 20 to 25 minutes, rotating sheet halfway through baking. Let bread cool in sheet for 10 minutes, then transfer to cutting board with metal spatula. Season with sea salt to taste, slice, and serve warm.

Stollen

Makes 2 loaves (**Serves** 20) MAKE AHEAD VEGETARIAN
Total Time 1¾ hours, plus 15½ hours rising and cooling

WHY THIS RECIPE WORKS Stollen is a rich, sweet yeasted bread served at Christmas throughout Germany and Austria. Unlike most breads, stollen improves over time, so you can enjoy it bit by bit or make extra loaves to give as gifts. We wanted our stollen to feature both dried and candied fruits as well as almonds and heady spirits. We enriched our dough with milk, brandy, egg, and butter, melting the butter before stirring it in to produce the short crumb we wanted. To make the traditional marzipan core, we softened our almond filling with butter and water and scented it with a pinch of nutmeg before shaping it into a rectangle and sealing it inside the dough. We do not recommend mixing this dough by hand. If the dough becomes too soft to work with at any point, refrigerate it until it's firm enough to easily handle. The texture and flavor of stollen improves over time; the bread is best eaten two weeks after baking.

FILLING

- 1 tube (7 ounces) almond paste, cut into 4 pieces
- 1 tablespoon unsalted butter, softened
- 1 tablespoon water
- Pinch nutmeg

DOUGH

- 1 cup raisins
- ½ cup brandy
- ½ cup chopped candied lemon peel
- ½ cup chopped candied orange peel
- ½ cup slivered almonds, toasted
- 3½ cups (17½ ounces) all-purpose flour
- 4 teaspoons instant or rapid-rise yeast
- 1¼ teaspoons table salt
- 1 cup whole milk, room temperature
- 10 tablespoons unsalted butter, melted, divided
- ½ cup (3½ ounces) granulated sugar
- 1 large egg, room temperature
- 1 teaspoon vanilla extract
- Confectioners' sugar

1. FOR THE FILLING Using stand mixer fitted with paddle, beat almond paste, butter, water, and nutmeg on medium speed until smooth, about 1 minute. Transfer to bowl, cover, and refrigerate until ready to use.

2. FOR THE DOUGH Microwave raisins and brandy in covered bowl until steaming, about 1 minute. Let stand until raisins have softened, about 15 minutes. Drain raisins and reserve brandy. Combine raisins, candied lemon peel, candied orange peel, and almonds in bowl.

3. Whisk flour, yeast, and salt together in clean, dry mixer bowl. Whisk milk, 8 tablespoons melted butter, granulated sugar, egg, vanilla, and reserved brandy in 4-cup liquid measuring cup until sugar has dissolved. Using paddle on low speed, slowly add milk mixture to flour mixture and mix until cohesive dough starts to form and no dry flour remains, about 2 minutes, scraping down bowl as needed. Slowly add fruit mixture and mix until incorporated, about 30 seconds. Transfer dough to

Za'atar Bread

Stollen

lightly greased large bowl or container, cover tightly with plastic wrap, and refrigerate for at least 12 hours or up to 24 hours.

4. Stack 2 rimmed baking sheets, line with aluminum foil, and spray with vegetable oil spray. Transfer filling to well-floured counter, divide in half, and press each half into 7 by 2-inch rectangle; set aside.

5. Transfer dough to well-floured counter, divide in half, and cover loosely with greased plastic. Using your well-floured hands, press 1 piece of dough into 10 by 8-inch rectangle (keep remaining piece covered), with short side parallel to counter edge. Place 1 piece of filling across top edge of dough, leaving 2-inch border at top. Fold dough away from you over filling until folded edge is snug against filling and dough extends 2 inches beyond top edge.

6. Fold top 2 inches of dough back toward center of loaf. Pinch side seams together to seal. Repeat with remaining dough and filling. Transfer loaves to prepared sheet, spaced about 4 inches apart. Cover loosely with greased plastic and let rest for 30 minutes.

7. Adjust oven rack to middle position and heat oven to 350 degrees. Bake until golden brown and loaves register 190 to 195 degrees, 40 to 45 minutes, rotating sheet halfway through baking. Brush loaves with remaining 2 tablespoons melted butter and dust liberally with confectioners' sugar. Transfer to wire rack and let cool completely, about 3 hours. Dust with additional confectioners' sugar before serving. (Stollen can be wrapped in plastic wrap and stored at room temperature for up to 1 month.)

Panettone

Makes 2 loaves (**Serves** 20)
Total Time 2 hours, plus 24 to 25 hours rising and cooling `MAKE AHEAD` `VEGETARIAN`

WHY THIS RECIPE WORKS Panettone is a sweet bread filled with candied and dried fruits; it was once the bread of emperors and popes and made only during the Christmas season. The abundance of fat in the dough—from butter, eggs, and extra yolks—can make the bread dense and crumbly; to remedy this, we used high-protein bread flour and kneaded the dough in a stand mixer before incorporating the softened butter to ensure that the dough had a strong gluten structure. Studded with golden raisins and candied orange peel and perfumed with orange zest, this panettone was certainly worthy of its regal history. You can find paper panettone molds online or at kitchen supply stores. Be sure to reduce the oven temperature immediately after putting the loaves in the oven.

Panettone

1¼ cups (6¼ ounces) golden raisins
1½ tablespoons grated orange zest plus ¼ cup juice
5 cups (27½ ounces) bread flour
2 tablespoons instant or rapid-rise yeast
1½ teaspoons table salt
2 cups whole milk, room temperature
4 large eggs plus 3 large yolks, room temperature
⅔ cup (4⅔ ounces) sugar
2 teaspoons vanilla extract
1 teaspoon almond extract
8 tablespoons unsalted butter, cut into 8 pieces and softened
1¼ cups (6 ounces) finely chopped candied orange peel

1. Microwave raisins and orange juice in covered bowl until steaming, about 1 minute. Let stand until raisins have softened, about 15 minutes. Drain raisins and reserve orange juice.

2. Whisk flour, yeast, and salt together in bowl of stand mixer. Whisk milk, eggs and yolks, sugar, vanilla, almond extract, and reserved orange juice in 4-cup liquid measuring cup until sugar has dissolved. Using dough hook on low speed, slowly add milk mixture to flour mixture and mix until cohesive dough starts to form and no dry flour remains, about 5 minutes, scraping down bowl as needed.

3. Increase speed to medium-low and knead until dough is elastic but still sticks to sides of bowl, about 8 minutes. With mixer running, add butter, 1 tablespoon at a time, and knead until butter is fully incorporated, about 4 minutes. Continue to knead until dough is satiny and elastic and very sticky, about 3 minutes. Reduce speed to low, slowly add candied orange peel, raisins, and orange zest and mix until incorporated, about 3 minutes. Transfer dough to lightly greased large bowl or container, cover tightly with plastic wrap, and let rise for 30 minutes.

4. Using greased bowl scraper (or your fingertips), fold dough over itself by gently lifting and folding edge of dough toward middle. Turn bowl 90 degrees and fold dough again; repeat turning bowl and folding dough 2 more times (total of 4 folds). Cover tightly with plastic and let dough rise for 30 minutes. Fold dough again, then cover bowl tightly with plastic and refrigerate for at least 16 hours or up to 2 days.

5. Let dough stand at room temperature for 1½ hours. Press down on dough to deflate. Transfer dough to well-floured counter, divide in half, and cover loosely with greased plastic. Press 1 piece of dough (keep remaining piece covered) into 6-inch round. Working around circumference of dough, fold edges toward center until ball forms. Flip ball seam side down and, using your cupped hands, drag in small circles on counter until dough feels taut and round and all seams are secured on underside. Repeat with remaining piece of dough.

6. Place dough rounds into two 6 by 4-inch paper panettone molds, pressing dough gently into corners. Transfer to wire rack set in rimmed baking sheet, cover loosely with greased plastic, and let rise until loaves reach 2 inches above lip of molds and dough springs back minimally when poked gently with your knuckle, 3 to 4 hours.

7. Adjust oven rack to middle position and heat oven to 400 degrees. Using sharp paring knife or single-edge razor blade, make two 5-inch-long, ¼-inch-deep slashes with swift, fluid motion along top of each loaf to form cross.

8. Place baking sheet in oven and reduce oven temperature to 350 degrees. Bake until loaves are deep golden brown, about 40 minutes, rotating sheet halfway through baking. Tent loaves with aluminum foil and continue to bake until loaves register 190 to 195 degrees, 20 to 30 minutes. Let loaves cool completely on wire rack, about 3 hours, before serving. (Panettone can be wrapped in double layer of plastic wrap and stored at room temperature for up to 5 days.)

Portuguese Sweet Bread

Portuguese Sweet Bread

Makes 1 loaf (**Serves** 10) | **Total Time** 1¼ hours, plus 7¾ to 8¾ hours rising and cooling VEGETARIAN

WHY THIS RECIPE WORKS Portuguese sweet bread is a mildly sweet enriched bread with a moderately compact yet delicate crumb and a thin, tender, mahogany-colored crust. It is baked both for holidays and as a daily bread; the bread is delicious on its own, dunked into coffee, slathered with jam, or made into French toast. Using three whole eggs plus one yolk in the dough gave us a tender, moist crumb, and we added just enough sugar—½ cup plus 1 tablespoon—to make our bread pleasingly sweet but mild enough to enjoy regularly. Portuguese sweet bread comes in many shapes, but we liked the simplicity of forming the dough into a round and baking it in a cake pan. This bread experiences a lot of oven spring that can cause it to tear on the sides, so we let it proof until the dough reached 1¾ inches above the lip of the pan before baking it so that the oven rise would be less dramatic. Slashing the loaf around its circumference was another way to eliminate tears by helping the loaf expand before its crust set.

4 cups (20 ounces) all-purpose flour

2¼ teaspoons instant or rapid-rise yeast

1 teaspoon table salt

¾ cup water, room temperature

3 large eggs plus 1 large yolk, room temperature

½ cup (4 ounces) plus 1 tablespoon sugar

½ teaspoon vanilla extract

4 tablespoons unsalted butter, softened

1 large egg, lightly beaten with 1 tablespoon water and pinch table salt

1. Whisk flour, yeast, and salt together in bowl of stand mixer. Whisk water, eggs and yolk, sugar, and vanilla in 4-cup liquid measuring cup until sugar has dissolved. Using dough hook on low speed, slowly add water mixture to flour mixture and mix until cohesive dough starts to form and no dry flour remains, about 2 minutes, scraping down bowl as needed.

2. Increase speed to medium-low and knead until dough begins to pull away from sides of bowl but sticks to bottom, about 5 minutes. With mixer running, add butter, 1 tablespoon at a time, and knead until butter is fully incorporated, about 2 minutes. Continue to knead until dough is elastic and slightly sticky, about 3 minutes.

3. Transfer dough to lightly floured counter and knead by hand to form smooth, round ball, about 30 seconds. Place dough seam side down in lightly greased large bowl or container, cover tightly with plastic wrap, and let rise until doubled in size, 2 to 2½ hours.

4. Generously grease 9-inch round cake pan. Press down on dough to deflate. Turn dough out onto clean counter (side of dough that was against bowl should now be facing up) and press into 10-inch round. Working around circumference of dough, fold edges toward center until ball forms.

5. Flip dough ball seam side down and, using your cupped hands, drag in small circles on counter until dough feels taut and round and all seams are secured on underside of loaf. Place loaf seam side down in prepared pan. Cover loosely with greased plastic and let rise until loaf reaches 1¾ inches above lip of pan and dough springs back minimally when poked gently with your knuckle, 2½ to 3 hours.

6. Adjust oven rack to lower-middle position and heat oven to 350 degrees. Using sharp paring knife or single-edge razor blade, make one ¼-inch-deep slash with swift, fluid motion around circumference of loaf, level with lip of pan. Lightly brush loaf with egg mixture and bake until deep golden brown and loaf registers 190 to 195 degrees, 30 to 35 minutes,

St. Lucia Buns

rotating pan halfway through baking. Let loaf cool in pan for 15 minutes. Remove loaf from pan and let cool completely on wire rack, about 3 hours, before serving.

St. Lucia Buns

Makes 16 buns | **Total Time** 1½ hours, plus 3 to 4 hours rising and cooling `MAKE AHEAD` `VEGETARIAN`

WHY THIS RECIPE WORKS Sunny yellow in color, Lussebullar—also known as St. Lucia buns—are a staple food of St. Lucia Day, which in Sweden is a festival of light that ushers in the winter holiday season. A mere ¼ teaspoon of precious saffron gave these sweet treats balanced flavor, and another yellow spice, turmeric, bolstered their color (the turmeric's flavor went undetected). Steeping the saffron and turmeric in boiling water for 15 minutes helped release the full potential of the saffron's water-soluble flavor compounds.

One-third cup each of sugar and currants (the customary mix-in) gave these buns just enough sweetness. There are many traditional shapes for these buns. We found that S-shaped buns were attractive and simple to achieve. Brushing the buns with an egg wash and giving each an optional sprinkling of pearled sugar created a glossy and festive finish. For an accurate measurement of boiling water, bring a full kettle of water to a boil and then measure out the desired amount. If the dough becomes too soft to work with at any point, refrigerate it until it's firm enough to easily handle.

¼ cup boiling water
¼ teaspoon saffron threads, crumbled
⅛ teaspoon ground turmeric
3½ cups (17½ ounces) all-purpose flour
2 teaspoons instant or rapid-rise yeast
¾ cup whole milk, room temperature
6 tablespoons unsalted butter, melted
⅓ cup (2⅓ ounces) granulated sugar
1 large egg, room temperature
1 teaspoon table salt
⅓ cup currants

1 large egg, lightly beaten with 1 tablespoon water and pinch table salt
¼ cup pearled sugar (optional)

1. Combine boiling water, saffron, and turmeric in small bowl and let steep for 15 minutes.

2. Whisk flour and yeast together in bowl of stand mixer. Whisk milk, melted butter, granulated sugar, egg, and saffron mixture in 4-cup liquid measuring cup until sugar has dissolved. Using dough hook on low speed, slowly add milk mixture to flour mixture and mix until cohesive dough starts to form and no dry flour remains, about 2 minutes, scraping down bowl as needed. Cover bowl and let dough stand for 10 minutes.

3. Add salt to dough and knead on medium-low speed until dough is smooth and elastic and clears sides of bowl but sticks to bottom, about 8 minutes. Reduce speed to low, slowly add currants, and mix until incorporated, about 2 minutes.

4. Transfer dough to lightly floured counter and knead by hand to form smooth, round ball, about 30 seconds. Place dough seam side down in lightly greased large bowl or container, cover tightly with greased plastic wrap, and let rise until increased in size by about half, 1½ to 2 hours.

5. Line 2 rimmed baking sheets with parchment paper. Press down on dough to deflate, then transfer to clean counter. Press and roll dough into 16 by 6-inch rectangle, with long side parallel to counter edge. Using pizza cutter or chef's knife, cut rectangle vertically into sixteen 6 by 1-inch strips and cover loosely with greased plastic.

6. Working with 1 dough strip at a time (keep remaining pieces covered), stretch and roll into 16-inch rope. (If dough resists stretching, let it relax for 5 to 10 minutes before trying to stretch it again.) Coil ends of rope in opposite directions to form tight S shape. Arrange buns on prepared sheets, spaced about 2½ inches apart. Cover loosely with greased plastic and let rise until puffy, 30 minutes to 1 hour.

7. Adjust oven racks to upper-middle and lower-middle positions and heat oven to 350 degrees. Gently brush buns with egg mixture and sprinkle with pearled sugar, if using. Bake until golden brown, 15 to 20 minutes, switching and rotating sheets halfway through baking. Transfer rolls to wire rack and let cool completely, about 1 hour, before serving. (St. Lucia Buns can be wrapped in double layer of plastic wrap and stored at room temperature for up to 5 days.)

SHAPING ST. LUCIA BUNS

1. Using pizza cutter or chef's knife, cut 16 by 6-inch dough rectangle vertically into sixteen 6 by 1-inch strips. Cover strips loosely with greased plastic wrap.

2. Working with 1 dough strip at a time (keep remaining pieces covered), stretch and roll into 16-inch rope.

3. Coil ends of rope in opposite directions to form tight S shape. Arrange buns on prepared sheets, spaced about 2½ inches apart.

Challah

Challah

Makes 1 loaf (**Serves** 10) | **Total Time** 2 hours, plus 6½ hours rising and cooling VEGETARIAN

WHY THIS RECIPE WORKS Enriched and braided challah is a cultural heavyweight, a fixture on many Jewish holiday tables. To make challah dough that was moist but malleable, we combined a short rest during kneading with a long fermentation; this built a sturdy but stretchy gluten network that made the dough easy to handle. We also employed the bread-mixing technique called tangzhong, incorporating a cooked flour-water paste that bound up water in the dough so that it was moist but not sticky. Ample amounts of oil and eggs made the baked bread plush. Braiding challah is an intimidating step for many novices, but pointing the four dough strands in different directions, rather than lining them up parallel to one another, made them easier to keep track of. Brushing an egg wash over the braided dough encouraged rich browning as the loaf baked. This dough will be firmer and drier than most bread doughs, which makes it easy to braid. Some friction is necessary for

rolling and braiding the ropes, so resist the urge to dust your counter with flour. If your counter is too narrow to stretch the ropes, slightly bend the pieces at the 12 o'clock and 6 o'clock positions. Bake this loaf on two nested baking sheets to keep the bottom of the loaf from getting too dark.

FLOUR PASTE
½ cup water
3 tablespoons bread flour

DOUGH
1 large egg plus 2 large yolks
¼ cup water
2 tablespoons vegetable oil
2¾ cups (15⅛ ounces) bread flour
1¼ teaspoons instant or rapid-rise yeast
¼ cup (1¾ ounces) sugar
1 teaspoon table salt
Vegetable oil spray

1 large egg, lightly beaten with pinch table salt
1 tablespoon sesame seeds or poppy seeds (optional)

1. FOR THE FLOUR PASTE Whisk water and flour in bowl until no lumps remain. Microwave, whisking every 20 seconds, until mixture thickens to stiff, smooth, pudding-like consistency that forms mound when dropped from end of whisk into bowl, 40 to 80 seconds.

2. FOR THE DOUGH In bowl of stand mixer, whisk flour paste, egg and yolks, water, and oil until well combined. Add flour and yeast. Fit mixer with dough hook and mix on low speed until all flour is moistened, 3 to 4 minutes. Let stand for 20 minutes.

3. Add sugar and salt and mix on medium speed for 9 minutes (dough will be quite firm and dry). Transfer dough to counter and lightly spray now-empty mixer bowl with oil spray. Knead dough briefly to form ball and return it to prepared bowl. Lightly spray dough with oil spray and cover bowl with plastic wrap. Let dough rise until about doubled in volume, about 1½ hours.

4. Line rimmed baking sheet with parchment paper and nest in second rimmed baking sheet. Transfer dough to counter and press into 8-inch square, expelling as much air as possible. Cut dough in half lengthwise to form 2 rectangles. Cut each rectangle in half lengthwise to form 4 equal strips of dough. Roll 1 strip of dough into 16-inch rope. Continue rolling, tapering ends, until rope is 18 inches long. Repeat with remaining dough strips. Arrange ropes in plus-sign shape, with

4 ends overlapping in center by ½ inch. Firmly press center of cross into counter to seal ropes to each other and to counter.

5. Lift rope at 12 o'clock, bring over center, and place in 5 o'clock position. Lift rope at 6 o'clock, bring over center, and place in 12 o'clock position.

6. Lift rope at 9 o'clock, bring over center, and place in 4 o'clock position. Lift rope at 3 o'clock and, working toward yourself, bring over braid and place in 8 o'clock position. Adjust ropes so they are at 12, 3, 6, and 9 o'clock positions.

7. Repeat steps 5 and 6, working toward yourself, until you can no longer braid. Loaf will naturally list to 1 side.

8. Pinch ends of ropes together and tuck both ends under braid. Carefully transfer braid to prepared sheets. Cover loosely with plastic and let rise until dough does not spring back fully when gently pressed with your knuckle, about 3 hours.

9. Thirty minutes before baking, adjust oven rack to middle position and heat oven to 350 degrees. Whisk together egg and salt. Brush loaf with egg wash and sprinkle with sesame seeds, if using. Bake until loaf is deep golden brown and registers at least 195 degrees, 35 to 40 minutes. Let cool on sheets for 20 minutes. Transfer loaf to wire rack and let cool completely, about 2 hours, before serving.

HOW TO BRAID CHALLAH

  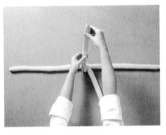 

1. Arrange ropes in plus-sign shape, with 4 ends overlapping in center by ½ inch. Firmly press center of cross into counter to seal ropes to each other and to counter.

2. Lift rope at 12 o'clock, bring over center, and place in 5 o'clock position.

3. Lift rope at 6 o'clock, bring over center, and place in 12 o'clock position.

4. Lift rope at 9 o'clock, bring over center, and place in 4 o'clock position.

 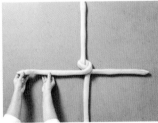  

5. Lift rope at 3 o'clock and, working toward yourself, bring over braid and place in 8 o'clock position.

6. Adjust ropes so they are at 12, 3, 6, and 9 o'clock positions. Repeat steps 2 through 6.

7. Continue braiding, working toward yourself, until you can no longer braid. Loaf will naturally list to 1 side.

8. Pinch ends of ropes together. Tuck both ends under braid.

Flavored Butters

Whipped Honey Butter

Makes about ½ cup | **Total Time** 30 minutes

  8 tablespoons unsalted butter, softened
  1 tablespoon honey
  1 pinch table salt

Using stand mixer fitted with whisk attachment, whip butter on medium speed until smooth, about 30 seconds. Add honey and salt and whip until combined, about 15 seconds, then increase speed to high and whip until very light and fluffy, about 2 minutes, scraping down bowl as needed. Cover with plastic wrap and let rest so flavors meld, about 10 minutes, or roll into log and refrigerate. (Butter can be refrigerated in airtight container for up to 4 days or frozen, wrapped tightly in plastic wrap, for up to 2 months.)

Molasses-Pecan Butter

Makes about 1 cup | **Total Time** 30 minutes

  8 tablespoons unsalted butter, softened
  ¼ cup pecans, toasted and chopped fine
  4 teaspoons light molasses
  2 teaspoons sugar
  ¼ teaspoon vanilla extract
     Pinch table salt

Using stand mixer fitted with whisk attachment, whip butter on medium speed until smooth, about 30 seconds. Add pecans, molasses, sugar, vanilla, and salt and whip until combined, about 15 seconds, then increase speed to high and whip until very light and fluffy, about 2 minutes, scraping down bowl as needed. Cover with plastic wrap and let rest so flavors meld, about 10 minutes, or roll into log and refrigerate. (Butter can be refrigerated in airtight container for up to 4 days or frozen, wrapped tightly in plastic wrap, for up to 2 months.)

Sweet Orange Butter

Makes about ½ cup | **Total Time** 30 minutes

  8 tablespoons unsalted butter, softened
  2 teaspoons sugar
  1 teaspoon orange zest
  ⅛ teaspoon vanilla extract
    Pinch table salt

Using stand mixer fitted with whisk attachment, whip butter on medium speed until smooth, about 30 seconds. Add sugar, orange zest, vanilla, and salt and whip until combined, about 15 seconds, then increase speed to high and whip until very light and fluffy, about 2 minutes, scraping down bowl as needed. Cover with plastic wrap and let rest so flavors meld, about 10 minutes, or roll into log and refrigerate. (Butter can be refrigerated in airtight container for up to 4 days or frozen, wrapped tightly in plastic wrap, for up to 2 months.)

Parsley-Lemon Butter

Makes about ¾ cup | **Total Time** 30 minutes

  8 tablespoons unsalted butter, softened
  ¼ cup minced fresh parsley
  4 teaspoons grated lemon zest
    Pinch table salt

Using stand mixer fitted with whisk attachment, whip butter on medium speed until smooth, about 30 seconds. Add parsley, zest, and salt, and whip until combined, about 15 seconds, then increase speed to high and whip until very light and fluffy, about 2 minutes, scraping down bowl as needed. Cover with plastic wrap and let rest so flavors meld, about 10 minutes, or roll into log and refrigerate. (Butter can be refrigerated in airtight container for up to 4 days or frozen, wrapped tightly in plastic wrap, for up to 2 months.)

Garlic-Herb Butter

Makes about 1 cup | **Total Time** 30 minutes

  8 tablespoons unsalted butter, softened
  2 tablespoons minced fresh sage or 1½ teaspoons dried
  1 tablespoon minced fresh parsley
  1 tablespoon minced fresh thyme or ¾ teaspoon dried
  2 garlic cloves, minced
  ¼ teaspoon table salt
  ¼ teaspoon pepper

Using stand mixer fitted with whisk attachment, whip butter on medium speed until smooth, about 30 seconds. Add sage, parsley, thyme, garlic, salt, and pepper, and whip until combined, about 15 seconds, then increase speed to high and whip until very light and fluffy, about 2 minutes, scraping down bowl as needed. Cover with plastic wrap and let rest so flavors meld, about 10 minutes, or roll into log and refrigerate. (Butter can be refrigerated in airtight container for up to 4 days or frozen, wrapped tightly in plastic wrap, for up to 2 months.)

NOTES FROM THE TEST KITCHEN

TWO SPEEDY WAYS TO SOFTEN BUTTER

Softening butter at room temperature is simple but requires patience, and sometimes we don't want to wait. One way to speed up the process is to cut the stick into 1-tablespoon pieces and set them on a plate; more exposed surface area helps the butter warm evenly, and the pieces will soften in about 20 minutes. This method is best when the butter will be creamed in baking applications. But if you just want to soften butter for spreading or for making flavored butters such as those listed here, there's an even quicker way: Microwave the pieces at 50 percent power in 10-second increments until the butter is still solid but yields completely to pressure. It's OK if the butter melts a little; simply stir it together until it's uniform. Just don't use the microwave method when baking, since over-softened butter can compromise baked goods.

cookies & cakes

■ MAKE AHEAD ▤ VEGETARIAN
Photo: Chocolate Crinkle Cookies

Easy Holiday Sugar Cookies

Vanilla Icebox Cookies

Easy Holiday Sugar Cookies

Makes about 40 cookies `MAKE AHEAD` `VEGETARIAN`
Total Time 2 hours, plus 1½ hours to dry icing

WHY THIS RECIPE WORKS Our holiday roll-and-cut sugar cookies taste as great as they are easy to make. Using superfine sugar, which we made by grinding granulated sugar in the food processor, was the key to crisp cookies without a hint of graininess. Instead of creaming together softened butter and sugar, we whizzed cold butter with sugar in the food processor. This technique meant that the just-made dough was cold enough to be rolled out immediately. Baking the cookies at a gentle 300 degrees on a rimless baking sheet (to allow for more airflow around the cookies) gave them an even, golden color, minimal browning, and a crisp, crunchy texture from edge to edge. In step 3, use a rolling pin and a combination of rolling and a pushing or smearing motion to form the soft dough into an oval. If you don't have a rimless cookie sheet, see "Cookie-Sheet Workaround" for an alternative. If desired, stir 1 or 2 drops of food coloring into the icing. For a pourable icing, whisk in milk, 1 teaspoon at a time, until the desired consistency is reached. You can also decorate the shapes with sanding sugar or sprinkles before baking.

COOKIES

- 1 large egg
- 1 teaspoon vanilla extract
- ¾ teaspoon table salt
- ¼ teaspoon almond extract
- 2½ cups (12½ ounces) all-purpose flour
- ¼ teaspoon baking powder
- ¼ teaspoon baking soda
- 1 cup (7 ounces) granulated sugar
- 16 tablespoons unsalted butter, cut into ½-inch pieces and chilled

ROYAL ICING

- 2⅔ cups (10⅔ ounces) confectioners' sugar
- 2 large egg whites
- ½ teaspoon vanilla extract
- ⅛ teaspoon table salt

1. FOR THE COOKIES Whisk egg, vanilla, salt, and almond extract together in small bowl. Whisk flour, baking powder, and baking soda together in second bowl.

2. Process sugar in food processor until finely ground, about 30 seconds. Add butter and process until uniform mass forms and no large pieces of butter are visible, about 30 seconds, scraping down sides of bowl as needed. Add egg mixture and process until mixture is smooth and paste-like, about 10 seconds. Add flour mixture and process until no dry flour remains but mixture remains crumbly, about 30 seconds, scraping down sides of bowl as needed.

3. Turn out dough onto counter and knead gently by hand until smooth, about 10 seconds. Divide dough in half. Place 1 piece of dough in center of large sheet of parchment paper and press into 7 by 9-inch oval. Place second large sheet of parchment over dough and roll dough into 10 by 14-inch oval of even ⅛-inch thickness. Transfer dough with parchment to rimmed baking sheet. Repeat pressing and rolling with second piece of dough, then stack on top of first piece on sheet. Refrigerate until dough is firm, at least 1½ hours (or freeze for 30 minutes). (Rolled dough can be wrapped in plastic wrap and refrigerated for up to 5 days.)

4. Adjust oven rack to lower-middle position and heat oven to 300 degrees. Line rimless cookie sheet with parchment. Working with 1 piece of rolled dough, gently peel off top layer of parchment. Replace parchment, loosely covering dough. (Peeling off parchment and returning it will make cutting and removing cookies easier.) Turn over dough and parchment and gently peel off and discard second piece of parchment. Using cookie cutter, cut dough into shapes. Transfer shapes to prepared cookie sheet, spacing them about ½ inch apart.

5. Bake until cookies are lightly and evenly browned around edges, 14 to 17 minutes, rotating sheet halfway through baking. Let cookies cool on sheet for 5 minutes. Using wide metal spatula, transfer cookies to wire rack; let cool completely. Repeat cutting and baking with remaining dough. (Dough scraps can be patted together, rerolled, and chilled once before cutting and baking.)

6. FOR THE ROYAL ICING Using stand mixer fitted with whisk attachment, whip all ingredients on medium-low speed until combined, about 1 minute. Increase speed to medium-high and whip until glossy, soft peaks form, 3 to 4 minutes, scraping down bowl as needed.

7. Spread icing onto cooled cookies. Let icing dry completely, about 1½ hours, before serving.

NOTES FROM THE TEST KITCHEN

COOKIE-SHEET WORKAROUND
Some cookies, like our Easy Holiday Sugar Cookies, benefit from the better air circulation provided by a rimless cookie sheet (versus a rimmed baking sheet), which results in more even baking across the sheet and more crisp cookies. Don't have a cookie sheet? No problem: Just flip over your rimmed baking sheet.

Vanilla Icebox Cookies

Makes about 40 cookies | **Total Time** 40 minutes, plus 2½ hours freezing and cooling

MAKE AHEAD VEGETARIAN

WHY THIS RECIPE WORKS Having slice-and-bake cookie dough in the refrigerator or freezer, ready to go, is the ultimate sweet convenience. These cookies are full of buttery vanilla flavor. First, we added as much butter as we could without causing the cookies to lose their crisp edge—12 tablespoons. Using just an egg yolk rather than a whole egg made the cookies firmer, and replacing some of the granulated sugar with light brown sugar added complexity. To achieve a dense shortbread texture, we had to be careful not to mix in too much air. Using a food processor to combine the ingredients rather than the traditional creaming method ensured that less air was whipped into the dough. To ensure uniformly sliced cookies, make sure the dough log is firm before slicing in step 4. For decorated edges like those in the photo, roll the dough log in sprinkles or finely chopped nuts before cutting the cookies.

- ⅓ cup (2⅓ ounces) granulated sugar
- 2 tablespoons packed light brown sugar
- ½ teaspoon table salt
- 12 tablespoons unsalted butter, cut into pieces and softened
- 1 large egg yolk
- 2 teaspoons vanilla extract
- 1½ cups (7½ ounces) all-purpose flour

1. Process granulated sugar, brown sugar, and salt in food processor until no lumps of brown sugar remain, about 30 seconds. Add butter, egg yolk, and vanilla and process until smooth and creamy, about 20 seconds. Scrape down bowl, add flour, and pulse until cohesive dough forms, about 20 pulses.

2. Transfer dough to lightly floured counter and roll into 10-inch log. Wrap log tightly in plastic wrap and refrigerate until firm, at least 2 hours or up to 3 days.

3. Adjust oven racks to upper-middle and lower-middle positions and heat oven to 350 degrees. Line 2 baking sheets with parchment paper.

4. Using chef's knife, slice dough into ¼-inch-thick rounds, rotating dough so that it won't become misshapen from weight of knife. Space cookies 1 inch apart on prepared baking sheets. Bake until edges are just golden, about 15 minutes, switching and rotating sheets halfway through baking. Let cookies cool on sheets for 10 minutes, then transfer to wire rack. Repeat with remaining dough. Let cookies cool completely before serving.

Brown Sugar–Walnut Icebox Cookies

Increase brown sugar to ¼ cup. Add 1 cup walnuts to food processor with sugars and salt in step 1 and process until walnuts are finely ground, about 1 minute.

Coconut-Lime Icebox Cookies

Add 2 cups sweetened shredded coconut and 2 teaspoons grated lime zest to food processor with sugars and salt in step 1.

Orange–Poppy Seed Icebox Cookies

Add ¼ cup poppy seeds and 1 tablespoon grated orange zest to food processor with sugars and salt in step 1.

Eggnog Snickerdoodles

Makes about 48 cookies `MAKE AHEAD` `VEGETARIAN`
Total Time 1 hour, plus 30 minutes cooling

WHY THIS RECIPE WORKS Traditional snickerdoodles are a cookie spread mainstay, both irresistibly tangy (thanks to acidic cream of tartar) and cinnamon sugar–sweet. To make them even more festive, we decided to infuse these cookies with the flavor of everyone's favorite holiday beverage: eggnog. Simply adding eggnog to the dough threw off the ratio of wet to dry ingredients, causing the cookies to spread too much and become cakey; not to mention, the flavor of the 'nog was not at all detectable in the finished cookies. Instead, we took the flavors that make eggnog what it is and isolated them, adding a shot of rum extract (straight rum didn't carry a strong enough flavor) to the dough and substituting nutmeg for snickerdoodles' customary cinnamon. We highly recommend enjoying these cookies alongside a chilled glass of eggnog. You can substitute rum for the rum extract, but the flavor won't be as pronounced.

2½ cups (12½ ounces) all-purpose flour
2 teaspoons cream of tartar
1 teaspoon baking soda
¼ teaspoon table salt
16 tablespoons unsalted butter, softened
1½ cups (10½ ounces) granulated sugar
2 large eggs
1½ teaspoons rum extract
½ cup confectioners' sugar
½ teaspoon ground nutmeg

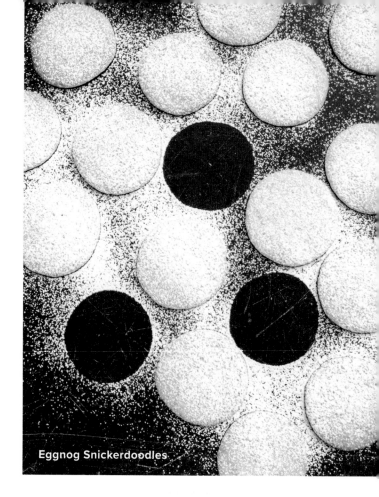

Eggnog Snickerdoodles

1. Adjust oven racks to upper-middle and lower-middle positions and heat oven to 400 degrees. Line 2 baking sheets with parchment paper. Whisk flour, cream of tartar, baking soda, and salt together in bowl.

2. Using stand mixer fitted with paddle, beat butter and granulated sugar on medium-high speed until fluffy, 3 to 6 minutes. Add eggs, one at a time, and rum extract and beat until incorporated. Reduce speed to low, slowly add flour mixture, and mix until just combined.

3. Working with 1 tablespoon dough at a time, roll into balls and space them 2 inches apart on prepared sheets. Using bottom of greased dry measuring cup, press each ball to even ½-inch thickness.

4. Bake cookies until edges are lightly browned, 8 to 10 minutes, switching and rotating sheets halfway through baking. Let cookies cool on sheets for 5 minutes, then transfer to wire rack. Repeat with remaining dough. Let cookies cool completely.

5. Whisk confectioners' sugar and nutmeg together in small bowl. Dust cookies with sugar-nutmeg mixture before serving. (Cookies can be stored in airtight container at room temperature for up to 3 days.)

Soft and Chewy Gingerbread People

Makes about 20 cookies | **Total Time** 45 minutes, plus 1½ hours chilling and cooling

`MAKE AHEAD` `VEGETARIAN`

WHY THIS RECIPE WORKS Piping decorating icing over a host of gingerbread people (and then, inevitably, biting off their heads) is a timeless activity the whole family can enjoy. These gingerbread cookies are soft, not crunchy, and brimming with the flavors of ginger and molasses. To put the chew in our gingerbread cookies, we added more fat than most recipes call for: 12 tablespoons of melted butter. Rolling the dough ¼ inch thick gave us cookies with just the right heft. We baked the cookies until they were just set around the edges and slightly puffed in the center. As they cooled, the slightly puffed cookies settled into sublime chewiness. Depending on your cookie cutter dimensions, all of the cookies may not fit on the sheets and a second round of baking may be required. We like to give our gingerbread people personality by decorating them with our Decorating Icing (page 340).

- 3 cups (15 ounces) all-purpose flour
- ¾ cup packed (5¼ ounces) dark brown sugar
- 1 tablespoon ground cinnamon
- 1 tablespoon ground ginger
- ¾ teaspoon baking soda
- ½ teaspoon ground cloves
- ½ teaspoon table salt
- 12 tablespoons unsalted butter, melted
- ¾ cup light molasses
- 2 tablespoons milk

1. Process flour, sugar, cinnamon, ginger, baking soda, cloves, and salt in food processor until combined, about 10 seconds. Add melted butter, molasses, and milk and process until soft dough forms and no streaks of flour remain, about 20 seconds, scraping down sides of bowl as needed.

2. Spray counter lightly with baking spray with flour, transfer dough to counter, and knead until dough forms cohesive ball, about 20 seconds. Divide dough in half. Form each half into 5-inch disk, wrap disks tightly in plastic wrap, and refrigerate for at least 1 hour or up to 24 hours.

3. Adjust oven racks to upper-middle and lower-middle positions and heat oven to 350 degrees. Line 2 baking sheets with parchment paper. Working with 1 disk of dough at a time, roll ¼ inch thick between 2 large sheets of parchment. (Keep second disk of dough refrigerated while rolling out

Soft and Chewy Gingerbread People

first.) Remove top piece of parchment. Using 3½-inch cookie cutter, cut dough into shapes. Peel away scraps from around cookies and space shapes ¾ inch apart on prepared sheets. Repeat rolling and cutting steps with dough scraps.

4. Bake cookies until puffy and just set around edges, 9 to 11 minutes, switching and rotating sheets halfway through baking. Let cookies cool on sheets for 10 minutes, then transfer to wire rack. Let cookies cool completely before serving. (Cookies can be stored in airtight container at room temperature, with sheet of parchment or waxed paper between each layer, for up to 3 days.)

NOTES FROM THE TEST KITCHEN

MORE SEASONAL COOKIE AND CAKE RECIPES
Pumpkin-Pecan Cookies, page 223
French Apple Cake, page 200
Cider-Glazed Apple Bundt Cake, page 201
Pumpkin–Chocolate Chip Snack Cake, page 220
Maple-Pumpkin Stack Cake, page 220
New York–Style Crumb Cake, page 298

Molasses Spice Cookies

Makes 24 cookies | **Total Time** 1¼ hours
`MAKE AHEAD` `VEGETARIAN`

WHY THIS RECIPE WORKS The best molasses spice cookies combine a homespun crinkled appearance with a chewy texture and a gently spiced, deep molasses flavor. We liked light (or mild) and dark (or robust) molasses equally in the dough: Light molasses imparted a mild flavor, while dark had a stronger presence, so the choice is up to you. (We found blackstrap molasses overpowering and bitter.) A modest amount of dark brown sugar added caramel notes. To complement these assertive sweeteners, we needed a powerful yet balanced team of spices. Cinnamon, ginger, cloves, allspice, and black pepper provided warmth and just enough bite, and a spoonful of vanilla smoothed out any rough edges. We found that dipping our hands in water before rolling the dough balls prevented the dough from sticking to them and also helped the granulated sugar adhere to the dough balls. For the best texture and appearance, be sure to bake the cookies one sheet at a time and pull them from the oven when they still look substantially underdone. They will continue to bake and harden as they cool.

2¼ cups (11¼ ounces) all-purpose flour
1½ teaspoons ground cinnamon
1½ teaspoons ground ginger
 1 teaspoon baking soda
½ teaspoon ground cloves
¼ teaspoon ground allspice
¼ teaspoon pepper
¼ teaspoon table salt
12 tablespoons unsalted butter, softened
⅓ cup packed (2⅓ ounces) dark brown sugar
⅓ cup (2⅓ ounces) granulated sugar, plus
 ½ cup for rolling
 1 large egg yolk
 1 teaspoon vanilla extract
½ cup mild or robust molasses

1. Adjust oven rack to middle position and heat oven to 375 degrees. Line 2 baking sheets with parchment paper. Whisk flour, cinnamon, ginger, baking soda, cloves, allspice, pepper, and salt together in bowl.

2. Using stand mixer fitted with paddle, beat butter, brown sugar, and ⅓ cup granulated sugar on medium speed until pale and fluffy, about 3 minutes. Reduce speed to medium-low, add egg yolk and vanilla, and beat until combined, about 30 seconds. Beat in molasses until incorporated, about 30 seconds, scraping down bowl as needed. Reduce speed to low and slowly add flour mixture until combined, about 30 seconds (dough will be soft). Give dough final stir by hand to ensure that no flour pockets remain.

3. Spread remaining ½ cup granulated sugar in shallow dish. Working with 2 tablespoons dough at a time, roll into balls with your dampened hands, then roll in sugar to coat; space dough balls 2 inches apart on prepared sheets. (Dough balls can be frozen for up to 1 month; bake frozen dough balls in 300-degree oven for 30 to 35 minutes.)

4. Bake cookies, 1 sheet at a time, until edges are set but centers are still soft, puffy, and cracked (cookies will look raw between cracks and seem underdone), 10 to 12 minutes, rotating sheet halfway through baking. Let cookies cool on sheet for 10 minutes. Serve warm or transfer to wire rack and let cool completely.

Molasses Spice Cookies with Dark Rum Glaze

Whisk 1 cup confectioners' sugar and 3 tablespoons dark rum in bowl until smooth. Drizzle glaze over cooled cookies and let dry for 10 to 15 minutes before serving.

Molasses Spice Cookies with Orange Essence

Add 1 teaspoon grated orange zest to dough with molasses in step 2. Process ⅔ cup granulated sugar with 2 teaspoons grated orange zest in food processor until fragrant, about 10 seconds; substitute orange sugar for granulated sugar when rolling cookies in step 3.

Chocolate Crinkle Cookies

Makes 22 cookies `MAKE AHEAD` `VEGETARIAN`
Total Time 1 hour, plus 30 minutes cooling

WHY THIS RECIPE WORKS Rolled in powdered sugar before baking, chocolate crinkle cookies (often called earthquakes) feature chocolaty fissures that break through the bright white surface as the cookies spread in the oven. A combination of cocoa powder and unsweetened chocolate (boosted with a few teaspoons of espresso powder) gave our cookies intense chocolate flavor, and replacing the granulated sugar with brown sugar added complexity. Three techniques worked in tandem to create the cookies' hallmark fissures. First, using both baking soda and baking powder in the dough produced lots of bubbles that quickly rose to the surface and burst during baking. Second, letting the dough sit at room temperature rather than baking the cookies straight from the refrigerator encouraged the cookies to spread slightly, leading to cracks in their surface. And finally, rolling the dough in granulated sugar before coating the balls in powdered sugar dried out the surface of the cookies, causing even more fissures to form. The result: Holiday cookies with picture-perfect powdery white exteriors broken up by striking chocolate stripes.

- 1 cup (5 ounces) all-purpose flour
- ½ cup (1½ ounces) unsweetened cocoa powder
- 1 teaspoon baking powder
- ¼ teaspoon baking soda
- ½ teaspoon table salt
- 1½ cups packed (10½ ounces) brown sugar
- 3 large eggs
- 4 teaspoons instant espresso powder (optional)
- 1 teaspoon vanilla extract
- 4 ounces unsweetened chocolate, chopped
- 4 tablespoons unsalted butter
- ½ cup (3½ ounces) granulated sugar
- ½ cup (2 ounces) confectioners' sugar

1. Adjust oven rack to middle position and heat oven to 325 degrees. Line 2 baking sheets with parchment paper. Whisk flour, cocoa, baking powder, baking soda, and salt together in bowl.

2. Whisk brown sugar; eggs; espresso powder, if using; and vanilla together in large bowl. Combine chocolate and butter in bowl and microwave at 50 percent power, stirring occasionally, until melted, 2 to 3 minutes.

3. Whisk chocolate mixture into egg mixture until combined. Fold in flour mixture until no dry streaks remain. Let dough stand at room temperature for 10 minutes.

4. Place granulated sugar and confectioners' sugar in separate shallow dishes. Working with 2 tablespoons dough (or #30 scoop) at a time, roll into balls. Drop each ball into granulated sugar directly after shaping and roll to coat. Transfer dough balls to confectioners' sugar and roll to coat evenly. Evenly space dough balls on prepared sheets, 11 dough balls per sheet.

5. Bake cookies, 1 sheet at a time, until puffed and cracked and edges have begun to set but centers are still soft (cookies will look raw between cracks and seem underdone), about 12 minutes, rotating sheet halfway through baking. Let cool completely on sheet before serving. (Cookies can be stored at room temperature in airtight container or zipper-lock bag for up to 5 days.)

Molasses Spice Cookies

Chocolate Crinkle Cookies

Cranberry, White Chocolate, and Macadamia Cookies

Cranberry, White Chocolate, and Macadamia Cookies

Makes about 32 cookies MAKE AHEAD VEGETARIAN
Total Time 1 hour, plus 30 minutes cooling

WHY THIS RECIPE WORKS The right balance of sweet, tart, crunchy, gooey, or savory mix-ins can make a cookie extraordinary. These cookies marry tart and chewy dried cranberries with sweet, melty white chocolate chips and mild, tender macadamia nuts. With a full cup of each mix-in in the dough, the cookies are loaded with flavor and contrasting texture in every bite. The method couldn't be simpler: We used a stand mixer to beat together melted butter and sugar, followed by eggs, vanilla for depth of flavor, and the dry ingredients, stirring in the mix-ins last until just incorporated. Slightly underbaking the cookies and allowing the residual heat of the baking sheet to finish cooking them ensured that they retained their fresh-baked chew once cool.

  2 cups (10 ounces) all-purpose flour
  ½ teaspoon baking soda
  ½ teaspoon table salt
 12 tablespoons unsalted butter, melted and cooled slightly
  1 cup packed (7 ounces) light brown sugar
  ½ cup (3½ ounces) granulated sugar
  1 large egg plus 1 large yolk
  2 teaspoons vanilla extract
  1 cup (6 ounces) white chocolate chips
  1 cup dried cranberries, chopped coarse
  1 cup macadamia nuts, chopped

1. Adjust oven rack to lower-middle position and heat oven to 325 degrees. Line 2 baking sheets with parchment paper. Whisk flour, baking soda, and salt together in bowl.

2. Using stand mixer fitted with paddle, beat melted butter, brown sugar, and granulated sugar on medium speed until smooth, 1 to 2 minutes. Add egg and yolk and vanilla and beat until combined, scraping down bowl as needed. Reduce speed to low, slowly add flour mixture, and mix until just combined. Add chocolate chips, cranberries, and macadamia nuts and mix until incorporated. (Dough can be portioned into 2 tablespoon–size balls and placed on parchment paper–lined baking sheets or large plates. Freeze until completely frozen, at least 30 minutes, then arrange cookies in layers in airtight storage container, using same parchment sheets to separate layers, and freeze for up to 2 months. To serve, bake cookies from frozen, increasing baking time in step 3 by 1 to 2 minutes.)

Peanut Butter Sandwich Cookies

3. Working with 2 tablespoons dough at a time, roll into balls and space 2 inches apart on prepared sheets. Bake, 1 sheet at a time, until edges are set but centers are still soft and puffy, 15 to 20 minutes, rotating sheet halfway through baking. Let cookies cool on sheet for 10 minutes, then transfer to wire rack. Let cookies cool completely before serving. (Cookies can be stored in airtight container at room temperature, with sheet of parchment or waxed paper between each layer, for up to 2 days. Recrisp cookies in 425-degree oven for 4 to 5 minutes and serve warm.)

Peanut Butter Sandwich Cookies

Makes 24 sandwich cookies | **Total Time** 2 hours, plus 1 hour setting MAKE AHEAD VEGETARIAN

WHY THIS RECIPE WORKS Our ideal peanut butter sandwich cookie features thin, crunchy cookies and a smooth, creamy filling, both packed with peanut flavor—essentially a Nutter Butter made better. The first task: giving the cookie rounds big flavor. In addition to the obvious inclusion of peanut butter in the dough, we cut a portion of the flour with finely chopped peanuts—a simple substitution that boosted flavor dramatically. To make the cookies thin and crisp, we added some milk; the increased moisture made a thinner dough that spread more readily during baking. Adding a full teaspoon of baking soda to the recipe encouraged the air bubbles within the dough to inflate so rapidly that they burst before the cookies set, leaving the cookies flat. Warming the creamy filling of peanut butter, confectioners' sugar, and butter in the microwave softened it so we were easily able to fill the cookie rounds. Do not use unsalted peanut butter in this recipe. Take care when processing the peanuts—you want to chop them, not turn them into a paste.

COOKIES

- 1¼ cups raw or dry-roasted peanuts, toasted and cooled
- ¾ cup (3¾ ounces) all-purpose flour
- 1 teaspoon baking soda
- ½ teaspoon table salt
- ½ cup creamy peanut butter
- ½ cup (3½ ounces) granulated sugar
- ½ cup (3½ ounces) light brown sugar
- 3 tablespoons unsalted butter, melted
- 3 tablespoons whole milk
- 1 large egg

FILLING

- ¾ cup creamy peanut butter
- 3 tablespoons unsalted butter
- 1 cup (4 ounces) confectioners' sugar

1. FOR THE COOKIES Adjust oven racks to upper-middle and lower-middle positions and heat oven to 350 degrees. Line 2 baking sheets with parchment paper. Pulse peanuts in food processor until finely chopped, about 8 pulses. Whisk flour, baking soda, and salt together in bowl. Whisk peanut butter, granulated sugar, brown sugar, melted butter, milk, and egg together in second bowl. Using rubber spatula, stir flour mixture into peanut butter mixture until combined. Stir in chopped peanuts until evenly distributed.

2. Using 1-tablespoon measure (or #60 scoop), drop 12 mounds evenly onto each prepared sheet. Using your dampened hand, press each mound until 2 inches in diameter.

3. Bake cookies until deep golden brown and firm to touch, 15 to 18 minutes, switching and rotating sheets halfway through baking. Let cookies cool on sheets for 5 minutes, then transfer to wire rack. Repeat with remaining dough. Let cookies cool completely.

4. FOR THE FILLING Microwave peanut butter and butter until melted and warm, about 40 seconds. Using rubber spatula, stir in confectioners' sugar until combined.

5. Place 1 tablespoon (or #60 scoop) warm filling in center of bottom of half of cookies, then top with remaining cookies, pressing gently until filling spreads to edges. Let filling set for 1 hour before serving. (Cookies can be stored in airtight container at room temperature for up to 3 days.)

Peanut Butter Sandwich Cookies with Honey-Cinnamon Filling

Omit butter from filling. Stir 5 tablespoons honey and ½ teaspoon ground cinnamon into warm peanut butter before adding confectioners' sugar.

Peanut Butter Sandwich Cookies with Milk Chocolate Filling

Reduce peanut butter in filling to ½ cup and omit butter from filling. Stir 6 ounces finely chopped milk chocolate into warm peanut butter until melted, microwaving for 10 seconds at a time if necessary, before adding confectioners' sugar.

Holiday Cookie Decorating

Easy All-Purpose Glaze

Makes about 1 cup | **Total Time** 5 minutes

This spreadable glaze easily coats the surface of a cookie. Spread this glaze onto completely cooled cookies using the back of a spoon or pipe the glaze onto cookies to form a pattern or design. Let the glaze dry completely, about 30 minutes, before serving.

    2 cups (8 ounces) confectioners' sugar
    3 tablespoons milk
    1 ounce cream cheese, softened
       Food coloring (optional)

Whisk all ingredients in bowl until smooth.

Citrus Glaze
Substitute lemon, lime, or orange juice for milk.

Coffee Glaze
Add 1¼ teaspoons instant espresso powder or instant coffee to glaze ingredients.

Decorating Icing

Makes 1⅓ cups
Total Time 5 minutes, plus 1½ hours to dry icing

Decorating icing is ideal for detailed piping work.

    2 large egg whites
2⅔ cups (10⅔ ounces) confectioners' sugar
       Food coloring (optional)

1. Using stand mixer fitted with whisk attachment, whip egg whites; sugar; and food coloring, if using, on medium-low speed until combined, about 1 minute. Increase speed to medium-high and whip until glossy, soft peaks form, 3 to 4 minutes, scraping down bowl as needed.

2. Transfer icing to pastry bag fitted with small round pastry tip. Decorate cookies and let icing harden, about 1½ hours, before serving.

Three Ways to Glaze

Our Easy All-Purpose Glaze spreads smoothly but doesn't hold as firm a line as stiffer Decorating Icing, so it's best used for simple decorating tips like those below. Be sure to start with completely cooled cookies; the glaze will liquefy and fail to set if it's piped onto warm cookies.

Spread Spoon a small amount of glaze in the center of the cookie, then spread it into an even layer. Spread the glaze outward from the center to ensure even coverage. Using the back of the spoon to spread the glaze will work, but you can also use a small offset spatula. Be sure to let the glaze dry before storing or serving the cookies.

Drag Two Glazes Together Glaze the entire cookie and then pipe small drops of a second glaze in a pattern. Drag a toothpick through the glazes to create a design. As long as both glazes are still wet, you can create a range of designs, from hearts to stars, wiggly lines, and swirls. This idea works best with glazes that are two very different hues.

Fill in Piped Borders For glazed cookies with cleaner edges than those made using the spreading technique, carefully pipe the glaze around the border of the cookie, then add more glaze to the center of the cookie and spread the extra glaze into an even layer. Use the same-colored glaze for both if you want to hide the piped edges, or use different-colored glazes to make the piped border stand out. Note that piping with glaze will be less detailed and neat than piping with decorating icing.

Taking Your Cookies to the Next Level

Our Decorating Icing is less runny and sets up more firmly than a glaze, so it's ideally suited for more intricate, detailed piping work. Here are a few of our favorite ways to step up your cookie decoration game by using icing and other embellishments.

Pipe To apply more intricate designs, such as dots or fine lines, to cookies, pipe the icing directly onto the cookie. Use a pastry bag fitted with a 1/16-inch or 1/8-inch round tip or a zipper-lock bag with a small snip in one corner to pipe the icing.

Layer Icing and Play with Patterns Create visual interest and a sense of depth by piping layers of icing over one another. Start by coating the cookie with a thin, smooth layer of icing. Let the first layer dry before piping dots, lines, or other patterns in a second layer on top. Play around with combinations of lines, dots, and swirls to make different patterns, from snowflake fractals to freeform loops to orderly rows.

Add Embellishments While the icing is still soft, place decorations on top and then allow it to dry. Small confections, such as shiny silver or gold balls known as dragées, can be used to dress up cookies. Other small candies—gumdrops, mini chocolate morsels, jelly beans—can be used in a similar fashion. Add these candies immediately after applying the icing. As the icing dries, it will affix the candies in place.

Linzer Sandwich Cookies

Linzer Sandwich Cookies

Makes about 24 sandwich cookies VEGETARIAN
Total Time 2 hours, plus 1 hour chilling and setting

WHY THIS RECIPE WORKS A Linzertorte is an Austrian confection consisting of a buttery, nutty dough topped with jam or preserves and then covered with lattice strips of the same base dough. Linzer cookies are a cookie plate classic strikingly similar to the torte but with a thinner, and thus more crisp, dough. The top cookie sports a small cutout in the center, which exposes the jam filling. We used ground toasted hazelnuts in our cookies and upped the nuttiness by also adding a dash of almond extract to the dough. While black currant jam is a traditional filling for Linzertorte, we liked the bright flavor of raspberry jam with the buttery hazelnut cookie. Starting with chilled butter gave us dough that was easy to work with and resulted in tender yet crisp cookies that complemented the soft jam center. Using confectioners' sugar as the sole sweetener gave our cookies an extraordinarily

tender texture and a fine crumb. For the best texture, serve the cookies immediately after the jam is set; letting them sit for longer will cause them to soften.

⅔ cup seedless raspberry jam
⅔ cup (2⅔ ounces) confectioners' sugar
½ cup hazelnuts, toasted and skinned
1 cup (5 ounces) all-purpose flour
6 tablespoons unsalted butter, cut into ½-inch pieces and chilled
¼ teaspoon table salt
1 large egg yolk
1 tablespoon heavy cream
½ teaspoon vanilla extract
¼ teaspoon almond extract

1. Simmer jam in small saucepan over medium heat, stirring frequently, until thickened and reduced to ½ cup, about 10 minutes; let cool completely, about 1 hour. Meanwhile, process sugar and hazelnuts in food processor until hazelnuts are finely ground, about 20 seconds. Add flour, butter, and salt and pulse until mixture resembles coarse meal, 15 to 20 pulses. Add egg yolk, cream, vanilla, and almond extract and process until dough forms ball, about 20 seconds. Transfer dough to counter. Form dough into disk, wrap disk tightly in plastic wrap, and refrigerate for 30 minutes.

2. Adjust oven racks to upper-middle and lower-middle positions and heat oven to 375 degrees. Line 2 baking sheets with parchment paper.

3. Roll dough ⅛ inch thick on counter. Using 2-inch fluted round cookie cutter, cut out rounds; space rounds ¾ inch apart on prepared sheets. Using smaller cutter, cut out centers of half of dough rounds. Gather and reroll scraps once. Bake until edges are lightly browned, 8 to 10 minutes, switching and rotating sheets halfway through baking. Let cookies cool on sheets for 5 minutes, then transfer to wire rack. Let cookies cool completely.

4. Spread bottom of each solid cookie with 1 teaspoon jam, then top with cutout cookie, pressing lightly to adhere. Let cookies set before serving, about 30 minutes.

Lemon Linzer Sandwich Cookies
Substitute ¾ cup sliced almonds, toasted, for hazelnuts. Omit raspberry jam and spread bottom of each solid cookie with ½ teaspoon lemon curd.

Pignoli

Makes about 18 cookies `MAKE AHEAD` `VEGETARIAN`
Total Time 40 minutes, plus 30 minutes cooling

WHY THIS RECIPE WORKS With an appealingly light texture from egg whites (no yolks) and a nutty flavor profile, the pine nut macaroons from southern Italy known as pignoli are standard after-dinner fare with espresso. Pignoli require only a few ingredients and are simple to make; plus, they are naturally gluten-free. For the base, most recipes we found relied on almond paste, but we achieved a deeper, richer almond flavor and more controlled sweetness by simply processing slivered almonds with granulated sugar. Many recipes call for lemon or orange zest, but we found that the flavors these ingredients brought distracted from the cookies' simple nuttiness, so we omitted them from our pignoli. Our base was a little sticky, but it was still easy enough to roll the dough into balls and coat them in pine nuts for the traditional finish. There was no need to toast the pine nuts ahead of time since they toasted as the cookies baked. If desired, the cookies can be dusted with confectioners' sugar just after they come out of the oven.

1⅔ cups slivered almonds
1⅓ cups (9⅓ ounces) sugar
  2 large egg whites
  1 cup pine nuts

1. Adjust oven racks to upper-middle and lower-middle positions and heat oven to 375 degrees. Line 2 baking sheets with parchment paper.

2. Process almonds and sugar in food processor until finely ground, about 30 seconds. Scrape down sides of bowl and add egg whites. Continue to process until smooth (dough will be wet), about 30 seconds; transfer mixture to bowl. Place pine nuts in shallow dish.

3. Working with 1 scant tablespoon dough at a time, roll into balls, roll in pine nuts to coat, and space 2 inches apart on prepared sheets.

4. Bake cookies until light golden brown, 13 to 15 minutes, switching and rotating sheets halfway through baking. Let cookies cool on sheets for 5 minutes, then transfer to wire rack. Let cookies cool completely before serving. (Cookies can be stored in airtight container at room temperature for up to 4 days.)

Pignoli

Rugelach with Raisin-Walnut Filling

Makes 32 rugelach | **Total Time** 1¾ hours, plus 1¾ hours chilling and cooling
`MAKE AHEAD` `VEGETARIAN`

WHY THIS RECIPE WORKS Part cookie, part pastry, rugelach are a traditional Jewish party snack. Their tight curls can contain a variety of bounteous sweet fillings; we settled on a generous combination of apricot preserves, raisins, and walnuts. The dough is made with tangy cream cheese and bakes up tender and flaky. To make the dough easier to work with, we added more flour to the dough than traditional recipes call for. A couple tablespoons of sour cream in addition to the cream cheese gave the cookies more punch. Be sure to stop processing the dough when the mixture resembles moist crumbs. If the dough gathers into a cohesive mass around the blade of the food processor, you have overprocessed it. If at any point during the cutting and rolling of the crescents the sheet of dough softens and becomes impossible to roll, slide it onto a baking sheet and freeze it until it is firm enough to handle. Feel free to substitute chopped pitted prunes, chopped dried apricots, or dried cranberries for the raisins in the filling.

DOUGH

2¼ cups (11¼ ounces) all-purpose flour
1½ tablespoons sugar
¼ teaspoon table salt
16 tablespoons unsalted butter, cut into ¼-inch pieces and chilled
8 ounces cream cheese, cut into ½-inch pieces and chilled
2 tablespoons sour cream

FILLING

⅔ cup apricot preserves
1 cup (7 ounces) sugar
1 tablespoon ground cinnamon
1 cup golden raisins, divided
2 cups walnuts, chopped fine, divided

GLAZE

2 large egg yolks
2 tablespoons milk

1. FOR THE DOUGH Pulse flour, sugar, and salt in food processor to combine, about 3 pulses. Add butter, cream cheese, and sour cream; process until dough comes together in small, uneven pebbles about size of cottage cheese curds, about 16 pulses. Turn out mixture onto counter, press into 9 by 6-inch log, and divide log into 4 equal pieces. Form each piece into 4½-inch disk. Place each disk between 2 sheets of plastic wrap and roll into 8½-inch round. Stack dough rounds on plate; freeze for 30 minutes.

2. FOR THE FILLING Meanwhile, process apricot preserves in food processor until smooth, about 10 seconds. Combine sugar and cinnamon in small bowl; set aside. Line rimmed baking sheet with parchment paper. Working with 1 round at a time, remove dough from freezer and spread 2½ tablespoons preserves, 2 tablespoons cinnamon sugar, ¼ cup raisins, and ½ cup walnuts over dough; pat down gently with your fingers. Cut dough round into 8 wedges. Roll each wedge into crescent shape. Space crescents ½ inch apart on prepared sheet. Cover sheet loosely with plastic and freeze crescents until firm, about 1¼ hours. (Crescents can be frozen for up to 6 weeks; transfer crescents to airtight container and cover tightly or wrap 2 or 3 crescents each in plastic and transfer to zipper-lock bags. Store remaining cinnamon sugar at room temperature.)

3. Adjust oven racks to upper-middle and lower-middle positions and heat oven to 375 degrees. Line 2 rimmed baking sheets with parchment paper. Space frozen crescents 2 inches apart on prepared sheets.

4. FOR THE GLAZE Whisk egg yolks and milk in small bowl until smooth. Brush tops and sides of frozen crescents with glaze.

5. Bake crescents until pale golden and slightly puffy, 25 to 30 minutes, switching and rotating sheets halfway through baking. Immediately sprinkle each cookie with scant teaspoon remaining cinnamon sugar; carefully transfer cookies to wire rack using wide metal spatula and let cool completely before serving. (Rugelach can be stored in airtight container at room temperature for up to 4 days.)

Cranberry Swirl Shortbread

Makes 16 wedges VEGETARIAN
Total Time 1¼ hours, plus 1½ hours cooling

WHY THIS RECIPE WORKS The "short" in shortbread refers to the butter-rich cookies' crumbly nature, a result of the way the fat in the butter coats the flour and prevents a strong gluten network from forming. While we love classic old-fashioned shortbread, here we decided to give it a festive, colorful spin by adding a cranberry swirl. The bright red spiral of pureed cranberries added a welcome tartness to the rich shortbread. We cooked the cranberries with orange and cinnamon to create another layer of flavor and then pureed them for a smooth texture and a filling that was easy to spread and pipe. In addition to spiraling the puree on top of the dough, we sandwiched a layer in the middle of the shortbread; this allowed us to incorporate more flavorful puree without weighing down the top and making the shortbread soggy. We baked the thick shortbread sandwich in two stages to crisp the bottom without drying out the cranberry swirl. For the ideal crisp texture, serve the shortbread immediately once it's cooled.

4 ounces (1 cup) fresh or frozen cranberries
½ cup (3½ ounces) granulated sugar, divided
½ teaspoon grated orange zest plus 2 tablespoons juice
¼ teaspoon ground cinnamon
2 cups (10 ounces) all-purpose flour
½ cup (2 ounces) confectioners' sugar
½ teaspoon table salt
14 tablespoons unsalted butter, cut into ½-inch pieces and chilled

1. Bring cranberries, ¼ cup granulated sugar, orange zest and juice, and cinnamon to boil in medium saucepan over medium-high heat. Cook, stirring frequently, until cranberries have burst and juice has just started to thicken, 2 to 4 minutes; let cool for 1 hour.

2. Meanwhile, adjust oven rack to middle position and heat oven to 375 degrees. Process flour, confectioners' sugar, salt, and remaining ¼ cup granulated sugar in food processor until combined, about 5 seconds. Scatter butter over top and process until dough starts to come together, about 1 minute. Gently knead dough by hand until no floury bits remain. Divide dough in half and roll each half into 9-inch circle on parchment paper; refrigerate dough for 20 minutes. Process cooled cranberry mixture in now-empty food processor until smooth, about 20 seconds.

3. Press 1 dough circle into 9-inch tart pan with removable bottom and poke all over with fork. Bake on baking sheet until edges are light golden brown, 15 to 17 minutes, rotating tart pan halfway through baking. Spread dough with ¼ cup cranberry puree, top with second dough circle, and poke all over with fork. Fill zipper-lock bag with remaining cranberry puree. Snip corner off bag and pipe remaining cranberry puree over dough in spiral shape. Score dough into 16 wedges. Between score marks, lightly run knife in opposite direction.

4. Bake shortbread until top is pale golden, 25 to 30 minutes, rotating tart pan halfway through baking. Let shortbread cool for 10 minutes, then remove outer ring of tart pan. Cut through score marks, transfer wedges to wire rack, and let cool completely before serving.

CREATING SWIRLS

1. After filling and topping parbaked shortbread base, fill zipper-lock bag with remaining cranberry puree, snip corner off bag, and pipe puree over dough in spiral shape.

2. Using paring knife, score dough into 16 wedges. Between score marks, lightly run knife in opposite direction.

Rugelach with Raisin-Walnut Filling

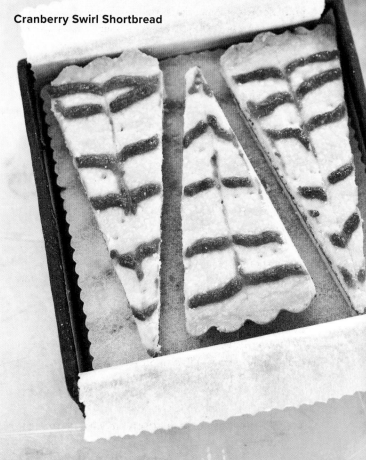

Cranberry Swirl Shortbread

Millionaire's Shortbread

Ultranutty Pecan Bars

Millionaire's Shortbread

Makes 40 cookies   `MAKE AHEAD`   `VEGETARIAN`
Total Time 1½ hours, plus 1½ hours cooling

WHY THIS RECIPE WORKS Millionaire's shortbread is a fitting name for this impressively rich British cookie, which consists of a buttery shortbread base topped with a caramel-like layer, which is in turn topped with a layer of shiny chocolate. It makes a beautiful holiday gift—as long as the top chocolate layer maintains an attractive tempered sheen and snap. For the crunchy shortbread base layer, we whisked together flour, sugar, and salt and stirred in melted butter. We then baked the dough until it was golden brown. Sweetened condensed milk gives the caramel portion of this cookie its luxurious creaminess. However, we found that the whey proteins in the condensed milk sometimes caused the caramel sauce to break. Adding fresh cream solved the problem, as its proteins haven't been damaged by processing. For the all-important top chocolate layer, our easy microwave tempering method resulted in a glossy, snappy blanket of chocolate on our shortbread. For a caramel filling with the right texture, monitor the temperature with an instant-read thermometer. For more information on making a foil sling, see page 225.

CRUST

2½ cups (12½ ounces) all-purpose flour
½ cup (3½ ounces) granulated sugar
¾ teaspoon table salt
16 tablespoons unsalted butter, melted

FILLING

1 (14-ounce) can sweetened condensed milk
1 cup packed (7 ounces) brown sugar
½ cup heavy cream
½ cup corn syrup
8 tablespoons unsalted butter
½ teaspoon table salt

8 ounces bittersweet chocolate (6 ounces chopped fine, 2 ounces grated)

1. FOR THE CRUST Adjust oven rack to lower-middle position and heat oven to 350 degrees. Make foil sling for 13 by 9-inch baking pan by folding 2 long sheets of aluminum foil; first sheet should be 13 inches wide and second sheet should be 9 inches wide. Lay sheets of foil in pan perpendicular to each other, with extra foil hanging over edges of pan. Push foil into corners and up sides of pan, smoothing foil flush to pan.

2. Combine flour, sugar, and salt in medium bowl. Add melted butter and stir with rubber spatula until flour is evenly moistened. Crumble dough evenly over bottom of prepared pan. Using your fingertips and palm of your hand, press and smooth dough into even thickness. Using fork, pierce dough at 1-inch intervals. Bake until light golden brown and firm to touch, 25 to 30 minutes. Transfer pan to wire rack. Using sturdy metal spatula, press on entire surface of warm crust to compress (this will make finished bars easier to cut). Let crust cool until it is just warm, at least 20 minutes.

3. FOR THE FILLING While crust cools, stir all ingredients together in large, heavy-bottomed saucepan. Cook over medium heat, stirring frequently, until mixture registers between 236 and 239 degrees (temperature will fluctuate), 16 to 20 minutes.

4. Pour over crust and spread to even thickness (mixture will be very hot). Let cool completely, about 1½ hours.

5. Microwave chopped chocolate in bowl at 50 percent power, stirring every 15 seconds, until melted but not much warmer than body temperature (check by holding bowl in palm of your hand), 1 to 2 minutes (chocolate should still be slightly lumpy). Stir in grated chocolate until melted and smooth, returning chocolate to microwave for no more than 5 seconds at a time, if needed, to complete melting. Spread chocolate evenly over surface of filling. Refrigerate shortbread until chocolate is just set, about 10 minutes.

6. Using foil overhang, lift shortbread out of pan and transfer to cutting board; discard foil. Using serrated knife and gentle sawing motion, cut shortbread in half crosswise to create two 6½ by 9-inch rectangles. Cut each rectangle in half to make four 3¼ by 9-inch strips. Cut each strip crosswise into 10 equal pieces, and serve. (Shortbread can be stored in airtight container at room temperature, between layers of parchment, for up to 1 week.)

Ultranutty Pecan Bars

Makes 24 bars `MAKE AHEAD` `VEGETARIAN`
Total Time 1 hour, plus 1½ hours cooling

WHY THIS RECIPE WORKS We think the ideal pecan bar should put the focus squarely on the star ingredient, with pecans piled high on a buttery crust and held in place by a not-too-sweet glaze. Corn syrup coated the nuts nicely but tasted flat, so we added brown sugar, melted butter, vanilla, and a good dose of salt to the mix. We then stirred a whole pound of toasted pecans into the glaze. With that many pecans, the nuts were layered on top of one another, allowing for a combination of textures in every bite—some nuts were slicked with glaze and chewy, while those sitting on the top

layer were crisp. Since the topping wasn't wet, we didn't need to parbake our crust to ensure that it didn't sog out. All that was needed was to pat the mixture of flour, sugar, and butter into the bottom of a baking pan, spread the pecans on top, and bake. For more information on making a foil sling, see page 225. The edges will be slightly firmer than the center. If desired, trim ¼ inch from the edges before cutting into bars.

CRUST

1¾ cups (8¾ ounces) all-purpose flour
6 tablespoons (2⅔ ounces) sugar
½ teaspoon table salt
8 tablespoons unsalted butter, melted

TOPPING

¾ cup packed (5¼ ounces) light brown sugar
½ cup light corn syrup
7 tablespoons unsalted butter, melted and hot
1 teaspoon vanilla extract
½ teaspoon table salt
4 cups (1 pound) pecans, toasted
½ teaspoon flake sea salt (optional)

1. FOR THE CRUST Adjust oven rack to lowest position and heat oven to 350 degrees. Make foil sling for 13 by 9-inch baking pan by folding 2 long sheets of aluminum foil; first sheet should be 13 inches wide and second sheet should be 9 inches wide. Lay sheets of foil in pan perpendicular to each other, with extra foil hanging over edges of pan. Push foil into corners and up sides of pan, smoothing foil flush to pan. Lightly spray foil with vegetable oil spray.

2. Whisk flour, sugar, and salt together in medium bowl. Add melted butter and stir with wooden spoon until dough begins to form. Using your hands, continue to combine until no dry flour remains and small portion of dough holds together when squeezed in palm of your hand. Evenly scatter tablespoon-size pieces of dough over surface of pan. Using your fingertips and palm of your hand, press and smooth dough into even thickness in bottom of pan.

3. FOR THE TOPPING Whisk sugar, corn syrup, melted butter, vanilla, and table salt in medium bowl until smooth (mixture will look separated at first but will become homogeneous), about 20 seconds. Fold pecans into sugar mixture until evenly coated.

4. Pour topping over crust. Using spatula, spread topping over crust, pushing to edges and into corners (there will be bare patches). Bake until topping is evenly distributed and rapidly bubbling across entire surface, 23 to 25 minutes.

5. Transfer pan to wire rack and lightly sprinkle with flake sea salt, if using. Let bars cool completely in pan on rack, about 1½ hours. Using foil overhang, lift bars out of pan and transfer to cutting board; discard foil. Cut into 24 bars. Serve. (Bars can be stored at room temperature for up to 5 days.)

Pear-Cherry Streusel Bars

Makes 24 bars VEGETARIAN
Total Time 1¼ hours, plus 2 hours cooling

WHY THIS RECIPE WORKS Apple- and berry-filled desserts abound, but pears never seem to get their due. The honey-sweet fruit plays well with a host of other flavors, so in these bars we matched the delicate, floral notes of pear with the tart but complementary punch of cherry. However, cramming two fruits into our bars weighed down the crust and made it soggy, so instead of using whole cherries we turned to cherry jam, which we spread over the bar base. And to eliminate excess moisture from the pears, we sautéed slices in butter with a little sugar before layering them on top of the jam. Cooking the pears also intensified their flavor, which we heightened further by adding lemon juice and vanilla extract. Parbaking the crust ensured that it stayed crisp below our lively fruit filling. Almonds complemented both the cherries and pears, and the caramel notes of brown sugar enhanced the streusel topping for a perfect finish to our unique bars. For more information on making a foil sling, see page 225.

2¼ cups (11¼ ounces) all-purpose flour
16 tablespoons unsalted butter, cut into 16 pieces and chilled, plus 2 tablespoons unsalted butter
⅔ cup (4⅔ ounces) plus 2 tablespoons granulated sugar, divided
½ teaspoon table salt
1 cup sliced almonds
¼ cup packed (1¾ ounces) light brown sugar
4 ripe but firm Bartlett or Bosc pears, peeled, halved, cored, and sliced ¼ inch thick
2 teaspoons lemon juice
1 teaspoon vanilla extract
¾ cup cherry jam

1. Adjust oven rack to middle position and heat oven to 375 degrees. Make foil sling for 13 by 9-inch baking pan by folding 2 long sheets of aluminum foil; first sheet should be 13 inches wide and second sheet should be 9 inches wide. Lay sheets of foil in pan perpendicular to each other, with extra foil hanging over edges of pan. Push foil into corners and up sides of pan, smoothing foil flush to pan. Lightly spray foil with vegetable oil spray.

2. Process flour, 16 tablespoons chilled butter, ⅔ cup granulated sugar, and salt in food processor until mixture resembles coarse meal, about 30 seconds. Set aside 1 cup flour mixture in bowl for topping. Sprinkle remaining mixture into prepared pan and press firmly into even layer. Bake until golden brown, about 20 minutes. Transfer pan to wire rack.

3. Return reserved flour mixture to now-empty food processor. Add almonds and brown sugar and pulse until just combined, 5 to 6 pulses.

4. Melt remaining 2 tablespoons butter in 12-inch skillet over medium-high heat. Add pears and remaining 2 tablespoons granulated sugar and cook until pears are light golden brown and dry, about 10 minutes. Stir in lemon juice and vanilla.

5. Spread jam evenly over warm crust, then top with even layer of pear mixture. Sprinkle with topping and bake until golden brown, 20 to 25 minutes. Let bars cool completely in pan on wire rack, about 2 hours. Using foil overhang, lift bars out of pan and transfer to cutting board; discard foil. Cut into 24 pieces before serving.

Fudgy Brownies

Makes 36 brownies MAKE AHEAD VEGETARIAN
Total Time 1 hour, plus 2 hours cooling

WHY THIS RECIPE WORKS Brownies are a controversial territory to chart: Some like them cakey and light in flavor; some like them moist and chewy; and others like them to be purely decadent—almost as dense as fudge and deliciously dark. We wanted to make intensely rich brownies that would be a chocolate lover's dream, so we started by using three forms of chocolate: unsweetened chocolate for oomph, cocoa powder for complexity, and bittersweet or semisweet chocolate for moisture and well-rounded flavor. Melting butter along with the chocolate was the key to a fudgy texture, and a generous three eggs contributed richness and structure. In addition to providing a clean sweetness, granulated sugar gave the baked brownies a delicate, shiny, crackly top crust. Tasters preferred the more complex flavor of bittersweet chocolate over semisweet, but either type works well here, as does 5 ounces of bittersweet or semisweet chocolate chips in place of the bar chocolate. Be sure to use a metal baking pan and not a glass baking dish in this recipe. For more information on making a foil sling, see page 225.

    5 ounces bittersweet or semisweet chocolate, chopped
    2 ounces unsweetened chocolate, chopped
    8 tablespoons unsalted butter, cut into 4 pieces
    3 tablespoons unsweetened cocoa powder
 1¼ cups (8¾ ounces) sugar
    3 large eggs
    2 teaspoons vanilla extract
    ½ teaspoon table salt
    1 cup (5 ounces) all-purpose flour

1. Adjust oven rack to middle position and heat oven to 350 degrees. Make foil sling for 8-inch square baking pan by folding 2 long sheets of aluminum foil so each is 8 inches wide. Lay sheets of foil in pan perpendicular to each other, with extra foil hanging over edges of pan. Push foil into corners and up sides of pan, smoothing foil flush to pan. Lightly spray foil with vegetable oil spray.

2. Microwave bittersweet and unsweetened chocolates in bowl at 50 percent power for 2 minutes. Stir in butter and continue to microwave, stirring often, until melted and smooth. Whisk in cocoa and let mixture cool slightly.

3. Whisk sugar, eggs, vanilla, and salt in large bowl until combined. Whisk chocolate mixture into sugar mixture until smooth. Using rubber spatula, stir in flour until no dry streaks remain. Transfer batter to prepared pan and smooth top. Bake until toothpick inserted in center comes out with few moist crumbs attached, 35 to 40 minutes, rotating pan halfway through baking.

4. Let brownies cool completely in pan on wire rack, about 2 hours. Using foil overhang, lift brownies out of pan and transfer to cutting board; discard foil. (Uncut brownies can be refrigerated for up to 3 days.) Cut into 36 pieces. Serve.

Fudgy Peppermint Surprise Brownies
In step 3, spread all but 1 cup batter in even layer in prepared pan. Space sixteen 1½-inch unwrapped York Peppermint Patty candies ½ inch apart on top of batter. Gently spread remaining batter over candies and smooth top. Continue with step 3, baking brownies as directed.

Pear-Cherry Streusel Bars

Fudgy Brownies

Cranberry–Sour Cream Pound Cake

Serves 8 `MAKE AHEAD` `VEGETARIAN`
Total Time 2¼ hours, plus 2¼ hours cooling

WHY THIS RECIPE WORKS Tart cranberries and tangy sour cream provide a welcome contrast to this rich, buttery cake. The bright cranberries also contribute a burst of color for an extra-special dessert. We wanted this pound cake to have a crumb that wasn't quite as tight as a classic all-butter pound cake, so we used all-purpose flour instead of cake flour and we thoroughly creamed the butter. We tamed the cranberries' sourness by tossing the coarsely chopped berries with confectioners' sugar before adding them to the batter; this also prevented them from sinking to the bottom of the pan. Baking the loaf slowly in a 300-degree oven ensured that the inside cooked through before the exterior became too brown. If you're using frozen cranberries, there's no need to thaw them first. The ideal temperature for the eggs and butter is 60 degrees. The test kitchen's preferred loaf pan measures 8½ by 4½ inches; if using a 9 by 5-inch loaf pan, start checking for doneness 5 minutes early.

Cranberry–Sour Cream Pound Cake

 5 large eggs, room temperature
 2 teaspoons vanilla extract
1¾ cups (8¾ ounces) all-purpose flour
 ¾ teaspoon plus ⅛ teaspoon table salt, divided
 ½ teaspoon baking powder
 ⅓ cup sour cream
 2 tablespoons milk
14 tablespoons unsalted butter, cut into 14 pieces and softened but still cool
1¼ cups (8¾ ounces) granulated sugar
 4 ounces (1 cup) fresh or frozen cranberries, chopped coarse
 1 tablespoon confectioners' sugar

1. Adjust oven rack to lower-middle position and heat oven to 300 degrees. Spray 8½ by 4½-inch loaf pan with baking spray with flour.

2. Whisk eggs and vanilla together in 2-cup liquid measuring cup. Sift flour, ¾ teaspoon salt, and baking powder into bowl. Whisk sour cream and milk together in second bowl.

3. Using stand mixer fitted with paddle, beat butter on medium-high speed until smooth and creamy, 2 to 3 minutes, scraping down bowl once. Reduce speed to medium and gradually add granulated sugar. Increase speed to medium-high and beat until pale and fluffy, 3 to 5 minutes, scraping down bowl as needed. Reduce speed to medium and gradually add egg mixture in slow, steady stream. Scrape down bowl and continue to mix on medium speed until uniform, about 1 minute (batter may look slightly curdled). Reduce speed to low and add flour mixture in 3 additions, alternating with sour cream mixture in 2 additions, scraping down bowl as needed. Give batter final stir by hand. Toss cranberries with confectioners' sugar and remaining ⅛ teaspoon salt in bowl until evenly coated, then gently but thoroughly fold into batter.

4. Transfer batter to prepared pan and gently tap pan on counter to release air bubbles. Bake until toothpick inserted in center comes out clean, 1¾ hours to 1 hour 55 minutes, rotating pan halfway through baking. Let cake cool in pan on wire rack for 15 minutes. Remove cake from pan and let cool completely on rack, about 2 hours. Serve. (Cake can be stored at room temperature for up to 3 days or frozen for up to 1 month; defrost cake at room temperature.)

Clementine Cake

Serves 8 `MAKE AHEAD` `VEGETARIAN`

Total Time 1¾ hours, plus 3 hours cooling and setting

WHY THIS RECIPE WORKS Clementine cakes are almost always tender single-layer cakes made with whole ground clementines and decorated with candied slices of their namesake fruit for an irresistible balance of sweet, sour, and floral sun-kissed flavors. Our recipe calls for a total of nine clementines: five pulverized and incorporated into the batter, and four sliced and candied to adorn the cake's surface. Microwaving the clementines for the batter before pureeing them softened the fruits and tamed the bitterness of their rinds. Ground almonds made up the base of the batter, giving the cake rich, nutty depth; adding a little all-purpose flour gave the crumb a lighter but sturdier texture. The cake's smooth white glaze perfectly set off the glimmering candied clementine slices, and required nothing more than finding the right ratio of confectioners' sugar to water to achieve a pourable but not-too-thin consistency. Look for clementines that are about 2 inches in diameter (about 1¾ ounces each). Use a mandoline to get consistent slices of clementine to arrange on top of the cake; you can also use a chef's knife. We found it easier to slice the clementines when they were cold.

CAKE

- 9 ounces clementines, unpeeled, stemmed (5 clementines)
- 2¼ cups (7½ ounces) sliced blanched almonds, toasted
- 1 cup (5 ounces) all-purpose flour
- 1¼ teaspoons baking powder
- ¼ teaspoon table salt
- 10 tablespoons unsalted butter, cut into 10 pieces and softened
- 1½ cups (10½ ounces) granulated sugar
- 5 large eggs

CANDIED CLEMENTINES

- 4 clementines, unpeeled, stemmed
- 1 cup water
- 1 cup (7 ounces) granulated sugar
- ⅛ teaspoon table salt

GLAZE

- 2 cups (8 ounces) confectioners' sugar
- 2½ tablespoons water, plus extra as needed
- Pinch table salt

Clementine Cake

1. FOR THE CAKE Adjust oven rack to middle position and heat oven to 325 degrees. Spray 9-inch springform pan with vegetable oil spray, line bottom with parchment paper, and spray parchment. Microwave clementines in covered bowl until softened and some juice is released, about 3 minutes. Discard juice and let clementines cool for 10 minutes.

2. Process almonds, flour, baking powder, and salt in food processor until almonds are finely ground, about 30 seconds; transfer to second bowl. Add clementines to now-empty processor and process until smooth, about 1 minute, scraping down sides of bowl as needed.

3. Using stand mixer fitted with paddle, beat butter and sugar on medium-high speed until pale and fluffy, about 3 minutes. Add eggs, one at a time, and beat until combined, scraping down bowl as needed. Add clementine puree and beat until incorporated, about 30 seconds.

4. Reduce speed to low and add almond mixture in 3 additions until just combined, scraping down bowl as needed. Using rubber spatula, give batter final stir by hand. Transfer batter to prepared pan and smooth top. Bake until toothpick inserted in center comes out clean, 55 minutes to 1 hour. Let cake cool completely in pan on wire rack, about 2 hours.

5. FOR THE CANDIED CLEMENTINES While cake cools, line baking sheet with triple layer of paper towels. Slice clementines ¼ inch thick perpendicular to stem; discard rounded ends. Bring water, sugar, and salt to simmer in small saucepan over medium heat and cook until sugar has dissolved, about 1 minute. Add clementines and cook until softened, about 6 minutes. Using tongs, transfer clementines to prepared sheet and let cool for at least 30 minutes, flipping halfway through cooling to blot away excess moisture.

6. FOR THE GLAZE Whisk sugar, water, and salt in bowl until smooth. Adjust consistency with extra water as needed, ½ teaspoon at a time, until glaze has consistency of thick craft glue and leaves visible trail in bowl when drizzled from whisk.

7. Carefully run paring knife around cake and remove side of pan. Using thin metal spatula, lift cake from pan bottom; discard parchment and transfer cake to serving platter. Pour glaze over cake and smooth top with offset spatula, allowing some glaze to drip down sides. Let stand for 1 hour to set.

8. Just before serving, select 8 uniform candied clementine slices (you will have more than 8 slices; reserve extra slices for another use) and blot away excess moisture with additional paper towels. Arrange slices around top edge of cake, evenly spaced. Serve. (Cake can be wrapped in plastic wrap and stored at room temperature for up to 2 days.)

Slow-Cooker Flourless Chocolate Cake

Slow-Cooker Flourless Chocolate Cake

Serves 8 `MAKE AHEAD` `VEGETARIAN`
Cooking Time 1 to 2 hours on High

WHY THIS RECIPE WORKS Most people think of flourless chocolate cake as a restaurant dessert, the type of rich confection that can only be whipped up by a skilled pastry chef. But in reality, it could hardly be easier. This decadent cake requires just a handful of ingredients (chocolate, butter, eggs, and coffee), is made in the slow cooker to keep your oven free, and can even be prepared ahead of time, making it perfect as a fuss-free dinner party finale. Removing the cake from the slow cooker when it was just slightly underdone (when it registered 140 degrees on an instant-read thermometer) was key because the cake continued to cook and firm up as it cooled. You will need a 6-inch springform pan for this recipe. Check the temperature of the cake after 1 hour of cooking and continue to monitor until it registers 140 degrees. To make neat slices, dip the knife blade into hot water and wipe it clean with a dish towel after each cut. You will need a 5-to 7-quart oval slow cooker for this recipe.

- 8 ounces bittersweet or semisweet chocolate, chopped
- 8 tablespoons unsalted butter
- 2 tablespoons brewed coffee
- 4 large eggs
  Confectioners' sugar

1. Fill slow cooker with ½ inch water (about 2 cups) and place aluminum foil rack in bottom. Grease 6-inch springform pan and line with parchment paper.

2. Microwave chocolate and butter in large bowl at 50 percent power, stirring occasionally, until melted, 1 to 2 minutes. Stir in coffee and let chocolate mixture cool slightly.

3. Using handheld mixer set at medium-low speed, whip eggs in separate bowl until foamy, about 1 minute. Increase speed to medium-high and whip eggs until very thick and pale yellow, 5 to 10 minutes. Gently fold one-third of whipped eggs into chocolate mixture until few streaks remain. Repeat folding twice more with remaining whipped eggs and continue to fold batter until no streaks remain. Scrape batter into prepared pan and smooth top. Set pan on prepared rack, cover, and cook until cake registers 140 degrees, 1 to 2 hours on high.

4. Transfer cake to wire rack. Run small knife around edge of cake and gently blot away condensation using paper towels. Let cake cool in pan to room temperature, about 1 hour. Cover with plastic wrap and refrigerate until well chilled, at least 3 hours or up to 3 days.

5. About 30 minutes before serving, run small knife around edge of cake, then remove sides of pan. Invert cake onto sheet of parchment paper. Peel off and discard parchment baked onto cake. Turn cake right side up onto serving dish. Dust with confectioners' sugar and serve.

MAKING A FOIL RACK

Loosely roll 24 by 12-inch piece of aluminum foil into 1-inch cylinder, then bend sides in to form oval ring that measures 8 inches long by 5 inches wide. After adding water to slow cooker, place foil rack in center.

Chocolate Lava Cake for a Crowd

Serves 12 | **Total Time** 2 hours `VEGETARIAN`

WHY THIS RECIPE WORKS Individual-size chocolate lava cakes feature moist chocolate cake surrounding a fudgy, molten center that acts like a sauce when the cake is cut open. We had a hunch that we could use our Dutch oven to make enough of this irresistibly chocolaty dessert to serve a crowd. We mixed the batter right in the Dutch oven, and then we sprinkled the batter with a mixture of granulated sugar, brown sugar, and cocoa powder and finished the assembly by pouring a combination of water and coffee over the top. The mixture didn't look very appealing at this stage, but a little over an hour in the oven produced a near-magical transformation. During baking, the sugar-cocoa mixture sank to the bottom and the cake rose to the top, creating just the fudgy layers we were looking for. The Dutch oven's heat-retaining walls kept the cake's center gooey and warm even as we went back for seconds. Serve with Whipped Cream (page 368).

- 12 tablespoons unsalted butter, cut into 12 pieces
- 4 ounces bittersweet chocolate, chopped coarse
- 1⅓ cups (4 ounces) unsweetened cocoa powder, divided
- 2 cups (14 ounces) granulated sugar, divided
- ⅔ cup packed (4⅔ ounces) light brown sugar
- 1½ cups brewed coffee
- 1½ cups water
- ⅔ cup whole milk
- 2 large egg yolks
- 2 tablespoons vanilla extract

Chocolate Lava Cake for a Crowd

- 4 teaspoons baking powder
- ½ teaspoon table salt
- 1½ cups (7½ ounces) all-purpose flour

1. Adjust oven rack to middle position and heat oven to 325 degrees. Melt butter, chocolate, and ⅔ cup cocoa in Dutch oven over low heat, stirring frequently, until smooth, 2 to 4 minutes. Remove pot from heat and let cool slightly.

2. Whisk ⅔ cup granulated sugar, brown sugar, and remaining ⅔ cup cocoa together in bowl, breaking up any large clumps of brown sugar with your fingers. In separate bowl, combine coffee and water.

3. Whisk milk, egg yolks, vanilla, baking powder, salt, and remaining 1⅓ cups granulated sugar into chocolate mixture. Whisk in flour until just combined. Sprinkle brown sugar mixture evenly over top, covering entire surface of batter. Pour coffee mixture gently over brown sugar mixture.

4. Scrape down exposed sides of pot, then transfer to oven. Bake, uncovered, until cake begins to pull away from sides of pot and top is just firm to touch, 1¼ to 1½ hours, rotating pot halfway through baking. Remove pot from oven and transfer to wire rack. Let cake cool for 15 minutes before serving.

Hot Cocoa Cake

Hot Cocoa Cake

Serves 10 to 12 `MAKE AHEAD`
Total Time 2¼ hours, plus 2 hours cooling

WHY THIS RECIPE WORKS Mounded with fluffy marshmallows and dusted with cocoa powder, this playful three-layer chocolate cake is sure to score smiles from kids and adults alike. Inspired by a steaming-hot mug of cocoa, the cake earns its name with its alternating layers of rich chocolate cake and gooey marshmallow filling. Rather than making the marshmallow filling from scratch, which would require closely monitoring a sugar mixture on the stove, we kept things easy by using store-bought marshmallow crème, which we stabilized with gelatin. Stirring in some butter and vanilla added creaminess and welcome flavor. We love a dollop of whipped cream on our mug of cocoa, so we figured a whipped cream frosting would be the perfect complement to this rich cake. We enhanced the whipped cream with cocoa powder and white chocolate for a stable, flavorful, and ultracreamy frosting. To finish, we topped the cake off just like the drink, with a garnish of marshmallows and cocoa powder. Do not substitute natural cocoa powder for the Dutch-processed cocoa powder here.

CAKE

- 4 ounces unsweetened chocolate, chopped coarse
- ½ cup hot water
- ¼ cup (¾ ounces) Dutch-processed cocoa powder
- 1¾ cups (12¼ ounces) sugar, divided
- 1¾ cups (8¾ ounces) all-purpose flour
- 1½ teaspoons baking soda
- 1 teaspoon table salt
- 1 cup buttermilk
- 2 teaspoons vanilla extract
- 4 large eggs plus 2 large yolks, room temperature
- 12 tablespoons unsalted butter, cut into 12 pieces and softened

FILLING

- 1 teaspoon unflavored gelatin
- ¼ cup water
- 6 tablespoons unsalted butter, cut into 6 pieces and softened
- 1 teaspoon vanilla extract
  Pinch table salt
- 2 cups marshmallow crème

FROSTING

½ cup (3 ounces) white chocolate chips
1½ cups heavy cream, divided
3 tablespoons Dutch-processed cocoa powder, plus extra for dusting
24 large marshmallows

1. FOR THE CAKE Adjust oven rack to middle position and heat oven to 350 degrees. Grease three 8-inch round cake pans, line with parchment paper, grease parchment, and flour pans.

2. Combine chocolate, hot water, and cocoa in medium heatproof bowl set over saucepan filled with 1 inch barely simmering water, making sure that water does not touch bottom of bowl and stirring with heat-resistant rubber spatula until chocolate is melted, about 2 minutes. Add ½ cup sugar to chocolate mixture and stir until thick and glossy, 1 to 2 minutes. Remove bowl from heat and set aside to cool.

3. Whisk flour, baking soda, and salt together in bowl. Combine buttermilk and vanilla in second bowl. Using stand mixer fitted with whisk attachment, whip eggs and yolks on medium-low speed until combined, about 10 seconds. Add remaining 1¼ cups sugar, increase speed to high, and whip until light and fluffy, 2 to 3 minutes.

4. Fit stand mixer with paddle. Add cooled chocolate mixture to egg mixture and mix on medium speed until thoroughly combined, 30 to 45 seconds, scraping down bowl as needed. Add butter, 1 piece at a time, mixing for about 10 seconds after each addition. Add flour mixture in 3 additions, alternating with buttermilk mixture in 2 additions, mixing until incorporated after each addition (about 15 seconds) and scraping down bowl as needed. Reduce speed to medium-low and mix until batter is thoroughly combined, about 15 seconds. Give batter final stir by hand.

5. Divide batter evenly between prepared pans and smooth tops with rubber spatula. Bake until toothpick inserted in center comes out with few moist crumbs attached, 15 to 20 minutes, switching and rotating pans halfway through baking. Let cakes cool in pans on wire rack for 10 minutes. Remove cakes from pans, discarding parchment, and let cool completely on rack, about 2 hours. (Cooled cakes can be stored at room temperature for up to 24 hours or frozen for up to 1 month; defrost cakes at room temperature.)

6. FOR THE FILLING Sprinkle gelatin over water in large bowl and let stand until gelatin softens, about 5 minutes. Microwave until mixture is bubbling around edges and gelatin dissolves, about 15 seconds. Stir in butter, vanilla, and salt until

combined. Let mixture cool until just warm to touch, about 5 minutes. Whisk in marshmallow crème until smooth; refrigerate filling until firm enough to spread, about 30 minutes.

7. FOR THE FROSTING Place chocolate chips in small bowl. Bring ½ cup cream and cocoa to simmer in small saucepan over medium-high heat, whisking until smooth. Pour cream mixture over chocolate chips and whisk until melted and smooth. Let chocolate mixture cool completely, about 30 minutes. Using stand mixer fitted with whisk attachment, whip remaining 1 cup cream with cooled chocolate mixture on medium-high speed until soft peaks form, 1 to 1½ minutes.

8. Line edges of cake platter with 4 strips of parchment paper to keep platter clean. Place 1 cake layer on platter. Spread half of filling evenly over top. Repeat with 1 more cake layer, press lightly to adhere, then spread with remaining filling. Top with remaining cake layer, pressing lightly to adhere. Spread frosting evenly over top and sides of cake. To smooth frosting, run edge of offset spatula around cake sides and over top. Arrange marshmallows on top of cake in large mound. Dust with extra cocoa. Serve.

HOW TO LINE AND FLOUR A CAKE PAN

1. Place cake pan on sheet of parchment paper and trace around bottom of pan. Cut out parchment circle.

2. Evenly spray bottom and sides of pan with vegetable oil spray or rub with butter.

3. Fit parchment into pan and spray or grease parchment. Sprinkle with several tablespoons of flour. Shake and rotate pan to coat it evenly, then shake out excess flour.

Gingerbread Layer Cake

Serves 12 to 16 | **Total Time** 1¾ hours, plus 2½ hours cooling and chilling `MAKE AHEAD` `VEGETARIAN`

WHY THIS RECIPE WORKS We wanted to transform homey gingerbread into a stately layer cake. The problem? Traditional recipes for gingerbread cake are too moist to be stacked four layers high. Instead of reducing the amount of molasses or coffee in our recipe, which would lighten the cake's color and dull its flavor, we added an ingredient that's unconventional in gingerbread: cocoa powder. Cocoa contains a high proportion of absorbent starch; just ¼ cup of it soaked up the cake's excess moisture. The cocoa also deepened the color and flavor of our gingerbread without making the cake taste chocolaty. Instead of a more assertive cream cheese frosting, our lush, silky Miracle Frosting let the spiced cake shine. Sprinkling chopped crystallized ginger over the top of the cake completed the holiday gingerbread revamp. Use a 2-cup liquid measuring cup to portion the cake batter. Do not use blackstrap molasses here as it is too bitter.

1¾ cups (8¾ ounces) all-purpose flour
¼ cup (¾ ounce) unsweetened cocoa powder
2 tablespoons ground ginger
1½ teaspoons baking powder
1 teaspoon ground cinnamon
¾ teaspoon table salt
½ teaspoon ground white pepper
⅛ teaspoon cayenne pepper
1 cup brewed coffee
¾ cup molasses
½ teaspoon baking soda
1½ cups (10½ ounces) sugar
¾ cup vegetable oil
3 large eggs, lightly beaten
2 tablespoons finely grated fresh ginger
1 recipe Miracle Frosting
¼ cup chopped crystallized ginger (optional)

1. Adjust oven rack to middle position and heat oven to 350 degrees. Grease and flour two 8-inch round cake pans and line pans with parchment paper. Whisk flour, cocoa, ground ginger, baking powder, cinnamon, salt, pepper, and cayenne together in large bowl. Whisk coffee, molasses, and baking soda in second large bowl until combined. Add sugar, oil, eggs, and fresh ginger to coffee mixture and whisk until smooth.

2. Whisk coffee mixture into flour mixture until smooth. Pour 1⅓ cups batter into each prepared pan. Bake until toothpick inserted in center comes out clean, 12 to 14 minutes. Let cakes cool in pans on wire rack for 10 minutes. Remove cakes from pan, discarding parchment, and let cool completely on rack, about 2 hours. Wipe pans clean with paper towels. Let pans cool completely, regrease and reflour pans, and line with fresh parchment. Repeat process with remaining batter.

3. Line edges of cake platter with 4 strips of parchment to keep platter clean. Place 1 cake layer on platter. Spread ¾ cup frosting evenly over top, right to edge of cake. Repeat with 2 more cake layers, pressing lightly to adhere and spreading ¾ cup frosting evenly over each layer. Top with remaining cake layer and spread remaining frosting evenly over top and sides of cake. Garnish top of cake with crystallized ginger, if using. Refrigerate until frosting is set, about 30 minutes, before serving. (Cake can be refrigerated for up to 2 days; let come to room temperature before serving.)

Miracle Frosting

Makes 5 cups (**Serves** 12 to 16)
Total Time 20 minutes, plus 2 hours cooling

1½ cups (10½ ounces) sugar
¼ cup (1¼ ounces) all-purpose flour
3 tablespoons cornstarch
½ teaspoon table salt
1½ cups milk
24 tablespoons (3 sticks) unsalted butter, softened
2 teaspoons vanilla extract

1. Whisk sugar, flour, cornstarch, and salt together in medium saucepan. Slowly whisk in milk until smooth. Cook over medium heat, whisking constantly and scraping corners of saucepan, until mixture boils and is very thick, 4 to 8 minutes. Transfer mixture to wide bowl and let cool completely, about 2 hours.

2. Using stand mixer fitted with paddle, beat butter on medium-high speed until light and fluffy, about 5 minutes. Reduce speed to medium, add cooled milk mixture and vanilla, and mix until combined, scraping down sides of bowl as needed. Increase speed to medium-high and beat until frosting is light and fluffy, 3 to 5 minutes. (Frosting can be refrigerated in airtight container for 1 week. When ready to use, let stand at room temperature until softened, about 2 hours. Beat with stand mixer on medium-high speed until light and fluffy, about 1 minute.)

Apricot and Cherry Modern Fruitcake

Serves 10 to 12 `MAKE AHEAD` `VEGETARIAN`
Total Time 2 hours, plus 3 hours cooling

WHY THIS RECIPE WORKS Fruitcake gets a bad rap: Many of us have experienced at least one bad one before swearing off of them forever. But it doesn't have to be this way. Our updated take offers balanced booziness, complementary fruits, and a moist but not overly dense texture. We skipped the candied fruits, instead hydrating dried apricots and tart dried cherries in ¼ cup of warm rum and then stirring this mixture into the batter. A rich, sturdy batter made with all-purpose flour and 2 eggs was able to support a full 2 cups of fruit as well as ¾ cup of crunchy walnuts. As the fruit cooked in the cake, the pieces turned translucent, giving them a naturally glacéed effect. A rum and orange juice soak gave the cake the boozy flavor we were looking for without being harsh or making the cake soggy. As a decorative touch we laid halved pieces of dried apricots around the bottom of the pan before pouring in the batter so that the finished cake would have a festive fruit crown, and we finished by brushing the cooled cake with a shiny apricot glaze.

CAKE

1½ cups (9 ounces) dried apricots (1 cup chopped fine, ½ cup halved crosswise)
¼ cup dark rum
1 cup dried cherries
1 cup (5 ounces) all-purpose flour
1¼ teaspoons baking powder
¾ teaspoon table salt
½ cup packed (3½ ounces) light brown sugar
⅓ cup (2⅓ ounces) granulated sugar
2 large eggs, room temperature
8 tablespoons unsalted butter, melted and cooled
1½ teaspoons vanilla extract
1 teaspoon grated lemon zest
1 teaspoon grated orange zest
¾ cup walnuts, toasted and chopped

SOAK AND GLAZE

⅓ cup dark rum
2 tablespoons orange juice
2 tablespoons apricot jam

1. FOR THE CAKE Adjust oven rack to middle position and heat oven to 350 degrees. Grease 8-inch round cake pan, line with parchment paper, grease parchment, and flour pan.

Gingerbread
Layer Cake

Apricot and Cherry
Modern Fruitcake

Arrange halved apricots cut side down, perpendicular to pan edge, in tightly packed ring around bottom of pan. Microwave rum in bowl until steaming, about 30 seconds, stir in chopped apricots and cherries and let stand for 20 minutes, stirring once halfway through cooling.

2. Whisk flour, baking powder, and salt together in bowl. Whisk brown sugar, granulated sugar, and eggs in large bowl until thoroughly combined and thick, about 45 seconds. Slowly whisk in melted butter until combined. Whisk in vanilla, lemon zest, and orange zest. Gently whisk in flour mixture until just combined. Using rubber spatula, fold in rum-soaked fruits and walnuts.

3. Pour batter into prepared pan and smooth top with rubber spatula. Bake until deep golden brown and skewer inserted in center comes out clean, 55 minutes to 1 hour 5 minutes, rotating pan halfway through baking. Let cake cool in pan on wire rack for 5 minutes. Run thin knife around edge of pan to loosen cake, invert cake onto wire rack set in rimmed baking sheet, and remove pan.

4. FOR THE SOAK AND GLAZE Combine rum and orange juice in bowl and microwave until steaming and fragrant, about 30 seconds. Measure out 2 tablespoons rum mixture and whisk with apricot jam. Strain mixture through fine-mesh strainer into small bowl, discarding solids, and set apricot glaze aside. Using skewer, poke 15 to 20 holes over cake. Brush warm cake with remaining rum mixture and let cool completely, at least 3 hours. Brush apricot glaze over cake and let stand for 10 minutes. Serve. (Cooled cake and glaze can be wrapped tightly in plastic wrap, separately, and stored at room temperature for up to 1 week. Brush with apricot glaze just before serving.)

Spiced-Citrus Bundt Cake

Serves 12 | **Total Time** 1¼ hours, plus 3½ hours cooling and setting `MAKE AHEAD` `VEGETARIAN`

WHY THIS RECIPE WORKS With the height and tender crumb of a chiffon cake and the richness of a pound cake, Bundt cakes are real crowd-pleasers. We wanted a spiced Bundt cake bursting with citrus flavor that we could proudly feature on our holiday table. For a light and even crumb, we creamed the butter and sugar, which aerated the batter and lightened the cake's texture. Using three eggs gave the cake all the structure it needed to rise up high. As for the citrus, we added a hefty amount of orange juice as well as a tablespoon of zest to the cake batter to create bold, unmistakable flavor. To round out the flavor profile, we added potent allspice,

licoricey anise seeds, and spicy ginger. Finally, we created a glaze that incorporated even more orange juice and zest for a final hit of sunny citrus.

CAKE

3	cups (15 ounces) all-purpose flour
2	teaspoons ground allspice
1½	teaspoon ground anise seeds
1½	teaspoons ground ginger
1	teaspoon table salt
1	teaspoon baking powder
½	teaspoon baking soda
1	tablespoon grated orange zest plus ¾ cup juice (2 oranges)
1	tablespoon vanilla extract
1	cup (7 ounces) granulated sugar
16	tablespoons unsalted butter, softened
3	large eggs

GLAZE

¾	cup plus 2 tablespoons (3½ ounces) confectioners' sugar
1	ounce cream cheese, softened
1	teaspoon grated orange zest plus 2 tablespoons juice

1. FOR THE CAKE Adjust oven rack to lower-middle position and heat oven to 350 degrees. Coat 12-cup nonstick Bundt pan heavily with baking spray with flour. Whisk flour, allspice, anise, ginger, salt, baking powder, and baking soda together in large bowl. In separate bowl, combine orange zest and juice and vanilla.

2. Using stand mixer fitted with paddle, beat sugar and butter on medium-high speed until pale and fluffy, about 3 minutes. Add eggs, one at a time, and beat until combined. Reduce speed to low and add flour mixture in 3 additions, alternating with juice mixture in 2 additions, scraping down bowl as needed. Give batter final stir by hand.

3. Scrape batter into prepared pan. Bake until skewer inserted in middle of cake comes out clean, 45 to 55 minutes, rotating pan halfway through baking.

4. Let cake cool in pan for 30 minutes. Using paring knife, loosen cake from sides of pan and invert onto wire rack. Let cool completely, about 2 hours, before glazing. (Cake can be wrapped tightly in plastic wrap and stored at room temperature for up to 2 days.)

5. FOR THE GLAZE Whisk sugar, cream cheese, and orange zest and juice together in bowl until smooth. Pour glaze over top of cake, letting it drip down sides. Let glaze set, about 1 hour, before serving.

Spiced-Citrus Bundt Cake

Cranberry-Orange Olive Oil Cake

Serves 10 to 12 | **Total Time** 5 hours

`MAKE AHEAD` `VEGETARIAN`

WHY THIS RECIPE WORKS This elegant cake featuring layers of contrasting flavors—tart cranberry, fruity olive oil, and silky vanilla buttercream—brings the magic of a snowy evening to the dinner table. The jewel-like sugared cranberries and rosemary sprigs give it a wintry feel. To achieve a super-moist cake full of citrusy flavor, we added orange zest and Grand Marnier to the batter and brushed the cake with a Grand Marnier soaking syrup. For a fresh, bright filling we turned to a cranberry curd; cooking the curd to 175 degrees gave us a filling that was creamy but firm enough to remain in a distinct layer in the cake. Instead of frosting the sides of our cake, we merely scraped them with a thin veil of our frosting so the lovely, sophisticated layers peeked through. You will need cake pans with at least 2-inch-tall sides for this recipe. For the best results, use a good-quality extra-virgin olive oil. You needn't thaw the cranberries before using them.

CRANBERRY CURD

- 12 ounces (3 cups) frozen cranberries
- 1 cup (7 ounces) sugar
- 2 teaspoons grated orange zest plus ¼ cup juice
- ¼ teaspoon table salt
- 2 large eggs plus 2 large yolks
- 8 tablespoons unsalted butter, cut into ½-inch pieces and chilled

CAKE

- 2⅔ cups (13⅓ ounces) all-purpose flour
- 1½ teaspoons baking powder
- 1¼ teaspoons table salt
- 4 large eggs plus 1 large yolk
- 2 cups (14 ounces) plus 2 tablespoons granulated sugar, divided
- 1 tablespoon grated orange zest
- 1⅓ cups extra-virgin olive oil
- 1 cup plus 2 tablespoons milk
- ½ cup Grand Marnier or other orange liqueur, divided

GARNISH

- 1¾ cups (12¼ ounces) granulated sugar, divided
- 2 (3- to 4-inch-long) fresh rosemary sprigs
- 10 ounces (2½ cups) frozen cranberries

BUTTERCREAM

- 20 tablespoons (2½ sticks) unsalted butter, softened
- 2½ cups (10 ounces) confectioners' sugar
- ⅛ teaspoon table salt
- 2 tablespoons heavy cream
- 2 teaspoons vanilla extract

1. FOR THE CRANBERRY CURD Cook cranberries, sugar, orange zest and juice, and salt in medium saucepan over medium-low heat, mashing occasionally with potato masher, until cranberries have mostly broken down and mixture measures 1¼ cups, 10 to 12 minutes. Strain cranberry mixture through fine-mesh strainer into bowl, pressing on solids with rubber spatula to extract as much puree as possible. Discard solids.

2. Whisk eggs and yolks into cranberry mixture in bowl. Return mixture to saucepan and cook over medium-low heat, stirring constantly with rubber spatula, until mixture is thickened and registers 175 degrees in multiple spots, 5 to 7 minutes.

3. Off heat, stir in butter until incorporated. Transfer curd to bowl, press piece of plastic wrap directly onto surface of curd, and refrigerate for at least 3 hours. (Curd can be refrigerated for up to 3 days.)

4. FOR THE CAKE Adjust oven rack to middle position and heat oven to 350 degrees. Grease three 9-inch round cake pans, line with parchment paper, grease parchment, and flour pans. Whisk flour, baking powder, and salt together in bowl.

5. Using stand mixer fitted with whisk attachment, whip eggs and yolk on medium speed until foamy, about 1 minute. Add 2 cups sugar and orange zest, increase speed to high, and whip until mixture is fluffy and pale yellow, about 3 minutes.

6. Reduce speed to medium and, with mixer running, slowly pour in oil. Mix until oil is fully incorporated, about 1 minute. Reduce speed to low, add half of flour mixture, and mix until incorporated, about 1 minute, scraping down bowl as needed. Add milk and ¼ cup Grand Marnier and mix until combined, about 30 seconds. Add remaining flour mixture and mix until just incorporated, about 1 minute.

7. Divide batter evenly among prepared pans and smooth tops with rubber spatula. Bake until cake is deep golden brown and toothpick inserted in center comes out with few crumbs attached, 40 to 45 minutes. Transfer pans to wire rack and let cool for 15 minutes. Loosen cakes from pans with paring knife, then invert onto greased wire rack and discard parchment. Invert cakes again and let cool completely on rack, about 1½ hours.

8. Bring ¼ cup water, remaining 2 tablespoons sugar, and remaining ¼ cup Grand Marnier to boil in small saucepan over medium heat; cook until sugar dissolves, about 3 minutes. Let cool completely, about 30 minutes. Once cooled, brush top and sides of cake layers with syrup.

9. FOR THE GARNISH Place ¾ cup sugar in shallow dish; set aside. Bring 1 cup water and remaining 1 cup granulated sugar to boil in medium saucepan over high heat; cook, stirring constantly, until sugar dissolves, about 3 minutes. Off heat, dip rosemary sprigs in sugar syrup, then roll in sugar in dish. Transfer to plate.

10. Stir cranberries into syrup and let syrup cool completely, about 30 minutes. (Cranberries in syrup can be refrigerated for up to 24 hours.) Drain cranberries in fine-mesh strainer; discard syrup. Working in 3 batches, roll cranberries in sugar in dish and transfer to large plate. Let stand at room temperature to dry, about 1 hour.

11. FOR THE BUTTERCREAM Using stand mixer fitted with whisk attachment, whip butter on medium-high speed until smooth, about 20 seconds. Add sugar and salt and mix on medium-low speed until most of sugar is moistened, about 45 seconds. Scrape down bowl. Add cream and vanilla and whip on medium-high speed until light and fluffy, about 4 minutes, scraping down bowl as needed.

Cranberry-Orange Olive Oil Cake

12. Fill pastry bag fitted with a ½-inch-wide straight tip with 1 cup buttercream. Place 1 cake layer on cake turntable. Using half of buttercream, pipe ½-inch-high ring of buttercream around top perimeter of cake layer. Spread half of cranberry curd (about 1 scant cup) evenly inside buttercream ring.

13. Place second cake layer on top, pressing lightly to adhere. Pipe another ½-inch-high ring of buttercream around top perimeter of cake layer with remaining buttercream in pastry bag. Spread remaining cranberry curd evenly inside buttercream ring. Top with remaining cake layer, pressing lightly to adhere. Refrigerate to allow buttercream to firm up, about 30 minutes.

14. Spread ¾ cup buttercream evenly over top of cake. Spread remaining buttercream evenly over sides of cake to cover with thin coat of buttercream. Run edge of offset spatula around cake sides to create sheer veil of buttercream so cake beneath is visible. Sprinkle ½ cup cranberries around bottom of cake. Pile remaining cranberries on top of 1 side of cake in half-moon shape. Place rosemary sprigs at base of cranberries. Serve.

Caramel-Espresso Yule Log

Serves 10 to 12 `MAKE AHEAD` `VEGETARIAN`

Total Time 2 hours, plus 2½ hours cooling and chilling

WHY THIS RECIPE WORKS A Yule log is one of the oldest finales to a Christmas feast: a moist, tender cake rolled around a creamy filling, coated in frosting, and often dusted with confectioners' sugar to resemble a snow-covered log. Choosing the right cake for the job is the first step, as it needs to be sturdy but flexible enough to roll without splitting. We used airy chiffon cake because its whipped eggs whites would make for a resilient crumb. To "train" the warm cake into a rolled shape, we rolled it into a clean, damp kitchen towel (coating the towel with sugar, as many recipes call for, dried out the cake's surface). For the filling, we opted for the bold flavors of caramel and espresso. Adding cream to the caramel allowed us to whip the mixture just like regular whipped cream. Finally, a simple bittersweet ganache made the perfect "bark." The filling must chill for at least 1½ hours before whipping, so make it before organizing the ingredients for the cake and ganache. A smooth dish towel works best for rolling the cake. Some of the cake may cling to the towel, but it washes out easily. We prefer to leave the cut surfaces of the log exposed, but there is enough ganache to cover them, if desired.

FILLING

- 2 cups heavy cream, divided
- 1 tablespoon instant espresso powder
- ¾ cup (5¼ ounces) granulated sugar
- ¼ cup water
- 1 tablespoon light corn syrup
- 4 ounces cream cheese, cut into 8 pieces and softened

CAKE

- 1⅓ cups (5⅓ ounces) cake flour
- ¾ cup (5¼ ounces) granulated sugar
- 1½ teaspoons baking powder
- ¼ teaspoon table salt
- 5 large eggs, separated
- ½ cup vegetable oil
- ¼ cup water
- 2 teaspoons vanilla extract
- ¼ teaspoon cream of tartar

GANACHE

- ¾ cup heavy cream
- 6 ounces bittersweet chocolate, chopped fine
- 2 teaspoons light corn syrup
  Confectioners' sugar (optional)

Caramel-Espresso Yule Log

1. FOR THE FILLING Pour 1 cup cream into wide bowl. Whisk together espresso powder and remaining 1 cup cream in small saucepan and bring to simmer over medium heat. Remove from heat and cover to keep hot. Bring sugar, water, and corn syrup to boil in large heavy-bottomed saucepan over medium-high heat. Cook, without stirring, until mixture is straw-colored, 6 to 8 minutes. Reduce heat to medium-low and continue to cook, swirling saucepan occasionally, until mixture is deep coppery brown and just starting to smoke, 4 to 7 minutes. Off heat, carefully whisk in hot cream mixture a little at a time (caramel will bubble and steam). Add cream cheese. Cover and let stand for 5 minutes. Whisk until mostly smooth (some small flecks of cream cheese are OK). Transfer mixture to bowl with cream and stir to combine. Cover and refrigerate until mixture registers 50 degrees or below, at least 1½ hours or up to 4 days.

2. FOR THE CAKE Adjust oven rack to middle position and heat oven to 350 degrees. Lightly grease 18 by 13-inch rimmed baking sheet, line with parchment paper, and lightly grease parchment. Whisk flour, sugar, baking powder, and salt together in large, wide bowl. Whisk egg yolks, oil, water, and vanilla into flour mixture until smooth batter forms.

3. Using stand mixer fitted with whisk attachment, whip egg whites and cream of tartar on medium-low speed until foamy, about 1 minute. Increase speed to medium-high and whip until stiff peaks form, 1½ to 2 minutes. Transfer one-third of whipped egg whites to batter and whisk gently until mixture is lightened. Using rubber spatula, gently fold remaining egg whites into batter. Pour batter into prepared sheet and spread evenly. Firmly tap sheet on counter 3 times to remove large air bubbles. Bake until cake springs back when pressed lightly in center, 12 to 14 minutes. While cake bakes, soak clean kitchen towel with water and wring out thoroughly.

4. Transfer sheet to wire rack. Immediately run knife around edge of sheet, then carefully invert cake onto second wire rack. Carefully remove parchment. Lay damp towel over cake and invert first wire rack over towel. Invert cake and remove rack. Starting from short side, gently roll cake and towel together into jelly roll shape. Let cake cool on rack, seam side down, for 1 hour.

5. **FOR THE GANACHE** Bring cream to simmer in small saucepan over medium heat. Place chocolate and corn syrup in bowl, pour cream over top, and let stand for 1 minute. Whisk mixture until smooth. Let cool until mixture has consistency of pudding, about 1 hour.

6. Transfer chilled filling to bowl of stand mixer fitted with whisk attachment. Whip on high speed until mixture is thick and fluffy and resembles buttercream frosting, 1½ to 2 minutes. Gently unroll cake with short side parallel to counter edge (innermost edge of cake will remain slightly curled; do not flatten). Spread filling evenly over cake, leaving ½-inch margin on each short side. Reroll cake, leaving towel behind as you roll. Wrap in plastic wrap and refrigerate for at least 20 minutes or up to 2 days.

7. Arrange two 12 by 4-inch strips of parchment 1 inch apart on serving platter. Unwrap cake and place on cutting board. Using sharp chef's knife, trim ½-inch slice from each end of log, wiping knife clean between cuts; discard trimmings. To make branch stump, cut 1 end of cake at 45-degree angle, starting 1½ inches from end of log (shorter side of stump will be 1½ inches long). Transfer larger cake piece to platter, centering it lengthwise on parchment. To attach stump, rest straight side of smaller piece against side of log. Fill in top of space between pieces with about 1 tablespoon ganache. Using offset spatula, gently spread remaining ganache over log, leaving cut ends exposed. Use tines of fork to make wood-grain pattern on surface of ganache. Carefully slide parchment from beneath cake (hold stump in place with your fingertip while sliding out parchment). Refrigerate cake, uncovered, to slightly set ganache, about 20 minutes. (Cake can be covered loosely and refrigerated for up to 24 hours; let stand at room temperature for 30 minutes before serving.) Dust lightly with confectioners' sugar, if using. To slice, dip sharp knife in very hot water and wipe dry between cuts. Serve.

ASSEMBLING A YULE LOG

1. Starting from short side, gently roll warm cake and damp kitchen towel together into jelly roll shape. Let cake cool seam side down for 1 hour.

2. Unroll cake. Spread filling evenly over cake, leaving ½-inch margin on each short side. Reroll cake without towel.

3. Trim ½-inch slice from each end of log. To make branch stump, cut 1 end of cake at 45-degree angle, starting 1½ inches from end. Transfer cake to platter and rest stump against log.

Maple Cheesecake

Serves 12 to 16 `MAKE AHEAD` `VEGETARIAN`
Total Time 4¾ hours, plus 8 hours cooling

WHY THIS RECIPE WORKS Wanting an autumnal twist on cheesecake, we wondered if it would be possible to replace the sugar with maple syrup without sacrificing the dessert's velvety-smooth texture. Real maple syrup (not corn syrup-based pancake syrup) was a must here for its inimitable flavor. For maximum impact, we landed on using a full 1¼ cups of syrup for 2 pounds of cream cheese. We simply combined the two ingredients in a food processor, adding eggs to the mixture to give it more stability once baked. Baking the cheesecake in a superlow 225-degree oven slowly set the cheesecake to a barely firm, custardy consistency with a crack-free surface without the need for a sloshy water bath. A border of crunchy granola plus an extra drizzle of maple syrup made this cheesecake look as stunning as it tastes. Do not substitute pancake syrup for the maple syrup. Reduce the oven temperature as soon as the crust is finished baking, and use an oven thermometer to check that it has dropped to 225 degrees before you bake the cheesecake. Thoroughly scrape the processor bowl as you make the filling to eliminate lumps.

CRUST

- 4 whole graham crackers, broken into pieces
- ¼ cup pecans
- ½ cup (2½ ounces) all-purpose flour
- ⅓ cup (2⅓ ounces) sugar
- ¼ teaspoon table salt
- 4 tablespoons unsalted butter, melted

CHEESECAKE

- 2 pounds cream cheese, softened
- 1¼ cups maple syrup
- 4 large eggs

TOPPING

- ⅓ cup granola
- ½ cup maple syrup

Maple Cheesecake

1. FOR THE CRUST Adjust oven rack to middle position and heat oven to 325 degrees. Grease bottom and side of 9-inch springform pan. Process cracker pieces and pecans in food processor until finely ground, about 30 seconds. Add flour, sugar, and salt and pulse to combine, about 2 pulses. Add melted butter and pulse until crumbs are evenly moistened, about 5 pulses.

2. Using your hands, press crumbs into even layer on prepared pan bottom. Using bottom of dry measuring cup, firmly pack crumbs into pan. Bake until crust smells toasty and is browned around edges, about 18 minutes. Reduce oven temperature to 225 degrees. Let crust cool completely.

3. FOR THE CHEESECAKE In clean, dry processor bowl, process cream cheese and maple syrup until smooth, about 2 minutes, scraping down sides of bowl as needed. With processor running, add eggs, one at a time, until just incorporated, about 30 seconds total. Pour batter onto cooled crust.

4. Firmly tap pan on counter and set aside for 10 minutes to allow air bubbles to rise to top. Gently draw tines of fork across surface of batter to pop air bubbles that have risen to surface.

5. Once oven has reached 225 degrees, bake cheesecake on aluminum foil–lined rimmed baking sheet until edges are set and center jiggles slightly when shaken and registers 165 degrees ½ inch below surface, about 3 hours.

6. Transfer pan to wire rack and let cool completely, about 2 hours. Refrigerate cheesecake, uncovered, until cold, about 6 hours. (Once fully chilled, cheesecake can be covered with plastic wrap and refrigerated for up to 4 days.)

7. To unmold cheesecake, run tip of paring knife between cake and side of pan; remove side of pan. Slide thin metal spatula between crust and pan bottom to loosen, then slide cheesecake onto serving platter. Let cheesecake stand at room temperature for 30 minutes.

8. FOR THE TOPPING Sprinkle granola around top edge of cheesecake. Drizzle maple syrup inside ring of granola. Spread with back of spoon, as needed, to fill area inside granola ring.

9. Warm knife under hot water, then wipe dry. Cut cheesecake into wedges and serve.

CHAPTER 14

pies, puddings, & fruit desserts

■ MAKE AHEAD ▥ VEGETARIAN

Photo: Cranberry Curd Tart with Almond Crust

Pecan Pie

Holiday Eggnog Custard Pie

Pecan Pie

Serves 8 `MAKE AHEAD` `VEGETARIAN`
Total Time 2 hours, plus 4 hours cooling

WHY THIS RECIPE WORKS Pecan pie is a holiday classic for good reason—rich, buttery pecans mingle with a custardy, deeply flavored sugar filling in a crisp crust for an irresistible treat. We used a simulated double-boiler setup to maintain gentle heat while cooking our filling, preventing the eggy custard from curdling. We found it important to add the hot filling to the warm parbaked pie crust to keep the crust from getting soggy. Finally, we avoided overbaking the pie by removing it from the oven when the center was still jiggly. As≈the pie cooled, the residual heat of the filling cooked the center through, so each slice of pie was silky and tender. We recommend chopping the toasted pecans by hand.

- 1 recipe Foolproof All-Butter Single-Crust Pie Dough (page 388)
- 6 tablespoons unsalted butter, cut into 1-inch pieces
- 1 cup packed (7 ounces) dark brown sugar
- ½ teaspoon table salt
- 3 large eggs
- ¾ cup light corn syrup
- 1 tablespoon vanilla extract
- 2 cups pecans, toasted and chopped fine

1. Roll dough into 12-inch circle on well-floured counter. Roll dough loosely around rolling pin and gently unroll it onto 9-inch pie plate, letting excess dough hang over edge. Ease dough into plate by gently lifting edge of dough with your hand while pressing into plate bottom with your other hand. Trim overhang to ½ inch beyond lip of plate. Tuck overhang under itself; folded edge should be flush with edge of plate. Crimp dough evenly around edge of plate. Wrap dough-lined plate loosely in plastic wrap and refrigerate until firm, about 30 minutes. Adjust oven rack to lowest position and heat oven to 425 degrees.

2. Line chilled pie shell with double layer of aluminum foil, covering edges to prevent burning, and fill with pie weights. Bake on foil-lined rimmed baking sheet until pie dough looks dry and is pale in color, about 15 minutes. Remove foil and weights, rotate sheet, and continue to bake until crust is light golden brown, 4 to 7 minutes. Transfer sheet to wire rack. (Crust must still be warm when filling is added.)

3. While crust is baking, melt butter in heatproof bowl set over saucepan filled with 1 inch of barely simmering water, making sure that water does not touch bottom of bowl. Off heat, stir in sugar and salt until butter is absorbed.

4. Whisk in eggs, then corn syrup and vanilla, until smooth. Return bowl to saucepan and stir until mixture is shiny, hot to touch, and registers 130 degrees. Off heat, stir in pecans.

5. As soon as pie crust comes out of oven, adjust oven rack to lower-middle position and reduce oven temperature to 275 degrees. With pie still on sheet, pour pecan mixture into warm crust.

6. Bake until filling looks set but yields like gelatin when gently pressed with back of spoon, 50 minutes to 1 hour, rotating sheet halfway through baking. Let pie cool completely on wire rack, about 4 hours. Serve.

To make ahead At end of step 5, cooled unbaked pie can be frozen until firm, then wrapped in double layer of plastic wrap followed by aluminum foil and frozen for up to 1 month. To bake, continue with step 6, increasing baking time at 275 degrees to 1½ hours. Baked pie can be held at room temperature for up to 8 hours or refrigerated for up to 2 days, although crust will be less crisp. If refrigerated, let come to room temperature before serving.

Holiday Eggnog Custard Pie

Serves 8 `MAKE AHEAD` `VEGETARIAN`
Total Time 1¾ hours, plus 4 hours cooling

WHY THIS RECIPE WORKS For a delicious eggnog, three elements need to be in balance: sweetness, richness, and the amount of alcohol. Here, we strike that balance in a custard pie inspired by the classic holiday drink. Adding cinnamon and nutmeg to a custard base gave it a subtle hint of spice, but in our opinion it wasn't truly eggnog without a little booze—just 2 tablespoons of dark rum did the trick. If you prefer your pie with a boozier punch, increase the rum to ¼ cup; if you prefer a nonalcoholic eggnog, you can omit the rum altogether and use regular Whipped Cream (page 368).

 1 recipe Foolproof All-Butter Single-Crust Pie Dough
   (page 388)
⅔ cup (4⅔ ounces) sugar
 3 large eggs
 3 tablespoons cornstarch
¼ teaspoon ground cinnamon, divided
⅛ teaspoon ground nutmeg
⅛ teaspoon table salt
 2 cups whole milk
 1 cup heavy cream

 2 tablespoons dark rum
 1 recipe Brown Sugar and Bourbon Whipped Cream
   (page 368)

1. Roll dough into 12-inch circle on well-floured counter. Roll dough loosely around rolling pin and gently unroll it onto 9-inch pie plate, letting excess dough hang over edge. Ease dough into plate by gently lifting edge of dough with your hand while pressing into plate bottom with your other hand.

2. Trim overhang to ½ inch beyond lip of plate. Tuck overhang under itself; folded edge should be flush with edge of plate. Crimp dough evenly around edge of plate. Wrap dough-lined plate loosely in plastic wrap and refrigerate until firm, about 30 minutes. Adjust oven rack to middle position and heat oven to 350 degrees. Line chilled pie shell with double layer of aluminum foil, covering edges to prevent burning, and fill with pie weights. Bake on foil-lined rimmed baking sheet until edges are set and just beginning to turn golden, 25 to 30 minutes, rotating sheet halfway through baking. Remove foil and weights, rotate sheet, and continue to bake crust until golden brown and crisp, 10 to 15 minutes longer. Transfer sheet to wire rack. (Crust must still be warm when filling is added.)

3. While crust bakes, whisk sugar, eggs, cornstarch, ⅛ teaspoon cinnamon, nutmeg, and salt together in bowl. Bring milk and cream to simmer in large saucepan over medium heat. Slowly whisk 1 cup of hot milk mixture into egg mixture to temper, then slowly whisk tempered egg mixture into remaining milk in saucepan. Cook over medium heat, whisking constantly, until mixture is thickened, bubbling, and registers 180 degrees, 30 to 90 seconds (custard should have consistency of thick pudding). Strain mixture through fine-mesh strainer into clean bowl, then stir in rum.

4. With pie still on sheet, pour custard into warm crust, smoothing top with clean spatula into even layer. Bake until center of pie registers 160 degrees, 14 to 18 minutes. Let pie cool completely on wire rack, about 4 hours. Spread whipped cream attractively over pie and dust with remaining ⅛ teaspoon cinnamon. Serve. (Pie can be wrapped tightly in plastic wrap and refrigerated for up to 2 days.)

NOTES FROM THE TEST KITCHEN

MORE SEASONAL PIE RECIPES
Classic Apple Tarte Tatin, page 204
Deep Dish Apple Pie, page 205
Salted Caramel Apple Pie, page 207
Pumpkin Pie, page 221
Rum Pumpkin Chiffon Pie, page 222

Orange-Chocolate Custard Pie

Serves 8 MAKE AHEAD VEGETARIAN
Total Time 1¾ hours, plus 4 hours cooling

WHY THIS RECIPE WORKS As the enduring popularity of chocolate oranges—foil-wrapped orange-shaped chocolates that pop up every year around the holidays—proves, chocolate and orange is a beloved flavor pairing that's hard to beat. We wanted to showcase the delectable way that sweet orange cuts through the richness of chocolate in an impressive custard pie. Instead of merely adding orange essence to chocolate cream filling, we decided to make a two-layer custard that would fill our pie shell with a stripe of chocolate and one of orange. The best way to do this was to cook one orange-scented custard, divide it in half, and add melted bittersweet chocolate to one half. We layered the more buoyant orange custard over the chocolate custard and baked the pie until just set. Topping the pie with orange whipped cream and chocolate shavings highlighted the flavors of the custards. Use a vegetable peeler to scrape chocolate shavings from a block of chocolate.

1 recipe Foolproof All-Butter Single-Crust Pie Dough (page 388)
⅔ cup (4⅔ ounces) sugar
3 large eggs
3 tablespoons cornstarch
1 tablespoon grated orange zest plus 1½ tablespoons juice
⅛ teaspoon table salt
2 cups whole milk
1 cup heavy cream
1 teaspoon vanilla extract
6 ounces bittersweet chocolate, chopped fine
1 recipe Orange Whipped Cream
Chocolate shavings

1. Roll dough into 12-inch circle on well-floured counter. Roll dough loosely around rolling pin and gently unroll it onto 9-inch pie plate, letting excess dough hang over edge. Ease dough into plate by gently lifting edge of dough with your hand while pressing into plate bottom with your other hand. Trim overhang to ½ inch beyond lip of plate.

2. Tuck overhang under itself; folded edge should be flush with edge of plate. Crimp dough evenly around edge of plate. Wrap dough-lined plate loosely in plastic wrap and refrigerate until firm, about 30 minutes. Adjust oven rack to middle position and heat oven to 350 degrees.

3. Line chilled pie shell with double layer of aluminum foil, covering edges to prevent burning, and fill with pie weights. Bake on foil-lined rimmed baking sheet until edges are set and just beginning to turn golden, 25 to 30 minutes, rotating sheet halfway through baking. Remove foil and weights, rotate sheet, and continue to bake crust until golden brown and crisp, 10 to 15 minutes. Transfer sheet to wire rack. (Crust must still be warm when filling is added.)

4. While crust bakes, whisk sugar, eggs, cornstarch, orange zest and juice, and salt together in bowl. Bring milk and cream to simmer in large saucepan over medium heat. Slowly whisk 1 cup of hot milk mixture into egg mixture to temper, then slowly whisk tempered egg mixture into remaining milk in saucepan. Cook over medium heat, whisking constantly, until mixture is thickened, bubbling, and registers 180 degrees, 30 to 90 seconds (mixture should have consistency of thick pudding). Strain mixture through fine-mesh strainer into clean bowl, then stir in vanilla. Transfer 1½ cups custard to second bowl; whisk in chocolate until smooth.

5. With pie still on sheet, pour chocolate mixture into warm crust, smoothing top with clean spatula into even layer. Gently pour remaining custard over chocolate layer, smoothing top with clean spatula into even layer. Bake until center of pie registers 160 degrees, 14 to 18 minutes. Let pie cool completely on wire rack, about 4 hours. Spread whipped cream attractively over pie and sprinkle with chocolate shavings. Serve. (Pie can be wrapped tightly in plastic wrap and refrigerated for up to 2 days.)

Maple Syrup Pie

Serves 8 `MAKE AHEAD` `VEGETARIAN`
Total Time 2¼ hours, plus 4 hours cooling

WHY THIS RECIPE WORKS Maple syrup pie was once common in the syrup-producing northern regions of the United States and in Canada. The best versions are sweetened with nothing but real maple syrup. For a pie that truly tasted of maple we found that a hefty dose of syrup was in order—a full 1¾ cups of dark amber syrup, in fact. But with maple flavor comes maple sweetness, and we wanted pie, not candy. Our solution was to add just a touch of cider vinegar. The vinegar's acidity balanced the syrup's sweetness and introduced a subtle tang. Some cornstarch, in addition to the custard's eggs, thickened the filling and helped the pie slice neatly. Make sure to use pure maple syrup in this recipe. We like to serve this rich pie with crème fraîche for sophistication and tang, or with unsweetened whipped cream.

  1 recipe Foolproof All-Butter Single-Crust Pie Dough (page 388)
1¾ cups maple syrup
  ⅔ cup heavy cream
  ¼ teaspoon table salt
  5 tablespoons unsalted butter, cut into 5 pieces
  2 tablespoons cornstarch
  3 large eggs plus 2 large yolks
  2 teaspoons cider vinegar

1. Roll dough into 12-inch circle on well-floured counter. Roll dough loosely around rolling pin and gently unroll it onto 9-inch pie plate, letting excess dough hang over edge. Ease dough into plate by gently lifting edge of dough with your hand while pressing into plate bottom with your other hand. Trim overhang to ½ inch beyond lip of plate.

Orange-Chocolate Custard Pie

Maple Syrup Pie

2. Tuck overhang under itself; folded edge should be flush with edge of plate. Crimp dough evenly around edge of plate. Wrap dough-lined plate loosely in plastic wrap and refrigerate until firm, about 30 minutes. Adjust oven rack to middle position and heat oven to 350 degrees.

3. Line chilled pie shell with double layer of aluminum foil, covering edges to prevent burning, and fill with pie weights. Bake on foil-lined rimmed baking sheet until edges are set and just beginning to turn golden, 25 to 30 minutes, rotating sheet halfway through baking. Remove foil and weights, rotate sheet, and continue to bake until center begins to look opaque and slightly drier, 3 to 6 minutes. Transfer sheet to wire rack and let cool completely, about 30 minutes.

4. Bring maple syrup, cream, and salt to boil in medium saucepan. Add butter and whisk until melted. Reduce heat to medium-low and whisk in cornstarch. Bring to simmer and cook for 1 minute, whisking frequently. Transfer to large bowl and let cool for at least 30 minutes. Whisk in eggs and yolks and vinegar until smooth. (Cooled filling can be refrigerated for up to 24 hours. Whisk to recombine and proceed with step 5, increasing baking time to 55 minutes to 1 hour 5 minutes.)

5. With pie still on sheet, pour filling into cooled crust. Bake until just set, 35 to 45 minutes. Let pie cool completely on wire rack, about 2 hours. Refrigerate pie until fully set, at least 2 hours or up to 24 hours. Serve cold or at room temperature.

Ginger-Cranberry-Pear Streusel Pie

Ginger-Cranberry-Pear Streusel Pie

Serves 8 VEGETARIAN
Total Time 1¾ hours, plus 4 hours cooling

WHY THIS RECIPE WORKS Ripe pears are filled with floral, honey-flavored juices. Those same juices stream from a pie when you try to make one with pears—much more so than with apples. We wanted a pear pie, perked up with complementary flavors, that wasn't a watery mess. To start, we microwaved the pears with sugar to release excess liquid, which we drained away. A loose streusel topping allowed for evaporation of pear juices during baking. Baking the pie on the bottom rack, closer to the heat source, also encouraged evaporation. By adding a little sugar, we were able to distribute 2 cups of cranberries throughout our pie without giving rise to mouth-puckering tartness. And for an alluring final component, we added 1 teaspoon of grated fresh ginger. Some ground ginger and chewy bits of crystallized ginger in the topping tied the components of our seasonal pie together.

1 recipe Foolproof All-Butter Single-Crust Pie Dough (page 388)
3 pounds ripe but firm Bartlett or Bosc pears, peeled, halved, cored, and sliced ¼ inch thick
½ cup (3½ ounces) granulated sugar, divided
¾ cup (3¾ ounces) all-purpose flour
¼ cup packed (1¾ ounces) light brown sugar
2 tablespoons crystallized ginger, chopped
¾ teaspoon ground ginger
⅛ teaspoon table salt
5 tablespoons unsalted butter, melted
8 ounces (2 cups) fresh or thawed frozen cranberries
1 teaspoon grated fresh ginger

1. Roll dough into 12-inch circle on well-floured counter. Roll dough loosely around rolling pin and gently unroll it onto 9-inch pie plate, letting excess dough hang over edge. Ease dough into plate by gently lifting edge of dough with your hand while pressing into plate bottom with your other hand. Trim overhang to ½ inch beyond lip of plate.

2. Tuck overhang under itself; folded edge should be flush with edge of plate. Crimp dough evenly around edge of plate. Wrap dough-lined plate loosely in plastic wrap and refrigerate until firm, about 30 minutes. Adjust oven rack to lowest position and heat oven to 400 degrees.

3. Toss pears with 2 tablespoons granulated sugar in large bowl. Microwave, covered, until pears turn translucent and release their juices, 4 to 8 minutes, stirring once halfway through microwaving. Uncover and let cool completely, about 30 minutes.

4. Combine flour, brown sugar, crystallized ginger, ground ginger, salt, and 2 tablespoons granulated sugar in bowl. Stir in melted butter until mixture is completely moistened; let stand for 10 minutes.

5. Combine cranberries, fresh ginger, and remaining ¼ cup granulated sugar in food processor and pulse until cranberries are coarsely chopped, about 5 pulses. Drain pears and discard liquid. Return pears to now-empty bowl and add cranberry mixture, stirring to combine. Spread mixture into dough-lined plate. Sprinkle topping over pear mixture, breaking apart any large clumps. Place pie on aluminum foil–lined rimmed baking sheet and bake until juices are bubbling and topping is deep golden brown, 45 to 55 minutes, rotating sheet halfway through baking. Let pie cool on wire rack until filling has set, about 4 hours. Serve.

Mulled Wine Quince Pie

Mulled Wine Quince Pie

Serves 8 VEGETARIAN
Total Time 4½ hours, plus 4 hours cooling

WHY THIS RECIPE WORKS A fall and winter orchard fruit, quince has a flavor somewhere between that of a pear and an apple, but it's quite tart when raw—sometimes downright astringent—with hard, dry flesh. But when cooked, quince softens into something unique and far more appealing, with a lush fragrance. We wanted to showcase quince's flavor in a sophisticated pie with seasonal appeal. First, we poached the quinces in spiced red wine, which softened the fruit and infused it with the heady warmth of mulled wine. We mashed half of the poached quinces and sliced the other half; quinces are a pectin powerhouse, so this technique was enough to create a pie that set up without an additional thickener. Some dried cherries underscored the fruity tartness. In lieu of a woven lattice top crust, we created a dramatic but deceptively simple arrangement of long triangles arranged in an overlapping free-form pattern. You can cut and arrange whatever shapes you like but it's important to anchor at least one side of each shape to the dough and not to overlap more than two shapes, or the top crust will bake up doughy. It's important to be fastidious when coring quinces, as the core remains tough even after cooking. Use a good-quality medium-bodied wine, such as a Côtes du Rhône or Pinot Noir. If you don't have cheesecloth, substitute a triple layer of disposable coffee filters.

- 4 (2-inch) strips orange zest
- 3 bay leaves
- 1 cinnamon stick
- 1 teaspoon allspice berries
- ¼ teaspoon black peppercorns
- 1 (750-ml) bottle red wine
- 2 cups water
- 1¼ cups (8¾ ounces) sugar, divided
- 3 pounds quinces, peeled, halved, and cored
- 1 recipe Foolproof All-Butter Double-Crust Pie Dough (page 389)
- ½ cup dried cherries
- ¼ teaspoon table salt
- 1 large egg, lightly beaten with 1 tablespoon water

1. Place orange zest, bay leaves, cinnamon stick, allspice, and peppercorns in triple layer of cheesecloth and tie closed with kitchen twine. Bring wine, water, ¾ cup sugar, and spice bundle to simmer in Dutch oven over medium-high heat, whisking to dissolve sugar. Add quinces and return to simmer. Reduce heat to medium-low and cook, covered, stirring occasionally, until quince is easily pierced with fork, about 2 hours.

2. While quinces cook, roll 1 disk of dough into 12-inch circle on well-floured counter. Roll dough loosely around rolling pin and gently unroll it onto 9-inch pie plate, letting excess dough hang over edge. Ease dough into plate by gently lifting edge of dough with your hand while pressing into plate bottom with your other hand. Leave any dough that overhangs plate in place. Wrap dough-lined plate loosely in plastic wrap and refrigerate until firm, about 30 minutes.

3. Roll other disk of dough into 13 by 10½-inch rectangle on floured counter, then transfer to parchment paper–lined rimmed baking sheet; cover loosely with plastic and refrigerate until firm, about 30 minutes.

4. Using pizza wheel or paring knife, cut dough into long triangles or other free-form shapes as desired. To match photo pattern, cut two 10½-inch-long by ½-inch wide triangles, three 10½-inch-long by 1-inch wide triangles, and three 10½-inch-long by 3-inch wide triangles. Cover loosely with plastic and refrigerate until firm, about 30 minutes. Adjust oven rack to middle position and heat oven to 400 degrees.

5. Off heat, discard spice bundle from pot. Using slotted spoon, transfer 4 quince halves to large bowl and mash into coarse paste with potato masher. Transfer remaining quince halves to cutting board; let stand until cool enough to handle, about 10 minutes (reserve cooking liquid). Cut quinces in half lengthwise, then slice ¼ inch thick crosswise. Add sliced quinces, ½ cup reserved cooking liquid, remaining ½ cup sugar, cherries, and salt to mashed quince mixture, stirring to combine. Spread quince filling into dough-lined plate.

6. Remove dough pieces from refrigerator; if too stiff to be workable, let stand at room temperature until softened slightly but still very cold. Arrange dough triangles decoratively over filling, with 1 end of each triangle placed at least ½ inch beyond edge of plate, and overlapping each triangle no more than once. (If dough becomes too soft to work with, refrigerate pie and dough triangles until firm.)

7. Trim overhang to ½ inch beyond lip of plate. Pinch edges of bottom crust and triangles together firmly to seal. Tuck overhang under itself; folded edge should be flush with edge of plate. Crimp dough evenly around edge of plate. (If dough is very soft, refrigerate for 10 minutes before baking.) Brush surface with egg wash.

8. Place pie on aluminum foil–lined rimmed baking sheet and bake until crust is light golden, 20 to 25 minutes. Reduce oven temperature to 350 degrees, rotate sheet, and continue to bake until juices are bubbling and crust is deep golden brown, 30 to 50 minutes. Let pie cool on wire rack until filling has set, about 4 hours.

9. Once pie is cooled, bring Dutch oven with remaining poaching liquid to boil over medium-high heat. Reduce until sauce has consistency of maple syrup and measures about ¾ cup, 15 to 20 minutes. Let cool slightly, about 20 minutes. Serve pie, passing sauce separately.

MAKING A FREE-FORM TOP CRUST DESIGN

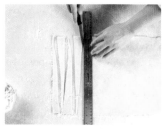   

1. Cut 13 by 10½-inch dough rectangle into two 10½-inch-long by ½-inch-wide triangles, three 10½-inch-long by 1-inch-wide triangles, and three 10½-inch-long by 3-inch-wide triangles. Chill for 30 minutes.

2. Arrange chilled dough triangles decoratively over top of filling, with 1 end of each triangle placed at least ½ inch beyond edge of plate and overlapping each triangle no more than once.

3. Trim overhang to ½ inch beyond lip of plate, then pinch edges of bottom crust and triangles together firmly to seal.

4. Tuck overhang under itself; folded edge should be flush with edge of plate. Crimp dough evenly around edge of plate.

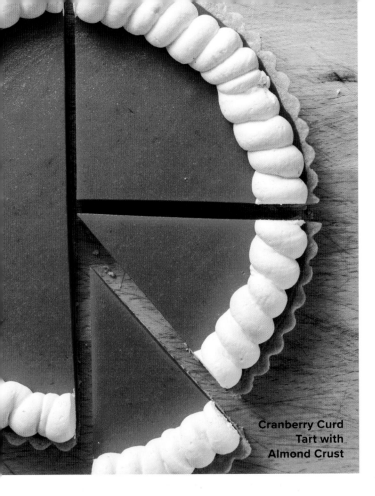

Cranberry Curd Tart with Almond Crust

Cranberry Curd Tart with Almond Crust

Serves 8 `MAKE AHEAD` `VEGETARIAN`
Total Time 1½ hours, plus 4 hours resting

WHY THIS RECIPE WORKS Our dazzling cranberry curd tart showcases cranberries' bold flavor and brilliant color while making use of their ample pectin content for thickening. We softened the berries and released their thickening pectin with a quick simmer and then immediately pureed them with egg yolks and cornstarch, using the berries' heat to cook the eggs and thicken the cornstarch. While the filling cooled, we mixed together and baked an almond flour tart crust. We then pureed butter into the cooled cranberry filling (which prevented it from developing a thick, rubbery skin), strained it, and poured the mixture over the crust. Finally, we whisked up a whipped cream topping stabilized by a small amount of the pectin-rich puree. This topping can be piped onto the tart hours in advance without breaking or weeping. You'll need a 9-inch tart pan with a removable bottom for this recipe.

We strongly recommend weighing the almond flour and cornstarch for the crust. If you prefer, you can use a stand mixer or handheld mixer to whip the cream in step 4.

FILLING
1 pound (4 cups) fresh or frozen cranberries
1¼ cups (8¾ ounces) plus 1 tablespoon sugar, divided
½ cup water
Pinch table salt
3 large egg yolks
2 teaspoons cornstarch
4 tablespoons unsalted butter, cut into 4 pieces and softened

CRUST
1 cup (4 ounces) almond flour
½ cup (2 ounces) cornstarch
⅓ cup (2⅓ ounces) sugar
½ teaspoon table salt
6 tablespoons unsalted butter, melted and cooled
¾ teaspoon almond extract

1 cup heavy cream

1. FOR THE FILLING Bring cranberries, 1¼ cups sugar, water, and salt to boil in medium saucepan over medium-high heat, stirring occasionally. Adjust heat to maintain very gentle simmer. Cover and cook until all cranberries have burst and started to shrivel, about 10 minutes. While cranberries cook, whisk egg yolks and cornstarch in bowl until smooth. Transfer hot cranberry mixture to food processor. Immediately add yolk mixture and process until smooth (small flecks of cranberry skin will be visible), about 1 minute, scraping down sides of bowl as necessary. Let mixture cool in processor bowl until skin forms and mixture registers 120 to 125 degrees, 45 minutes to 1 hour. While mixture cools, make crust.

2. FOR THE CRUST Adjust oven rack to middle position and heat oven to 350 degrees. Whisk flour, cornstarch, sugar, and salt in bowl until well combined. Add melted butter and almond extract and stir with wooden spoon until uniform dough forms. Crumble two-thirds of mixture over bottom of 9-inch tart pan with removable bottom. Press dough to even thickness in bottom of pan. Crumble remaining dough and scatter evenly around edge of pan. Press crumbled dough into sides of pan. Press edges to even thickness. Place pan on rimmed baking sheet and bake until crust is golden brown, about 20 minutes, rotating pan halfway through baking.

3. Add softened butter to cranberry puree and process until fully combined, about 30 seconds. Strain mixture through fine-mesh strainer set over bowl, pressing on solids with rubber spatula to extract puree. Transfer 2 tablespoons puree to medium bowl, then stir in cream and remaining 1 tablespoon sugar. Cover and refrigerate. Transfer remaining puree to crust (it's OK if crust is still warm) and smooth into even layer. Let tart stand at room temperature for at least 4 hours. (Cover tart with large bowl and refrigerate after 4 hours if making ahead. Tart can be made up to 3 days ahead, crust will be more tender.)

4. Whisk cream mixture until stiff peaks form, 1 to 3 minutes. Transfer to pastry bag fitted with pastry tip. Pipe decorative border around edge of tart. Transfer any remaining whipped cream to small serving bowl.

5. Remove outer metal ring of tart pan. Slide thin metal spatula between tart and pan bottom to loosen tart. Carefully slide tart onto serving platter. (Tart can be covered and refrigerated for up to 3 days.) Slice into wedges, wiping knife clean between cuts if necessary, and serve, passing extra whipped cream separately.

HOW TO PIPE DECORATIVE DESIGNS WITH STABILIZED WHIPPED CREAM

Confetti Border

Hold filled pastry bag fitted with ¾- to 1-inch round tip at 90-degree angle about ½ inch above tart. Squeeze gently to create 1-inch dots around perimeter (about eight to 12 in total). With each dot, as you stop squeezing, pull bag straight up to create peak. Fill in empty areas around perimeter with smaller peaked dots by holding bag about ¼ inch above tart.

Zigzag Border

Hold filled pastry bag fitted with ½- to ¾-inch round tip at 90-degree angle about ½ inch above tart. Pipe 1- to 1½-inch-wide, slightly overlapped zigzag pattern around tart perimeter, rotating tart frequently (about every one-eighth of the way around) to keep pattern even.

Poached Pear and Almond Tart

Serves 10 to 12 **MAKE AHEAD** **VEGETARIAN**
Total Time 3¼ hours, plus 3 hours cooling

WHY THIS RECIPE WORKS Sliced poached pears, fanned atop light, nutty frangipane (a sweetened, custardy paste of ground almonds) and contained within a sweet crust is a stunning classic French tart. The process of poaching doesn't just tenderize the pears; it perfumes them with flavor that complements the almond filling. White wine spiced with a cinnamon stick, black peppercorns, whole cloves, and a vanilla bean created our fragrant poaching liquid. For the frangipane, we processed blanched slivered almonds in a food processor with sugar; incorporating the sugar at this point allowed us to grind the almonds superfine without the risk of them transforming into greasy almond butter. We made sure to dry the pears before setting them on the frangipane; otherwise, their moisture made the dessert sticky and wet. Glazing the pears with jelly gave them a beautiful sheen. We like the bright, crisp flavor of pears poached in Sauvignon Blanc. Chardonnay-poached pears have a deeper, oakier flavor that we also like.

POACHED PEARS
- 1 (750-ml) bottle white wine
- ⅔ cup (4⅔ ounces) sugar
- 5 (2-inch) strips lemon zest plus 2 tablespoons juice
- 1 cinnamon stick
- 15 black peppercorns
- 3 cloves
- ⅛ teaspoon table salt
- ½ vanilla bean (optional)
- 4 ripe but firm Bosc or Bartlett pears (8 ounces each), peeled, halved, and cored

FILLING
- 1 cup slivered almonds
- ½ cup (3½ ounces) sugar
- ⅛ teaspoon table salt
- 1 large egg plus 1 large white
- ½ teaspoon almond extract
- ½ teaspoon vanilla extract
- 6 tablespoons unsalted butter, cut into 6 pieces and softened

- 1 recipe Classic Tart Dough (page 389)
- ¼ cup apple jelly

1. FOR THE POACHED PEARS Combine wine, sugar, lemon zest and juice, cinnamon stick, peppercorns, cloves, and salt in large saucepan. If using, cut vanilla bean in half lengthwise, then, using tip of paring knife, scrape out seeds and add seeds and pod to saucepan. Bring mixture to simmer, stirring occasionally to dissolve sugar. Slide pear halves into simmering wine mixture. Return to simmer, then reduce heat to low, cover, and cook pears, covered, turning them occasionally, until tender and skewer can be inserted into pear with very little resistance, about 10 minutes. Off heat, let pears cool in liquid, partially covered, until pears have turned translucent and are cool enough to handle, about 1 hour. (Pears and liquid can be refrigerated for up to 3 days; transfer to bowl, let cool completely, and cover before refrigerating.)

2. FOR THE FILLING Pulse almonds, sugar, and salt in food processor until finely ground, about 25 pulses. Continue to process until nut mixture is as finely ground as possible, about 10 seconds. Add egg and white, almond extract, and vanilla and process until combined, about 10 seconds. Add butter and process until no lumps remain, about 20 seconds, scraping down bowl as needed. (Filling can be refrigerated for up to 3 days. Let filling stand at room temperature until softened, about 10 minutes, stirring 3 or 4 times, before using.)

3. Roll dough into 11-inch circle on lightly floured counter, then transfer to parchment paper–lined rimmed baking sheet; cover loosely with plastic wrap and refrigerate until firm but pliable, about 10 minutes.

4. Roll dough loosely around rolling pin and gently unroll it onto 9-inch tart pan with removable bottom, letting excess dough hang over edge. Ease dough into plate by gently lifting edge of dough with your hand while pressing into corners and fluted sides of pan with your other hand. Run rolling pin over top of pan to remove any excess dough. Wrap loosely in plastic, place on large plate, and freeze until fully chilled and firm, about 30 minutes. (Dough-lined tart pan can be frozen for up to 1 month.) Adjust oven rack to middle position and heat oven to 375 degrees.

5. Line chilled tart shell with double layer of aluminum foil and fill with pie weights. Bake on foil-lined rimmed baking sheet until tart shell is golden and set, about 30 minutes, rotating sheet halfway through baking. Remove foil and weights. Transfer sheet to wire rack and let cool completely, about 1 hour. Reduce oven temperature to 350 degrees.

6. Spread filling evenly over bottom of cooled tart shell. Remove pears from poaching liquid and pat dry with paper towels. Cut 1 poached pear half crosswise into ⅜-inch slices, leaving pear half intact on cutting board (do not separate

Poached Pear and Almond Tart

slices). Pat dry again with paper towels to absorb excess moisture. Discard first 4 slices from narrow end of sliced pear half. Slide spatula under sliced pear and, steadying it with your hand, slide pear off spatula onto center of tart. Cut and dry another pear half. Slide spatula under pear and gently press pear to fan slices toward narrow end. Slide fanned pear half onto filling, narrow end toward center, almost touching center pear. Repeat slicing, fanning, and placing remaining pear halves, spacing them evenly and making flower petal pattern around center pear.

7. Bake tart on sheet until crust is deep golden brown and almond filling is puffed, browned, and firm to the touch, about 45 minutes, rotating sheet halfway through baking. Transfer sheet to wire rack and let tart cool for 10 minutes.

8. Melt jelly in small saucepan over medium-high heat, stirring occasionally to smooth out lumps. Using pastry brush, gently dab jelly over fruit, avoiding crust. Let tart cool completely, about 2 hours. Remove outer ring of tart pan, slide thin metal spatula between tart and tart pan bottom, and carefully slide tart onto serving platter or cutting board. Serve.

Chocolate,
Matcha, and
Pomegranate Tart

Sticky Toffee Pudding

Chocolate, Matcha, and Pomegranate Tart

Serves 8 to 10 `MAKE AHEAD` `VEGETARIAN`
Total Time 1¾ hours, plus 2 hours cooling and chilling

WHY THIS RECIPE WORKS The flavors of this stunning dessert are complex: bittersweet, tart, and herbaceous. There's a buttery tart shell, green tea–spiked whipped cream, and tart pomegranate seeds, but the star is the ganache, a dairy-free version inspired by one developed by French chemist Hervé This. Without the cream found in a standard ganache, the result is a layer of chocolate intense enough to compete with the pleasantly strong flavor and umami notes of the matcha. We adorned the top of the tart with pomegranate seeds for looks but also to provide contrasting tartness and crunch against the creamy and silky layers. Be sure to use chocolate containing 70 percent cacao or higher; using chocolate with a lower percentage will result in a loose, grainy chocolate layer. You can make your tart look like the one in the photograph with a piping bag, or you can simply spread the matcha whipped cream over the tart.

1 recipe Classic Tart Dough (page 389)

CHOCOLATE FILLING
2½ cups plus 1 tablespoon water, divided
4 cups ice cubes
5⅓ ounces bittersweet chocolate (70 percent cacao or higher), chopped
3 tablespoons plus 1 teaspoon granulated sugar
⅛ teaspoon table salt

MATCHA WHIPPED CREAM
1 cup heavy cream
½ cup (2 ounces) confectioners' sugar
⅛ teaspoon table salt
1 tablespoon matcha, plus 1 teaspoon for serving
⅓ cup pomegranate seeds

1. Roll dough into 11-inch circle on lightly floured counter, then transfer to parchment paper–lined rimmed baking sheet; cover loosely with plastic wrap and refrigerate until firm but pliable, about 10 minutes.

2. Roll dough loosely around rolling pin and gently unroll it onto 9-inch tart pan with removable bottom, letting excess dough hang over edge. Ease dough into pan by gently lifting edge of dough with your hand while pressing into corners and fluted sides of pan with your other hand. Run rolling pin over top of pan to remove any excess dough. Wrap loosely in plastic, place on large plate, and freeze until fully chilled and firm, about 30 minutes. (Dough-lined tart pan can be frozen for up to 1 month.) Adjust oven rack to middle position and heat oven to 375 degrees.

3. Line chilled tart shell with double layer of aluminum foil and fill with pie weights. Bake on foil-lined rimmed baking sheet until tart shell is golden brown and set, about 30 minutes, rotating sheet halfway through baking. Remove foil and weights and continue to bake tart shell until it is fully baked and golden, 5 to 10 minutes. Transfer sheet to wire rack and let shell cool completely, about 1 hour.

4. FOR THE CHOCOLATE FILLING Fill large bowl with 2 cups water and ice cubes. Place chocolate, ½ cup plus 1 tablespoon water, sugar, and salt in large heatproof bowl over saucepan filled with 1 inch barely simmering water, making sure that water does not touch bottom of bowl. Cook, stirring frequently with rubber spatula, until chocolate is fully melted and smooth, about 5 minutes. Transfer bowl to ice bath and chill, stirring constantly, until mixture is slightly thickened and registers between 75 and 80 degrees, 30 seconds to 1 minute. Remove bowl from ice bath and continue to stir 30 seconds. Transfer filling to cooled tart shell and tap baking sheet lightly on counter to release air bubbles; refrigerate tart until set, about 1 hour. (Tart can be refrigerated for up to 24 hours.)

5. FOR THE MATCHA WHIPPED CREAM Using stand mixer fitted with whisk attachment, whip cream, sugar, and salt on high speed until soft peaks form. Add 1 tablespoon matcha, reduce speed to medium, and whip until stiff peaks form. Remove tart from refrigerator. Remove outer ring of tart pan, slide thin metal spatula between tart and tart pan bottom, and carefully slide tart onto serving platter or cutting board. Spread whipped cream evenly over chocolate layer. Using fine-mesh strainer, dust tart with 1 teaspoon matcha. Sprinkle with pomegranate seeds. Serve.

Sticky Toffee Pudding

Serves 8 | **Total Time** 1¾ hours VEGETARIAN

WHY THIS RECIPE WORKS This British dessert features a moist date-studded cake soaked in toffee sauce. Treacle, a sweetener similar to molasses, is traditionally used; substituting molasses overwhelmed the dates' delicate caramel flavor, so instead we opted to use brown sugar. We also boosted the flavor of the dates by first soaking them in baking soda–laced water (to soften their skins) and then using that soaking liquid in the batter rather than water. Pulverizing half of the dates

before mixing them in guaranteed that every bite was laced with date flavor. We needed a fairly sturdy cake that would stand up to the sauce, so we employed the quick-bread technique, mixing dry and wet ingredients separately and then combining them, to produce a dense-yet-springy crumb. Baking the cakes in a water bath ensured they remained moist. Be sure to form a tight seal with the foil before baking the cakes. You will need eight 6-ounce ramekins for this recipe.

CAKES

- 8 ounces pitted dates, cut crosswise into ¼-inch-thick slices (1⅓ cups), divided
- ¾ cup warm water (110 degrees)
- ½ teaspoon baking soda
- 1¼ cups (6¼ ounces) all-purpose flour
- ½ teaspoon baking powder
- ½ teaspoon table salt
- ¾ cup packed (5¼ ounces) brown sugar
- 2 large eggs
- 4 tablespoons unsalted butter, melted
- 1½ tablespoons vanilla extract

SAUCE

- 4 tablespoons unsalted butter
- 1 cup packed (7 ounces) brown sugar
- ¼ teaspoon table salt
- 1 cup heavy cream, divided
- 1 tablespoon rum
- ¼ teaspoon lemon juice

1. FOR THE CAKES Adjust oven rack to middle position and heat oven to 350 degrees. Grease and flour eight 6-ounce ramekins. Fold dish towel in half and place in bottom of large roasting pan. Place prepared ramekins on top of towel; set aside pan. Bring kettle of water to boil.

2. Combine half of dates, warm water, and baking soda in 2-cup liquid measuring cup (dates should be submerged beneath water); soak dates for 5 minutes. Meanwhile, whisk flour, baking powder, and salt together in large bowl.

3. Process sugar and remaining dates in food processor until no large chunks remain and mixture has texture of damp, coarse sand, about 45 seconds, scraping down sides of bowl as needed. Drain soaked dates and add soaking liquid to processor. Add eggs, melted butter, and vanilla and process until smooth, about 15 seconds. Transfer sugar mixture to bowl with flour mixture and sprinkle soaked dates on top. Using rubber spatula or wooden spoon, gently fold sugar mixture into flour mixture until just combined and date pieces are evenly dispersed.

4. Divide batter evenly among prepared ramekins (ramekins should be two-thirds full). Quickly pour enough boiling water into roasting pan to come ¼ inch up sides of ramekins. Cover pan tightly with aluminum foil, crimping edges to seal. Bake until cakes are puffed and surfaces are spongy, firm, and moist to touch, about 40 minutes. Immediately transfer ramekins from water bath to wire rack and let cool for 10 minutes.

5. FOR THE SAUCE While cakes cool, melt butter in medium saucepan over medium-high heat. Whisk in sugar and salt until smooth. Continue to cook, stirring occasionally, until sugar is dissolved and slightly darkened, 3 to 4 minutes. Stir in ⅓ cup cream until smooth, about 30 seconds. Slowly pour in rum and remaining ⅔ cup cream, whisking constantly until smooth. Reduce heat to low; simmer until frothy, about 3 minutes. Remove from heat and stir in lemon juice.

6. Using toothpick, poke 25 holes in top of each cake and spoon 1 tablespoon toffee sauce over each cake. Let cakes stand until sauce is absorbed, about 5 minutes. Invert each ramekin onto plate or shallow bowl; lift off ramekin. Divide remaining toffee sauce evenly among cakes and serve immediately.

Slow-Cooker Bourbon Bread Pudding

Slow-Cooker Bourbon Bread Pudding

Serves 8 to 10 `VEGETARIAN`
Cooking Time 3 to 4 hours on Low

WHY THIS RECIPE WORKS This bread pudding boasts tender bread cubes enveloped by a rich custard accented with sweetly spiced cardamom and a toasty pecan topping. Making it in the slow cooker allowed the low, even heat to gently set the pudding to a moist, luxurious consistency in a few totally hands-off hours. We liked using buttery challah as the pudding's base. Using staled bread was key, as it was much better at soaking up the custard. Occasionally pressing on the challah as it soaked ensured that every bit was evenly saturated with custard. Hearty white sandwich bread can be substituted for the challah. If you don't have stale bread, you can dry fresh bread pieces by baking them on a rimmed baking sheet in a 225-degree oven for about 40 minutes, stirring occasionally. You will need an oval 5- to 7-quart slow cooker for this recipe.

2½ cups heavy cream
2½ cups whole milk
 9 large egg yolks
 ¾ cup packed (5¼ ounces) plus 2 tablespoons packed brown sugar, divided
 ⅓ cup bourbon
 1 tablespoon vanilla extract
 ¾ teaspoon table salt
 ¼ teaspoon cardamom
 1 pound challah, cut into 1-inch pieces (12 cups), staled overnight
 ½ cup pecans, toasted and chopped

1. Line slow cooker with aluminum foil collar and lightly coat with vegetable oil spray. Whisk cream, milk, egg yolks, ¾ cup sugar, bourbon, vanilla, salt, and cardamom in large bowl until sugar has dissolved. Stir in challah and let stand, pressing on bread occasionally, until custard is mostly absorbed, about 10 minutes.

2. Transfer challah mixture to prepared slow cooker and spread into even layer. Sprinkle with remaining 2 tablespoons sugar. Cover and cook until center of bread pudding is set, 3 to 4 hours on low.

3. Turn off slow cooker and let bread pudding cool, covered, for 30 minutes. Discard foil collar. Serve, sprinkling individual portions with pecans.

MAKING A FOIL COLLAR

Fold sheets of aluminum foil to make six-layered foil rectangle that measures roughly 16 inches long by 4 inches wide. Press collar into back side of slow cooker; food will help hold collar in place.

Chocolate Soufflé

Slow-Cooker Chocolate Fondue

Serves 8 to 10   MAKE AHEAD   VEGETARIAN
Cooking Time 1 to 2 hours on Low

WHY THIS RECIPE WORKS Chocolate fondue is a party pleaser: Dipping a piece of fruit, cake, or crusty bread into warm melted chocolate is guaranteed to make just about anybody happy. The slow cooker not only warms the ingredients gently, but its warm or low setting can also be used to keep the fondue perfectly dippable for hours. We combined semisweet chocolate with heavy cream, 1 tablespoon of corn syrup to give the fondue a satiny consistency and a beautiful gloss, and a pinch of salt to bring out the flavors. After heating the mixture for about an hour in the slow cooker, all we needed to do was whisk it until smooth and velvety. We found that semisweet chocolate produced both the most reliable consistency and the best flavor to pair with an array of accompaniments. We don't recommend using white, milk, or bittersweet chocolate here. For dipping, we like to use bite-size pieces of fruit, pound cake, or bread; make sure you have long skewers on hand to make things easy. You will need a 1½- to 7-quart slow cooker for this recipe.

12   ounces semisweet chocolate, chopped
1⅓   cups heavy cream, plus extra as needed
1   tablespoon light corn syrup
     Pinch table salt

Combine all ingredients in slow cooker. Cover and cook until chocolate has melted and mixture is hot, 1 to 2 hours on low. Whisk chocolate mixture together until smooth and serve. (Fondue can be held on warm or low setting for up to 2 hours; adjust consistency with extra hot cream as needed.)

Chocolate Soufflé

Serves 6 to 8 | **Total Time** 1 hour   VEGETARIAN

WHY THIS RECIPE WORKS Ethereally light and rising to impressively tall heights, a well-made chocolate soufflé is a thing of beauty—and good taste. We wanted to create a foolproof chocolate soufflé that would offer decadent chocolate flavor without compromising the requisite light, creamy texture and dramatic rise. Instead of starting with a classic béchamel base (we found that the flour and milk in the béchamel muted the chocolate flavor), we relied entirely on eggs to make up the soufflé's foundation. After beating six egg yolks with sugar, we folded them into a mixture of melted chocolate and butter scented with orange liqueur. The whites we whipped to stiff peaks (adding two more for extra volume) and then folded into the chocolate mixture. The eggs provided enough structure to support an entire half a pound of chocolate, yielding an airy yet decadently chocolaty confection. Soufflé waits for no one, so be ready to serve it immediately. Or see the brilliant make-ahead variation that can be frozen up to 1 month ahead and go directly from your freezer to the oven.

1 tablespoon softened butter plus 4 tablespoons unsalted butter, cut into ½-inch pieces, divided
1 tablespoon plus ⅓ cup (2⅓ ounces) sugar, divided
8 ounces bittersweet or semisweet chocolate, chopped
1 tablespoon orange-flavored liqueur, such as Grand Marnier
½ teaspoon vanilla extract
⅛ teaspoon table salt
6 large eggs, separated, plus 2 large whites
¼ teaspoon cream of tartar

1. Adjust oven rack to lower-middle position and heat oven to 375 degrees. Grease 2-quart soufflé dish with 1 tablespoon softened butter, then coat dish evenly with 1 tablespoon sugar; refrigerate until ready to use.

2. Microwave chocolate and remaining 4 tablespoons butter in large bowl at 50 percent power, stirring occasionally, until melted and smooth, 2 to 4 minutes. Stir in liqueur, vanilla, and salt; set aside.

3. Using stand mixer fitted with paddle, beat egg yolks and remaining ⅓ cup sugar on medium speed until thick and pale yellow, about 3 minutes. Fold into chocolate mixture.

4. Using clean, dry mixer bowl and whisk attachment, whip egg whites and cream of tartar on medium-low speed until foamy, about 1 minute. Increase speed to medium-high and whip until stiff peaks form, 3 to 4 minutes.

5. Using rubber spatula, vigorously stir one-quarter of whipped whites into chocolate mixture. Gently fold remaining whites into chocolate mixture until just incorporated. Transfer mixture to prepared dish. Bake until fragrant, fully risen, and exterior is set but interior is still a bit loose and creamy, about 25 minutes. (Use 2 large spoons to gently pull open top and peek inside.) Serve immediately.

Make-Ahead Individual Chocolate Soufflés

Omit 2-quart soufflé dish. Grease eight 8-ounce ramekins with 1 tablespoon butter, then coat dishes evenly with 1 tablespoon sugar. In step 3, bring remaining ⅓ cup sugar and 2 tablespoons water to boil in small saucepan, then reduce heat and simmer until sugar dissolves. With mixer running, slowly add sugar syrup to egg yolks and beat until mixture triples in volume, about 3 minutes. Whip egg whites as directed, beating in 2 table-spoons confectioners' sugar. Stir and fold into chocolate base as directed. Fill each chilled ramekin almost to rim, wiping each rim clean with wet paper towel. Cover each ramekin tightly with plastic wrap and freeze until firm, at least 3 hours or up to 1 month. (Do not thaw before baking.) To serve, heat oven to 400 degrees and reduce baking time to 16 to 18 minutes.

Baked Alaska

Baked Alaska

Serves 8   MAKE AHEAD   VEGETARIAN
Total Time 2½ hours, plus 2 hours chilling

WHY THIS RECIPE WORKS A conversation starter and showstopper, baked Alaska is a unicorn among desserts: We've all heard of it, but few have seen one. While this delightfully antithetical creation—cake and ice cream cloaked in meringue, then baked or blowtorched (or set aflame) to crisp the exterior without melting the ice cream—may intimidate, it's no more difficult than any other ice cream cake. We encased the ice cream in a thin layer of cake, permitting us to decrease the amount of meringue without sacrificing heat resistance. We used a superhot oven to turn the meringue's peaks golden brown. We liked the contrast that slightly bitter coffee ice cream offered to the sweet meringue and chocolate cake, but other flavors may be substituted, if desired. A high-quality ice cream such as Häagen-Dazs works best because it is slower to melt. See page 382 for more on how to assemble baked Alaska. To ensure the proper texture when serving, it is necessary to remove the cake from the freezer before making the meringue.

2 (1-pint) containers coffee ice cream

CAKE

1 cup (4 ounces) cake flour
⅓ cup (1 ounce) unsweetened cocoa powder
⅔ cup (4⅔ ounces) sugar, divided
1½ teaspoons baking powder
¼ teaspoon table salt
4 large eggs, separated
½ cup vegetable oil
6 tablespoons water

MERINGUE

¾ cup (5¼ ounces) sugar
⅓ cup light corn syrup
3 large egg whites
2 tablespoons water
Pinch table salt
1 teaspoon vanilla extract

1. Lay 12-inch square sheet of plastic wrap on counter and remove lids from ice cream. Use scissors to cut cardboard tubs from top to bottom. Peel away cardboard and discard. Place ice cream blocks on their sides in center of plastic with wider ends facing each other. Grasp each side of plastic and firmly press blocks together to form barrel shape. Wrap plastic tightly around ice cream and roll briefly on counter to form uniform cylinder. Place cylinder, standing on end, in freezer until completely solid, at least 1 hour.

2. FOR THE CAKE Adjust oven rack to middle position and heat oven to 350 degrees. Lightly grease 18 by 13-inch rimmed baking sheet, line with parchment paper, and lightly grease parchment. Whisk flour, cocoa, ⅓ cup sugar, baking powder, and salt together in large bowl. Whisk egg yolks, oil, and water into flour mixture until smooth batter forms.

3. Using stand mixer fitted with whisk attachment, whip egg whites on medium-low speed until foamy, about 1 minute. Increase speed to medium-high and whip whites to soft, billowy mounds, about 1 minute. Gradually add remaining ⅓ cup sugar and whip until glossy, soft peaks form, 1 to 2 minutes. Transfer one-third of egg whites to batter; whisk gently until mixture is lightened. Using rubber spatula, gently fold remaining whites into batter until just incorporated.

4. Pour batter into prepared sheet; spread evenly. Bake until cake springs back when pressed lightly in center, 10 to 13 minutes. Transfer cake to wire rack and let cool for 5 minutes. Run knife around edge of sheet, then invert cake onto wire rack. Carefully remove parchment, then reinvert cake onto second wire rack. Let cool completely, at least 15 minutes.

5. Transfer cake to cutting board with long side of rectangle parallel to edge of counter. Using serrated knife, trim ¼ inch off left side of cake and discard. Using ruler, measure 4½ inches from cut edge and make mark with knife. Using mark as guide, cut 4½-inch-wide rectangle from cake. Trim piece to create 4½ by 11-inch rectangle and set aside. (Depending on pan size and how much cake has shrunk during baking, it may not be necessary to trim piece to measure 11 inches.) Measure 4 inches from new cut edge and make mark. Using mark as guide, cut 4-inch-wide rectangle from cake. Trim piece to create 4 by 10-inch rectangle, wrap rectangle in plastic, and set aside. Cut 3½-inch round from remaining cake and set aside (biscuit cutter works well).

6. Unwrap ice cream. Trim cylinder to 4½ inches in length. Place ice cream cylinder on 4½ by 11-inch cake rectangle and wrap cake around ice cream. (Cake may crack slightly.) Place cake circle on 1 end of cylinder. Wrap entire cylinder tightly in plastic. Freeze cylinder, standing on cake-covered end, until cake is firm, at least 30 minutes.

7. Unwrap cylinder; place on cutting board, standing on cake-covered end, and cut in half lengthwise. Unwrap reserved 4 by 10-inch cake rectangle and place halves on top, ice cream side down, with open ends meeting in middle. Wrap tightly in plastic and press ends gently to close gap between halves. Freeze cake for at least 2 hours or up to 2 weeks.

8. FOR THE MERINGUE Adjust oven rack to upper-middle position and heat oven to 500 degrees. Spray wire rack set in rimmed baking sheet with vegetable oil spray. Unwrap cake and place on rack. Combine sugar, corn syrup, egg whites, water, and salt in bowl of stand mixer; place bowl over saucepan filled with 1 inch simmering water, making sure that water does not touch bottom of bowl. Whisking gently but constantly, heat until sugar is dissolved and mixture registers 160 degrees, 5 to 8 minutes.

9. Place bowl in stand mixer fitted with whisk attachment. Beat mixture on medium speed until bowl is only slightly warm to touch, about 5 minutes. Increase speed to high and beat until mixture begins to lose its gloss and forms stiff peaks, about 5 minutes. Add vanilla and beat until combined.

10. Using offset spatula, spread meringue over top and sides of cake, avoiding getting meringue on rack. Use back of spoon to create peaks all over meringue.

11. Bake until browned and crisp, about 5 minutes. Slide offset spatula or thin knife under dessert to loosen from rack, then use 2 spatulas to transfer to serving platter.

12. Slice dessert, dipping sharp knife in very hot water and wiping dry after each cut. Serve immediately.

ASSEMBLING BAKED ALASKA

1. Place ice cream cylinder on 4½ by 11-inch cake rectangle and wrap cake around ice cream.

2. Place cake circle on 1 end of cylinder. Wrap entire cylinder tightly in plastic. Place cylinder, standing on cake-covered end, in freezer until cake is firm, at least 30 minutes.

3. Unwrap cylinder. Place on cutting board, standing on cake-covered end, and cut in half lengthwise.

4. Place halves on top of reserved 4 by 10-inch cake rectangle, ice cream side down, with open ends meeting in middle. Wrap tightly in plastic and press ends gently to close gap.

Tiramisu

Serves 10 to 12 MAKE AHEAD VEGETARIAN
Total Time 40 minutes, plus 6 hours chilling

WHY THIS RECIPE WORKS Holiday-season tip: Make this creamy, coffee-flavored, rum-spiked tiramisu; store it in your freezer; and you have a grand dessert at the ready, needing only to be defrosted before serving. A good tiramisu is a seamless union of flavors and textures—it's difficult to tell where cookie ends and cream begins, where bitter espresso gives over to the bite of alcohol. For our version, instead of making a custard filling, we simply whipped egg yolks, sugar, salt, rum, and mascarpone together and lightened it with whipped cream. A mixture of coffee, espresso powder, and more rum moistened the ladyfingers. We prefer a tiramisu with a pronounced rum flavor; for a less potent dessert, reduce the amount of rum in the coffee mixture. Brandy or whiskey can be substituted for the rum. Don't let the mascarpone warm to room temperature before whipping it. Dried ladyfingers are also called savoiardi; you will need between 42 and 60, depending on their size and the brand.

2½ cups strong brewed coffee, room temperature
9 tablespoons dark rum, divided
1½ tablespoons instant espresso powder
6 large egg yolks
⅔ cup (4⅔ ounces) sugar
¼ teaspoon table salt
1½ pounds mascarpone cheese (3 cups)
¾ cup heavy cream, chilled
14 ounces dried ladyfingers (savoiardi)
3½ tablespoons Dutch-processed cocoa, divided
¼ cup grated semisweet or bittersweet chocolate (optional)

1. Stir coffee, 5 tablespoons rum, and espresso in wide bowl or baking dish until espresso dissolves; set aside.

2. Using stand mixer fitted with whisk, whip egg yolks on low speed until just combined. Add sugar and salt and whip on medium-high speed until pale yellow, 1½ to 2 minutes, scraping down bowl once or twice. Add remaining ¼ cup rum and whip on medium speed until just combined, 20 to 30 seconds; scrape down bowl. Add mascarpone and whip on medium speed until no lumps remain, 30 to 45 seconds, scraping down bowl once or twice. Transfer mixture to large bowl and set aside.

3. In now-empty mixer bowl, whip cream on medium-low speed until foamy, about 1 minute. Increase speed to high and whip until stiff peaks form, 1 to 3 minutes. Using rubber spatula, fold one-third of whipped cream into mascarpone mixture to lighten, then gently fold in remaining whipped cream until no white streaks remain. Set mascarpone mixture aside.

4. Working with one at a time, drop half of ladyfingers into coffee mixture, roll to coat, remove, and transfer to 13 by 9-inch glass or ceramic baking dish. (Do not submerge ladyfingers in coffee mixture; entire process should take no longer than 2 to 3 seconds for each cookie.) Arrange soaked cookies in single layer in baking dish, breaking or trimming ladyfingers as needed to fit neatly into dish.

5. Spread half of mascarpone mixture over ladyfingers with spatula, spreading mixture to sides and into corners of dish, then smooth surface. Place 2 tablespoons cocoa in fine-mesh strainer and dust cocoa over mascarpone.

Chocolate–Peanut Butter Crème Brûlée

creamy peanut butter to our custard base in addition to 4 ounces of bittersweet chocolate, which made the custard chocolaty without adversely affecting the texture or obscuring the peanut butter flavor. We've found that the key to a soft, supple crème brûlée, rather than a bouncy one, is to use just egg yolks rather than whole eggs. We replaced a portion of the cream with milk to prevent the custard from becoming overly rich from the added fat from the chocolate and peanut butter. The traditional sugar crust provided a nice crunch against the creamy custard, but we doubled down on the crunch for this new spin, topping the caramelized sugar with toasty, sweet-salty candied peanuts that reinforced the flavor of the peanut butter. You will need a kitchen torch and eight 6-ounce ramekins (or shallow fluted dishes) for this recipe.

2¾ cups heavy cream, divided
½ cup (3½ ounces) granulated sugar
4 ounces bittersweet chocolate, chopped fine
¼ cup creamy peanut butter
1 cup whole milk
10 large egg yolks
3 tablespoons turbinado sugar or Demerara sugar
1 recipe Candied Peanuts (page 384)

1. Adjust oven rack to lower-middle position and heat oven to 300 degrees. Place dish towel in bottom of large baking dish or roasting pan. Set eight 6-ounce ramekins (or shallow fluted dishes) on towel. Bring kettle of water to boil.

2. Combine 2 cups cream and granulated sugar in medium saucepan. Bring mixture to boil over medium heat, stirring occasionally to dissolve sugar. Off heat, whisk in chocolate and peanut butter until melted and smooth. Stir in milk and remaining ¾ cup heavy cream. Meanwhile, whisk egg yolks in large bowl until uniform. Whisk about 1 cup chocolate mixture into yolks; repeat with 1 cup more chocolate mixture. Whisk in remaining chocolate mixture until thoroughly combined. Strain custard through fine-mesh strainer into 4-cup liquid measuring cup; discard solids. Divide custard evenly among ramekins.

3. Set baking dish on oven rack. Taking care not to splash water into ramekins, pour enough boiling water into dish to reach two-thirds up sides of ramekins. Bake until centers of custards are just barely set and register 170 to 175 degrees, 25 to 35 minutes depending on ramekin type, checking temperature 5 minutes early. Transfer ramekins to wire rack and let cool completely, about 2 hours. Set ramekins on baking sheet, cover tightly with plastic wrap, and refrigerate until cold, at least 4 hours or up to 3 days.

6. Repeat dipping and arrangement of ladyfingers; spread remaining mascarpone mixture over ladyfingers and dust with remaining 1½ tablespoons cocoa. Wipe edges of dish clean with paper towel. Cover with plastic wrap and refrigerate for at least 6 hours or up to 24 hours. Garnish with grated chocolate, if using, and serve chilled. (Tiramisu can be refrigerated for up to 24 hours or frozen for up to 1 month; if frozen, thaw completely in refrigerator before serving.)

Chocolate–Peanut Butter Crème Brûlée

Serves 8   MAKE AHEAD   VEGETARIAN
Total Time 1 hour, plus 6½ hours cooling and chilling

WHY THIS RECIPE WORKS We love the creaminess and textural contrasts of crème brûlée, but the ubiquitous version flavored only with vanilla bean can be a bit, well, vanilla. We reinvented this classic French dessert by giving it a very American chocolate-peanut profile. We added ¼ cup of

4. Uncover ramekins and gently blot tops dry with paper towels. Sprinkle each with 1 to 1½ teaspoons turbinado sugar (depending on ramekin type). Tilt and tap each ramekin to distribute sugar evenly, then dump out excess sugar and wipe rims of ramekins clean. Caramelize sugar with torch until deep golden brown, continually sweeping flame about 2 inches above ramekin. Rechill custards for 30 minutes. Sprinkle with candied peanuts before serving.

Candied Peanuts

Makes about 1 cup | **Total Time** 20 minutes

1 cup peanuts, toasted
¼ cup (1¾ ounces) sugar
¼ cup water
½ teaspoon table salt

1. Line rimmed baking sheet with parchment paper. Bring all ingredients to boil in medium saucepan over medium heat. Cook, stirring constantly, until water evaporates and sugar appears dry, opaque, and somewhat crystallized and evenly coats nuts, about 5 minutes.

2. Reduce heat to low and continue to stir nuts until sugar is amber-colored, about 2 minutes. Transfer nuts to prepared sheet and spread in even layer. Let cool completely, about 10 minutes.

Autumn Pear Crumble

Serves 8 | **Total Time** 1½ hours
`MAKE AHEAD` `VEGETARIAN`

WHY THIS RECIPE WORKS Many cooks shy away from using pears in baked desserts because of the amount of moisture they release when cooked, but it doesn't have to be this way. In this crumble, we compensated for the pears' moisture by cooking the fruit and crumble separately. Precooking the pears in a Dutch oven allowed them to release their juices and become tender; a teaspoon of cornstarch thickened those juices into a velvety glaze. Tart dried cranberries balanced the pears' sweetness. We baked our crumble mixture (more cookie than streusel, with lots of sugar and butter) on a rimmed baking sheet until it was lightly golden, crisp, and nutty-tasting before sprinkling it onto individual bowls of cooked fruit. A final pass in the oven browned the topping and helped it cling to the bubbling filling. Be careful not to overbake the topping in step 4, or it may get too dark when baked again with the filling in step 5. You will need eight 6-ounce ramekins for this recipe. Serve with vanilla ice cream or Whipped Cream (page 368).

FRUIT FILLING
4 pounds Bosc or Bartlett pears, peeled, cored, and cut into ½-inch pieces
5 tablespoons (2¼ ounces) granulated sugar
1 tablespoon brandy
1 tablespoon lemon juice
1 teaspoon cornstarch
½ teaspoon cinnamon
⅛ teaspoon table salt
1 cup dried cranberries

CRUMBLE
1 cup (5 ounces) all-purpose flour
¼ cup (1¾ ounces) plus 1 tablespoon granulated sugar
¼ cup packed (1¾ ounces) brown sugar
2 teaspoons vanilla extract
⅛ teaspoon table salt
6 tablespoons unsalted butter, cut into 6 pieces and softened
½ cup sliced almonds, divided

1. FOR THE FRUIT FILLING Combine pears, sugar, brandy, lemon juice, cornstarch, cinnamon, and salt in Dutch oven. Cover and cook over medium heat, stirring often, until pears are tender when poked with fork but still hold their shape, 15 to 20 minutes. Off heat, gently stir in cranberries. Divide mixture among eight 6-ounce ramekins and set on rimmed baking sheet. (Fruit filling can be refrigerated for up to 2 days.)

2. FOR THE CRUMBLE Adjust oven rack to middle position and heat oven to 350 degrees. Line rimmed baking sheet with parchment paper.

3. Pulse flour, ¼ cup granulated sugar, brown sugar, vanilla, and salt in food processor until combined, about 5 pulses. Sprinkle butter and ¼ cup almonds over top and process until mixture clumps together into large crumbly balls, about 30 seconds. Sprinkle remaining ¼ cup almonds over top and pulse to incorporate, about 2 pulses.

4. Spread mixture out onto prepared baking sheet, breaking it into ¼-inch pieces (with some smaller loose bits). Bake until lightly browned, 10 to 15 minutes. (Topping can be stored at room temperature for up to 3 days.)

5. Sprinkle topping evenly over filling in ramekins, breaking up any large pieces. Sprinkle with remaining 1 tablespoon granulated sugar. Bake crumble until topping is well browned and fruit is bubbling around edges, 23 to 27 minutes, rotating baking sheet halfway through baking. Let cool for 10 minutes before serving.

Bananas Foster

Serves 3 to 4 | **Total Time** 20 minutes `VEGETARIAN`

WHY THIS RECIPE WORKS Bananas Foster is an ingenious dessert composed of bananas caramelized in a butterscotch sauce, flambéed with liqueur, and usually paired with scoops of vanilla ice cream. To complement the caramelized flavors that developed from the flambéing, we kept the amounts of butter and brown sugar in check so the sauce was rich, thick, and not overly sweet. We added just ¼ cup of rum, enough to impart a robust rum taste without overwhelming booziness, using a little in the sauce and the rest to flambé the bananas. As for the bananas, we cooked them in the sauce until soft, flipping them over halfway through cooking so they turned out perfectly tender.

- 4 tablespoons unsalted butter
- ½ cup packed (3½ ounces) dark brown sugar
- 1 cinnamon stick
- 1 (2-inch) strip lemon zest
- ¼ cup dark rum, divided
- 2 large, firm, ripe bananas, peeled, halved crosswise, then halved lengthwise
- 1 pint vanilla ice cream

1. Combine butter, sugar, cinnamon stick, lemon zest, and 1 tablespoon rum in 12-inch skillet. Cook over medium-high heat, stirring constantly, until sugar dissolves and mixture has thickened, about 2 minutes.

2. Reduce heat to medium and add bananas to pan, spooning some sauce over each quarter. Cook until bananas are glossy and golden on bottom, about 1½ minutes. Flip bananas; continue to cook until very soft but not mushy or falling apart, about 1½ minutes.

3. Off heat, add remaining 3 tablespoons rum and allow rum to warm slightly, about 5 seconds. Wave lit fireplace match or wooden skewer over pan until rum ignites, shaking pan to distribute flame over entire pan. After flames subside, 15 to 30 seconds, discard cinnamon stick and lemon zest. Divide ice cream among individual bowls and top with bananas and sauce. Serve.

Autumn Pear Crumble

Bananas Foster

Roasted Oranges in
Spiced Syrup

Roasted Figs with Balsamic
Glaze and Mascarpone

Roasted Oranges in Spiced Syrup

Serves 6 | **Total Time** 1 hour VEGETARIAN

WHY THIS RECIPE WORKS Light and fragrant, a dessert of glazed oranges is a simple but sophisticated way to end a rich meal. Our method capitalizes on the caramelized flavor of roasted oranges. Slicing the oranges into thick rounds meant exposing more of the fruit to the oven's heat, concentrating its flavor. To avoid drying out the fruit during roasting, we arranged the slices in a shallow pool of caramel syrup in a baking dish. Our syrupy sauce—a simple reduction of sugar and water—came together easily on the stovetop, and steeping a cinnamon stick and cloves in it gave the sweet sauce spicy warmth. Adding fresh orange juice to the sauce reinforced the citrus flavor. We roasted the oranges for 20 minutes, just until they were appealingly soft and tender. Serve with ice cream, pound cake, or yogurt.

7 oranges (6 whole, 1 juiced to yield ½ cup)
¾ cup (5¼ ounces) sugar
½ cup water
2 whole cloves
1 cinnamon stick

1. Adjust oven rack to middle position and heat oven to 450 degrees. Cut away peel and pith from 6 oranges, then slice crosswise into ½-inch-thick rounds. Arrange oranges evenly in 13 by 9-inch baking dish, overlapping rounds as needed.

2. Combine sugar, water, cloves, and cinnamon stick in medium saucepan. Bring to boil over medium-high heat and cook, without stirring, until mixture is amber colored, 8 to 10 minutes. Reduce heat to low and continue to cook, swirling saucepan occasionally, until dark amber, 2 to 5 minutes. (Caramel will register 350 degrees.)

3. Off heat, carefully stir in orange juice (mixture will bubble and steam). Return saucepan to medium heat and cook, stirring frequently, until caramel dissolves completely into orange juice and turns syrupy, about 2 minutes.

4. Pour syrup and spices over orange slices. Roast until syrup is bubbling and oranges are slightly wilted, 18 to 20 minutes. Transfer dish to wire rack and let cool slightly. Discard cloves and cinnamon stick. Serve warm or at room temperature.

Roasted Oranges in Vanilla-Anise Syrup

Cut vanilla bean in half lengthwise. Using tip of paring knife, scrape out seeds. Substitute vanilla bean and seeds and 2 star anise pods for cloves and cinnamon stick.

MORE RUSTIC FRUIT DESSERT RECIPES
Cranberry-Pecan-Stuffed Baked Apples, page 197
Skillet Apple Crisp, page 198
Apple Pandowdy, page 199

Roasted Figs with Balsamic Glaze and Mascarpone

Serves 6 | **Total Time** 35 minutes VEGETARIAN

WHY THIS RECIPE WORKS Fresh figs, a start-of-autumn treat, turn wonderfully tender and rich when roasted. We turned simple roasted figs into an elegant dessert by infusing them with the complex sweetness of balsamic vinegar and the floral notes of honey. Reducing the vinegar on the stovetop turned it viscous and syrupy (much like the texture of high-end drizzling balsamics), and adding honey to it banished any harshness. Roasting figs on their own can yield dry, scorched fruit, so instead we roasted the figs in the oven in the balsamic glaze. As the figs roasted, they grew tender and lent their natural sweetness to the surrounding syrup. To finish with flair, we dolloped each fig with honeyed mascarpone cheese and sprinkled them with toasted pistachios for crunch. You will need a 12-inch ovensafe skillet for this recipe.

½ cup balsamic vinegar
¼ cup honey, divided
1 tablespoon unsalted butter
1½ pounds fresh figs, stemmed and halved
4 ounces (½ cup) mascarpone cheese
½ teaspoon grated lemon zest
⅓ cup shelled pistachios, toasted and chopped

1. Adjust oven rack to middle position and heat oven to 450 degrees. Bring vinegar, 3 tablespoons honey, and butter to simmer in 12-inch ovensafe skillet over medium-high heat and cook until reduced to ⅓ cup, about 3 minutes. Off heat, add figs and toss to coat. Transfer skillet to oven and roast until figs are tender, 8 to 10 minutes

2. Remove skillet from oven and let figs rest for 5 minutes. Combine mascarpone, lemon zest, and remaining 1 tablespoon honey in bowl. Divide figs among individual bowls. Dollop with mascarpone mixture, drizzle with balsamic syrup, and sprinkle with pistachios. Serve.

Slow-Cooker White Wine–Poached Pears

Serves 6 | **Cooking Time** 3 to 4 hours on Low or 2 to 3 hours on High MAKE AHEAD   VEGETARIAN

WHY THIS RECIPE WORKS A classic French dessert, poached pears are surprisingly simple to make at home, especially when using the gentle, controlled heat of a slow cooker. We liked Bosc and Bartlett pears here because of their honeyed sweetness and clean appearance when poached; cutting the pears in half ensured that they cooked evenly. Using sweetened white wine enhanced with lemon and mint as the poaching liquid infused the pears with bright yet nuanced fruitiness. Thyme added an intriguing hint of wood-siness. Once the pears were tender, we reduced the poaching liquid to make a sauce. Refrigerating the pears and sauce together allowed the fruit to absorb even more flavor while taking on a lovely translucent appearance. We recommend a medium-bodied dry white wine such as Sauvignon Blanc. You will need an oval 4- to 7-quart slow cooker for this recipe.

1 (750-ml) bottle dry white wine
¾ cup (5¼ ounces) sugar
½ vanilla bean
6 (2-inch) strips lemon zest
5 sprigs fresh mint
3 sprigs fresh thyme
½ cinnamon stick
⅛ teaspoon table salt
6 ripe but firm Bosc or Bartlett pears (8 ounces each), peeled, halved, and cored

1. Whisk wine and sugar together in slow cooker until sugar has dissolved. Cut vanilla bean in half lengthwise. Using tip of paring knife, scrape out seeds. Stir vanilla bean and seeds, lemon zest, mint sprigs, thyme sprigs, cinnamon stick, and salt into wine mixture. Nestle pears into slow cooker, cover, and cook until skewer inserted into pears meets little resistance, 3 to 4 hours on low or 2 to 3 hours on high.

2. Using slotted spoon, transfer pears to shallow casserole dish. Strain cooking liquid into large saucepan. Bring to simmer over medium heat and cook until thickened and measures about 1⅓ cups, about 15 minutes. Pour sauce over pears, cover, and refrigerate until well chilled, at least 2 hours or up to 3 days. Serve.

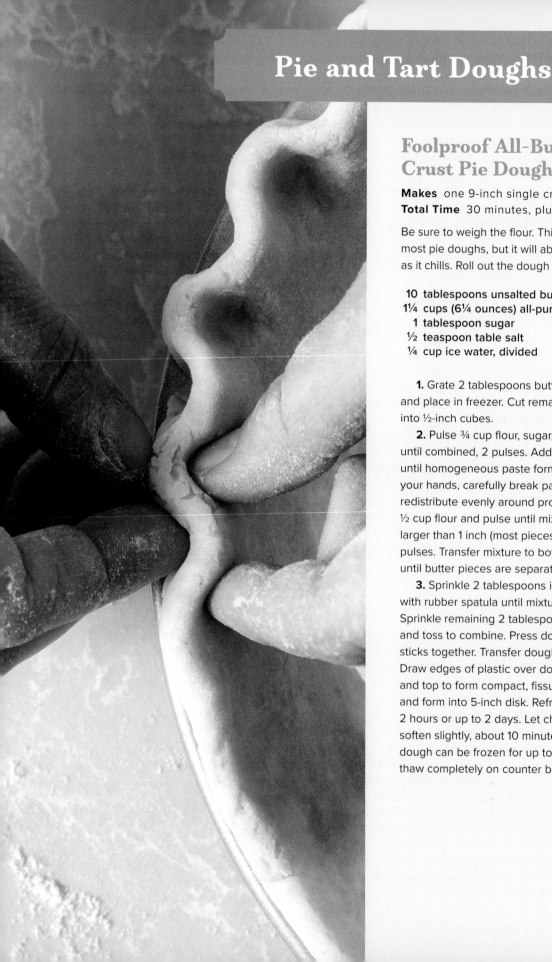

Foolproof All-Butter Single-Crust Pie Dough

Makes one 9-inch single crust
Total Time 30 minutes, plus 2 hours chilling

Be sure to weigh the flour. This dough will be moister than most pie doughs, but it will absorb a lot of excess moisture as it chills. Roll out the dough on a well-floured counter.

10 tablespoons unsalted butter, chilled, divided
1¼ cups (6¼ ounces) all-purpose flour, divided
1 tablespoon sugar
½ teaspoon table salt
¼ cup ice water, divided

1. Grate 2 tablespoons butter on large holes of box grater and place in freezer. Cut remaining 8 tablespoons butter into ½-inch cubes.

2. Pulse ¾ cup flour, sugar, and salt in food processor until combined, 2 pulses. Add cubed butter and process until homogeneous paste forms, about 30 seconds. Using your hands, carefully break paste into 2-inch chunks and redistribute evenly around processor blade. Add remaining ½ cup flour and pulse until mixture is broken into pieces no larger than 1 inch (most pieces will be much smaller), 4 to 5 pulses. Transfer mixture to bowl. Add grated butter and toss until butter pieces are separated and coated with flour.

3. Sprinkle 2 tablespoons ice water over mixture. Toss with rubber spatula until mixture is evenly moistened. Sprinkle remaining 2 tablespoons ice water over mixture and toss to combine. Press dough with spatula until dough sticks together. Transfer dough to sheet of plastic wrap. Draw edges of plastic over dough and press firmly on sides and top to form compact, fissure-free mass. Wrap in plastic and form into 5-inch disk. Refrigerate dough for at least 2 hours or up to 2 days. Let chilled dough sit on counter to soften slightly, about 10 minutes, before rolling. (Wrapped dough can be frozen for up to 1 month. If frozen, let dough thaw completely on counter before rolling.)

Foolproof All-Butter Double-Crust Pie Dough

Makes one 9-inch double crust
Total Time 30 minutes, plus 2 hours chilling

Be sure to weigh the flour. This dough will be moister than most pie doughs, but it will absorb a lot of excess moisture as it chills. Roll out the dough on a well-floured counter.

 20 tablespoons (2½ sticks) unsalted butter, chilled, divided
2½ cups (12½ ounces) all-purpose flour, divided
  2 tablespoons sugar
  1 teaspoon table salt
 ½ cup (4 ounces) ice water, divided

1. Grate 4 tablespoons butter on large holes of box grater and place in freezer. Cut remaining 16 tablespoons butter into ½-inch cubes.

2. Pulse 1½ cups flour, sugar, and salt in food processor until combined, 2 pulses. Add cubed butter and process until homogeneous paste forms, 40 to 50 seconds. Using your hands, carefully break paste into 2-inch chunks and redistribute evenly around processor blade. Add remaining 1 cup flour and pulse until mixture is broken into pieces no larger than 1 inch (most pieces will be much smaller), 4 to 5 pulses. Transfer mixture to bowl. Add grated butter and toss until butter pieces are separated and coated with flour.

3. Sprinkle ¼ cup ice water over mixture. Toss with rubber spatula until mixture is evenly moistened. Sprinkle remaining ¼ cup ice water over mixture and toss to combine. Press dough with spatula until dough sticks together. Using spatula, divide dough into 2 equal portions. Transfer each portion to sheet of plastic wrap. Working with 1 portion at a time, draw edges of plastic over dough and press firmly on sides and top to form compact, fissure-free mass. Wrap in plastic and form into 5-inch disk. Refrigerate dough for at least 2 hours or up to 2 days. Let chilled dough sit on counter to soften slightly, about 10 minutes, before rolling. (Wrapped dough can be frozen for up to 1 month. If frozen, let dough thaw completely on counter before rolling.)

Classic Tart Dough

Makes one 9-inch tart crust
Total Time 20 minutes, plus 1 hour chilling

You need only to lightly flour the counter when rolling out this supple dough.

  1 large egg yolk
  1 tablespoon heavy cream
 ½ teaspoon vanilla extract
1¼ cups (6¼ ounces) all-purpose flour
 ⅔ cup (2⅔ ounces) confectioners' sugar
 ¼ teaspoon table salt
  8 tablespoons unsalted butter, cut into ¼-inch pieces and chilled

1. Whisk egg yolk, cream, and vanilla together in bowl. Process flour, sugar, and salt in food processor until combined, about 5 seconds. Scatter butter over top and pulse until mixture resembles coarse cornmeal, about 15 pulses. With processor running, add egg yolk mixture and continue to process until dough just comes together around processor blade, about 12 seconds.

2. Transfer dough to sheet of plastic wrap and form into 6-inch disk. Wrap tightly in plastic and refrigerate for at least 1 hour or up to 2 days. Let chilled dough sit on counter to soften slightly, about 10 minutes, before rolling. (Wrapped dough can be frozen for up to 1 month. If frozen, let dough thaw completely on counter before rolling.)

TRANSFERRING DOUGH TO PIE PLATE

1. Roll dough loosely around rolling pin. Gently unroll onto 9-inch pie plate, letting excess dough hang over edge.

2. Ease dough into plate by gently lifting edge of dough with your hand while pressing into plate bottom with your other hand.

food gifts

■ MAKE AHEAD ▦ VEGETARIAN

Photo: Chocolate Fudge

Spiced Pecans with Rum Glaze

Cherry-Almond
Chocolate Granola

Spiced Pecans with Rum Glaze

Makes about 2 cups | **Total Time** 30 minutes

`MAKE AHEAD` `VEGETARIAN`

WHY THIS RECIPE WORKS Toasty, warmly spiced nuts sparkling with crystallized sugar are good enough to eat by the handful—or to give away as a thoughtful homemade favor. We started by toasting raw pecans, which took less than 10 minutes in the oven to become deeply fragrant. The sweetly spiced coating is what takes these nuts to the next level, so we wanted to ensure that the spices and sugar stuck to the nuts without clumping or leaving a sticky mess. Common methods call for boiling the nuts, tossing them with butter, or coating them with an egg white mixture to get the spices to stick, but what worked best for us was stirring the pecans into a light glaze made from a very small amount of liquid (we liked the headiness of rum, but you can use water if preferred), butter, and brown sugar, with a little vanilla extract for depth. This left the nuts just tacky enough to pick up an even, light coating when tossed with the spice mixture.

2 cups raw pecan halves

SPICE MIX

2 tablespoons sugar
¾ teaspoon table salt
½ teaspoon ground cinnamon
⅛ teaspoon ground cloves
⅛ teaspoon ground allspice

RUM GLAZE

1 tablespoon rum, preferably dark, or water
1 tablespoon unsalted butter
2 teaspoons vanilla extract
1 teaspoon brown sugar

1. Adjust oven rack to middle position and heat oven to 350 degrees. Line rimmed baking sheet with parchment paper and spread pecans on it in even layer. Toast until pecans are fragrant and color deepens slightly, about 8 minutes, rotating sheet halfway through toasting. Transfer baking sheet with nuts to wire rack.

2. FOR THE SPICE MIX While nuts toast, combine all ingredients in medium bowl and set aside.

3. FOR THE RUM GLAZE Bring all ingredients to boil in medium saucepan over medium-high heat, whisking constantly. Stir in pecans and cook, stirring constantly with wooden spoon, until almost all liquid has evaporated, about 1½ minutes.

4. Transfer pecans to bowl with spice mix and toss well to coat. Return pecans to parchment-lined baking sheet and let cool completely before serving. (Spiced nuts can be stored in airtight container at room temperature for up to 5 days.)

Chocolate Granola

Makes about 9 cups · MAKE AHEAD · VEGETARIAN
Total Time 1 hour, plus 1 hour cooling

WHY THIS RECIPE WORKS Who could turn down homemade chocolate granola? Not us. We wanted the focus to be squarely on the chocolate, so we kept the other ingredients basic: just oats, maple syrup and brown sugar for complex sweetness, vanilla and salt for depth, vegetable oil to help the oats clump together and crisp, and walnuts for crunch and subtle balancing bitterness. We stirred cocoa powder into the wet ingredients before adding the oats and walnuts to ensure that each and every oat picked up chocolate flavor. We waited to add the chopped chocolate until after baking so the pieces would stay intact and give each bite of granola an intense chocolaty burst. We firmly packed the mixture into a rimmed baking sheet before popping it into the oven; after the baked granola cooled, we were able to break it up into large, satisfying, crunchy clusters. Do not use quick oats here. Chop the nuts and chocolate by hand for even texture.

½ cup vegetable oil
⅓ cup maple syrup
⅓ cup (1 ounce) unsweetened cocoa powder
⅓ cup packed (2⅓ ounces) light brown sugar
4 teaspoons vanilla extract
½ teaspoon table salt
5 cups (15 ounces) old-fashioned rolled oats
2 cups (8 ounces) walnuts, chopped
6 ounces bittersweet or semisweet chocolate, chopped

1. Adjust oven rack to upper-middle position and heat oven to 325 degrees. Line rimmed baking sheet with parchment paper and spray with vegetable oil spray.

2. Whisk oil, maple syrup, cocoa, sugar, vanilla, and salt together in large bowl. Fold in oats and walnuts until thoroughly combined.

3. Transfer oat mixture to prepared sheet and spread across entire surface of sheet in even layer. Using stiff metal spatula, press down firmly on oat mixture until very compact. Bake until fragrant and granola gives little resistance when pressed, 35 to 40 minutes, rotating sheet halfway through baking.

4. Transfer sheet to wire rack and let granola cool completely, about 1 hour. Break cooled granola into pieces of desired size and transfer to large bowl. Add chocolate and gently toss to combine. Serve. (Granola can be stored in airtight container at room temperature for up to 2 weeks.)

Cherry-Almond Chocolate Granola

Substitute whole almonds for walnuts. Add 1 cup chopped dried cherries to granola with chocolate.

Coconut-Cashew Chocolate Granola

Substitute raw cashews for walnuts. Add 1 cup unsweetened flaked coconut to granola with chocolate.

Chocolate Truffles

Makes 24 truffles · MAKE AHEAD · VEGETARIAN
Total Time 20 minutes, plus 1¾ hours chilling

WHY THIS RECIPE WORKS Bite-size and decadently rich, chocolate truffles are elegant and irresistible treats. But making the chocolate ganache base, waiting for it to firm up, shaping it into balls, waiting again, and coating the balls with cocoa or nuts can take up an entire afternoon. We came up with a method that produced two dozen truffles with just 20 minutes of hands-on time and a couple short chilling periods. To start, we made a supersimple ganache with just bittersweet chocolate, heavy cream, and salt (the salt amplified the chocolate's complex flavors). For the silkiest ganache, we used a rubber spatula to carefully combine the ingredients, since the spatula didn't incorporate a lot of air into the mix. Some recipes call for cooling the ganache for as long as 4 hours before shaping it into balls, but we found that just 45 minutes in the refrigerator was enough. After we portioned out the mixture using a teaspoon measure, a short 30-minute chilling period firmed the ganache before we rolled it quickly into truffles. Wear latex gloves when forming the truffles to keep your hands clean.

¼ cup (¾ ounce) unsweetened cocoa powder
1 tablespoon confectioners' sugar
8 ounces bittersweet chocolate, chopped fine
½ cup heavy cream
Pinch table salt

Chocolate Truffles

Chocolate-Almond Truffles

Substitute 1 cup sliced almonds, toasted and chopped fine, for cocoa mixture coating. Add ½ teaspoon almond extract to chocolate mixture before microwaving in step 1.

Chocolate-Spice Truffles

Sift ¼ teaspoon ground cinnamon with cocoa powder and sugar for coating. Add 1 teaspoon ground cinnamon and ⅛ teaspoon cayenne pepper to chocolate mixture before microwaving in step 1.

Chocolate-Ginger Truffles

Add 2 teaspoons ground ginger to chocolate mixture before microwaving in step 1.

Chocolate-Lemon Truffles

Add 1 teaspoon grated lemon zest to chocolate mixture before microwaving in step 1.

Wintermint Bark

Makes about 1 pound MAKE AHEAD   VEGETARIAN
Total Time 20 minutes, plus 1 hour chilling

WHY THIS RECIPE WORKS The red, green, and white colors and festive flavors of this simple confection make it a perfect holiday gift. Anything but fussy to make, it requires a mere three ingredients and a straightforward method. Making the bark was as simple as melting white bar chocolate; stirring in green pistachios and crunchy, cooling bits of crushed peppermint candies; and then allowing the bark to firm up in the refrigerator. Lining a baking pan with an aluminum foil sling before spreading the white chocolate mixture over the bottom ensured that we had an easy way to lift the cooled bark out of the pan without risking breaking it into pieces. For more information on making a foil sling, see page 225. Unsalted pumpkin seeds can be substituted for the pistachios.

  1 cup unsalted pistachios
  1 pound white chocolate, chopped
  12 round red-and-white-striped hard peppermint candies, crushed in food processor

1. Sift cocoa and sugar through fine-mesh strainer into pie plate. Microwave chocolate, cream, and salt in bowl at 50 percent power, stirring occasionally with rubber spatula, until melted, about 1 minute. Stir truffle mixture until fully combined; transfer to 8-inch square baking dish and refrigerate until set, about 45 minutes.

2. Using heaping teaspoon measure, scoop truffle mixture into 24 portions, transfer to large plate, and refrigerate until firm, about 30 minutes. Roll each truffle between your hands to form uniform balls (balls needn't be perfect).

3. Transfer truffles to cocoa mixture and roll to evenly coat. Lightly shake truffles in your hand over pie plate to remove excess coating and transfer to platter. Refrigerate for 30 minutes. Let stand at room temperature for 10 minutes before serving. (Truffles can be refrigerated along with excess cocoa mixture in airtight container for up to 1 week. Shake truffles in your hand to remove excess coating and let stand at room temperature for 10 minutes before serving.)

1. Make foil sling for 8-inch square baking pan by folding 2 long sheets of aluminum foil so each is 8 inches wide. Lay sheets of foil in pan perpendicular to each other, with extra foil hanging over edges of pan. Push foil into corners and up sides of pan, smoothing foil flush to pan.

2. Microwave chocolate in bowl at 50 percent power, stirring occasionally with rubber spatula, until melted and smooth, 2 to 4 minutes. Stir pistachios into chocolate, scrape mixture into prepared pan, and smooth top. Sprinkle peppermint candies on top and refrigerate until firm, about 1 hour.

3. Using foil overhang, remove bark from pan and transfer to cutting board. Peel away and discard foil. Cut bark into rough chunks with chef's knife and serve. (Pieces can be layered between waxed paper in airtight container and refrigerated for up to 2 weeks.)

Rocky Road Bark

Makes 16 pieces | **Total Time** 1 hour
`MAKE AHEAD`

WHY THIS RECIPE WORKS This playful bark incorporates all the elements of rocky road candy. We used nutty-tasting graham crackers as the bark's base, fitting them into a baking pan in a single layer. Instead of making caramel on the stovetop, we poured a mixture of melted butter and just-dissolved brown sugar over the crackers and then popped the pan into the oven, where the even heat turned the butter-sugar mixture into an easy caramel. The caramel's bubbling was our visual cue that it would set to just the right texture. We then scattered finely chopped chocolate over the still-hot surface to melt and sprinkled on mini marshmallows and pecans to give the bark pleasant chew, buttery crunch, and the rocky appearance suggested by the candy's name. For more information on making a foil sling, see page 225. You can substitute 1 cup semisweet chocolate chips for the semisweet chocolate. Since graham cracker sizes can vary slightly from brand to brand, use the amount necessary to fit the pan.

5–6 whole graham crackers
   6 tablespoons unsalted butter
   ¼ cup packed (1¾ ounces) light brown sugar
   ½ teaspoon table salt
   6 ounces semisweet chocolate, chopped fine
   ¾ cup mini marshmallows
   ½ cup pecans, walnuts, or almonds, toasted and chopped

Wintermint Bark

Rocky Road Bark

1. Adjust oven rack to middle position and heat oven to 375 degrees. Make foil sling for 8-inch square baking pan by folding 2 long sheets of aluminum foil so each is 8 inches wide. Lay sheets of foil in pan perpendicular to each other, with extra foil hanging over edges of pan. Push foil into corners and up sides of pan, smoothing foil flush to pan.

2. Line bottom of pan with single layer of graham crackers, breaking them as needed to fit. Cook butter, sugar, and salt together in small saucepan over low heat, stirring constantly, until butter is melted and sugar has dissolved, about 2 minutes. Pour mixture over graham crackers and smooth with spatula to cover crackers completely. Bake until caramel is bubbling, about 8 minutes.

3. Transfer pan to wire rack, sprinkle chocolate over caramel, and let melt for 5 minutes. Using spatula, smooth chocolate into even layer. Sprinkle with marshmallows and nuts and press lightly to adhere. Freeze, uncovered, until chocolate has hardened, about 13 minutes.

4. Using foil overhang, remove bark from pan and transfer to cutting board. Peel away and discard foil. Cut bark into 16 squares and serve, or transfer to refrigerator until serving time. (Pieces can be layered between waxed paper in airtight container and refrigerated for up to 2 weeks.)

Chocolate Fudge

Makes about 3 pounds | **Total Time** 40 minutes, plus 4 hours cooling and chilling MAKE AHEAD

WHY THIS RECIPE WORKS Whether you're looking for a thoughtful gift for the person who has everything or just want to satisfy your own sweet tooth, you can't go wrong with a box of fudge. We were after a creamy, rich, ultrachocolaty fudge that didn't take hours or an arm workout to put together. Cooking a brown sugar syrup to a temperature between 234 and 238 degrees (what candymakers call "soft-ball stage") ensured fudge that was firm yet pliable after cooling. Marshmallows guaranteed a smooth, melt-in-your-mouth texture. Bittersweet, rather than milk or unsweetened, chocolate was sweet enough to taste like candy but also deeply and satisfyingly chocolaty. For more information on making a foil sling, see page 225. You will need a digital or candy thermometer for this recipe. You can substitute semi-sweet chocolate bars or bars labeled "dark chocolate" for the bittersweet chocolate, but we do not recommend using chocolate that's 85 percent cacao or higher. If you're using an electric stove, the mixture will likely take longer than 5 minutes to reach 234 degrees in step 2.

3 cups packed (21 ounces) light brown sugar
12 tablespoons unsalted butter, cut into 12 pieces
⅔ cup evaporated milk
½ teaspoon table salt
12 ounces bittersweet chocolate, chopped
5 ounces large marshmallows (about 3 cups)
1½ cups walnuts, toasted and chopped coarse (optional)

1. Make foil sling for 8-inch square baking pan by folding 2 long sheets of aluminum foil so each is 8 inches wide. Lay sheets of foil in pan perpendicular to each other, with extra foil hanging over edges of pan. Push foil into corners and up sides of pan, smoothing foil flush to pan. Spray foil with vegetable oil spray.

2. Combine sugar, butter, evaporated milk, and salt in large saucepan. Bring to boil over medium-high heat, stirring frequently. Once boiling, reduce heat to medium-low and simmer, stirring frequently, until mixture registers 234 degrees, 3 to 5 minutes.

3. Off heat, add chocolate and marshmallows and whisk until smooth and all marshmallows are fully melted, about 2 minutes (fudge will thicken to consistency of frosting). Stir in walnuts, if using. Transfer mixture to prepared pan. Let cool completely, about 2 hours. Cover and refrigerate until set, about 2 hours.

4. Using foil overhang, lift fudge out of pan and transfer to cutting board. Peel away and discard foil. Cut into 1-inch cubes. Let stand at room temperature for 15 minutes before serving. (Fudge can be stored in airtight container at room temperature for up to 2 weeks.)

Chocolate-Peppermint Fudge

Omit walnuts. Add 1 teaspoon peppermint extract with chocolate and marshmallows in step 3. After transferring fudge to prepared pan, sprinkle with ¼ cup crushed soft peppermint candies before letting fudge cool.

Chocolate-Toffee Fudge

Omit walnuts. Add 1½ tablespoons instant espresso powder with chocolate and marshmallows in step 3. Stir ¼ cup Heath Toffee Bits into fudge before transferring to prepared pan. After transferring fudge to prepared pan, sprinkle with additional ¼ cup toffee bits before letting fudge cool.

Oreo Mint Balls

Makes 15 balls | **Total Time** 45 minutes

MAKE AHEAD VEGETARIAN

WHY THIS RECIPE WORKS We took one of America's most recognizable cookies and transformed it into something completely different: a no-bake treat that's part cookie and part candy. We reached for Oreo Mint Creme cookies for a cookie ball that was both richly chocolaty and cooling, mixing the ground Oreos with cream cheese and then rolling the mixture into balls. After the balls spent 20 minutes in the freezer, they were firm enough to dip in chocolate. We melted the chocolate in the microwave along with a little oil, which gave the coating a velvety consistency. After we dipped them, we quickly topped the balls with sprinkles before the chocolate had a chance to set and returned them to the freezer again until the chocolate hardened. The end result? Tasty, minty, adorable little treats sure to disappear in as little time as they take to make. For the proper texture, be sure to serve the mint balls chilled. You can substitute 1 cup semisweet chocolate chips for the semisweet chocolate, but we found bar chocolate to melt more consistently.

14 Oreo Mint Creme cookies
 3 ounces cream cheese, softened
 6 ounces semisweet chocolate, chopped
1½ tablespoons vegetable oil
 1 tablespoon green sprinkles

1. Line large plate with parchment paper. Process cookies in food processor until finely ground, about 1 minute. Stir cream cheese and cookies in bowl until uniform. Roll mixture into fifteen 1-inch balls and space them evenly on prepared plate. Freeze, uncovered, until firm, about 20 minutes.

2. Microwave chocolate and oil in bowl at 50 percent power, stirring occasionally, until melted and smooth, 2 to 4 minutes. Using toothpick, dip mint ball into melted chocolate to coat, letting excess chocolate drip back into bowl. Return mint ball to plate, remove toothpick, and immediately decorate with sprinkles. Repeat with remaining mint balls and chocolate. Freeze mint balls, uncovered, until chocolate has hardened, about 10 minutes. Store in refrigerator until ready to serve. (Oreo balls can be refrigerated in airtight container for up to 1 week.)

Chocolate-Peppermint Fudge

Oreo Mint Balls

Bourbon Balls

2½ cups (6 ounces) vanilla wafers
  1 cup pecans, toasted
 ½ cup (2 ounces) confectioners' sugar
  6 tablespoons bourbon
  3 tablespoons light corn syrup
1½ tablespoons unsweetened cocoa powder
 ½ cup granulated sugar

1. Process vanilla wafers and pecans in food processor until finely ground, about 15 seconds; transfer to large bowl. Stir in confectioners' sugar, bourbon, corn syrup, and cocoa.

2. Spread granulated sugar in shallow dish. Working with 1 heaping tablespoon at a time, roll wafer mixture into balls, then roll in granulated sugar to coat. Transfer balls to large plate and refrigerate until firm, at least 1 hour, before serving. (Bourbon balls can be refrigerated in airtight container for up to 1 week.)

White Chocolate–Coconut Candies

Makes 30 balls | **Total Time** 1 hour
MAKE AHEAD   VEGETARIAN

WHY THIS RECIPE WORKS Combining coconut, white chocolate, and almonds, these irresistible bites are a perfect present for the sweet-toothed among us. A splash of bourbon gives the no-cook candies a grown-up vibe. We created the candies' no-fuss filling by microwaving white chocolate with cream, essentially making a rich, smooth white chocolate ganache. After stirring in the almonds and bourbon, we poured the mixture into a baking pan and transferred it to the freezer to firm up. To make even-size candies, we cut the firmed ganache into squares before rolling each piece into a ball. Finally, rolling the balls in finely processed toasted coconut gave them an attractive golden-flaked finish. For more information on making a foil sling, see page 225. You can use either white bar chocolate or white chocolate chips, but we found bar chocolate to melt more consistently. The balls will soften as they sit, so it's best to serve them chilled.

  2 tablespoons toasted slivered almonds
1⅓ cups (4 ounces) sweetened shredded
    coconut, toasted
  8 ounces white chocolate, chopped
 ¼ cup heavy cream
  1 tablespoon bourbon or dark rum

Bourbon Balls

Makes about 24 balls MAKE AHEAD   VEGETARIAN
Total Time 20 minutes, plus 1 hour chilling

WHY THIS RECIPE WORKS There are many things to love about these truffle-like treats, from how quick and easy they are to make (no eggs, no butter, and no baking) to the fact that almost all their ingredients are common pantry items. Oh, and the adult appeal of their unmistakable bourbon flavor doesn't hurt, either. The combination of ground vanilla wafers and toasted nuts contributed a unique crunch, which helped distinguish these confections from most candies. The sweet, buttery flavor of pecans was a perfect match for the caramel-y, slightly smoky notes of the bourbon. A small amount of cocoa powder brought bittersweet complexity (and helped bind the mixture) without making the bourbon balls taste chocolaty. Since these treats aren't baked, granulated or brown sugar wouldn't have a chance to melt, so we used confectioners' sugar to sweeten the balls without making them gritty. But we welcomed a little crunch on the exterior, so the finishing touch was a roll in sparkly granulated sugar.

1. Make foil sling for 8-inch square baking pan by folding 2 long sheets of aluminum foil so each is 8 inches wide. Lay sheets of foil in pan perpendicular to each other, with extra foil hanging over edges of pan. Push foil into corners and up sides of pan, smoothing foil flush to pan.

2. Process almonds in food processor to fine crumbs, about 15 seconds; transfer to bowl. Process coconut in food processor to fine crumbs, about 15 seconds; spread in shallow dish.

3. Combine chocolate and cream in large bowl. Microwave, covered, at 50 percent power, stirring occasionally, until melted and smooth, about 2 minutes. Stir in bourbon and almonds. Transfer mixture to prepared pan and press firmly into even layer with greased spatula. Freeze, uncovered, for 15 minutes.

4. Using foil overhang, lift chilled mixture out of pan and transfer to cutting board. Peel away and discard foil. Cut into 30 squares, then roll squares into balls. Roll balls in coconut to coat and transfer to platter. Freeze, uncovered, until firm, about 10 minutes. Store in refrigerator until ready to serve. (Candies can be refrigerated in airtight container for up to 1 week.)

Caramel Apples

Makes 6 apples | **Total Time** 35 minutes

`MAKE AHEAD` `VEGETARIAN`

WHY THIS RECIPE WORKS No take on the iconic pairing of apple and caramel is as whimsical as a chewy caramel apple. We knew that the caramel would be the sticking point (perhaps literally): It needed to be firm enough to cling to the apples, but soft enough that we could take a bite without our teeth getting lodged. Starting by melting down soft-yet-set caramel candies ensured that the caramel would firm up into the same ideal consistency when it cooled. Since the apples last for up to three days after they're made, they make a great party favor—and you can watch your friends' faces light up when they catch a glimpse of the nostalgic treats. We used Granny Smiths in this recipe, but you can substitute any apple variety. You will need six Popsicle sticks for this recipe. If you can't find Popsicle sticks at the grocery store, check a craft store.

- 6 Granny Smith apples, stems removed
- 1 (14-ounce) bag caramel candies
- 2 tablespoons water
- 1 cup dry-roasted peanuts, chopped (optional)

1. Insert Popsicle stick into stem end of each apple and set aside. Line rimmed baking sheet with parchment paper, coat parchment with vegetable oil spray, and set aside.

Caramel Apples

2. Combine caramels and water in double boiler or in bowl set over saucepan filled with inch of water. Cook over medium-low heat, stirring occasionally, until caramels have melted to smooth consistency, about 10 minutes.

3. Dip apples, one at a time, into caramel, spooning caramel over apple to ensure even coverage. Allow excess caramel to drip back into double boiler. Transfer apples to prepared baking sheet and sprinkle with peanuts, if using. Let cool for 15 minutes before serving. (Coated apples can be stored in airtight container and refrigerated for up to 3 days.)

Chocolate-Caramel Apples

Once caramel apples have cooled, microwave 8 ounces chopped bittersweet chocolate in medium bowl, whisking often, until melted and smooth, 1 to 3 minutes. Carefully tilt bowl and dip caramel apples, one at a time, into chocolate, spooning chocolate over apple to ensure even coverage. Transfer chocolate-covered caramel apples back to baking sheet and refrigerate until chocolate sets, about 30 minutes.

Homemade Almond Butter

Chocolate-Hazelnut
Spread

Homemade Almond Butter

Makes 2¼ cups | **Total Time** 1 hour
`MAKE AHEAD` `VEGETARIAN`

WHY THIS RECIPE WORKS A jar of homemade nut butter, customized as desired with your choice of nut and optional ground spices, is a wonderful gift for friends who don't know how simple it is to make using a food processor. Roasting the nuts prior to processing them boosted their flavor and also warmed their oils so they broke down more quickly. Salt brought out more flavor, and a single teaspoon of honey added light sweetness. You can use blanched, skin-on, raw, or preroasted almonds here, but do not use salted almonds. You can customize your almond butter by adding ¼ to ½ teaspoon of ground cinnamon, nutmeg, or ginger or ⅛ teaspoon of cayenne pepper to the almonds before processing in step 2.

    4 cups (1¼ pounds) whole almonds
    1 teaspoon honey, plus extra for seasoning
    ¾ teaspoon kosher salt

1. Adjust oven rack to middle position and heat oven to 375 degrees. Spread almonds in single layer on rimmed baking sheet and roast until fragrant and slightly darkened, 10 to 12 minutes, rotating sheet halfway through roasting. (If using preroasted almonds, place in oven for 5 minutes to warm.) Transfer sheet to wire rack and let almonds cool slightly, about 10 minutes.

2. Process almonds in food processor until oil is released and paste begins to form, scraping down sides of bowl often. Add honey and salt and continue to process to desired smoothness, 18 to 20 minutes. Season with extra honey and salt to taste. If butter is thicker than desired, thin by adding vegetable oil, 1 teaspoon at a time, pulsing 3 times after each addition, until desired consistency is reached. If butter is thinner than desired, thicken by adding water, 1 teaspoon at a time, pulsing 3 times after each addition, until desired consistency is reached. Transfer to jar with tight-fitting lid. (Butter can be stored at room temperature or refrigerated for up to 2 months.)

Homemade Pistachio Butter

You can use raw or preroasted pistachios here, but do not use salted pistachios. Substitute 4 cups (1¼ pounds) shelled pistachios for almonds.

Homemade Pecan Butter

You can use raw or preroasted pecans here, but do not use salted pecans. Substitute 4 cups (1 pound) pecans for almonds.

Homemade Cashew Butter

You can use raw or preroasted cashews here, but do not use salted cashews. Substitute 4 cups (1¼ pounds) cashews for almonds.

Homemade Peanut Butter

You can use raw or preroasted peanuts here, but do not use salted peanuts. Substitute 4 cups (1¼ pounds) peanuts for almonds.

Homemade Hazelnut Butter

You can use raw or preroasted hazelnuts here, but do not use salted hazelnuts. Substitute 4 cups (1 pound) hazelnuts for almonds.

Chocolate-Hazelnut Spread

Makes 1½ cups | **Total Time** 45 minutes

MAKE AHEAD VEGETARIAN

WHY THIS RECIPE WORKS Nutella, the queen of nut butters, brims with toasty nuttiness and is richly chocolaty and silky-smooth—a morning-treat favorite spread on toast or rolled up in a sweet crepe. But once you taste our home-made version, you'll realize that the stuff from the store is actually a little plasticky and wan. Our not-too-sweet chocolate-hazelnut spread is made using freshly toasted hazelnuts, intense unsweetened cocoa powder, and a food processor. Hazelnut skins can mar the smooth texture of the spread, so we blanched the nuts in a baking soda solution; after blanching, we were easily able to rub off the skins using a kitchen towel. A quick roast in the oven toasted the hazelnuts and warmed their fragrant oils, promoting a quicker break-down in the food processor. A bit of vanilla and salt accented the main flavors. Hazelnut oil is available in high-end grocery stores and gourmet shops. Walnut oil also works well. If you cannot find either, use vegetable oil.

  2 cups hazelnuts
  6 tablespoons baking soda
  1 cup (4 ounces) confectioners' sugar
  ⅓ cup (1 ounce) unsweetened cocoa powder
  2 tablespoons hazelnut oil
  1 teaspoon vanilla extract
  ⅛ teaspoon table salt

1. Adjust oven rack to middle position and heat oven to 375 degrees. Fill large bowl halfway with ice and water. Bring 4 cups water to boil. Add hazelnuts and baking soda and boil for 3 minutes. Transfer hazelnuts to ice bath with slotted spoon, drain, and rub skins off with kitchen towel.

2. Place hazelnuts in single layer on rimmed baking sheet and roast until fragrant and golden brown, 12 to 15 minutes, rotating sheet halfway through roasting.

3. Process hazelnuts in food processor until oil is released and smooth, loose paste forms, about 5 minutes, scraping down sides of bowl often.

4. Add sugar, cocoa, oil, vanilla, and salt and process until fully incorporated and mixture begins to loosen slightly and becomes glossy, about 2 minutes, scraping down sides of bowl as needed. (Spread can be stored at room temperature or refrigerated for up to 1 month.)

Hot Fudge Sauce

Makes about 2 cups | **Total Time** 20 minutes

MAKE AHEAD VEGETARIAN

WHY THIS RECIPE WORKS Treat the chocolate lovers in your life to a jar of intensely chocolaty homemade hot fudge sauce and they may never be able to go back to the store-bought stuff. This luxurious, grown-up sauce instantly transforms a simple scoop of ice cream into a decadent dessert. Dense and rich, the sauce relies of cocoa powder and unsweetened chocolate for its wallop of chocolate flavor. We added just enough sugar to temper the chocolate's bitterness without making the sauce too sweet. Cream dulled the chocolate's flavor, so instead we used milk and butter, which gave the sauce an attractive sheen. The result was a fudge sauce so irresistibly chocolaty that you may decide to keep it all for yourself.

  1¼ cups (8¾ ounces) sugar
  ⅔ cup whole milk
  ¼ teaspoon table salt
  ⅓ cup (1 ounce) unsweetened cocoa powder, sifted
  3 ounces unsweetened chocolate, chopped fine
  4 tablespoons unsalted butter, cut into 8 pieces and chilled
  1 teaspoon vanilla extract

1. Heat sugar, milk, and salt in medium saucepan over medium-low heat, whisking gently, until sugar has dissolved, and liquid starts to bubble around edges of saucepan, about 6 minutes. Reduce heat to low, add cocoa, and whisk until smooth.

2. Off heat, stir in chocolate and let stand for 3 minutes. Whisk sauce until smooth and chocolate is fully melted. Whisk in butter and vanilla until fully incorporated and sauce thickens slightly. (Sauce can be refrigerated for up to 1 month; gently warm in microwave, stirring every 10 seconds, until pourable, before using.)

Sugar Cookie Mix

Makes 42 ounces mix; enough for 48 cookies
Total Time for Mix 10 minutes | **Total Time for Cookies Made from Mix** 35 minutes, plus 30 minutes cooling `MAKE AHEAD` `VEGETARIAN`

WHY THIS RECIPE WORKS A homemade dry cookie mix is a casual home baker's secret weapon. The ingredients are fresher and simpler than those in most store-bought mixes, and since the dry ingredients are premeasured and the wet ingredients are kitchen staples, you're just a few steps away from freshly baked cookies at any given moment. (It also makes a wonderful holiday favor for a sweet-toothed friend.) When you're ready for cookies, you simply measure out some of the mix (all-purpose flour, sugar, salt, baking soda, and vanilla powder), combine it with butter and an egg, and reap the rewards: fresh, crisp, vanilla-scented sugar cookies. You can find vanilla powder in the baking aisle at some grocery stores, or you can order it online. If you can't find vanilla powder, you can add 1 teaspoon vanilla extract along with the melted butter and egg when baking a batch of cookies. If giving this mix as a gift, be sure to include instructions for baking the cookies; see steps 3 through 5.

SUGAR COOKIE MIX
    4 cups (20 ounces) all-purpose flour
    3 cups (21 ounces) sugar
    1 teaspoon table salt
    4 teaspoons vanilla powder
    1 teaspoon baking soda

COOKIES
    4 tablespoons unsalted butter, melted and cooled
    1 large egg
1½ cups (10 ounces) Sugar Cookie Mix

Sugar Cookie Mix

1. **FOR THE SUGAR COOKIE MIX** In extra-large bowl, combine flour, sugar, and salt. Whisk until well combined. Set fine-mesh strainer over bowl. Add vanilla powder and baking soda to fine-mesh strainer and tap side of strainer to sift mixture into bowl.

2. Whisk until very well combined, about 1 minute. Transfer cookie mix to large airtight storage container. (Cookie mix can be stored at room temperature for at least 2 months.)

3. **TO MAKE ONE BATCH OF COOKIES** Adjust oven rack to middle position and heat oven to 325 degrees. Line rimmed baking sheet with parchment paper.

4. In large bowl, whisk melted butter and egg until combined. Add cookie mix and use rubber spatula to stir and press mixture until soft dough forms and no dry mix is visible. Use your hands to roll dough into 12 balls (about 1 heaping tablespoon each). Place dough balls on prepared baking sheet, leaving space between them.

5. Use your fingers to gently press and flatten each dough ball into 2-inch-wide circle. Bake until edges of cookies are just beginning to brown and centers are still soft, 14 to 16 minutes. Let cookies cool completely on sheet on cooling rack, about 30 minutes. Serve.

Chocolate Layer Cake Mix

Makes 64 ounces mix; enough for 3 layer cakes
Total Time for Mix 10 minutes | **Total Time for Cake**
Made from Mix 1¼ hours, plus 1 hour cooling

`MAKE AHEAD` `VEGETARIAN`

WHY THIS RECIPE WORKS This chocolate cake mix is the
ideal present for someone accustomed to using store-bought
mixes to satisfy their dessert cravings. The method is much the
same, but the flavor difference made by using fresh ingredients
won't escape their notice. We whipped up the shelf-stable mix
using all-purpose flour, sugar, Dutch-processed cocoa powder
(cocoa powder that's treated with an alkali to darken its
color and mellow its more astringent notes), salt, and baking
powder and soda for leavening. When we were ready to bake,
we simply stirred in the wet ingredients (milk, oil, and eggs),
divided the batter between two cake pans, and popped both
into the oven. If giving this mix as a gift, be sure to include
instructions for baking the cake; see steps 3 through 7.
Before measuring out the dry cake mix to make the cake,
give the mixture a whisk inside the container to ensure that
the ingredients are evenly distributed. For a playful touch,
you can decorate the assembled cake with sprinkles.

Chocolate
Layer Cake Mix

CHOCOLATE LAYER CAKE MIX

4½ cups (22½ ounces) all-purpose flour
4½ cups (31½ ounces) sugar
3 cups (9 ounces) Dutch-processed cocoa powder
1½ teaspoons table salt
1 tablespoon baking powder
1½ teaspoons baking soda

CAKE

1½ cups (12 ounces) milk
¾ cup vegetable oil
2 large eggs
3¼ cups (21 ounces) Chocolate Layer Cake Mix
5 cups store-bought vanilla frosting

1. FOR THE CHOCOLATE LAYER CAKE MIX In
extra-large bowl, whisk flour, sugar, cocoa, and salt until
well combined. Set fine-mesh strainer over bowl. Add baking
powder and baking soda to fine-mesh strainer and tap side
of strainer to sift mixture into bowl.

2. Whisk until very well combined, about 1 minute.
Transfer cake mix to large airtight storage container. (Cake
mix can be stored at room temperature for at least 2 months.)

3. TO MAKE ONE 9-INCH LAYER CAKE Adjust oven
rack to middle position and heat oven to 325 degrees. Grease
two 9-inch round cake pans and line with parchment paper.

4. In large bowl, whisk milk, oil, and eggs until combined.
Add cake mix and stir until just combined and no dry mix is
visible. Divide batter evenly between prepared cake pans and
smooth tops.

5. Bake until toothpick inserted in center of each cake
comes out clean, 34 to 36 minutes. Place cake pans on cooling
rack and let cakes cool completely in pans, about 1 hour.

6. Run butter knife around edge of cakes to loosen them
from pans. Remove cakes from pans and discard parchment.
Place 1 cake layer on serving platter or cake stand. Spread
1 cup frosting over top of cake. Top with second cake layer
and press down gently to set.

7. Spread remaining 4 cups frosting evenly over top and
sides of cake. To smooth frosting, run edge of offset spatula
around cake sides and over top. Serve.

Hot Chocolate Mix

Vanilla Extract

Hot Chocolate Mix

Makes 3 cups mix; enough for twelve 1-cup servings
Total Time for Mix 10 minutes | **Total Time for Hot Chocolate Made from Mix** 10 minutes

`MAKE AHEAD` `VEGETARIAN`

WHY THIS RECIPE WORKS A steaming mug of hot chocolate is bliss on a cold day and the perfect beverage for sipping on a cozy night in with a book. Preparing a home-made mix ahead of time means that at a moment's notice you can make yourself a mug of hot chocolate that's deeper and more intensely chocolaty than any version made with a store-bought mix. To this end, we used unsweetened choco-late, not just cocoa powder, in the mix. The cocoa butter in the unsweetened chocolate gave the hot chocolate a lush, not dusty, texture. Whizzing the chocolate in the food processor along with the other mix ingredients broke it up into tiny pieces that melted instantly when stirred into hot milk. If giving this mix as a gift, be sure to include instructions for making the hot chocolate; see step 2. You can use skim milk to make the hot chocolate, but the hot chocolate will not be as rich.

HOT CHOCOLATE MIX

  1 cup (7 ounces) sugar
  6 ounces unsweetened chocolate, chopped fine
  1 cup (3 ounces) unsweetened cocoa powder
  ½ cup (1½ ounces) nonfat dry milk powder
  5 teaspoons cornstarch
  1 teaspoon vanilla extract
  ¾ teaspoon kosher salt

HOT CHOCOLATE

  1 cup milk
  ¼ cup Hot Chocolate Mix
     Whipped cream (optional)
     Marshmallows (optional)

1. FOR THE HOT CHOCOLATE MIX Process all ingredients in food processor until ground to powder, 30 to 60 seconds. Transfer to airtight storage container. (Mix can be stored at room temperature for up to 2 months.)

2. TO MAKE ONE SERVING OF HOT CHOCOLATE Heat milk in small saucepan over medium heat until it starts to steam and bubbles appear around edge of saucepan. Add hot chocolate mix and continue to heat, whisking constantly, until mixture is simmering, 2 to 3 minutes. Pour hot chocolate into mug and serve with whipped cream or marshmallows, if desired.

Malted Hot Chocolate Mix

Substitute malted milk powder for nonfat dry milk powder and reduce sugar to ¾ cup.

Mexican Hot Chocolate Mix

Add 1 teaspoon ground cinnamon, ¾ teaspoon ancho chile powder, and pinch cayenne pepper to processor with other ingredients.

Mint Hot Chocolate Mix

Substitute mint extract for vanilla.

Mocha Hot Chocolate Mix

Add ⅓ cup instant espresso powder to processor with other ingredients.

Vanilla Extract

Makes 1 cup MAKE AHEAD VEGETARIAN
Total Time 10 minutes, plus 6 weeks steeping

WHY THIS RECIPE WORKS Making vanilla extract at home gives you the ability to customize this essential baking ingredient. Want to experiment with subtle flavor profiles? Try making several batches using different types of beans. Want a more assertive vanilla flavor? Steep the beans in the alcohol (we used neutral-tasting vodka) for longer to extract more flavor. Splitting the pods and scraping out the beans helped speed along the extraction process, as did gently heating the vodka. Since the seeds and pod settled to the bottom of the jar after a while, shaking the jar weekly encouraged more full and even extraction. For a classic, all-purpose extract, use Madagascar vanilla beans. Tahitian beans will produce a more floral extract, and Mexican beans one that's bolder. The longer the mixture sits in step 2, the fuller the flavor will be.

 8 vanilla beans (1 ounce)
 1 cup vodka

1. Cut vanilla beans in half lengthwise. Using tip of paring knife or spoon, scrape out seeds and transfer to small saucepan. Cut bean pods into 1-inch pieces and add to saucepan. Add vodka, cover, and cook over medium-low heat until mixture is hot and steaming, about 2 minutes. (Caution: Do not open lid while pot is over flame or alcohol will ignite.)

2. Pour mixture into jar with tight-fitting lid and let cool completely. Cover with lid and store in dark place for at least 6 weeks or up to 10 weeks, shaking jar gently once a week.

3. Line fine-mesh strainer with 2 coffee filters and set over liquid measuring cup. Strain vanilla through filters, then transfer from measuring cup to clean jar with tight-fitting lid. (Vanilla extract will keep indefinitely.)

Sweet Vermouth

Makes about 32 ounces | **Total Time** 40 minutes, plus 12½ hours steeping and cooling
MAKE AHEAD VEGETARIAN

WHY THIS RECIPE WORKS Sweet vermouth plays a special role in defining how good (or how mediocre) many classic cocktails can be. For our homemade version, we added golden raisins for their concentrated fruity sweetness, and we emphasized the vermouth's warmer spices and floral flavors while keeping the herbal notes in balance. To sweeten the vermouth and enrich its color, we made an easy stovetop caramel syrup, adding it to our mixture of aromatized wine and vodka. We prefer to use Pinot Grigio (Pinot Gris in

Sweet Vermouth

French), but you can substitute your favorite unoaked dry white wine. You can purchase dried wormwood, chamomile flowers, hibiscus flowers, and quassia bark chips online or in specialty spice shops; look for chips that are approximately ¼ inch in size. The hibiscus flowers bring this vermouth closer to the garnet shade of commercial vermouths, but they may be omitted. For an accurate measurement of boiling water, bring a full kettle of water to a boil and then measure out the desired amount. You will need a quart-size glass jar with a tight-fitting lid for this recipe.

    6 ounces vodka
    ½ cup golden raisins, chopped
    2 (3-inch) strips orange zest
    1 bay leaf
    1 teaspoon dried wormwood
    1 teaspoon dried chamomile flowers
    6 juniper berries, lightly crushed
    ½ teaspoon quassia bark chips
    ½ teaspoon coriander seeds
    ½ teaspoon dried sage
    ½ teaspoon dried thyme
    ¼ teaspoon black peppercorns
    4 whole cloves
    2 green cardamom pods
    ½ star anise pod
    2 teaspoons dried hibiscus flowers (optional)
    6 ounces boiling water, divided
    ¾ cup sugar
    20 ounces Pinot Grigio

    1. Combine vodka, raisins, orange zest, bay leaf, wormwood, chamomile flowers, juniper berries, quassia bark chips, coriander seeds, sage, thyme, peppercorns, cloves, cardamom pods, and star anise pod in quart-size glass jar. Cover and store jar in cool, dark place for at least 12 hours or up to 24 hours.

    2. Set fine-mesh strainer in medium bowl and line with triple layer of cheesecloth. Strain vodka mixture through prepared strainer, pressing on solids to extract as much liquid as possible; discard solids. Set aside.

    3. If using hibiscus, combine flowers and 4 ounces boiling water in bowl and let steep for 5 minutes. Strain through fine-mesh strainer into separate bowl, pressing on solids to extract as much liquid as possible.

    4. Combine sugar and 2 ounces boiling water in medium saucepan. Bring to boil over medium-high heat and cook, without stirring, until mixture is amber-colored around edges of saucepan. Reduce heat to low and continue to cook, swirling

saucepan occasionally, until caramel is evenly dark amber, 3 to 5 minutes. Off heat, carefully whisk in either hibiscus tea or remaining 4 ounces boiling water (mixture will bubble and steam) until syrup is smooth. Immediately transfer caramel to large bowl and let cool completely, about 30 minutes.

    5. Add infused vodka, wine, and caramel to clean jar, cover, and gently shake to combine. (Vermouth can be refrigerated for up to 3 months. Shake gently before using.)

Limoncello

Makes about 32 ounces MAKE AHEAD VEGETARIAN
Total Time 45 minutes, plus 1 week steeping

WHY THIS RECIPE WORKS Italians often end grand, leisurely meals with a small chilled glass of this refreshing, palate-cleansing liqueur. Making limoncello is a simple process in which strips of lemon zest are steeped in a neutral-tasting spirit to extract the zest's flavors and aromas. Traditionally this takes a month or longer, but we wanted speedier gratification—without compromising flavor—so we turned to the blender. Because alcohol is so efficient at extracting soluble compounds from flavoring agents, we found that processing the zest with vodka in the blender served both to extract these flavor compounds mechanically and to create more surface area on which the alcohol could act to extract flavors more quickly. After just one week, our processed zest yielded as much flavor as strips that had been steeped for a month. Over time, a fine sediment of innocuous pith residue may form on the surface of the liqueur; if you like, repeat straining the liqueur through cheesecloth, or simply shake it. You will need a quart-size glass jar with a tight-fitting lid for this recipe.

    40 (3-inch) strips lemon zest (4 large lemons)
    10 ounces vodka
    1½ cups sugar
    18 ounces water

    1. Process lemon zest and vodka in blender until finely ground, about 30 seconds. Transfer mixture to quart-size glass jar. Cover and store in cool, dark place for 1 week, shaking mixture once every other day.

    2. Set fine-mesh strainer in medium bowl and line with triple layer of cheesecloth. Strain vodka mixture through prepared strainer, pressing on solids to extract as much liquid as possible; discard solids. Return infused vodka to clean jar.

3. Heat sugar and water in small saucepan over medium heat, whisking often, until sugar has dissolved, about 5 minutes; do not boil. Let cool completely, about 30 minutes; add to jar with vodka mixture. Cover and gently shake to combine. Refrigerate to chill before serving. (Limoncello can be refrigerated for up to 1 year. Shake gently before using.)

Crema di Limoncello
Substitute 16 ounces of half-and-half for 16 ounces of water.

Arancello
Substitute forty 3-inch strips of sour orange zest (4 oranges) for lemon zest. Sour oranges (also known as Seville, bigarade, bitter, or marmalade oranges) can be found in Latin American and Caribbean grocery stores. If you can't find sour oranges, substitute twenty 3-inch strips of sweet orange zest (such as navel), ten 3-inch strips of lemon zest, and eight 2-inch strips of lime zest for sour orange zest.

Lavender Liqueur
Makes about 16 ounces `MAKE AHEAD` `VEGETARIAN`
Total Time 10 minutes, plus 2 days steeping

WHY THIS RECIPE WORKS Used in a variety of different cocktails, a homemade floral liqueur (or a selection of a few) is just the thing to give to the aspiring home bartenders in your life. Dried flowers are easy to work with, they are readily available online and in specialty shops, and they infuse quickly into a spirit. Since elderflower liqueur is somewhat ubiquitous, we decided to focus on lesser-used blossoms. Lavender liqueur led the pack, and we also loved chamomile, jasmine, and rose. We found that in each case, a single strip of lemon zest balanced the floral fragrances with just a hint of fresh citrus aroma. Lavender liqueur can be used as a substitute for crème de violette, and we love the chamomile liqueur in the Highlander (page 260). Be sure to use food-grade dried flowers (available online or in specialty spice shops) to make these liqueurs; other types likely have been sprayed with pesticides or treated with chemicals. You will need a pint-size glass jar with a tight-fitting lid for this recipe.

    1 tablespoon (¼ ounce) dried lavender flowers
    1 (3-inch) strip lemon zest
   14 ounces vodka
    2 ounces Simple Syrup (page 261)

Limoncello

Floral Liqueurs

1. Place flowers, lemon zest, and vodka in pint-size glass jar. Cover tightly and shake to combine. Store jar in cool, dark place for 2 days, shaking mixture occasionally.

2. Set fine-mesh strainer in medium bowl and line with triple layer of cheesecloth. Strain vodka mixture through prepared strainer, pressing on solids to extract as much liquid as possible; discard solids. Return infused vodka to clean jar and add simple syrup. Cover and gently shake to combine. (Liqueur can be stored in cool, dark place for up to 1 year. Shake gently before using.)

Chamomile Liqueur

Substitute dried chamomile flowers for lavender.

Jasmine Liqueur

Substitute dried jasmine flowers for lavender.

Rose Liqueur

Substitute dried rose petals for lavender.

Fruits of the Forest Liqueur

Makes about 16 ounces **MAKE AHEAD** **VEGETARIAN**
Total Time 10 minutes, plus 1 week steeping

WHY THIS RECIPE WORKS Inspired by such iconic berry liqueurs as Chambord (made from black raspberries) and crème de cassis (made from black currants), we set out to create an intensely flavored yet balanced berry liqueur that could be used whenever these luxurious liqueurs are called for. We started by making batches of liqueurs using the berries we could find most easily at the grocery store—raspberries, blackberries, blueberries, and strawberries—trying fresh, frozen, and freeze-dried forms of all these berries in our liqueur. We strongly preferred the bright, intense flavors of the liqueurs made from freeze-dried berries; that they are available in this form year-round was a bonus. And while we liked each of the liqueurs made exclusively from individual berry types, the liqueurs made with combinations of at least two types of berries were bursting with complex, exquisite flavors that were far more interesting than liqueurs made using just any one type of berry. Try this liqueur in Holiday Punch (page 271) or the Royal Berry (page 265); if you're planning to gift the

Fruits of the
Forest Liqueur

liqueur, we suggest writing out and including one of these cocktail recipes along with your gift. You will need a pint-size glass jar with a tight-fitting lid for this recipe.

- 1 ounce freeze-dried blackberries, blueberries, and/or raspberries
- ½ ounce freeze-dried strawberries
- 12 ounces vodka
- 4 ounces Simple Syrup (page 261)

1. Place blackberries, strawberries, and vodka in pint-size glass jar. Cover tightly and shake to combine. Store jar in cool, dark place for 1 week, shaking mixture once every other day.

2. Set fine-mesh strainer in medium bowl and line with triple layer of cheesecloth. Strain vodka mixture through prepared strainer, pressing on solids to extract as much liquid as possible; discard solids. Return infused vodka to clean jar and add simple syrup. Cover and gently shake to combine. (Liqueur can be stored in cool, dark place for up to 1 year. Shake gently before using.)

Ancho Chile Liqueur

Makes about 16 ounces `MAKE AHEAD` `VEGETARIAN`
Total time 10 minutes, plus 1 week steeping

WHY THIS RECIPE WORKS Fruity, smoky, and mildly spicy, ancho chiles are a natural fit for infusing into tequila. This liqueur is great in our Old Poblano (page 268) and is a delicious substitute for tequila in other tequila-based cocktails. We found that adding a hint of cinnamon deepened the spicy complexity of the liqueur. The simple syrup tempered and balanced the heat of the chiles; adding the syrup after the infusion process was complete avoided diluting the alcohol during extraction. We used blanco tequila (white tequila, also known as silver) because of its clean, comparatively neutral flavor and its price point. You can substitute more expensive reposado (rested) tequila or añejo (aged) tequila in this recipe, but we recommend using either of these only if you plan to sip your liqueur on its own (over ice is nice), where its flavors can be fully enjoyed. Although our favorite base spirit for this liqueur is tequila, vodka or bourbon will also work well. For a spicier liqueur, include the chile seeds when steeping. You will need a pint-size glass jar with a tight-fitting lid for this recipe. Experiment with flavors by substituting an equal weight of dried guajillo, pasilla, or New Mexico chiles for the ancho.

½ dried ancho chile (¼ ounce), stemmed, seeded, and torn into 1-inch pieces
¼ cinnamon stick
12 ounces blanco tequila
4 ounces Simple Syrup (page 261)

1. Place ancho, cinnamon stick, and tequila in pint-size glass jar. Cover tightly and shake to combine. Store jar in cool, dark place for 1 week, shaking mixture once every other day.

2. Set fine-mesh strainer in medium bowl and line with triple layer of cheesecloth. Strain tequila mixture through prepared strainer, pressing on solids to extract as much liquid as possible; discard solids. Return infused tequila to clean jar and add simple syrup. Cover and gently shake to combine. (Liqueur can be stored in cool, dark place for up to 1 year. Shake gently before using.)

Mole Chile Liqueur
Add ½ teaspoon of cacao nibs and 1 teaspoon of coffee beans to jar with ancho chile.

Orgeat Syrup

Orgeat Syrup

Makes about 8 ounces `MAKE AHEAD` `VEGETARIAN`
Total Time 30 minutes, plus 12 hours steeping

WHY THIS RECIPE WORKS Orgeat gets its name from the French word for barley, orge, which was its original ingredient. Over time, almonds were added to the mix, and they eventually prevailed over the barley. Today, creamy, lightly perfumed almond-based orgeat syrup adds a compelling je ne sais quoi element to otherwise straightforward combinations of fruit juices and rum; we like to use it in House Punch (page 271). We started by heating sugar and water in a saucepan until the sugar dissolved. We then added finely chopped blanched toasted almonds, letting the almonds sit in the sugar syrup overnight before straining them out. The resulting syrup was thick, milky, and full of almond flavor, far superior to cloyingly sweet or artificially almond-y store-bought versions. A little orange blossom water (a traditional ingredient) lent an enchanting hint of floral aroma; look for it in the international aisle of well-stocked supermarkets or in Indian or Middle Eastern markets.

5 ounces blanched whole, sliced, or slivered almonds, toasted and cooled
1 cup sugar
8 ounces water
¼ teaspoon orange blossom water

1. Pulse almonds in food processor until finely chopped, about 30 pulses. Heat sugar and water in small saucepan over medium heat, whisking often, until sugar has dissolved, about 5 minutes; do not boil. Off heat, stir in almonds, cover, and let stand at least 12 hours or up to 24 hours.

2. Set fine-mesh strainer over medium bowl and line with triple layer of cheesecloth that overhangs edges. Transfer almond mixture to prepared strainer and let drain until liquid no longer runs freely, about 10 minutes. Pull edges of cheesecloth together to form pouch, then firmly squeeze pouch to extract as much syrup from pulp as possible; discard pulp. Stir in orange blossom water. (Syrup can be refrigerated in airtight container for up to 1 month. Shake gently before using.)

Cranberry Shrub Syrup

Makes about 8 ounces | **Total Time** 50 minutes
MAKE AHEAD VEGETARIAN

WHY THIS RECIPE WORKS Sweetened vinegar-and-fruit syrups, shrubs date back centuries. The version popping up in modern American glasses is believed to have evolved from the fruit-and-vinegar preserves American colonists used to preserve seasonal fruit. We wanted to develop a simple shrub recipe that was bursting with clean, bright, tangy fruit flavor. Bracingly tart cranberries served as our base. We simply simmered them with sugar and water until they began to break down, and then strained out the solids before adding a dash of white wine vinegar to the cranberry-flavored syrup. This shrub syrup can be enjoyed mixed with seltzer for a simple shrub soda, as in the New Englander (page 262), or it can contribute to the nuances of more complex cocktails.

2 cups fresh or frozen cranberries
1 cup sugar
6 ounces water
1 ounce white wine vinegar

1. Bring cranberries, sugar, and water to boil in large saucepan over high heat. Reduce heat to medium-low, cover, and simmer until cranberries are beginning to break down, about 5 minutes.

2. Remove saucepan from heat and use potato masher to crush cranberries. Set fine-mesh strainer over medium bowl and line with triple layer of cheesecloth that overhangs edges. Transfer cranberry mixture to prepared strainer and let drain until liquid no longer runs freely and mixture is cool enough to touch, about 30 minutes. Pull edges of cheesecloth together to form pouch, then gently squeeze pouch to extract as much syrup as possible; discard solids. Whisk in vinegar. (Syrup can be stored in an airtight container for up to 1 month. Shake well before using.)

Peach Shrub Syrup

Substitute 1¾ cups frozen peaches, thawed and chopped, for cranberries and 2 ounces cider vinegar for white wine vinegar. In step 1, simmer, stirring occasionally, until peaches are soft and beginning to break down, about 10 minutes. In step 2, omit triple layer of cheesecloth. Press on solids to extract as much liquid as possible; discard solids.

Old-Fashioned Aromatic Bitters

Makes about 16 ounces MAKE AHEAD VEGETARIAN
Total Time 20 minutes, plus 2 weeks steeping

WHY THIS RECIPE WORKS Intensely concentrated botanical elixirs added to cocktails in tiny amounts, bitters have the power to elevate a cocktail to a refined, distinctive libation. These bitters are woodsy and earthy, with notes of dried fruit plus just a hint of warm spice, which we achieved by infusing high-proof alcohol with flavoring agents—barks, roots, spices, herbs, flowers, fruits, and nuts. If you can't find 100-proof vodka, substitute 80-proof vodka, but add 1 week to the infusion time. We recommend storing your bitters in a cool, dark place to prevent oxidation. Gentian root chips and dried mugwort are bittering agents; you can purchase them, along with dried orange peel, online or in specialty spice shops; look for ¼-inch chips. You will need a quart-size glass jar with a tight-fitting lid for this recipe.

¼ cup raisins, chopped
2 tablespoons (½ ounce) dried orange peel
2 tablespoons (½ ounce) gentian root chips
2 tablespoons dried mugwort
8 green cardamom pods
10 allspice berries, lightly crushed

4 whole cloves

16 ounces 100-proof vodka

1 ounce Simple Syrup (page 261)

1. Place raisins, orange peel, gentian root chips, mugwort, cardamom pods, allspice berries, and cloves in quart-size glass jar. Add vodka, cover, and shake to combine. Store jar in cool, dark place for 2 weeks, shaking mixture once every other day.

2. Set fine-mesh strainer in medium bowl and line with triple layer of cheesecloth. Strain vodka through prepared strainer, pressing on solids to extract as much liquid as possible; discard solids. Return infused vodka mixture to clean jar and add simple syrup. Cover and shake gently to combine. (Bitters can be stored in cool, dark place for up to 1 year.)

Shrub Syrups

NOTES FROM THE TEST KITCHEN

WRAPPING FOOD GIFTS

When you're bustling around in the kitchen making homemade treats to give away, it can be easy to forget about a key element: presentation. A thoughtful wrapping job can give your offering a personal touch and make it feel truly special—and it doesn't have to be complicated.

First, make sure to pack your treats in an appropriate container. This doesn't have to mean buying a fancy holiday cookie tin from the craft store (although you can if you want). If you're giving away fudge or bark, a simple card stock box lined with waxed paper or parchment paper and tied with a ribbon works beautifully. If you're gifting something liquid, like our Homemade Almond Butter (page 400) or one of our homemade liqueurs (pages 407–409), a tightly sealed mason jar adorned with a ribbon or bow is perfect.

Second, consider whether the gift receiver will need any extra information to enjoy their gift. You may want to label your gift with the recipe name, or include the recipe with the gift in case they feel inspired to make more. And some homemade gifts, such as our dry baking mixes (pages 402–403), may require the receiver to do some of the work themselves (mixing in the wet ingredients and then baking to make cookies, for instance). In this case, be sure to pass along the instructions they'll need to make the recipe successfully, including a list of the necessary ingredients as well as the recipe steps.

Old-Fashioned Aromatic Bitters

cooking charts

Salting, brining, and properly cooking meat and grains are basic skills you can build any number of meals upon. The following charts include all you need to know about brining and salting various proteins, cooking meat to your preferred level of doneness, and achieving tender, intact whole grains every time.

Salting Meat and Poultry

Salting deeply seasons meat and helps dry out its surface for better browning. Compared to brining, salting is the best choice for meats that are already relatively juicy and/or well marbled. We prefer to use kosher salt for salting because it's easier to distribute the salt evenly. We use Diamond Crystal Kosher Salt; if using Morton Kosher Salt, reduce the amounts listed by 33 percent (e.g., use ⅔ teaspoon Morton Kosher Salt or 1 teaspoon Diamond Crystal).

CUTS	TIME	KOSHER SALT	METHOD
Meat			
Steaks Lamb Chops, Pork Chops	1 hour	¾ teaspoon per 8-ounce chop or steak	Apply salt evenly over surface and let rest at room temperature, uncovered, on wire rack set in rimmed baking sheet.
Beef, Lamb, and Pork Roasts	At least 6 hours and up to 24 hours	1 teaspoon per pound	Apply salt evenly over surface, wrap tightly with plastic wrap, and let rest in refrigerator.
Poultry			
Whole Chicken	At least 6 hours and up to 24 hours	1 teaspoon per pound	Apply salt evenly inside cavity and under skin of breast and legs and let rest in refrigerator on wire rack set in rimmed baking sheet. (Wrap with plastic wrap if salting for longer than 12 hours.)
Bone-In Chicken Pieces, Boneless or Bone-In Turkey Breast	At least 6 hours and up to 24 hours	¾ teaspoon per pound	If poultry is skin-on, apply salt evenly between skin and meat, leaving skin attached, and let rest in refrigerator on wire rack set in rimmed baking sheet. (Wrap with plastic wrap if salting for longer than 12 hours.)
Whole Turkey	At least 24 hours and up to 2 days	1 teaspoon per pound	Apply salt evenly inside cavity and under skin of breast and legs, wrap tightly with plastic wrap, and let rest in refrigerator.

Brining Poultry and Pork

Brining means soaking meat in a solution of water and salt (and sometimes sugar) before cooking. The meat absorbs some of this brine as it soaks and then retains it during cooking, which improves both its flavor and tenderness. It works especially well with lean cuts of meat, like chicken, turkey, and pork; do not brine kosher birds or enhanced pork. We prefer to use table salt for brining because it dissolves quickly and has a standard crystal size that measures uniformly from brand to brand.

BRINING DIRECTIONS

Dissolve the salt in the water in a container or bowl large enough to hold the brine and meat, following the amounts in the chart. Submerge the meat completely in the brine. Cover and refrigerate, following the times in the chart (do not brine for longer or the meat will become overly salty). Remove the meat from the brine and pat dry with paper towels.

CUTS	COLD WATER	TABLE SALT	TIME
Chicken			
1 (3- to 8-pound) whole chicken	2 quarts	½ cup	1 hour
2 (3- to 8-pound) whole chickens	3 quarts	¾ cup	1 hour
4 pounds bone-in chicken pieces (whole breasts, split breasts, whole legs, thighs, and/or drumsticks)	2 quarts	½ cup	½ to 1 hour
Boneless, skinless chicken breasts (up to 6 breasts)	1½ quarts	3 tablespoons	½ to 1 hour
Turkey			
1 (12- to 17-pound) whole turkey	2 gallons	1 cup	6 to 12 hours
1 (18- to 24-pound) whole turkey	3 gallons	1½ cups	6 to 12 hours
Bone-in turkey breast	1 gallon	½ cup	3 to 6 hours
Pork			
Bone-in pork chops (up to 6)	1½ quarts	3 tablespoons	½ to 1 hour
Boneless pork chops (up to 6)	1½ quarts	3 tablespoons	½ to 1 hour
1 (2½- to 6-pound) pork roast	2 quarts	¼ cup	1½ to 2 hours

Doneness Temperatures for Meat, Poultry, and Fish

Do not guess at doneness: Use a thermometer. We list below the final cooking temperatures of meat, poultry, and fish. Note that the temperature of beef and pork (but not poultry or fish) will continue to rise after the meat is removed from the heat source (this is known as carryover cooking). For this reason, we list both the cooking and serving temperatures.

USING A THERMOMETER

When temping a whole bird, you should take the temperature of both the breast meat and thigh meat. To temp the breast meat, insert the thermometer from the neck end, holding the thermometer parallel to the bird. To temp the thigh meat, insert the thermometer at an angle into the area between the drumstick and breast, taking care not to hit bone. When taking the temperature of thin steaks or pork chops, use kitchen tongs to hold the meat away from the cooking surface and insert the thermometer through the side of the meat and into the center, taking care not to hit bone. For large roasts, we recommend taking the temperature in a few places and finding the lowest temperature because there are often hotter and cooler spots; the lowest temperature should be your guide.

FOR THIS INGREDIENT...	COOK TO THIS TEMPERATURE
Beef and Lamb	
Chops, Steaks, and Roasts	
Rare	115 to 120 degrees (120 to 125 degrees after resting)
Medium-Rare	120 to 125 degrees (125 to 130 degrees after resting)
Medium	130 to 135 degrees (135 to 140 degrees after resting)
Medium-Well	140 to 145 degrees (145 to 150 degrees after resting)
Well-Done	150 to 155 degrees (155 to 160 degrees after resting)
Pork	
Chops and Tenderloins	
Medium-Well	145 degrees (150 degrees after resting)
Well-Done	160 degrees
Loin Roasts	
Medium-Well	140 degrees (145 degrees after resting)
Well-Done	160 degrees
Poultry	
Breasts	160 degrees
Thighs and Drumsticks	175 degrees
Fish	
Rare	110 degrees (for tuna only)
Medium-Rare	125 degrees (for tuna or salmon)
Medium	135 to 140 degrees (for white-fleshed fish)

Cooking Whole Grains

Here in the test kitchen we have homed in on three basic methods for cooking grains and determined which are best for each type of grain. While some grains, such as bulgur, take well to any cooking method, others will turn out best when cooked with a specific method.

BOILING DIRECTIONS

Bring water to boil in large saucepan. Stir in grain and salt. Return to boil, then reduce to simmer and cook until grain is tender, following cooking times given in chart below. Drain.

PILAF-STYLE DIRECTIONS

Rinse and then dry grain on towel. Heat 1 tablespoon oil in medium saucepan (preferably nonstick) over medium-high heat until shimmering. Stir in grain and toast until lightly golden and fragrant, 2 to 3 minutes. Stir in water and salt. Bring mixture to simmer, then reduce heat to low, cover, and continue to simmer until grain is tender and has absorbed all of water, following cooking times given below. Off heat, let grain stand for 10 minutes, then fluff with fork.

MICROWAVE DIRECTIONS

Rinse grain. Combine water, grain, 1 tablespoon oil, and salt in bowl. Cover and cook following times given below. Remove from microwave and fluff with fork. Cover bowl with plastic wrap, poke several vent holes with tip of knife, and let sit until grain is completely tender, about 5 minutes.

TYPE OF GRAIN	COOKING METHOD	AMOUNT OF GRAIN	AMOUNT OF WATER	AMOUNT OF SALT	COOKING TIME
Pearl Barley	Pilaf-Style	1 cup	1⅔ cups	¼ teaspoon	20 to 40 minutes
	Boiling	1 cup	4 quarts	1 tablespoon	20 to 40 minutes
Bulgur (Medium- to Coarse-Grind)	Pilaf-Style *	1 cup	1½ cups	¼ teaspoon	16 to 18 minutes
	Boiling	1 cup	4 quarts	1½ teaspoons	5 minutes
	Microwave	1 cup	1 cup	¼ teaspoon	5 to 10 minutes
Farro	Boiling	1 cup	4 quarts	1 tablespoon	15 to 30 minutes
Freekeh	Boiling	1 cup	4 quarts	1 tablespoon	30 to 45 minutes
Long-Grain Brown Rice	Pilaf-Style	1 cup	1¾ cups	¼ teaspoon	40 to 50 minutes
	Boiling	1 cup	4 quarts	1 tablespoon	25 to 30 minutes
	Microwave	1 cup	2 cups	¼ teaspoon	25 to 30 minutes
Quinoa	Pilaf-Style	1 cup	1 cup plus 3 tablespoons	¼ teaspoon	18 to 20 minutes
	Microwave	1 cup	2 cups	¼ teaspoon	5 minutes on medium, then 5 minutes on high
Wheat Berries	Boiling	1 cup	4 quarts	1½ teaspoons	1 hour to 1 hour 10 minutes

* If cooking bulgur using the pilaf-style method, do not rinse, and skip the toasting step, instead adding the grain to the pot with the liquid.

nutritional information for our recipes

To calculate the nutritional values of our recipes per serving, we used The Food Processor SQL by ESHA research. When using this program, we entered all the ingredients, using weights wherever possible. We also used our preferred brands in these analyses. Any ingredient listed as "optional" was excluded from the analyses. If there is a range in the serving size, we used the highest number of servings to calculate nutritional values. We did not include additional salt or pepper for food that's seasoned to taste.

	CALORIES	TOTAL FAT (G)	SAT FAT (G)	CHOL (MG)	SODIUM (MG)	TOTAL CARB (G)	DIETARY FIBER (G)	TOTAL SUGARS (G)	PROTEIN (G)
Soups, Stews, and Chilis									
Classic Chicken Noodle Soup	445	26	6	172	1309	17	2	1	34
Pressure-Cooker Spiced Chicken Soup with Squash and Chickpeas	190	7	1	60	700	16	4	3	20
Turkey Barley Soup	181	3	1	36	309	25	5	2	14
Kimchi, Beef, and Tofu Soup	481	27	8	81	1305	16	5	4	36
Pressure-Cooker Hawaiian Oxtail Soup	520	29	10	170	1090	14	4	4	53
Harira	310	13	3	35	850	25	6	5	24
Miso Soup with Halibut	280	8	1	85	1120	13	4	3	39
Rich and Velvety Shrimp Bisque	521	27	13	255	1973	17	2	5	34
French Onion Soup	604	31	15	68	1762	50	6	17	28
Creamless Creamy Tomato Soup	161	8	1	0	714	18	5	8	5
Creamy Chestnut Soup	305	8	4	21	842	50	2	9	7
Pureed Carrot Soup with Nutmeg	137	6	3	15	511	16	4	9	4
Red Lentil and Squash Soup	528	19	4	11	1217	71	11	12	24
Classic Croutons	70	3.5	2	10	55	8	0	1	1
Sweet Potato and Peanut Soup	280	14	4	10	940	33	6	10	7
Wild Rice and Mushroom Soup	260	12	7	30	890	29	2	4	7
Lentil and Escarole Soup	270	10	1.5	0	890	36	9	5	10
Beet and Wheat Berry Soup with Dill Cream	240	11	2	10	1690	32	6	7	5
Chicken and Dumplings	588	30	17	170	740	42	4	5	35
Vegetable Broth Base (per 1 tablespoon)	10	0	0	0	380	2	0	1	0
Doro Wat	1120	60	18	490	770	15	2	4	103
Easy-Peel Hard-Cooked Eggs	70	5	1.5	185	70	0	0	0	6
Stifado	469	29	11	129	869	9	1	4	39

	CALORIES	TOTAL FAT (G)	SAT FAT (G)	CHOL (MG)	SODIUM (MG)	TOTAL CARB (G)	DIETARY FIBER (G)	TOTAL SUGARS (G)	PROTEIN (G)
Soups, Stews, and Chilis (cont.)									
Beef Stew with Parsnips, Kale, and Mushrooms	630	33	12	135	730	38	8	10	36
Lamb Stew with Turnips and Carrots	510	24	8	135	920	27	5	11	44
Seafood and Chorizo Stew	447	22	7	217	1614	15	6	7	47
Tuscan White Bean Stew	330	9	2.5	15	920	43	22	5	19
Swiss Chard and Butternut Squash Stew	310	20	11	0	1190	34	6	7	6
Hearty Beef and Vegetable Chili	710	43	15	175	1180	34	5	8	45
Pressure-Cooker Easy Beef Chili	380	18	5	50	1030	33	8	10	23
Slow-Cooker White Chicken Chili	613	22	4	163	1334	55	14	5	50
Pressure-Cooker Black Bean Chili	410	8	0.5	0	420	66	5	17	20
Butternut Squash and Peanut Chili with Quinoa	580	38	15	0	660	55	11	10	13
Weeknight Dinners									
Pan-Roasted Chicken Breasts with Root Vegetables	460	10	1.5	160	750	39	6	8	54
Za'atar Chicken with Pistachios, Brussels Sprouts, and Pomegranate	680	44	9	145	760	17	6	6	53
Pomegranate Molasses	60	0	0	0	30	16	0	13	0
Pressure-Cooker Chicken with Spiced Whole Parsnips and Scallion-Mint Relish	620	39	8	120	810	43	11	14	25
Chicken Schnitzel with Apple-Fennel Rémoulade	653	40	4	159	534	34	2	2	38
Apple-Fennel Rémoulade	78	6	1	3	192	7	2	4	1
Chicken, Spinach, and Artichoke Pot Pie	508	31	16	188	1063	23	8	4	39
Rustic Turkey Tart	251	15	8	50	412	21	4	13	10
Thanksgiving Quinoa Bowl	600	24	4	85	830	65	7	13	33
Creamy Roasted Garlic Dressing	130	9	1.5	0	95	11	1	2	2
Steak Salad with Beets, Walnuts, and Creamy Horseradish Dressing	360	21	5	80	420	8	2	5	36
Steak Tips with Wilted Spinach, Goat Cheese, and Pear Salad	600	38	12	160	650	12	3	6	52
Pressure-Cooker Steak Tips with Warm Potato and Green Bean Salad	430	20	5	80	730	33	5	6	29
Roasted Pork Chops and Vegetables with Parsley Vinaigrette	810	36	8	190	1470	39	5	8	80
Harissa-Glazed Pork Tenderloin with Couscous Salad	711	37	10	165	1049	41	4	12	54
Crunchy Parmesan-Crusted Pork Chops with Glazed Winter Squash	1050	40	13	230	1340	111	7	62	60

	CALORIES	TOTAL FAT (G)	SAT FAT (G)	CHOL (MG)	SODIUM (MG)	TOTAL CARB (G)	DIETARY FIBER (G)	TOTAL SUGARS (G)	PROTEIN (G)
Weeknight Dinners (cont.)									
Italian Sausage with Grapes and Balsamic Vinegar	258	12	4	34	650	18	1	13	19
Stuffed Veal Cutlets with Prosciutto and Fontina	499	36	20	228	609	20	1	1	25
Lamb Meatballs with Orzo, Tomatoes, and Feta	990	52	23	190	1610	77	2	9	49
One-Pan Roasted Salmon with White Beans, Fennel, and Tomatoes	972	52	18	155	982	67	19	12	60
Roasted Snapper and Vegetables with Mustard Sauce	530	26	4	65	960	29	5	7	41
Braised Halibut with Coriander, Carrots, and Pearl Couscous	670	22	13	135	620	67	3	8	42
Palak Dal	276	8	4	16	348	41	8	4	15
Farro, White Bean, and Broccoli Rabe Gratin	390	13	3.5	15	780	51	9	4	22
Hoppin' John	478	17	6	56	932	56	7	5	23
Garlicky Spaghetti with Basil and Broiled Tomatoes	420	15	3	5	520	60	1	4	14
Pasta with Sautéed Wild Mushrooms	560	22	11	50	550	75	3	8	19
Pasta alla Norcina	430	19	9	50	300	46	1	2	15
Unstuffed Shells with Butternut Squash and Leeks	530	25	14	65	550	59	5	6	19
Bulgur-Stuffed Acorn Squash with Ras el Hanout	450	23	8	30	740	61	8	15	7
Roasted Cabbage Wedges with Stewed Tomatoes and Chickpeas	490	29	2.5	0	1250	52	17	10	15
Herbed Yogurt Sauce	40	2	1.5	10	30	3	0	3	2
Weekend Roasting and Braising									
Roast Chicken with Cranberry-Walnut Stuffing	780	45	16	205	1140	36	3	13	57
Spice-Roasted Chicken with Chili and Oregano	696	51	13	217	1091	3	1	0	54
One-Pan Roast Turkey Breast with Herb Stuffing	940	36	13	270	1640	43	1	7	101
Deviled Beef Short Ribs	440	20	9	100	1420	31	1	14	33
Maple-Glazed Pork Roast	300	13	4	80	360	18	0	16	26
Roast Pork Loin with Sweet Potatoes and Cilantro Sauce	690	35	6	145	700	36	6	11	54
Harissa-Rubbed Roast Boneless Leg of Lamb with Warm Cauliflower Salad	340	13	4	110	440	15	2	11	38
Prosciutto-Wrapped Cod with Lemon-Caper Butter	340	19	9	125	950	2	0	0	39
Roasted Salmon with Orange Beurre Blanc	450	36	14	115	300	2	0	1	27
Faster Coq au Vin	560	27	11	220	860	10	1	4	42
Hunter's-Style Chicken	743	51	14	227	1060	8	2	4	58
Chicken Tagine with Fennel, Chickpeas, and Apricots	764	39	10	257	448	44	9	13	59
Chicken in a Pot with Red Potatoes, Carrots, and Shallots	958	54	17	233	1971	53	9	13	61
Pot Roast with Root Vegetables	805	39	14	174	1853	57	12	16	56
Slow-Cooker Beef Burgundy	796	48	19	211	1291	18	2	6	61
Braised Short Ribs with Daikon and Shiitakes	500	19	7	90	1600	38	4	19	35
Braised Steaks with Root Vegetables	400	14	5	115	510	28	6	7	38
Pressure-Cooker Boneless Short Rib and Cauliflower Puttanesca	550	38	15	130	970	19	6	9	37
Red-Cooked Beef	602	43	18	165	1117	10	0	6	42
Shizi Tou (Lion's Head Meatballs)	530	34	12	140	1150	22	2	5	31

	CALORIES	TOTAL FAT (G)	SAT FAT (G)	CHOL (MG)	SODIUM (MG)	TOTAL CARB (G)	DIETARY FIBER (G)	TOTAL SUGARS (G)	PROTEIN (G)
Weekend Roasting and Braising (cont.)									
Roman Braised Oxtails	707	49	18	153	1187	15	3	8	47
Milk-Braised Pork Roast	330	15	6	120	650	8	0	6	36
Slow-Cooker Pork Loin with Fennel, Oranges, and Olives	362	18	3	107	735	9	3	4	37
Goan Pork Vindaloo	304	20	6	87	600	6	1	1	25
Carne Adovada	438	27	9	134	1107	9	1	7	38
Choucroute Garnie	732	62	22	133	1864	10	4	3	29
Salmon en Cocotte with Leeks and White Wine	610	41	11	132	707	8	1	2	44
Pressure-Cooker Braised Whole Cauliflower with Olives, Raisins, and Pine Nuts	340	15	2	5	1090	44	11	24	12
Mediterranean Braised Green Beans with Potatoes and Basil	230	12	1.5	0	1080	28	4	7	4
Stuffed Cabbage Rolls	740	43	14	125	2420	53	10	32	35
Mushroom Ragu	180	6	3.5	15	550	20	4	10	7
Chana Masala	291	11	1	0	578	39	11	8	11
Pistachio Dukkah (per 1 tablespoon)	15	1	0	0	7	1	0	0	1
Hazelnut-Nigella Dukkah (per 1 tablespoon)	12	1	0	0	6	1	0	0	0
Five-Spice Powder (per 1 teaspoon)	7	0	0	0	1	1	1	0	0
Garam Masala (per 1 teaspoon)	6	0	0	0	1	1	1	0	0
Ras el Hanout (per 1 teaspoon)	7	0	0	0	7	1	1	0	0
Harissa (per 1 tablespoon)	100	11	1.5	0	37	2	1	0	1
Za'atar (per 2 teaspoons)	8	0	0	0	0	1	1	0	0
Centerpieces for a Crowd									
Twin Roast Chickens with Root Vegetables and Tarragon Vinaigrette	908	56	15	231	1664	39	8	10	62
Boneless Turkey Breast with Gravy	260	10	4	140	720	4	0	1	36
Two-Hour Turkey and Gravy	571	24	6	254	1396	7	2	2	76
Simple Grill-Roasted Turkey	430	18	5	240	1390	0	0	0	63
Turkey and Gravy for a Crowd	564	27	10	222	981	9	1	2	66
Balsamic-Glazed Cornish Game Hens	880	49	14	350	760	46	0	46	60
Whole Roast Ducks with Cherry Sauce	1378	125	42	241	960	24	1	21	37
Rosemary-Garlic Top Sirloin Roast	370	17	4.5	140	890	1	0	0	51
Slow-Roasted Chuck Roast with Horseradish–Sour Cream Sauce	927	62	27	292	1448	12	1	4	77
Best Roast Prime Rib	650	34	13	235	1090	0	0	0	80
Herb-Crusted Roast Beef Tenderloin	390	21	6	120	510	5	0	1	43
Horseradish Sauce	80	9	1.5	5	90	0	0	0	0
Braised Brisket with Pomegranate, Cumin, and Cilantro	370	11	2.5	110	1060	28	3	16	40
Pomegranate-Glazed Roast Bone-In Leg of Lamb	330	12	4	125	380	14	0	13	40
Spiced Lamb Pot Roast with Figs	430	18	7	120	520	15	2	10	38
Porchetta	469	35	10	118	634	4	2	0	34

	CALORIES	TOTAL FAT (G)	SAT FAT (G)	CHOL (MG)	SODIUM (MG)	TOTAL CARB (G)	DIETARY FIBER (G)	TOTAL SUGARS (G)	PROTEIN (G)
Centerpieces for a Crowd (cont.)									
Crown Roast of Pork	694	41	17	188	1189	23	3	7	55
Pork Pernil	543	37	11	156	801	4	1	1	47
Glazed Spiral-Sliced Ham	480	19	7	135	2910	37	0	33	40
Roasted Whole Side of Salmon	390	24	6	100	433	4	0	3	37
Vegetable Moussaka	443	19	8	30	1366	55	13	17	17
Mushroom Lasagna	390	21	9	45	790	33	2	11	17
Simple Cheese Lasagna	440	22	13	90	1670	33	3	10	29
Eggplant Parmesan	320	25	7	25	680	18	7	10	11
Mushroom and Leek Galette with Gorgonzola	370	23	13	75	430	34	3	4	9
Swiss Chard Pie	380	25	14	75	730	27	3	2	11
Double-Crust Chicken Pot Pie	540	31	18	160	830	42	2	4	22
Chicken B'stilla	420	24	4	165	440	27	2	4	24
Simple Cranberry Sauce	80	0	0	0	50	20	1	18	0
Cranberry Sauce with Pears and Ginger	100	0	0	0	50	25	2	21	0
Spiced Apple Chutney	25	0	0	0	0	6	0	5	0
Cherry-Port Sauce	160	0	0	0	20	27	1	24	0
Grapefruit-Basil Relish	20	0.5	0	0	0	4	2	3	0
Onion-Balsamic Relish	100	8	1	0	120	5	0	3	0
Our Favorite Turkey Gravy	100	5	3	18	205	8	1	2	5
All-Purpose Gravy	70	4.5	2.5	10	290	5	0	1	1
Vegetable Sides									
Roquefort Salad with Apple, Celery, and Hazelnuts	270	22	7	25	620	11	2	7	8
Citrus and Radicchio Salad with Dates and Smoked Almonds	260	13	1.5	0	270	36	7	27	4
Butternut Squash and Apple Pita Salad	310	19	2.5	0	460	33	4	7	4
Pan-Roasted Pear Salad with Frisée, Goat Cheese, and Almonds	160	8	2	5	150	21	4	13	3
Pressure-Cooker Beet and Watercress Salad with Orange and Dill	180	10	4	10	340	18	5	12	7
Easy-Peel Soft-Cooked Eggs	70	5	1.5	185	70	0	0	0	6
Braised Beets with Lemon and Almonds	120	6	0.5	0	360	13	4	8	4
Braised Bok Choy with Garlic	60	5	0	0	115	3	1	1	2
Skillet-Roasted Brussels Sprouts with Lemon and Pecorino Romano	230	20	4	5	280	9	4	2	5
Brussels Sprout Gratin	300	23	13	65	460	16	5	4	10
Braised Savoy Cabbage with Pancetta	180	12	5	25	536	12	4	4	7
Celery Root Puree for a Crowd	156	9	6	28	396	17	3	3	3
Shallot, Sage, and Black Pepper Topping	43	4	2	10	26	2	1	0	0
Southern-Style Collard Greens	260	15	6	80	1030	6	3	2	23

	CALORIES	TOTAL FAT (G)	SAT FAT (G)	CHOL (MG)	SODIUM (MG)	TOTAL CARB (G)	DIETARY FIBER (G)	TOTAL SUGARS (G)	PROTEIN (G)
Vegetable Sides (cont.)									
Corn Pudding	346	24	14	92	339	31	2	9	5
Roasted Fennel with Rye Crumble	180	13	8	35	700	13	4	4	4
Extra-Crunchy Green Bean Casserole	493	33	17	78	709	41	5	7	9
Creamed Kale with Chestnuts	535	31	18	92	1027	52	9	10	20
Slow-Cooker Braised Kale with Garlic and Chorizo	291	19	6	35	610	17	6	4	17
Roasted Kohlrabi with Crunchy Seeds	100	8	1	0	310	7	4	3	2
Sautéed Mushrooms with Red Wine and Rosemary	97	4	2	9	199	9	2	5	6
Roasted King Trumpet Mushrooms	140	11	7	30	300	7	0	5	3
Red Wine–Miso Sauce	100	3	2	10	430	7	0	4	1
Browned Butter–Lemon Vinaigrette	110	11	7	30	180	2	0	1	0
Sautéed Parsnips with Ginger, Maple, and Fennel Seeds	210	9	0.5	0	480	32	7	11	3
Creamy Mashed Potatoes	390	26	17	75	250	33	0	1	5
Cheesy Mashed Potato Casserole	450	29	18	85	660	33	0	2	14
Potato Galette	180	7	4.5	20	300	26	2	0	3
Braised Red Potatoes with Lemon and Chives	130	6	3.5	15	310	19	2	2	2
Slow-Cooker Lemon-Herb Fingerling Potatoes	160	4.5	0.5	0	400	28	4	1	3
Cider-Glazed Root Vegetables with Apples and Tarragon	201	6	4	15	638	31	6	15	3
Slow-Cooker Mashed Sweet Potatoes	180	5	3.5	15	320	31	5	10	3
Sweet Potato Fritters with Cheddar, Chipotle, and Cilantro	386	25	5	76	450	32	4	5	9
Candied Sweet Potato Casserole	450	20	6	20	432	67	7	35	5
Sautéed Swiss Chard with Currants and Pine Nuts	160	12	1.5	0	440	12	3	7	4
Roasted Turnips, Shallots, and Garlic with Rosemary	130	6	3.5	15	390	17	4	8	3
Roasted Delicata Squash	150	12	3	10	220	11	2	2	1
Roasted Kabocha Squash with Maple and Sage	240	14	2	0	290	28	4	13	4
Grain and Bean Sides									
Walk-Away Herbed White Rice	190	0.5	0	0	290	40	1	0	3
Pressure-Cooker Spiced Rice Pilaf with Sweet Potatoes and Pomegranate	320	10	1.5	0	500	52	3	5	8
Mexican Red Rice	111	10	1	0	334	6	1	2	2
Chelow (Persian-Style Rice with Golden Crust)	375	17	4	12	216	50	1	1	5
Brown Rice Pilaf with Dates and Pistachios	269	7	1	0	498	48	4	8	6
Baked Wild Rice	154	2	1	3	298	30	2	1	6
Barley with Lemon and Herbs	186	6	1	0	146	31	7	1	4
Farro Salad with Butternut Squash, Radicchio, and Blue Cheese	306	13	4	8	388	40	7	5	10
Pressure-Cooker Wild Mushroom Farrotto	280	10	2.5	5	630	35	4	2	13
Freekeh Pilaf with Dates and Cauliflower	360	13	2	0	240	53	12	13	10
Quinoa Pilaf with Herbs and Lemon	196	6	3	10	298	29	3	1	6
Wheat Berry Salad with Figs, Pine Nuts, and Goat Cheese	330	14	2.5	5	260	45	8	8	9

	CALORIES	TOTAL FAT (G)	SAT FAT (G)	CHOL (MG)	SODIUM (MG)	TOTAL CARB (G)	DIETARY FIBER (G)	TOTAL SUGARS (G)	PROTEIN (G)
Grain and Bean Sides (cont.)									
Hearty Pearl Couscous with Eggplant, Spinach, and Beans	370	12	1.5	0	650	55	5	5	11
Polenta with Cheese and Butter	210	11	6	25	500	15	2	0	14
Rustic Bread Stuffing with Cranberries and Walnuts	360	14	3.5	10	680	53	3	20	8
Classic Sausage-Herb Cornbread Dressing	376	16	8	132	650	41	2	9	16
Dried Fruit and Nut Wild Rice Dressing	494	31	13	92	318	48	6	13	11
Egg Noodles with Browned Butter and Caraway	150	9	5	35	135	14	0	0	3
Creamy Orzo with Peas and Parmesan	160	4.6	2	10	810	14	1	2	13
Make-Ahead Creamy Macaroni and Cheese	742	49	29	146	682	48	2	3	29
Savory Noodle Kugel	269	9	2	150	274	36	2	3	11
Slow-Cooker Pinto Beans with Chipotle	350	5	0.5	0	430	55	18	7	17
Spiced Red Lentils	340	11	4	15	20	45	11	7	18
Slow-Cooker Lentil Salad with Dill, Orange, and Spinach	500	17	2	0	610	59	13	12	25
French Lentils with Carrots and Parsley	160	5	0.5	0	220	23	6	3	7
Gigante Beans with Spinach and Feta	310	16	4.5	20	670	32	7	7	12
Cannellini Beans with Roasted Red Peppers and Kale	350	17	3	5	840	33	9	7	15
Spicy Chickpeas with Turnips	210	7	0.5	0	650	31	7	9	8
Basic Black Beans	450	12	3	45	1100	54	2	9	28
Cranberry Beans with Tequila, Green Chiles, and Pepitas	340	18	4	10	600	29	8	5	12
Quick Pickled Shallot and Radishes	30	0	0	0	150	8	1	4	1
Black-Eyed Peas with Walnuts and Pomegranate	240	14	2	0	440	22	5	5	7
All Things Apple									
Bibb and Frisée Salad with Apple and Celery	119	11	2	0	95	5	2	3	1
Curried Butternut Squash and Apple Soup	250	15	9	45	410	29	5	9	3
Celery Root, Fennel, and Apple Chowder	200	8	4.5	20	700	27	4	8	3
Caraway-Crusted Pork Tenderloin with Sauerkraut and Apples	405	14	3	123	1049	29	7	19	41
Cider-Braised Pork Roast with Apples	598	35	11	147	1063	28	2	21	42
Apple-Cinnamon Muffins	294	8	2	37	273	51	2	27	5
Apple Cider Doughnuts	250	9	3	25	150	39	0	21	3
Apple Fritters	310	9	2	45	380	55	0	37	4
Cranberry-Pecan-Stuffed Baked Apples	380	16	7	30	35	66	1	55	2
Skillet Apple Crisp	475	22	10	38	156	68	6	45	4
Apple Pandowdy	420	18	11	70	310	66	6	46	3
French Apple Cake	411	24	2	21	208	46	2	31	3
Cider-Glazed Apple Bundt Cake	500	16	20	85	380	82	1	46	6
Apple Turnovers	146	3	1	0	55	30	3	23	1
Apple Strudel with Pine Nuts	360	16	9	35	270	52	3	24	4
Classic Apple Tarte Tatin	480	24	15	85	110	65	4	44	3

	CALORIES	TOTAL FAT (G)	SAT FAT (G)	CHOL (MG)	SODIUM (MG)	TOTAL CARB (G)	DIETARY FIBER (G)	TOTAL SUGARS (G)	PROTEIN (G)
All Things Apple (cont.)									
Deep Dish Apple Pie	630	28	18	75	370	91	6	50	5
Salted Caramel Apple Pie	580	28	17	145	390	75	2	53	7
Applesauce	225	1	0	0	44	60	8	48	1
Apple Butter	80	0	0	0	20	17	1	15	0
Everyone Loves Pumpkin									
Pumpkin Seed Dip	130	11	2	4	95	4	1	1	5
Slow-Cooker Creamy Pumpkin-Chai Soup	230	10	5	25	530	33	5	25	6
Pumpkin Cappellacci	500	28	16	160	540	48	2	3	14
Roasted Sugar Pumpkin Wedges	80	5	0	0	440	8	1	3	1
Mashed Spiced Pumpkin	180	8	5	20	300	29	2	16	3
Chicken with Pumpkin Seed Sauce	410	22	2.5	125	930	9	3	4	45
Homemade Pumpkin Puree	96	0	0	0	4	24	2	10	4
Pumpkin Bread	283	12	3	56	236	41	2	25	4
Pumpkin Spice Muffins	406	13	8	62	236	68	2	40	5
Pumpkin Spice Waffles	450	17	2.5	80	630	59	7	17	16
Pumpkin–Chocolate Chip Snack Cake	184	9	2	23	130	24	1	16	2
Maple-Pumpkin Stack Cake	370	21	12	100	360	42	2	27	5
Pumpkin Pie	530	29	18	195	520	58	2	37	8
Rum Pumpkin Chiffon Pie	380	24	15	70	310	35	2	28	4
Pumpkin-Pecan Cookies	130	7	3.5	15	20	16	1	8	1
Pumpkin Cheesecake Bars	201	12	7	62	169	22	1	17	3
Pumpkin–Cream Cheese Brownies	210	12	4.5	30	120	26	2	18	3
Pumpkin Streusel Bars	250	12	5	35	75	32	2	20	4
Appetizers and Starters									
Parsnip Hummus	140	10	1.5	0	230	11	3	2	2
Herbed Spinach Dip	186	19	4	17	232	3	1	1	2
Slow-Cooker Creamy Crab Dip	225	19	8	97	465	2	0	1	12
Buffalo Chicken Dip	560	48	21	155	1520	6	0	3	28
Slow-Cooker Beer and Cheddar Fondue	221	17	10	50	407	4	0	0	11
Cheddar Cheese Log with Everything Bagel Blend	182	17	8	39	351	2	1	1	6
Everything Bagel Blend	9	1	0	0	80	1	0	0	0
Baked Brie en Croûte with Mango-Peach Chutney	260	14	7	50	250	28	0	13	8
Mango-Peach Chutney	100	2	0	0	0	22	0	13	0
Chicken Liver Pâté	160	11	6	180	210	3	0	2	8
Crostini	25	1	0	0	45	3	0	0	1
Cheese Straws	200	13	6	5	400	20	1	1	7
Slow-Cooker Party Mix	306	15	6	20	446	40	5	4	8
Spiced Nuts	460	41	3.5	0	300	24	6	18	6

	CALORIES	TOTAL FAT (G)	SAT FAT (G)	CHOL (MG)	SODIUM (MG)	TOTAL CARB (G)	DIETARY FIBER (G)	TOTAL SUGARS (G)	PROTEIN (G)
Appetizers and Starters (cont.)									
Herbed Deviled Eggs	50	4	1	95	85	0	0	0	3
Cheddar and Chutney Canapés with Walnut Bread	290	12	6	30	370	36	0	14	11
Easy Melted Brie with Honey and Herbs	160	13	8	45	290	2	0	2	9
Boursin–Cheddar Cheese Spread	150	15	8	35	240	1	0	1	5
Sun-Dried Tomato Tapenade with Farmer's Cheese	180	16	5	15	250	4	1	0	6
Baked Goat Cheese with Olive Oil and Herbs	200	18	7	20	270	1	0	1	8
Stuffed Mushrooms	33	3	1	1	42	1	0	1	1
Shrimp Cocktail with Horseradish Cocktail Sauce	100	0.5	0	70	630	15	0	11	8
Garlicky Roasted Shrimp with Parsley and Anise	265	19	6	211	858	3	0	0	21
Broiled Bacon-Wrapped Sea Scallops	90	6	2	20	340	2	0	0	7
Fried Brussels Sprouts with Lemon-Chive Dipping Sauce	260	24	2.5	5	140	10	4	2	4
Cauliflower Buffalo Bites	430	37	14	20	780	25	2	4	2
Ranch Dressing	120	14	2	5	170	0	0	0	0
Slow-Cooker Swedish Meatballs	300	21	10	105	450	8	0	1	17
Baked Jalapeño Poppers	92	8	4	27	130	1	0	1	4
Korean Fried Chicken Wings	440	30	7	150	220	16	0	4	26
Oven-Fried Chicken Wings	660	48	17	356	1116	4	0	3	53
Buffalo Wing Sauce	80	8	5	20	499	3	0	3	0
Smoky Barbecue Wing Sauce	25	0	0	0	123	6	0	5	0
Sweet and Spicy Wing Sauce	95	2	0	0	477	19	0	18	0
Pizza Monkey Bread	640	30	11	45	1337	66	5	6	26
Tomato Sauce	80	6	1	0	330	8	2	4	2
Oysters on the Half-Shell with Ginger Mignonette Sauce	260	7	2	150	321	18	1	0	29
Crispy Potato Latkes	140	7	1	35	250	17	1	1	3
Savory Applesauce with Beets and Horseradish	40	0	0	0	70	10	1	8	0
Buckwheat Blini with Smoked Salmon	130	7	3	35	480	10	1	3	9
Smoked Salmon and Leek Tart	290	18	10	90	470	22	1	3	9
Camembert, Sun-Dried Tomato, and Potato Tart	360	22	13	60	700	31	1	2	10
Press-In Tart Dough	180	11	7	30	150	18	0	2	2
Festive Drinks									
Autumn in New England	203	1	1	0	3	14	4	7	1
Fireside	239	0	0	0	5	53	1	50	0
Pumpkin Pie Spice Rim Sugar (per ¼ teaspoon)	420	0.5	0	0	0	107	3	101	0
Highlander	190	0	0	0	0	13	0	13	0
Simple Syrup	35	0	0	0	0	9	0	9	0
Herb Syrup	35	0	0	0	0	10	0	9	0
Citrus Syrup	35	0	0	0	0	9	0	9	0
Spiced Syrup	35	0	0	0	0	9	0	9	0

	CALORIES	TOTAL FAT (G)	SAT FAT (G)	CHOL (MG)	SODIUM (MG)	TOTAL CARB (G)	DIETARY FIBER (G)	TOTAL SUGARS (G)	PROTEIN (G)
Festive Drinks (cont.)									
Ginger Syrup	35	0	0	0	0	10	0	9	0
Grapefruit-Rosemary Spritzer	70	0	0	0	0	19	0	18	0
New Englander	80	0	0	0	35	22	1	20	0
Cocochai	280	24	21	0	15	18	0	15	2
Champagne Cocktail	149	0	0	0	9	8	1	4	0
DIY Bitters Sugar Cubes	10	0	0	0	0	2	0	2	0
Mimosa	135	0	0	0	6	14	0	10	1
Sicilian Sojourn	110	0	0	0	25	26	0	23	1
Espresso Martini	213	0	0	0	7	14	0	12	0
Whiskey Sour	190	0	0	0	0	12	0	11	0
Old Poblano	195	0	0	0	3	14	0	11	0
Moscow Mule	220	0	0	0	0	23	0	21	0
Negroni	165	0	0	0	2	1	0	0	0
Practically Clear Ice	0	0	0	0	0	0	0	0	0
Big-Batch Boulevardiers	250	0	0	0	5	16	0	14	0
House Punch	266	0	0	0	8	34	1	28	0
Holiday Punch	219	0	0	0	11	12	1	9	0
Bloody Marys for a Crowd	120	0	0	0	357	7	1	4	1
Eggnog	320	23	13	209	135	16	0	15	6
Mulled Cider	125	0	0	0	8	22	1	18	0
Mulled Wine	236	0	0	0	9	22	1	17	0
Irish Coffee	300	20	13	65	15	13	0	13	2
Hot Toddy	175	0	0	0	8	22	0	19	0
Make-Ahead Hot Chocolate	245	19	12	33	71	22	2	19	2
Masala Chai	100	3.5	2	10	75	13	0	13	3
Brunch									
Broccoli and Feta Frittata	237	16	7	390	463	5	0	2	17
Spicy Chilaquiles with Fried Eggs	750	45	11	400	1320	61	4	6	26
Green Shakshuka	410	27	7	385	1260	22	8	6	23
24-Hour "Omelet"	439	28	15	250	576	24	2	7	23
Savory Bread Pudding with Turkey Sausage and Kale	872	63	34	478	986	45	5	13	34
Leek and Goat Cheese Quiche	370	28	15	155	333	22	1	4	9
Shrimp Skewers with Cheesy Grits	501	22	12	200	1135	42	3	5	31
Gravlax	170	9	2	37	176	7	0	7	14
Carrot and Smoked Salmon Salad	210	11	1.5	10	710	19	6	9	9
Mango, Orange, and Jicama Salad	120	0.5	0	0	30	30	6	22	2
Home Fries	256	10	3	11	564	39	3	3	5
Sheet-Pan Hash Browns	294	14	2	0	401	40	5	2	5

	CALORIES	TOTAL FAT (G)	SAT FAT (G)	CHOL (MG)	SODIUM (MG)	TOTAL CARB (G)	DIETARY FIBER (G)	TOTAL SUGARS (G)	PROTEIN (G)
Brunch (cont.)									
Oven-Fried Bacon	100	9	4	15	340	0	0	0	5
Classic Buttermilk Pancakes	122	4	2	32	147	17	0	3	4
Butter-Pecan Maple Syrup (per ¼ cup)	230	8	2	10	25	31	1	37	1
Apple-Cinnamon Maple Syrup (per ¼ cup)	140	0	0	0	20	37	0	33	0
Berry Maple Syrup (per ¼ cup)	180	0	0	0	30	47	0	42	0
Apple-Cranberry Topping (per ½ cup)	74	0	0	0	26	18	2	14	0
Maple Butter (per 1 tablespoon)	115	12	7	31	45	3	0	3	0
Savory Dutch Baby with Burrata and Prosciutto	530	36	12	240	940	30	0	4	27
Yeasted Waffles	333	17	10	94	315	36	1	5	8
French Toast Casserole	385	11	4	151	397	55	5	26	17
Blueberry Swirl Muffins with Frozen Blueberries	300	10	3	42	268	49	1	28	5
Mixed Berry Scones	463	22	14	79	364	59	2	17	8
Ultimate Banana Bread	318	12	6	62	263	51	2.5	24	5
New York–Style Crumb Cake	383	17	11	80	147	53	1	26	4
Ultimate Cinnamon Buns	868	31	18	149	558	137	3	77	12
Chocolate Babka	260	15	9	75	115	28	0	7	5
Breads									
Easiest-Ever Biscuits	347	20	12	71	224	36	1	3	5
Pat-in-the-Pan Buttermilk Biscuits	340	16	10	43	291	42	1	3	6
Parker House Rolls	161	8	5	27	110	20	1	2	3
Fluffy Dinner Rolls	162	6	3	28	140	23	1	3	4
Oatmeal Dinner Rolls	170	3	2	21	145	31	2	5	5
Really Good Garlic Bread	258	14	8	31	350	29	2	1	5
Southern-Style Skillet Cornbread	260	16	7	60	320	25	1	4	4
Cranberry-Walnut Loaf	250	8	1	20	470	39	3	12	7
English Muffin Bread	140	1.5	0.5	5	310	25	1	2	6
Almost No-Knead Bread	168	1	0	0	174	33	1	0	4
Oatmeal-Raisin Bread	239	6	3	11	231	41	3	6	7
No-Knead Brioche	264	14	8	112	185	27	1	4	7
Classic Italian Bread	260	3.5	0.5	0	440	44	2	0	8
Fig and Fennel Bread	333	2	0	0	347	60	6	9	10
Rosemary Focaccia	251	7	1	0	245	41	2	0	6
Za'atar Bread	430	18	2.5	0	590	53	3	1	10
Stollen	290	10	4.5	25	20	41	1	21	5
Panettone	273	9	5	53	209	42	2	15	6
Portuguese Sweet Bread	280	7	3.5	105	260	46	0	11	8

	CALORIES	TOTAL FAT (G)	SAT FAT (G)	CHOL (MG)	SODIUM (MG)	TOTAL CARB (G)	DIETARY FIBER (G)	TOTAL SUGARS (G)	PROTEIN (G)
Breads (cont.)									
St. Lucia Buns	203	6	3	46	140	33	1	9	5
Challah	247	7	3.5	68	196	39	1.5	5	7
Whipped Honey Butter (per 1 tablespoon)	109	11	7	30	20	2	0	2	0
Molasses-Pecan Butter (per 1 tablespoon)	70	7	3.5	15	10	2	0	2	0
Sweet Orange Butter (per 1 tablespoon)	50	6	3.5	15	10	1	0	1	0
Parsley-Lemon Butter (per 1 tablespoon)	70	7	4.5	20	0	0	0	0	0
Garlic-Herb Butter (per 1 tablespoon)	70	7	4.5	20	0	0	0	0	0
Cookies and Cakes									
Easy Holiday Sugar Cookies	125	5	3	17	67	19	0	12	1
Vanilla Icebox Cookies	86	4	3	18	25	11	0	6	1
Eggnog Snickerdoodles	90	4	3	18	42	13	0	7	1
Soft and Chewy Gingerbread People	166	6	4	15	95	26	1	12	2
Molasses Spice Cookies	159	7	4	25	88	24	1	12	2
Chocolate Crinkle Cookies	155	6	3	31	96	24	2	17	3
Cranberry, White Chocolate, and Macadamia Cookies	173	9	4	18	65	21	1	13	2
Peanut Butter Sandwich Cookies	214	14	4	16	104	19	1	14	6
Easy All-Purpose Glaze (per 1 teaspoon)	20	0	0	0	0	5	0	5	0
Decorating Icing (per 1 teaspoon)	20	0	0	0	0	5	0	5	0
Linzer Sandwich Cookies	100	5	2	15	25	14	0	9	1
Pignoli	170	10	1	0	5	18	2	15	4
Rugelach with Raisin-Walnut Filling	171	9	5	35	50	22	1	13	2
Cranberry Swirl Shortbread	196	10	6	27	75	24	1	10	2
Millionaire's Shortbread	198	11	7	26	92	25	1	18	2
Ultranutty Pecan Bars	282	21	6	19	123	24	2	14	3
Pear-Cherry Streusel Bars	198	10	5	20	54	26	1	13	2
Fudgy Brownies	100	5	3	20	40	13	0	7	1
Cranberry–Sour Cream Pound Cake	490	25	15	175	344	58	1	33	8
Clementine Cake	776	32	11	154	239	117	4	97	12
Slow-Cooker Flourless Chocolate Cake	277	22	13	124	40	19	2	16	4
Chocolate Lava Cake for a Crowd	420	17	10	60	250	68	1	45	4
Hot Cocoa Cake	530	32	20	115	221	58	3	35	7
Gingerbread Layer Cake	632	34	14	95	333	80	1	61	5
Miracle Frosting	250	17	11	45	85	23	0	20	1
Apricot and Cherry Modern Fruitcake	350	13	5	50	210	48	2	32	5
Spiced-Citrus Bundt Cake	470	18	11	105	330	70	0	43	6
Cranberry-Orange Olive Oil Cake	987	55	22	170	414	113	4	84	8
Caramel-Espresso Yule Log	561	39	18	163	183	50	1	39	6
Maple Cheesecake	454	29	15	133	323	43	1	32	7

	CALORIES	TOTAL FAT (G)	SAT FAT (G)	CHOL (MG)	SODIUM (MG)	TOTAL CARB (G)	DIETARY FIBER (G)	TOTAL SUGARS (G)	PROTEIN (G)
Pies, Puddings, and Fruit Desserts									
Pecan Pie	690	43	16	130	350	71	3	52	7
Holiday Eggnog Custard Pie	650	43	26	203	307	56	1	37	8
Whipped Cream (per ¼ cup)	110	11	7	35	25	2	0	2	1
Orange-Chocolate Custard Pie	472	33	19	157	148	41	2	35	7
Maple Syrup Pie	360	17	10	116	131	50	0	42	3
Ginger-Cranberry-Pear Streusel Pie	544	23	12	42	192	79	8	40	5
Mulled Wine Quince Pie	356	2	0	23	111	70	4	38	2
Cranberry Curd Tart with Almond Crust	548	34	17	148	183	59	4	44	5
Poached Pear and Almond Tart	483	22	11	75	120	57	4	37	5
Chocolate, Matcha, and Pomegranate Tart	496	26	15	81	201	64	3	40	5
Sticky Toffee Pudding	550	23	14	110	360	81	2	62	5
Slow-Cooker Bourbon Bread Pudding	520	34	17	277	406	38	2	17	10
Slow-Cooker Chocolate Fondue	279	22	13	43	32	24	2	21	2
Chocolate Soufflé	301	19	11	157	102	29	2	26	7
Baked Alaska	472	21	4	108	252	67	2	53	8
Tiramisu	481	31	17	248	316	37	1	15	9
Chocolate–Peanut Butter Crème Brûlée	620	51	26	325	120	34	2	24	12
Candied Peanuts	130	12	1.5	0	150	10	2	7	4
Autumn Pear Crumble	410	11	5	25	80	73	7	46	4
Bananas Foster	418	19	12	59	62	54	2	45	3
Roasted Oranges in Spiced Syrup	170	0	0	0	0	45	3	38	1
Roasted Figs with Balsamic Glaze and Mascarpone	300	14	6	30	10	42	4	36	4
Slow-Cooker White Wine–Poached Pears	335	0	0	0	60	60	8	46	1
Foolproof All-Butter Single-Crust Pie Dough	210	14	9	40	150	18	0	2	2
Foolproof All-Butter Double-Crust Pie Dough	410	28	18	75	290	35	0	3	5
Classic Tart Dough	230	12	8	55	75	26	0	9	3
Food Gifts									
Spiced Pecans with Rum Glaze (per ¼ cup)	210	19	2.5	5	220	7	2	5	2
Chocolate Granola	310	20	4	0	65	31	4	8	6
Chocolate Truffles	66	5	3	7	9	7	1	6	1
Wintermint Bark	170	11	5	10	135	19	0	13	2
Rocky Road Bark	170	11	5	10	135	19	0	13	2
Chocolate Fudge	298	14	9	23	93	45	1	41	2
Oreo Mint Balls	92	7	3	7	24	9	1	7	1
Bourbon Balls	104	4	1	0	24	14	1	9	1
White Chocolate–Coconut Candies	70	4.5	3.5	0	15	7	0	7	1
Caramel Apples	220	3	1	0	85	48	5	38	2

	CALORIES	TOTAL FAT (G)	SAT FAT (G)	CHOL (MG)	SODIUM (MG)	TOTAL CARB (G)	DIETARY FIBER (G)	TOTAL SUGARS (G)	PROTEIN (G)
Food Gifts (cont.)									
Homemade Almond Butter	205	18	1	0	83	8	4	2	8
Chocolate-Hazelnut Spread	182	14	1	0	25	14	3	10	3
Hot Fudge Sauce	300	15	9	20	38	46	3	42	2
Sugar Cookie Mix	120	4	2.5	80	20	0	13	13	2
Chocolate Layer Cake Mix	460	29	14	160	48	0	40	39	3
Hot Chocolate Mix	194	9	6	4	100	27	5	18	4
Vanilla Extract	10	0	0	0	0	0	0	0	0
Sweet Vermouth (per 1 ounce)	20	0	0	0	1	2	2	1	0
Limoncello (per 1 ounce)	58	0	0	0	0	10	0	10	0
Lavender Liqueur (per 1 ounce)	95	0	0	0	1	10	0	10	0
Fruits of the Forest Liqueur (per 1 ounce)	87	0	0	0	1	10	0	10	0
Ancho Chile Liqueur (per 1 ounce)	87	0	0	0	1	10	0	10	0
Orgeat Syrup (per 1 ounce)	200	9	0.5	0	1	29	2	26	4
Cranberry Shrub Syrup (per 1 ounce)	110	0	0	0	2	28	1.5	26	0
Old-Fashioned Aromatic Bitters (per 1 ounce)	8	0	0	0	0	2	0	1	0

conversions & equivalents

Some say cooking is a science and an art. We would say that geography has a hand in it, too. Flours and sugars manufactured in the United Kingdom and elsewhere will feel and taste different from those manufactured in the United States. So we cannot promise that the loaf of bread you bake in Canada or England will taste the same as a loaf baked in the States, but we can offer guidelines for converting weights and measures. We also recommend that you rely on your instincts when making our recipes. Refer to the visual cues provided. If the dough hasn't "come together in a ball" as described, you may need to add more flour—even if the recipe doesn't tell you to. You be the judge.

The recipes in this book were developed using standard U.S. measures following U.S. government guidelines. The charts below offer equivalents for U.S. and metric measures. All conversions are approximate and have been rounded up or down to the nearest whole number.

EXAMPLE

1 teaspoon = 4.9292 milliliters, rounded up to 5 milliliters

1 ounce = 28.3495 grams, rounded down to 28 grams

Volume Conversions

U.S.	METRIC
1 teaspoon	5 milliliters
2 teaspoons	10 milliliters
1 tablespoon	15 milliliters
2 tablespoons	30 milliliters
¼ cup	59 milliliters
⅓ cup	79 milliliters
½ cup	118 milliliters
¾ cup	177 milliliters
1 cup	237 milliliters
1¼ cups	296 milliliters
1½ cups	355 milliliters
2 cups (1 pint)	473 milliliters
2½ cups	591 milliliters
3 cups	710 milliliters
4 cups (1 quart)	0.946 liter
1.06 quarts	1 liter
4 quarts (1 gallon)	3.8 liters

Weight Conversions

OUNCES	GRAMS
½	14
¾	21
1	28
1½	43
2	57
2½	71
3	85
3½	99
4	113
4½	128
5	142
6	170
7	198
8	227
9	255
10	283
12	340
16 (1 pound)	454

Conversions for Common Baking Ingredients

Baking is an exacting science. Because measuring by weight is far more accurate than measuring by volume, and thus more likely to produce reliable results, in our recipes we provide ounce measures in addition to cup measures for many ingredients. Refer to the chart below to convert these measures into grams.

INGREDIENT	OUNCES	GRAMS
Flour		
1 cup all-purpose flour*	5	142
1 cup cake flour	4	113
1 cup whole-wheat flour	5½	156
Sugar		
1 cup granulated (white) sugar	7	198
1 cup packed brown sugar (light or dark)	7	198
1 cup confectioners' sugar	4	113
Cocoa Powder		
1 cup cocoa powder	3	85
Butter†		
4 tablespoons (½ stick or ¼ cup)	2	57
8 tablespoons (1 stick or ½ cup)	4	113
16 tablespoons (2 sticks or 1 cup)	8	227

* U.S. all-purpose flour, the most frequently used flour in this book, does not contain leaveners, as some European flours do. These leavened flours are called self-rising or self-raising. If you are using self-rising flour, take this into consideration before adding leaveners to a recipe.

† In the United States, butter is sold both salted and unsalted. We generally recommend unsalted butter. If you are using salted butter, take this into consideration before adding salt to a recipe.

Oven Temperatures

FAHRENHEIT	CELSIUS	GAS MARK
225	105	¼
250	120	½
275	135	1
300	150	2
325	165	3
350	180	4
375	190	5
400	200	6
425	220	7
450	230	8
475	245	9

Converting Temperatures from an Instant-Read Thermometer

We include doneness temperatures in many of the recipes in this book. We recommend an instant-read thermometer for the job. Use this simple formula to convert Fahrenheit degrees to Celsius:

Subtract 32 degrees from the Fahrenheit reading, then divide the result by 1.8 to find the Celsius reading.

EXAMPLE

"Roast chicken until thighs register 175 degrees."

To convert:

175°F − 32 =	143°
143° ÷ 1.8 =	79.44°C, rounded down to 79°C

index

K

Kale

Creamed, with Chestnuts, 149–50

Parsnips, and Mushrooms, Beef Stew with ■, 36, *36*

and Roasted Red Peppers, Cannellini Beans with ■ ■, 183–84, *184*

Slow-Cooker Braised, with Garlic and Chorizo, 150

and Turkey Sausage, Savory Bread Pudding with, 283–84

Tuscan White Bean Stew ■, 38, *39*

Kidney Beans

Pressure-Cooker Easy Beef Chili ■, 41

Pressure-Cooker Easy Five-Alarm Chili, 41

Pressure-Cooker Easy Turkey Chili, 41

Kimchi, Beef, and Tofu Soup, 20–21

Knives, slicing/carving, 13

Kohlrabi

buying and preparing, 151

Roasted, with Crunchy Seeds ■, *150,* 150–51

Korean Fried Chicken Wings ■, 248, *248*

Kugel, Savory Noodle ■, 180

L

Lamb

doneness temperatures, 414

Harira ■, *22,* 22–23

Harissa-Rubbed Roast Boneless Leg of, with Warm Cauliflower Salad, *77,* 77–78

Meatballs with Orzo, Tomatoes, and Feta ■, 59, *59*

Pot Roast, Spiced, with Figs, 117, *117*

Roast Bone-In Leg of, Pomegranate-Glazed, 116–17

salting, 412

Stew with Turnips and Carrots ■, 37

Lasagna

Cheese, Simple ■ ■, 125

Mushroom ■ ■, *124,* 124–25

Latkes, Crispy Potato ■ ■, *252,* 252–53

Lattetini, Espresso, 267

Lavender Liqueur ■ ■, *407,* 407–8

Leek(s)

and Butternut Squash, Unstuffed Shells with ■, *66,* 67–68

and Goat Cheese Quiche ■ ■, 284

and Mushroom Galette with Gorgonzola ■ ■, 126–27, *127*

and Smoked Salmon Tart, 254, *255*

and White Wine, Salmon en Cocotte with, 95, *95*

Lemon

and Almonds, Braised Beets with ■, 142

–Browned Butter Vinaigrette, 152

-Caper Butter, Prosciutto-Wrapped Cod with, 78, *79*

-Chive Dipping Sauce, Fried Brussels Sprouts with ■, *244,* 245

and Chives, Braised Red Potatoes with ■, 156

-Chocolate Truffles, 394

Crema di Limoncello, 407

-Herb Fingerling Potatoes, Slow-Cooker ■, 156, *157*

Limoncello ■ ■, 406–7, *407*

Linzer Sandwich Cookies, 342

-Parsley Butter, 329

Stollen ■ ■, 320–21, *321*

Lentil(s)

and Escarole Soup ■, 30, *31*

French, with Carrots and Parsley ■ ■, 182, *183*

Harira ■, *22,* 22–23

Palak Dal ■, 62–63, *63*

Red, and Squash Soup ■ ■, 28

Red, Spiced ■, 181, *181*

Salad, Slow-Cooker, with Dill, Orange, and Spinach ■, 182

Lettuce

Bibb and Arugula Salad with Apple and Goat Cheese, 190

Bibb and Frisée Salad with Apple and Celery ■, 190, *190*

Roquefort Salad with Apple, Celery, and Hazelnuts ■, 138, *139*

Lettuce *(cont.)*

Roquefort Salad with Fennel, Dried Cherries, and Walnuts, 138

Steak Salad with Beets, Walnuts, and Creamy Horseradish Dressing, 52, *53*

Lime

-Coconut Icebox Cookies, 334

House Punch ■ ■, 271, *271*

New Englander ■ ■, 262

New Englander with Vodka, 262

and Pepitas, Braised Beets with, 142

Limoncello ■ ■, 406–7, *407*

Linzer Sandwich Cookies ■, 342, *342*

Linzer Sandwich Cookies, Lemon, 342

Liqueurs

Ancho Chile ■ ■, 409

Arancello, 407

Chamomile, *407,* 408

Crema di Limoncello, 407

Fruits of the Forest ■ ■, 408, *408*

Jasmine, *407,* 408

Lavender ■ ■, *407,* 407–8

Limoncello ■ ■, 406–7, *407*

Mole Chile, 409

Rose, *407,* 408

Liver, Chicken, Pâté ■, 236, *236*

Loaf pan, 13

M

Macadamia

Cranberry, and White Chocolate Cookies ■ ■, *338,* 338–39

–Dried Fig-Stuffed Baked Apples, 198

Macaroni and Cheese, Creamy Make-Ahead ■ ■, *178,* 179

Make-Ahead Autumn in New Englands for Four, 258

Make-Ahead Creamy Macaroni and Cheese ■ ■, *178,* 179

Make-Ahead Espresso Martinis for Four, 267

Make-Ahead Firesides for Four, 259

Make-Ahead Highlanders for Four, 260

Make-Ahead Hot Chocolate ■ ■, 276–77